D1586330

COLLINS GEM

THESAURUS

IN A-Z FORM

COLLINS GEM

THESAURUS

IN A-Z FORM

Collins Gem

An Imprint of HarperCollins*Publishers*

First Edition 1987

Second Edition 1994

Third Edition 1999
Reprinted 1999

10 9 8 7 6 5 4 3 2

© HarperCollins Publishers 1987, 1994, 1999

The HarperCollins website address is
www.**fire**and**water**.com

ISBN 0 00 472207-8

A catalogue record for this book
is available from the British Library.

Typeset by Stewart C. Russell

Printed and bound in Great Britain by
Caledonian International Book Manufacturing Ltd, Glasgow, G64

EDITORIAL STAFF

Editorial Director
Diana Treffry

Editors
Ian Brookes
Lorna Gilmour

Editorial Assistance
Susan Dunsmore

Computing Staff
Stewart C. Russell
Jane Creevy

FOREWORD

Collins Gem Thesaurus, which was first published in 1987, has proved itself to be an immensely popular language resource. It allows you to look up a word and find a wide selection of alternatives that can replace it. It is, therefore, tremendously helpful when you are trying to find different ways of expressing yourself, as well as being an invaluable aid for crosswords and puzzles.

Collins thesauruses have always been designed to give the user as much help as possible in finding the right word for any occasion. Collins pioneered the A-Z arrangement of main entry words. This lets you go straight to any word without having to resort to an index, just as if you were looking up a word in a dictionary. This arrangement is continued in this new edition, but the number of main entry words has been increased, thus giving you an even greater chance of finding the word you want. At the same time, the list of alternative words (synonyms) for each main entry word has been reviewed so that the most helpful alternatives are included in each case. The new edition also takes account of recent changes in the language, with new terms like *gridlock*, *nerd*, and *Internet* included as main entry words for the first time, and words like *wannabe*, *stakeholder*, and *luvvie* being found among the synonyms.

This new edition further demonstrates Collins' commitment to helping the user. As part of an innovative design, key synonyms have been underlined and placed first in each list. This layout enables you to see immediately which sense of the word is referred to. This is particularly helpful when a main entry word has a number of different senses. It also gives you an idea of which synonym is the closest alternative to the word you have looked up.

These innovations mean that **Collins Gem Thesaurus** continues to provide the user with a treasury of useful words arranged in the most helpful format possible.

HOW TO USE THIS BOOK

Main Entry Words

Main entry words are printed in large bold type. They are arranged in alphabetical order, so you can go straight to the word for which you want to find an alternative.

> **absolute**
>
> **absolutely**
>
> **absolution**

When the main entry word has been borrowed from a foreign language, it is given in italics.

> *femme fatale*

Parts of Speech

The part of speech of each main entry word is indicated in italic letters.

> **famine** *noun*

The symbol ♦ is used to indicate that the following sense or senses of the main entry word refer to a different part of speech.

> **farm** *noun* 1 <u>smallholding</u> ... ♦ *verb*
> 2 <u>cultivate</u>

Sometimes the synonyms that are given can refer to more than one part of speech.

> **tweak** *verb, noun* <u>twist</u>, jerk, pinch,
> pull, squeeze

Synonyms

The alternative words for the headword are listed in alphabetical order, except for the most useful synonym, which is placed first and underlined to give it special prominence.

> **fertilizer** *noun* <u>compost</u>, dressing,
> dung, manure

When a word has more than one sense, separate numbered lists of synonyms are given for each sense.

HOW TO USE THIS BOOK

> **field** *noun* **1** <u>meadow</u>, grassland,
> green, lea (*poetic*), pasture
> **2** <u>competitors</u>, applicants,
> candidates, competition, contestants,
> entrants, possibilities, runners
> **3** <u>speciality</u>, area, department, discipline,
> domain, line, province, territory

When a synonym has been borrowed from a foreign language, it is given in italics.

> **flower** *noun* ... **2** <u>elite</u>, best, cream,
> *crème de la crème*, pick

Phrases and Idioms

Short idiomatic phrases are given in small bold type and included under the most appropriate main entry word from the phrase. Such phrases appear after other senses of the main entry word which refer to the same part of speech.

> **fort** *noun* **1** <u>fortress</u>, blockhouse,
> camp, castle, citadel, fortification,
> garrison, stronghold **2 hold the**
> **fort** <u>stand in</u>, carry on, keep things
> on an even keel, take over the reins

When a particular sense of a word is usually found only in a certain phrase, that phrase is shown.

> **mince** *verb* **1** <u>cut</u>, chop, crumble,
> grind, hash **2** *As in* **mince one's**
> **words** <u>tone down</u>, moderate,
> soften, spare, weaken

Cross-references

Cross-references to other main entry words are shown in small capital letters.

> **enquire** *see* INQUIRE

HOW TO USE THIS BOOK

Labels

Many words and senses are labelled to indicate that their use is restricted to a certain subject, a certain geographical area, or a certain style of language.

> **overture** *noun* **1** *Music* ...
>
> **scupper** *verb Brit. slang* ...
>
> **wimp** *noun Informal* ...

An italic label in brackets refers only to the synonym preceding it, and gives you guidance about the appropriate context for using that particular alternative to the main entry word.

> **faint** ... ♦ *verb* **4** <u>pass out</u>, black out, collapse, flake out (*informal*), keel over (*informal*), lose consciousness, swoon (*literary*)

A a

abandon verb **1** leave, desert, forsake, strand **2** give up, relinquish, surrender, yield ♦ noun **3** wildness, recklessness

abandonment noun leaving, dereliction, desertion, forsaking

abashed adjective embarrassed, ashamed, chagrined, disconcerted, dismayed, humiliated, mortified, shamefaced, taken aback

abate verb decrease, decline, diminish, dwindle, fade, lessen, let up, moderate, relax, slacken, subside, weaken

abbey noun monastery, convent, friary, nunnery, priory

abbreviate verb shorten, abridge, compress, condense, contract, cut, reduce, summarize

abbreviation noun shortening, abridgment, contraction, reduction, summary, synopsis

abdicate verb give up, abandon, quit, relinquish, renounce, resign, step down (informal)

abdication noun giving up, abandonment, quitting, renunciation, resignation, retirement, surrender

abduct verb kidnap, carry off, seize, snatch (slang)

abduction noun kidnapping, carrying off, seizure

aberration noun oddity, abnormality, anomaly, defect, irregularity, lapse, peculiarity, quirk

abet verb help, aid, assist, connive at, support

abeyance noun in abeyance shelved, hanging fire, on ice (informal), pending, suspended

abhor verb hate, abominate, detest, loathe, shrink from, shudder at

abhorrent adjective hateful, abominable, disgusting, distasteful, hated, horrid, loathsome, offensive, repulsive

abide verb tolerate, accept, bear, endure, put up with, stand, suffer

abide by verb obey, agree to, comply with, conform to, follow, observe, submit to

abiding adjective everlasting, continuing, enduring, lasting, permanent, persistent, unchanging

ability noun skill, aptitude, capability, competence, expertise, proficiency, talent

abject adjective **1** miserable, deplorable, forlorn, hopeless, pitiable, wretched **2** servile, cringing, degraded, fawning, grovelling, submissive

ablaze adjective on fire, aflame, alight, blazing, burning, fiery, flaming, ignited, lighted

able adjective capable, accomplished, competent, efficient, proficient, qualified, skilful

able-bodied adjective strong, fit, healthy, robust, sound, sturdy

abnormal adjective unusual, atypical, exceptional,

extraordinary, irregular, odd, peculiar, strange, uncommon

abnormality noun oddity, deformity, exception, irregularity, peculiarity, singularity, strangeness

abode noun home, domicile, dwelling, habitat, habitation, house, lodging, pad (slang), quarters, residence

abolish verb do away with, annul, cancel, destroy, eliminate, end, eradicate, put an end to, quash, rescind, revoke, stamp out

abolition noun ending, cancellation, destruction, elimination, end, extermination, termination, wiping out

abominable adjective terrible, despicable, detestable, disgusting, hateful, horrible, horrid, repulsive, revolting, vile

abort verb 1 terminate (a pregnancy), miscarry 2 stop, arrest, axe (informal), call off, check, end, fail, halt, terminate

abortion noun termination, deliberate miscarriage, miscarriage

abortive adjective failed, fruitless, futile, ineffectual, miscarried, unsuccessful, useless, vain

abound verb be plentiful, flourish, proliferate, swarm, swell, teem, thrive

abounding adjective plentiful, abundant, bountiful, copious, full, profuse, prolific, rich

about preposition 1 regarding, as regards, concerning, dealing with, on, referring to, relating to 2 near, adjacent to, beside, circa (used with dates), close to, nearby

♦ adverb 3 nearly, almost, approaching, approximately, around, close to, more or less, roughly

above preposition over, beyond, exceeding, higher than, on top of, upon

abrasion noun Medical graze, chafe, scrape, scratch, scuff, surface injury

abrasive adjective 1 unpleasant, caustic, cutting, galling, grating, irritating, rough, sharp 2 rough, chafing, grating, scraping, scratchy

abreast adjective 1 alongside, beside, side by side 2 abreast of informed about, acquainted with, au courant with, au fait with, conversant with, familiar with, in the picture about, in touch with, keeping one's finger on the pulse of, knowledgeable about, up to date with, up to speed with

abridge verb shorten, abbreviate, condense, cut, decrease, reduce, summarize

abroad adverb overseas, in foreign lands, out of the country

abrupt adjective 1 sudden, precipitate, quick, surprising, unexpected 2 curt, brusque, gruff, impatient, rude, short, terse

abscond verb flee, clear out, disappear, escape, make off, run off, steal away

absence noun 1 nonattendance, absenteeism, truancy 2 lack, deficiency, need, omission, unavailability, want

absent adjective 1 missing, away, elsewhere, gone, nonexistent,

out, unavailable
2 absent-minded blank, distracted, inattentive, oblivious, preoccupied, vacant, vague ◆ *verb* **3 absent oneself** stay away, keep away, play truant, withdraw

absent-minded *adjective* vague, distracted, dreaming, forgetful, inattentive, preoccupied, unaware

absolute *adjective* **1** total, complete, outright, perfect, pure, sheer, thorough, utter **2** supreme, full, sovereign, unbounded, unconditional, unlimited, unrestricted

absolutely *adverb* totally, completely, entirely, fully, one hundred per cent, perfectly, utterly, wholly

absolution *noun* forgiveness, deliverance, exculpation, exoneration, mercy, pardon, release

absolve *verb* forgive, deliver, exculpate, excuse, let off, pardon, release, set free

absorb *verb* **1** soak up, consume, digest, imbibe, incorporate, receive, suck up, take in **2** preoccupy, captivate, engage, engross, fascinate, rivet

absorbed *adjective*
1 preoccupied, captivated, engrossed, fascinated, immersed, involved, lost, rapt, riveted, wrapped up **2** digested, assimilated, incorporated, received, soaked up

absorbent *adjective* permeable, porous, receptive, spongy

absorbing *adjective* fascinating, captivating, engrossing, gripping, interesting, intriguing,

riveting, spellbinding

absorption *noun* **1** soaking up, assimilation, consumption, digestion, incorporation, sucking up **2** concentration, fascination, immersion, intentness, involvement, preoccupation

abstain *verb* refrain, avoid, decline, deny (oneself), desist, fast, forbear, forgo, give up, keep from

abstemious *adjective* self-denying, ascetic, austere, frugal, moderate, sober, temperate

abstention *noun* refusal, abstaining, abstinence, avoidance, forbearance, refraining, self-control, self-restraint

abstinence *noun* self-denial, abstemiousness, avoidance, forbearance, moderation, self-restraint, soberness, teetotalism, temperance

abstinent *adjective* self-denying, abstaining, abstemious, forbearing, moderate, self-controlled, sober, temperate

abstract *adjective* **1** theoretical, abstruse, general, hypothetical, indefinite, notional, recondite ◆ *noun* **2** summary, abridgment, digest, epitome, outline, précis, résumé, synopsis ◆ *verb* **3** summarize, abbreviate, abridge, condense, digest, epitomize, outline, précis, shorten **4** remove, detach, extract, isolate, separate, take away, take out, withdraw

abstraction *noun* **1** idea, concept, formula, generalization, hypothesis, notion, theorem,

theory, thought
2 <u>absent-mindedness</u>, absence, dreaminess, inattention, pensiveness, preoccupation, remoteness, woolgathering

abstruse *adjective* <u>obscure</u>, arcane, complex, deep, enigmatic, esoteric, recondite, unfathomable, vague

absurd *adjective* <u>ridiculous</u>, crazy (*informal*), farcical, foolish, idiotic, illogical, inane, incongruous, irrational, ludicrous, nonsensical, preposterous, senseless, silly, stupid, unreasonable

absurdity *noun* <u>ridiculousness</u>, farce, folly, foolishness, incongruity, joke, nonsense, silliness, stupidity

abundance *noun* <u>plenty</u>, affluence, bounty, copiousness, exuberance, fullness, profusion

abundant *adjective* <u>plentiful</u>, ample, bountiful, copious, exuberant, filled, full, luxuriant, profuse, rich, teeming

abuse *noun* **1** <u>ill-treatment</u>, damage, exploitation, harm, hurt, injury, maltreatment, manhandling **2** <u>insults</u>, blame, castigation, censure, defamation, derision, disparagement, invective, reproach, scolding, vilification **3** <u>misuse</u>, misapplication ◆ *verb* **4** <u>ill-treat</u>, damage, exploit, harm, hurt, injure, maltreat, misuse, take advantage of **5** <u>insult</u>, castigate, curse, defame, disparage, malign, scold, vilify

abusive *adjective* **1** <u>insulting</u>, censorious, defamatory, disparaging, libellous, offensive,

reproachful, rude, scathing
2 <u>harmful</u>, brutal, cruel, destructive, hurtful, injurious, rough

abysmal *adjective* <u>terrible</u>, appalling, awful, bad, dire, dreadful

abyss *noun* <u>pit</u>, chasm, crevasse, fissure, gorge, gulf, void

academic *adjective* **1** <u>scholarly</u>, bookish, erudite, highbrow, learned, literary, studious **2** <u>hypothetical</u>, abstract, conjectural, impractical, notional, speculative, theoretical ◆ *noun* **3** <u>scholar</u>, academician, don, fellow, lecturer, master, professor, tutor

accede *verb* **1** <u>agree</u>, accept, acquiesce, admit, assent, comply, concede, concur, consent, endorse, grant **2** <u>inherit</u>, assume, attain, come to, enter upon, succeed, succeed to (*as heir*)

accelerate *verb* <u>speed up</u>, advance, expedite, further, hasten, hurry, quicken

acceleration *noun* <u>speeding up</u>, hastening, hurrying, quickening, stepping up (*informal*)

accent *noun* **1** <u>pronunciation</u>, articulation, brogue, enunciation, inflection, intonation, modulation, tone **2** <u>emphasis</u>, beat, cadence, force, pitch, rhythm, stress, timbre ◆ *verb* **3** <u>emphasize</u>, accentuate, stress, underline, underscore

accentuate *verb* <u>emphasize</u>, accent, draw attention to, foreground, highlight, stress, underline, underscore

accept *verb* **1** <u>receive</u>, acquire,

gain, get, obtain, secure, take
2 agree to, admit, approve,
believe, concur with, consent to,
cooperate with, recognize

acceptable *adjective* satisfactory,
adequate, admissible, all right,
fair, moderate, passable, tolerable

acceptance *noun* **1** accepting,
acquiring, gaining, getting,
obtaining, receipt, securing,
taking **2** agreement,
acknowledgment, acquiescence,
admission, adoption, approval,
assent, concurrence, consent,
cooperation, recognition

accepted *adjective* agreed,
acknowledged, approved,
common, conventional,
customary, established, normal,
recognized, traditional

access *noun* entrance, admission,
admittance, approach, entry,
passage, path, road

accessibility *noun* **1** handiness,
availability, nearness, possibility,
readiness **2** approachability,
affability, cordiality, friendliness,
informality **3** openness,
susceptibility

accessible *adjective* **1** handy,
achievable, at hand, attainable,
available, near, nearby,
obtainable, reachable
2 approachable, affable,
available, cordial, friendly,
informal **3** open, exposed, liable,
susceptible, vulnerable,
wide-open

accessory *noun* **1** addition,
accompaniment, adjunct,
adornment, appendage,
attachment, decoration, extra,
supplement, trimming
2 accomplice, abettor, assistant,

associate (*in crime*), colleague,
confederate, helper, partner

accident *noun* **1** misfortune,
calamity, collision, crash,
disaster, misadventure, mishap
2 chance, fate, fluke, fortuity,
fortune, hazard, luck

accidental *adjective*
unintentional, casual, chance,
fortuitous, haphazard,
inadvertent, incidental, random,
unexpected, unforeseen,
unlooked-for, unplanned

accidentally *adverb*
unintentionally, by accident, by
chance, fortuitously,
haphazardly, inadvertently,
incidentally, randomly,
unwittingly

acclaim *verb* **1** praise, applaud,
approve, celebrate, cheer, clap,
commend, exalt, hail, honour,
salute ♦ *noun* **2** praise,
acclamation, applause, approval,
celebration, commendation,
honour, kudos

acclamation *noun* praise,
acclaim, adulation, approval,
ovation, plaudit, tribute

acclimatization *noun*
adaptation, adjustment,
habituation, inurement,
naturalization

acclimatize *verb* adapt,
accommodate, accustom, adjust,
get used to, habituate, inure,
naturalize

accolade *noun* praise, acclaim,
applause, approval,
commendation, compliment,
ovation, recognition, tribute

accommodate *verb* **1** house,
cater for, entertain, lodge, put
up, shelter **2** help, aid, assist,

oblige, serve **3** adapt, adjust, comply, conform, fit, harmonize, modify, reconcile, settle

accommodating adjective
helpful, considerate, cooperative, friendly, hospitable, kind, obliging, polite, unselfish, willing

accommodation noun housing, board, digs (Brit. informal), house, lodging(s), quarters, shelter

accompaniment noun
1 supplement, accessory, companion, complement **2** backing music, backing

accompany verb **1** go with, attend, chaperon, conduct, convoy, escort, hold (someone's) hand **2** occur with, belong to, come with, follow, go together with, supplement

accompanying adjective
additional, associated, attached, attendant, complementary, related, supplementary

accomplice noun helper, abettor, accessory, ally, assistant, associate, collaborator, colleague, henchman, partner

accomplish verb do, achieve, attain, bring about, carry out, complete, effect, execute, finish, fulfil, manage, perform, produce

accomplished adjective skilled, expert, gifted, masterly, polished, practised, proficient, talented

accomplishment noun
1 completion, bringing about, carrying out, conclusion, execution, finishing, fulfilment, performance **2** achievement, act, coup, deed, exploit, feat, stroke, triumph

accord noun **1** agreement, conformity, correspondence, harmony, rapport, sympathy, unison ♦ verb **2** fit, agree, conform, correspond, harmonize, match, suit, tally

accordingly adverb
1 appropriately, correspondingly, fitly, properly, suitably **2** consequently, as a result, ergo, hence, in consequence, so, therefore, thus

according to adverb **1** as stated by, as believed by, as maintained by, in the light of, on the authority of, on the report of **2** in keeping with, after, after the manner of, consistent with, in accordance with, in compliance with, in line with, in the manner of

accost verb approach, buttonhole, confront, greet, hail

account noun **1** description, explanation, narrative, report, statement, story, tale, version **2** Commerce statement, balance, bill, books, charge, invoice, reckoning, register, score, tally **3** importance, consequence, honour, note, significance, standing, value, worth ♦ verb **4** consider, count, estimate, judge, rate, reckon, regard, think, value

accountability noun
responsibility, answerability, chargeability, culpability, liability

accountable adjective
responsible, amenable, answerable, charged with, liable, obligated, obliged

accountant noun auditor, bean counter (informal), book-keeper

account for verb explain, answer for, clarify, clear up, elucidate, illuminate, justify, rationalize

accredited adjective authorized, appointed, certified, empowered, endorsed, guaranteed, licensed, official, recognized

accrue verb increase, accumulate, amass, arise, be added, build up, collect, enlarge, flow, follow, grow

accumulate verb collect, accrue, amass, build up, gather, hoard, increase, pile up, store

accumulation noun collection, build-up, gathering, heap, hoard, increase, mass, pile, stack, stock, stockpile, store

accuracy noun exactness, accurateness, authenticity, carefulness, closeness, correctness, fidelity, precision, strictness, truthfulness, veracity

accurate adjective exact, authentic, close, correct, faithful, precise, scrupulous, spot-on (*Brit. informal*), strict, true, unerring

accurately adverb exactly, authentically, closely, correctly, faithfully, precisely, scrupulously, strictly, to the letter, truly, unerringly

accursed adjective **1** cursed, bewitched, condemned, damned, doomed, hopeless, ill-fated, ill-omened, jinxed, unfortunate, unlucky, wretched **2** hateful, abominable, despicable, detestable, execrable, hellish, horrible

accusation noun charge, allegation, complaint, denunciation, incrimination, indictment, recrimination

accuse verb charge, blame, censure, denounce, impeach, impute, incriminate, indict

accustom verb adapt, acclimatize, acquaint, discipline, exercise, familiarize, train

accustomed adjective **1** usual, common, conventional, customary, established, everyday, expected, habitual, normal, ordinary, regular, traditional **2** used, acclimatized, acquainted, adapted, familiar, familiarized, given to, in the habit of, trained

ace noun **1** Cards, dice, etc. one, single point **2** Informal expert, champion, dab hand (*Brit. informal*), master, star, virtuoso, wizard (*informal*) ◆ adjective **3** Informal excellent, awesome (*slang*), brilliant, fine, great, outstanding, superb

ache verb **1** hurt, pain, pound, smart, suffer, throb, twinge ◆ noun **2** pain, hurt, pang, pounding, soreness, suffering, throbbing

achieve verb attain, accomplish, acquire, bring about, carry out, complete, do, execute, fulfil, gain, get, obtain, perform

achievement noun accomplishment, act, deed, effort, exploit, feat, feather in one's cap, stroke

acid adjective **1** sour, acerbic, acrid, pungent, tart, vinegary **2** sharp, biting, bitter, caustic, cutting, harsh, trenchant, vitriolic

acidity noun **1** sourness, acerbity, pungency, tartness **2** sharpness, bitterness, harshness

acknowledge verb 1 <u>accept</u>, admit, allow, concede, confess, declare, grant, own, profess, recognize, grant 2 <u>greet</u>, address, hail, notice, recognize, salute 3 <u>reply to</u>, answer, notice, react to, recognize, respond to, return

acknowledged adjective <u>accepted</u>, accredited, approved, confessed, declared, professed, recognized, returned

acknowledgment noun 1 <u>acceptance</u>, admission, allowing, confession, declaration, profession, realization, yielding 2 <u>greeting</u>, addressing, hail, hailing, notice, recognition, salutation, salute 3 <u>appreciation</u>, answer, credit, gratitude, reaction, recognition, reply, response, return, thanks

acquaint verb <u>tell</u>, disclose, divulge, enlighten, familiarize, inform, let (someone) know, notify, reveal

acquaintance noun 1 <u>associate</u>, colleague, contact 2 <u>knowledge</u>, awareness, experience, familiarity, fellowship, relationship, understanding

acquainted with adjective <u>familiar with</u>, alive to, apprised of, au fait with, aware of, conscious of, experienced in, informed of, knowledgeable about, versed in

acquiesce verb <u>agree</u>, accede, accept, allow, approve, assent, comply, concur, conform, consent, give in, go along with, submit, yield

acquiescence noun <u>agreement</u>, acceptance, approval, assent, compliance, conformity,

consent, giving in, obedience, submission, yielding

acquire verb <u>get</u>, amass, attain, buy, collect, earn, gain, gather, obtain, receive, secure, win

acquisition noun 1 <u>possession</u>, buy, gain, prize, property, purchase 2 <u>acquiring</u>, attainment, gaining, procurement

acquisitive adjective <u>greedy</u>, avaricious, avid, covetous, grabbing, grasping, predatory, rapacious

acquit verb 1 <u>clear</u>, discharge, free, liberate, release, vindicate 2 <u>behave</u>, bear, comport, conduct, perform

acquittal noun <u>clearance</u>, absolution, deliverance, discharge, exoneration, liberation, release, relief, vindication

acrid adjective <u>pungent</u>, bitter, caustic, harsh, sharp, vitriolic

acrimonious adjective <u>bitter</u>, caustic, irascible, petulant, rancorous, spiteful, splenetic, testy

acrimony noun <u>bitterness</u>, harshness, ill will, irascibility, rancour, virulence

act noun 1 <u>deed</u>, accomplishment, achievement, action, exploit, feat, performance ♦ undertaking 2 <u>law</u>, bill, decree, edict, enactment, measure, ordinance, resolution, statute 3 <u>performance</u>, routine, show, sketch, turn 4 <u>pretence</u>, affectation, attitude, front, performance, pose, posture, show ♦ verb 5 <u>do</u>, carry out, enact, execute, function, operate, perform, take effect, work **6** perform, act out, impersonate, mimic, play, play or take the part of, portray, represent

act for verb stand in for, cover for, deputize for, fill in for, replace, represent, substitute for, take the place of

acting noun **1** performance, characterization, impersonation, performing, playing, portrayal, stagecraft, theatre ◆ adjective **2** temporary, interim, pro tem, provisional, substitute, surrogate

action noun **1** deed, accomplishment, achievement, act, exploit, feat, performance **2** lawsuit, case, litigation, proceeding, prosecution, suit **3** energy, activity, force, liveliness, spirit, vigour, vim, vitality **4** movement, activity, functioning, motion, operation, process, working **5** battle, clash, combat, conflict, contest, encounter, engagement, fight, skirmish, sortie

activate verb start, arouse, energize, galvanize, initiate, mobilize, move, rouse, set in motion, stir

active adjective **1** busy, bustling, hard-working, involved, occupied, on the go (informal), on the move, strenuous **2** energetic, alert, animated, industrious, lively, quick, sprightly, spry, vigorous **3** in operation, acting, at work, effectual, in action, in force, operative, working

activist noun militant, organizer, partisan

activity noun **1** action,

animation, bustle, exercise, exertion, hustle, labour, motion, movement **2** pursuit, hobby, interest, pastime, project, scheme

actor noun performer, actress, luvvie (informal), player, Thespian

actress noun performer, actor, leading lady, player, starlet, Thespian

actual adjective definite, concrete, factual, physical, positive, real, substantial, tangible

actually adverb really, as a matter of fact, indeed, in fact, in point of fact, in reality, in truth, literally, truly

acumen noun judgment, astuteness, cleverness, ingenuity, insight, intelligence, perspicacity, shrewdness

acute adjective **1** serious, critical, crucial, dangerous, grave, important, severe, urgent **2** sharp, excruciating, fierce, intense, piercing, powerful, severe, shooting, violent **3** perceptive, astute, clever, insightful, keen, observant, sensitive, sharp, smart

acuteness noun **1** seriousness, gravity, importance, severity, urgency **2** perceptiveness, astuteness, cleverness, discrimination, insight, perspicacity, sharpness

adamant adjective determined, firm, fixed, obdurate, resolute, stubborn, unbending, uncompromising

adapt verb adjust, acclimatize, accommodate, alter, change, conform, convert, modify, remodel, tailor

adaptability noun flexibility, changeability, resilience, versatility

adaptable adjective flexible, adjustable, changeable, compliant, easy-going, plastic, pliant, resilient, versatile

adaptation noun
1 acclimatization, familiarization, naturalization **2** conversion, adjustment, alteration, change, modification, transformation, variation

add verb **1** count up, add up, compute, reckon, total, tot up **2** include, adjoin, affix, append, attach, augment, supplement

addendum noun addition, appendage, appendix, attachment, extension, extra, postscript, supplement

addict noun **1** junkie (informal), fiend (informal), freak (informal) **2** fan, adherent, buff (informal), devotee, enthusiast, follower, nut (slang)

addicted adjective hooked (slang), absorbed, accustomed, dedicated, dependent, devoted, habituated

addiction noun dependence, craving, enslavement, habit, obsession

addition noun **1** inclusion, adding, amplification, attachment, augmentation, enlargement, extension, increasing **2** extra, addendum, additive, appendage, appendix, extension, gain, increase, increment, supplement **3** counting up, adding up, computation, totalling, totting up **4 in addition (to)** as well (as),

additionally, also, besides, into the bargain, moreover, over and above, to boot, too

additional adjective extra, added, fresh, further, new, other, spare, supplementary

address noun **1** location, abode, dwelling, home, house, residence, situation, whereabouts **2** speech, discourse, dissertation, lecture, oration, sermon, talk ♦ verb **3** speak to, approach, greet, hail, talk to **4 address (oneself) to** concentrate on, apply (oneself), attend to, devote (oneself) to, engage in, focus on, take care of

add up verb count up, add, compute, count, reckon, total, tot up

adept adjective **1** skilful, able, accomplished, adroit, expert, practised, proficient, skilled, versed ♦ noun **2** expert, dab hand (Brit. informal), genius, hotshot (informal), master

adequacy noun sufficiency, capability, competence, fairness, suitability, tolerability

adequate adjective enough, competent, fair, satisfactory, sufficient, tolerable, up to scratch (informal)

adhere verb stick, attach, cleave, cling, fasten, fix, glue, hold fast, paste

adherent noun supporter, admirer, devotee, disciple, fan, follower, upholder

adhesive adjective **1** sticky, clinging, cohesive, gluey, glutinous, tenacious ♦ noun **2** glue, cement, gum, paste

adieu noun goodbye, farewell, leave-taking, parting, valediction

adjacent adjective next, adjoining, beside, bordering, cheek by jowl, close, near, neighbouring, next door, touching

adjoin verb connect, border, join, link, touch

adjoining adjective connecting, abutting, adjacent, bordering, neighbouring, next door, touching

adjourn verb postpone, defer, delay, discontinue, interrupt, put off, suspend

adjournment noun postponement, delay, discontinuation, interruption, putting off, recess, suspension

adjudicate verb judge, adjudge, arbitrate, decide, determine, mediate, referee, settle, umpire

adjudication noun judgment, arbitration, conclusion, decision, finding, pronouncement, ruling, settlement, verdict

adjust verb alter, accustom, adapt, make conform, modify

adjustable adjective alterable, adaptable, flexible, malleable, modifiable, movable

adjustment noun 1 alteration, adaptation, modification, redress, regulation, tuning 2 acclimatization, orientation, settling in

ad-lib verb 1 improvise, busk, extemporize, make up, speak off the cuff, wing it (informal)

administer verb 1 manage, conduct, control, direct, govern, handle, oversee, run, supervise 2 give, apply, dispense, impose, mete out, perform, provide

administration noun management, application, conduct, control, direction, government, running, supervision

administrative adjective managerial, directorial, executive, governmental, organizational, regulatory, supervisory

administrator noun manager, bureaucrat, executive, official, organizer, supervisor

admirable adjective excellent, commendable, exquisite, fine, laudable, praiseworthy, wonderful, worthy

admiration noun regard, amazement, appreciation, approval, esteem, praise, respect, wonder

admire verb 1 respect, appreciate, approve, esteem, look up to, praise, prize, think highly of, value 2 marvel at, appreciate, delight in, take pleasure in, wonder at

admirer noun 1 suitor, beau, boyfriend, lover, sweetheart, wooer 2 fan, devotee, disciple, enthusiast, follower, partisan, supporter

admissible adjective permissible, acceptable, allowable, passable, tolerable

admission noun 1 entrance, acceptance, access, admittance, entrée, entry, initiation, introduction 2 confession, acknowledgment, allowance, declaration, disclosure, divulgence, revelation

admit verb 1 confess, acknowledge, declare, disclose, divulge, own, reveal 2 allow, agree, grant, let, permit, recognize 3 let in, accept, allow, give access, initiate, introduce, receive, take in

admonish verb reprimand, berate, chide, rebuke, scold, slap on the wrist (informal)

adolescence noun 1 youth, boyhood, girlhood, minority, teens 2 youthfulness, childishness, immaturity

adolescent adjective 1 young, boyish, girlish, immature, juvenile, puerile, teenage, youthful ♦ noun 2 youth, juvenile, minor, teenager, youngster

adopt verb 1 foster, take in 2 choose, assume, espouse, follow, maintain, take up

adoption noun 1 fostering, adopting, taking in 2 choice, appropriation, assumption, embracing, endorsement, espousal, selection, taking up

adorable adjective lovable, appealing, attractive, charming, cute, dear, delightful, fetching, pleasing

adore verb love, admire, cherish, dote on, esteem, exalt, glorify, honour, idolize, revere, worship

adoring adjective loving, admiring, affectionate, devoted, doting, fond

adorn verb decorate, array, embellish, festoon

adornment noun decoration, accessory, embellishment, festoon, frill, frippery, ornament, supplement, trimming

adrift adjective 1 drifting, afloat, unanchored, unmoored 2 aimless, directionless, goalless, purposeless ♦ adverb 3 wrong, amiss, astray, off course

adroit adjective skilful, adept, clever, deft, dexterous, expert, masterful, neat, proficient, skilled

adulation noun worship, fawning, fulsome praise, servile flattery, sycophancy

adult noun 1 grown-up, grown or grown-up person (man or woman), person of mature age ♦ adjective 2 fully grown, full grown, fully developed, grown-up, mature, of age, ripe

advance verb 1 progress, come forward, go on, hasten, make inroads, proceed, speed 2 benefit, further, improve, prosper 3 suggest, offer, present, proffer, put forward, submit 4 lend, pay beforehand, supply on credit ♦ noun 5 progress, advancement, development, forward movement, headway, inroads, onward movement 6 improvement, breakthrough, gain, growth, progress, promotion, step 7 loan, credit, deposit, down payment, prepayment, retainer 8 advances overtures, approach, approaches, moves, proposals, proposition ♦ adjective 9 prior, beforehand, early, forward, in front 10 in advance beforehand, ahead, earlier, previously

advanced adjective foremost, ahead, avant-garde, forward, higher, leading, precocious, progressive

advancement noun promotion, betterment, gain, improvement, preferment, progress, rise

advantage noun benefit, ascendancy, dominance, good, help, lead, precedence, profit, superiority, sway

advantageous adjective **1** beneficial, convenient, expedient, helpful, of service, profitable, useful, valuable, worthwhile **2** superior, dominant, dominating, favourable

adventure noun escapade, enterprise, experience, exploit, incident, occurrence, undertaking, venture

adventurer noun **1** mercenary, charlatan, fortune-hunter, gambler, opportunist, rogue, speculator **2** hero, daredevil, heroine, knight-errant, traveller, voyager

adventurous adjective daring, bold, daredevil, enterprising, intrepid, reckless

adversary noun opponent, antagonist, competitor, contestant, enemy, foe, rival

adverse adjective unfavourable, contrary, detrimental, hostile, inopportune, negative, opposing

adversity noun hardship, affliction, bad luck, disaster, distress, hard times, misfortune, reverse, trouble

advert noun Brit. informal advertisement, ad (informal), announcement, blurb, commercial, notice, plug (informal), poster

advertise verb publicize,

announce, inform, make known, notify, plug (informal), promote, tout

advertisement noun advert (Brit. informal), ad (informal), announcement, blurb, commercial, notice, plug (informal), poster

advice noun guidance, counsel, help, opinion, recommendation, suggestion

advisability noun wisdom, appropriateness, aptness, desirability, expediency, fitness, propriety, prudence, suitability

advisable adjective wise, appropriate, desirable, expedient, fitting, politic, prudent, recommended, seemly, sensible

advise verb **1** recommend, admonish, caution, commend, counsel, prescribe, suggest, urge **2** notify, acquaint, apprise, inform, make known, report, tell, warn

adviser noun guide, aide, confidant, consultant, counsellor, helper, mentor, right-hand man

advisory adjective advising, consultative, counselling, helping, recommending

advocate verb **1** recommend, advise, argue for, campaign for, champion, commend, encourage, promote, propose, support, uphold ♦ noun **2** supporter, campaigner, champion, counsellor, defender, promoter, proponent, spokesman, upholder **3** Law lawyer, attorney, barrister, counsel, solicitor

affable adjective friendly, amiable,

amicable, approachable, congenial, cordial, courteous, genial, pleasant, sociable, urbane

affair noun 1 event, activity, business, episode, happening, incident, matter, occurrence 2 relationship, amour, intrigue, liaison, romance

affect[1] verb 1 influence, act on, alter, bear upon, change, concern, impinge upon, relate to 2 move, disturb, overcome, perturb, stir, touch, upset

affect[2] verb put on, adopt, aspire to, assume, contrive, feign, imitate, pretend, simulate

affectation noun pretence, act, artificiality, assumed manners, façade, insincerity, pose, pretentiousness, show

affected adjective pretended, artificial, contrived, feigned, insincere, mannered, phoney or phony (informal), put-on, unnatural

affecting adjective moving, pathetic, pitiful, poignant, sad, touching

affection noun fondness, attachment, care, feeling, goodwill, kindness, liking, love, tenderness, warmth

affectionate adjective fond, attached, caring, devoted, doting, friendly, kind, loving, tender, warm-hearted

affiliate verb join, ally, amalgamate, associate, band together, combine, incorporate, link, unite

affinity noun 1 attraction, fondness, inclination, leaning, liking, partiality, rapport,

sympathy 2 similarity, analogy, closeness, connection, correspondence, kinship, likeness, relationship, resemblance

affirm verb declare, assert, certify, confirm, maintain, pronounce, state, swear, testify

affirmation noun declaration, assertion, certification, confirmation, oath, pronouncement, statement, testimony

affirmative adjective agreeing, approving, assenting, concurring, confirming, consenting, corroborative, favourable, positive

afflict verb torment, distress, grieve, harass, hurt, oppress, pain, plague, trouble

affliction noun suffering, adversity, curse, disease, hardship, misfortune, ordeal, plague, scourge, torment, trial, trouble, woe

affluence noun wealth, abundance, fortune, opulence, plenty, prosperity, riches

affluent adjective wealthy, loaded (slang), moneyed, opulent, prosperous, rich, well-heeled (informal), well-off, well-to-do

afford verb 1 As in can afford spare, bear, manage, stand, sustain 2 give, offer, produce, provide, render, supply, yield

affordable adjective inexpensive, cheap, economical, low-cost, moderate, modest, reasonable

affront noun 1 insult, offence, outrage, provocation, slap in the face (informal), slight, slur ◆ verb

2 <u>offend</u>, anger, annoy, displease, insult, outrage, provoke, slight

aflame *adjective* <u>burning</u>, ablaze, alight, blazing, fiery, flaming, lit, on fire

afoot *adverb* <u>going on</u>, abroad, brewing, current, happening, in preparation, in progress, on the go (*informal*), up (*informal*)

afraid *adjective* 1 <u>scared</u>, apprehensive, cowardly, faint-hearted, fearful, frightened, nervous 2 <u>sorry</u>, regretful, unhappy

afresh *adverb* <u>again</u>, anew, newly, once again, once more, over again

after *adverb* <u>following</u>, afterwards, behind, below, later, subsequently, succeeding, thereafter

aftermath *noun* <u>effects</u>, aftereffects, consequences, end result, outcome, results, sequel, upshot, wake

again *adverb* 1 <u>once more</u>, afresh, anew, another time 2 <u>also</u>, besides, furthermore, in addition, moreover

against *preposition* 1 <u>beside</u>, abutting, facing, in contact with, on, opposite to, touching, upon 2 <u>opposed to</u>, anti (*informal*), averse to, hostile to, in defiance of, in opposition to, resisting, versus 3 <u>in preparation for</u>, in anticipation of, in expectation of, in provision for

age *noun* 1 <u>time</u>, date, day(s), duration, epoch, era, generation, lifetime, period, span 2 <u>old age</u>, advancing years, decline (*of life*), majority, maturity, senescence,

senility, seniority ♦ *verb* 3 <u>grow old</u>, decline, deteriorate, mature, mellow, ripen

aged *adjective* <u>old</u>, ancient, antiquated, antique, elderly, getting on, grey

agency *noun* 1 <u>business</u>, bureau, department, office, organization 2 *Old-fashioned* <u>medium</u>, activity, means, mechanism

agenda *noun* <u>list</u>, calendar, diary, plan, programme, schedule, timetable

agent *noun* 1 <u>representative</u>, envoy, go-between, negotiator, rep (*informal*), surrogate 2 <u>worker</u>, author, doer, mover, operator, performer 3 <u>force</u>, agency, cause, instrument, means, power, vehicle

aggravate *verb* 1 <u>make worse</u>, exacerbate, exaggerate, increase, inflame, intensify, magnify, worsen 2 *Informal* <u>annoy</u>, bother, get on one's nerves (*informal*), irritate, nettle, provoke

aggravation *noun* 1 <u>worsening</u>, exacerbation, exaggeration, heightening, increase, inflaming, intensification, magnification 2 *Informal* <u>annoyance</u>, exasperation, gall, grief (*informal*), hassle (*informal*), irritation, provocation

aggregate *noun* 1 <u>total</u>, accumulation, amount, body, bulk, collection, combination, mass, pile, sum, whole ♦ *adjective* 2 <u>total</u>, accumulated, collected, combined, composite, cumulative, mixed ♦ *verb* 3 <u>combine</u>, accumulate, amass, assemble, collect, heap, mix, pile

aggression *noun* 1 <u>hostility</u>,

antagonism, belligerence, destructiveness, pugnacity **2** attack, assault, injury, invasion, offensive, onslaught, raid

aggressive adjective **1** hostile, belligerent, destructive, offensive, pugnacious, quarrelsome **2** forceful, assertive, bold, dynamic, energetic, enterprising, militant, pushy (informal), vigorous

aggressor noun attacker, assailant, assaulter, invader

aggrieved adjective hurt, afflicted, distressed, disturbed, harmed, injured, unhappy, wronged

aghast adjective horrified, amazed, appalled, astonished, astounded, awestruck, confounded, shocked, startled, stunned

agile adjective **1** nimble, active, brisk, lithe, quick, sprightly, spry, supple, swift **2** acute, alert, bright (informal), clever, lively, quick-witted, sharp

agility noun nimbleness, litheness, liveliness, quickness, suppleness, swiftness

agitate verb **1** upset, disconcert, distract, excite, fluster, perturb, trouble, unnerve, worry **2** stir, beat, convulse, disturb, rouse, shake, toss

agitation noun **1** turmoil, clamour, commotion, confusion, disturbance, excitement, ferment, trouble, upheaval **2** turbulence, convulsion, disturbance, shaking, stirring, tossing

agitator noun troublemaker, agent provocateur, firebrand, instigator, rabble-rouser, revolutionary, stirrer (informal)

agog adjective eager, avid, curious, enthralled, enthusiastic, excited, expectant, impatient, in suspense

agonize verb suffer, be distressed, be in agony, be in anguish, go through the mill, labour, strain, struggle, worry

agony noun suffering, anguish, distress, misery, pain, throes, torment, torture

agree verb **1** consent, assent, be of the same opinion, comply, concur, see eye to eye **2** get on (together), coincide, conform, correspond, match, tally

agreeable adjective **1** pleasant, delightful, enjoyable, gratifying, likable or likeable, pleasing, satisfying, to one's taste **2** consenting, amenable, approving, complying, concurring, in accord, onside (informal), sympathetic, well-disposed, willing

agreement noun **1** assent, agreeing, compliance, concord, concurrence, consent, harmony, union, unison **2** correspondence, compatibility, conformity, congruity, consistency, similarity **3** contract, arrangement, bargain, covenant, deal (informal), pact, settlement, treaty, understanding

agricultural adjective farming, agrarian, country, rural, rustic

agriculture noun farming, cultivation, culture, husbandry, tillage

aground adverb beached, ashore, foundered, grounded, high and dry, on the rocks, stranded, stuck

ahead adverb in front, at an advantage, at the head, before, in advance, in the lead, leading, to the fore, winning

aid noun 1 help, assistance, benefit, encouragement, favour, promotion, relief, service, support ◆ verb 2 help, assist, encourage, favour, promote, serve, subsidize, support, sustain

aide noun assistant, attendant, helper, right-hand man, second, supporter

ailing adjective ill, indisposed, infirm, poorly, sick, under the weather (informal), unwell, weak

ailment noun illness, affliction, complaint, disease, disorder, infirmity, malady, sickness

aim verb 1 intend, attempt, endeavour, mean, plan, point, propose, seek, set one's sights on, strive, try ◆ noun 2 intention, ambition, aspiration, desire, goal, objective, plan, purpose, target

aimless adjective purposeless, directionless, pointless, random, stray

air noun 1 atmosphere, heavens, sky 2 wind, breeze, draught, zephyr 3 manner, appearance, atmosphere, aura, demeanour, impression, look, mood 4 tune, aria, lay, melody, song ◆ verb 5 publicize, circulate, display, exhibit, express, give vent to, make known, make public, reveal, voice 6 ventilate, aerate, expose, freshen

airborne adjective flying, floating, gliding, hovering, in flight, in the air, on the wing

airing noun 1 ventilation, aeration, drying, freshening 2 exposure, circulation, display, dissemination, expression, publicity, utterance, vent

airless adjective stuffy, close, heavy, muggy, oppressive, stifling, suffocating, sultry

airs plural noun affectation, arrogance, haughtiness, hauteur, pomposity, pretensions, superciliousness, swank (informal)

airy adjective 1 well-ventilated, fresh, light, open, spacious, uncluttered 2 light-hearted, blithe, cheerful, high-spirited, jaunty, lively, sprightly

aisle noun passageway, alley, corridor, gangway, lane, passage, path

alacrity noun eagerness, alertness, enthusiasm, promptness, quickness, readiness, speed, willingness, zeal

alarm noun 1 fear, anxiety, apprehension, consternation, fright, nervousness, panic, scare, trepidation 2 danger signal, alarm bell, alert, bell, distress signal, hooter, siren, warning ◆ verb 3 frighten, daunt, dismay, distress, give (someone) a turn (informal), panic, scare, startle, unnerve

alarming adjective frightening, daunting, distressing, disturbing, scaring, shocking, startling, unnerving

alcoholic noun 1 drunkard, dipsomaniac, drinker, drunk, inebriate, tippler, toper, wino (informal) ◆ adjective 2 intoxicating, brewed, distilled, fermented, hard, strong

alcove noun 1 recess, bay, compartment, corner, cubbyhole, cubicle, niche, nook

alert adjective 1 watchful, attentive, awake, circumspect, heedful, observant, on guard, on one's toes, on the lookout, vigilant, wide-awake ♦ noun 2 warning, alarm, signal, siren ♦ verb 3 warn, alarm, forewarn, inform, notify, signal

alertness noun watchfulness, attentiveness, heedfulness, liveliness, vigilance

alias adverb 1 also known as, also called, otherwise, otherwise known as ♦ noun 2 pseudonym, assumed name, nom de guerre, nom de plume, pen name, stage name

alibi noun excuse, defence, explanation, justification, plea, pretext, reason

alien adjective 1 foreign, exotic, incongruous, strange, unfamiliar ♦ noun 2 foreigner, newcomer, outsider, stranger

alienate verb set against, disaffect, estrange, make unfriendly, turn away

alienation noun setting against, disaffection, estrangement, remoteness, separation, turning away

alight¹ verb 1 get off, descend, disembark, dismount, get down 2 land, come down, come to rest, descend, light, perch, settle, touch down

alight² adjective 1 on fire, ablaze, aflame, blazing, burning, fiery, flaming, lighted, lit 2 lit up, bright, brilliant, illuminated, shining

align verb 1 ally, affiliate, agree, associate, cooperate, join, side, sympathize 2 line up, even up, order, range, regulate, straighten

alignment noun 1 alliance, affiliation, agreement, association, cooperation, sympathy, union 2 lining up, adjustment, arrangement, evening up, order, straightening up

alike adjective 1 similar, akin, analogous, corresponding, identical, of a piece, parallel, resembling, the same ♦ adverb 2 similarly, analogously, correspondingly, equally, evenly, identically, uniformly

alive adjective 1 living, animate, breathing, in the land of the living (informal), subsisting 2 in existence, active, existing, extant, functioning, in force, operative 3 lively, active, alert, animated, energetic, full of life, vital, vivacious

all adjective 1 the whole of, every bit of, the complete, the entire, the sum of 2 every, each and every, every one of, every single 3 complete, entire, full, greatest, perfect, total, utter ♦ adverb 4 completely, altogether, entirely, fully, totally, utterly, wholly ♦ noun 5 whole amount, aggregate, entirety, everything, sum total, total, totality, utmost

allegation noun claim, accusation, affirmation, assertion, charge, declaration, statement

allege verb claim, affirm, assert, charge, declare, maintain, state

alleged adjective 1 stated,

affirmed, asserted, declared, described, designated
2 <u>supposed</u>, doubtful, dubious, ostensible, professed, purported, so-called, unproved

allegiance noun <u>loyalty</u>, constancy, devotion, faithfulness, fidelity, obedience

allegorical adjective <u>symbolic</u>, emblematic, figurative, symbolizing

allegory noun <u>symbol</u>, fable, myth, parable, story, symbolism, tale

allergic adjective <u>sensitive</u>, affected by, hypersensitive, susceptible

allergy noun <u>sensitivity</u>, antipathy, hypersensitivity, susceptibility

alleviate verb <u>ease</u>, allay, lessen, lighten, moderate, reduce, relieve, soothe

alley noun <u>passage</u>, alleyway, backstreet, lane, passageway, pathway, walk

alliance noun <u>union</u>, affiliation, agreement, association, coalition, combination, confederation, connection, federation, league, marriage, pact, partnership, treaty

allied adjective <u>united</u>, affiliated, associated, combined, connected, in league, linked, related

allocate verb <u>assign</u>, allot, allow, apportion, budget, designate, earmark, mete, set aside, share out

allocation noun <u>assignment</u>, allotment, allowance, lot, portion, quota, ration, share

allot verb <u>assign</u>, allocate, apportion, budget, designate, earmark, mete, set aside, share out

allotment noun **1** <u>plot</u>, kitchen garden, patch, tract
2 <u>assignment</u>, allocation, allowance, grant, portion, quota, ration, share, stint

all-out adjective <u>total</u>, complete, exhaustive, full, full-scale, maximum, thoroughgoing, undivided, unremitting, unrestrained

allow verb **1** <u>permit</u>, approve, authorize, enable, endure, let, sanction, stand, suffer, tolerate
2 <u>give</u>, allocate, allot, assign, grant, provide, set aside, spare
3 <u>acknowledge</u>, admit, concede, confess, grant, own

allowable adjective <u>permissible</u>, acceptable, admissible, all right, appropriate, suitable, tolerable

allowance noun **1** <u>portion</u>, allocation, amount, grant, lot, quota, ration, share, stint
2 <u>concession</u>, deduction, discount, rebate, reduction

allow for verb <u>take into account</u>, consider, make allowances for, make concessions for, make provision for, plan for, provide for, take into consideration

alloy noun **1** <u>mixture</u>, admixture, amalgam, blend, combination, composite, compound, hybrid
♦ verb **2** <u>mix</u>, amalgamate, blend, combine, compound, fuse

all right adjective **1** <u>satisfactory</u>, acceptable, adequate, average, fair, O.K. or okay (informal), standard, up to scratch (informal)
2 <u>O.K. or okay</u> (informal),

healthy, safe, sound, unharmed, uninjured, well, whole

allude verb <u>refer</u>, hint, imply, intimate, mention, suggest, touch upon

allure noun **1** <u>attractiveness</u>, appeal, attraction, charm, enchantment, enticement, glamour, lure, persuasion, seductiveness, temptation ♦ verb **2** <u>attract</u>, captivate, charm, enchant, entice, lure, persuade, seduce, tempt, win over

alluring adjective <u>attractive</u>, beguiling, captivating, come-hither, fetching, glamorous, seductive, tempting

allusion noun <u>reference</u>, casual remark, hint, implication, innuendo, insinuation, intimation, mention, suggestion

ally noun **1** <u>partner</u>, accomplice, associate, collaborator, colleague, friend, helper ♦ verb **2** <u>unite</u>, associate, collaborate, combine, join, join forces, unify

almighty adjective **1** <u>all-powerful</u>, absolute, invincible, omnipotent, supreme, unlimited **2** Informal <u>great</u>, enormous, excessive, intense, loud, severe, terrible

almost adverb <u>nearly</u>, about, approximately, close to, just about, not quite, on the brink of, practically, virtually

alone adjective <u>by oneself</u>, apart, detached, isolated, lonely, only, on one's tod (slang), separate, single, solitary, unaccompanied

aloof adjective <u>distant</u>, detached, haughty, remote, standoffish, supercilious, unapproachable, unfriendly

aloud adverb <u>out loud</u>, audibly, clearly, distinctly, intelligibly, plainly

already adverb <u>before now</u>, at present, before, by now, by then, even now, heretofore, just now, previously

also adverb <u>too</u>, additionally, and, as well, besides, further, furthermore, in addition, into the bargain, moreover, to boot

alter verb <u>change</u>, adapt, adjust, amend, convert, modify, reform, revise, transform, turn, vary

alteration noun <u>change</u>, adaptation, adjustment, amendment, conversion, difference, modification, reformation, revision, transformation, variation

alternate verb **1** <u>change</u>, act reciprocally, fluctuate, interchange, oscillate, rotate, substitute, take turns ♦ adjective **2** <u>every other</u>, alternating, every second, interchanging, rotating

alternative noun **1** <u>choice</u>, option, other (of two), preference, recourse, selection, substitute ♦ adjective **2** <u>different</u>, alternate, another, other, second, substitute

alternatively adverb <u>or</u>, as an alternative, if not, instead, on the other hand, otherwise

although conjunction <u>though</u>, albeit, despite the fact that, even if, even though, notwithstanding, while

altogether adverb **1** <u>completely</u>, absolutely, fully, perfectly, quite, thoroughly, totally, utterly, wholly **2** <u>on the whole</u>, all in all, all things considered, as a whole,

altruistic *adjective* selfless, benevolent, charitable, generous, humanitarian, philanthropic, public-spirited, self-sacrificing, unselfish

always *adverb* continually, consistently, constantly, eternally, evermore, every time, forever, invariably, perpetually, repeatedly, without exception

amalgamate *verb* combine, ally, blend, fuse, incorporate, integrate, merge, mingle, unite

amalgamation *noun* combination, blend, coalition, compound, fusion, joining, merger, mixture, union

amass *verb* collect, accumulate, assemble, compile, gather, hoard, pile up

amateur *noun* nonprofessional, dabbler, dilettante, layman

amateurish *adjective* unprofessional, amateur, bungling, clumsy, crude, inexpert, unaccomplished

amaze *verb* astonish, alarm, astound, bewilder, dumbfound, shock, stagger, startle, stun, surprise

amazement *noun* astonishment, admiration, bewilderment, confusion, perplexity, shock, surprise, wonder

amazing *adjective* astonishing, astounding, breathtaking, eye-opening, overwhelming, staggering, startling, stunning, surprising

collectively, generally, in general **3** in total, all told, everything included, in all, in sum, taken together

ambassador *noun* representative, agent, consul, deputy, diplomat, envoy, legate, minister

ambiguity *noun* vagueness, doubt, dubiousness, equivocation, obscurity, uncertainty

ambiguous *adjective* unclear, dubious, enigmatic, equivocal, inconclusive, indefinite, indeterminate, obscure, vague

ambition *noun* **1** enterprise, aspiration, desire, drive, eagerness, longing, striving, yearning, zeal **2** goal, aim, aspiration, desire, dream, hope, intent, objective, purpose, wish

ambitious *adjective* enterprising, aspiring, avid, eager, hopeful, intent, purposeful, striving, zealous

ambivalent *adjective* undecided, contradictory, doubtful, equivocal, in two minds, uncertain, wavering

amble *verb* stroll, dawdle, meander, mosey (*informal*), ramble, saunter, walk, wander

ambush *noun* **1** trap, lying in wait, waylaying ♦ *verb* **2** trap, attack, bushwhack (*U.S.*), ensnare, surprise, waylay

amenable *adjective* receptive, able to be influenced, acquiescent, agreeable, open, persuadable, responsive, susceptible

amend *verb* change, alter, correct, fix, improve, mend, modify, reform, remedy, repair, revise

amendment *noun* **1** change,

alteration, correction, emendation, improvement, modification, reform, remedy, repair, revision **2** alteration, addendum, addition, attachment, clarification

amends plural noun As in **make amends for** compensation, atonement, recompense, redress, reparation, restitution, satisfaction

amenity noun facility, advantage, comfort, convenience, service

amiable adjective pleasant, affable, agreeable, charming, congenial, engaging, friendly, genial, likable or likeable, lovable

amicable adjective friendly, amiable, civil, cordial, courteous, harmonious, neighbourly, peaceful, sociable

amid, amidst preposition in the middle of, among, amongst, in the midst of, in the thick of, surrounded by

amiss adverb **1** wrongly, erroneously, improperly, inappropriately, incorrectly, mistakenly, unsuitably **2** As in **take (something) amiss** as an insult, as offensive, out of turn, wrongly ♦ adjective **3** wrong, awry, faulty, incorrect, mistaken, untoward

ammunition noun munitions, armaments, explosives, powder, rounds, shells, shot

amnesty noun general pardon, absolution, dispensation, forgiveness, immunity, remission (of penalty), reprieve

amok, amuck adverb As in **run amok** madly, berserk, destructively, ferociously, in a frenzy, murderously, savagely,

uncontrollably, violently, wildly

among, amongst preposition **1** in the midst of, amid, amidst, in the middle of, in the thick of, surrounded by, together with, with **2** in the group of, in the class of, in the company of, in the number of, out of **3** to each of, between

amorous adjective loving, erotic, impassioned, in love, lustful, passionate, tender

amount noun quantity, expanse, extent, magnitude, mass, measure, number, supply, volume

amount to verb add up to, become, come to, develop into, equal, mean, total

ample adjective plenty, abundant, bountiful, copious, expansive, extensive, full, generous, lavish, plentiful, profuse

amplify verb **1** explain, develop, elaborate, enlarge, expand, flesh out, go into detail **2** increase, enlarge, expand, extend, heighten, intensify, magnify, strengthen, widen

amply adverb fully, abundantly, completely, copiously, generously, profusely, richly

amputate verb cut off, curtail, lop, remove, separate, sever, truncate

amuck see AMOK

amuse verb entertain, charm, cheer, delight, interest, please, tickle

amusement noun **1** entertainment, cheer, enjoyment, fun, merriment, mirth, pleasure **2** entertainment, diversion, game, hobby, joke, pastime, recreation, sport

amusing *adjective* <u>funny</u>, comical, droll, enjoyable, entertaining, humorous, interesting, witty

anaemic *adjective* <u>pale</u>, ashen, colourless, feeble, pallid, sickly, wan, weak

anaesthetic *noun* **1** <u>painkiller</u>, analgesic, anodyne, narcotic, opiate, sedative, soporific
♦ *adjective* **2** <u>pain-killing</u>, analgesic, anodyne, deadening, dulling, numbing, sedative, soporific

analogy *noun* <u>similarity</u>, comparison, correlation, correspondence, likeness, parallel, relation, resemblance

analyse *verb* **1** <u>examine</u>, evaluate, investigate, research, test, work over **2** <u>break down</u>, dissect, divide, resolve, separate, think through

analysis *noun* <u>examination</u>, breakdown, dissection, inquiry, investigation, scrutiny, sifting, test

analytic, analytical *adjective* <u>rational</u>, inquiring, inquisitive, investigative, logical, organized, problem-solving, systematic

anarchic *adjective* <u>lawless</u>, chaotic, disorganized, rebellious, riotous, ungoverned

anarchist *noun* <u>revolutionary</u>, insurgent, nihilist, rebel, terrorist

anarchy *noun* <u>lawlessness</u>, chaos, confusion, disorder, disorganization, revolution, riot

anatomy *noun* **1** <u>examination</u>, analysis, dissection, division, inquiry, investigation, study

2 <u>structure</u>, build, composition, frame, framework, make-up

ancestor *noun* <u>forefather</u>, forebear, forerunner, precursor, predecessor

ancient *adjective* <u>old</u>, aged, antique, archaic, old-fashioned, primeval, primordial, timeworn

ancillary *adjective* <u>supplementary</u>, additional, auxiliary, extra, secondary, subordinate, subsidiary, supporting

and *conjunction* <u>also</u>, along with, as well as, furthermore, in addition to, including, moreover, plus, together with

anecdote *noun* <u>story</u>, reminiscence, short story, sketch, tale, urban legend, yarn

angel *noun* **1** <u>divine messenger</u>, archangel, cherub, seraph **2** *Informal* <u>dear</u>, beauty, darling, gem, jewel, paragon, saint, treasure

angelic *adjective* **1** <u>pure</u>, adorable, beautiful, entrancing, lovely, saintly, virtuous **2** <u>heavenly</u>, celestial, cherubic, ethereal, seraphic

anger *noun* **1** <u>rage</u>, annoyance, displeasure, exasperation, fury, ire, outrage, resentment, temper, wrath ♦ *verb* **2** <u>madden</u>, annoy, displease, enrage, exasperate, gall, incense, infuriate, outrage, rile, vex

angle[1] *noun* **1** <u>intersection</u>, bend, corner, crook, edge, elbow, nook, point **2** <u>point of view</u>, approach, aspect, outlook, perspective, position, side, slant, standpoint, viewpoint

angle[2] *verb* <u>fish</u>, cast

angry *adjective* furious, annoyed, cross, displeased, enraged, exasperated, incensed, infuriated, irate, mad (*informal*), outraged, resentful

angst *noun* anxiety, apprehension, unease, worry

anguish *noun* suffering, agony, distress, grief, heartache, misery, pain, sorrow, torment, woe

animal *noun* 1 creature, beast, brute 2 *Applied to a person* brute, barbarian, beast, monster, savage, wild man ♦ *adjective* 3 physical, bestial, bodily, brutish, carnal, gross, sensual

animate *verb* 1 enliven, energize, excite, fire, inspire, invigorate, kindle, move, stimulate ♦ *adjective* 2 living, alive, alive and kicking, breathing, live, moving

animated *adjective* lively, ebullient, energetic, enthusiastic, excited, passionate, spirited, vivacious

animation *noun* liveliness, ebullience, energy, enthusiasm, excitement, fervour, passion, spirit, verve, vivacity, zest

animosity *noun* hostility, acrimony, antipathy, bitterness, enmity, hatred, ill will, malevolence, malice, rancour, resentment

annals *plural noun* records, accounts, archives, chronicles, history

annex *verb* 1 seize, acquire, appropriate, conquer, occupy, take over 2 join, add, adjoin, attach, connect, fasten

annihilate *verb* destroy, abolish, eradicate, exterminate, extinguish, obliterate, wipe out

announce *verb* make known, advertise, broadcast, declare, disclose, proclaim, report, reveal, tell

announcement *noun* statement, advertisement, broadcast, bulletin, communiqué, declaration, proclamation, report, revelation

announcer *noun* presenter, broadcaster, commentator, master of ceremonies, newscaster, newsreader, reporter

annoy *verb* irritate, anger, bother, displease, disturb, exasperate, get on one's nerves (*informal*), hassle (*informal*), madden, molest, pester, plague, trouble, vex

annoyance *noun* 1 irritation, anger, bother, hassle (*informal*), nuisance, trouble 2 nuisance, bore, bother, drag (*informal*), pain (*informal*)

annoying *adjective* irritating, disturbing, exasperating, maddening, troublesome

annual *adjective* yearly, once a year, yearlong

annually *adverb* yearly, by the year, once a year, per annum, per year

annul *verb* invalidate, abolish, cancel, declare or render null and void, negate, nullify, repeal, retract

anoint *verb* consecrate, bless, hallow, sanctify

anomalous *adjective* unusual, abnormal, eccentric, exceptional, incongruous, inconsistent, irregular, odd, peculiar

anomaly noun irregularity, abnormality, eccentricity, exception, incongruity, inconsistency, oddity, peculiarity

anonymous adjective unnamed, incognito, nameless, unacknowledged, uncredited, unidentified, unknown, unsigned

answer verb 1 reply, explain, react, resolve, respond, retort, return, solve ♦ noun 2 reply, comeback, defence, explanation, reaction, rejoinder, response, retort, return, riposte, solution

answerable adjective, usually with **for** or **to** responsible, accountable, amenable, chargeable, liable, subject, to blame

answer for verb be responsible for, be accountable for, be answerable for, be chargeable for, be liable for, be to blame for

antagonism noun hostility, antipathy, conflict, discord, dissension, friction, opposition, rivalry

antagonist noun opponent, adversary, competitor, contender, enemy, foe, rival

antagonistic adjective hostile, at odds, at variance, conflicting, incompatible, in dispute, opposed, unfriendly

antagonize verb annoy, anger, get on one's nerves (informal), hassle (informal), irritate, offend

anthem noun 1 hymn, canticle, carol, chant, chorale, psalm 2 song of praise, paean

anthology noun collection, compendium, compilation,

miscellany, selection, treasury

anticipate verb expect, await, foresee, foretell, hope for, look forward to, predict, prepare for

anticipation noun expectation, expectancy, foresight, forethought, premonition, prescience

anticlimax noun disappointment, bathos, comedown (informal), letdown

antics plural noun clowning, escapades, horseplay, mischief, playfulness, pranks, tomfoolery, tricks

antidote noun cure, countermeasure, remedy

antipathy noun hostility, aversion, bad blood, dislike, enmity, hatred, ill will

antiquated adjective obsolete, antique, archaic, dated, old-fashioned, out-of-date, passé

antique noun 1 period piece, bygone, heirloom, relic ♦ adjective 2 vintage, antiquarian, classic, olden 3 old-fashioned, archaic, obsolete, outdated

antiquity noun 1 old age, age, ancientness, elderliness, oldness 2 distant past, ancient times, olden days, time immemorial

antiseptic adjective 1 hygienic, clean, germ-free, pure, sanitary, sterile, uncontaminated ♦ noun 2 disinfectant, germicide, purifier

antisocial adjective 1 unsociable, alienated, misanthropic, reserved, retiring, uncommunicative, unfriendly, withdrawn 2 disruptive, antagonistic, belligerent, disorderly, hostile, menacing, rebellious, uncooperative

antithesis noun <u>opposite</u>, contrary, contrast, converse, inverse, reverse

anxiety noun <u>uneasiness</u>, angst, apprehension, concern, foreboding, misgiving, nervousness, tension, trepidation, worry

anxious adjective 1 <u>uneasy</u>, apprehensive, concerned, fearful, in suspense, nervous, on tenterhooks, tense, troubled, worried 2 <u>eager</u>, desirous, impatient, intent, itching, keen, yearning

apart adverb 1 <u>to pieces</u>, asunder, in bits, in pieces, to bits 2 <u>separate</u>, alone, aside, away, by oneself, isolated, to one side 3 **apart from** <u>except for</u>, aside from, besides, but, excluding, not counting, other than, save

apartment noun <u>room</u>, accommodation, flat, living quarters, penthouse, quarters, rooms, suite

apathetic adjective <u>uninterested</u>, cool, indifferent, passive, phlegmatic, unconcerned

apathy noun <u>lack of interest</u>, coolness, indifference, inertia, nonchalance, passivity, torpor, unconcern

apex noun <u>highest point</u>, crest, crown, culmination, peak, pinnacle, point, summit, top

apiece adverb <u>each</u>, for each, from each, individually, respectively, separately, to each

aplomb noun <u>self-possession</u>, calmness, composure, confidence, level-headedness, poise, sang-froid, self-assurance, self-confidence

apocryphal adjective <u>dubious</u>, doubtful, legendary, mythical, questionable, unauthenticated, unsubstantiated

apologetic adjective <u>regretful</u>, contrite, penitent, remorseful, rueful, sorry

apologize verb <u>say sorry</u>, ask forgiveness, beg pardon, express regret

apology noun 1 <u>defence</u>, acknowledgment, confession, excuse, explanation, justification, plea 2 *As in* **an apology for** <u>mockery</u>, caricature, excuse, imitation, travesty

apostle noun 1 <u>evangelist</u>, herald, messenger, missionary, preacher 2 <u>supporter</u>, advocate, champion, pioneer, propagandist, proponent

apotheosis noun <u>deification</u>, elevation, exaltation, glorification, idealization, idolization

appal verb <u>horrify</u>, alarm, daunt, dishearten, dismay, frighten, outrage, shock, unnerve

appalling adjective <u>horrifying</u>, alarming, awful, daunting, dreadful, fearful, frightful, horrible, shocking, terrifying

apparatus noun 1 <u>equipment</u>, appliance, contraption (*informal*), device, gear, machinery, mechanism, tackle, tools 2 <u>organization</u>, bureaucracy, chain of command, hierarchy, network, setup (*informal*), structure, system

apparent adjective 1 <u>obvious</u>,

discernible, distinct, evident, manifest, marked, unmistakable, visible 2 seeming, ostensible, outward, superficial

apparently adverb it appears that, it seems that, on the face of it, ostensibly, outwardly, seemingly, superficially

apparition noun ghost, chimera, phantom, spectre, spirit, wraith

appeal verb 1 plead, ask, beg, call upon, entreat, pray, request 2 attract, allure, charm, entice, fascinate, interest, please, tempt ♦ noun 3 plea, application, entreaty, petition, prayer, request, supplication 4 attraction, allure, beauty, charm, fascination

appealing adjective attractive, alluring, charming, desirable, engaging, winsome

appear verb 1 come into view, be present, come out, come to light, crop up (informal), emerge, occur, show up (informal), surface, turn up 2 look (like or as if), occur, seem, strike one as

appearance noun 1 arrival, coming, emergence, introduction, presence 2 look, demeanour, expression, figure, form, looks, manner, mien (literary) 3 impression, front, guise, illusion, image, outward show, pretence, semblance

appease verb 1 pacify, calm, conciliate, mollify, placate, quiet, satisfy, soothe 2 ease, allay, alleviate, calm, relieve, soothe

appeasement noun 1 pacification, accommodation, compromise, concession, conciliation, mollification,

placation 2 easing, alleviation, lessening, relieving, soothing

appendage noun attachment, accessory, addition, supplement

appendix noun supplement, addendum, addition, adjunct, appendage, postscript

appetite noun desire, craving, demand, hunger, liking, longing, passion, relish, stomach, taste, yearning

appetizing adjective delicious, appealing, inviting, mouthwatering, palatable, succulent, tasty, tempting

applaud verb clap, acclaim, approve, cheer, commend, compliment, encourage, extol, praise

applause noun ovation, accolade, approval, big hand, cheers, clapping, hand, praise

appliance noun device, apparatus, gadget, implement, instrument, machine, mechanism, tool

applicable adjective appropriate, apt, fitting, pertinent, relevant, suitable, useful

applicant noun candidate, claimant, inquirer

application noun 1 request, appeal, claim, inquiry, petition, requisition 2 effort, commitment, dedication, diligence, hard work, industry, perseverance

apply verb 1 request, appeal, claim, inquire, petition, put in, requisition 2 use, bring to bear, carry out, employ, exercise, exert, implement, practise, utilize 3 put on, cover with, lay on, paint, place, smear, spread on **4** be relevant, be applicable, be appropriate, bear upon, be fitting, fit, pertain, refer, relate **5** apply oneself try, be diligent, buckle down (*informal*), commit oneself, concentrate, dedicate oneself, devote oneself, persevere, work hard

appoint verb **1** assign, choose, commission, delegate, elect, name, nominate, select **2** decide, allot, arrange, assign, choose, designate, establish, fix, set **3** equip, fit out, furnish, provide, supply

appointed adjective **1** assigned, chosen, delegated, elected, named, nominated, selected **2** decided, allotted, arranged, assigned, chosen, designated, established, fixed, set **3** equipped, fitted out, furnished, provided, supplied

appointment noun **1** meeting, arrangement, assignation, date, engagement, interview, rendezvous **2** selection, assignment, choice, election, naming, nomination **3** job, assignment, office, place, position, post, situation **4** appointments fittings, fixtures, furnishings, gear, outfit, paraphernalia, trappings

apportion verb divide, allocate, allot, assign, dispense, distribute, dole out, ration out, share

apportionment noun division, allocation, allotment, assignment, dispensing, distribution, doling out, rationing out, sharing

apposite adjective appropriate,

applicable, apt, fitting, pertinent, relevant, suitable, to the point

appraisal noun assessment, estimate, estimation, evaluation, judgment, opinion

appraise verb assess, estimate, evaluate, gauge, judge, rate, review, value

appreciable adjective significant, considerable, definite, discernible, evident, marked, noticeable, obvious, pronounced, substantial

appreciate verb **1** value, admire, enjoy, like, prize, rate highly, respect, treasure **2** be aware of, perceive, realize, recognize, sympathize with, take account of, understand **3** be grateful for, be appreciative, be indebted, be obliged, be thankful for, give thanks for **4** increase, enhance, gain, grow, improve, rise

appreciation noun **1** gratitude, acknowledgment, gratefulness, indebtedness, obligation, thankfulness, thanks **2** awareness, admiration, comprehension, enjoyment, perception, realization, recognition, sensitivity, sympathy, understanding **3** increase, enhancement, gain, growth, improvement, rise

appreciative adjective **1** grateful, beholden, indebted, obliged, thankful **2** aware, admiring, enthusiastic, respectful, responsive, sensitive, sympathetic, understanding

apprehend verb **1** arrest, capture, catch, nick (*slang, chiefly Brit.*), seize, take prisoner **2** understand, comprehend, conceive, get the picture, grasp, perceive, realize, recognize

apprehension noun 1 <u>anxiety</u>, alarm, concern, dread, fear, foreboding, suspicion, trepidation, worry 2 <u>arrest</u>, capture, catching, seizure, taking 3 <u>awareness</u>, comprehension, grasp, perception, understanding

apprehensive adjective <u>anxious</u>, concerned, foreboding, nervous, uneasy, worried

apprentice noun <u>trainee</u>, beginner, learner, novice, probationer, pupil, student

approach verb 1 <u>move towards</u>, come close, come near, draw near, near, reach 2 <u>make a proposal to</u>, appeal to, apply to, make overtures to, sound out 3 <u>set about</u>, begin work on, commence, embark on, enter upon, make a start, undertake ◆ noun 4 <u>coming</u>, advance, arrival, drawing near, nearing 5 often plural <u>proposal</u>, advance, appeal, application, invitation, offer, overture, proposition 6 <u>access</u>, avenue, entrance, passage, road, way 7 <u>way</u>, manner, means, method, style, technique 8 <u>likeness</u>, approximation, semblance

approachable adjective 1 <u>friendly</u>, affable, congenial, cordial, open, sociable 2 <u>accessible</u>, attainable, reachable

appropriate adjective 1 <u>suitable</u>, apt, befitting, fitting, pertinent, relevant, to the point, well-suited ◆ verb 2 <u>seize</u>, commandeer, confiscate, impound, take possession of, usurp 3 <u>steal</u>, embezzle, filch, misappropriate,

pilfer, pocket 4 <u>set aside</u>, allocate, allot, apportion, assign, devote, earmark

approval noun 1 <u>consent</u>, agreement, assent, authorization, blessing, endorsement, permission, recommendation, sanction 2 <u>favour</u>, acclaim, admiration, applause, appreciation, esteem, good opinion, praise, respect

approve verb 1 <u>favour</u>, admire, commend, have a good opinion of, like, praise, regard highly, respect 2 <u>agree to</u>, allow, assent to, authorize, consent to, endorse, pass, permit, recommend, sanction

approximate adjective 1 <u>close</u>, near 2 <u>rough</u>, estimated, inexact, loose ◆ verb 3 <u>come close</u>, approach, border on, come near, reach, resemble, touch, verge on

approximately adverb <u>almost</u>, about, around, circa (used with dates), close to, in the region of, just about, more or less, nearly, roughly

approximation noun <u>guess</u>, conjecture, estimate, estimation, guesswork, rough calculation, rough idea

apron noun <u>pinny</u> (informal), pinafore

apt adjective 1 <u>inclined</u>, disposed, given, liable, likely, of a mind, prone, ready 2 <u>appropriate</u>, fitting, pertinent, relevant, suitable, to the point 3 <u>gifted</u>, clever, quick, sharp, smart, talented

aptitude noun 1 <u>tendency</u>, inclination, leaning, predilection, proclivity, propensity 2 <u>gift</u>, ability, capability, faculty, intelligence, proficiency, talent

arable adjective <u>productive</u>, farmable, fertile, fruitful

arbiter noun 1 <u>judge</u>, adjudicator, arbitrator, referee, umpire 2 <u>authority</u>, controller, dictator, expert, governor, lord, master, pundit, ruler

arbitrary adjective <u>random</u>, capricious, chance, erratic, inconsistent, personal, subjective, whimsical

arbitrate verb <u>settle</u>, adjudicate, decide, determine, judge, mediate, pass judgment, referee, umpire

arbitration noun <u>settlement</u>, adjudication, decision, determination, judgment

arbitrator noun <u>judge</u>, adjudicator, arbiter, referee, umpire

arc noun <u>curve</u>, arch, bend, bow, crescent, half-moon

arcade noun <u>gallery</u>, cloister, colonnade, portico

arcane adjective <u>mysterious</u>, esoteric, hidden, occult, recondite, secret

arch[1] noun 1 <u>curve</u>, archway, dome, span, vault 2 <u>curve</u>, arc, bend, bow, hump, semicircle
♦ verb 3 <u>curve</u>, arc, bend, bow, bridge, span

arch[2] adjective <u>playful</u>, frolicsome, mischievous, pert, roguish, saucy, sly, waggish

archaic adjective 1 <u>old</u>, ancient, antique, bygone, olden (archaic), primitive 2 <u>old-fashioned</u>, antiquated, behind the times,

obsolete, outmoded, out of date, passé

archetypal adjective 1 <u>typical</u>, classic, ideal, model, standard 2 <u>original</u>, prototypic or prototypical

archetype noun 1 <u>standard</u>, model, paradigm, pattern, prime example 2 <u>original</u>, prototype

architect noun <u>designer</u>, master builder, planner

architecture noun 1 <u>design</u>, building, construction, planning 2 <u>structure</u>, construction, design, framework, make-up, style

archive noun 1 <u>record office</u>, museum, registry, repository 2 **archives** <u>records</u>, annals, chronicles, documents, papers, rolls

arctic adjective Informal <u>freezing</u>, chilly, cold, frigid, frozen, glacial, icy

Arctic adjective <u>polar</u>, far-northern, hyperborean

ardent adjective 1 <u>passionate</u>, amorous, hot-blooded, impassioned, intense, lusty 2 <u>enthusiastic</u>, avid, eager, keen, zealous

ardour noun 1 <u>passion</u>, fervour, intensity, spirit, vehemence, warmth 2 <u>enthusiasm</u>, avidity, eagerness, keenness, zeal

arduous adjective <u>difficult</u>, exhausting, fatiguing, gruelling, laborious, onerous, punishing, rigorous, strenuous, taxing, tiring

area noun 1 <u>region</u>, district, locality, neighbourhood, zone 2 <u>part</u>, portion, section, sector 3 <u>field</u>, department, domain, province, realm, sphere, territory

arena noun 1 ring, amphitheatre, bowl, enclosure, field, ground, stadium 2 sphere, area, domain, field, province, realm, sector, territory

argue verb 1 discuss, assert, claim, debate, dispute, maintain, reason, remonstrate 2 quarrel, bicker, disagree, dispute, fall out (informal), fight, squabble

argument noun 1 quarrel, clash, controversy, disagreement, dispute, feud, fight, row, squabble 2 discussion, assertion, claim, debate, dispute, plea, questioning, remonstration 3 reason, argumentation, case, defence, dialectic, ground(s), line of reasoning, logic, polemic, reasoning

argumentative adjective quarrelsome, belligerent, combative, contentious, contrary, disputatious, litigious, opinionated

arid adjective 1 dry, barren, desert, parched, sterile, torrid, waterless 2 boring, dreary, dry, dull, tedious, tiresome, uninspired, uninteresting

arise verb 1 happen, begin, emerge, ensue, follow, occur, result, start, stem 2 Old-fashioned get up, get to one's feet, go up, rise, stand up, wake up

aristocracy noun upper class, elite, gentry, nobility, patricians, peerage, ruling class

aristocrat adjective noble, aristo (informal), grandee, lady, lord, patrician, peer, peeress

aristocratic noun upper-class, blue-blooded, elite, gentlemanly, lordly, noble, patrician, titled

arm[1] noun upper limb, appendage, limb

arm[2] verb Especially with weapons equip, accoutre, array, deck out, furnish, issue with, provide, supply

armada noun fleet, flotilla, navy, squadron

armaments plural noun weapons, ammunition, arms, guns, materiel, munitions, ordnance, weaponry

armed adjective carrying weapons, equipped, fitted out, primed, protected

armistice noun truce, ceasefire, peace, suspension of hostilities

armour noun protection, armour plate, covering, sheathing, shield

armoured adjective protected, armour-plated, bombproof, bulletproof, ironclad, mailed, steel-plated

arms plural noun 1 weapons, armaments, firearms, guns, instruments of war, ordnance, weaponry 2 heraldry, blazonry, crest, escutcheon, insignia

army noun 1 soldiers, armed force, legions, military, military force, soldiery, troops 2 vast number, array, horde, host, multitude, pack, swarm, throng

aroma noun scent, bouquet, fragrance, odour, perfume, redolence, savour, smell

aromatic adjective fragrant, balmy, perfumed, pungent, redolent, savoury, spicy, sweet-scented, sweet-smelling

around preposition 1 surrounding, about, encircling, enclosing, encompassing, on all sides of,

on every side of
2 <u>approximately</u>, about, circa (*used with dates*), roughly ♦ *adverb* **3** <u>everywhere</u>, about, all over, here and there, in all directions, on all sides, throughout, to and fro **4** <u>near</u>, at hand, close, close at hand, nearby, nigh (*archaic or dialect*)

arouse *verb* **1** <u>stimulate</u>, excite, incite, instigate, provoke, spur, stir up, summon up, whip up **2** <u>awaken</u>, rouse, waken, wake up

arrange *verb* **1** <u>plan</u>, construct, contrive, devise, fix up, organize, prepare **2** <u>agree</u>, adjust, come to terms, compromise, determine, settle **3** <u>put in order</u>, classify, group, line up, order, organize, position, sort **4** <u>adapt</u>, instrument, orchestrate, score

arrangement *noun* **1** *often plural* <u>plan</u>, organization, planning, preparation, provision, schedule **2** <u>agreement</u>, adjustment, compact, compromise, deal, settlement, terms **3** <u>order</u>, alignment, classification, form, organization, structure, system **4** <u>adaptation</u>, instrumentation, interpretation, orchestration, score, version

array *noun* **1** <u>arrangement</u>, collection, display, exhibition, formation, line-up, parade, show, supply **2** *Poetic* <u>clothing</u>, apparel, attire, clothes, dress, finery, garments, regalia ♦ *verb* **3** <u>arrange</u>, display, exhibit, group, parade, range, show **4** <u>dress</u>, adorn, attire, clothe, deck, decorate, festoon

arrest *verb* **1** <u>capture</u>, apprehend, catch, detain, nick

(*slang, chiefly Brit.*), seize, take prisoner **2** <u>stop</u>, block, delay, end, inhibit, interrupt, obstruct, slow, suppress **3** <u>grip</u>, absorb, engage, engross, fascinate, hold, intrigue, occupy ♦ *noun* **4** <u>capture</u>, bust (*informal*), cop (*slang*), detention, seizure **5** <u>stopping</u>, blockage, delay, end, hindrance, interruption, obstruction, suppression

arresting *adjective* <u>striking</u>, engaging, impressive, noticeable, outstanding, remarkable, stunning, surprising

arrival *noun* **1** <u>coming</u>, advent, appearance, arriving, entrance, happening, occurrence, taking place **2** <u>newcomer</u>, caller, entrant, incomer, visitor

arrive *verb* **1** <u>come</u>, appear, enter, get to, reach, show up (*informal*), turn up **2** *Informal* <u>succeed</u>, become famous, make good, make it (*informal*), make the grade (*informal*)

arrogance *noun* <u>conceit</u>, disdainfulness, haughtiness, high-handedness, insolence, pride, superciliousness, swagger

arrogant *adjective* <u>conceited</u>, disdainful, haughty, high-handed, overbearing, proud, scornful, supercilious

arrow *noun* **1** <u>dart</u>, bolt, flight, quarrel, shaft (*archaic*) **2** <u>pointer</u>, indicator

arsenal *noun* <u>armoury</u>, ammunition dump, arms depot, ordnance depot, stockpile, store, storehouse, supply

art *noun* <u>skill</u>, craft, expertise, ingenuity, mastery, virtuosity

artful *adjective* <u>cunning</u>, clever,

crafty, shrewd, sly, smart, wily

article noun **1** piece, composition, discourse, essay, feature, item, paper, story, treatise **2** thing, commodity, item, object, piece, substance, unit **3** clause, item, paragraph, part, passage, point, portion, section

articulate adjective **1** expressive, clear, coherent, eloquent, fluent, lucid, well-spoken ♦ verb **2** express, enunciate, pronounce, say, speak, state, talk, utter, voice

artifice noun **1** trick, contrivance, device, machination, manoeuvre, stratagem, subterfuge, tactic **2** cleverness, ingenuity, inventiveness, skill

artificial adjective **1** synthetic, man-made, manufactured, non-natural, plastic **2** fake, bogus, counterfeit, imitation, mock, sham, simulated **3** insincere, affected, contrived, false, feigned, forced, phoney or phony (informal), unnatural

artillery noun big guns, battery, cannon, cannonry, gunnery, ordnance

artisan noun craftsman, journeyman, mechanic, skilled workman, technician

artistic adjective creative, aesthetic, beautiful, cultured, elegant, refined, sophisticated, stylish, tasteful

artistry noun skill, brilliance, craftsmanship, creativity, finesse, mastery, proficiency, virtuosity

artless adjective **1** straightforward, frank, guileless, open, plain **2** natural, plain, pure, simple, unadorned,

unaffected, unpretentious

as conjunction **1** when, at the time that, during the time that, just as, while **2** in the way that, in the manner that, like **3** what, that which **4** since, because, considering that, seeing that **5** for instance, like, such as ♦ preposition **6** being, in the character of, in the role of, under the name of

ascend verb move up, climb, go up, mount, scale

ascent noun **1** rise, ascending, ascension, climb, mounting, rising, scaling, upward movement **2** upward slope, gradient, incline, ramp, rise, rising ground

ascertain verb find out, confirm, determine, discover, establish, learn

ascetic noun **1** monk, abstainer, hermit, nun, recluse ♦ adjective **2** self-denying, abstinent, austere, celibate, frugal, puritanical, self-disciplined

ascribe verb attribute, assign, charge, credit, impute, put down, refer, set down

ashamed adjective embarrassed, distressed, guilty, humiliated, mortified, remorseful, shamefaced, sheepish, sorry

ashen adjective pale, colourless, grey, leaden, like death warmed up (informal), pallid, wan, white

ashore adverb on land, aground, landwards, on dry land, on the beach, on the shore, shorewards, to the shore

aside adverb **1** to one side, apart, beside, on one side, out of the way, privately, separately, to the side ♦ *noun* **2** interpolation, parenthesis

asinine *adjective* stupid, fatuous, foolish, idiotic, imbecilic, moronic, senseless

ask *verb* **1** inquire, interrogate, query, question, quiz **2** request, appeal, beg, demand, plead, seek **3** invite, bid, summon

askew *adverb* **1** crookedly, aslant, awry, obliquely, off-centre, to one side ♦ *adjective* **2** crooked, awry, cockeyed (*informal*), lopsided, oblique, off-centre, skewwhiff (*Brit. informal*)

asleep *adjective* sleeping, dormant, dozing, fast asleep, napping, slumbering, snoozing (*informal*), sound asleep

aspect *noun* **1** feature, angle, facet, side **2** position, outlook, point of view, prospect, scene, situation, view **3** appearance, air, attitude, bearing, condition, demeanour, expression, look, manner

asphyxiate *verb* suffocate, choke, smother, stifle, strangle, strangulate, throttle

aspiration *noun* aim, ambition, desire, dream, goal, hope, objective, wish

aspire *verb* aim, desire, dream, hope, long, seek, set one's heart on, wish

aspiring *adjective* hopeful, ambitious, eager, longing, wannabe (*informal*), would-be

ass *noun* **1** donkey, moke (*slang*) **2** fool, blockhead, halfwit, idiot, jackass, numbskull *or* numskull,

oaf, twit (*informal, chiefly Brit.*)

assail *verb* attack, assault, fall upon, lay into (*informal*), set upon

assailant *noun* attacker, aggressor, assailer, assaulter, invader

assassin *noun* murderer, executioner, hatchet man (*slang*), hit man (*slang*), killer, liquidator, slayer

assassinate *verb* murder, eliminate (*slang*), hit (*slang*), kill, liquidate, slay, take out (*slang*)

assault *noun* **1** attack, charge, invasion, offensive, onslaught ♦ *verb* **2** attack, beset, fall upon, lay into (*informal*), set about, set upon, strike at

assemble *verb* **1** gather, amass, bring together, call together, collect, come together, congregate, meet, muster, rally **2** put together, build up, connect, construct, fabricate, fit together, join, piece together, set up

assembly *noun* **1** gathering, collection, company, conference, congress, council, crowd, group, mass, meeting **2** putting together, building up, connecting, construction, piecing together, setting up

assent *noun* **1** agreement, acceptance, approval, compliance, concurrence, consent, permission, sanction ♦ *verb* **2** agree, allow, approve, consent, grant, permit

assert *verb* **1** state, affirm, declare, maintain, profess, pronounce, swear **2** insist upon, claim, defend, press, put forward, stand up for, stress, uphold **3 assert oneself** be forceful, exert one's influence, make one's presence felt, put oneself forward, put one's foot down (informal)

assertion noun **1** statement, claim, declaration, pronouncement **2** insistence, maintenance, stressing

assertive adjective confident, aggressive, domineering, emphatic, feisty (informal, chiefly U.S. & Canad.), forceful, insistent, positive, pushy (informal), strong-willed

assess verb **1** judge, appraise, estimate, evaluate, rate, size up (informal), value, weigh **2** evaluate, fix, impose, levy, rate, tax, value

assessment noun **1** judgment, appraisal, estimate, evaluation, rating, valuation **2** evaluation, charge, fee, levy, rating, toll, valuation

asset noun **1** benefit, advantage, aid, blessing, boon, feather in one's cap, help, resource, service **2** assets property, capital, estate, funds, goods, money, possessions, resources, wealth

assiduous adjective diligent, hard-working, indefatigable, industrious, persevering, persistent, unflagging

assign verb **1** select, appoint, choose, delegate, designate, name, nominate **2** give, allocate, allot, apportion, consign, distribute, give out, grant **3** attribute, accredit, ascribe, put down

assignation noun **1** secret

meeting, clandestine meeting, illicit meeting, rendezvous, tryst (archaic) **2** selection, appointment, assignment, choice, delegation, designation, nomination

assignment noun task, appointment, commission, duty, job, mission, position, post, responsibility

assimilate verb **1** learn, absorb, digest, incorporate, take in **2** adjust, adapt, blend in, mingle

assist verb help, abet, aid, cooperate, lend a helping hand, serve, support

assistance noun help, aid, backing, cooperation, helping hand, support

assistant noun helper, accomplice, aide, ally, colleague, right-hand man, second, supporter

associate verb **1** connect, ally, combine, identify, join, link, lump together **2** mix, accompany, consort, hobnob, mingle, socialize ♦ noun **3** partner, collaborator, colleague, confederate, co-worker **4** friend, ally, companion, comrade, mate (informal)

association noun **1** group, alliance, band, club, coalition, federation, league, organization, society **2** connection, blend, combination, joining, juxtaposition, mixture, pairing, union

assorted adjective various, different, diverse, miscellaneous, mixed, motley, sundry, varied

assortment noun variety, array,

assume verb 1 take for granted, believe, expect, fancy, imagine, infer, presume, suppose, surmise, think 2 take on, accept, enter upon, put on, shoulder, take over 3 put on, adopt, affect, feign, imitate, impersonate, mimic, pretend to, simulate

assumed adjective 1 false, bogus, counterfeit, fake, fictitious, made-up, make-believe 2 taken for granted, accepted, expected, hypothetical, presumed, presupposed, supposed, surmised

assumption noun
1 presumption, belief, conjecture, guess, hypothesis, inference, supposition, surmise
2 taking on, acceptance, acquisition, adoption, entering upon, putting on, shouldering, takeover, taking on 3 taking, acquisition, appropriation, seizure, takeover

assurance noun 1 assertion, declaration, guarantee, oath, pledge, promise, statement, vow, word 2 confidence, boldness, certainty, conviction, faith, nerve, poise, self-confidence

assure verb 1 promise, certify, confirm, declare confidently, give one's word to, guarantee, pledge, swear, vow 2 convince, comfort, embolden, encourage, hearten, persuade, reassure 3 make certain, clinch, complete, confirm, ensure, guarantee, make sure, seal, secure

assured adjective 1 confident,
certain, poised, positive, self-assured, self-confident, sure of oneself 2 certain, beyond doubt, confirmed, ensured, fixed, guaranteed, in the bag (slang), secure, settled, sure

astonish verb amaze, astound, bewilder, confound, daze, dumbfound, stagger, stun, surprise

astonishing adjective amazing, astounding, bewildering, breathtaking, brilliant, sensational (informal), staggering, stunning, surprising

astonishment noun amazement, awe, bewilderment, confusion, consternation, surprise, wonder, wonderment

astounding adjective amazing, astonishing, bewildering, breathtaking, brilliant, impressive, sensational (informal), staggering, stunning, surprising

astray adjective, adverb off the right track, adrift, amiss, lost, off, off course, off the mark, off the subject

astute adjective intelligent, canny, clever, crafty, cunning, perceptive, sagacious, sharp, shrewd, subtle

asylum noun 1 refuge, harbour, haven, preserve, retreat, safety, sanctuary, shelter 2 Old-fashioned mental hospital, hospital, institution, madhouse (informal), psychiatric hospital

atheism noun nonbelief, disbelief, godlessness, heathenism, infidelity, irreligion, paganism, scepticism, unbelief

atheist noun nonbeliever, disbeliever, heathen, infidel, pagan, sceptic, unbeliever

athlete noun <u>sportsperson</u>, competitor, contestant, gymnast, player, runner, sportsman, sportswoman

athletic adjective <u>fit</u>, active, energetic, muscular, powerful, strapping, strong, sturdy

athletics plural noun <u>sports</u>, contests, exercises, gymnastics, races, track and field events

atmosphere noun **1** <u>air</u>, aerosphere, heavens, sky **2** <u>feeling</u>, ambience, character, climate, environment, mood, spirit, surroundings, tone

atom noun <u>particle</u>, bit, dot, molecule, speck, spot, trace

atone verb, usually with **for** <u>make amends</u>, compensate, do penance, make redress, make reparation, make up for, pay for, recompense, redress

atonement noun <u>amends</u>, compensation, penance, recompense, redress, reparation, restitution

atrocious adjective **1** <u>cruel</u>, barbaric, brutal, fiendish, infernal, monstrous, savage, vicious, wicked **2** Informal <u>shocking</u>, appalling, detestable, grievous, horrible, horrifying, terrible

atrocity noun **1** <u>cruelty</u>, barbarity, brutality, fiendishness, horror, savagery, viciousness, wickedness **2** <u>act of cruelty</u>, abomination, crime, evil, horror, outrage

attach verb **1** <u>connect</u>, add, couple, fasten, fix, join, link, secure, stick, tie **2** <u>put</u>, ascribe,

assign, associate, attribute, connect

attached adjective **1** <u>spoken for</u>, accompanied, engaged, married, partnered **2** **attached to** <u>fond of</u>, affectionate towards, devoted to, full of regard for

attachment noun **1** <u>fondness</u>, affection, affinity, attraction, liking, regard **2** <u>accessory</u>, accoutrement, extension, extra, fitting, fixture, supplement

attack verb **1** <u>assault</u>, invade, lay into (informal), raid, set upon, storm, strike (at) **2** <u>criticize</u>, abuse, blame, censure, have a go (at) (informal), put down, vilify ♦ noun **3** <u>assault</u>, campaign, charge, foray, incursion, invasion, offensive, onslaught, raid, strike **4** <u>criticism</u>, abuse, blame, censure, denigration, stick (slang), vilification **5** <u>bout</u>, convulsion, fit, paroxysm, seizure, spasm, stroke

attacker noun <u>assailant</u>, aggressor, assaulter, intruder, invader, raider

attain verb <u>achieve</u>, accomplish, acquire, complete, fulfil, gain, get, obtain, reach

attainment noun <u>achievement</u>, accomplishment, completion, feat

attempt verb **1** <u>try</u>, endeavour, seek, strive, undertake, venture ♦ noun **2** <u>try</u>, bid, crack (informal), effort, go (informal), shot (informal), stab (informal), trial

attend verb **1** <u>be present</u>, appear, frequent, go to, haunt, put in an appearance, show oneself, turn up, visit **2** <u>look after</u>, care for, mind, minister to, nurse, take

care of, tend **3** pay attention,
hear, heed, listen, mark, note,
observe, pay heed **4 attend to**
apply oneself to, concentrate on,
devote oneself to, get to work
on, look after, occupy oneself
with, see to, take care of

attendance noun **1** presence,
appearance, attending, being
there **2** turnout, audience,
crowd, gate, house, number
present

attendant noun **1** assistant, aide,
companion, escort, follower,
guard, helper, servant ♦ adjective
2 accompanying, accessory,
associated, concomitant,
consequent, related

attention noun **1** concentration,
deliberation, heed, intentness,
mind, scrutiny, thinking, thought
2 notice, awareness,
consciousness, consideration,
observation, recognition, regard
3 care, concern, looking after,
ministration, treatment

attentive adjective **1** intent, alert,
awake, careful, concentrating,
heedful, mindful, observant,
studious, watchful **2** considerate,
courteous, helpful, kind,
obliging, polite, respectful,
thoughtful

attic noun loft, garret

attire noun clothes, apparel,
costume, dress, garb, garments,
outfit, robes, wear

attitude noun **1** disposition,
approach, frame of mind, mood,
opinion, outlook, perspective,
point of view, position, stance
2 position, pose, posture, stance

attract verb appeal to, allure,
charm, draw, enchant, entice,

lure, pull (informal), tempt

attraction noun appeal, allure,
charm, enticement, fascination,
lure, magnetism, pull (informal),
temptation

attractive adjective appealing,
alluring, charming, fair, fetching,
good-looking, handsome,
inviting, lovely, pleasant, pretty,
tempting

attribute verb **1** ascribe, assign,
charge, credit, put down to,
refer, set down to, trace to
♦ noun **2** quality, aspect,
character, characteristic, facet,
feature, peculiarity, property, trait

attune verb accustom, adapt,
adjust, familiarize, harmonize,
regulate

audacious adjective **1** daring,
bold, brave, courageous, fearless,
intrepid, rash, reckless **2** cheeky,
brazen, defiant, impertinent,
impudent, insolent,
presumptuous, shameless

audacity noun **1** daring,
boldness, bravery, courage,
fearlessness, nerve, rashness,
recklessness **2** cheek, chutzpah
(U.S. & Canad. informal),
effrontery, impertinence,
impudence, insolence, nerve

audible adjective clear,
detectable, discernible, distinct,
hearable, perceptible

audience noun **1** spectators,
assembly, crowd, gallery,
gathering, listeners, onlookers,
turnout, viewers **2** interview,
consultation, hearing, meeting,
reception

aura noun air, ambience,
atmosphere, feeling, mood,
quality, tone

auspicious adjective favourable, bright, encouraging, felicitous, hopeful, promising

austere adjective 1 stern, forbidding, formal, serious, severe, solemn, strict 2 ascetic, abstemious, puritanical, self-disciplined, sober, solemn, strait-laced, strict 3 plain, bleak, harsh, simple, spare, Spartan, stark

austerity noun 1 sternness, formality, inflexibility, rigour, seriousness, severity, solemnity, stiffness, strictness 2 asceticism, puritanism, self-denial, self-discipline, sobriety 3 plainness, simplicity, starkness

authentic adjective genuine, actual, authoritative, bona fide, legitimate, pure, real, true-to-life, valid

authenticity noun genuineness, accuracy, certainty, faithfulness, legitimacy, purity, truthfulness, validity

author noun 1 writer, composer, creator 2 creator, architect, designer, father, founder, inventor, originator, producer

authoritarian adjective 1 strict, autocratic, dictatorial, doctrinaire, dogmatic, severe, tyrannical ♦ noun 2 disciplinarian, absolutist, autocrat, despot, dictator, tyrant

authoritative adjective 1 reliable, accurate, authentic, definitive, dependable, trustworthy, valid 2 commanding, assertive, imperious, imposing, masterly, self-assured

authority noun 1 power, command, control, direction, influence, supremacy, sway, weight 2 usually plural powers that be, administration, government, management, officialdom, police, the Establishment 3 expert, connoisseur, judge, master, professional, specialist

authorization noun permission, a blank cheque, approval, leave, licence, permit, warrant

authorize verb 1 empower, accredit, commission, enable, entitle, give authority 2 permit, allow, approve, give authority for, license, sanction, warrant

autocracy noun dictatorship, absolutism, despotism, tyranny

autocrat noun dictator, absolutist, despot, tyrant

autocratic adjective dictatorial, absolute, all-powerful, despotic, domineering, imperious, tyrannical

automatic adjective 1 mechanical, automated, mechanized, push-button, self-propelling 2 involuntary, instinctive, mechanical, natural, reflex, spontaneous, unconscious, unwilled

autonomous adjective self-ruling, free, independent, self-determining, self-governing, sovereign

autonomy noun independence, freedom, home rule, self-determination, self-government, self-rule, sovereignty

auxiliary adjective 1 supplementary, back-up, emergency, fall-back, reserve, secondary, subsidiary, substitute

2 supporting, accessory, aiding, ancillary, assisting, helping ♦ *noun* **3** backup, reserve **4** helper, assistant, associate, companion, subordinate, supporter

avail *verb* **1** benefit, aid, assist, be of advantage, be useful, help, profit ♦ *noun* **2** benefit, advantage, aid, good, help, profit, use

availability *noun* accessibility, attainability, handiness, readiness

available *adjective* accessible, at hand, at one's disposal, free, handy, on tap, ready, to hand

avalanche *noun* **1** snow-slide, landslide, landslip **2** flood, barrage, deluge, inundation, torrent

avant-garde *adjective* progressive, experimental, ground-breaking, innovative, pioneering, unconventional

avarice *noun* greed, covetousness, meanness, miserliness, niggardliness, parsimony, stinginess

avaricious *adjective* grasping, covetous, greedy, mean, miserly, niggardly, parsimonious, tight

avenge *verb* get revenge for, get even for (*informal*), get one's own back, hit back, punish, repay, retaliate

avenue *noun* street, approach, boulevard, course, drive, passage, path, road, route, way

average *noun* **1** usual, mean, medium, midpoint, norm, normal, par, standard **2 on average** usually, as a rule, for the most part, generally,

normally, typically ♦ *adjective* **3** usual, commonplace, fair, general, normal, ordinary, regular, standard, typical **4** mean, intermediate, median, medium, middle ♦ *verb* **5** make on average, balance out to, be on average, do on average, even out to

averse *adjective* opposed, disinclined, hostile, ill-disposed, loath, reluctant, unwilling

aversion *noun* hatred, animosity, antipathy, disinclination, dislike, hostility, revulsion, unwillingness

avert *verb* **1** turn away, turn aside **2** ward off, avoid, fend off, forestall, frustrate, preclude, prevent, stave off

aviator *noun* pilot, aeronaut, airman, flyer

avid *adjective* **1** enthusiastic, ardent, devoted, eager, fanatical, intense, keen, passionate, zealous **2** insatiable, grasping, greedy, hungry, rapacious, ravenous, thirsty, voracious

avoid *verb* **1** refrain from, dodge, duck (out of) (*informal*), eschew, fight shy of, shirk **2** prevent, avert **3** keep away from, bypass, dodge, elude, escape, evade, shun, steer clear of

avoidance *noun* evasion, dodging, eluding, escape, keeping away, shunning, steering clear

avowed *adjective* **1** declared, open, professed, self-proclaimed, sworn **2** confessed, acknowledged, admitted

await *verb* **1** wait for, abide, anticipate, expect, look for, look forward to, stay for **2** be in store for, attend, be in readiness for, be prepared for, be ready for, wait for

awake *adjective* **1** not sleeping, aroused, awakened, aware, conscious, wakeful, wide-awake **2** alert, alive, attentive, aware, heedful, observant, on the lookout, vigilant, watchful ♦ *verb* **3** wake up, awaken, rouse, wake **4** alert, arouse, kindle, provoke, revive, stimulate, stir up

awaken *verb* **1** awake, arouse, revive, rouse, wake **2** alert, kindle, provoke, stimulate, stir up

awakening *noun* waking up, arousal, revival, rousing, stimulation, stirring up

award *verb* **1** give, bestow, confer, endow, grant, hand out, present ♦ *noun* **2** prize, decoration, gift, grant, trophy

aware *adjective* **1** aware of knowing about, acquainted with, conscious of, conversant with, familiar with, mindful of **2** informed, enlightened, in the picture, knowledgeable

awareness *noun* knowledge, consciousness, familiarity, perception, realization, recognition, understanding

away *adverb* **1** off, abroad, elsewhere, from here, from home, hence **2** at a distance, apart, far, remote **3** aside, out of the way, to one side **4** continuously, incessantly, interminably, relentlessly, repeatedly, uninterruptedly, unremittingly ♦ *adjective* **5** not present, abroad, absent, elsewhere, gone, not at home, not here, out

awe *noun* **1** wonder, admiration, amazement, astonishment, dread, fear, horror, respect, reverence, terror ♦ *verb* **2** impress, amaze, astonish, frighten, horrify, intimidate, stun, terrify

awesome *adjective* awe-inspiring, amazing, astonishing, breathtaking, formidable, impressive, intimidating, stunning

awful *adjective* **1** terrible, abysmal, appalling, deplorable, dreadful, frightful, ghastly, horrendous **2** *Obsolete* awe-inspiring, awesome, fearsome, majestic, solemn

awfully *adverb* **1** badly, disgracefully, dreadfully, reprehensibly, unforgivably, unpleasantly, woefully, wretchedly **2** *Informal* very, dreadfully, exceedingly, exceptionally, extremely, greatly, immensely, terribly

awkward *adjective* **1** clumsy, gauche, gawky, inelegant, lumbering, uncoordinated, ungainly **2** unmanageable, clunky (*informal*), cumbersome, difficult, inconvenient, troublesome, unwieldy **3** embarrassing, delicate, difficult, ill at ease, inconvenient, uncomfortable

awkwardness *noun* **1** clumsiness, gawkiness, inelegance, ungainliness **2** unwieldiness, difficulty, inconvenience **3** embarrassment, delicacy, difficulty, inconvenience

axe *noun* **1** hatchet, adze, chopper **2** the axe *Informal* the sack (*informal*), dismissal, termination, the boot (*slang*), the chop (*slang*) ◆ *verb* 3 *Informal* cut back, cancel, dismiss, dispense with, eliminate, fire (*informal*), get rid of, remove, sack (*informal*)

axiom *noun* principle, adage, aphorism, dictum, maxim, precept, truism

axiomatic *adjective* self-evident, accepted, assumed, certain, given, granted, manifest, understood

axis *noun* pivot, axle, centre line, shaft, spindle

axle *noun* shaft, axis, pin, pivot, rod, spindle

B b

babble *verb* 1 gabble, burble, chatter, jabber, prattle, waffle (*informal, chiefly Brit.*) 2 gibber, gurgle ◆ *noun* 3 gabble, burble, drivel, gibberish, waffle (*informal, chiefly Brit.*)

baby *noun* 1 infant, babe, babe in arms, bairn (*Scot.*), child, newborn child ◆ *adjective* 2 small, little, mini, miniature, minute, teeny-weeny, tiny, wee

babyish *adjective* childish, foolish, immature, infantile, juvenile, puerile, sissy, spoiled

back *noun* 1 rear, end, far end, hind part, hindquarters, reverse, stern, tail end 2 behind one's back secretly, covertly, deceitfully, sneakily, surreptitiously ◆ *verb* 3 move back, back off, backtrack, go back, retire, retreat, reverse, turn tail, withdraw 4 support,

advocate, assist, champion, endorse, promote, sponsor ◆ *adjective* 5 rear, end, hind, hindmost, posterior, tail 6 previous, delayed, earlier, elapsed, former, overdue, past

backbiting *noun* slander, bitchiness (*slang*), cattiness (*informal*), defamation, disparagement, gossip, malice, scandalmongering, spitefulness

backbone *noun* 1 *Medical* spinal column, spine, vertebrae, vertebral column 2 strength of character, character, courage, determination, fortitude, grit, nerve, pluck, resolution

backbreaking *adjective* exhausting, arduous, crushing, gruelling, hard, laborious, punishing, strenuous

back down *verb* give in, accede, admit defeat, back-pedal, concede, surrender, withdraw, yield

backer *noun* supporter, advocate, angel (*informal*), benefactor, patron, promoter, second, sponsor, subscriber

backfire *verb* fail, boomerang, disappoint, flop (*informal*), miscarry, rebound, recoil

background *noun* history, circumstances, culture, education, environment, grounding, tradition, upbringing

backing *noun* support, aid, assistance, encouragement, endorsement, moral support, patronage, sponsorship

backlash *noun* reaction, counteraction, recoil, repercussion, resistance, response, retaliation

backlog noun <u>build-up</u>, accumulation, excess, hoard, reserve, stock, supply

back out verb, often with **of** <u>withdraw</u>, abandon, cancel, give up, go back on, resign, retreat

backslide verb <u>relapse</u>, go astray, go wrong, lapse, revert, slip, stray, weaken

backslider noun <u>relapser</u>, apostate, deserter, recidivist, recreant, renegade, turncoat

back up verb <u>support</u>, aid, assist, bolster, confirm, corroborate, reinforce, second, stand by, substantiate

backward adjective <u>slow</u>, behind, dull, retarded, subnormal, underdeveloped, undeveloped

backwards, backward adverb <u>towards the rear</u>, behind, in reverse, rearward

bacteria plural noun <u>microorganisms</u>, bacilli, bugs (slang), germs, microbes, pathogens, viruses

bad adjective 1 <u>inferior</u>, defective, faulty, imperfect, inadequate, poor, substandard, unsatisfactory 2 <u>harmful</u>, damaging, dangerous, deleterious, detrimental, hurtful, ruinous, unhealthy 3 <u>evil</u>, corrupt, criminal, immoral, mean, sinful, wicked, wrong 4 <u>naughty</u>, disobedient, mischievous, unruly 5 <u>rotten</u>, decayed, mouldy, off, putrid, rancid, sour, spoiled 6 <u>unfavourable</u>, adverse, distressing, gloomy, grim, troubled, unfortunate, unpleasant

badge noun <u>mark</u>, brand, device, emblem, identification, insignia, sign, stamp, token

badger verb <u>pester</u>, bully, goad, harass, hound, importune, nag, plague, torment

badinage noun <u>wordplay</u>, banter, mockery, pleasantry, repartee, teasing

badly adverb 1 <u>poorly</u>, carelessly, imperfectly, inadequately, incorrectly, ineptly, wrongly 2 <u>unfavourably</u>, unfortunately, unsuccessfully 3 <u>severely</u>, deeply, desperately, exceedingly, extremely, greatly, intensely, seriously

baffle verb <u>puzzle</u>, bewilder, confound, confuse, flummox, mystify, nonplus, perplex, stump

bag noun <u>container</u>, receptacle, sac, sack ♦ verb 2 <u>catch</u>, acquire, capture, kill, land, shoot, trap

baggage noun <u>luggage</u>, accoutrements, bags, belongings, equipment, gear, paraphernalia, suitcases, things

baggy adjective <u>loose</u>, bulging, droopy, floppy, ill-fitting, oversize, roomy, sagging, slack

bail noun Law <u>security</u>, bond, guarantee, pledge, surety, warranty

bail out see BALE OUT

bait noun 1 <u>lure</u>, allurement, attraction, decoy, enticement, incentive, inducement, snare, temptation ♦ verb 2 <u>tease</u>, annoy, bother, harass, hassle (informal), hound, irritate, persecute, torment, wind up (Brit. slang)

baked adjective <u>dry</u>, arid, desiccated, parched, scorched, seared, sun-baked, torrid

balance noun 1 <u>stability</u>,

composure, equanimity, poise, self-control, self-possession, steadiness **2** equilibrium, correspondence, equity, equivalence, evenness, parity, symmetry **3** remainder, difference, residue, rest, surplus ♦ *verb* **4** stabilize, level, match, parallel, steady **5** compare, assess, consider, deliberate, estimate, evaluate, weigh **6** *Accounting* calculate, compute, settle, square, tally, total

balcony *noun* **1** terrace, veranda **2** upper circle, gallery, gods

bald *adjective* **1** hairless, baldheaded, depilated **2** plain, blunt, direct, forthright, straightforward, unadorned, unvarnished

balderdash *noun* nonsense, claptrap (*informal*), drivel, garbage (*informal*), gibberish, hogwash, hot air (*informal*), rubbish

baldness *noun* **1** hairlessness, alopecia (*Pathology*), baldheadedness **2** plainness, austerity, bluntness, severity, simplicity

bale out, bail out *verb* **1** *Informal* help, aid, relieve, rescue, save (someone's) bacon (*informal, chiefly Brit.*) **2** escape, quit, retreat, withdraw

balk, baulk *verb* **1** recoil, evade, flinch, hesitate, jib, refuse, resist, shirk, shrink from **2** foil, check, counteract, defeat, frustrate, hinder, obstruct, prevent, thwart

ball *noun* sphere, drop, globe, globule, orb, pellet, spheroid

ballast *noun* counterbalance, balance, counterweight,

equilibrium, sandbag, stability, stabilizer, weight

balloon *verb* swell, billow, blow up, dilate, distend, expand, grow rapidly, inflate, puff out

ballot *noun* vote, election, poll, polling, voting

ballyhoo *noun* *Informal* fuss, babble, commotion, hubbub, hue and cry, hullabaloo, noise, racket, to-do

balm *noun* **1** ointment, balsam, cream, embrocation, emollient, lotion, salve, unguent **2** comfort, anodyne, consolation, curative, palliative, restorative, solace

balmy *adjective* mild, clement, pleasant, summery, temperate

bamboozle *verb* *Informal* **1** cheat, con (*informal*), deceive, dupe, fool, hoodwink, swindle, trick **2** puzzle, baffle, befuddle, confound, confuse, mystify, perplex, stump

ban *verb* **1** prohibit, banish, bar, block, boycott, disallow, disqualify, exclude, forbid, outlaw ♦ *noun* **2** prohibition, boycott, disqualification, embargo, restriction, taboo

banal *adjective* unoriginal, hackneyed, humdrum, mundane, pedestrian, stale, stereotyped, trite, unimaginative

band[1] *noun* **1** ensemble, combo, group, orchestra **2** gang, body, company, group, party, posse (*informal*)

band[2] *noun* strip, belt, bond, chain, cord, ribbon, strap

bandage *noun* **1** dressing, compress, gauze, plaster ♦ *verb* **2** dress, bind, cover, swathe

bandit noun robber, brigand, desperado, highwayman, marauder, outlaw, thief

bane noun plague, bête noire, curse, nuisance, pest, ruin, scourge, torment

bang noun 1 explosion, clang, clap, clash, pop, slam, thud, thump 2 blow, bump, cuff, knock, punch, smack, stroke, whack ♦ verb 3 hit, belt (informal), clatter, knock, slam, strike, thump 4 explode, boom, clang, resound, thump, thunder ♦ adverb 5 hard, abruptly, headlong, noisily, suddenly 6 straight, precisely, slap, smack

banish verb 1 expel, deport, eject, evict, exile, outlaw 2 get rid of, ban, cast out, discard, dismiss, oust, remove

banishment noun expulsion, deportation, exile, expatriation, transportation

banisters plural noun railing, balusters, balustrade, handrail, rail

bank[1] noun 1 storehouse, depository, repository 2 store, accumulation, fund, hoard, reserve, reservoir, savings, stock, stockpile ♦ verb 3 save, deposit, keep

bank[2] noun 1 mound, banking, embankment, heap, mass, pile, ridge 2 side, brink, edge, margin, shore ♦ verb 3 pile, amass, heap, mass, mound, stack 4 tilt, camber, cant, heel, incline, pitch, slant, slope, tip

bank[3] noun row, array, file, group, line, rank, sequence, series, succession

bankrupt adjective insolvent,

broke (informal), destitute, impoverished, in queer street, in the red, ruined, wiped out (informal)

bankruptcy noun insolvency, disaster, failure, liquidation, ruin

banner noun flag, colours, ensign, pennant, placard, standard, streamer

banquet noun feast, dinner, meal, repast, revel, treat

banter verb 1 joke, jest, kid (informal), rib (informal), taunt, tease ♦ noun 2 joking, badinage, jesting, kidding (informal), repartee, teasing, wordplay

baptism noun Christianity christening, immersion, purification, sprinkling

baptize verb Christianity purify, cleanse, immerse

bar noun 1 rod, paling, palisade, pole, rail, shaft, stake, stick 2 obstacle, barricade, barrier, block, deterrent, hindrance, impediment, obstruction, stop 3 public house, boozer (Brit., Austral. & N.Z. informal), canteen, counter, inn, pub (informal, chiefly Brit.), saloon, tavern, watering hole (facetious slang) ♦ verb 4 fasten, barricade, bolt, latch, lock, secure 5 obstruct, hinder, prevent, restrain 6 exclude, ban, black, blackball, forbid, keep out, prohibit

Bar noun the Bar Law barristers, body of lawyers, counsel, court, judgment, tribunal

barb noun 1 dig, affront, cut, gibe, insult, sarcasm, scoff, sneer 2 point, bristle, prickle, prong, quill, spike, spur, thorn

barbarian noun 1 <u>savage</u>, brute, yahoo 2 <u>lout</u>, bigot, boor, philistine

barbaric adjective 1 <u>uncivilized</u>, primitive, rude, wild 2 <u>brutal</u>, barbarous, coarse, crude, cruel, fierce, inhuman, savage

barbarism noun <u>savagery</u>, coarseness, crudity

barbarous adjective 1 <u>uncivilized</u>, barbarian, brutish, primitive, rough, rude, savage, uncouth, wild 2 <u>brutal</u>, barbaric, cruel, ferocious, heartless, inhuman, monstrous, ruthless, vicious

barbed adjective 1 <u>cutting</u>, critical, hostile, hurtful, nasty, pointed, scathing, unkind 2 <u>spiked</u>, hooked, jagged, prickly, spiny, thorny

bare adjective 1 <u>naked</u>, nude, stripped, unclad, unclothed, uncovered, undressed, without a stitch on (informal) 2 <u>plain</u>, bald, basic, sheer, simple, stark, unembellished 3 <u>simple</u>, austere, spare, spartan, unadorned, unembellished

barefaced adjective 1 <u>obvious</u>, blatant, flagrant, open, transparent, unconcealed 2 <u>shameless</u>, audacious, bold, brash, brazen, impudent, insolent

barely adverb <u>only just</u>, almost, at a push, by the skin of one's teeth, hardly, just, scarcely

bargain noun 1 <u>agreement</u>, arrangement, contract, pact, pledge, promise 2 <u>good buy</u>, (cheap) purchase, discount, giveaway, good deal, reduction, snip (informal), steal (informal) ♦ verb 3 <u>negotiate</u>, agree, contract, covenant, promise, stipulate, transact

barge noun <u>canal boat</u>, flatboat, lighter, narrow boat

bark¹ noun, verb <u>yap</u>, bay, growl, howl, snarl, woof, yelp

bark² noun <u>covering</u>, casing, cortex (Anatomy, botany), crust, husk, rind, skin

barmy adjective 1 Slang <u>insane</u>, crazy, daft (informal), foolish, idiotic, nuts (slang), out of one's mind, stupid

barracks plural noun <u>camp</u>, billet, encampment, garrison, quarters

barrage noun 1 <u>torrent</u>, burst, deluge, hail, mass, onslaught, plethora, stream 2 Military <u>bombardment</u>, battery, cannonade, fusillade, gunfire, salvo, shelling, volley

barren adjective 1 <u>infertile</u>, childless, sterile 2 <u>unproductive</u>, arid, desert, desolate, dry, empty, unfruitful, waste

barricade noun 1 <u>barrier</u>, blockade, bulwark, fence, obstruction, palisade, rampart, stockade ♦ verb 2 <u>bar</u>, block, blockade, defend, fortify, obstruct, protect, shut in

barrier noun 1 <u>barricade</u>, bar, blockade, boundary, fence, obstacle, obstruction, wall 2 <u>hindrance</u>, difficulty, drawback, handicap, hurdle, obstacle, restriction, stumbling block

barter verb <u>trade</u>, bargain, drive a hard bargain, exchange, haggle, sell, swap, traffic

base¹ noun 1 <u>bottom</u>, bed, foot, foundation, pedestal, rest, stand, support 2 <u>basis</u>, core, essence,

base heart, key, origin, root, source **3** <u>centre</u>, camp, headquarters, home, post, settlement, starting point, station ♦ **verb 4** <u>found</u>, build, construct, depend, derive, establish, ground, hinge **5** <u>place</u>, locate, post, station

base² adjective **1** <u>dishonourable</u>, contemptible, despicable, disreputable, evil, immoral, shameful, sordid, wicked **2** <u>counterfeit</u>, alloyed, debased, fake, forged, fraudulent, impure

baseless adjective <u>unfounded</u>, groundless, unconfirmed, uncorroborated, ungrounded, unjustified, unsubstantiated, unsupported

bash verb **1** Informal <u>hit</u>, belt (informal), smash, sock (slang), strike, wallop (informal) ♦ noun **2** Informal <u>attempt</u>, crack (informal), go (informal), shot (informal), stab (informal), try

bashful adjective <u>shy</u>, blushing, coy, diffident, reserved, reticent, retiring, timid

basic adjective <u>essential</u>, elementary, fundamental, key, necessary, primary, vital

basically adverb <u>essentially</u>, at heart, fundamentally, inherently, in substance, intrinsically, mostly, primarily

basics plural noun <u>essentials</u>, brass tacks (informal), fundamentals, nitty-gritty (informal), nuts and bolts (informal), principles, rudiments

basis noun <u>foundation</u>, base, bottom, footing, ground, groundwork, support

bask verb <u>lie in</u>, laze, loll, lounge, relax, sunbathe, swim in

bass adjective <u>deep</u>, deep-toned, low, low-pitched, resonant, sonorous

bastard noun **1** Informal, offensive <u>rogue</u>, blackguard, miscreant, reprobate, scoundrel, villain, wretch **2** <u>illegitimate child</u>, love child, natural child

bastion noun <u>stronghold</u>, bulwark, citadel, defence, fortress, mainstay, prop, rock, support, tower of strength

bat noun, verb <u>hit</u>, bang, smack, strike, swat, thump, wallop (informal), whack

batch noun <u>group</u>, amount, assemblage, bunch, collection, crowd, lot, pack, quantity, set

bath noun **1** <u>wash</u>, cleansing, douche, scrubbing, shower, soak, tub ♦ verb **2** <u>wash</u>, bathe, clean, douse, scrub down, shower, soak

bathe verb **1** <u>swim</u> **2** <u>wash</u>, cleanse, rinse **3** <u>cover</u>, flood, immerse, steep, suffuse

baton noun <u>stick</u>, club, crook, mace, rod, sceptre, staff, truncheon, wand

batten verb, usually with down <u>fasten</u>, board up, clamp down, cover up, fix, nail down, secure, tighten

batter verb <u>beat</u>, buffet, clobber (slang), pelt, pound, pummel, thrash, wallop (informal)

battery noun <u>artillery</u>, cannon, cannonry, gun emplacements, guns

battle noun **1** <u>fight</u>, action, attack, combat, encounter, engagement, hostilities, skirmish **2** <u>conflict</u>, campaign, contest, crusade, dispute, struggle ♦ *verb* **3** struggle, argue, clamour, dispute, fight, lock horns, strive, war

battlefield *noun* battleground, combat zone, field, field of battle, front

battleship *noun* warship, gunboat, man-of-war

batty *adjective* crazy, daft (*informal*), dotty (*slang, chiefly Brit.*), eccentric, mad, odd, peculiar, potty (*Brit. informal*), touched

bauble *noun* trinket, bagatelle, gewgaw, gimcrack, knick-knack, plaything, toy, trifle

baulk *see* BALK

bawdy *adjective* rude, coarse, dirty, indecent, lascivious, lecherous, lewd, ribald, salacious, smutty

bawl *verb* **1** cry, blubber, sob, wail, weep **2** shout, bellow, call, clamour, howl, roar, yell

bay¹ *noun* inlet, bight, cove, gulf, natural harbour, sound

bay² *noun* recess, alcove, compartment, niche, nook, opening

bay³ *verb* howl, bark, clamour, cry, growl, yelp

bazaar *noun* **1** fair, bring-and-buy, fête, sale of work **2** market, exchange, marketplace

be *verb* exist, be alive, breathe, inhabit, live

beach *noun* shore, coast, sands, seashore, seaside, water's edge

beached *adjective* stranded, abandoned, aground, ashore, deserted, grounded, high and dry, marooned, wrecked

beacon *noun* signal, beam, bonfire, flare, lighthouse, sign, watchtower

bead *noun* drop, blob, bubble, dot, droplet, globule, pellet, pill

beady *adjective* bright, gleaming, glinting, glittering, sharp, shining

beak *noun* **1** bill, mandible, neb (*archaic or dialect*), nib **2** *Slang* nose, proboscis, snout

beam *noun* **1** smile, grin **2** ray, gleam, glimmer, glint, glow, shaft, streak, stream **3** rafter, girder, joist, plank, spar, support, timber ♦ *verb* **4** smile, grin **5** radiate, glare, gleam, glitter, glow, shine **6** send out, broadcast, emit, transmit

bear *verb* **1** support, have, hold, maintain, possess, shoulder, sustain, uphold **2** carry, bring, convey, hump (*Brit. slang*), move, take, transport **3** produce, beget, breed, bring forth, engender, generate, give birth to, yield **4** tolerate, abide, allow, brook, endure, permit, put up with (*informal*), stomach, suffer

bearable *adjective* tolerable, admissible, endurable, manageable, passable, sufferable, supportable, sustainable

bearer *noun* carrier, agent, conveyor, messenger, porter, runner, servant

bearing *noun* **1** *usually with* **on** *or* **upon** relevance, application, connection, import, pertinence, reference, relation, significance **2** manner, air, aspect, attitude, behaviour, demeanour, deportment, posture

bearings *plural noun* position,

aim, course, direction, location, orientation, situation, track, way, whereabouts

bear out verb support, confirm, corroborate, endorse, justify, prove, substantiate, uphold, vindicate

beast noun 1 animal, brute, creature 2 brute, barbarian, fiend, monster, ogre, sadist, savage, swine

beastly adjective unpleasant, awful, disagreeable, horrid, mean, nasty, rotten

beat verb 1 hit, bang, batter, buffet, knock, pound, strike, thrash 2 flap, flutter 3 throb, palpitate, pound, pulsate, quake, thump, vibrate 4 defeat, conquer, outdo, overcome, overwhelm, surpass, vanquish ♦ noun 5 throb, palpitation, pulsation, pulse 6 route, circuit, course, path, rounds, way 7 rhythm, accent, cadence, metre, stress, time

beaten adjective 1 stirred, blended, foamy, frothy, mixed, whipped, whisked 2 defeated, cowed, overcome, overwhelmed, thwarted, vanquished

beat up verb Informal assault, attack, batter, beat the living daylights out of (informal), knock about or around, thrash

beau noun 1 Chiefly U.S. boyfriend, admirer, fiancé, lover, suitor, sweetheart 2 dandy, coxcomb, fop, gallant, ladies' man

beautiful adjective attractive, charming, delightful, exquisite, fair, fine, gorgeous, handsome, lovely, pleasing

beautify verb make beautiful, adorn, decorate, embellish, festoon, garnish, glamorize, ornament

beauty noun 1 attractiveness, charm, comeliness, elegance, exquisiteness, glamour, grace, handsomeness, loveliness 2 belle, good-looker, lovely (slang), stunner (informal)

becalmed adjective still, motionless, settled, stranded, stuck

because conjunction since, as, by reason of, in that, on account of, owing to, thanks to

beckon verb gesture, bid, gesticulate, motion, nod, signal, summon, wave at

become verb 1 come to be, alter to, be transformed into, change into, develop into, grow into, mature into, ripen into 2 suit, embellish, enhance, fit, flatter, set off

becoming adjective 1 appropriate, compatible, fitting, in keeping, proper, seemly, suitable, worthy 2 flattering, attractive, comely, enhancing, graceful, neat, pretty, tasteful

bed noun 1 bedstead, berth, bunk, cot, couch, divan 2 plot, area, border, garden, patch, row, strip 3 bottom, base, foundation, groundwork

bedevil verb 1 torment, afflict, distress, harass, plague, trouble, vex, worry 2 confuse, confound

bedlam noun pandemonium, chaos, commotion, confusion, furore, tumult, turmoil, uproar

bedraggled adjective messy, dirty, dishevelled, disordered, muddied, unkempt, untidy

bedridden adjective confined to bed, confined, flat on one's back, incapacitated, laid up (informal)

bedrock noun 1 bottom, bed, foundation, rock bottom, substratum, substructure 2 basics, basis, core, essentials, fundamentals, nuts and bolts (informal), roots

beefy adjective Informal brawny, bulky, hulking, muscular, stocky, strapping, sturdy, thickset

befall verb Archaic or literary happen, chance, come to pass, fall, occur, take place, transpire (informal)

befitting adjective appropriate, apposite, becoming, fit, fitting, proper, right, seemly, suitable

before preposition 1 ahead of, in advance of, in front of 2 earlier than, in advance of, prior to 3 in the presence of, in front of ♦ adverb 4 previously, ahead, earlier, formerly, in advance, sooner 5 in front, ahead

beforehand adverb in advance, ahead of time, already, before, earlier, in anticipation, previously, sooner

befriend verb help, aid, assist, back, encourage, side with, stand by, support, welcome

beg verb 1 scrounge, cadge, seek charity, solicit charity, sponge on, touch (someone) for (slang) 2 implore, beseech, entreat, petition, plead, request, solicit

beggar noun tramp, bag lady

(chiefly U.S.), bum (informal), down-and-out, pauper, vagrant

beggarly adjective poor, destitute, impoverished, indigent, needy, poverty-stricken

begin verb 1 start, commence, embark on, initiate, instigate, institute, prepare, set about 2 happen, appear, arise, come into being, emerge, originate, start

beginner noun novice, amateur, apprentice, learner, neophyte, starter, trainee, tyro

beginning noun 1 start, birth, commencement, inauguration, inception, initiation, onset, opening, origin, outset 2 seed, fount, germ, root

begrudge verb resent, be jealous, be reluctant, be stingy, envy, grudge

beguile verb 1 fool, cheat, deceive, delude, dupe, hoodwink, mislead, take for a ride (informal), trick 2 charm, amuse, distract, divert, engross, entertain, occupy

beguiling adjective charming, alluring, attractive, bewitching, captivating, enchanting, enthralling, intriguing

behave verb 1 act, function, operate, perform, run, work 2 conduct oneself properly, act correctly, keep one's nose clean, mind one's manners

behaviour noun 1 conduct, actions, bearing, demeanour, deportment, manner, manners, ways 2 action, functioning, operation, performance

behind preposition 1 after, at the

back of, at the heels of, at the rear of, following, later than **2** *causing*, at the bottom of, initiating, instigating, responsible for **3** *supporting*, backing, for, in agreement, on the side of
♦ *adverb* **4** *after*, following, in the wake (of), next, subsequently **5** *overdue*, behindhand, in arrears, in debt
♦ *noun* **6** *Informal* bottom, butt (U.S. & Canad. informal), buttocks, posterior

behold *verb Archaic or literary* look at, observe, perceive, regard, survey, view, watch, witness

beholden *adjective* indebted, bound, grateful, obliged, owing, under obligation

being *noun* **1** existence, life, reality **2** nature, entity, essence, soul, spirit, substance **3** creature, human being, individual, living thing

belated *adjective* late, behindhand, behind time, delayed, late in the day, overdue, tardy

belch *verb* **1** burp (informal), hiccup **2** emit, discharge, disgorge, erupt, give off, spew forth, vent

beleaguered *adjective*
1 harassed, badgered, hassled (informal), persecuted, pestered, plagued, put upon, vexed
2 besieged, assailed, beset, blockaded, hemmed in, surrounded

belief *noun* **1** trust, assurance, confidence, conviction, feeling, impression, judgment, notion, opinion **2** faith, credo, creed, doctrine, dogma, ideology,

principles, tenet

believable *adjective* credible, authentic, imaginable, likely, plausible, possible, probable, trustworthy

believe *verb* **1** accept, be certain of, be convinced of, credit, depend on, have faith in, rely on, swear by, trust **2** think, assume, gather, imagine, judge, presume, reckon, speculate, suppose

believer *noun* follower, adherent, convert, devotee, disciple, supporter, upholder, zealot

belittle *verb* disparage, decry, denigrate, deprecate, deride, scoff at, scorn, sneer at

belligerent *adjective*
1 aggressive, bellicose, combative, hostile, pugnacious, unfriendly, warlike, warring
♦ *noun* **2** fighter, combatant, warring nation

bellow *noun, verb* shout, bawl, cry, howl, roar, scream, shriek, yell

belly *noun* **1** stomach, abdomen, corporation (informal), gut, insides (informal), paunch, potbelly, tummy ♦ *verb* **2** swell out, billow, bulge, fill, spread, swell

bellyful *noun* surfeit, enough, excess, glut, plateful, plenty, satiety, too much

belonging *noun* relationship, acceptance, affinity, association, attachment, fellowship, inclusion, loyalty, rapport

belongings *plural noun* possessions, accoutrements, chattels, effects, gear, goods, paraphernalia, personal property, stuff, things

belong to verb 1 be the property of, be at the disposal of, be held by, be owned by 2 be a member of, be affiliated to, be allied to, be associated with, be included in

beloved adjective dear, admired, adored, darling, loved, pet, precious, prized, treasured, worshipped

below preposition 1 lesser, inferior, subject, subordinate 2 less than, lower than ◆adverb 3 lower, beneath, down, under, underneath

belt noun 1 waistband, band, cummerbund, girdle, girth, sash 2 Geography zone, area, district, layer, region, stretch, strip, tract

bemoan verb lament, bewail, deplore, grieve for, mourn, regret, rue, weep for

bemused adjective puzzled, at sea, bewildered, confused, flummoxed, muddled, nonplussed, perplexed

bench noun 1 seat, form, pew, settle, stall 2 worktable, board, counter, table, trestle table, workbench 3 the bench court, courtroom, judges, judiciary, magistrates, tribunal

benchmark noun reference point, criterion, gauge, level, measure, model, norm, par, standard, yardstick

bend verb 1 curve, arc, arch, bow, lean, turn, twist, veer ◆noun 2 curve, angle, arc, arch, bow, corner, loop, turn, twist

beneath preposition 1 under,

below, lower than, underneath 2 inferior to, below, less than 3 unworthy of, unbefitting ◆adverb 4 underneath, below, in a lower place

benefactor noun supporter, backer, donor, helper, patron, philanthropist, sponsor, well-wisher

beneficial adjective helpful, advantageous, benign, favourable, profitable, useful, valuable, wholesome

beneficiary noun recipient, heir, inheritor, payee, receiver

benefit noun 1 help, advantage, aid, asset, assistance, favour, good, profit ◆verb 2 help, aid, assist, avail, enhance, further, improve, profit

benevolent adjective kind, altruistic, benign, caring, charitable, generous, philanthropic

benign adjective 1 kindly, amiable, friendly, genial, kind, obliging, sympathetic 2 Medical harmless, curable, remediable

bent adjective 1 curved, angled, arched, bowed, crooked, hunched, stooped, twisted 2 bent on determined to, disposed to, fixed on, inclined to, insistent on, predisposed to, resolved on, set on ◆noun 3 inclination, ability, aptitude, leaning, penchant, preference, propensity, tendency

bequeath verb leave, bestow, endow, entrust, give, grant, hand down, impart, pass on, will

bequest noun legacy, bestowal, endowment, estate, gift, inheritance, settlement

berate verb scold, castigate, censure, chide, criticize, harangue, rebuke, reprimand, reprove, tell off (informal), upbraid

bereavement noun loss, affliction, death, deprivation, misfortune, tribulation

bereft adjective deprived, devoid, lacking, parted from, robbed of, wanting

berserk adverb crazy, amok, enraged, frantic, frenzied, mad, raging, wild

berth noun bunk, bed, billet, hammock 2 Nautical anchorage, dock, harbour, haven, pier, port, quay, wharf ♦ verb 3 Nautical anchor, dock, drop anchor, land, moor, tie up

beseech verb beg, ask, call upon, entreat, implore, plead, pray, solicit

beset verb plague, bedevil, harass, pester, trouble

beside preposition 1 next to, abreast of, adjacent to, alongside, at the side of, close to, near, nearby, neighbouring 2 beside oneself distraught, apoplectic, at the end of one's tether, demented, desperate, frantic, frenzied, out of one's mind, unhinged

besides adverb 1 too, also, as well, further, furthermore, in addition, into the bargain, moreover, otherwise, what's more ♦ preposition 2 apart from, barring, excepting, excluding, in addition to, other than, over and above, without

besiege verb 1 surround, blockade, encircle, hem in, lay siege to, shut in 2 harass, badger, harry, hassle (informal), hound, nag, pester, plague

besotted adjective infatuated, doting, hypnotized, smitten, spellbound

best adjective 1 finest, foremost, leading, most excellent, outstanding, pre-eminent, principal, supreme, unsurpassed ♦ adverb 2 most highly, extremely, greatly, most deeply, most fully ♦ noun 3 finest, cream, crème de la crème, elite, flower, pick, prime, top

bestial adjective brutal, barbaric, beastly, brutish, inhuman, savage, sordid

bestow verb present, award, commit, give, grant, hand out, impart, lavish

bet noun 1 gamble, long shot, risk, speculation, stake, venture, wager ♦ verb 2 gamble, chance, hazard, risk, speculate, stake, venture, wager

betoken verb indicate, bode, denote, promise, represent, signify, suggest

betray verb 1 be disloyal, be treacherous, be unfaithful, break one's promise, double-cross (informal), inform on or against, sell out (informal), stab in the back 2 give away, disclose, divulge, expose, let slip, reveal, uncover, unmask

betrayal noun 1 disloyalty, deception, double-cross (informal), sell-out (informal), treachery, treason, trickery 2 giving away, disclosure, divulgence, revelation

better adjective 1 superior,

excelling, finer, greater, higher-quality, more desirable, preferable, surpassing **2** well, cured, fully recovered, on the mend (*informal*), recovering, stronger ♦ *adverb* **3** in a more excellent manner, in a superior way, more advantageously, more attractively, more competently, more effectively **4** to a greater degree, more completely, more thoroughly ♦ *verb* **5** improve, enhance, further, raise

between *preposition* amidst, among, betwixt, in the middle of, mid

beverage *noun* drink, liquid, liquor, refreshment

bevy *noun* group, band, bunch (*informal*), collection, company, crowd, gathering, pack, troupe

bewail *verb* lament, bemoan, cry over, deplore, grieve for, moan, mourn, regret

beware *verb* be careful, be cautious, be wary, guard against, heed, look out, mind, take heed, watch out

bewilder *verb* confound, baffle, bemuse, confuse, flummox, mystify, nonplus, perplex, puzzle

bewildered *adjective* confused, at a loss, at sea, baffled, flummoxed, mystified, nonplussed, perplexed, puzzled

bewitch *verb* enchant, beguile, captivate, charm, enrapture, entrance, fascinate, hypnotize

bewitched *adjective* enchanted, charmed, entranced, fascinated, mesmerized, spellbound, under a spell

beyond *preposition* **1** past, above, apart from, at a distance, away from, over **2** exceeding, out of reach of, superior to, surpassing

bias *noun* **1** prejudice, favouritism, inclination, leaning, partiality, tendency ♦ *verb* **2** prejudice, distort, influence, predispose, slant, sway, twist, warp, weight

biased *adjective* prejudiced, distorted, one-sided, partial, slanted, weighted

bicker *verb* quarrel, argue, disagree, dispute, fight, row (*informal*), squabble, wrangle

bid *verb* **1** offer, proffer, propose, submit, tender **2** say, call, greet, tell, wish **3** tell, ask, command, direct, instruct, order, require ♦ *noun* **4** offer, advance, amount, price, proposal, sum, tender **5** attempt, crack (*informal*), effort, go (*informal*), stab (*informal*), try

bidding *noun* order, beck and call, command, direction, instruction, request, summons

big *adjective* **1** large, enormous, extensive, great, huge, immense, massive, substantial, vast **2** important, eminent, influential, leading, main, powerful, prominent, significant **3** grown-up, adult, elder, grown, mature **4** generous, altruistic, benevolent, gracious, magnanimous, noble, unselfish

bighead *noun Informal* boaster, braggart, know-all (*informal*)

bigheaded *adjective* boastful, arrogant, cocky, conceited, egotistic, immodest, overconfident, swollen-headed

bigot *noun* fanatic, racist,

sectarian, zealot

bigoted *adjective* <u>intolerant</u>, biased, dogmatic, narrow-minded, opinionated, prejudiced, sectarian

bigotry *noun* <u>intolerance</u>, bias, discrimination, dogmatism, fanaticism, narrow-mindedness, prejudice, sectarianism

bigwig *noun Informal* <u>important person</u>, big shot (*informal*), celebrity, dignitary, mogul, personage, somebody, V.I.P.

bill¹ *noun* 1 <u>charges</u>, account, invoice, reckoning, score, statement, tally 2 <u>proposal</u>, measure, piece of legislation, projected law 3 <u>advertisement</u>, bulletin, circular, handbill, handout, leaflet, notice, placard, poster 4 <u>list</u>, agenda, card, catalogue, inventory, listing, programme, roster, schedule ♦ *verb* 5 <u>charge</u>, debit, invoice 6 <u>advertise</u>, announce, give advance notice of, post

bill² *noun* <u>beak</u>, mandible, neb (*archaic or dialect*), nib

billet *verb* 1 <u>quarter</u>, accommodate, berth, station ♦ *noun* 2 <u>quarters</u>, accommodation, barracks, lodging

billow *noun* 1 <u>wave</u>, breaker, crest, roller, surge, swell, tide ♦ *verb* 2 <u>surge</u>, balloon, belly, puff up, rise up, roll, swell

bind *verb* 1 <u>secure</u>, fasten, hitch, lash, stick, strap, tie, wrap 2 <u>oblige</u>, compel, constrain, engage, force, necessitate, require ♦ *noun* 3 *Informal* <u>nuisance</u>, bore, difficulty, dilemma, drag (*informal*), pain in the neck (*informal*), quandary, spot (*informal*)

binding *adjective* <u>compulsory</u>, indissoluble, irrevocable, mandatory, necessary, obligatory, unalterable

binge *noun Informal* <u>bout</u>, bender (*informal*), feast, fling, orgy, spree

biography *noun* <u>life story</u>, account, curriculum vitae, CV, life, memoir, profile, record

birth *noun* 1 <u>childbirth</u>, delivery, nativity, parturition 2 <u>ancestry</u>, background, blood, breeding, lineage, parentage, pedigree, stock

bisect *verb* <u>cut in two</u>, cross, cut across, divide in two, halve, intersect, separate, split

bit¹ *noun* <u>piece</u>, crumb, fragment, grain, morsel, part, scrap, speck

bit² *noun* <u>curb</u>, brake, check, restraint, snaffle

bitchy *adjective Informal* <u>spiteful</u>, backbiting, catty (*informal*), mean, nasty, snide, vindictive

bite *verb* 1 <u>cut</u>, chew, gnaw, nip, pierce, pinch, snap, tear, wound ♦ *noun* 2 <u>wound</u>, nip, pinch, prick, smarting, sting, tooth marks 3 <u>snack</u>, food, light meal, morsel, mouthful, piece, refreshment, taste

biting *adjective* 1 <u>piercing</u>, bitter, cutting, harsh, penetrating, sharp 2 <u>sarcastic</u>, caustic, cutting, incisive, mordant, scathing, stinging, trenchant, vitriolic

bitter *adjective* 1 <u>sour</u>, acid, acrid, astringent, harsh, sharp, tart, unsweetened, vinegary 2 <u>resentful</u>, acrimonious, begrudging, hostile, sore, sour, sullen **3** freezing, biting, fierce, intense, severe, stinging

bitterness noun **1** sourness, acerbity, acidity, sharpness, tartness **2** resentment, acrimony, animosity, asperity, grudge, hostility, rancour, sarcasm

bizarre adjective strange, eccentric, extraordinary, fantastic, freakish, ludicrous, outlandish, peculiar, unusual, weird, zany

blab verb tell, blurt out, disclose, divulge, give away, let slip, let the cat out of the bag, reveal, spill the beans (informal)

black adjective **1** dark, dusky, ebony, jet, raven, sable, swarthy **2** hopeless, depressing, dismal, foreboding, gloomy, ominous, sad, sombre **3** angry, furious, hostile, menacing, resentful, sullen, threatening **4** wicked, bad, evil, iniquitous, nefarious, villainous ◆ verb **5** boycott, ban, bar, blacklist

blacken verb **1** darken, befoul, begrime, cloud, dirty, make black, smudge, soil **2** discredit, defame, denigrate, malign, slander, smear, smirch, vilify

blackguard noun scoundrel, bastard (offensive), bounder (old-fashioned Brit. slang), rascal, rogue, swine, villain

blacklist verb exclude, ban, bar, boycott, debar, expel, reject, snub

black magic noun witchcraft, black art, diabolism, necromancy, sorcery, voodoo, wizardry

blackmail noun **1** threat,

extortion, hush money (slang), intimidation, ransom ◆ verb **2** threaten, coerce, compel, demand, extort, hold to ransom, intimidate, squeeze

blackness noun darkness, duskiness, gloom, murkiness, swarthiness

blackout noun
1 unconsciousness, coma, faint, loss of consciousness, oblivion, swoon **2** noncommunication, censorship, radio silence, secrecy, suppression, withholding news

black sheep noun disgrace, bad egg (old-fashioned informal), dropout, ne'er-do-well, outcast, prodigal, renegade, reprobate, wastrel

blame verb **1** hold responsible, accuse, censure, chide, condemn, criticize, find fault with, reproach ◆ noun
2 responsibility, accountability, culpability, fault, guilt, liability, onus

blameless adjective innocent, above suspicion, clean, faultless, guiltless, immaculate, impeccable, irreproachable, perfect, unblemished, virtuous

blameworthy adjective reprehensible, discreditable, disreputable, indefensible, inexcusable, iniquitous, reproachable, shameful

bland adjective dull, boring, flat, humdrum, insipid, tasteless, unexciting, uninspiring, vapid

blank adjective **1** unmarked, bare, clean, clear, empty, plain, void, white **2** expressionless, deadpan, empty, impassive, poker-faced

blanket (*informal*), vacant, vague ♦ *noun* 3 empty space, emptiness, gap, nothingness, space, vacancy, vacuum, void

blanket *noun* 1 cover, coverlet, rug 2 covering, carpet, cloak, coat, layer, mantle, sheet ♦ *verb* 3 cover, cloak, coat, conceal, hide, mask, obscure, suppress

blare *verb* sound out, blast, clamour, clang, resound, roar, scream, trumpet

blarney *noun* flattery, blandishment, cajolery, coaxing, soft soap (*informal*), spiel, sweet talk (*informal*), wheedling

blasé *adjective* indifferent, apathetic, lukewarm, nonchalant, offhand, unconcerned

blaspheme *verb* curse, abuse, damn, desecrate, execrate, profane, revile, swear

blasphemous *adjective* irreverent, godless, impious, irreligious, profane, sacrilegious, ungodly

blasphemy *noun* irreverence, cursing, desecration, execration, impiety, profanity, sacrilege, swearing

blast *noun* 1 explosion, bang, burst, crash, detonation, discharge, eruption, outburst, salvo, volley 2 gust, gale, squall, storm, strong breeze, tempest 3 blare, blow, clang, honk, peal, scream, toot, wail ♦ *verb* 4 blow up, break up, burst, demolish, destroy, explode, put paid to, ruin, shatter

blastoff *noun* launch, discharge, expulsion, firing, launching, liftoff, projection, shot

blatant *adjective* obvious, brazen, conspicuous, flagrant, glaring, obtrusive, ostentatious, overt

blaze *noun* 1 fire, bonfire, conflagration, flames 2 glare, beam, brilliance, flare, flash, gleam, glitter, glow, light, radiance ♦ *verb* 3 burn, fire, flame 4 shine, beam, flare, flash, glare, gleam, glow

bleach *verb* whiten, blanch, fade, grow pale, lighten, wash out

bleak *adjective* 1 exposed, bare, barren, desolate, unsheltered, weather-beaten, windswept 2 dismal, cheerless, depressing, discouraging, dreary, gloomy, grim, hopeless, joyless, sombre

bleary *adjective* dim, blurred, blurry, foggy, fuzzy, hazy, indistinct, misty, murky

bleed *verb* 1 lose blood, flow, gush, ooze, run, shed blood, spurt 2 draw or take blood, extract, leech 3 *Informal* extort, drain, exhaust, fleece, milk, squeeze

blemish *noun* 1 mark, blot, defect, disfigurement, fault, flaw, imperfection, smudge, stain, taint ♦ *verb* 2 stain, damage, disfigure, impair, injure, mar, mark, spoil, sully, taint, tarnish

blend *verb* 1 mix, amalgamate, combine, compound, merge, mingle, unite 2 go well, complement, fit, go with, harmonize, suit ♦ *noun* 3 mixture, alloy, amalgamation, combination, compound, concoction, mix, synthesis, union

bless *verb* 1 sanctify, anoint, consecrate, dedicate, exalt, hallow, ordain 2 grant, bestow, favour, give, grace, provide

blessed adjective holy, adored, beatified, divine, hallowed, revered, sacred, sanctified

blessing noun **1** benediction, benison, commendation, consecration, dedication, grace, invocation, thanksgiving **2** approval, backing, consent, favour, good wishes, leave, permission, sanction, support **3** benefit, favour, gift, godsend, good fortune, help, kindness, service, windfall

blight noun **1** curse, affliction, bane, contamination, corruption, evil, plague, pollution, scourge, woe **2** disease, canker, decay, fungus, infestation, mildew, pest, pestilence, rot **3** frustrate, crush, dash, disappoint, mar, ruin, spoil, undo, wreck

blind adjective **1** sightless, eyeless, unseeing, unsighted, visionless **2** unaware of, careless, heedless, ignorant, inattentive, inconsiderate, indifferent, insensitive, oblivious, unconscious of **3** unreasoning, indiscriminate, prejudiced ◆ noun **4** cover, camouflage, cloak, façade, feint, front, mask, masquerade, screen, smoke screen

blindly adverb **1** thoughtlessly, carelessly, heedlessly, inconsiderately, recklessly, senselessly **2** aimlessly, at random, indiscriminately, instinctively

blink verb **1** wink, bat, flutter **2** flicker, flash, gleam, glimmer, shine, twinkle, wink ◆ noun **3 on the blink** Slang not working

(properly), faulty, malfunctioning, out of action, out of order, playing up

bliss noun joy, beatitude, blessedness, blissfulness, ecstasy, euphoria, felicity, gladness, happiness, heaven, nirvana, paradise, rapture

blissful adjective joyful, ecstatic, elated, enraptured, euphoric, happy, heavenly (informal), rapturous

blister noun sore, abscess, boil, carbuncle, cyst, pimple, pustule, swelling

blithe adjective heedless, careless, casual, indifferent, nonchalant, thoughtless, unconcerned, untroubled

blitz noun attack, assault, blitzkrieg, bombardment, campaign, offensive, onslaught, raid, strike

blizzard noun snowstorm, blast, gale, squall, storm, tempest

bloat verb puff up, balloon, blow up, dilate, distend, enlarge, expand, inflate, swell

blob noun drop, ball, bead, bubble, dab, droplet, globule, lump, mass

bloc noun group, alliance, axis, coalition, faction, league, union

block noun **1** piece, bar, brick, chunk, hunk, ingot, lump, mass **2** obstruction, bar, barrier, blockage, hindrance, impediment, jam, obstacle ◆ verb **3** obstruct, bung up (informal), choke, clog, close, plug, stem the flow, stop up **4** stop, bar, check, halt, hinder, impede, obstruct, thwart

blockade noun stoppage, barricade, barrier, block, hindrance, impediment, obstacle, obstruction, restriction, siege

blockage noun obstruction, block, impediment, occlusion, stoppage

blockhead noun idiot, chump (informal), dunce, fool, nitwit, numbskull or numskull, thickhead, twit (informal, chiefly Brit.)

bloke noun Informal man, chap, character (informal), fellow, guy (informal), individual, person

blond, blonde adjective fair, fair-haired, fair-skinned, flaxen, golden-haired, light, tow-headed

blood noun 1 lifeblood, gore, vital fluid 2 family, ancestry, birth, descent, extraction, kinship, lineage, relations

bloodcurdling adjective terrifying, appalling, chilling, dreadful, fearful, frightening, hair-raising, horrendous, horrifying, scaring, spine-chilling

bloodshed noun killing, blood bath, blood-letting, butchery, carnage, gore, massacre, murder, slaughter, slaying

bloodthirsty adjective cruel, barbarous, brutal, cut-throat, ferocious, gory, murderous, savage, vicious, warlike

bloody adjective 1 bloodstained, bleeding, blood-soaked, blood-spattered, gaping, raw 2 cruel, ferocious, fierce, sanguinary, savage

bloom noun 1 flower, blossom, blossoming, bud, efflorescence, opening (of flowers) 2 prime, beauty, flourishing, freshness, glow, health, heyday, lustre, radiance, vigour ♦ verb 3 blossom, blow, bud, burgeon, open, sprout 4 flourish, develop, fare well, grow, prosper, succeed, thrive, wax

blossom noun 1 flower, bloom, bud, floret, flowers ♦ verb 2 flower, bloom, burgeon 3 grow, bloom, develop, flourish, mature, progress, prosper, thrive

blot noun 1 spot, blotch, mark, patch, smear, smudge, speck, splodge 2 stain, blemish, defect, fault, flaw, scar, spot, taint ♦ verb 3 stain, disgrace, mark, smirch, smudge, spoil, spot, sully, tarnish 4 soak up, absorb, dry, take up 5 blot out a obliterate, darken, destroy, eclipse, efface, obscure, shadow b erase, cancel, expunge

blow¹ verb 1 carry, buffet, drive, fling, flutter, move, sweep, waft 2 exhale, breathe, pant, puff 3 play, blare, mouth, pipe, sound, toot, trumpet, vibrate

blow² noun 1 knock, bang, clout (informal), punch, smack, sock (slang), stroke, thump, wallop (informal), whack 2 setback, bombshell, calamity, catastrophe, disappointment, disaster, misfortune, reverse, shock

blow out verb 1 put out, extinguish, snuff 2 burst, erupt, explode, rupture, shatter

blow up verb 1 explode, blast, blow sky-high, bomb, burst, detonate, rupture, shatter

2 inflate, bloat, distend, enlarge, expand, fill, puff up, pump up, swell **3** Informal lose one's temper, become angry, erupt, fly off the handle (informal), hit the roof (informal), rage, see red (informal)

bludgeon noun **1** club, cosh (Brit.), cudgel, truncheon ♦ verb **2** club, beat up, cosh (Brit.), cudgel, knock down, strike **3** bully, bulldoze (informal), coerce, force, railroad (informal), steamroller

blue adjective **1** azure, cerulean, cobalt, cyan, navy, sapphire, sky-coloured, ultramarine **2** depressed, dejected, despondent, downcast, low, melancholy, sad, unhappy **3** smutty, indecent, lewd, obscene, risqué, X-rated (informal)

blueprint noun plan, design, draft, outline, pattern, pilot scheme, prototype, sketch

blues plural noun depression, doldrums, dumps (informal), gloom, low spirits, melancholy, unhappiness

bluff[1] verb **1** deceive, con, delude, fake, feign, mislead, pretend, pull the wool over someone's eyes ♦ noun **2** deception, bluster, bravado, deceit, fraud, humbug, pretence, sham, subterfuge

bluff[2] noun **1** precipice, bank, cliff, crag, escarpment, headland, peak, promontory, ridge ♦ adjective **2** hearty, blunt, blustering, genial, good-natured, open, outspoken, plain-spoken

blunder noun **1** mistake, bloomer

(Brit. informal), clanger (informal), faux pas, gaffe, howler (informal), indiscretion **2** error, fault, inaccuracy, mistake, oversight, slip, slip-up (informal) ♦ verb **3** make a mistake, botch, bungle, err, put one's foot in it (informal), slip up (informal) **4** stumble, bumble, flounder

blunt adjective **1** dull, dulled, edgeless, pointless, rounded, unsharpened **2** forthright, bluff, brusque, frank, outspoken, plain-spoken, rude, straightforward, tactless ♦ verb **3** dull, dampen, deaden, numb, soften, take the edge off, water down, weaken

blur verb **1** make indistinct, cloud, darken, make hazy, make vague, mask, obscure ♦ noun **2** indistinctness, confusion, fog, haze, obscurity

blurt out verb exclaim, disclose, let the cat out of the bag, reveal, spill the beans (informal), tell all, utter suddenly

blush verb **1** turn red, colour, flush, go red (as a beetroot), redden, turn scarlet ♦ noun **2** reddening, colour, flush, glow, pink tinge, rosiness, rosy tint, ruddiness

bluster verb **1** roar, bully, domineer, hector, rant, storm ♦ noun **2** hot air (informal), bluff, bombast, bravado

blustery adjective gusty, boisterous, inclement, squally, stormy, tempestuous, violent, wild, windy

board noun **1** plank, panel, piece of timber, slat, timber **2** directors, advisers, committee,

conclave, council, panel, trustees
3 meals, daily meals, provisions,
victuals ♦ *verb* **4 get on**, embark,
enter, mount **5 lodge**, put up,
quarter, room

boast *verb* **1** brag, blow one's
own trumpet, crow, strut,
swagger, talk big (*slang*), vaunt
2 possess, be proud of,
congratulate oneself on, exhibit,
flatter oneself, pride oneself on,
show off ♦ *noun* **3** brag, avowal

boastful *adjective* bragging,
cocky, conceited, crowing,
egotistical, full of oneself,
swaggering, swollen-headed,
vaunting

bob *verb* duck, bounce, hop,
nod, oscillate, waggle, wobble

bode *verb* portend, augur, be an
omen of, forebode, foretell,
predict, signify, threaten

bodily *adjective* physical, actual,
carnal, corporal, corporeal,
material, substantial, tangible

body *noun* **1** physique, build,
figure, form, frame, shape
2 torso, trunk **3 corpse**, cadaver,
carcass, dead body, remains, stiff
(*slang*) **4 organization**,
association, band, bloc,
collection, company,
confederation, congress,
corporation, society **5 main part**,
bulk, essence, mass, material,
matter, substance

boffin *noun Brit. informal* expert,
brainbox, egghead, genius,
intellectual, inventor, mastermind

bog *noun* marsh, fen, mire,
morass, quagmire, slough,
swamp, wetlands

bogey *noun* bugbear, bête noire,
bugaboo, nightmare

bogus *adjective* fake, artificial,
counterfeit, false, forged,
fraudulent, imitation, phoney *or*
phony (*informal*), sham

bohemian *adjective*
1 unconventional, alternative,
artistic, arty (*informal*), left bank,
nonconformist, offbeat,
unorthodox ♦ *noun*
2 nonconformist, beatnik,
dropout, hippy, iconoclast

boil[1] *verb* bubble, effervesce, fizz,
foam, froth, seethe

boil[2] *noun* pustule, blister,
carbuncle, gathering, swelling,
tumour, ulcer

boisterous *adjective* unruly,
disorderly, loud, noisy, riotous,
rollicking, rowdy, unrestrained,
vociferous, wild

bold *adjective* **1** fearless,
adventurous, audacious, brave,
courageous, daring, enterprising,
heroic, intrepid, valiant
2 impudent, barefaced, brazen,
cheeky, confident, forward,
insolent, rude, shameless

bolster *verb* support, augment,
boost, help, reinforce, shore up,
strengthen

bolt *noun* **1** bar, catch, fastener,
latch, lock, sliding bar **2** pin,
peg, rivet, rod ♦ *verb* **3** run
away, abscond, dash, escape,
flee, fly, make a break (for it),
run for it **4** lock, bar, fasten,
latch, secure **5** gobble, cram,
devour, gorge, gulp, guzzle,
stuff, swallow whole, wolf

bomb *noun* **1** explosive, device,
grenade, mine, missile,
projectile, rocket, shell, torpedo
♦ *verb* **2** blow up, attack, blow
sky-high, bombard, destroy,

shell, strafe, torpedo

bombard verb **1** bomb, assault, blitz, fire upon, open fire, pound, shell, strafe **2** attack, assail, beset, besiege, harass, hound, pester

bombardment noun bombing, assault, attack, barrage, blitz, fusillade, shelling

bombastic adjective grandiloquent, grandiose, high-flown, inflated, pompous, verbose, wordy

bona fide adjective genuine, actual, authentic, honest, kosher (informal), legitimate, real, true

bond noun **1** fastening, chain, cord, fetter, ligature, manacle, shackle, tie **2** tie, affiliation, affinity, attachment, connection, link, relation, union **3** agreement, contract, covenant, guarantee, obligation, pledge, promise, word ♦ verb **4** hold together, bind, connect, fasten, fix together, glue, paste

bondage noun slavery, captivity, confinement, enslavement, imprisonment, subjugation

bonus noun extra, dividend, gift, icing on the cake, plus, premium, prize, reward

bony adjective thin, emaciated, gaunt, lean, scrawny, skin and bone, skinny

book noun **1** work, publication, title, tome, tract, volume **2** notebook, album, diary, exercise book, jotter, pad ♦ verb **3** reserve, arrange for, charter, engage, make reservations, organize, programme, schedule **4** note, enter, list, log, mark down, put down, record,

register, write down

booklet noun brochure, leaflet, pamphlet

boom verb **1** bang, blast, crash, explode, resound, reverberate, roar, roll, rumble, thunder **2** flourish, develop, expand, grow, increase, intensify, prosper, strengthen, swell, thrive ♦ noun **3** bang, blast, burst, clap, crash, explosion, roar, rumble, thunder **4** expansion, boost, development, growth, improvement, increase, jump, upsurge, upswing, upturn

boon noun benefit, advantage, blessing, favour, gift, godsend, manna from heaven, windfall

boorish adjective loutish, churlish, coarse, crude, oafish, uncivilized, uncouth, vulgar

boost noun **1** help, encouragement, praise, promotion **2** rise, addition, expansion, improvement, increase, increment, jump ♦ verb **3** increase, add to, amplify, develop, enlarge, expand, heighten, raise **4** advertise, encourage, foster, further, hype, plug (informal), praise, promote

boot verb kick, drive, drop-kick, knock, punt, put the boot in(to) (slang), shove

booty noun plunder, gains, haul, loot, prey, spoils, swag (slang), takings, winnings

border noun **1** frontier, borderline, boundary, line, march **2** edge, bounds, brink, limits, margin, rim, verge ♦ verb **3** edge, bind, decorate, fringe, hem, rim, trim

bore[1] verb drill, burrow, gouge

out, mine, penetrate, perforate, pierce, sink, tunnel

bore² verb **1** tire, be tedious, fatigue, jade, pall on, send to sleep, wear out, weary ♦ noun **2** nuisance, anorak (informal), pain (informal), yawn (informal)

bored adjective fed up, listless, tired, uninterested, wearied

boredom noun tedium, apathy, ennui, flatness, monotony, sameness, tediousness, weariness, world-weariness

boring adjective uninteresting, dull, flat, humdrum, mind-numbing, monotonous, tedious, tiresome

borrow verb **1** take on loan, cadge, scrounge (informal), touch (someone) for (slang), use temporarily **2** steal, adopt, copy, obtain, plagiarize, take, usurp

bosom noun **1** breast, bust, chest ♦ adjective **2** intimate, boon, cherished, close, confidential, dear, very dear

boss¹ noun head, chief, director, employer, gaffer (informal, chiefly Brit.), leader, manager, master, supervisor

boss² noun stud, knob, point, protuberance, tip

boss around verb Informal domineer, bully, dominate, oppress, order, push around (slang)

bossy adjective domineering, arrogant, authoritarian, autocratic, dictatorial, hectoring, high-handed, imperious, overbearing, tyrannical

botch verb **1** spoil, blunder, bungle, cock up (Brit. slang), make a pig's ear of (informal), mar, mess up, screw up (informal) ♦ noun **2** mess, blunder, bungle, cock-up (Brit. slang), failure, hash, pig's ear (informal)

bother verb **1** trouble, alarm, concern, disturb, harass, hassle (informal), inconvenience, pester, plague, worry ♦ noun **2** trouble, difficulty, fuss, hassle (informal), inconvenience, irritation, nuisance, problem, worry

bottleneck noun hold-up, block, blockage, congestion, impediment, jam, obstacle, obstruction, snarl-up (informal, chiefly Brit.)

bottle up verb suppress, check, contain, curb, keep back, restrict, shut in, trap

bottom noun **1** lowest part, base, bed, depths, floor, foot, foundation **2** underside, lower side, sole, underneath **3** buttocks, backside, behind (informal), posterior, rear, rump, seat ♦ adjective **4** lowest, last

bottomless adjective unlimited, boundless, deep, fathomless, immeasurable, inexhaustible, infinite, unfathomable

bounce verb **1** rebound, bob, bound, jump, leap, recoil, ricochet, spring ♦ noun **2** Informal life, dynamism, energy, go (informal), liveliness, vigour, vivacity, zip (informal) **3** springiness, elasticity, give, recoil, resilience, spring

bound¹ adjective **1** tied, cased, fastened, fixed, pinioned, secured, tied up **2** certain, destined, doomed, fated, sure

3 obliged, beholden, committed, compelled, constrained, duty-bound, forced, pledged, required

bound² verb limit, confine, demarcate, encircle, enclose, hem in, restrain, restrict, surround

bound³ verb, noun leap, bob, bounce, gambol, hurdle, jump, skip, spring, vault

boundary noun limits, barrier, border, borderline, brink, edge, extremity, fringe, frontier, margin

boundless adjective unlimited, endless, immense, incalculable, inexhaustible, infinite, unconfined, untold, vast

bounds plural noun boundary, border, confine, edge, extremity, limit, rim, verge

bountiful adjective Literary **1** plentiful, abundant, ample, bounteous, copious, exuberant, lavish, luxuriant, prolific **2** generous, liberal, magnanimous, open-handed, prodigal, unstinting

bounty noun Literary **1** generosity, benevolence, charity, kindness, largesse or largess, liberality, philanthropy **2** reward, bonus, gift, present

bouquet noun **1** bunch of flowers, buttonhole, corsage, garland, nosegay, posy, spray, wreath **2** aroma, fragrance, perfume, redolence, savour, scent

bourgeois adjective middle-class, conventional, hidebound, materialistic, traditional

bout noun **1** period, fit, spell, stint, term, turn **2** fight, boxing

match, competition, contest, encounter, engagement, match, set-to, struggle

bow¹ verb **1** bend, bob, droop, genuflect, nod, stoop **2** give in, acquiesce, comply, concede, defer, kowtow, relent, submit, succumb, surrender, yield ♦ noun **3** bending, bob, genuflexion, kowtow, nod, obeisance

bow² noun Nautical prow, beak, fore, head, stem

bowels plural noun **1** guts, entrails, innards (informal), insides (informal), intestines, viscera, vitals **2** depths, belly, core, deep, hold, inside, interior

bowl¹ noun basin, dish, vessel

bowl² verb throw, fling, hurl, pitch

box¹ noun **1** container, carton, case, casket, chest, pack, package, receptacle, trunk ♦ verb **2** pack, package, wrap

box² verb fight, exchange blows, spar

boxer noun fighter, prizefighter, pugilist, sparring partner

boy noun lad, fellow, junior, schoolboy, stripling, youngster, youth

boycott verb embargo, ban, bar, black, exclude, outlaw, prohibit, refuse, reject

boyfriend noun sweetheart, admirer, beau, date, lover, man, suitor

boyish adjective youthful, adolescent, childish, immature, juvenile, puerile, young

brace noun **1** support, bolster, bracket, buttress, prop, reinforcement, stay, strut, truss ♦ verb **2** support, bolster, buttress, fortify, reinforce, steady, strengthen

bracing adjective <u>refreshing</u>, brisk, crisp, exhilarating, fresh, invigorating, stimulating

brag verb <u>boast</u>, blow one's own trumpet, bluster, crow, swagger, talk big (slang), vaunt

braggart noun <u>boaster</u>, bigmouth (slang), bragger, show-off (informal)

braid verb <u>interweave</u>, entwine, interlace, intertwine, lace, plait, twine, weave

brainless adjective <u>stupid</u>, foolish, idiotic, inane, mindless, senseless, thoughtless, witless

brains plural noun <u>intelligence</u>, intellect, sense, understanding

brainwave noun <u>idea</u>, bright idea, stroke of genius, thought

brainy adjective Informal <u>intelligent</u>, bright, brilliant, clever, smart

brake noun 1 <u>control</u>, check, constraint, curb, rein, restraint ♦ verb 2 <u>slow</u>, check, decelerate, halt, moderate, reduce speed, slacken, stop

branch noun 1 <u>bough</u>, arm, limb, offshoot, shoot, spray, sprig 2 <u>division</u>, chapter, department, office, part, section, subdivision, subsection, wing

brand noun 1 <u>label</u>, emblem, hallmark, logo, mark, marker, sign, stamp, symbol, trademark 2 <u>kind</u>, cast, class, grade, make, quality, sort, species, type, variety ♦ verb 3 <u>mark</u>, burn, burn in, label, scar, stamp 4 <u>stigmatize</u>, censure, denounce, discredit, disgrace, expose, mark

brandish verb <u>wave</u>, display, exhibit, flaunt, flourish, parade, raise, shake, swing, wield

brash adjective <u>bold</u>, brazen, cocky, impertinent, impudent, insolent, pushy (informal), rude

bravado noun <u>swagger</u>, bluster, boastfulness, boasting, bombast, swashbuckling, vaunting

brave adjective 1 <u>courageous</u>, bold, daring, fearless, heroic, intrepid, plucky, resolute, valiant ♦ verb 2 <u>confront</u>, defy, endure, face, stand up to, suffer, tackle, withstand

bravery noun <u>courage</u>, boldness, daring, fearlessness, fortitude, heroism, intrepidity, mettle, pluck, spirit, valour

brawl noun 1 <u>fight</u>, affray (Law), altercation, clash, dispute, fracas, fray, melee or mêlée, punch-up (Brit. informal), rumpus, scuffle, skirmish ♦ verb 2 <u>fight</u>, scrap (informal), scuffle, tussle, wrestle

brawn noun <u>muscle</u>, beef (informal), might, muscles, power, strength, vigour

brawny adjective <u>muscular</u>, beefy (informal), hefty (informal), lusty, powerful, strapping, strong, sturdy, well-built

brazen adjective <u>bold</u>, audacious, barefaced, brash, defiant, impudent, insolent, shameless, unabashed, unashamed

breach noun 1 <u>nonobservance</u>, contravention, infraction, infringement, noncompliance, transgression, trespass, violation 2 <u>crack</u>, cleft, fissure, gap, opening, rift, rupture, split

bread noun 1 <u>food</u>, fare,

nourishment, sustenance **2** *Slang* money, cash, dough (*slang*)

breadth noun **1** width, broadness, latitude, span, spread, wideness **2** extent, compass, expanse, range, scale, scope

break verb **1** separate, burst, crack, destroy, disintegrate, fracture, fragment, shatter, smash, snap, split, tear **2** disobey, breach, contravene, disregard, infringe, renege on, transgress, violate **3** reveal, announce, disclose, divulge, impart, inform, let out, make public, proclaim, tell **4** stop, abandon, cut, discontinue, give up, interrupt, pause, rest, suspend **5** weaken, demoralize, dispirit, subdue, tame, undermine **6** *Of a record, etc.* beat, better, exceed, excel, go beyond, outdo, outstrip, surpass, top ♦ *noun* **7** division, crack, fissure, fracture, gap, hole, opening, split, tear **8** rest, breather (*informal*), hiatus, interlude, intermission, interruption, interval, let-up (*informal*), lull, pause, respite **9** *Informal* stroke of luck, advantage, chance, fortune, opening, opportunity

breakable adjective fragile, brittle, crumbly, delicate, flimsy, frail, frangible, friable

breakdown noun collapse, disintegration, disruption, failure, mishap, stoppage

break down verb **1** collapse, come unstuck, fail, seize up, stop, stop working **2** be overcome, crack up (*informal*),

go to pieces

break-in noun burglary, breaking and entering, robbery

break off verb **1** detach, divide, part, pull off, separate, sever, snap off, splinter **2** stop, cease, desist, discontinue, end, finish, halt, pull the plug on, suspend, terminate

break out verb begin, appear, arise, commence, emerge, happen, occur, set in, spring up, start

breakthrough noun development, advance, discovery, find, invention, leap, progress, quantum leap, step forward

break up verb **1** separate, dissolve, divide, divorce, part, scatter, sever, split **2** stop, adjourn, disband, dismantle, end, suspend, terminate

breast noun bosom, bust, chest, front, teat, udder

breath noun respiration, breathing, exhalation, gasp, gulp, inhalation, pant, wheeze

breathe verb **1** inhale and exhale, draw in, gasp, gulp, pant, puff, respire, wheeze **2** whisper, murmur, sigh

breather noun *Informal* rest, break, breathing space, halt, pause, recess, respite

breathless adjective **1** out of breath, gasping, gulping, panting, short-winded, spent, wheezing **2** excited, eager, on tenterhooks, open-mouthed, with bated breath

breathtaking adjective amazing, astonishing, awe-inspiring, exciting, impressive, magnificent, sensational, stunning (*informal*), thrilling

breed verb 1 reproduce, bear, bring forth, hatch, multiply, procreate, produce, propagate 2 bring up, cultivate, develop, nourish, nurture, raise, rear 3 produce, arouse, bring about, cause, create, generate, give rise to, stir up ♦ noun 4 variety, pedigree, race, species, stock, strain, type 5 kind, brand, sort, stamp, type, variety

breeding noun 1 upbringing, ancestry, cultivation, development, lineage, nurture, raising, rearing, reproduction, training 2 refinement, conduct, courtesy, cultivation, culture, polish, sophistication, urbanity

breeze noun 1 light wind, air, breath of wind, current of air, draught, gust, waft, zephyr ♦ verb 2 move briskly, flit, glide, hurry, pass, sail, sweep

breezy adjective 1 windy, airy, blowy, blustery, fresh, gusty, squally 2 carefree, blithe, casual, easy-going, free and easy, jaunty, light-hearted, lively, sprightly

brevity noun 1 shortness, briefness, impermanence, transience, transitoriness 2 conciseness, crispness, curtness, economy, pithiness, succinctness, terseness

brew verb 1 make (*beer*), boil, ferment, infuse (*tea*), soak, steep, stew 2 develop, foment, form, gather, start, stir up ♦ noun 3 drink, beverage, blend, concoction, infusion, liquor,

mixture, preparation

bribe verb 1 buy off, corrupt, grease the palm or hand of (*slang*), pay off (*informal*), reward, suborn ♦ noun 2 inducement, allurement, backhander (*slang*), enticement, kickback (*U.S.*), pay-off (*informal*), sweetener (*slang*)

bribery noun buying off, corruption, inducement, palm-greasing (*slang*), payola (*informal*)

bric-a-brac noun knick-knacks, baubles, curios, ornaments, trinkets

bridal adjective matrimonial, conjugal, connubial, marital, marriage, nuptial, wedding

bridge noun 1 arch, flyover, overpass, span, viaduct ♦ verb 2 connect, join, link, span

bridle noun 1 curb, check, control, rein, restraint ♦ verb 2 get angry, be indignant, bristle, draw (oneself) up, get one's back up, raise one's hackles, rear up

brief adjective 1 short, ephemeral, fleeting, momentary, quick, short-lived, swift, transitory ♦ noun 2 summary, abridgment, abstract, epitome, outline, précis, sketch, synopsis ♦ verb 3 inform, advise, explain, fill in (*informal*), instruct, keep posted, prepare, prime, put (someone) in the picture (*informal*)

briefing noun instructions, conference, directions, guidance, information, preparation, priming, rundown

briefly adverb shortly, concisely,

hastily, hurriedly, in a nutshell, in brief, momentarily, quickly

brigade noun group, band, company, corps, force, organization, outfit, squad, team, troop, unit

brigand noun bandit, desperado, freebooter, gangster, highwayman, marauder, outlaw, plunderer, robber

bright adjective 1 shining, brilliant, dazzling, gleaming, glowing, luminous, lustrous, radiant, shimmering, vivid 2 intelligent, astute, aware, clever, inventive, quick-witted, sharp, smart, wide-awake 3 sunny, clear, cloudless, fair, limpid, lucid, pleasant, translucent, transparent, unclouded

brighten verb make brighter, gleam, glow, illuminate, lighten, light up, shine

brightness noun shine, brilliance, glare, incandescence, intensity, light, luminosity, radiance, vividness 2 intelligence, acuity, cleverness, quickness, sharpness, smartness

brilliance, brilliancy noun 1 brightness, dazzle, intensity, luminosity, lustre, radiance, sparkle, vividness 2 talent, cleverness, distinction, excellence, genius, greatness, inventiveness, wisdom 3 splendour, éclat, glamour, grandeur, illustriousness, magnificence

brilliant adjective 1 shining, bright, dazzling, glittering, intense, luminous, radiant, sparkling, vivid 2 splendid,

celebrated, famous, glorious, illustrious, magnificent, notable, outstanding, superb 3 intelligent, clever, expert, gifted, intellectual, inventive, masterly, penetrating, profound, talented

brim noun 1 rim, border, brink, edge, lip, margin, skirt, verge ◆ verb 2 be full, fill, fill up, hold no more, overflow, run over, spill, well over

bring verb 1 take, bear, carry, conduct, convey, deliver, escort, fetch, guide, lead, transfer, transport 2 cause, contribute to, create, effect, inflict, occasion, produce, result in, wreak

bring about verb cause, accomplish, achieve, create, effect, generate, give rise to, make happen, produce

bring off verb accomplish, achieve, carry off, execute, perform, pull off, succeed

bring up verb 1 rear, breed, develop, educate, form, nurture, raise, support, teach, train 2 mention, allude to, broach, introduce, move, propose, put forward, raise

brink noun edge, border, boundary, brim, fringe, frontier, limit, lip, margin, rim, skirt, threshold, verge

brisk adjective lively, active, bustling, busy, energetic, quick, sprightly, spry, vigorous

briskly adverb quickly, actively, apace, efficiently, energetically, promptly, rapidly, readily, smartly

bristle noun 1 hair, barb, prickle, spine, stubble, thorn, whisker ◆ verb 2 stand up, rise, stand on end **3** be angry, bridle, flare up, rage, see red, seethe

bristly adjective **1** hairy, prickly, rough, stubbly

brittle adjective fragile, breakable, crisp, crumbling, crumbly, delicate, frail, frangible, friable

broach verb **1** bring up, introduce, mention, open up, propose, raise the subject, speak of, suggest, talk of, touch on **2** open, crack, draw off, pierce, puncture, start, tap, uncork

broad adjective **1** wide, ample, expansive, extensive, generous, large, roomy, spacious, vast, voluminous, widespread **2** general, all-embracing, comprehensive, encyclopedic, inclusive, sweeping, wide, wide-ranging

broadcast noun **1** transmission, programme, show, telecast ♦ verb **2** transmit, air, beam, cable, put on the air, radio, relay, show, televise **3** make public, advertise, announce, circulate, proclaim, publish, report, spread

broaden verb expand, develop, enlarge, extend, increase, spread, stretch, supplement, swell, widen

broad-minded adjective tolerant, free-thinking, indulgent, liberal, open-minded, permissive, unbiased, unbigoted, unprejudiced

broadside noun attack, assault, battering, bombardment, censure, criticism, denunciation, diatribe

brochure noun booklet, advertisement, circular, folder, handbill, hand-out, leaflet, mailshot, pamphlet

broke adjective Informal penniless, bankrupt, bust (informal), down and out, impoverished, insolvent, in the red, ruined, short, skint (Brit. slang)

broken adjective **1** smashed, burst, fractured, fragmented, ruptured, separated, severed, shattered **2** interrupted, discontinuous, erratic, fragmentary, incomplete, intermittent, spasmodic **3** not working, defective, imperfect, kaput (informal), on the blink (slang), out of order **4** imperfect, disjointed, halting, hesitating, stammering

brokenhearted adjective heartbroken, desolate, devastated, disconsolate, grief-stricken, inconsolable, miserable, sorrowful, wretched

broker noun dealer, agent, factor, go-between, intermediary, middleman, negotiator

bronze adjective reddish-brown, brownish, chestnut, copper, rust, tan

brood noun **1** offspring, clutch, family, issue, litter, progeny ♦ verb **2** think upon, agonize, dwell upon, mope, mull over, muse, ponder, ruminate

brook noun stream, beck, burn, rill, rivulet, watercourse

brother noun **1** sibling, blood brother, kin, kinsman, relation, relative **2** monk, cleric, friar

brotherhood noun **1** fellowship, brotherliness, camaraderie, companionship, comradeship,

friendliness, kinship
2 association, alliance, community, fraternity, guild, league, order, society, union

brotherly adjective kind, affectionate, altruistic, amicable, benevolent, cordial, fraternal, friendly, neighbourly, philanthropic, sympathetic

browbeat verb bully, badger, coerce, dragoon, hector, intimidate, ride roughshod over, threaten, tyrannize

brown adjective **1** brunette, auburn, bay, bronze, chestnut, chocolate, coffee, dun, hazel, sunburnt, tan, tanned, tawny, umber ◆ verb **2** fry, cook, grill, sauté, seal, sear

browse verb **1** skim, dip into, examine cursorily, flip through, glance at, leaf through, look round, look through, peruse, scan, survey **2** graze, eat, feed, nibble

bruise verb **1** discolour, damage, injure, mar, mark, pound ◆ noun **2** discoloration, black mark, blemish, contusion, injury, mark, swelling

brunt noun full force, burden, force, impact, pressure, shock, strain, stress, thrust, violence

brush[1] noun **1** broom, besom, sweeper **2** encounter, clash, conflict, confrontation, skirmish, tussle ◆ verb **3** clean, buff, paint, polish, sweep, wash **4** touch, flick, glance, graze, kiss, scrape, stroke, sweep

brush[2] noun shrubs, brushwood, bushes, copse, scrub, thicket, undergrowth

brush off verb Slang ignore,

disdain, dismiss, disregard, reject, repudiate, scorn, snub, spurn

brush up verb revise, bone up (informal), cram, go over, polish up, read up, refresh one's memory, relearn, study

brusque adjective curt, abrupt, discourteous, gruff, impolite, sharp, short, surly, terse

brutal adjective **1** cruel, bloodthirsty, heartless, inhuman, ruthless, savage, uncivilized, vicious **2** harsh, callous, gruff, impolite, insensitive, rough, rude, severe

brutality noun cruelty, atrocity, barbarism, bloodthirstiness, ferocity, inhumanity, ruthlessness, savagery, viciousness

brute noun **1** savage, barbarian, beast, devil, fiend, monster, sadist, swine **2** animal, beast, creature, wild animal ◆ adjective **3** mindless, bodily, carnal, fleshly, instinctive, physical, senseless, unthinking

bubble noun **1** air ball, bead, blister, blob, drop, droplet, globule ◆ verb **2** foam, boil, effervesce, fizz, froth, percolate, seethe, sparkle **3** gurgle, babble, burble, murmur, ripple, trickle

bubbly adjective **1** lively, animated, bouncy, elated, excited, happy, merry, sparky **2** frothy, carbonated, effervescent, fizzy, foamy, sparkling

buccaneer noun pirate, corsair, freebooter, privateer, sea-rover

buckle noun **1** fastener, catch, clasp, clip, hasp ◆ verb **2** fasten, clasp, close, hook, secure

3 distort, bend, bulge, cave in, collapse, contort, crumple, fold, twist, warp

bud *noun* **1** shoot, embryo, germ, sprout ◆ *verb* **2** develop, burgeon, burst forth, grow, shoot, sprout

budding *adjective* developing, beginning, burgeoning, embryonic, fledgling, growing, incipient, nascent, potential, promising

budge *verb* move, dislodge, push, shift, stir

budget *noun* **1** allowance, allocation, cost, finances, funds, means, resources ◆ *verb* **2** plan, allocate, apportion, cost, estimate, ration

buff[1] *adjective* **1** yellowish-brown, sandy, straw, tan, yellowish ◆ *verb* **2** polish, brush, burnish, rub, shine, smooth

buff[2] *noun Informal* expert, addict, admirer, aficionado, connoisseur, devotee, enthusiast, fan

buffer *noun* safeguard, bulwark, bumper, cushion, fender, intermediary, screen, shield, shock absorber

buffet[1] *noun* snack bar, brasserie, café, cafeteria, refreshment counter, sideboard

buffet[2] *verb* batter, beat, bump, knock, pound, pummel, strike, thump, wallop (*informal*)

buffoon *noun* clown, comedian, comic, fool, harlequin, jester, joker, wag

bug *noun* **1** *Informal* illness, disease, infection, lurgy (*informal*), virus **2** fault, defect, error, flaw, glitch, gremlin ◆ *verb*

3 *Informal* annoy, bother, disturb, get on one's nerves (*informal*), hassle (*informal*), irritate, pester, vex **4** tap, eavesdrop, listen in, spy

bugbear *noun* pet hate, bane, bête noire, bogey, dread, horror, nightmare

build *verb* **1** construct, assemble, erect, fabricate, form, make, put up, raise ◆ *noun* **2** physique, body, figure, form, frame, shape, structure

building *noun* structure, domicile, dwelling, edifice, house

build-up *noun* increase, accumulation, development, enlargement, escalation, expansion, gain, growth

bulbous *adjective* bulging, bloated, convex, rounded, swelling, swollen

bulge *noun* **1** swelling, bump, hump, lump, projection, protrusion, protuberance **2** increase, boost, intensification, rise, surge ◆ *verb* **3** swell out, dilate, distend, expand, project, protrude, puff out, stick out

bulk *noun* **1** size, dimensions, immensity, largeness, magnitude, substance, volume, weight **2** main part, better part, body, lion's share, majority, mass, most, nearly all, preponderance

bulky *adjective* large, big, cumbersome, heavy, hulking, massive, substantial, unwieldy, voluminous, weighty

bulldoze *verb* demolish, flatten, level, raze

bullet *noun* projectile, ball,

missile, pellet, shot, slug

bulletin noun <u>announcement</u>, account, communication, communiqué, dispatch, message, news flash, notification, report, statement

bully noun 1 <u>persecutor</u>, browbeater, bully boy, coercer, intimidator, oppressor, ruffian, tormentor, tough ♦ verb 2 <u>persecute</u>, browbeat, coerce, domineer, hector, intimidate, oppress, push around (slang), terrorize, tyrannize

bulwark noun 1 <u>fortification</u>, bastion, buttress, defence, embankment, partition, rampart 2 <u>defence</u>, buffer, guard, mainstay, safeguard, security, support

bumbling adjective <u>clumsy</u>, awkward, blundering, bungling, incompetent, inefficient, inept, maladroit, muddled

bump verb 1 <u>knock</u>, bang, collide (with), crash, hit, slam, smash into, strike 2 <u>jerk</u>, bounce, jolt, rattle, shake ♦ noun 3 <u>knock</u>, bang, blow, collision, crash, impact, jolt, thud, thump 4 <u>lump</u>, bulge, contusion, hump, nodule, protuberance, swelling

bumper adjective <u>exceptional</u>, abundant, bountiful, excellent, jumbo (informal), massive, whopping (informal)

bumpkin noun <u>yokel</u>, country bumpkin, hick (informal, chiefly U.S. & Canad.), hillbilly, peasant, rustic

bumptious adjective <u>cocky</u>, arrogant, brash, conceited, forward, full of oneself, overconfident, pushy (informal), self-assertive

bumpy adjective <u>rough</u>, bouncy, choppy, jarring, jerky, jolting, rutted, uneven

bunch noun 1 <u>number</u>, assortment, batch, bundle, clump, cluster, collection, heap, lot, mass, pile 2 <u>group</u>, band, crowd, flock, gang, gathering, party, team ♦ verb 3 <u>group</u>, assemble, bundle, cluster, collect, huddle, mass, pack

bundle noun 1 <u>bunch</u>, assortment, batch, collection, group, heap, mass, pile, stack ♦ verb 2 with out, off, into, etc. <u>push</u>, hurry, hustle, rush, shove, throw, thrust

bundle up verb <u>wrap up</u>, swathe

bungle verb <u>mess up</u>, blow (slang), blunder, botch, foul up, make a mess of, muff, ruin, spoil

bungling adjective <u>incompetent</u>, blundering, cack-handed (informal), clumsy, ham-fisted (informal), inept, maladroit

bunk, bunkum noun Informal <u>nonsense</u>, balderdash, baloney (informal), garbage (informal), hogwash, hot air (informal), moonshine, poppycock (informal), rubbish, stuff and nonsense, twaddle

buoy noun 1 <u>marker</u>, beacon, float, guide, signal ♦ verb 2 **buoy up** <u>encourage</u>, boost, cheer, cheer up, hearten, keep afloat, lift, raise, support, sustain

buoyancy noun 1 <u>lightness</u>, weightlessness 2 <u>cheerfulness</u>, animation, bounce (informal), good humour, high spirits, liveliness

buoyant adjective **1** floating, afloat, light, weightless **2** cheerful, carefree, chirpy (informal), happy, jaunty, light-hearted, upbeat (informal)

burden noun **1** load, encumbrance, weight **2** trouble, affliction, millstone, onus, responsibility, strain, weight, worry ♦ verb **3** weigh down, bother, handicap, load, oppress, saddle with, tax, worry

bureau noun **1** office, agency, branch, department, division, service **2** desk, writing desk

bureaucracy noun **1** government, administration, authorities, civil service, corridors of power, officials, the system **2** red tape, officialdom, regulations

bureaucrat noun official, administrator, civil servant, functionary, mandarin, officer, public servant

burglar noun housebreaker, cat burglar, filcher, pilferer, robber, sneak thief, thief

burglary noun breaking and entering, break-in, housebreaking, larceny, robbery, stealing, theft, thieving

burial noun interment, entombment, exequies, funeral, obsequies

buried adjective **1** interred, entombed, laid to rest **2** hidden, concealed, private, sequestered, tucked away

burlesque noun **1** parody, caricature, mockery, satire, send-up (Brit. informal), spoof (informal), takeoff (informal), travesty ♦ verb **2** satirize, ape,

caricature, exaggerate, imitate, lampoon, make a monkey out of, make fun of, mock, parody, ridicule, send up (Brit. informal), spoof (informal), take off (informal), take the piss out of (taboo slang), travesty

burly adjective brawny, beefy (informal), big, bulky, hefty, hulking, stocky, stout, sturdy, thickset, well-built

burn verb **1** be on fire, be ablaze, blaze, flame, flare, glow, go up in flames, smoke **2** set on fire, char, ignite, incinerate, kindle, light, parch, scorch, sear, singe, toast **3** be passionate, be angry, be aroused, be inflamed, fume, seethe, simmer, smoulder

burning adjective **1** intense, ardent, eager, fervent, impassioned, passionate, vehement **2** crucial, acute, compelling, critical, essential, important, pressing, significant, urgent, vital **3** blazing, fiery, flaming, flashing, gleaming, glowing, illuminated, scorching, smouldering

burnish verb polish, brighten, buff, furbish, glaze, rub up, shine, smooth

burrow noun **1** hole, den, lair, retreat, shelter, tunnel ♦ verb **2** dig, delve, excavate, hollow out, scoop out, tunnel

burst verb **1** explode, blow up, break, crack, puncture, rupture, shatter, split, tear apart **2** rush, barge, break, break out, erupt, gush forth, run, spout ♦ noun **3** explosion, bang, blast, blowout, break, crack, discharge, rupture, split **4** rush, gush, gust, outbreak, outburst, outpouring, spate, spurt, surge, torrent ♦ *adjective* **5** ruptured, flat, punctured, rent, split

bury *verb* **1** inter, consign to the grave, entomb, inhume, lay to rest **2** embed, engulf, submerge **3** hide, conceal, cover, enshroud, secrete, stow away

bush *noun* **1** shrub, hedge, plant, shrubbery, thicket **2 the bush** the wild, backwoods, brush, scrub, scrubland, woodland

bushy *adjective* thick, bristling, fluffy, fuzzy, luxuriant, rough, shaggy, unruly

busily *adverb* actively, assiduously, briskly, diligently, energetically, industriously, purposefully, speedily, strenuously

business *noun* **1** trade, bargaining, commerce, dealings, industry, manufacturing, selling, transaction **2** establishment, company, concern, corporation, enterprise, firm, organization, venture **3** profession, career, employment, function, job, line, occupation, trade, vocation, work **4** concern, affair, assignment, duty, pigeon (*informal*), problem, responsibility, task

businesslike *adjective* efficient, methodical, orderly, organized, practical, professional, systematic, thorough, well-ordered

businessman *noun* executive, capitalist, employer, entrepreneur, financier, industrialist, merchant, tradesman, tycoon

bust¹ *noun* bosom, breast, chest, front, torso

bust² *Informal* ♦ *verb* **1** break, burst, fracture, rupture **2** arrest, catch, raid, search ♦ *adjective* **3 go bust** go bankrupt, become insolvent, be ruined, fail

bustle *verb* **1** hurry, fuss, hasten, rush, scamper, scurry, scuttle ♦ *noun* **2** activity, ado, commotion, excitement, flurry, fuss, hurly-burly, stir, to-do

bustling *adjective* busy, active, buzzing, crowded, full, humming, lively, swarming, teeming

busy *adjective* **1** occupied, active, employed, engaged, hard at work, industrious, on duty, rushed off one's feet, working **2** lively, energetic, exacting, full, hectic, hustling ♦ *verb* **3** occupy, absorb, employ, engage, engross, immerse, interest

busybody *noun* nosy parker (*informal*), gossip, meddler, snooper, stirrer (*informal*), troublemaker

but *conjunction* **1** however, further, moreover, nevertheless, on the contrary, on the other hand, still, yet ♦ *preposition* **2** except, bar, barring, excepting, excluding, notwithstanding, save, with the exception of ♦ *adverb* **3** only, just, merely, simply, singly, solely

butcher *noun* **1** murderer, destroyer, killer, slaughterer, slayer ♦ *verb* **2** slaughter, carve, clean, cut, cut up, dress, joint, prepare **3** kill, assassinate, cut down, destroy, exterminate, liquidate, massacre, put to the sword, slaughter, slay

butt[1] *noun* **1** end, haft, handle, hilt, shaft, shank, stock **2** stub, fag end (*informal*), leftover, tip

butt[2] *noun* target, Aunt Sally, dupe, laughing stock, victim

butt[3] *verb, noun* With or of the head or horns knock, bump, poke, prod, push, ram, shove, thrust ♦ *verb* **2** butt in interfere, chip in (*informal*), cut in, interrupt, intrude, meddle, put one's oar in, stick one's nose in

butt[4] *noun* cask, barrel

buttonhole *verb* detain, accost, bore, catch, grab, importune, take aside, waylay

buttress *noun* **1** support, brace, mainstay, prop, reinforcement, stanchion, strut ♦ *verb* **2** support, back up, bolster, prop up, reinforce, shore up, strengthen, sustain, uphold

buxom *adjective* plump, ample, bosomy, busty, curvaceous, healthy, voluptuous, well-rounded

buy *verb* **1** purchase, acquire, get, invest in, obtain, pay for, procure, shop for ♦ *noun* **2** purchase, acquisition, bargain, deal

by *preposition* **1** via, by way of, over **2** through, through the agency of **3** near, along, beside, close to, next to, past ♦ *adverb* **4** near, at hand, close, handy, in reach **5** past, aside, away, to one side

bygone *adjective* past, antiquated, extinct, forgotten, former, lost, of old, olden

bypass *verb* go round, avoid, circumvent, depart from, detour round, deviate from, get round, give a wide berth to, pass round

bystander *noun* onlooker, eyewitness, looker-on, observer, passer-by, spectator, viewer, watcher, witness

byword *noun* saying, adage, maxim, motto, precept, proverb, slogan

C c

cab *noun* taxi, hackney carriage, minicab, taxicab

cabal *noun* **1** clique, caucus, conclave, faction, league, party, set **2** plot, conspiracy, intrigue, machination, scheme

cabin *noun* **1** room, berth, compartment, quarters **2** hut, chalet, cottage, lodge, shack, shanty, shed

cabinet *noun* cupboard, case, chiffonier, closet, commode, dresser, escritoire, locker

Cabinet *noun* council, administration, assembly, counsellors, ministry

cad *noun Old-fashioned, informal* scoundrel, bounder (*old-fashioned Brit. slang*), heel (*slang*), rat (*informal*), rotter (*slang, chiefly Brit.*)

caddish *adjective* ungentlemanly, despicable, ill-bred, low, unmannerly

café *noun* snack bar, brasserie, cafeteria, coffee bar, coffee shop, lunchroom, restaurant, tearoom

cage *noun* enclosure, pen, pound

cagey, cagy *adjective Informal*

wary, careful, cautious, chary, discreet, guarded, noncommittal, shrewd, wily

cajole verb persuade, coax, flatter, seduce, sweet-talk (informal), wheedle

cake noun 1 block, bar, cube, loaf, lump, mass, slab ♦ verb 2 encrust, bake, coagulate, congeal, solidify

calamitous adjective disastrous, cataclysmic, catastrophic, deadly, devastating, dire, fatal, ruinous, tragic

calamity noun disaster, cataclysm, catastrophe, misadventure, misfortune, mishap, ruin, tragedy, tribulation

calculate verb 1 work out, compute, count, determine, enumerate, estimate, figure, reckon 2 plan, aim, design, intend

calculated adjective deliberate, considered, intended, intentional, planned, premeditated, purposeful

calculating adjective scheming, crafty, cunning, devious, Machiavellian, manipulative, sharp, shrewd, sly

calculation noun 1 working out, answer, computation, estimate, forecast, judgment, reckoning, result 2 planning, contrivance, deliberation, discretion, foresight, forethought, precaution

calibre noun 1 worth, ability, capacity, distinction, merit, quality, stature, talent 2 diameter, bore, gauge, measure

call verb 1 name, christen,

describe as, designate, dub, entitle, label, style, term 2 cry, arouse, hail, rouse, shout, yell 3 phone, ring up (informal, chiefly Brit.), telephone 4 summon, assemble, convene, gather, muster, rally ♦ noun 5 cry, hail, scream, shout, signal, whoop, yell 6 summons, appeal, command, demand, invitation, notice, order, plea, request 7 need, cause, excuse, grounds, justification, occasion, reason

call for verb 1 require, demand, entail, involve, necessitate, need, occasion, suggest 2 fetch, collect, pick up

calling noun profession, career, life's work, mission, trade, vocation

call on verb visit, drop in on, look in on, look up, see

callous adjective heartless, cold, hard-bitten, hardened, hardhearted, insensitive, uncaring, unfeeling

callow adjective inexperienced, green, guileless, immature, naive, raw, unsophisticated

calm adjective cool, collected, composed, dispassionate, relaxed, sedate, self-possessed, unemotional 2 still, balmy, mild, quiet, serene, smooth, tranquil, windless ♦ noun 3 peacefulness, hush, peace, quiet, repose, serenity, stillness ♦ verb 4 quieten, hush, mollify, placate, relax, soothe

calmness noun 1 coolness, composure, cool (slang), equanimity, impassivity, poise, sang-froid, self-possession 2 peacefulness, calm, hush, quiet, repose, restfulness, serenity, stillness, tranquillity

camouflage noun 1 disguise, blind, cloak, concealment, cover, mask, masquerade, screen, subterfuge ♦ verb 2 disguise, cloak, conceal, cover, hide, mask, obfuscate, obscure, screen, veil

camp¹ noun camp site, bivouac, camping ground, encampment, tents

camp² adjective Informal effeminate, affected, artificial, mannered, ostentatious, posturing

campaign noun operation, attack, crusade, drive, expedition, movement, offensive, push

canal noun waterway, channel, conduit, duct, passage, watercourse

cancel verb 1 call off, abolish, abort, annul, delete, do away with, eliminate, erase, expunge, obliterate, repeal, revoke 2 cancel out make up for, balance out, compensate for, counterbalance, neutralize, nullify, offset

cancellation noun abandonment, abolition, annulment, deletion, elimination, repeal, revocation

cancer noun growth, corruption, malignancy, pestilence, sickness, tumour

candid adjective honest, blunt, forthright, frank, open, outspoken, plain, straightforward, truthful

candidate noun contender,

applicant, claimant, competitor, contestant, entrant, nominee, runner

candour noun honesty, directness, forthrightness, frankness, openness, outspokenness, straightforwardness, truthfulness

canker noun disease, bane, blight, cancer, corruption, infection, rot, scourge, sore, ulcer

cannon noun gun, big gun, field gun, mortar

canny adjective shrewd, astute, careful, cautious, clever, judicious, prudent, wise

canon noun 1 rule, criterion, dictate, formula, precept, principle, regulation, standard, statute, yardstick 2 list, catalogue, roll

canopy noun awning, covering, shade, sunshade

cant¹ noun 1 hypocrisy, humbug, insincerity, lip service, pretence, pretentiousness, sanctimoniousness 2 jargon, argot, lingo, patter, slang, vernacular

cant² verb tilt, angle, bevel, incline, rise, slant, slope

cantankerous adjective bad-tempered, choleric, contrary, disagreeable, grumpy, irascible, irritable, testy, waspish

canter noun 1 jog, amble, dogtrot, lope ♦ verb 2 jog, amble, lope

canvass verb 1 campaign, electioneer, solicit, solicit votes 2 poll, examine, inspect, investigate, scrutinize, study ♦ noun 3 poll, examination, investigation, scrutiny, survey, tally

cap verb Informal **beat**, better, crown, eclipse, exceed, outdo, outstrip, surpass, top, transcend

capability noun **ability**, capacity, competence, means, potential, power, proficiency, qualification(s), wherewithal

capable adjective **able**, accomplished, competent, efficient, gifted, proficient, qualified, talented

capacious adjective **spacious**, broad, commodious, expansive, extensive, roomy, sizable or sizeable, substantial, vast, voluminous, wide

capacity noun 1 **size**, amplitude, compass, dimensions, extent, magnitude, range, room, scope, space, volume 2 **ability**, aptitude, aptness, capability, competence, facility, genius, gift 3 **function**, office, position, post, province, role, sphere

cape noun **headland**, head, peninsula, point, promontory

caper noun 1 **escapade**, antic, high jinks, jape, lark (informal), mischief, practical joke, prank, stunt ♦ verb 2 **dance**, bound, cavort, frolic, gambol, jump, skip, spring, trip

capital noun 1 **money**, assets, cash, finances, funds, investment(s), means, principal, resources, wealth, wherewithal ♦ adjective 2 **principal**, cardinal, major, prime, vital 3 Old-fashioned **first-rate**, excellent, fine, splendid, sterling, superb

capitalism noun **private**

enterprise, free enterprise, laissez faire or laisser faire, private ownership

capitalize on verb **take advantage of**, benefit from, cash in on (informal), exploit, gain from, make the most of, profit from

capitulate verb **give in**, come to terms, give up, relent, submit, succumb, surrender, yield

caprice noun **whim**, fad, fancy, fickleness, impulse, inconstancy, notion, whimsy

capricious adjective **unpredictable**, changeful, erratic, fickle, fitful, impulsive, inconsistent, inconstant, mercurial, variable, wayward, whimsical

capsize verb **overturn**, invert, keel over, tip over, turn over, turn turtle, upset

capsule noun 1 **pill**, lozenge, tablet 2 Botany **pod**, case, receptacle, seed case, sheath, shell, vessel

captain noun **leader**, boss, chief, commander, head, master, skipper

captivate verb **charm**, allure, attract, beguile, bewitch, enchant, enrapture, enthral, entrance, fascinate, infatuate, mesmerize

captive noun 1 **prisoner**, convict, detainee, hostage, internee, prisoner of war, slave ♦ adjective 2 **confined**, caged, enslaved, ensnared, imprisoned, incarcerated, locked up, penned, restricted, subjugated

captivity noun **confinement**,

bondage, custody, detention, imprisonment, incarceration, internment, slavery

capture verb 1 catch, apprehend, arrest, bag, collar (informal), secure, seize, take, take prisoner ◆noun 2 catching, apprehension, arrest, imprisonment, seizure, taking, taking captive, trapping

car noun 1 vehicle, auto (U.S.), automobile, jalopy (informal), machine, motor, motorcar, wheels (informal) 2 U.S. & Canad. (railway) carriage, buffet car, cable car, coach, dining car, sleeping car, van

carcass noun body, cadaver (Medical), corpse, dead body, framework, hulk, remains, shell, skeleton

cardinal adjective principal, capital, central, chief, essential, first, fundamental, key, leading, main, paramount, primary

care verb 1 be concerned, be bothered, be interested, mind ◆noun 2 caution, attention, carefulness, consideration, forethought, heed, management, pains, prudence, vigilance, watchfulness 3 protection, charge, control, custody, guardianship, keeping, management, supervision 4 worry, anxiety, concern, disquiet, perplexity, pressure, responsibility, stress, trouble

career noun 1 occupation, calling, employment, life's work, livelihood, pursuit, vocation ◆verb 2 rush, barrel (along) (informal, chiefly U.S. & Canad.), bolt, dash, hurtle, race, speed, tear

care for verb 1 look after, attend, foster, mind, minister to, nurse, protect, provide for, tend, watch over 2 like, be fond of, desire, enjoy, love, prize, take to, want

carefree adjective untroubled, blithe, breezy, cheerful, easy-going, halcyon, happy-go-lucky, light-hearted

careful adjective 1 cautious, chary, circumspect, discreet, prudent, scrupulous, thoughtful, thrifty 2 thorough, conscientious, meticulous, painstaking, particular, precise

careless adjective 1 slapdash, cavalier, inaccurate, irresponsible, lackadaisical, neglectful, offhand, slipshod, sloppy (informal) 2 negligent, absent-minded, forgetful, hasty, remiss, thoughtless, unthinking 3 nonchalant, artless, casual, unstudied

carelessness noun negligence, indiscretion, irresponsibility, laxity, neglect, omission, slackness, sloppiness (informal), thoughtlessness

caress verb 1 stroke, cuddle, embrace, fondle, hug, kiss, neck (informal), nuzzle, pet ◆noun 2 stroke, cuddle, embrace, fondling, hug, kiss, pat

caretaker noun warden, concierge, curator, custodian, janitor, keeper, porter, superintendent, watchman

cargo noun load, baggage, consignment, contents, freight, goods, merchandise, shipment

caricature noun 1 parody, burlesque, cartoon, distortion, farce, lampoon, satire, send-up

(*Brit. informal*), takeoff (*informal*), travesty ♦ *verb* 2 parody, burlesque, distort, lampoon, mimic, mock, ridicule, satirize, send up (*Brit. informal*), take off (*informal*)

carnage *noun* slaughter, blood bath, bloodshed, butchery, havoc, holocaust, massacre, mass murder, murder, shambles

carnal *adjective* sexual, erotic, fleshly, lascivious, lewd, libidinous, lustful, sensual

carnival *noun* festival, celebration, fair, fête, fiesta, gala, holiday, jamboree, jubilee, merrymaking, revelry

carol *noun* song, chorus, ditty, hymn, lay

carp *verb* find fault, cavil, complain, criticize, pick holes, quibble, reproach

carpenter *noun* joiner, cabinet-maker, woodworker

carriage *noun* 1 vehicle, cab, coach, conveyance 2 bearing, air, behaviour, comportment, conduct, demeanour, deportment, gait, manner, posture

carry *verb* 1 transport, bear, bring, conduct, convey, fetch, haul, lug, move, relay, take, transfer 2 win, accomplish, capture, effect, gain, secure

carry on *verb* 1 continue, endure, keep going, last, maintain, perpetuate, persevere, persist 2 *Informal* make a fuss, create (*slang*), misbehave, raise Cain

carry out *verb* perform, accomplish, achieve, carry

through, effect, execute, fulfil, implement, realize

carton *noun* box, case, container, pack, package, packet

cartoon *noun* 1 drawing, caricature, comic strip, lampoon, parody, satire, sketch, takeoff (*informal*) 2 animation, animated cartoon, animated film

cartridge *noun* 1 shell, charge, round 2 container, capsule, case, cassette, cylinder, magazine

carve *verb* cut, chip, chisel, engrave, etch, hew, mould, sculpt, slice, whittle

cascade *noun* 1 waterfall, avalanche, cataract, deluge, downpour, falls, flood, fountain, outpouring, shower, torrent ♦ *verb* 2 flow, descend, fall, flood, gush, overflow, pitch, plunge, pour, spill, surge, teem, tumble

case[1] *noun* 1 instance, example, illustration, occasion, occurrence, specimen 2 situation, circumstance(s), condition, context, contingency, event, position, state 3 *Law* lawsuit, action, dispute, proceedings, suit, trial

case[2] *noun* 1 container, box, canister, casket, chest, crate, holder, receptacle, suitcase, tray 2 covering, capsule, casing, envelope, jacket, sheath, shell, wrapper

cash *noun* money, brass (*Northern English dialect*), coinage, currency, dough (*slang*), funds, notes, ready money, silver

cashier[1] *noun* teller, bank clerk, banker, bursar, clerk, purser, treasurer

cashier² verb dismiss, discard, discharge, drum out, expel, give the boot to (slang)

casket noun box, case, chest, coffer, jewel box

cast noun 1 actors, characters, company, dramatis personae, players, troupe 2 type, complexion, manner, stamp, style ♦ verb 3 choose, allot, appoint, assign, name, pick, select 4 give out, bestow, deposit, diffuse, distribute, emit, radiate, scatter, shed, spread 5 found, mould, mould, set, shape 6 throw, fling, hurl, launch, pitch, sling, thrust, toss

caste noun class, estate, grade, order, rank, social order, status, stratum

castigate verb reprimand, berate, censure, chastise, criticize, diffuse, lambast(e), rebuke, scold

cast-iron adjective certain, copper-bottomed, definite, established, fixed, guaranteed, settled

castle noun fortress, chateau, citadel, keep, palace, stronghold, tower

cast-off adjective 1 unwanted, discarded, rejected, scrapped, surplus to requirements, unneeded, useless ♦ noun 2 reject, discard, failure, outcast, second

castrate verb neuter, emasculate, geld

casual adjective 1 careless, blasé, cursory, lackadaisical, nonchalant, offhand, relaxed, unconcerned 2 occasional, accidental, chance, incidental, irregular, random, unexpected

3 informal, non-dressy, sporty

casualty noun victim, death, fatality, loss, sufferer, wounded

cat noun feline, kitty (informal), moggy (slang), puss (informal), pussy (informal), tabby

catacombs plural noun vault, crypt, tomb

catalogue noun 1 list, directory, gazetteer, index, inventory, record, register, roll, roster, schedule ♦ verb 2 list, accession, alphabetize, classify, file, index, inventory, register, tabulate

catapult noun 1 sling, slingshot (U.S.) ♦ verb 2 shoot, heave, hurl, pitch, plunge, propel

catastrophe noun disaster, adversity, calamity, cataclysm, fiasco, misfortune, tragedy, trouble

catcall noun jeer, boo, gibe, hiss, raspberry, whistle

catch verb 1 seize, clutch, get, grab, grasp, grip, lay hold of, snatch, take 2 capture, apprehend, arrest, ensnare, entrap, snare 3 discover, catch in the act, detect, expose, find out, surprise, take unawares, unmask 4 contract, develop, get, go down with, incur, succumb to, suffer from 5 make out, comprehend, discern, get, grasp, hear, perceive, recognize, sense, take in ♦ noun 6 fastener, bolt, clasp, clip, hook, latch 7 Informal drawback, disadvantage, fly in the ointment, hitch, snag, stumbling block, trap, trick

catching adjective infectious, communicable, contagious, transferable, transmittable

catch on verb Informal understand, comprehend, find out, get the picture, grasp, see, see through, twig (Brit. informal)

catchword noun slogan, byword, motto, password, watchword

catchy adjective memorable, captivating, haunting, popular

categorical adjective absolute, downright, emphatic, explicit, express, positive, unambiguous, unconditional, unequivocal, unqualified, unreserved

category noun class, classification, department, division, grade, grouping, heading, section, sort, type

cater verb provide, furnish, outfit, purvey, supply

cattle plural noun cows, beasts, bovines, livestock, stock

catty adjective spiteful, backbiting, bitchy (informal), malevolent, malicious, rancorous, shrewish, snide, venomous

cause noun 1 origin, agent, beginning, creator, genesis, mainspring, maker, producer, root, source, spring 2 reason, basis, grounds, incentive, inducement, justification, motivation, motive, purpose 3 aim, belief, conviction, enterprise, ideal, movement, principle ♦ verb 4 produce, bring about, create, generate, give rise to, incite, induce, lead to, result in

caustic adjective 1 burning, acrid, astringent, biting, corroding, corrosive, mordant, vitriolic 2 sarcastic, acrimonious, cutting, pungent, scathing, stinging, trenchant, virulent, vitriolic

caution noun 1 care, alertness, carefulness, circumspection, deliberation, discretion, forethought, heed, prudence, vigilance, watchfulness 2 warning, admonition, advice, counsel, injunction ♦ verb 3 warn, admonish, advise, tip off, urge

cautious adjective careful, cagey (informal), chary, circumspect, guarded, judicious, prudent, tentative, wary

cavalcade noun parade, array, march-past, procession, spectacle, train

cavalier adjective haughty, arrogant, disdainful, lofty, lordly, offhand, scornful, supercilious

cavalry noun horsemen, horse, mounted troops

cave noun hollow, cavern, cavity, den, grotto

cavern noun cave, hollow, pothole

cavernous adjective deep, hollow, sunken, yawning

cavity noun hollow, crater, dent, gap, hole, pit

cease verb stop, break off, conclude, discontinue, end, finish, halt, leave off, refrain, terminate

ceaseless adjective continual, constant, endless, eternal, everlasting, incessant, interminable, never-ending, nonstop, perpetual, unremitting

cede verb surrender, concede, hand over, make over, relinquish, renounce, resign, transfer, yield

celebrate verb 1 rejoice,

commemorate, drink to, keep, kill the fatted calf, observe, put the flags out, toast **2** perform, bless, honour, solemnize

celebrated adjective well-known, acclaimed, distinguished, eminent, famous, illustrious, notable, popular, prominent, renowned

celebration noun **1** party, festival, festivity, gala, jubilee, merrymaking, red-letter day, revelry **2** performance, anniversary, commemoration, honouring, observance, remembrance, solemnization

celebrity noun **1** personality, big name, big shot (informal), dignitary, luminary, star, superstar, V.I.P. **2** fame, distinction, notability, prestige, prominence, renown, reputation, repute, stardom

celestial adjective heavenly, angelic, astral, divine, ethereal, spiritual, sublime, supernatural

celibacy noun chastity, continence, purity, virginity

cell noun **1** room, cavity, chamber, compartment, cubicle, dungeon, stall **2** unit, caucus, core, coterie, group, nucleus

cement noun **1** mortar, adhesive, glue, gum, paste, plaster, sealant ◆ verb **2** stick together, attach, bind, bond, combine, glue, join, plaster, seal, unite, weld

cemetery noun graveyard, burial ground, churchyard, God's acre, necropolis

censor verb cut, blue-pencil, bowdlerize, expurgate

censorious adjective critical, captious, carping, cavilling, condemnatory, disapproving, disparaging, fault-finding, hypercritical, scathing, severe

censure noun **1** disapproval, blame, condemnation, criticism, obloquy, rebuke, reprimand, reproach, reproof, stick (slang) ◆ verb **2** criticize, blame, castigate, condemn, denounce, rap over the knuckles, rebuke, reprimand, reproach, scold, slap on the wrist

central adjective **1** middle, inner, interior, mean, median, mid **2** main, chief, essential, focal, fundamental, key, primary, principal

centralize verb unify, concentrate, condense, incorporate, rationalize, streamline

centre noun **1** middle, core, focus, heart, hub, kernel, midpoint, nucleus, pivot ◆ verb **2** focus, cluster, concentrate, converge, revolve

ceremonial adjective **1** ritual, formal, liturgical, ritualistic, solemn, stately ◆ noun **2** ritual, ceremony, formality, rite, solemnity

ceremonious adjective formal, civil, courteous, deferential, dignified, punctilious, solemn, stately, stiff

ceremony noun **1** ritual, commemoration, function, observance, parade, rite, service, show, solemnities **2** formality, ceremonial, decorum, etiquette, niceties, pomp, propriety, protocol

certain adjective **1** sure, assured,

confident, convinced, positive, satisfied **2** <u>known</u>, conclusive, incontrovertible, irrefutable, true, undeniable, unequivocal **3** <u>inevitable</u>, bound, definite, destined, fated, inescapable, sure **4** <u>fixed</u>, decided, definite, established, settled

certainly adverb <u>definitely</u>, assuredly, indisputably, indubitably, surely, truly, undeniably, undoubtedly, without doubt

certainty noun **1** <u>sureness</u>, assurance, confidence, conviction, faith, positiveness, trust, validity **2** <u>fact</u>, reality, sure thing (informal), truth

certificate noun <u>document</u>, authorization, credential(s), diploma, licence, testimonial, voucher, warrant

certify verb <u>confirm</u>, assure, attest, authenticate, declare, guarantee, testify, validate, verify

chafe verb **1** <u>rub</u>, abrade, rasp, scrape, scratch **2** <u>be annoyed</u>, be impatient, fret, fume, rage, worry

chaff[1] noun <u>waste</u>, dregs, husks, refuse, remains, rubbish, trash

chaff[2] verb <u>tease</u>, mock, rib (informal), ridicule, scoff, taunt

chain noun **1** <u>link</u>, bond, coupling, fetter, manacle, shackle **2** <u>series</u>, progression, sequence, set, string, succession, train ♦ verb **3** <u>bind</u>, confine, enslave, fetter, handcuff, manacle, restrain, shackle, tether

chairman noun <u>director</u>, chairperson, chairwoman, master of ceremonies, president, speaker, spokesman

challenge noun **1** <u>test</u>, confrontation, provocation, question, trial, ultimatum ♦ verb **2** <u>test</u>, confront, defy, dispute, object to, question, tackle, throw down the gauntlet

chamber noun **1** <u>room</u>, apartment, bedroom, compartment, cubicle, enclosure, hall **2** <u>council</u>, assembly, legislative body, legislature

champion noun **1** <u>winner</u>, conqueror, hero, title holder, victor **2** <u>defender</u>, backer, guardian, patron, protector, upholder ♦ verb **3** <u>support</u>, advocate, back, commend, defend, encourage, espouse, fight for, promote, uphold

chance noun **1** <u>probability</u>, likelihood, odds, possibility, prospect **2** <u>opportunity</u>, occasion, opening, time **3** <u>luck</u>, accident, coincidence, destiny, fate, fortune, providence **4** <u>risk</u>, gamble, hazard, jeopardy, speculation, uncertainty ♦ verb **5** <u>risk</u>, endanger, gamble, hazard, jeopardize, stake, try, venture, wager

change noun **1** <u>alteration</u>, difference, innovation, metamorphosis, modification, mutation, revolution, transformation, transition **2** <u>variety</u>, break (informal), departure, diversion, novelty, variation **3** <u>exchange</u>, conversion, interchange, substitution, swap, trade ♦ verb **4** <u>alter</u>, convert, modify, mutate, reform, reorganize, restyle, shift, transform, vary **5** <u>exchange</u>, barter, convert, interchange, replace, substitute, swap, trade

changeable adjective variable, erratic, fickle, inconstant, irregular, mobile, mutable, protean, shifting, unsettled, unstable, volatile, wavering

channel noun 1 route, approach, artery, avenue, course, means, medium, path, way 2 passage, canal, conduit, duct, furrow, groove, gutter, route, strait ◆ verb 3 direct, conduct, convey, guide, transmit

chant verb 1 sing, carol, chorus, descant, intone, recite, warble ◆ noun 2 song, carol, chorus, melody, psalm

chaos noun disorder, anarchy, bedlam, confusion, disorganization, lawlessness, mayhem, pandemonium, tumult

chaotic adjective disordered, anarchic, confused, deranged, disorganized, lawless, riotous, topsy-turvy, tumultuous, uncontrolled

chap noun Informal fellow, bloke (Brit. informal), character, guy (informal), individual, man, person

chaperone noun 1 escort, companion ◆ verb 2 escort, accompany, attend, protect, safeguard, shepherd, watch over

chapter noun section, clause, division, episode, part, period, phase, stage, topic

character noun 1 nature, attributes, calibre, complexion, disposition, personality, quality, temperament, type 2 reputation, honour, integrity, rectitude, strength, uprightness 3 role, part, persona, portrayal

4 eccentric, card (informal), oddball (informal), original 5 symbol, device, figure, hieroglyph, letter, mark, rune, sign

characteristic noun 1 feature, attribute, faculty, idiosyncrasy, mark, peculiarity, property, quality, quirk, trait ◆ adjective 2 typical, distinctive, distinguishing, idiosyncratic, individual, peculiar, representative, singular, special, symbolic, symptomatic

characterize verb identify, brand, distinguish, indicate, mark, represent, stamp, typify

charade noun pretence, fake, farce, pantomime, parody, travesty

charge verb 1 accuse, arraign, blame, impeach, incriminate, indict 2 rush, assail, assault, attack, stampede, storm 3 fill, load 4 Formal command, bid, commit, demand, entrust, instruct, order, require ◆ noun 5 price, amount, cost, expenditure, expense, outlay, payment, rate, toll 6 accusation, allegation, imputation, indictment 7 rush, assault, attack, onset, onslaught, sortie, stampede 8 care, custody, duty, office, responsibility, safekeeping, trust 9 ward 10 instruction, command, demand, direction, injunction, mandate, order, precept

charisma noun charm, allure, attraction, lure, magnetism, personality

charismatic adjective charming, alluring, attractive, enticing, influential, magnetic

charitable adjective **1** tolerant, considerate, favourable, forgiving, humane, indulgent, kindly, lenient, magnanimous, sympathetic, understanding **2** generous, beneficent, benevolent, bountiful, kind, lavish, liberal, philanthropic

charity noun **1** donations, assistance, benefaction, contributions, endowment, fund, gift, hand-out, help, largesse or largess, philanthropy, relief **2** kindness, altruism, benevolence, compassion, fellow feeling, generosity, goodwill, humanity, indulgence

charlatan noun fraud, cheat, con man (informal), fake, impostor, phoney or phony (informal), pretender, quack, sham, swindler

charm noun **1** attraction, allure, appeal, fascination, magnetism **2** spell, enchantment, magic, sorcery **3** talisman, amulet, fetish, trinket ◆ verb **4** attract, allure, beguile, bewitch, captivate, delight, enchant, enrapture, entrance, fascinate, mesmerize, win over

charming adjective attractive, appealing, captivating, cute, delightful, fetching, likable or likeable, pleasing, seductive, winsome

chart noun **1** table, blueprint, diagram, graph, map, plan ◆ verb **2** plot, delineate, draft, map out, outline, shape, sketch

charter noun **1** document, contract, deed, licence, permit, prerogative ◆ verb **2** hire, commission, employ, lease, rent **3** authorize, sanction

chase verb **1** pursue, course, follow, hunt, run after, track **2** drive away, drive, expel, hound, put to flight ◆ noun **3** pursuit, hunt, hunting, race

chasm noun gulf, abyss, crater, crevasse, fissure, gap, gorge, ravine

chaste adjective pure, immaculate, innocent, modest, simple, unaffected, undefiled, virtuous

chasten verb subdue, chastise, correct, discipline, humble, humiliate, put in one's place, tame

chastise verb **1** scold, berate, castigate, censure, correct, discipline, upbraid **2** Old-fashioned beat, flog, lash, lick (informal), punish, scourge, whip

chastity noun purity, celibacy, continence, innocence, maidenhood, modesty, virginity, virtue

chat noun **1** talk, chatter, chinwag (Brit. informal), conversation, gossip, heart-to-heart, natter, tête-à-tête ◆ verb **2** talk, chatter, gossip, jaw (slang), natter

chatter noun **1** prattle, babble, blather, chat, gab (informal), gossip, natter ◆ verb **2** prattle, babble, blather, chat, gab (informal), gossip, natter, rabbit (on) (Brit. informal), schmooze (slang)

cheap adjective **1** inexpensive, bargain, cut-price, economical, keen, low-cost, low-priced, reasonable, reduced **2** inferior, common, poor, second-rate, shoddy, tatty, tawdry, two a penny, worthless **3** *Informal* despicable, contemptible, mean

cheapen *verb* degrade, belittle, debase, demean, denigrate, depreciate, devalue, discredit, disparage, lower

cheat *verb* **1** deceive, beguile, con (*informal*), defraud, double-cross (*informal*), dupe, fleece, fool, mislead, rip off (*slang*), swindle, trick ♦ *noun* **2** deceiver, charlatan, con man (*informal*), double-crosser (*informal*), shark, sharper, swindler, trickster **3** deception, deceit, fraud, rip-off (*slang*), scam (*slang*), swindle, trickery

check *verb* **1** examine, inquire into, inspect, investigate, look at, make sure, monitor, research, scrutinize, study, test, vet **2** stop, delay, halt, hinder, impede, inhibit, limit, obstruct, restrain, retard ♦ *noun* **3** examination, inspection, investigation, once-over (*informal*), research, scrutiny, test **4** stoppage, constraint, control, curb, damper, hindrance, impediment, limitation, obstacle, obstruction, restraint

cheek *noun Informal* impudence, audacity, chutzpah (*U.S. & Canad. informal*), disrespect, effrontery, impertinence, insolence, lip (*slang*), nerve, temerity

cheeky *adjective* impudent, audacious, disrespectful, forward, impertinent, insolent, insulting, pert, saucy

cheer *verb* **1** applaud, acclaim,

clap, hail **2** cheer up, brighten, buoy up, comfort, encourage, gladden, hearten, uplift ♦ *noun* **3** applause, acclamation, ovation, plaudits

cheerful *adjective* happy, buoyant, cheery, chirpy (*informal*), enthusiastic, jaunty, jolly, light-hearted, merry, optimistic, upbeat (*informal*)

cheerfulness *noun* happiness, buoyancy, exuberance, gaiety, geniality, good cheer, good humour, high spirits, jauntiness, light-heartedness

cheerless *adjective* gloomy, bleak, desolate, dismal, drab, dreary, forlorn, miserable, sombre, woeful

cheer up *verb* **1** comfort, encourage, enliven, gladden, hearten, jolly along (*informal*) **2** take heart, buck up (*informal*), perk up, rally

cheery *adjective* cheerful, breezy, carefree, chirpy (*informal*), genial, good-humoured, happy, jovial, upbeat (*informal*)

chemist *noun* pharmacist, apothecary (*obsolete*), dispenser

cherish *verb* **1** cling to, cleave to, encourage, entertain, foster, harbour, hold dear, nurture, prize, sustain, treasure **2** care for, comfort, hold dear, love, nurse, shelter, support

chest *noun* box, case, casket, coffer, crate, strongbox, trunk

chew *verb* bite, champ, chomp, crunch, gnaw, grind, masticate, munch

chewy *adjective* tough, as tough as old boots, leathery

chic adjective stylish, elegant, fashionable, smart, trendy (Brit. informal)

chide verb Old-fashioned scold, admonish, berate, censure, criticize, lecture, rebuke, reprimand, reproach, reprove, tell off (informal)

chief noun 1 head, boss (informal), captain, commander, director, governor, leader, manager, master, principal, ruler ♦ adjective 2 primary, highest, key, leading, main, predominant, pre-eminent, premier, prime, principal, supreme, uppermost

chiefly adverb 1 especially, above all, essentially, primarily, principally 2 mainly, in general, in the main, largely, mostly, on the whole, predominantly, usually

child noun youngster, babe, baby, bairn (Scot.), infant, juvenile, kid (informal), offspring, toddler, tot

childbirth noun child-bearing, confinement, delivery, labour, lying-in, parturition, travail

childhood noun youth, boyhood or girlhood, immaturity, infancy, minority, schooldays

childish adjective immature, boyish or girlish, foolish, infantile, juvenile, puerile, young

childlike adjective innocent, artless, guileless, ingenuous, naive, simple, trusting

chill noun 1 cold, bite, coldness, coolness, crispness, frigidity, nip, rawness, sharpness ♦ verb 2 cool, freeze, refrigerate 3 dishearten, dampen, deject, depress, discourage, dismay ♦ adjective

4 cold, biting, bleak, chilly, freezing, frigid, raw, sharp, wintry

chilly adjective 1 cool, brisk, crisp, draughty, fresh, nippy, penetrating, sharp 2 unfriendly, frigid, hostile, unresponsive, unsympathetic, unwelcoming

chime verb, noun ring, clang, jingle, peal, sound, tinkle, toll

china noun pottery, ceramics, crockery, porcelain, service, tableware, ware

chink noun opening, aperture, cleft, crack, cranny, crevice, fissure, gap

chip noun 1 scratch, fragment, nick, notch, shard, shaving, sliver, wafer ♦ verb 2 nick, chisel, damage, gash, whittle

chirp verb chirrup, cheep, peep, pipe, tweet, twitter, warble

chivalrous adjective courteous, bold, brave, courageous, gallant, gentlemanly, honourable, valiant

chivalry noun courtesy, courage, gallantry, gentlemanliness, knight-errantry, knighthood, politeness

choice noun 1 option, alternative, pick, preference, say 2 selection, range, variety ♦ adjective 3 best, elite, excellent, exclusive, prime, rare, select

choke verb 1 strangle, asphyxiate, gag, overpower, smother, stifle, suffocate, suppress, throttle 2 block, bung, clog, congest, constrict, obstruct, stop

choose verb pick, adopt, designate, elect, opt for, prefer, select, settle upon

choosy adjective Informal fussy,

discriminating, faddy, fastidious, finicky, particular, picky (*informal*), selective

chop *verb* cut, cleave, fell, hack, hew, lop, sever

chore *noun* task, burden, duty, errand, job

chortle *verb*, *noun* chuckle, cackle, crow, guffaw

chorus *noun* **1** choir, choristers, ensemble, singers, vocalists **2** refrain, burden, response, strain **3** unison, accord, concert, harmony

christen *verb* **1** baptize **2** name, call, designate, dub, style, term, title

Christmas *noun* festive season, Noel, Xmas (*informal*), Yule (*archaic*), Yuletide (*archaic*)

chronicle *noun* **1** record, account, annals, diary, history, journal, narrative, register, story ♦ *verb* **2** record, enter, narrate, put on record, recount, register, relate, report, set down, tell

chubby *adjective* plump, buxom, flabby, podgy, portly, rotund, round, stout, tubby

chuck *verb* Informal throw, cast, fling, heave, hurl, pitch, sling, toss

chuckle *verb* laugh, chortle, crow, exult, giggle, snigger, titter

chum *noun* Informal friend, companion, comrade, crony, mate (*informal*), pal (*informal*)

chunk *noun* piece, block, dollop (*informal*), hunk, lump, mass, nugget, portion, slab

churlish *adjective* rude, brusque, harsh, ill-tempered, impolite, sullen, surly, uncivil

churn *verb* stir up, agitate, beat, convulse, swirl, toss

cinema *noun* films, big screen (*informal*), flicks (*slang*), motion pictures, movies, pictures

cipher *noun* **1** code, cryptograph **2** nobody, nonentity

circle *noun* **1** ring, disc, globe, orb, sphere **2** group, clique, club, company, coterie, set, society ♦ *verb* **3** go round, circumnavigate, circumscribe, encircle, enclose, envelop, ring, surround

circuit *noun* course, journey, lap, orbit, revolution, route, tour, track

circuitous *adjective* indirect, labyrinthine, meandering, oblique, rambling, roundabout, tortuous, winding

circular *adjective* **1** round, ring-shaped, rotund, spherical **2** orbital, circuitous, cyclical ♦ *noun* **3** advertisement, notice

circulate *verb* **1** spread, broadcast, disseminate, distribute, issue, make known, promulgate, publicize, publish **2** flow, gyrate, radiate, revolve, rotate

circulation *noun* **1** bloodstream **2** flow, circling, motion, rotation **3** distribution, currency, dissemination, spread, transmission

circumference *noun* boundary, border, edge, extremity, limits, outline, perimeter, periphery, rim

circumstance *noun* event, accident, condition, contingency, happening, incident, occurrence, particular, respect, situation

circumstances *plural noun* situation, means, position, state, state of affairs, station, status

cistern *noun* tank, basin, reservoir, sink, vat

citadel *noun* fortress, bastion, fortification, keep, stronghold, tower

cite *verb* quote, adduce, advance, allude to, enumerate, extract, mention, name, specify

citizen *noun* inhabitant, denizen, dweller, resident, subject, townsman

city *noun* town, conurbation, metropolis, municipality

civic *adjective* public, communal, local, municipal

civil *adjective* 1 civic, domestic, municipal, political 2 polite, affable, courteous, obliging, refined, urbane, well-mannered

civilization *noun* 1 culture, advancement, cultivation, development, education, enlightenment, progress, refinement, sophistication 2 society, community, nation, people, polity

civilize *verb* cultivate, educate, enlighten, refine, sophisticate, tame

civilized *adjective* cultured, educated, enlightened, humane, polite, sophisticated, tolerant, urbane

claim *verb* 1 assert, allege, challenge, insist, maintain, profess, uphold 2 demand, ask, call for, insist, need, require ◆ *noun* 3 assertion, affirmation, allegation, pretension, privilege,

protestation 4 demand, application, call, petition, request, requirement 5 right, title

clairvoyant *noun* 1 psychic, diviner, fortune-teller, visionary ◆ *adjective* 2 psychic, extrasensory, second-sighted, telepathic, visionary

clamber *verb* climb, claw, scale, scrabble, scramble, shin

clammy *adjective* moist, close, damp, dank, sticky, sweaty

clamour *noun* noise, commotion, din, hubbub, outcry, racket, shouting, uproar

clamp *noun* 1 vice, bracket, fastener, grip, press ◆ *verb* 2 fasten, brace, fix, make fast, secure

clan *noun* family, brotherhood, faction, fraternity, group, society, tribe

clandestine *adjective* secret, cloak-and-dagger, concealed, covert, furtive, private, stealthy, surreptitious, underground

clap *verb* applaud, acclaim, cheer

clarification *noun* explanation, elucidation, exposition, illumination, interpretation, simplification

clarify *verb* explain, clear up, elucidate, illuminate, interpret, make plain, simplify, throw or shed light on

clarity *noun* clearness, definition, limpidity, lucidity, precision, simplicity, transparency

clash *verb* 1 conflict, cross swords, feud, grapple, lock horns, quarrel, war, wrangle 2 crash, bang, clang, clank, clatter, jangle, jar, rattle ◆ *noun*

3 conflict, brush, collision, confrontation, difference of opinion, disagreement, fight, showdown (*informal*)

clasp noun 1 fastening, brooch, buckle, catch, clip, fastener, grip, hook, pin 2 grasp, embrace, grip, hold, hug ♦ verb 3 grasp, clutch, embrace, grip, hold, hug, press, seize, squeeze 4 fasten, connect

class noun 1 group, category, division, genre, kind, set, sort, type ♦ verb 2 classify, brand, categorize, designate, grade, group, label, rank, rate

classic adjective 1 definitive, archetypal, exemplary, ideal, model, quintessential, standard 2 typical, characteristic, regular, standard, time-honoured, usual 3 best, consummate, finest, first-rate, masterly, world-class 4 lasting, abiding, ageless, deathless, enduring, immortal, undying ♦ noun 5 standard, exemplar, masterpiece, model, paradigm, prototype

classical adjective pure, elegant, harmonious, refined, restrained, symmetrical, understated, well-proportioned

classification noun categorization, analysis, arrangement, grading, sorting, taxonomy

classify verb categorize, arrange, catalogue, grade, pigeonhole, rank, sort, systematize, tabulate

classy adjective Informal high-class, elegant, exclusive, posh (*informal, chiefly Brit.*), stylish, superior, top-drawer, up-market

clause noun section, article, chapter, condition, paragraph, part, passage

claw noun 1 nail, pincer, talon, tentacle ♦ verb 2 scratch, dig, lacerate, maul, rip, scrape, tear

clean adjective 1 pure, flawless, fresh, immaculate, impeccable, spotless, unblemished, unsullied 2 hygienic, antiseptic, decontaminated, purified, sterile, sterilized, uncontaminated, unpolluted 3 moral, chaste, decent, good, honourable, innocent, pure, respectable, upright, virtuous 4 complete, conclusive, decisive, entire, final, perfect, thorough, total, unimpaired, whole ♦ verb 5 cleanse, disinfect, launder, purge, purify, rinse, sanitize, scour, scrub, wash

cleanse verb clean, absolve, clear, purge, purify, rinse, scour, scrub, wash

cleanser noun detergent, disinfectant, purifier, scourer, soap, solvent

clear adjective 1 certain, convinced, decided, definite, positive, resolved, satisfied, sure 2 obvious, apparent, blatant, comprehensible, conspicuous, distinct, evident, manifest, palpable, plain, pronounced, recognizable, unmistakable 3 transparent, crystalline, glassy, limpid, pellucid, see-through, translucent 4 bright, cloudless, fair, fine, light, luminous, shining, sunny, unclouded 5 unobstructed, empty, free, open, smooth, unhindered, unimpeded 6 unblemished, clean, immaculate, innocent, pure, untarnished ♦ *verb* **7** unblock, disentangle, extricate, free, loosen, open, rid, unload **8** pass over, jump, leap, miss, vault **9** brighten, break up, lighten **10** clean, cleanse, erase, purify, refine, sweep away, tidy (up), wipe **11** absolve, acquit, excuse, exonerate, justify, vindicate **12** gain, acquire, earn, make, reap, secure

clear-cut *adjective* straightforward, black-and-white, cut-and-dried (*informal*), definite, explicit, plain, precise, specific, unambiguous, unequivocal

clearly *adverb* obviously, beyond doubt, distinctly, evidently, markedly, openly, overtly, undeniably, undoubtedly

clergy *noun* priesthood, churchmen, clergymen, clerics, holy orders, ministry, the cloth

clergyman *noun* minister, chaplain, cleric, man of God, man of the cloth, padre, parson, pastor, priest, vicar

clever *adjective* intelligent, bright, gifted, ingenious, knowledgeable, quick-witted, resourceful, shrewd, smart, talented

cleverness *noun* intelligence, ability, brains, ingenuity, quick wits, resourcefulness, shrewdness, smartness

cliché *noun* platitude, banality, commonplace, hackneyed phrase, stereotype, truism

client *noun* customer, applicant, buyer, consumer, patient, patron, shopper

clientele *noun* customers,

business, clients, following, market, patronage, regulars, trade

cliff *noun* rock face, bluff, crag, escarpment, overhang, precipice, scar, scarp

climactic *adjective* crucial, critical, decisive, paramount, peak

climate *noun* weather, temperature

climax *noun* culmination, height, highlight, high point, peak, summit, top, zenith

climb *verb* ascend, clamber, mount, rise, scale, shin up, soar, top

climb down *verb* **1** descend, dismount **2** back down, eat one's words, retract, retreat

clinch *verb* settle, conclude, confirm, decide, determine, seal, secure, set the seal on, sew up (*informal*)

cling *verb* stick, adhere, clasp, clutch, embrace, grasp, grip, hug

clinical *adjective* unemotional, analytic, cold, detached, dispassionate, impersonal, objective, scientific

clip¹ *verb* **1** trim, crop, curtail, cut, pare, prune, shear, shorten, snip ♦ *noun*, *verb* **2** *Informal* smack, clout (*informal*), cuff, knock, punch, strike, thump, wallop (*informal*), whack

clip² *verb* attach, fasten, fix, hold, pin, staple

clique *noun* group, cabal, circle, coterie, faction, gang, set

cloak *noun* **1** cape, coat, mantle, wrap ♦ *verb* **2** cover, camouflage, conceal, disguise, hide, mask, obscure, screen, veil

clog verb <u>obstruct</u>, block, congest, hinder, impede, jam

close[1] verb 1 <u>shut</u>, bar, block, lock, plug, seal, secure, stop up 2 <u>end</u>, cease, complete, conclude, finish, shut down, terminate, wind up 3 <u>connect</u>, come together, couple, fuse, join, unite ♦ noun 4 <u>end</u>, completion, conclusion, culmination, denouement, ending, finale, finish

close[2] adjective 1 <u>near</u>, adjacent, adjoining, at hand, cheek by jowl, handy, impending, nearby, neighbouring, nigh 2 <u>intimate</u>, attached, confidential, dear, devoted, familiar, inseparable, loving 3 <u>careful</u>, detailed, intense, minute, painstaking, rigorous, thorough 4 <u>compact</u>, congested, crowded, dense, impenetrable, jam-packed, packed, tight 5 <u>stifling</u>, airless, heavy, humid, muggy, oppressive, stuffy, suffocating, sweltering 6 <u>secretive</u>, private, reticent, secret, taciturn, uncommunicative 7 <u>mean</u>, miserly, stingy

closed adjective 1 <u>shut</u>, fastened, locked, out of service, sealed 2 <u>exclusive</u>, restricted 3 <u>finished</u>, concluded, decided, ended, over, resolved, settled, terminated

cloth noun <u>fabric</u>, material, textiles

clothe verb <u>dress</u>, apparel, array, attire, cover, drape, equip, fit out, garb, robe, swathe

clothes plural noun <u>clothing</u>, apparel, attire, costume, dress, garb, garments, gear (informal), outfit, wardrobe, wear

clothing noun <u>clothes</u>, apparel, attire, costume, dress, garb, garments, gear (informal), outfit, wardrobe, wear

cloud noun 1 <u>mist</u>, gloom, haze, murk, vapour ♦ verb 2 <u>obscure</u>, becloud, darken, dim, eclipse, obfuscate, overshadow, shade, shadow, veil 3 <u>confuse</u>, disorient, distort, impair, muddle, muddy the waters

cloudy adjective 1 <u>dull</u>, dim, gloomy, leaden, louring or lowering, overcast, sombre, sunless 2 <u>opaque</u>, muddy, murky

clout Informal ♦ noun 1 <u>influence</u>, authority, power, prestige, pull, weight ♦ verb 2 <u>hit</u>, clobber (slang), punch, sock (slang), strike, thump, wallop (informal)

clown noun 1 <u>comedian</u>, buffoon, comic, fool, harlequin, jester, joker, prankster ♦ verb 2 <u>play the fool</u>, act the fool, jest, mess about

club noun 1 <u>association</u>, company, fraternity, group, guild, lodge, set, society, union 2 <u>stick</u>, bat, bludgeon, cosh (Brit.), cudgel, truncheon ♦ verb 3 <u>beat</u>, bash, batter, bludgeon, cosh (Brit.), hammer, pummel, strike

clue noun <u>indication</u>, evidence, hint, lead, pointer, sign, suggestion, suspicion, trace

clueless adjective <u>stupid</u>, dim, dozy (Brit. informal), dull, half-witted, simple, slow, thick, unintelligent, witless

clump noun 1 <u>cluster</u>, bunch, bundle, group, mass ♦ verb 2 <u>stomp</u>, lumber, plod, thud, thump, tramp

clumsy adjective <u>awkward</u>,

bumbling, gauche, gawky, ham-fisted (*informal*), lumbering, maladroit, ponderous, uncoordinated, ungainly, unwieldy

cluster noun 1 gathering, assemblage, batch, bunch, clump, collection, group, knot ♦ verb 2 gather, assemble, bunch, collect, flock, group

clutch verb seize, catch, clasp, cling to, embrace, grab, grasp, grip, snatch

clutches plural noun power, claws, control, custody, grasp, grip, hands, keeping, possession, sway

clutter verb 1 litter, scatter, strew ♦ noun 2 untidiness, confusion, disarray, disorder, hotchpotch, jumble, litter, mess, muddle

coach noun 1 bus, car, carriage, charabanc, vehicle 2 instructor, handler, teacher, trainer, tutor ♦ verb 3 instruct, drill, exercise, prepare, train, tutor

coalesce verb blend, amalgamate, combine, fuse, incorporate, integrate, merge, mix, unite

coalition noun alliance, amalgamation, association, bloc, combination, confederation, conjunction, fusion, merger, union

coarse adjective 1 rough, crude, homespun, impure, unfinished, unpolished, unprocessed, unpurified, unrefined 2 vulgar, earthy, improper, indecent, indelicate, ribald, rude, smutty

coarseness noun 1 roughness, crudity, unevenness 2 vulgarity, bawdiness, crudity, earthiness, indelicacy, ribaldry, smut, uncouthness

coast noun 1 shore, beach, border, coastline, seaboard, seaside ♦ verb 2 cruise, drift, freewheel, glide, sail, taxi

coat noun 1 fur, fleece, hair, hide, pelt, skin, wool 2 layer, coating, covering, overlay ♦ verb 3 cover, apply, plaster, smear, spread

coax verb persuade, allure, cajole, entice, prevail upon, sweet-talk (*informal*), talk into, wheedle

cocktail noun mixture, blend, combination, mix

cocky adjective overconfident, arrogant, brash, cocksure, conceited, egotistical, full of oneself, swaggering, vain

code noun 1 cipher, cryptograph 2 principles, canon, convention, custom, ethics, etiquette, manners, maxim, regulations, rules, system

cogent adjective convincing, compelling, effective, forceful, influential, potent, powerful, strong, weighty

cogitate verb think, consider, contemplate, deliberate, meditate, mull over, muse, ponder, reflect, ruminate

coherent adjective 1 consistent, logical, lucid, meaningful, orderly, organized, rational, reasoned, systematic 2 intelligible, articulate, comprehensible

coil verb wind, curl, loop, snake, spiral, twine, twist, wreathe, writhe

coin noun 1 money, cash,

change, copper, silver, specie
♦ verb 2 invent, create, fabricate, forge, make up, mint, mould, originate

coincide verb 1 occur simultaneously, be concurrent, coexist, synchronize 2 agree, accord, concur, correspond, harmonize, match, square, tally

coincidence noun 1 chance, accident, fluke, happy accident, luck, stroke of luck 2 coinciding, concurrence, conjunction, correlation, correspondence

coincidental adjective chance, accidental, casual, fluky (informal), fortuitous, unintentional, unplanned

cold adjective 1 chilly, arctic, bleak, cool, freezing, frigid, frosty, frozen, icy, wintry 2 unfriendly, aloof, distant, frigid, indifferent, reserved, standoffish ♦ noun 3 coldness, chill, frigidity, frostiness, iciness

cold-blooded adjective callous, dispassionate, heartless, ruthless, steely, stony-hearted, unemotional, unfeeling

collaborate verb 1 work together, cooperate, join forces, participate, play ball (informal), team up 2 conspire, collude, cooperate, fraternize

collaboration noun teamwork, alliance, association, cooperation, partnership

collaborator noun 1 co-worker, associate, colleague, confederate, partner, team-mate 2 traitor, fraternizer, quisling, turncoat

collapse verb 1 fall down, cave in, crumple, fall, fall apart at the seams, give way, subside 2 fail, come to nothing, fold, founder, go belly-up (informal) ♦ noun 3 falling down, cave-in, disintegration, falling apart, ruin, subsidence 4 failure, downfall, flop, slump 5 faint, breakdown, exhaustion, prostration

collar verb Informal seize, apprehend, arrest, capture, catch, grab, nab (informal), nail (informal)

colleague noun fellow worker, ally, assistant, associate, collaborator, comrade, helper, partner, team-mate, workmate

collect verb 1 assemble, cluster, congregate, convene, converge, flock together, rally 2 gather, accumulate, amass, assemble, heap, hoard, save, stockpile

collected adjective calm, composed, cool, poised, self-possessed, serene, unperturbed, unruffled

collection noun 1 accumulation, anthology, compilation, heap, hoard, mass, pile, set, stockpile, store 2 group, assembly, assortment, cluster, company, crowd 3 contribution, alms, offering, offertory

collective adjective combined, aggregate, composite, corporate, cumulative, joint, shared, unified, united

collide verb 1 crash, clash, come into collision, meet head-on 2 conflict, clash

collision noun 1 crash, accident, bump, impact, pile-up (informal), prang (informal), smash 2 conflict, clash, confrontation, encounter, opposition, skirmish

colloquial *adjective* informal, conversational, demotic, everyday, familiar, idiomatic, vernacular

colony *noun* settlement, community, dependency, dominion, outpost, possession, province, satellite state, territory

colossal *adjective* huge, enormous, gigantic, immense, mammoth, massive, monumental, prodigious, vast

colour *noun* 1 hue, colorant, dye, paint, pigment, shade, tint ◆ *verb* 2 paint, dye, stain, tinge, tint 3 blush, flush, redden

colourful *adjective* 1 bright, brilliant, multicoloured, psychedelic, variegated 2 interesting, distinctive, graphic, lively, picturesque, rich, vivid

colourless *adjective* 1 drab, achromatic, anaemic, ashen, bleached, faded, wan, washed out 2 uninteresting, characterless, dreary, dull, insipid, lacklustre, vapid

column *noun* 1 pillar, obelisk, post, shaft, support, upright 2 line, cavalcade, file, procession, rank, row

coma *noun* unconsciousness, oblivion, stupor, trance

comb *verb* 1 untangle, arrange, dress, groom 2 search, forage, hunt, rake, ransack, rummage, scour, sift

combat *noun* 1 fight, action, battle, conflict, contest, encounter, engagement, skirmish, struggle, war, warfare ◆ *verb* 2 fight, defy, do battle with, oppose, resist, withstand

combatant *noun* fighter, adversary, antagonist, enemy, opponent, soldier, warrior

combination *noun* 1 mixture, amalgamation, blend, coalescence, composite, connection, mix 2 association, alliance, coalition, confederation, consortium, federation, syndicate, union

combine *verb* join together, amalgamate, blend, connect, integrate, link, merge, mix, pool, unite

come *verb* 1 move towards, advance, approach, draw near, near 2 arrive, appear, enter, materialize, reach, show up (*informal*), turn up (*informal*) 3 happen, fall, occur, take place 4 result, arise, emanate, emerge, flow, issue, originate 5 reach, extend 6 be available, be made, be offered, be on offer, be produced

come about *verb* happen, arise, befall, come to pass, occur, result, take place, transpire (*informal*)

come across *verb* find, bump into (*informal*), chance upon, discover, encounter, meet, notice, stumble upon, unearth

comeback *noun* 1 *Informal* return, rally, rebound, recovery, resurgence, revival, triumph 2 response, rejoinder, reply, retaliation, retort, riposte

come back *verb* return, reappear, recur, re-enter

comedian *noun* comic, card (*informal*), clown, funny man, humorist, jester, joker, wag, wit

comedown *noun* 1 decline,

deflation, demotion, reverse
2 *Informal* disappointment,
anticlimax, blow, humiliation,
letdown

comedy *noun* humour, farce,
fun, hilarity, jesting, joking, light
entertainment

comeuppance *noun Informal*
punishment, chastening, deserts,
due reward, recompense,
retribution

comfort *noun* **1** luxury, cosiness,
ease, opulence, snugness,
wellbeing **2** relief, compensation,
consolation, help, succour,
support ◆ *verb* **3** console,
commiserate with, hearten,
reassure, soothe

comfortable *adjective* **1** relaxing,
agreeable, convenient, cosy,
homely, pleasant, restful, snug
2 happy, at ease, at home,
contented, gratified, relaxed,
serene **3** *Informal* well-off,
affluent, in clover (*informal*),
prosperous, well-to-do

comforting *adjective* consoling,
cheering, consolatory,
encouraging, heart-warming,
reassuring, soothing

comic *adjective* **1** funny, amusing,
comical, droll, farcical,
humorous, jocular, witty ◆ *noun*
2 comedian, buffoon, clown,
funny man, humorist, jester,
wag, wit

comical *adjective* funny, amusing,
comic, droll, farcical, hilarious,
humorous, priceless, side-splitting

coming *adjective* **1** approaching,
at hand, forthcoming, imminent,
impending, in store, near, nigh
◆ *noun* **2** arrival, advent, approach

command *verb* **1** order, bid,

charge, compel, demand, direct,
require **2** have authority over,
control, dominate, govern,
handle, head, lead, manage,
rule, supervise ◆ *noun* **3** order,
commandment, decree,
demand, directive, instruction,
requirement, ultimatum
4 authority, charge, control,
government, management,
mastery, power, rule, supervision

commandeer *verb* seize,
appropriate, confiscate,
requisition, sequester, sequestrate

commander *noun* officer, boss,
captain, chief, commanding
officer, head, leader, ruler

commanding *adjective*
controlling, advantageous,
decisive, dominant, dominating,
superior

commemorate *verb* remember,
celebrate, honour, immortalize,
pay tribute to, salute

commemoration *noun*
remembrance, ceremony,
honouring, memorial service,
tribute

commence *verb* begin, embark
on, enter upon, initiate, open,
originate, start

commend *verb* praise, acclaim,
applaud, approve, compliment,
extol, recommend, speak highly
of

commendable *adjective*
praiseworthy, admirable,
creditable, deserving, estimable,
exemplary, laudable,
meritorious, worthy

commendation *noun* praise,
acclaim, acclamation,
approbation, approval, credit,
encouragement, good opinion,

panegyric, recommendation

comment noun 1 <u>remark</u>, observation, statement 2 <u>note</u>, annotation, commentary, explanation, exposition, illustration ◆ verb 3 <u>remark</u>, mention, note, observe, point out, say, utter 4 <u>annotate</u>, elucidate, explain, interpret

commentary noun 1 <u>narration</u>, description, voice-over 2 <u>notes</u>, analysis, critique, explanation, review, treatise

commentator noun 1 <u>reporter</u>, special correspondent, sportscaster 2 <u>critic</u>, annotator, interpreter

commerce noun <u>trade</u>, business, dealing, exchange, traffic

commercial adjective 1 <u>mercantile</u>, trading 2 <u>materialistic</u>, mercenary, profit-making

commiserate verb <u>sympathize</u>, console, feel for, pity

commission noun 1 <u>duty</u>, errand, mandate, mission, task 2 <u>fee</u>, cut, percentage, rake-off (slang), royalties 3 <u>committee</u>, board, commissioners, delegation, deputation, representatives ◆ verb 4 <u>appoint</u>, authorize, contract, delegate, depute, empower, engage, nominate, order, select

commit verb 1 <u>do</u>, carry out, enact, execute, perform, perpetrate 2 <u>put in custody</u>, confine, imprison

commitment noun 1 <u>dedication</u>, devotion, involvement, loyalty 2 <u>responsibility</u>, duty, engagement, liability, obligation, tie

common adjective 1 <u>average</u>, commonplace, conventional, customary, everyday, familiar, frequent, habitual, ordinary, regular, routine, standard, stock, usual 2 <u>popular</u>, accepted, general, prevailing, prevalent, universal, widespread 3 <u>collective</u>, communal, popular, public, social 4 <u>vulgar</u>, coarse, inferior, plebeian

commonplace adjective 1 <u>everyday</u>, banal, common, humdrum, mundane, obvious, ordinary, run-of-the-mill, widespread ◆ noun 2 <u>cliché</u>, banality, platitude, truism

common sense noun <u>good sense</u>, gumption (Brit. informal), horse sense, level-headedness, native intelligence, prudence, sound judgment, wit

commotion noun <u>disturbance</u>, disorder, excitement, furore, fuss, hue and cry, rumpus, tumult, turmoil, upheaval, uproar

communal adjective <u>public</u>, collective, general, joint, shared

commune noun <u>community</u>, collective, cooperative, kibbutz

commune with verb <u>contemplate</u>, meditate on, muse on, ponder, reflect on

communicate verb <u>make known</u>, convey, declare, disclose, impart, inform, pass on, proclaim, transmit

communication noun 1 <u>passing on</u>, contact, conversation, correspondence, dissemination, link, transmission 2 <u>message</u>, announcement, disclosure, dispatch, information, news, report, statement, word

communicative adjective
talkative, chatty, expansive,
forthcoming, frank, informative,
loquacious, open, outgoing,
voluble

Communism noun socialism,
Bolshevism, collectivism,
Marxism, state socialism

Communist noun socialist,
Bolshevik, collectivist, Marxist,
Red (informal)

community noun society,
brotherhood, commonwealth,
company, general public,
people, populace, public,
residents, state

commuter noun daily traveller,
straphanger (informal),
suburbanite

compact[1] adjective 1 closely
packed, compressed, condensed,
dense, pressed together, solid,
thick 2 brief, compendious,
concise, succinct, terse, to the
point ♦ verb 3 pack closely,
compress, condense, cram, stuff,
tamp

compact[2] noun agreement,
arrangement, bargain, bond,
contract, covenant, deal, pact,
treaty, understanding

companion noun 1 friend,
accomplice, ally, associate,
colleague, comrade, consort,
mate (informal), partner 2 escort,
aide, assistant, attendant,
chaperon, squire

companionship noun fellowship,
camaraderie, company,
comradeship, conviviality, esprit
de corps, friendship, rapport,
togetherness

company noun 1 business,
association, concern,

corporation, establishment, firm,
house, partnership, syndicate
2 group, assembly, band,
collection, community, crowd,
gathering, party, set 3 guests,
callers, party, visitors

comparable adjective 1 on a par,
a match for, as good as,
commensurate, equal,
equivalent, in a class with,
proportionate, tantamount
2 similar, akin, alike, analogous,
cognate, corresponding, cut
from the same cloth, of a piece,
related

comparative adjective relative,
by comparison, qualified

compare verb 1 weigh, balance,
contrast, juxtapose, set against
2 usually with **with** be on a par
with, approach, bear
comparison, be in the same class
as, be the equal of, compete
with, equal, hold a candle to,
match 3 **compare to** liken to,
correlate to, equate to, identify
with, mention in the same
breath as, parallel, resemble

comparison noun 1 contrast,
distinction, juxtaposition
2 similarity, analogy,
comparability, correlation,
likeness, resemblance

compartment noun section,
alcove, bay, berth, booth,
carriage, cubbyhole, cubicle,
locker, niche, pigeonhole

compass noun range, area,
boundary, circumference, extent,
field, limit, reach, realm, scope

compassion noun sympathy,
condolence, fellow feeling,
humanity, kindness, mercy, pity,
sorrow, tender-heartedness,

tenderness, understanding

compassionate adjective
<u>sympathetic</u>, benevolent,
charitable, humane,
humanitarian, kind-hearted,
merciful, pitying, tender-hearted,
understanding

compatibility noun <u>harmony</u>,
affinity, agreement, concord,
empathy, like-mindedness,
rapport, sympathy

compatible adjective
<u>harmonious</u>, adaptable,
congruous, consistent, in
harmony, in keeping, suitable

compel verb <u>force</u>, coerce,
constrain, dragoon, impel, make,
oblige, railroad (informal)

compelling adjective
1 <u>fascinating</u>, enchanting,
enthralling, gripping, hypnotic,
irresistible, mesmeric,
spellbinding 2 <u>pressing</u>, binding,
coercive, imperative, overriding,
peremptory, unavoidable, urgent
3 <u>convincing</u>, cogent,
conclusive, forceful, irrefutable,
powerful, telling, weighty

compensate verb 1 <u>recompense</u>,
atone, make amends, make
good, refund, reimburse,
remunerate, repay 2 <u>cancel</u>
(out), balance, counteract,
counterbalance, make up for,
offset, redress

compensation noun
<u>recompense</u>, amends,
atonement, damages,
reimbursement, remuneration,
reparation, restitution, satisfaction

compete verb <u>contend</u>, be in the
running, challenge, contest,
fight, strive, struggle, vie

competence noun <u>ability</u>,

capability, capacity, expertise,
fitness, proficiency, skill, suitability

competent adjective <u>able</u>,
adequate, capable, fit, proficient,
qualified, suitable

competition noun 1 <u>rivalry</u>,
opposition, strife, struggle
2 <u>contest</u>, championship, event,
head-to-head, puzzle, quiz,
tournament 3 <u>opposition</u>,
challengers, field, rivals

competitive adjective
1 <u>cut-throat</u>, aggressive,
antagonistic, at odds,
dog-eat-dog, opposing, rival
2 <u>ambitious</u>, combative

competitor noun <u>contestant</u>,
adversary, antagonist,
challenger, opponent, rival

compilation noun <u>collection</u>,
accumulation, anthology,
assemblage, assortment, treasury

compile verb <u>put together</u>,
accumulate, amass, collect, cull,
garner, gather, marshal, organize

complacency noun
<u>self-satisfaction</u>, contentment,
satisfaction, smugness

complacent adjective
<u>self-satisfied</u>, contented, pleased
with oneself, resting on one's
laurels, satisfied, serene, smug,
unconcerned

complain verb <u>find fault</u>,
bemoan, bewail, carp, deplore,
groan, grouse, grumble, lament,
moan, whine, whinge (informal)

complaint noun 1 <u>criticism</u>,
charge, grievance, gripe
(informal), grouse, grumble,
lament, moan, protest 2 <u>illness</u>,
affliction, ailment, disease,
disorder, malady, sickness, upset

complement noun
1 completion, companion, consummation, counterpart, finishing touch, rounding-off, supplement 2 total, aggregate, capacity, entirety, quota, totality, wholeness ◆ verb 3 complete, cap (informal), crown, round off, set off

complementary adjective completing, companion, corresponding, interdependent, interrelating, matched, reciprocal

complete adjective 1 total, absolute, consummate, outright, perfect, thorough, thoroughgoing, utter 2 finished, accomplished, achieved, concluded, ended 3 entire, all, faultless, full, intact, plenary, unbroken, whole ◆ verb 4 finish, close, conclude, crown, end, finalize, round off, settle, wrap up (informal)

completely adverb totally, absolutely, altogether, entirely, every inch, fully, hook, line and sinker, in full, lock, stock and barrel, one hundred per cent, perfectly, thoroughly, utterly, wholly

completion noun finishing, bitter end, close, conclusion, culmination, end, fruition, fulfilment

complex adjective 1 compound, composite, heterogeneous, manifold, multifarious, multiple 2 complicated, convoluted, elaborate, intricate, involved, labyrinthine, tangled, tortuous ◆ noun 3 structure, aggregate, composite, network, organization, scheme, system

4 Informal obsession, fixation, fixed idea, idée fixe, phobia, preoccupation

complexion noun 1 skin, colour, colouring, hue, pigmentation, skin tone 2 nature, appearance, aspect, character, guise, light, look, make-up

complexity noun complication, elaboration, entanglement, intricacy, involvement, ramification

complicate verb make difficult, confuse, entangle, involve, muddle, ravel

complicated adjective 1 difficult, involved, perplexing, problematic, puzzling, troublesome 2 involved, complex, convoluted, elaborate, intricate, labyrinthine

complication noun
1 complexity, confusion, entanglement, intricacy, web 2 problem, difficulty, drawback, embarrassment, obstacle, snag

compliment noun 1 praise, bouquet, commendation, congratulations, eulogy, flattery, honour, tribute ◆ verb 2 praise, commend, congratulate, extol, flatter, pay tribute to, salute, speak highly of

complimentary adjective
1 flattering, appreciative, approving, commendatory, congratulatory, laudatory 2 free, courtesy, donated, gratis, gratuitous, honorary, on the house

compliments plural noun greetings, good wishes, regards, remembrances, respects, salutation

comply verb obey, abide by, acquiesce, adhere to, conform to, follow, observe, submit, toe the line

component noun 1 part, constituent, element, ingredient, item, piece, unit ♦ adjective 2 constituent, inherent, intrinsic

compose verb 1 put together, build, comprise, constitute, construct, fashion, form, make, make up 2 create, contrive, devise, invent, produce, write 3 calm, collect, control, pacify, placate, quiet, soothe 4 arrange, adjust

composed adjective calm, at ease, collected, cool, level-headed, poised, relaxed, sedate, self-possessed, serene, unflappable

composition noun 1 creation, compilation, fashioning, formation, formulation, making, production, putting together 2 design, arrangement, configuration, formation, layout, make-up, organization, structure 3 essay, exercise, literary work, opus, piece, treatise, work

composure noun calmness, aplomb, equanimity, poise, sang-froid, self-assurance, self-possession, serenity

compound noun 1 combination, alloy, amalgam, blend, composite, fusion, medley, mixture, synthesis ♦ verb 2 combine, amalgamate, blend, intermingle, mix, synthesize, unite 3 intensify, add to, aggravate, augment, complicate, exacerbate, heighten, magnify, worsen ♦ adjective 4 complex,

composite, intricate, multiple

comprehend verb understand, apprehend, conceive, fathom, grasp, know, make out, perceive, see, take in

comprehensible adjective understandable, clear, coherent, conceivable, explicit, intelligible, plain

comprehension noun understanding, conception, discernment, grasp, intelligence, perception, realization

comprehensive adjective broad, all-embracing, all-inclusive, blanket, complete, encyclopedic, exhaustive, full, inclusive, thorough

compress verb squeeze, abbreviate, concentrate, condense, contract, crush, press, shorten, squash

comprise verb 1 be composed of, consist of, contain, embrace, encompass, include, take in 2 make up, compose, constitute, form

compromise noun 1 give-and-take, accommodation, adjustment, agreement, concession, settlement, trade-off ♦ verb 2 meet halfway, adjust, agree, concede, give and take, go fifty-fifty (informal), settle, strike a balance 3 dishonour, discredit, embarrass, expose, jeopardize, prejudice, weaken

compulsion noun 1 urge, drive, necessity, need, obsession, preoccupation 2 force, coercion, constraint, demand, duress, obligation, pressure, urgency

compulsive adjective irresistible,

compelling, driving, neurotic, obsessive, overwhelming, uncontrollable, urgent

compulsory *adjective* <u>obligatory</u>, binding, de rigueur, forced, imperative, mandatory, required, requisite

compute *verb* <u>calculate</u>, add up, count, enumerate, figure out, reckon, tally, total

comrade *noun* <u>companion</u>, ally, associate, colleague, co-worker, fellow, friend, partner

con *Informal* ♦ *noun* 1 <u>swindle</u>, deception, fraud, scam (*slang*), sting (*informal*), trick ♦ *verb* 2 <u>swindle</u>, cheat, deceive, defraud, double-cross (*informal*), dupe, hoodwink, rip off (*slang*), trick

concave *adjective* <u>hollow</u>, indented

conceal *verb* <u>hide</u>, bury, camouflage, cover, disguise, mask, obscure, screen

concede *verb* 1 <u>admit</u>, accept, acknowledge, allow, confess, grant, own 2 <u>give up</u>, cede, hand over, relinquish, surrender, yield

conceit *noun* 1 <u>self-importance</u>, arrogance, egotism, narcissism, pride, swagger, vanity 2 *Archaic* <u>fancy</u>, fantasy, image, whim, whimsy

conceited *adjective* <u>self-important</u>, arrogant, bigheaded (*informal*), cocky, egotistical, full of oneself, immodest, narcissistic, too big for one's boots *or* breeches, vain

conceivable *adjective* <u>imaginable</u>, believable, credible, possible, thinkable

conceive *verb* 1 <u>imagine</u>, believe, comprehend, envisage, fancy, suppose, think, understand 2 <u>think up</u>, contrive, create, design, devise, formulate 3 <u>become pregnant</u>, become impregnated

concentrate *verb* 1 <u>focus one's attention on</u>, be engrossed in, put one's mind to, rack one's brains 2 <u>focus</u>, bring to bear, centre, cluster, converge 3 <u>gather</u>, accumulate, cluster, collect, congregate, huddle

concentrated *adjective* 1 <u>intense</u>, all-out (*informal*), deep, hard, intensive 2 <u>condensed</u>, boiled down, evaporated, reduced, rich, thickened, undiluted

concentration *noun* 1 <u>single-mindedness</u>, absorption, application, heed 2 <u>focusing</u>, bringing to bear, centralization, centring, consolidation, convergence, intensification 3 <u>convergence</u>, accumulation, aggregation, cluster, collection, horde, mass

concept *noun* <u>idea</u>, abstraction, conception, conceptualization, hypothesis, image, notion, theory, view

conception *noun* 1 <u>idea</u>, concept, design, image, notion, plan 2 <u>impregnation</u>, fertilization, germination, insemination

concern *noun* 1 <u>worry</u>, anxiety, apprehension, burden, care, disquiet, distress 2 <u>importance</u>, bearing, interest, relevance 3 <u>business</u>, affair, interest, job, responsibility, task 4 <u>business</u>, company, corporation, enterprise, establishment, firm, organization ♦ verb 5 <u>worry</u>, bother, disquiet, distress, disturb, make anxious, perturb, trouble 6 <u>be relevant to</u>, affect, apply to, bear on, interest, involve, pertain to, regard, touch

concerned adjective 1 <u>involved</u>, active, implicated, interested, mixed up, privy to 2 <u>worried</u>, anxious, bothered, distressed, disturbed, troubled, uneasy, upset

concerning preposition <u>regarding</u>, about, apropos of, as regards, on the subject of, re, relating to, respecting, touching, with reference to

concession noun 1 <u>grant</u>, adjustment, allowance, boon, compromise, indulgence, permit, privilege, sop 2 <u>conceding</u>, acknowledgment, admission, assent, confession, surrender, yielding

conciliate verb <u>pacify</u>, appease, clear the air, mediate, mollify, placate, reconcile, soothe, win over

conciliation noun <u>pacification</u>, appeasement, mollification, placation, reconciliation, soothing

conciliatory adjective <u>pacifying</u>, appeasing, mollifying, pacific, peaceable, placatory

concise adjective <u>brief</u>, compendious, condensed, laconic, pithy, short, succinct, terse

conclude verb 1 <u>decide</u>, assume, deduce, gather, infer, judge, surmise, work out 2 <u>end</u>, cease, close, complete, finish, round

off, terminate, wind up 3 <u>accomplish</u>, bring about, carry out, effect, pull off

conclusion noun 1 <u>decision</u>, conviction, deduction, inference, judgment, opinion, verdict 2 <u>end</u>, bitter end, close, completion, ending, finale, finish, result, termination 3 <u>outcome</u>, consequence, culmination, end result, result, upshot

conclusive adjective <u>decisive</u>, clinching, convincing, definite, final, irrefutable, ultimate, unanswerable

concoct verb <u>make up</u>, brew, contrive, devise, formulate, hatch, invent, prepare, think up

concoction noun <u>mixture</u>, blend, brew, combination, compound, creation, preparation

concrete adjective 1 <u>specific</u>, definite, explicit 2 <u>real</u>, actual, factual, material, sensible, substantial, tangible

concur verb <u>agree</u>, acquiesce, assent, consent

condemn verb 1 <u>disapprove</u>, blame, censure, damn, denounce, reproach, reprove, upbraid 2 <u>sentence</u>, convict, damn, doom, pass sentence on

condemnation noun 1 <u>disapproval</u>, blame, censure, denunciation, reproach, reproof, stricture 2 <u>sentence</u>, conviction, damnation, doom, judgment

condensation noun 1 <u>distillation</u>, liquefaction, precipitate, precipitation 2 <u>abridgment</u>, contraction, digest, précis, synopsis 3 <u>concentration</u>, compression, consolidation, crystallization, curtailment, reduction

condense verb **1** abridge, abbreviate, compress, concentrate, epitomize, shorten, summarize **2** concentrate, boil down, reduce, thicken

condensed adjective **1** abridged, compressed, concentrated, shortened, shrunken, slimmed-down, summarized **2** concentrated, boiled down, reduced, thickened

condescend verb **1** patronize, talk down to **2** lower oneself, bend, deign, humble or demean oneself, see fit, stoop

condescending adjective patronizing, disdainful, lofty, lordly, snobbish, snooty (informal), supercilious, superior, toffee-nosed (slang, chiefly Brit.)

condition noun **1** state, circumstances, lie of the land, position, shape, situation, state of affairs **2** requirement, limitation, prerequisite, proviso, qualification, restriction, rider, stipulation, terms **3** health, fettle, fitness, kilter, order, shape, state of health, trim **4** ailment, complaint, infirmity, malady, problem, weakness ◆ verb **5** accustom, adapt, equip, prepare, ready, tone up, train, work out

conditional adjective dependent, contingent, limited, provisional, qualified, subject to, with reservations

conditions plural noun circumstances, environment, milieu, situation, surroundings, way of life

condone verb overlook, excuse, forgive, let pass, look the other way, make allowance for, pardon, turn a blind eye to

conduct noun **1** behaviour, attitude, bearing, demeanour, deportment, manners, ways **2** management, administration, control, direction, guidance, handling, organization, running, supervision ◆ verb **3** carry out, administer, control, direct, handle, manage, organize, preside over, run, supervise **4** behave, acquit, act, carry, comport, deport **5** accompany, convey, escort, guide, lead, steer, usher

confederacy noun union, alliance, coalition, confederation, federation, league

confer verb **1** discuss, consult, converse, deliberate, discourse, talk **2** grant, accord, award, bestow, give, hand out, present

conference noun meeting, colloquium, congress, consultation, convention, discussion, forum, seminar, symposium

confess verb **1** admit, acknowledge, come clean (informal), concede, confide, disclose, divulge, own up **2** declare, affirm, assert, confirm, profess, reveal

confession noun admission, acknowledgment, disclosure, exposure, revelation, unbosoming

confidant, confidante noun close friend, alter ego, bosom friend, crony, familiar, intimate

confide verb **1** tell, admit, confess, disclose, divulge, impart, reveal, whisper **2** *Formal* entrust, commend, commit, consign

confidence *noun* **1** trust, belief, credence, dependence, faith, reliance **2** self-assurance, aplomb, assurance, boldness, courage, firmness, nerve, self-possession **3 in confidence** in secrecy, between you and me (and the gatepost), confidentially, privately

confident *adjective* **1** certain, convinced, counting on, positive, satisfied, secure, sure **2** self-assured, assured, bold, dauntless, fearless, self-reliant

confidential *adjective* secret, classified, hush-hush (*informal*), intimate, off the record, private, privy

confidentially *adverb* in secret, behind closed doors, between ourselves, in camera, in confidence, personally, privately, sub rosa

confine *verb* restrict, cage, enclose, hem in, hold back, imprison, incarcerate, intern, keep, limit, shut up

confinement *noun* **1** imprisonment, custody, detention, incarceration, internment, porridge (*slang*) **2** childbirth, childbed, labour, lying-in, parturition

confines *plural noun* limits, boundaries, bounds, circumference, edge, precincts

confirm *verb* **1** prove, authenticate, bear out, corroborate, endorse, ratify, substantiate, validate, verify **2** strengthen, buttress, establish, fix, fortify, reinforce

confirmation *noun* **1** proof, authentication, corroboration, evidence, substantiation, testimony, validation, verification **2** sanction, acceptance, agreement, approval, assent, endorsement, ratification

confirmed *adjective* long-established, chronic, dyed-in-the-wool, habitual, hardened, ingrained, inveterate, seasoned

confiscate *verb* seize, appropriate, commandeer, impound, sequester, sequestrate

confiscation *noun* seizure, appropriation, forfeiture, impounding, sequestration, takeover

conflict *noun* **1** opposition, antagonism, difference, disagreement, discord, dissension, friction, hostility, strife **2** battle, clash, combat, contest, encounter, fight, strife, war ♦ *verb* **3** be incompatible, be at variance, clash, collide, differ, disagree, interfere

conflicting *adjective* incompatible, antagonistic, clashing, contradictory, contrary, discordant, inconsistent, opposing, paradoxical

conform *verb* **1** comply, adapt, adjust, fall in with, follow, obey, toe the line **2** agree, accord, correspond, harmonize, match, suit, tally

conformist *noun* traditionalist, stick-in-the-mud (*informal*), yes man

conformity *noun* compliance, conventionality, observance, orthodoxy, traditionalism

confound verb bewilder, astound, baffle, confuse, dumbfound, flummox, mystify, nonplus, perplex

confront verb face, accost, challenge, defy, encounter, oppose, stand up to, tackle

confrontation noun conflict, contest, encounter, fight, head-to-head, set-to (informal), showdown (informal)

confuse verb 1 mix up, disarrange, disorder, jumble, mingle, muddle, ravel 2 bewilder, baffle, bemuse, faze, flummox, mystify, nonplus, perplex, puzzle 3 disconcert, discompose, disorient, fluster, rattle (informal), throw off balance, unnerve, upset

confused adjective 1 bewildered, at sea, baffled, disorientated, flummoxed, muddled, nonplussed, perplexed, puzzled, taken aback 2 disordered, chaotic, disorganized, higgledy-piggledy (informal), in disarray, jumbled, mixed up, topsy-turvy, untidy

confusing adjective bewildering, baffling, contradictory, disconcerting, misleading, perplexing, puzzling, unclear

confusion noun 1 bewilderment, disorientation, mystification, perplexity, puzzlement 2 disorder, chaos, commotion, jumble, mess, muddle, shambles, turmoil, untidiness, upheaval

congenial adjective 1 pleasant, affable, agreeable, companionable, favourable, friendly, genial, kindly

2 compatible, kindred, like-minded, sympathetic, well-suited

congenital adjective inborn, immanent, inbred, inherent, innate, natural

congested adjective 1 overcrowded, crowded, teeming 2 clogged, blocked-up, crammed, jammed, overfilled, overflowing, packed, stuffed

congestion noun 1 overcrowding, crowding 2 clogging, bottleneck, jam, surfeit

congratulate verb compliment, pat on the back, wish joy to

congratulations plural noun, interjection good wishes, best wishes, compliments, felicitations, greetings

congregate verb come together, assemble, collect, convene, converge, flock, gather, mass, meet

congregation noun assembly, brethren, crowd, fellowship, flock, multitude, throng

congress noun meeting, assembly, conclave, conference, convention, council, legislature, parliament

conjecture noun 1 guess, hypothesis, shot in the dark, speculation, supposition, surmise, theory ♦ verb 2 guess, hypothesize, imagine, speculate, suppose, surmise, theorize

conjugal adjective marital, bridal, connubial, married, matrimonial, nuptial, wedded

conjure verb perform tricks, juggle

conjure up verb bring to mind, contrive, create, evoke, produce as if by magic, recall, recollect

conjuror, conjurer noun magician, illusionist, sorcerer, wizard

connect verb link, affix, attach, couple, fasten, join, unite

connected adjective linked, affiliated, akin, allied, associated, combined, coupled, joined, related, united

connection noun 1 association, affinity, bond, liaison, link, relationship, relevance, tie-in 2 link, alliance, association, attachment, coupling, fastening, junction, tie, union 3 contact, acquaintance, ally, associate, friend, sponsor

connivance noun collusion, abetting, complicity, conspiring, tacit consent

connive verb 1 conspire, collude, cook up (informal), intrigue, plot, scheme 2 connive at turn a blind eye to, abet, disregard, let pass, look the other way, overlook, wink at

connoisseur noun expert, aficionado, appreciator, authority, buff (informal), devotee, judge

conquer verb 1 defeat, beat, crush, get the better of, master, overcome, overpower, overthrow, quell, subjugate, vanquish 2 seize, acquire, annex, obtain, occupy, overrun, win

conqueror noun winner, conquistador, defeater, master, subjugator, vanquisher, victor

conquest noun 1 defeat,

mastery, overthrow, rout, triumph, victory 2 takeover, annexation, coup, invasion, occupation, subjugation

conscience noun principles, moral sense, scruples, sense of right and wrong, still small voice

conscientious adjective thorough, careful, diligent, exact, faithful, meticulous, painstaking, particular, punctilious

conscious adjective 1 aware, alert, alive to, awake, responsive, sensible, sentient 2 deliberate, calculated, intentional, knowing, premeditated, self-conscious, studied, wilful

consciousness noun awareness, apprehension, knowledge, realization, recognition, sensibility

consecrate verb sanctify, dedicate, devote, hallow, ordain, set apart, venerate

consecutive adjective successive, in sequence, in turn, running, sequential, succeeding, uninterrupted

consensus noun agreement, assent, common consent, concord, general agreement, harmony, unanimity, unity

consent noun 1 agreement, acquiescence, approval, assent, compliance, go-ahead (informal), O.K. or okay (informal), permission, sanction ♦ verb 2 agree, acquiesce, allow, approve, assent, concur, permit

consequence noun 1 result, effect, end result, issue, outcome, repercussion, sequel, upshot 2 importance, account, concern, import, moment, significance, value, weight

consequent *adjective* following, ensuing, resultant, resulting, subsequent, successive

consequently *adverb* as a result, accordingly, ergo, hence, subsequently, therefore, thus

conservation *noun* protection, guardianship, husbandry, maintenance, preservation, safeguarding, safekeeping, saving, upkeep

conservative *adjective*
1 traditional, cautious, conventional, die-hard, hidebound, reactionary, sober ♦ *noun* **2** traditionalist, reactionary, stick-in-the-mud (*informal*)

Conservative *adjective* **1** Tory, right-wing ♦ *noun* **2** Tory, right-winger

conserve *verb* protect, hoard, husband, keep, nurse, preserve, save, store up, take care of, use sparingly

consider *verb* **1** think, believe, deem, hold to be, judge, rate, regard as **2** think about, cogitate, contemplate, deliberate, meditate, ponder, reflect, ruminate, turn over in one's mind, weigh **3** bear in mind, keep in view, make allowance for, reckon with, remember, respect, take into account

considerable *adjective* large, appreciable, goodly, great, marked, noticeable, plentiful, sizable *or* sizeable, substantial

considerably *adverb* greatly, appreciably, markedly, noticeably, remarkably,

significantly, substantially, very much

considerate *adjective* thoughtful, attentive, concerned, kindly, mindful, obliging, patient, tactful, unselfish

consideration *noun* **1** thought, analysis, deliberation, discussion, examination, reflection, review, scrutiny **2** factor, concern, issue, point **3** thoughtfulness, concern, considerateness, kindness, respect, tact **4** payment, fee, recompense, remuneration, reward, tip

considering *preposition* taking into account, in the light of, in view of

consignment *noun* shipment, batch, delivery, goods

consist *verb* **1** consist of be made up of, amount to, be composed of, comprise, contain, embody, include, incorporate, involve **2** consist in lie in, be expressed by, be found *or* contained in, inhere in, reside in

consistency *noun* **1** texture, compactness, density, firmness, thickness, viscosity **2** constancy, evenness, regularity, steadfastness, steadiness, uniformity

consistent *adjective*
1 unchanging, constant, dependable, persistent, regular, steady, true to type, undeviating **2** agreeing, coherent, compatible, congruous, consonant, harmonious, logical

consolation *noun* comfort, cheer, encouragement, help, relief, solace, succour, support

console *verb* comfort, calm,

cheer, encourage, express sympathy for, soothe

consolidate verb 1 strengthen, fortify, reinforce, secure, stabilize 2 combine, amalgamate, federate, fuse, join, unite

consort verb 1 associate, fraternize, go around with, hang about, around or out with, keep company, mix ◆ noun 2 spouse, companion, husband, partner, wife

conspicuous adjective 1 obvious, blatant, clear, evident, noticeable, patent, salient 2 noteworthy, illustrious, notable, outstanding, prominent, remarkable, salient, signal, striking

conspiracy noun 1 plot, collusion, intrigue, machination, scheme, treason

conspirator noun 1 plotter, conspirer, intriguer, schemer, traitor

conspire verb 1 plot, contrive, intrigue, machinate, manoeuvre, plan, scheme 2 work together, combine, concur, contribute, cooperate, tend

constant adjective 1 continuous, ceaseless, incessant, interminable, nonstop, perpetual, sustained, unrelenting 2 unchanging, even, fixed, invariable, permanent, stable, steady, uniform, unvarying 3 faithful, devoted, loyal, stalwart, staunch, true, trustworthy, trusty

constantly adverb continuously, all the time, always, continually, endlessly, incessantly, interminably, invariably,

nonstop, perpetually

consternation noun dismay, alarm, anxiety, distress, dread, fear, trepidation

constituent noun 1 voter, elector 2 component, element, factor, ingredient, part, unit ◆ adjective 3 component, basic, elemental, essential, integral

constitute verb make up, compose, comprise, establish, form, found, set up

constitution noun 1 health, build, character, disposition, physique 2 structure, composition, form, make-up, nature

constitutional adjective 1 statutory, chartered, vested ◆ noun 2 walk, airing, stroll, turn

constrain verb 1 force, bind, coerce, compel, impel, necessitate, oblige, pressurize 2 restrict, check, confine, constrict, curb, restrain, straiten

constraint noun 1 restriction, check, curb, deterrent, hindrance, limitation, rein 2 force, coercion, compulsion, necessity, pressure, restraint

construct verb build, assemble, compose, create, fashion, form, make, manufacture, put together, shape

construction noun 1 building, composition, creation, edifice 2 Formal interpretation, explanation, inference, reading, rendering

constructive adjective helpful, positive, practical, productive, useful, valuable

consult verb ask, compare notes,

confer, pick (someone's) brains, question, refer to, take counsel, turn to

consultant noun specialist, adviser, authority

consultation noun seminar, appointment, conference, council, deliberation, dialogue, discussion, examination, hearing, interview, meeting, session

consume verb 1 eat, devour, eat up, gobble (up), put away, swallow 2 use up, absorb, dissipate, exhaust, expend, spend, squander, waste 3 destroy, annihilate, demolish, devastate, lay waste, ravage 4 often passive obsess, absorb, dominate, eat up, engross, monopolize, preoccupy

consumer noun buyer, customer, purchaser, shopper, user

consummate verb 1 complete, accomplish, conclude, crown, end, finish, fulfil ♦ adjective 2 skilled, accomplished, matchless, perfect, polished, practised, superb, supreme 3 complete, absolute, conspicuous, extreme, supreme, total, utter

consumption noun 1 using up, depletion, diminution, dissipation, exhaustion, expenditure, loss, waste 2 Old-fashioned tuberculosis, T.B.

contact noun 1 communication, association, connection 2 touch, contiguity 3 acquaintance, connection ♦ verb 4 get or be in touch with, approach, call, communicate with, reach, speak to, write to

contagious adjective infectious,

catching, communicable, spreading, transmissible

contain verb 1 hold, accommodate, enclose, have capacity for, incorporate, seat 2 include, comprehend, comprise, consist of, embody, embrace, involve 3 restrain, control, curb, hold back, hold in, keep a tight rein on, repress, stifle

container noun holder, receptacle, repository, vessel

contaminate verb pollute, adulterate, befoul, corrupt, defile, infect, stain, taint, tarnish

contamination noun pollution, contagion, corruption, defilement, impurity, infection, poisoning, taint

contemplate verb 1 think about, consider, deliberate, meditate, muse over, ponder, reflect upon, ruminate (upon) 2 consider, envisage, expect, foresee, intend, plan, think of 3 look at, examine, eye up, gaze at, inspect, regard, stare at, study, survey, view

contemporary adjective 1 coexisting, concurrent, contemporaneous 2 modern, à la mode, current, newfangled, present, present-day, recent, up-to-date ♦ noun 3 peer, fellow

contempt noun scorn, derision, disdain, disregard, disrespect, mockery, neglect, slight

contemptible adjective despicable, detestable, ignominious, measly, paltry, pitiful, shameful, worthless

contemptuous adjective scornful, arrogant,

condescending, derisive, disdainful, haughty, sneering, supercilious, withering

contend *verb* **1** compete, clash, contest, fight, jostle, strive, struggle, vie **2** argue, affirm, allege, assert, dispute, hold, maintain

content[1] *noun* **1** meaning, essence, gist, significance, substance **2** amount, capacity, load, measure, size, volume

content[2] *adjective* **1** satisfied, agreeable, at ease, comfortable, contented, fulfilled, willing to accept ♦ *verb* **2** satisfy, appease, humour, indulge, mollify, placate, please ♦ *noun* **3** satisfaction, comfort, contentment, ease, gratification, peace of mind, pleasure

contented *adjective* satisfied, comfortable, content, glad, gratified, happy, pleased, serene, thankful

contentious *adjective* argumentative, bickering, captious, cavilling, disputatious, quarrelsome, querulous, wrangling

contentment *noun* satisfaction, comfort, content, ease, equanimity, fulfilment, happiness, peace, pleasure, serenity

contents *plural noun* constituents, elements, ingredients, load

contest *noun* **1** competition, game, match, tournament, trial **2** struggle, battle, combat, conflict, controversy, dispute, fight ♦ *verb* **3** dispute, argue, call in *or* into question, challenge,

debate, doubt, object to, oppose, question **4** compete, contend, fight, strive, vie

contestant *noun* competitor, candidate, contender, entrant, participant, player

context *noun* **1** circumstances, ambience, conditions, situation **2** frame of reference, background, connection, framework, relation

contingency *noun* possibility, accident, chance, emergency, event, eventuality, happening, incident

continual *adjective* constant, frequent, incessant, interminable, recurrent, regular, repeated, unremitting

continually *adverb* constantly, all the time, always, forever, incessantly, interminably, nonstop, persistently, repeatedly

continuation *noun* **1** continuing, perpetuation, prolongation, resumption **2** addition, extension, furtherance, postscript, sequel, supplement

continue *verb* **1** remain, abide, carry on, endure, last, live on, persist, stay, survive **2** keep on, carry on, go on, maintain, persevere, persist in, stick at, sustain **3** resume, carry on, pick up where one left off, proceed, recommence, return to, take up

continuing *adjective* lasting, enduring, in progress, ongoing, sustained

continuity *noun* sequence, cohesion, connection, flow, progression, succession

continuous *adjective* constant,

extended, prolonged, unbroken, unceasing, undivided, uninterrupted

contraband noun 1 smuggling, black-marketing, bootlegging, trafficking ♦ adjective 2 smuggled, banned, bootleg, forbidden, hot (informal), illegal, illicit, prohibited, unlawful

contract noun 1 agreement, arrangement, bargain, commitment, covenant, pact, settlement ♦ verb 2 agree, bargain, come to terms, commit oneself, covenant, negotiate, pledge 3 shorten, abbreviate, curtail, diminish, dwindle, lessen, narrow, reduce, shrink, shrivel 4 catch, acquire, be afflicted with, develop, get, go down with, incur

contraction noun shortening, abbreviation, compression, narrowing, reduction, shrinkage, shrivelling, tightening

contradict verb deny, be at variance with, belie, challenge, controvert, fly in the face of, negate, rebut

contradiction noun denial, conflict, contravention, incongruity, inconsistency, negation, opposite

contradictory adjective inconsistent, conflicting, contrary, incompatible, opposed, opposite, paradoxical

contraption noun Informal device, apparatus, contrivance, gadget, instrument, mechanism

contrary noun 1 opposite, antithesis, converse, reverse ♦ adjective 2 opposed, adverse, clashing, contradictory, counter,

discordant, hostile, inconsistent, opposite, paradoxical 3 perverse, awkward, cantankerous, difficult, disobliging, intractable, obstinate, stroppy (Brit. slang), unaccommodating

contrast noun 1 difference, comparison, disparity, dissimilarity, distinction, divergence, foil, opposition ♦ verb 2 differentiate, compare, differ, distinguish, oppose, set in opposition, set off

contribute verb 1 give, add, bestow, chip in (informal), donate, provide, subscribe, supply 2 contribute to be partly responsible for, be conducive to, be instrumental in, help, lead to, tend to

contribution noun gift, addition, donation, grant, input, offering, subscription

contributor noun giver, donor, patron, subscriber, supporter

contrite adjective sorry, chastened, conscience-stricken, humble, penitent, regretful, remorseful, repentant, sorrowful

contrivance noun 1 device, apparatus, appliance, contraption, gadget, implement, instrument, invention, machine, mechanism 2 plan, intrigue, machination, plot, ruse, scheme, stratagem, trick

contrive verb 1 bring about, arrange, effect, manage, manoeuvre, plan, plot, scheme, succeed 2 devise, concoct, construct, create, design, fabricate, improvise, invent, manufacture

contrived adjective forced,

artificial, elaborate, laboured, overdone, planned, strained, unnatural

control noun 1 <u>power</u>, authority, charge, command, guidance, management, oversight, supervision, supremacy 2 <u>restraint</u>, brake, check, curb, limitation, regulation ♦ verb 3 <u>have power over</u>, administer, command, direct, govern, handle, have charge of, manage, manipulate, supervise 4 <u>restrain</u>, check, constrain, contain, curb, hold back, limit, repress, subdue

controls plural noun <u>instruments</u>, console, control panel, dash, dashboard, dials

controversial adjective <u>disputed</u>, at issue, contentious, debatable, disputable, open to question, under discussion

controversy noun <u>argument</u>, altercation, debate, dispute, quarrel, row, squabble, wrangling

convalescence noun <u>recovery</u>, improvement, recuperation, rehabilitation, return to health

convalescent adjective <u>recovering</u>, getting better, improving, mending, on the mend, recuperating

convene verb <u>gather</u>, assemble, bring together, call, come together, congregate, convoke, meet, summon

convenience noun 1 <u>availability</u>, accessibility, advantage, appropriateness, benefit, fitness, suitability, usefulness, utility 2 <u>appliance</u>, amenity, comfort, facility, help, labour-saving device

convenient adjective 1 <u>useful</u>, appropriate, fit, handy, helpful,

labour-saving, serviceable, suitable, timely 2 <u>nearby</u>, accessible, at hand, available, close at hand, handy, just round the corner, within reach

convention noun 1 <u>custom</u>, code, etiquette, practice, propriety, protocol, tradition, usage 2 <u>agreement</u>, bargain, contract, pact, protocol, treaty 3 <u>assembly</u>, conference, congress, convocation, council, meeting

conventional adjective 1 <u>ordinary</u>, accepted, customary, normal, orthodox, regular, standard, traditional, usual 2 <u>unoriginal</u>, banal, hackneyed, prosaic, routine, run-of-the-mill, stereotyped

converge verb <u>come together</u>, coincide, combine, gather, join, meet, merge

conversation noun <u>talk</u>, chat, conference, dialogue, discourse, discussion, gossip, tête-à-tête

converse[1] verb <u>talk</u>, chat, commune, confer, discourse, exchange views

converse[2] noun 1 <u>opposite</u>, antithesis, contrary, obverse, other side of the coin, reverse ♦ adjective 2 <u>opposite</u>, contrary, counter, reverse, reversed, transposed

conversion noun 1 <u>change</u>, metamorphosis, transformation 2 <u>adaptation</u>, alteration, modification, reconstruction, remodelling, reorganization

convert verb 1 <u>change</u>, alter, transform, transpose, turn 2 <u>adapt</u>, apply, customize, modify, remodel, reorganize, restyle, revise **3** reform, convince, proselytize ♦ *noun* **4** neophyte, disciple, proselyte

convex *adjective* rounded, bulging, gibbous, protuberant

convey *verb* **1** communicate, disclose, impart, make known, relate, reveal, tell **2** carry, bear, bring, conduct, fetch, guide, move, send, transport

convict *verb* **1** find guilty, condemn, imprison, pronounce guilty, sentence ♦ *noun* **2** prisoner, criminal, culprit, felon, jailbird, lag (*slang*)

conviction *noun* **1** belief, creed, faith, opinion, persuasion, principle, tenet, view **2** confidence, assurance, certainty, certitude, firmness, reliance

convince *verb* persuade, assure, bring round, prevail upon, satisfy, sway, win over

convincing *adjective* persuasive, cogent, conclusive, credible, impressive, plausible, powerful, telling

convulse *verb* shake, agitate, churn up, derange, disorder, disturb, twist, work

convulsion *noun* spasm, contraction, cramp, fit, paroxysm, seizure

cool *adjective* **1** cold, chilled, chilly, nippy, refreshing **2** calm, collected, composed, relaxed, sedate, self-controlled, self-possessed, unemotional, unruffled **3** unfriendly, aloof, distant, indifferent, lukewarm, offhand, standoffish, unenthusiastic, unwelcoming ♦ *verb* **4** chill, cool off, freeze,

lose heat, refrigerate ♦ *noun* **5** *Slang* calmness, composure, control, poise, self-control, self-discipline, self-possession, temper

cooperate *verb* work together, collaborate, combine, conspire, coordinate, join forces, pool resources, pull together

cooperation *noun* teamwork, collaboration, combined effort, esprit de corps, give-and-take, unity

cooperative *adjective* **1** helpful, accommodating, obliging, onside (*informal*), responsive, supportive **2** shared, collective, combined, joint

coordinate *verb* bring together, harmonize, integrate, match, organize, synchronize, systematize

cope *verb* **1** manage, carry on, get by (*informal*), hold one's own, make the grade, struggle through, survive **2** cope with deal with, contend with, grapple with, handle, struggle with, weather, wrestle with

copious *adjective* abundant, ample, bountiful, extensive, full, lavish, plentiful, profuse

copy *noun* **1** reproduction, counterfeit, duplicate, facsimile, forgery, imitation, likeness, model, replica ♦ *verb* **2** reproduce, counterfeit, duplicate, replicate, transcribe **3** imitate, ape, emulate, follow, mimic, mirror, repeat

cord *noun* rope, line, string, twine

cordial *adjective* warm, affable, agreeable, cheerful, congenial, friendly, genial, hearty, sociable

cordon noun **1** chain, barrier, line, ring ♦ verb **2 cordon off** surround, close off, encircle, enclose, fence off, isolate, picket, separate

core noun centre, crux, essence, gist, heart, kernel, nub, nucleus, pith

corner noun **1** angle, bend, crook, joint **2** space, hideaway, hide-out, nook, retreat ♦ verb **3** trap, run to earth **4** As in **corner the market** monopolize, dominate, engross, hog (slang)

corny adjective Slang unoriginal, hackneyed, old-fashioned, old hat, stale, stereotyped, trite

corporation noun **1** business, association, corporate body, society **2** town council, civic authorities, council, municipal authorities **3** Informal paunch, beer belly (informal), middle-age spread (informal), potbelly, spare tyre (Brit. slang), spread (informal)

corps noun team, band, company, detachment, division, regiment, squadron, troop, unit

corpse noun body, cadaver, carcass, remains, stiff (slang)

correct adjective **1** true, accurate, exact, faultless, flawless, O.K. or okay (informal), precise, right **2** proper, acceptable, appropriate, fitting, kosher (informal), O.K. or okay (informal), seemly, standard ♦ verb **3** rectify, adjust, amend, cure, emend, redress, reform, remedy, right **4** punish, admonish, chasten, chastise, chide, discipline, rebuke, reprimand, reprove

correction noun **1** rectification,

adjustment, alteration, amendment, emendation, improvement, modification **2** punishment, admonition, castigation, chastisement, discipline, reformation, reproof

correctly adverb rightly, accurately, perfectly, precisely, properly, right

correctness noun **1** truth, accuracy, exactitude, exactness, faultlessness, fidelity, preciseness, precision, regularity **2** decorum, civility, good breeding, propriety, seemliness

correspond verb **1** be consistent, accord, agree, conform, fit, harmonize, match, square, tally **2** communicate, exchange letters, keep in touch, write

correspondence noun **1** letters, communication, mail, post, writing **2** relation, agreement, coincidence, comparison, conformity, correlation, harmony, match, similarity

correspondent noun **1** letter writer, pen friend or pal **2** reporter, contributor, journalist

corresponding adjective related, analogous, answering, complementary, equivalent, matching, reciprocal, similar

corridor noun passage, aisle, alley, hallway, passageway

corroborate verb support, authenticate, back up, bear out, confirm, endorse, ratify, substantiate, validate

corrode verb eat away, consume, corrupt, erode, gnaw, oxidize, rust, wear away

corrosive adjective corroding,

caustic, consuming, erosive, virulent, vitriolic, wasting, wearing

corrupt adjective 1 dishonest, bent (slang), bribable, crooked (informal), fraudulent, unprincipled, unscrupulous, venal 2 depraved, debased, degenerate, dissolute, profligate, vicious 3 distorted, altered, doctored, falsified ♦ verb 4 bribe, buy off, entice, fix (informal), grease (someone's palm) (slang), lure, suborn 5 deprave, debauch, pervert, subvert 6 distort, doctor, tamper with

corruption noun 1 dishonesty, bribery, extortion, fraud, shady dealings (informal), unscrupulousness, venality 2 depravity, decadence, evil, immorality, perversion, vice, wickedness 3 distortion, doctoring, falsification

corset noun girdle, belt, bodice

cosmetic adjective beautifying, nonessential, superficial, surface

cosmic adjective universal, stellar

cosmopolitan adjective 1 sophisticated, broad-minded, catholic, open-minded, universal, urbane, well-travelled, worldly-wise ♦ noun 2 man or woman of the world, jet-setter, sophisticate

cost noun 1 price, amount, charge, damage (informal), expense, outlay, payment, worth 2 loss, damage, detriment, expense, harm, hurt, injury, penalty, sacrifice, suffering ♦ verb 3 sell at, come to, command a price of, set (someone) back (informal) 4 lose, do disservice

to, harm, hurt, injure

costly adjective 1 expensive, dear, exorbitant, extortionate, highly-priced, steep (informal), stiff 2 damaging, catastrophic, deleterious, disastrous, harmful, loss-making, ruinous

costs plural noun expenses, budget, outgoings, overheads

costume noun outfit, apparel, attire, clothing, dress, ensemble, garb, livery, uniform

cosy adjective snug, comfortable, comfy (informal), homely, intimate, sheltered, tucked up, warm

cottage noun cabin, chalet, hut, lodge, shack

cough noun 1 frog or tickle in one's throat, bark, hack ♦ verb 2 clear one's throat, bark, hack

council noun governing body, assembly, board, cabinet, committee, conference, congress, convention, panel, parliament

counsel noun 1 advice, direction, guidance, information, recommendation, suggestion, warning 2 legal adviser, advocate, attorney, barrister, lawyer, solicitor ♦ verb 3 advise, advocate, exhort, instruct, recommend, urge, warn

count verb 1 add (up), calculate, compute, enumerate, number, reckon, tally, tot up 2 matter, be important, carry weight, rate, signify, tell, weigh 3 consider, deem, judge, look upon, rate, regard, think 4 take into account or consideration, include, number among ♦ noun 5 calculation, computation, enumeration, numbering, poll, reckoning, sum, tally

counter verb 1 retaliate, answer, hit back, meet, oppose, parry, resist, respond, ward off ♦ adverb 2 opposite to, against, at variance with, contrariwise, conversely, in defiance of, versus

counteract verb act against, foil, frustrate, negate, neutralize, offset, resist, thwart

counterbalance verb offset, balance, compensate, make up for, set off

counterfeit adjective 1 fake, bogus, false, forged, imitation, phoney or phony (informal), sham, simulated ♦ noun 2 fake, copy, forgery, fraud, imitation, phoney or phony (informal), reproduction, sham ♦ verb 3 fake, copy, fabricate, feign, forge, imitate, impersonate, pretend, sham, simulate

countermand verb cancel, annul, override, repeal, rescind, retract, reverse, revoke

counterpart noun opposite number, complement, equal, fellow, match, mate, supplement, tally, twin

countless adjective innumerable, endless, immeasurable, incalculable, infinite, legion, limitless, myriad, numberless, untold

count on or **upon** verb depend on, bank on, believe (in), lean on, pin one's faith on, reckon on, rely on, take for granted, take on trust, trust

country noun 1 nation, commonwealth, kingdom, people, realm, state 2 territory, land, region, terrain 3 people, citizens, community, inhabitants, nation, populace, public, society 4 countryside, backwoods, farmland, green belt, outback (Austral. & N.Z.), provinces, sticks (informal)

countryside noun country, farmland, green belt, outback (Austral. & N.Z.), outdoors, sticks (informal)

count up verb add, reckon up, sum, tally, total

county noun province, shire

coup noun masterstroke, accomplishment, action, deed, exploit, feat, manoeuvre, stunt

couple noun 1 pair, brace, duo, two, twosome ♦ verb 2 link, connect, hitch, join, marry, pair, unite, wed, yoke

coupon noun slip, card, certificate, ticket, token, voucher

courage noun bravery, daring, fearlessness, gallantry, heroism, mettle, nerve, pluck, resolution, valour

courageous adjective brave, bold, daring, fearless, gallant, gritty, intrepid, lion-hearted, stouthearted, valiant

courier noun 1 guide, representative 2 messenger, bearer, carrier, envoy, runner

course noun 1 classes, curriculum, lectures, programme, schedule 2 progression, development, flow, movement, order, progress, sequence, unfolding 3 route, direction, line, passage, path, road, track, trajectory, way 4 racecourse, cinder track, circuit

5 procedure, behaviour, conduct, manner, method, mode, plan, policy, programme **6** period, duration, lapse, passage, passing, sweep, term, time **7 of course** naturally, certainly, definitely, indubitably, needless to say, obviously, undoubtedly, without a doubt ♦ verb **8** run, flow, gush, race, speed, stream, surge **9** hunt, chase, follow, pursue

court noun **1** law court, bar, bench, tribunal **2** courtyard, cloister, piazza, plaza, quad (informal), quadrangle, square, yard **3** palace, hall, manor **4** royal household, attendants, cortege, entourage, retinue, suite, train ♦ verb **5** woo, date, go (out) with, run after, serenade, set one's cap at, take out, walk out with **6** cultivate, curry favour with, fawn upon, flatter, pander to, seek, solicit **7** invite, attract, bring about, incite, prompt, provoke, seek

courteous adjective polite, affable, attentive, civil, gallant, gracious, refined, respectful, urbane, well-mannered

courtesy noun **1** politeness, affability, civility, courteousness, gallantry, good manners, graciousness, urbanity **2** favour, indulgence, kindness

courtier noun attendant, follower, squire

courtly adjective ceremonious, chivalrous, dignified, elegant, formal, gallant, polished, refined, stately, urbane

courtyard noun yard, enclosure, quad, quadrangle

cove noun bay, anchorage, inlet, sound

covenant noun **1** promise, agreement, arrangement, commitment, contract, pact, pledge ♦ verb **2** promise, agree, contract, pledge, stipulate, undertake

cover verb **1** clothe, dress, envelop, put on, wrap **2** overlay, coat, daub, encase, envelop **3** submerge, engulf, flood, overrun, wash over **4** conceal, cloak, disguise, enshroud, hide, mask, obscure, shroud, veil **5** travel over, cross, pass through or over, traverse **6** protect, defend, guard, shield **7** report, describe, investigate, narrate, relate, tell of, write up ♦ noun **8** covering, canopy, case, coating, envelope, jacket, lid, top, wrapper **9** disguise, façade, front, mask, pretext, screen, smoke screen, veil **10** protection, camouflage, concealment, defence, guard, shelter, shield **11** insurance, compensation, indemnity, protection, reimbursement

covering adjective **1** explanatory, accompanying, descriptive, introductory ♦ noun **2** cover, blanket, casing, coating, layer, wrapping

cover-up noun concealment, complicity, conspiracy, front, smoke screen, whitewash (informal)

cover up verb conceal, draw a veil over, hide, hush up, suppress, sweep under the carpet, whitewash (informal)

covet verb long for, aspire to,

crave, desire, envy, lust after, set one's heart on, yearn for

covetous *adjective* <u>envious</u>, acquisitive, avaricious, close-fisted, grasping, greedy, jealous, rapacious, yearning

coward *noun* <u>wimp</u> (*informal*), chicken (*slang*), scaredy-cat (*informal*), yellow-belly (*slang*)

cowardice *noun* <u>faint-heartedness</u>, fearfulness, spinelessness, weakness

cowardly *adjective* <u>faint-hearted</u>, chicken (*slang*), craven, fearful, scared, soft, spineless, timorous, weak, yellow (*informal*)

cowboy *noun* <u>cowhand</u>, cattleman, drover, gaucho (*S. American*), herdsman, rancher, stockman

cower *verb* <u>cringe</u>, draw back, flinch, grovel, quail, shrink, tremble

coy *adjective* <u>shy</u>, bashful, demure, modest, reserved, retiring, shrinking, timid

crack *verb* **1** <u>break</u>, burst, cleave, fracture, snap, splinter, split **2** <u>snap</u>, burst, crash, detonate, explode, pop, ring **3** <u>give in</u>, break down, collapse, give way, go to pieces, lose control, succumb, yield **4** *Informal* <u>hit</u>, clip (*informal*), clout (*informal*), cuff, slap, smack, whack **5** <u>solve</u>, decipher, fathom, get the answer to, work out ◆ *noun* **6** <u>snap</u>, burst, clap, crash, explosion, pop, report **7** <u>break</u>, chink, cleft, cranny, crevice, fissure, fracture, gap, rift **8** *Informal* <u>blow</u>, clip (*informal*), clout (*informal*), cuff, slap, smack, whack **9** *Informal* <u>joke</u>, dig, funny remark, gag (*informal*), jibe, quip, wisecrack, witticism ◆ *adjective* **10** *Slang* <u>first-class</u>, ace, choice, elite, excellent, first-rate, hand-picked, superior, world-class

crackdown *noun* <u>suppression</u>, clampdown, crushing, repression

cracked *adjective* <u>broken</u>, chipped, damaged, defective, faulty, flawed, imperfect, split

cradle *noun* **1** <u>crib</u>, bassinet, cot, Moses basket **2** <u>birthplace</u>, beginning, fount, fountainhead, origin, source, spring, wellspring ◆ *verb* **3** <u>hold</u>, lull, nestle, rock, support

craft *noun* **1** <u>occupation</u>, business, employment, handicraft, pursuit, trade, vocation, work **2** <u>skill</u>, ability, aptitude, art, artistry, expertise, ingenuity, know-how (*informal*), technique, workmanship **3** <u>vessel</u>, aircraft, boat, plane, ship, spacecraft

craftsman *noun* <u>skilled worker</u>, artisan, maker, master, smith, technician, wright

craftsmanship *noun* <u>workmanship</u>, artistry, expertise, mastery, technique

crafty *adjective* <u>cunning</u>, artful, calculating, devious, sharp, shrewd, sly, subtle, wily

crag *noun* <u>rock</u>, bluff, peak, pinnacle, tor

cram *verb* **1** <u>stuff</u>, compress, force, jam, pack in, press, shove, squeeze **2** <u>overeat</u>, glut, gorge, satiate, stuff **3** <u>study</u>, bone up (*informal*), mug up (*slang*), revise, swot

cramp[1] noun spasm, ache, contraction, convulsion, pain, pang, stitch, twinge

cramp[2] verb restrict, constrain, hamper, handicap, hinder, impede, inhibit, obstruct

cramped adjective closed in, confined, congested, crowded, hemmed in, overcrowded, packed, uncomfortable

cranny noun crevice, chink, cleft, crack, fissure, gap, hole, opening

crash noun 1 collision, accident, bump, pile-up (informal), prang (informal), smash, wreck 2 smash, bang, boom, clang, clash, clatter, din, racket, thunder 3 collapse, debacle, depression, downfall, failure, ruin ♦ verb 4 collide, bump (into), crash-land (an aircraft), drive into, have an accident, hit, plough into, wreck 5 collapse, be ruined, fail, fold, fold up, go belly up (informal), go bust (informal), go to the wall, go under 6 hurtle, fall headlong, give way, lurch, overbalance, plunge, topple

crass adjective insensitive, boorish, gross, indelicate, oafish, stupid, unrefined, witless

crate noun container, box, case, packing case, tea chest

crater noun hollow, depression, dip

crave verb 1 long for, desire, hanker after, hope for, lust after, want, yearn for 2 Informal beg, ask, beseech, entreat, implore, petition, plead for, pray for, seek, solicit, supplicate

craving noun longing, appetite, desire, hankering, hope, hunger, thirst, yearning, yen (informal)

crawl verb 1 creep, advance slowly, inch, slither, worm one's way, wriggle, writhe 2 grovel, creep, fawn, humble oneself, toady 3 be full of, be alive, be overrun (slang), swarm, teem

craze noun fad, enthusiasm, fashion, infatuation, mania, rage, trend, vogue

crazy adjective 1 Informal ridiculous, absurd, foolish, idiotic, ill-conceived, ludicrous, nonsensical, preposterous, senseless 2 fanatical, devoted, enthusiastic, infatuated, mad, passionate, wild (informal) 3 insane, crazed, demented, deranged, mad, nuts (slang), out of one's mind, unbalanced

creak verb squeak, grate, grind, groan, scrape, scratch, screech

cream noun 1 lotion, cosmetic, emulsion, essence, liniment, oil, ointment, paste, salve, unguent 2 best, crème de la crème, elite, flower, pick, prime ♦ adjective 3 off-white, yellowish-white

creamy adjective smooth, buttery, milky, rich, soft, velvety

crease noun 1 line, corrugation, fold, groove, ridge, wrinkle ♦ verb 2 wrinkle, corrugate, crumple, double up, fold, rumple, screw up

create verb 1 make, compose, devise, formulate, invent, originate, produce, spawn 2 cause, bring about, lead to, occasion 3 appoint, constitute, establish, install, invest, make, set up

creation noun 1 making, conception, formation,

generation, genesis, procreation
2 setting up, development,
establishment, formation,
foundation, inception,
institution, production
3 invention, achievement,
brainchild (*informal*), concoction,
handiwork, magnum opus, *pièce
de résistance*, production
4 universe, cosmos, nature, world

creative *adjective* imaginative,
artistic, clever, gifted, ingenious,
inspired, inventive, original,
visionary

creativity *noun* imagination,
cleverness, ingenuity, inspiration,
inventiveness, originality

creator *noun* maker, architect,
author, designer, father,
inventor, originator, prime mover

creature *noun* **1** living thing,
animal, beast, being, brute
2 person, human being,
individual, man, mortal, soul,
woman

credentials *plural noun*
certification, authorization,
document, licence, papers,
passport, reference(s), testimonial

credibility *noun* believability,
integrity, plausibility, reliability,
trustworthiness

credible *adjective* **1** believable,
conceivable, imaginable, likely,
plausible, possible, probable,
reasonable, thinkable **2** reliable,
dependable, honest, sincere,
trustworthy, trusty

credit *noun* **1** praise, acclaim,
acknowledgment, approval,
commendation, honour, kudos,
recognition, tribute **2** *As in* **be a
credit to** source of satisfaction or
pride, feather in one's cap,

honour **3** prestige, esteem, good
name, influence, position,
regard, reputation, repute,
standing, status **4** belief,
confidence, credence, faith,
reliance, trust **5** **on credit** on
account, by deferred payment,
by instalments, on hire-purchase,
on (the) H.P., on the slate
(*informal*), on tick (*informal*)
♦ *verb* **6** believe, accept, have
faith in, rely on, trust **7** **credit
with** attribute to, ascribe to,
assign to, impute to

creditable *adjective* praiseworthy,
admirable, commendable,
honourable, laudable, reputable,
respectable, worthy

credulity *noun* gullibility, blind
faith, credulousness, naïveté

creed *noun* belief, articles of
faith, catechism, credo, doctrine,
dogma, principles

creek *noun* **1** inlet, bay, bight,
cove, firth *or* frith (*Scot.*) **2** *U.S.,
Canad., Austral., & N.Z.* stream,
bayou, brook, rivulet, runnel,
tributary, watercourse

creep *verb* **1** sneak, approach
unnoticed, skulk, slink, steal,
tiptoe **2** crawl, glide, slither,
squirm, wriggle, writhe ♦ *noun*
3 *Slang* bootlicker (*informal*),
crawler (*slang*), sneak,
sycophant, toady

creeper *noun* climbing plant,
rambler, runner, trailing plant,
vine (*chiefly U.S.*)

creeps *plural noun* **give one the
creeps** *Informal* disgust, frighten,
make one's hair stand on end,
make one squirm, repel, repulse,
scare

creepy *adjective* *Informal*

disturbing, eerie, frightening, hair-raising, macabre, menacing, scary (*informal*), sinister

crescent *noun* meniscus, new moon, sickle

crest *noun* **1** top, apex, crown, highest point, peak, pinnacle, ridge, summit **2** tuft, comb, crown, mane, plume **3** emblem, badge, bearings, device, insignia, symbol

crestfallen *adjective* disappointed, dejected, depressed, despondent, discouraged, disheartened, downcast, downhearted

crevice *noun* gap, chink, cleft, crack, cranny, fissure, hole, opening, slit

crew *noun* **1** (ship's) company, hands, (ship's) complement **2** team, corps, gang, posse, squad **3** *Informal* crowd, band, bunch (*informal*), gang, horde, mob, pack, set

crib *noun* **1** *Informal* translation, key **2** cradle, bassinet, bed, cot **3** manger, rack, stall ♦ *verb* **4** *Informal* copy, cheat, pirate, plagiarize, purloin, steal

crime *noun* **1** offence, felony, misdeed, misdemeanour, transgression, trespass, unlawful act, violation **2** lawbreaking, corruption, illegality, misconduct, vice, wrongdoing

criminal *noun* **1** lawbreaker, convict, crook (*informal*), culprit, felon, offender, sinner, villain ♦ *adjective* **2** unlawful, corrupt, crooked (*informal*), illegal, illicit, immoral, lawless, wicked, wrong **3** *Informal* disgraceful, deplorable, foolish, preposterous,

ridiculous, scandalous, senseless

cringe *verb* **1** shrink, cower, draw back, flinch, recoil, shy, wince **2** grovel, bootlick (*informal*), crawl, creep, fawn, kowtow, pander to, toady

cripple *verb* **1** disable, hamstring, incapacitate, lame, maim, paralyse, weaken **2** damage, destroy, impair, put out of action, paid to, ruin, spoil

crippled *adjective* disabled, handicapped, incapacitated, laid up (*informal*), lame, paralysed

crisis *noun* **1** critical point, climax, crunch (*informal*), crux, culmination, height, moment of truth, turning point **2** emergency, deep water, dire straits, meltdown (*informal*), panic stations (*informal*), plight, predicament, trouble

crisp *adjective* **1** crunchy, brittle, crispy, crumbly, firm, fresh **2** clean, neat, smart, spruce, tidy, trim, well-groomed, well-pressed **3** bracing, brisk, fresh, invigorating, refreshing

criterion *noun* standard, bench mark, gauge, measure, principle, rule, test, touchstone, yardstick

critic *noun* **1** judge, analyst, authority, commentator, connoisseur, expert, pundit, reviewer **2** fault-finder, attacker, detractor, knocker (*informal*)

critical *adjective* **1** crucial, all-important, decisive, pivotal, precarious, pressing, serious, urgent, vital **2** disparaging, captious, censorious, derogatory, disapproving, fault-finding, nagging, nit-picking (*informal*), scathing **3** analytical, discerning, discriminating, fastidious, judicious, penetrating, perceptive

criticism noun **1** fault-finding, bad press, censure, character assassination, disapproval, disparagement, flak (informal), stick (slang) **2** analysis, appraisal, appreciation, assessment, comment, commentary, critique, evaluation, judgment

criticize verb find fault with, carp, censure, condemn, disapprove of, disparage, knock (informal), put down, slate (informal)

croak verb squawk, caw, grunt, utter or speak huskily, wheeze

crook noun Informal criminal, cheat, racketeer, robber, rogue, shark, swindler, thief, villain

crooked adjective **1** bent, curved, deformed, distorted, hooked, irregular, misshapen, out of shape, twisted, warped, zigzag **2** at an angle, askew, awry, lopsided, off-centre, skewwhiff (Brit. informal), slanting, squint, uneven **3** Informal dishonest, bent (slang), corrupt, criminal, fraudulent, illegal, shady (informal), underhand, unlawful

croon verb sing, hum, purr, warble

crop noun **1** produce, fruits, gathering, harvest, reaping, vintage, yield ◆ verb **2** cut, clip, lop, pare, prune, shear, snip, trim **3** graze, browse, nibble

crop up verb Informal happen, appear, arise, emerge, occur, spring up, turn up

cross verb **1** go across, bridge, cut across, extend over, move across, pass over, span, traverse **2** intersect, crisscross, intertwine **3** oppose, block, impede, interfere, obstruct, resist **4** interbreed, blend, crossbreed, cross-fertilize, cross-pollinate, hybridize, intercross, mix, mongrelize ◆ noun **5** crucifix, rood **6** crossroads, crossing, intersection, junction **7** mixture, amalgam, blend, combination **8** trouble, affliction, burden, grief, load, misfortune, trial, tribulation, woe, worry ◆ adjective **9** angry, annoyed, grumpy, ill-tempered, in a bad mood, irascible, put out, short **10** transverse, crosswise, diagonal, intersecting, oblique

cross-examine verb question, grill (informal), interrogate, pump, quiz

cross out or **off** verb strike off or out, blue-pencil, cancel, delete, eliminate, score off or out

crouch verb bend down, bow, duck, hunch, kneel, squat, stoop

crow verb gloat, blow one's own trumpet, boast, brag, exult, strut, swagger, triumph

crowd noun **1** multitude, army, horde, host, mass, mob, pack, swarm, throng **2** group, bunch (informal), circle, clique, lot, set **3** audience, attendance, gate, house, spectators ◆ verb **4** flock, congregate, gather, mass, stream, surge, swarm, throng **5** squeeze, bundle, congest, cram, pack, pile

crowded adjective packed, busy, congested, cramped, full, jam-packed, swarming, teeming

crown noun **1** coronet, circlet, diadem, tiara **2** laurel wreath, garland, honour, laurels, prize, trophy, wreath **3** high point, apex, crest, pinnacle, summit, tip, top ♦ *verb* **4** honour, adorn, dignify, festoon **5** cap, be the climax *or* culmination of, complete, finish, perfect, put the finishing touch to, round off, top **6** *Slang* strike, belt (*informal*), biff (*slang*), box, cuff, hit over the head, punch

Crown *noun* **1** monarchy, royalty, sovereignty **2** monarch, emperor *or* empress, king *or* queen, ruler, sovereign

crucial *adjective* **1** *Informal* vital, essential, high-priority, important, momentous, pressing, urgent **2** critical, central, decisive, pivotal

crucify *verb* execute, persecute, torment, torture

crude *adjective* **1** primitive, clumsy, makeshift, rough, rough-and-ready, rudimentary, unpolished **2** vulgar, coarse, dirty, gross, indecent, obscene, smutty, tasteless, uncouth **3** unrefined, natural, raw, unprocessed

crudely *adverb* vulgarly, bluntly, coarsely, impolitely, roughly, rudely, tastelessly

crudity *noun* **1** roughness, clumsiness, crudeness **2** vulgarity, coarseness, impropriety, indecency, indelicacy, obscenity, smuttiness

cruel *adjective* **1** brutal, barbarous, callous, hard-hearted, heartless, inhumane, malevolent, sadistic, spiteful, unkind, vicious **2** merciless, pitiless, ruthless, unrelenting

cruelly *adverb* **1** brutally, barbarously, callously, heartlessly, in cold blood, mercilessly, pitilessly, sadistically, spitefully **2** bitterly, deeply, fearfully, grievously, monstrously, severely

cruelty *noun* brutality, barbarity, callousness, depravity, fiendishness, inhumanity, mercilessness, ruthlessness, spitefulness

cruise *noun* **1** sail, boat trip, sea trip, voyage ♦ *verb* **2** sail, coast, voyage **3** travel along, coast, drift, keep a steady pace

crumb *noun* bit, fragment, grain, morsel, scrap, shred, soupçon

crumble *verb* **1** disintegrate, collapse, decay, degenerate, deteriorate, fall apart, go to pieces, go to wrack and ruin, tumble down **2** crush, fragment, granulate, grind, pound, powder, pulverize

crumple *verb* **1** crush, crease, rumple, screw up, scrumple, wrinkle **2** collapse, break down, cave in, fall, give way, go to pieces

crunch *verb* **1** chomp, champ, chew noisily, grind, munch ♦ *noun* **2** *Informal* critical point, crisis, crux, emergency, moment of truth, test

crusade *noun* campaign, cause, drive, movement, push

crush *verb* **1** squash, break, compress, press, pulverize, squeeze **2** overcome, conquer, overpower, overwhelm, put down, quell, stamp out, subdue **3** humiliate, abash, mortify, put down (*slang*), quash, shame

♦ *noun* 4 crowd, huddle, jam

crust *noun* layer, coating, covering, shell, skin, surface

crusty *adjective* 1 crispy, hard 2 irritable, cantankerous, cross, gruff, prickly, short-tempered, testy

cry *verb* 1 weep, blubber, shed tears, snivel, sob 2 shout, bawl, bellow, call out, exclaim, howl, roar, scream, shriek, yell ♦ *noun* 3 weeping, blubbering, snivelling, sob, sobbing, weep 4 shout, bellow, call, exclamation, howl, roar, scream, screech, shriek, yell 5 appeal, plea

cry off *verb Informal* back out, excuse oneself, quit, withdraw

cub *noun* young, offspring, whelp

cuddle *verb* hug, bill and coo, cosset, embrace, fondle, pet, snuggle

cudgel *noun* club, baton, bludgeon, cosh (*Brit.*), stick, truncheon

cue *noun* signal, catchword, hint, key, prompting, reminder, sign, suggestion

cul-de-sac *noun* dead end, blind alley

culminate *verb* end up, climax, close, come to a climax, come to a head, conclude, finish, wind up

culmination *noun* climax, acme, conclusion, consummation, finale, peak, pinnacle, zenith

culpable *adjective* blameworthy, at fault, found wanting, guilty, in the wrong, to blame, wrong

culprit *noun* offender, criminal, evildoer, felon, guilty party,

miscreant, transgressor, wrongdoer

cult *noun* 1 sect, clique, faction, religion, school 2 devotion, idolization, worship

cultivate *verb* 1 farm, plant, plough, tend, till, work 2 develop, foster, improve, promote, refine 3 court, dance attendance upon, run after, seek out

cultivation *noun* 1 farming, gardening, husbandry, planting, ploughing, tillage 2 development, encouragement, fostering, furtherance, nurture, patronage, promotion, support

cultural *adjective* artistic, civilizing, edifying, educational, enlightening, enriching, humane, liberal

culture *noun* 1 civilization, customs, lifestyle, mores, society, way of life 2 refinement, education, enlightenment, good taste, sophistication, urbanity 3 farming, cultivation, husbandry

cultured *adjective* refined, educated, enlightened, highbrow, sophisticated, urbane, well-informed, well-read

culvert *noun* drain, channel, conduit, gutter, watercourse

cumbersome *adjective* awkward, bulky, burdensome, heavy, unmanageable, unwieldy, weighty

cunning *adjective* 1 crafty, artful, devious, Machiavellian, sharp, shifty, sly, wily 2 skilful, imaginative, ingenious ♦ *noun* 3 craftiness, artfulness, deviousness, guile, slyness, trickery 4 skill, artifice, cleverness, ingenuity, subtlety

cup noun **1** <u>mug</u>, beaker, bowl, chalice, goblet, teacup **2** <u>trophy</u>

cupboard noun <u>cabinet</u>, press

curb noun **1** <u>restraint</u>, brake, bridle, check, control, deterrent, limitation, rein ♦ verb **2** <u>restrain</u>, check, control, hinder, impede, inhibit, restrict, retard, suppress

cure verb **1** <u>make better</u>, correct, ease, heal, mend, relieve, remedy, restore **2** <u>preserve</u>, dry, pickle, salt, smoke ♦ noun **3** <u>remedy</u>, antidote, medicine, nostrum, panacea, treatment

curiosity noun **1** <u>inquisitiveness</u>, interest, nosiness (*informal*), prying, snooping (*informal*) **2** <u>oddity</u>, freak, novelty, phenomenon, rarity, sight, spectacle, wonder

curious adjective **1** <u>inquiring</u>, inquisitive, interested, questioning, searching **2** <u>inquisitive</u>, meddling, nosy (*informal*), prying **3** <u>unusual</u>, bizarre, extraordinary, mysterious, novel, odd, peculiar, rare, strange, unexpected

curl verb **1** <u>twirl</u>, bend, coil, curve, loop, spiral, turn, twist, wind ♦ noun **2** <u>twist</u>, coil, kink, ringlet, spiral, whorl

curly adjective <u>curling</u>, crinkly, curled, frizzy, fuzzy, wavy, winding

currency noun **1** <u>money</u>, coinage, coins, notes **2** <u>acceptance</u>, circulation, exposure, popularity, prevalence, vogue

current adjective **1** <u>present</u>, contemporary, fashionable, in fashion, in vogue, present-day, trendy (*Brit. informal*), up-to-date **2** <u>prevalent</u>, accepted, common, customary, in circulation, popular, topical, widespread ♦ noun **3** <u>flow</u>, course, draught, jet, progression, river, stream, tide, undertow **4** <u>mood</u>, atmosphere, feeling, tendency, trend, undercurrent

curse verb **1** <u>swear</u>, blaspheme, cuss (*informal*), take the Lord's name in vain **2** <u>damn</u>, anathematize, excommunicate ♦ noun **3** <u>oath</u>, blasphemy, expletive, obscenity, swearing, swearword **4** <u>denunciation</u>, anathema, ban, excommunication, hoodoo (*informal*), jinx **5** <u>affliction</u>, bane, hardship, plague, scourge, torment, trouble

cursed adjective <u>damned</u>, accursed, bedevilled, doomed, ill-fated

curt adjective <u>short</u>, abrupt, blunt, brief, brusque, gruff, monosyllabic, succinct, terse

curtail verb <u>cut short</u>, cut back, decrease, diminish, dock, lessen, reduce, shorten, truncate

curtain noun <u>hanging</u>, drape (*chiefly U.S.*)

curve noun **1** <u>bend</u>, arc, curvature, loop, trajectory, turn ♦ verb **2** <u>bend</u>, arc, arch, coil, hook, spiral, swerve, turn, twist, wind

curved adjective <u>bent</u>, arched, bowed, rounded, serpentine, sinuous, twisted

cushion noun **1** <u>pillow</u>, beanbag, bolster, hassock, headrest, pad ♦ verb **2** <u>soften</u>, dampen, deaden, muffle, stifle, suppress

cushy adjective Informal easy, comfortable, soft, undemanding

custody noun 1 safekeeping, care, charge, keeping, protection, supervision 2 imprisonment, confinement, detention, incarceration

custom noun 1 tradition, convention, policy, practice, ritual, rule, usage 2 habit, practice, procedure, routine, way, wont 3 customers, patronage, trade

customary adjective usual, accepted, accustomed, common, conventional, established, normal, ordinary, routine, traditional

customer noun client, buyer, consumer, patron, purchaser, regular (informal), shopper

customs plural noun duty, import charges, tariff, tax, toll

cut verb 1 penetrate, chop, pierce, score, sever, slash, slice, slit, wound 2 divide, bisect, dissect, slice, split 3 trim, clip, hew, lop, mow, pare, prune, shave, snip 4 abridge, abbreviate, condense, curtail, delete, shorten 5 reduce, contract, cut back, decrease, diminish, lower, slash, slim (down) 6 shape, carve, chisel, engrave, fashion, form, sculpt, whittle 7 hurt, insult, put down, snub, sting, wound 8 Informal ignore, avoid, cold-shoulder, slight, spurn, turn one's back on ♦ noun 9 incision, gash, laceration, nick, slash, slit, stroke, wound 10 reduction, cutback, decrease, fall, lowering, saving

11 Informal share, percentage, piece, portion, section, slice **12** style, fashion, look, shape

cutback noun reduction, cut, decrease, economy, lessening, retrenchment

cut down verb 1 fell, hew, level, lop 2 reduce, decrease, lessen, lower

cute adjective appealing, attractive, charming, delightful, engaging, lovable, sweet, winning, winsome

cut in verb interrupt, break in, butt in, intervene, intrude

cut off verb 1 separate, isolate, sever 2 interrupt, disconnect, intercept

cut out verb stop, cease, give up, refrain from

cutthroat adjective 1 competitive, dog-eat-dog, fierce, relentless, ruthless, unprincipled ♦ noun 2 murderer, assassin, butcher, executioner, hit man (slang), killer

cutting adjective hurtful, acrimonious, barbed, bitter, caustic, malicious, sarcastic, scathing, vitriolic, wounding

cycle noun era, circle, period, phase, revolution, rotation

cynic noun sceptic, doubter, misanthrope, misanthropist, pessimist, scoffer

cynical adjective sceptical, contemptuous, derisive, distrustful, misanthropic, mocking, pessimistic, scoffing, scornful, unbelieving

cynicism noun scepticism, disbelief, doubt, misanthropy, pessimism

D d

dab *verb* **1** pat, daub, stipple, tap, touch ♦ *noun* **2** spot, bit, drop, pat, smudge, speck **3** pat, flick, stroke, tap, touch

dabble *verb* **1** play at, dip into, potter, tinker, trifle (with) **2** splash, dip

daft *adjective Informal, chiefly Brit.* **1** foolish, absurd, asinine, crackpot (*informal*), crazy, idiotic, silly, stupid, witless **2** crazy, crackers (*Brit. slang*), demented, deranged, insane, nuts (*slang*), touched, unhinged

dagger *noun* knife, bayonet, dirk, stiletto

daily *adjective* **1** everyday, diurnal, quotidian ♦ *adverb* **2** every day, day by day, once a day

dainty *adjective* delicate, charming, elegant, exquisite, fine, graceful, neat, petite, pretty

dam *noun* **1** barrier, barrage, embankment, obstruction, wall ♦ *verb* **2** block up, barricade, hold back, obstruct, restrict

damage *verb* **1** harm, hurt, impair, injure, ruin, spoil, weaken, wreck ♦ *noun* **2** harm, destruction, detriment, devastation, hurt, injury, loss, suffering **3** *Informal* cost, bill, charge, expense

damages *plural noun Law* compensation, fine, reimbursement, reparation, satisfaction

damaging *adjective* harmful,

deleterious, detrimental, disadvantageous, hurtful, injurious, ruinous

dame *noun* noblewoman, baroness, dowager, *grande dame*, lady, peeress

damn *verb* **1** condemn, blast, censure, criticize, denounce, put down **2** sentence, condemn, doom

damnation *noun* condemnation, anathema, damning, denunciation, doom

damned *adjective* **1** doomed, accursed, condemned, lost **2** *Slang* detestable, confounded, hateful, infernal, loathsome

damp *adjective* **1** moist, clammy, dank, dewy, drizzly, humid, soggy, sopping, wet ♦ *noun* **2** moisture, dampness, dankness, drizzle ♦ *verb* **3** moisten, dampen, wet **4** damp down reduce, allay, check, curb, diminish, inhibit, pour cold water on, stifle

dampen *verb* **1** reduce, check, dull, lessen, moderate, restrain, stifle **2** moisten, make damp, spray, wet

damper *noun As in* put a damper on discouragement, cold water (*informal*), hindrance, restraint, wet blanket (*informal*)

dance *verb* **1** prance, hop, jig, skip, sway, trip, whirl ♦ *noun* **2** ball, disco, discotheque, hop (*informal*), knees-up (*Brit. informal*), social

dancer *noun* ballerina, Terpsichorean

danger *noun* peril, hazard, jeopardy, menace, pitfall, risk, threat, vulnerability

dangerous *adjective* perilous, breakneck, chancy (*informal*), hazardous, insecure, precarious, risky, unsafe, vulnerable

dangerously *adverb* perilously, alarmingly, hazardously, precariously, recklessly, riskily, unsafely

dangle *verb* 1 hang, flap, hang down, sway, swing, trail 2 wave, brandish, flaunt, flourish

dapper *adjective* neat, natty (*informal*), smart, soigné *or* soignée, spruce, spry, trim, well-groomed, well turned out

dare *verb* 1 risk, hazard, make bold, presume, venture 2 challenge, defy, goad, provoke, taunt, throw down the gauntlet ♦ *noun* 3 challenge, provocation, taunt

daredevil *noun* 1 adventurer, desperado, exhibitionist, madcap, show-off (*informal*), stunt man ♦ *adjective* 2 daring, adventurous, audacious, bold, death-defying, madcap, reckless

daring *adjective* 1 brave, adventurous, audacious, bold, daredevil, fearless, intrepid, reckless, venturesome ♦ *noun* 2 bravery, audacity, boldness, bottle (*Brit. slang*), courage, fearlessness, nerve (*informal*), pluck, temerity

dark *adjective* 1 dim, dingy, murky, shadowy, shady, sunless, unlit 2 black, dark-skinned, dusky, ebony, sable, swarthy 3 gloomy, bleak, dismal, grim, morose, mournful, sad, sombre 4 evil, foul, infernal, sinister, vile, wicked 5 secret, concealed,

hidden, mysterious ♦ *noun* 6 darkness, dimness, dusk, gloom, murk, obscurity, semi-darkness 7 night, evening, nightfall, night-time, twilight

darken *verb* make dark, blacken, dim, obscure, overshadow

darkness *noun* dark, blackness, duskiness, gloom, murk, nightfall, shade, shadows

darling *noun* 1 beloved, dear, dearest, love, sweetheart, truelove ♦ *adjective* 2 beloved, adored, cherished, dear, precious, treasured

darn *verb* 1 mend, cobble up, patch, repair, sew up, stitch ♦ *noun* 2 mend, invisible repair, patch, reinforcement

dart *verb* dash, fly, race, run, rush, shoot, spring, sprint, tear

dash *verb* 1 rush, bolt, fly, hurry, race, run, speed, sprint, tear 2 throw, cast, fling, hurl, slam, sling 3 crash, break, destroy, shatter, smash, splinter 4 frustrate, blight, foil, ruin, spoil, thwart, undo ♦ *noun* 5 rush, dart, race, run, sortie, sprint, spurt 6 little, bit, drop, hint, pinch, soupçon, sprinkling, tinge, touch 7 style, brio, élan, flair, flourish, panache, spirit, verve

dashing *adjective* 1 bold, debonair, gallant, lively, spirited, swashbuckling 2 stylish, elegant, flamboyant, jaunty, showy, smart, sporty

data *noun* information, details, facts, figures, statistics

date *noun* 1 time, age, epoch, era, period, stage 2 appointment, assignation, engagement, meeting, rendezvous, tryst **3** partner, escort, friend ♦ *verb* **4** put a date on, assign a date to, fix the period of **5** become old-fashioned, be dated, show one's age **6** date from *or* date back to come from, bear a date of, belong to, exist from, originate in

dated *adjective* old-fashioned, obsolete, old hat, outdated, outmoded, out of date, passé, unfashionable

daub *verb* smear, coat, cover, paint, plaster, slap on (*informal*)

daunting *adjective* intimidating, alarming, demoralizing, disconcerting, discouraging, disheartening, frightening, off-putting (*Brit. informal*), unnerving

dauntless *adjective* fearless, bold, doughty, gallant, indomitable, intrepid, resolute, stouthearted, undaunted, unflinching

dawdle *verb* waste time, dally, delay, drag one's feet *or* heels, hang about, idle, loaf, loiter, trail

dawn *noun* **1** daybreak, aurora (*poetic*), cockcrow, crack of dawn, daylight, morning, sunrise, sunup **2** beginning, advent, birth, emergence, genesis, origin, rise, start ♦ *verb* **3** grow light, break, brighten, lighten **4** begin, appear, develop, emerge, originate, rise, unfold **5** dawn on *or* upon hit, become apparent, come into one's head, come to mind, occur, register (*informal*), strike

day *noun* **1** twenty-four hours, daylight, daytime **2** point in

time, date, time **3** time, age, epoch, era, heyday, period, zenith

daybreak *noun* dawn, break of day, cockcrow, crack of dawn, first light, morning, sunrise, sunup

daydream *noun* **1** fantasy, dream, fancy, imagining, pipe dream, reverie, wish ♦ *verb* **2** fantasize, dream, envision, fancy, imagine, muse

daylight *noun* sunlight, light of day, sunshine

daze *verb* **1** stun, benumb, numb, paralyse, shock, stupefy ♦ *noun* **2** shock, bewilderment, confusion, distraction, stupor, trance, trancelike state

dazed *adjective* shocked, bewildered, confused, disorientated, dizzy, muddled, punch-drunk, staggered, stunned

dazzle *verb* **1** impress, amaze, astonish, bowl over (*informal*), overpower, overwhelm, take one's breath away **2** blind, bedazzle, blur, confuse, daze ♦ *noun* **3** splendour, brilliance, glitter, magnificence, razzmatazz (*slang*), sparkle

dazzling *adjective* splendid, brilliant, glittering, glorious, scintillating, sensational (*informal*), sparkling, stunning, virtuoso

dead *adjective* **1** deceased, defunct, departed, extinct, late, passed away, perished **2** not working, inactive, inoperative, stagnant, unemployed, useless **3** numb, inert, paralysed **4** total, absolute, complete, outright, thorough, unqualified, utter

5 *Informal* exhausted, dead beat
(*informal*), spent, tired, worn out
6 boring, dull, flat, uninteresting
♦ *noun* **7** middle, depth, midst
♦ *adverb* **8** exactly, absolutely, completely, directly,
entirely, totally

deaden *verb* reduce, alleviate,
blunt, cushion, diminish, dull,
lessen, muffle, smother, stifle,
suppress, weaken

deadline *noun* time limit, cutoff
point, limit, target date

deadlock *noun* impasse, dead
heat, draw, gridlock, stalemate,
standoff, standstill, tie

deadlocked *adjective* even,
equal, level, neck and neck

deadly *adjective* **1** lethal,
dangerous, death-dealing,
deathly, fatal, malignant, mortal
2 *Informal* boring, dull,
mind-numbing, monotonous,
tedious, tiresome, uninteresting,
wearisome

deadpan *adjective* expressionless,
blank, impassive, inexpressive,
inscrutable, poker-faced,
straight-faced

deaf *adjective* **1** hard of hearing,
stone deaf, without hearing
2 oblivious, indifferent,
unconcerned, unhearing,
unmoved

deafen *verb* make deaf, din,
drown out, split *or* burst the
eardrums

deafening *adjective* ear-piercing,
booming, ear-splitting,
overpowering, piercing,
resounding, ringing, thunderous

deal *noun* **1** *Informal* agreement,
arrangement, bargain, contract,

pact, transaction, understanding
2 amount, degree, extent,
portion, quantity, share ♦ *verb*
3 sell, bargain, buy and sell, do
business, negotiate, stock, trade,
traffic

dealer *noun* trader, merchant,
purveyor, supplier, tradesman,
wholesaler

deal out *verb* distribute, allot,
apportion, assign, dispense, dole
out, give, mete out, share

deal with *verb* **1** handle, attend
to, cope with, get to grips with,
manage, see to, take care of,
treat **2** be concerned with,
consider

dear *noun* **1** beloved, angel,
darling, loved one, precious,
treasure ♦ *adjective* **2** beloved,
cherished, close, favourite,
intimate, precious, prized,
treasured **3** expensive, at a
premium, costly, high-priced,
overpriced, pricey (*informal*)

dearly *adverb* **1** very much,
extremely, greatly, profoundly
2 at great cost, at a high price

dearth *noun* scarcity, deficiency,
inadequacy, insufficiency, lack,
paucity, poverty, shortage, want

death *noun* **1** dying, demise,
departure, end, exit, passing
2 destruction, downfall,
extinction, finish, ruin, undoing

deathly *adjective* deathlike,
ghastly, grim, pale, pallid, wan

debacle *noun* disaster,
catastrophe, collapse, defeat,
fiasco, reversal, rout

debase *verb* degrade, cheapen,
devalue, lower, reduce

debatable *adjective* doubtful,

arguable, controversial, dubious, moot, problematical, questionable, uncertain

debate noun 1 <u>discussion</u>, argument, contention, controversy, dispute ♦ verb 2 <u>discuss</u>, argue, dispute, question 3 <u>consider</u>, deliberate, ponder, reflect, ruminate, weigh

debauchery noun <u>depravity</u>, dissipation, dissoluteness, excess, indulgence, intemperance, lewdness, overindulgence

debonair adjective <u>elegant</u>, charming, courteous, dashing, refined, smooth, suave, urbane, well-bred

debrief verb <u>interrogate</u>, cross-examine, examine, probe, question, quiz

debris noun <u>remains</u>, bits, detritus, fragments, rubble, ruins, waste, wreckage

debt noun 1 <u>debit</u>, commitment, liability, obligation 2 **in debt** <u>owing</u>, in arrears, in the red (informal), liable

debtor noun <u>borrower</u>, mortgagor

debunk verb Informal <u>expose</u>, cut down to size, deflate, disparage, mock, ridicule, show up

debut noun <u>introduction</u>, beginning, bow, coming out, entrance, first appearance, initiation, presentation

decadence noun <u>degeneration</u>, corruption, decay, decline, deterioration, dissipation, dissolution

decadent adjective <u>degenerate</u>, corrupt, decaying, declining, dissolute, immoral, self-indulgent

decapitate verb <u>behead</u>, execute, guillotine

decay verb 1 <u>decline</u>, crumble, deteriorate, disintegrate, dwindle, shrivel, wane, waste away, wither 2 <u>rot</u>, corrode, decompose, perish, putrefy ♦ noun 3 <u>decline</u>, collapse, degeneration, deterioration, fading, failing, wasting, withering 4 <u>rot</u>, caries, decomposition, gangrene, putrefaction

decease noun Formal <u>death</u>, demise, departure, dying, release

deceased adjective <u>dead</u>, defunct, departed, expired, former, late, lifeless

deceit noun <u>dishonesty</u>, cheating, chicanery, deception, fraud, lying, pretence, treachery, trickery

deceitful adjective <u>dishonest</u>, deceptive, false, fraudulent, sneaky, treacherous, two-faced, untrustworthy

deceive verb <u>take in</u> (informal), cheat, con (informal), dupe, fool, hoodwink, mislead, swindle, trick

deceiver noun <u>liar</u>, cheat, con man (informal), double-dealer, fraud, impostor, swindler, trickster

decency noun <u>respectability</u>, civility, correctness, courtesy, decorum, etiquette, modesty, propriety

decent adjective 1 <u>reasonable</u>, adequate, ample, fair, passable, satisfactory, sufficient, tolerable 2 <u>respectable</u>, chaste, decorous, modest, proper, pure 3 <u>proper</u>, appropriate, becoming, befitting, fitting, seemly, suitable 4 Informal <u>kind</u>, accommodating, courteous, friendly, generous, gracious, helpful, obliging, thoughtful

deception noun 1 trickery, cunning, deceit, fraud, guile, legerdemain, treachery 2 trick, bluff, decoy, hoax, illusion, lie, ruse, subterfuge

deceptive adjective misleading, ambiguous, deceitful, dishonest, false, fraudulent, illusory, unreliable

decide verb reach or come to a decision, adjudge, adjudicate, choose, conclude, determine, make up one's mind, resolve

decidedly adverb definitely, clearly, distinctly, downright, positively, unequivocally, unmistakably

decimate verb devastate, ravage, wreak havoc on

decipher verb figure out (informal), crack, decode, deduce, interpret, make out, read, solve

decision noun 1 judgment, arbitration, conclusion, finding, resolution, ruling, sentence, verdict 2 decisiveness, determination, firmness, purpose, resolution, resolve, strength of mind or will

decisive adjective 1 influential, conclusive, critical, crucial, fateful, momentous, significant 2 resolute, decided, determined, firm, forceful, incisive, strong-minded, trenchant

deck verb decorate, adorn, array, beautify, clothe, dress, embellish, festoon

declaim verb 1 orate, harangue,

hold forth, lecture, proclaim, rant, recite, speak 2 **declaim against** protest against, attack, decry, denounce, inveigh, rail

declaration noun 1 statement, acknowledgment, affirmation, assertion, avowal, disclosure, protestation, revelation, testimony 2 announcement, edict, notification, proclamation, profession, pronouncement

declare verb 1 state, affirm, announce, assert, claim, maintain, proclaim, profess, pronounce, swear, utter 2 make known, confess, disclose, reveal, show

decline verb 1 lessen, decrease, diminish, dwindle, ebb, fade, fall off, shrink, sink, wane 2 deteriorate, decay, degenerate, droop, languish, pine, weaken, worsen 3 refuse, abstain, avoid, reject, say 'no', turn down ♦ noun 4 lessening, downturn, drop, dwindling, falling off, recession, slump 5 deterioration, decay, degeneration, failing, weakening, worsening

decode verb decipher, crack, decrypt, interpret, solve, unscramble, work out

decompose verb rot, break up, crumble, decay, fall apart, fester, putrefy

decor noun decoration, colour scheme, furnishing style, ornamentation

decorate verb 1 adorn, beautify, embellish, festoon, grace, ornament, trim 2 do up (informal), colour, furbish, paint, paper, renovate, wallpaper 3 pin a medal on, cite, confer an honour on *or* upon

decoration noun **1** adornment, beautification, elaboration, embellishment, enrichment, ornamentation, trimming **2** ornament, bauble, frill, garnish, trimmings **3** medal, award, badge, ribbon, star

decorative adjective ornamental, beautifying, fancy, nonfunctional, pretty

decorous adjective proper, becoming, correct, decent, dignified, fitting, polite, seemly, well-behaved

decorum noun propriety, decency, dignity, etiquette, good manners, politeness, protocol, respectability

decoy noun **1** lure, bait, enticement, inducement, pretence, trap ♦ verb **2** lure, deceive, ensnare, entice, entrap, seduce, tempt

decrease verb **1** lessen, cut down, decline, diminish, drop, dwindle, lower, reduce, shrink, subside ♦ noun **2** lessening, contraction, cutback, decline, dwindling, falling off, loss, reduction, subsidence

decree noun **1** law, act, command, edict, order, proclamation, ruling, statute ♦ verb **2** order, command, demand, ordain, prescribe, proclaim, pronounce, rule

decrepit adjective **1** weak, aged, doddering, feeble, frail, infirm **2** worn-out, battered, beat-up (*informal*), broken-down, dilapidated, ramshackle, rickety, run-down, tumbledown, weather-beaten

decry verb condemn, belittle, criticize, denigrate, denounce, discredit, disparage, put down, run down

dedicate verb **1** devote, commit, give over to, pledge, surrender **2** inscribe, address

dedicated adjective devoted, committed, enthusiastic, purposeful, single-minded, wholehearted, zealous

dedication noun **1** devotion, adherence, allegiance, commitment, faithfulness, loyalty, single-mindedness, wholeheartedness **2** inscription, address, message

deduce verb conclude, draw, gather, glean, infer, reason, take to mean, understand

deduct verb subtract, decrease by, knock off (*informal*), reduce by, remove, take away, take off

deduction noun **1** subtraction, decrease, diminution, discount, reduction, withdrawal **2** conclusion, assumption, finding, inference, reasoning, result

deed noun **1** action, achievement, act, exploit, fact, feat, performance **2** *Law* document, contract, title

deep adjective **1** wide, bottomless, broad, far, profound, unfathomable, yawning **2** mysterious, abstract, abstruse, arcane, esoteric, hidden, obscure, recondite, secret **3** intense, extreme, grave, great, profound, serious (*informal*), unqualified **4** absorbed, engrossed, immersed, lost, preoccupied, rapt **5** dark, intense, rich, strong, vivid **6** low, bass, booming, low-pitched, resonant, sonorous ♦ *noun* **7 the deep** *Poetic* ocean, briny (*informal*), high seas, main, sea

deepen *verb* intensify, grow, increase, magnify, reinforce, strengthen

deeply *adverb* **1** thoroughly, completely, gravely, profoundly, seriously, severely, to the core, to the heart, to the quick **2** intensely, acutely, affectingly, distressingly, feelingly, mournfully, movingly, passionately, sadly

deface *verb* vandalize, damage, deform, disfigure, mar, mutilate, spoil, tarnish

de facto *adverb* **1** in fact, actually, in effect, in reality, really ♦ *adjective* **2** actual, existing, real

defame *verb* slander, bad-mouth (*slang, chiefly U.S. & Canad.*), cast aspersions on, denigrate, discredit, disparage, knock (*informal*), libel, malign, smear

default *noun* **1** failure, deficiency, dereliction, evasion, lapse, neglect, nonpayment, omission ♦ *verb* **2** fail, dodge, evade, neglect

defeat *verb* **1** beat, conquer, crush, master, overwhelm, rout, trounce, vanquish, wipe the floor with (*informal*) **2** frustrate, baffle, balk, confound, foil, get the better of, ruin, thwart ♦ *noun* **3** conquest, beating, overthrow, pasting (*slang*), rout **4** frustration, failure, rebuff, reverse, setback, thwarting

defeatist *noun* **1** pessimist, prophet of doom, quitter ♦ *adjective* **2** pessimistic

defect *noun* **1** imperfection, blemish, blotch, error, failing, fault, flaw, spot, taint ♦ *verb* **2** desert, abandon, change sides, go over, rebel, revolt, walk out on (*informal*)

defection *noun* desertion, apostasy, rebellion

defective *adjective* faulty, broken, deficient, flawed, imperfect, not working, on the blink (*slang*), out of order

defector *noun* deserter, apostate, renegade, turncoat

defence *noun* **1** protection, cover, guard, immunity, resistance, safeguard, security, shelter **2** shield, barricade, bulwark, buttress, fortification, rampart **3** argument, excuse, explanation, justification, plea, vindication **4** *Law* plea, alibi, denial, rebuttal, testimony

defenceless *adjective* helpless, exposed, naked, powerless, unarmed, unguarded, unprotected, vulnerable, wide open

defend *verb* **1** protect, cover, guard, keep safe, preserve, safeguard, screen, shelter, shield **2** support, champion, endorse, justify, speak up for, stand up for, stick up for (*informal*), uphold, vindicate

defendant *noun* the accused, defence, offender, prisoner at the bar, respondent

defender *noun* **1** protector, bodyguard, escort, guard **2** supporter, advocate, champion, sponsor

defensive adjective on guard, on the defensive, protective, uptight (informal), watchful

defer[1] verb postpone, delay, hold over, procrastinate, put off, put on ice, shelve, suspend

defer[2] verb comply, accede, bow, capitulate, give in, give way to, submit, yield

deference noun respect, attention, civility, consideration, courtesy, honour, politeness, regard, reverence

deferential adjective respectful, ingratiating, obedient, obeisant, obsequious, polite, reverential, submissive

defiance noun resistance, confrontation, contempt, disobedience, disregard, insolence, insubordination, opposition, rebelliousness

defiant adjective resisting, audacious, bold, daring, disobedient, insolent, insubordinate, mutinous, provocative, rebellious

deficiency noun 1 lack, absence, dearth, deficit, scarcity, shortage 2 failing, defect, demerit, fault, flaw, frailty, imperfection, shortcoming, weakness

deficient adjective 1 lacking, inadequate, insufficient, meagre, scant, scarce, short, skimpy, wanting 2 unsatisfactory, defective, faulty, flawed, impaired, imperfect, incomplete, inferior, weak

deficit noun shortfall, arrears, deficiency, loss, shortage

define verb 1 describe,

characterize, designate, explain, expound, interpret, specify, spell out 2 mark out, bound, circumscribe, delineate, demarcate, limit, outline

definite adjective 1 clear, black-and-white, cut-and-dried (informal), exact, fixed, marked, particular, precise, specific 2 certain, assured, decided, guaranteed, positive, settled, sure

definitely adverb certainly, absolutely, categorically, clearly, positively, surely, undeniably, unmistakably, unquestionably, without doubt

definition noun 1 explanation, clarification, elucidation, exposition, statement of meaning 2 sharpness, clarity, contrast, distinctness, focus, precision

definitive adjective 1 final, absolute, complete, conclusive, decisive 2 authoritative, exhaustive, perfect, reliable, ultimate

deflate verb 1 collapse, empty, exhaust, flatten, puncture, shrink 2 humiliate, chasten, disconcert, dispirit, humble, mortify, put down (slang), squash 3 Economics reduce, depress, devalue, diminish

deflect verb turn aside, bend, deviate, diverge, glance off, ricochet, swerve, veer

deflection noun deviation, bend, divergence, swerve

deform verb 1 distort, buckle, contort, gnarl, mangle, misshape, twist, warp 2 disfigure, deface, maim, mar, mutilate, ruin, spoil

deformity noun abnormality, defect, disfigurement, malformation

defraud verb cheat, con (informal), diddle (informal), embezzle, fleece, pilfer, rip off (slang), swindle, trick

deft adjective skilful, adept, adroit, agile, dexterous, expert, neat, nimble, proficient

defunct adjective 1 dead, deceased, departed, extinct, gone 2 obsolete, bygone, expired, inoperative, invalid, nonexistent, out of commission

defy verb resist, brave, confront, disregard, flout, scorn, slight, spurn

degenerate adjective 1 depraved, corrupt, debauched, decadent, dissolute, immoral, low, perverted ♦ verb 2 worsen, decay, decline, decrease, deteriorate, fall off, lapse, sink, slip

degradation noun 1 disgrace, discredit, dishonour, humiliation, ignominy, mortification, shame 2 deterioration, decline, degeneration, demotion, downgrading

degrade verb 1 disgrace, debase, demean, discredit, dishonour, humble, humiliate, shame 2 demote, downgrade, lower

degrading adjective demeaning, dishonourable, humiliating, infra dig (informal), shameful, undignified, unworthy

degree noun stage, grade, notch, point, rung, step, unit

deity noun god, divinity, goddess, godhead, idol,

immortal, supreme being

dejected adjective downhearted, crestfallen, depressed, despondent, disconsolate, disheartened, downcast, glum, miserable, sad

dejection noun low spirits, depression, despair, despondency, doldrums, downheartedness, gloom, melancholy, sadness, sorrow, unhappiness

de jure adverb legally, by right, rightfully

delay verb 1 put off, defer, hold over, postpone, procrastinate, shelve, suspend 2 hold up, bog down, detain, hinder, hold back, impede, obstruct, set back, slow up ♦ noun 3 putting off, deferment, postponement, procrastination, suspension 4 hold-up, hindrance, impediment, interruption, interval, setback, stoppage, wait

delegate noun 1 representative, agent, ambassador, commissioner, deputy, envoy, legate ♦ verb 2 entrust, assign, consign, devolve, give, hand over, pass on, transfer 3 appoint, accredit, authorize, commission, depute, designate, empower, mandate

delegation noun 1 deputation, commission, contingent, embassy, envoys, legation, mission 2 devolution, assignment, commissioning, committal

delete verb remove, cancel, cross out, efface, erase, expunge, obliterate, rub out, strike out

deliberate adjective 1 intentional,

calculated, conscious, planned, prearranged, premeditated, purposeful, wilful **2** unhurried, careful, cautious, circumspect, measured, methodical, ponderous, slow, thoughtful ♦ verb **3** consider, cogitate, consult, debate, discuss, meditate, ponder, reflect, think, weigh

deliberately adverb intentionally, by design, calculatingly, consciously, in cold blood, knowingly, on purpose, wilfully, wittingly

deliberation noun
1 consideration, calculation, circumspection, forethought, meditation, reflection, thought **2** discussion, conference, consultation, debate

delicacy noun **1** fineness, accuracy, daintiness, elegance, exquisiteness, lightness, precision, subtlety **2** fragility, flimsiness, frailty, slenderness, tenderness, weakness **3** treat, dainty, luxury, savoury, titbit **4** fastidiousness, discrimination, finesse, purity, refinement, sensibility, taste **5** sensitivity, sensitiveness, tact

delicate adjective **1** fine, deft, elegant, exquisite, graceful, precise, skilled, subtle **2** subtle, choice, dainty, delicious, fine, savoury, tender **3** fragile, flimsy, frail, slender, slight, tender, weak **4** considerate, diplomatic, discreet, sensitive, tactful

delicately adverb **1** finely, daintily, deftly, elegantly, exquisitely, gracefully, precisely, skilfully, subtly **2** tactfully,

diplomatically, sensitively

delicious adjective delectable, appetizing, choice, dainty, mouthwatering, savoury, scrumptious (informal), tasty, toothsome

delight noun **1** pleasure, ecstasy, enjoyment, gladness, glee, happiness, joy, rapture ♦ verb **2** please, amuse, charm, cheer, enchant, gratify, thrill **3** delight in take pleasure in, appreciate, enjoy, feast on, like, love, relish, revel in, savour

delighted adjective pleased, ecstatic, elated, enchanted, happy, joyous, jubilant, overjoyed, thrilled

delightful adjective pleasant, agreeable, charming, delectable, enchanting, enjoyable, pleasurable, rapturous, thrilling

delinquent noun criminal, culprit, lawbreaker, miscreant, offender, villain, wrongdoer

delirious adjective **1** mad, crazy, demented, deranged, incoherent, insane, raving, unhinged **2** ecstatic, beside oneself, carried away, excited, frantic, frenzied, hysterical, wild

delirium noun **1** madness, derangement, hallucination, insanity, raving **2** frenzy, ecstasy, fever, hysteria, passion

deliver verb **1** carry, bear, bring, cart, convey, distribute, transport **2** hand over, commit, give up, grant, make over, relinquish, surrender, transfer, turn over, yield **3** give, announce, declare, present, read, utter **4** release, emancipate, free, liberate, loose, ransom, rescue, save **5** strike, administer, aim, deal, direct, give, inflict, launch

deliverance noun <u>release</u>, emancipation, escape, liberation, ransom, redemption, rescue, salvation

delivery noun 1 <u>handing over</u>, consignment, conveyance, dispatch, distribution, surrender, transfer, transmission 2 <u>speech</u>, articulation, elocution, enunciation, intonation, utterance 3 <u>childbirth</u>, confinement, labour, parturition

delude verb <u>deceive</u>, beguile, dupe, fool, hoodwink, kid (informal), mislead, take in (informal), trick

deluge noun 1 <u>flood</u>, cataclysm, downpour, inundation, overflowing, spate, torrent 2 <u>rush</u>, avalanche, barrage, flood, spate, torrent ♦ verb 3 <u>flood</u>, douse, drench, drown, inundate, soak, submerge, swamp 4 <u>overwhelm</u>, engulf, inundate, overload, overrun, swamp

delusion noun <u>misconception</u>, error, fallacy, false impression, fancy, hallucination, illusion, misapprehension, mistake

de luxe adjective <u>luxurious</u>, costly, exclusive, expensive, grand, opulent, select, special, splendid, superior

delve verb <u>research</u>, burrow, explore, ferret out, forage, investigate, look into, probe, rummage, search

demagogue noun <u>agitator</u>, firebrand, rabble-rouser

demand verb 1 <u>request</u>, ask, challenge, inquire, interrogate, question 2 <u>require</u>, call for, cry out for, entail, involve, necessitate, need, want 3 <u>claim</u>, exact, expect, insist on, order ♦ noun 4 <u>request</u>, inquiry, order, question, requisition 5 <u>need</u>, call, claim, market, requirement, want

demanding adjective <u>difficult</u>, challenging, exacting, hard, taxing, tough, trying, wearing

demarcation noun <u>delimitation</u>, differentiation, distinction, division, separation

demean verb <u>lower</u>, abase, debase, degrade, descend, humble, stoop

demeanour noun <u>behaviour</u>, air, bearing, carriage, comportment, conduct, deportment, manner

demented adjective <u>mad</u>, crazed, crazy, deranged, frenzied, insane, maniacal, unbalanced, unhinged

demise noun 1 <u>failure</u>, collapse, downfall, end, fall, ruin 2 Euphemistic <u>death</u>, decease, departure

democracy noun <u>self-government</u>, commonwealth, republic

democratic adjective <u>self-governing</u>, autonomous, egalitarian, popular, populist, representative

demolish verb 1 <u>knock down</u>, bulldoze, destroy, dismantle, flatten, level, raze, tear down 2 <u>defeat</u>, annihilate, destroy, overthrow, overturn, undo, wreck

demolition noun <u>knocking down</u>, bulldozing, destruction, explosion, levelling, razing, tearing down, wrecking

demon noun **1** evil spirit, devil, fiend, ghoul, goblin, malignant spirit **2** wizard, ace (*informal*), fiend, master

demonic, demoniac, demoniacal adjective **1** devilish, diabolic, diabolical, fiendish, hellish, infernal, satanic **2** frenzied, crazed, frantic, frenetic, furious, hectic, maniacal, manic

demonstrable adjective provable, evident, irrefutable, obvious, palpable, self-evident, unmistakable, verifiable

demonstrate verb **1** prove, display, exhibit, indicate, manifest, show, testify to **2** show how, describe, explain, illustrate, make clear, teach **3** march, parade, picket, protest, rally

demonstration noun **1** march, mass lobby, parade, picket, protest, rally, sit-in **2** explanation, description, exposition, presentation, test, trial **3** proof, confirmation, display, evidence, exhibition, expression, illustration, testimony

demoralize verb dishearten, deject, depress, discourage, dispirit, undermine, unnerve, weaken

demote verb downgrade, degrade, kick downstairs (*slang*), lower in rank, relegate

demur verb **1** object, balk, dispute, hesitate, protest, refuse, take exception, waver ♦ noun **2** As in *without demur* objection, compunction, dissent, hesitation, misgiving, protest, qualm

demure adjective shy, diffident, modest, reserved, reticent, retiring, sedate, unassuming

den noun **1** lair, cave, cavern, haunt, hide-out, hole, shelter **2** *Chiefly U.S.* study, cubbyhole, hideaway, retreat, sanctuary, sanctum

denial noun **1** negation, contradiction, dissent, renunciation, repudiation, retraction **2** refusal, prohibition, rebuff, rejection, repulse, veto

denigrate verb disparage, bad-mouth (*slang, chiefly U.S. & Canad.*), belittle, knock (*informal*), malign, rubbish (*informal*), run down, slander, vilify

denomination noun **1** religious group, belief, creed, persuasion, school, sect **2** unit, grade, size, value

denote verb indicate, betoken, designate, express, imply, mark, mean, show, signify

denounce verb condemn, accuse, attack, censure, denunciate, revile, stigmatize, vilify

dense adjective **1** thick, close-knit, compact, condensed, heavy, impenetrable, opaque, solid **2** *Informal* stupid, dozy (*Brit. informal*), dull, obtuse, slow-witted, stolid, thick

density noun tightness, bulk, compactness, consistency, denseness, impenetrability, mass, solidity, thickness

dent noun **1** hollow, chip, crater, depression, dimple, dip, impression, indentation, pit ♦ verb **2** make a dent in, gouge, hollow, press in, push in

deny verb 1 contradict, disagree with, disprove, rebuff, rebut, refute 2 refuse, begrudge, disallow, forbid, reject, turn down, withhold 3 renounce, disclaim, disown, recant, repudiate, retract

depart verb 1 leave, absent (oneself), disappear, exit, go, go away, quit, retire, retreat, withdraw 2 deviate, differ, digress, diverge, stray, swerve, turn aside, vary, veer

department noun section, branch, bureau, division, office, station, subdivision, unit

departure noun 1 leaving, exit, exodus, going, going away, leave-taking, removal, retirement, withdrawal 2 divergence, deviation, digression, variation 3 shift, change, difference, innovation, novelty, whole new ball game (informal)

depend verb 1 trust in, bank on, count on, lean on, reckon on, rely upon, turn to 2 be determined by, be based on, be contingent on, be subject to, be subordinate to, hang on, hinge on, rest on, revolve around

dependable adjective reliable, faithful, reputable, responsible, staunch, steady, sure, trustworthy, trusty, unfailing

dependant noun relative, child, minor, protégé, subordinate

dependent adjective 1 relying on, defenceless, helpless, reliant, vulnerable, weak 2 dependent on or upon determined by, conditional on, contingent on, depending on, influenced by, subject to

depict verb 1 draw, delineate, illustrate, outline, paint, picture, portray, sketch 2 describe, characterize, narrate, outline, represent

depiction noun representation, delineation, description, picture, portrayal, sketch

deplete verb use up, consume, drain, empty, exhaust, expend, impoverish, lessen, reduce

deplorable adjective 1 regrettable, grievous, lamentable, pitiable, sad, unfortunate, wretched 2 disgraceful, dishonourable, reprehensible, scandalous, shameful

deplore verb disapprove of, abhor, censure, condemn, denounce, object to, take a dim view of

deploy verb position, arrange, set out, station, use, utilize

deployment noun position, arrangement, organization, spread, stationing, use, utilization

deport verb 1 expel, banish, exile, expatriate, extradite, oust 2 deport oneself behave, acquit oneself, act, bear oneself, carry oneself, comport oneself, conduct oneself, hold oneself

depose verb 1 remove from office, demote, dethrone, dismiss, displace, oust 2 Law testify, avouch, declare, make a deposition

deposit verb 1 put, drop, lay, locate, place 2 store, bank, consign, entrust, lodge ♦ noun 3 down payment, instalment, part payment, pledge, retainer, security, stake **4** <u>sediment</u>, accumulation, dregs, lees, precipitate, silt

depot noun **1** <u>storehouse</u>, depository, repository, warehouse **2** *Chiefly U.S. & Canad.* <u>bus station</u>, garage, terminus

depraved adjective <u>corrupt</u>, degenerate, dissolute, evil, immoral, sinful, vicious, vile, wicked

depravity noun <u>corruption</u>, debauchery, evil, immorality, sinfulness, vice, wickedness

depreciate verb **1** <u>devalue</u>, decrease, deflate, lessen, lose value, lower, reduce **2** <u>disparage</u>, belittle, denigrate, deride, detract, run down, scorn, sneer at

depreciation noun **1** <u>devaluation</u>, deflation, depression, drop, fall, slump **2** <u>disparagement</u>, belittlement, denigration, deprecation, detraction

depress verb **1** <u>sadden</u>, deject, discourage, dishearten, dispirit, make despondent, oppress, weigh down **2** <u>lower</u>, cheapen, depreciate, devalue, diminish, downgrade, lessen, reduce **3** <u>press down</u>, flatten, level, lower, push down

depressed adjective **1** <u>low-spirited</u>, blue, dejected, despondent, discouraged, dispirited, downcast, downhearted, fed up, sad, unhappy **2** <u>poverty-stricken</u>, deprived, disadvantaged, needy, poor, run-down **3** <u>lowered</u>,

cheapened, depreciated, devalued, weakened **4** <u>sunken</u>, concave, hollow, indented, recessed

depressing adjective <u>bleak</u>, discouraging, disheartening, dismal, dispiriting, gloomy, harrowing, sad, saddening

depression noun **1** <u>low spirits</u>, dejection, despair, despondency, downheartedness, dumps (*informal*), gloominess, melancholy, sadness, the blues **2** <u>recession</u>, economic decline, hard or bad times, inactivity, slump, stagnation **3** <u>hollow</u>, bowl, cavity, dent, dimple, dip, indentation, pit, valley

deprivation noun **1** <u>withholding</u>, denial, dispossession, expropriation, removal, withdrawal **2** <u>want</u>, destitution, distress, hardship, need, privation

deprive verb <u>withhold</u>, bereave, despoil, dispossess, rob, strip

deprived adjective <u>poor</u>, bereft, destitute, disadvantaged, down at heel, in need, lacking, needy

depth noun **1** <u>deepness</u>, drop, extent, measure **2** <u>insight</u>, astuteness, discernment, penetration, profoundness, profundity, sagacity, wisdom

deputation noun <u>delegation</u>, commission, embassy, envoys, legation

deputize verb <u>stand in for</u>, act for, take the place of, understudy

deputy noun <u>substitute</u>, delegate, legate, lieutenant, number two, proxy, representative, second-in-command, surrogate

deranged adjective <u>mad</u>, crazed,

crazy, demented, distracted, insane, irrational, unbalanced, unhinged

derelict adjective 1 <u>abandoned</u>, deserted, dilapidated, discarded, forsaken, neglected, ruined ♦ noun 2 <u>tramp</u>, bag lady, down-and-out, outcast, vagrant

deride verb <u>mock</u>, disdain, disparage, insult, jeer, ridicule, scoff, scorn, sneer, taunt

derisory adjective <u>ridiculous</u>, contemptible, insulting, laughable, ludicrous, outrageous, preposterous

derivation noun <u>origin</u>, beginning, foundation, root, source

derive from verb <u>come from</u>, arise from, emanate from, flow from, issue from, originate from, proceed from, spring from, stem from

derogatory adjective <u>disparaging</u>, belittling, defamatory, offensive, slighting, uncomplimentary, unfavourable, unflattering

descend verb 1 <u>move down</u>, drop, fall, go down, plummet, plunge, sink, subside, tumble 2 <u>slope</u>, dip, incline, slant 3 <u>lower oneself</u>, degenerate, deteriorate, stoop 4 **be descended** <u>originate</u>, be handed down, be passed down, derive, issue, proceed, spring 5 **descend on** <u>attack</u>, arrive, invade, raid, swoop

descent noun 1 <u>coming down</u>, drop, fall, plunge, swoop 2 <u>slope</u>, declivity, dip, drop, incline, slant 3 <u>ancestry</u>, extraction, family tree, genealogy, lineage, origin,

parentage 4 <u>decline</u>, degeneration, deterioration

describe verb 1 <u>relate</u>, depict, explain, express, narrate, portray, recount, report, tell 2 <u>trace</u>, delineate, draw, mark out, outline

description noun 1 <u>account</u>, depiction, explanation, narrative, portrayal, report, representation, sketch 2 <u>kind</u>, brand, category, class, order, sort, type, variety

descriptive adjective <u>graphic</u>, detailed, explanatory, expressive, illustrative, pictorial, picturesque, vivid

desert[1] noun <u>wilderness</u>, solitude, waste, wasteland, wilds

desert[2] verb <u>abandon</u>, abscond, forsake, jilt, leave, leave stranded, maroon, quit, strand, walk out on (informal)

deserted adjective <u>abandoned</u>, derelict, desolate, empty, forsaken, neglected, unoccupied, vacant

deserter noun <u>defector</u>, absconder, escapee, fugitive, renegade, runaway, traitor, truant

desertion noun <u>abandonment</u>, absconding, apostasy, betrayal, defection, dereliction, escape, evasion, flight, relinquishment

deserve verb <u>merit</u>, be entitled to, be worthy of, earn, justify, rate, warrant

deserved adjective <u>well-earned</u>, due, earned, fitting, justified, merited, proper, rightful, warranted

deserving adjective <u>worthy</u>, commendable, estimable, laudable, meritorious, praiseworthy, righteous

design verb 1 plan, draft, draw, outline, sketch, trace 2 create, conceive, fabricate, fashion, invent, originate, think up 3 intend, aim, mean, plan, propose, purpose ♦ noun 4 plan, blueprint, draft, drawing, model, outline, scheme, sketch 5 arrangement, construction, form, organization, pattern, shape, style 6 intention, aim, end, goal, object, objective, purpose, target

designate verb 1 name, call, dub, entitle, label, style, term 2 appoint, assign, choose, delegate, depute, nominate, select

designation noun name, description, label, mark, title

designer noun creator, architect, deviser, inventor, originator, planner

desirable adjective 1 worthwhile, advantageous, advisable, beneficial, good, preferable, profitable 2 attractive, adorable, alluring, fetching, glamorous, seductive, sexy (informal)

desire verb 1 want, crave, hanker after, hope for, long for, set one's heart on, thirst for, wish for, yearn for ♦ noun 2 wish, aspiration, craving, hankering, hope, longing, thirst, want 3 lust, appetite, libido, passion

desist verb stop, break off, cease, discontinue, end, forbear, leave off, pause, refrain from

desolate adjective 1 uninhabited, bare, barren, bleak, dreary, godforsaken, solitary, wild 2 miserable, dejected,

despondent, disconsolate, downcast, forlorn, gloomy, wretched ♦ verb 3 lay waste, depopulate, despoil, destroy, devastate, lay low, pillage, plunder, ravage, ruin 4 deject, depress, discourage, dishearten, dismay, distress, grieve

desolation noun 1 ruin, destruction, devastation, havoc 2 bleakness, barrenness, isolation, solitude 3 misery, anguish, dejection, despair, distress, gloom, sadness, woe, wretchedness

despair noun 1 despondency, anguish, dejection, depression, desperation, gloom, hopelessness, misery, wretchedness ♦ verb 2 lose hope, give up, lose heart

despairing adjective hopeless, dejected, desperate, despondent, disconsolate, frantic, grief-stricken, inconsolable, miserable, wretched

despatch see DISPATCH

desperado noun criminal, bandit, lawbreaker, outlaw, villain

desperate adjective 1 reckless, audacious, daring, frantic, furious, risky 2 grave, drastic, extreme, urgent

desperately adverb 1 gravely, badly, dangerously, perilously, seriously, severely 2 hopelessly, appallingly, fearfully, frightfully, shockingly

desperation noun 1 recklessness, foolhardiness, frenzy, impetuosity, madness, rashness 2 misery, agony, anguish, despair, hopelessness, trouble, unhappiness, worry

despicable adjective
contemptible, detestable,
disgraceful, hateful, mean,
shameful, sordid, vile, worthless,
wretched

despise verb look down on,
abhor, detest, loathe, revile,
scorn

despite preposition in spite of,
against, even with, in the face
of, in the teeth of,
notwithstanding, regardless of,
undeterred by

despondency noun dejection,
depression, despair, desperation,
gloom, low spirits, melancholy,
misery, sadness

despondent adjective dejected,
depressed, disconsolate,
disheartened, dispirited,
downhearted, glum, in despair,
sad, sorrowful

despot noun tyrant, autocrat,
dictator, oppressor

despotic adjective tyrannical,
authoritarian, autocratic,
dictatorial, domineering,
imperious, oppressive

despotism noun tyranny,
autocracy, dictatorship,
oppression, totalitarianism

destination noun journey's end,
haven, resting-place, station,
stop, terminus

destined adjective fated, bound,
certain, doomed, intended,
meant, predestined

destiny noun fate, doom,
fortune, karma, kismet, lot,
portion

destitute adjective penniless,
down and out, impoverished,
indigent, insolvent, moneyless,
penurious, poor, poverty-stricken

destroy verb ruin, annihilate,
crush, demolish, devastate,
eradicate, shatter, wipe out,
wreck

destruction noun ruin,
annihilation, demolition,
devastation, eradication,
extermination, havoc, slaughter,
wreckage

destructive adjective damaging,
calamitous, catastrophic, deadly,
devastating, fatal, harmful,
lethal, ruinous

detach verb separate, cut off,
disconnect, disengage, divide,
remove, sever, tear off, unfasten

detached adjective 1 separate,
disconnected, discrete,
unconnected 2 uninvolved,
disinterested, dispassionate,
impartial, impersonal, neutral,
objective, reserved, unbiased

detachment noun 1 indifference,
aloofness, coolness,
nonchalance, remoteness,
unconcern 2 impartiality,
fairness, neutrality, objectivity
3 Military unit, body, force,
party, patrol, squad, task force

detail noun 1 point, aspect,
component, element, fact,
factor, feature, particular, respect
2 fine point, nicety, particular,
triviality 3 Military party,
assignment, body, detachment,
duty, fatigue, force, squad ◆ verb
4 list, catalogue, enumerate,
itemize, recite, recount, rehearse,
relate, tabulate 5 appoint,
allocate, assign, charge,
commission, delegate, send

detailed adjective comprehensive,
blow-by-blow, exhaustive, full,

intricate, minute, particular, thorough

detain verb 1 delay, check, hinder, hold up, impede, keep back, retard, slow up (or down) 2 hold, arrest, confine, intern, restrain

detect verb 1 notice, ascertain, identify, note, observe, perceive, recognize, spot 2 discover, find, track down, uncover, unmask

detective noun investigator, cop (slang), gumshoe (U.S. slang), private eye, private investigator, sleuth (informal)

detention noun imprisonment, confinement, custody, incarceration, quarantine

deter verb discourage, dissuade, frighten, inhibit from, intimidate, prevent, put off, stop, talk out of

detergent noun cleaner, cleanser

deteriorate verb decline, degenerate, go downhill (informal), lower, slump, worsen

determination noun tenacity, dedication, doggedness, fortitude, perseverance, persistence, resolve, single-mindedness, steadfastness, willpower

determine verb 1 settle, conclude, decide, end, finish, ordain, regulate 2 find out, ascertain, detect, discover, learn, verify, work out 3 decide, choose, elect, make up one's mind, resolve

determined adjective resolute, dogged, firm, intent, persevering, persistent, single-minded, steadfast, tenacious, unwavering

deterrent noun discouragement, check, curb, disincentive, hindrance, impediment, obstacle, restraint

detest verb hate, abhor, abominate, despise, dislike intensely, loathe, recoil from

detonate verb explode, blast, blow up, discharge, set off, trigger

detour noun diversion, bypass, indirect course, roundabout way

detract verb lessen, devaluate, diminish, lower, reduce, take away from

detriment noun damage, disadvantage, disservice, harm, hurt, impairment, injury, loss

detrimental adjective damaging, adverse, deleterious, destructive, disadvantageous, harmful, prejudicial, unfavourable

devastate verb destroy, demolish, lay waste, level, ravage, raze, ruin, sack, wreck

devastating adjective overwhelming, cutting, overpowering, savage, trenchant, vitriolic, withering

devastation noun destruction, demolition, desolation, havoc, ruin

develop verb 1 advance, evolve, flourish, grow, mature, progress, prosper, ripen 2 form, breed, establish, generate, invent, originate 3 expand, amplify, augment, broaden, elaborate, enlarge, unfold, work out

development noun 1 growth, advance, evolution, expansion, improvement, increase, progress, spread 2 event, happening,

deviant adjective **1** perverted, kinky (slang), sick (informal), twisted, warped ♦ noun **2** pervert, freak, misfit

deviate verb differ, depart, diverge, stray, swerve, veer, wander

deviation noun departure, digression, discrepancy, disparity, divergence, inconsistency, irregularity, shift, variation

device noun **1** gadget, apparatus, appliance, contraption, implement, instrument, machine, tool **2** ploy, gambit, manoeuvre, plan, scheme, stratagem, trick, wile

devil noun **1 the Devil** Satan, Beelzebub, Evil One, Lucifer, Mephistopheles, Old Nick (informal), Prince of Darkness **2** brute, beast, demon, fiend, monster, ogre, terror **3** scamp, rascal, rogue, scoundrel **4** person, beggar, creature, thing, wretch

devilish adjective fiendish, atrocious, damnable, detestable, diabolical, hellish, infernal, satanic, wicked

devious adjective **1** sly, calculating, deceitful, dishonest, double-dealing, insincere, scheming, surreptitious, underhand, wily **2** indirect, circuitous, rambling, roundabout

devise verb work out, conceive, construct, contrive, design, dream up, formulate, invent, think up

devoid adjective lacking, bereft, deficient, destitute, empty, free from, wanting, without

devote verb dedicate, allot, apply, assign, commit, give, pledge, reserve, set apart

devoted adjective dedicated, ardent, committed, constant, devout, faithful, loyal, staunch, steadfast, true

devotee noun enthusiast, adherent, admirer, aficionado, buff (informal), disciple, fan, fanatic, follower, supporter

devotion noun **1** dedication, adherence, allegiance, commitment, constancy, faithfulness, fidelity, loyalty **2** love, affection, attachment, fondness, passion **3** devoutness, godliness, holiness, piety, reverence, spirituality **4 devotions** prayers, church service, divine office, religious observance

devour verb **1** eat, consume, gobble, gulp, guzzle, polish off (informal), swallow, wolf **2** destroy, annihilate, consume, ravage, waste, wipe out **3** enjoy, read compulsively or voraciously, take in

devout adjective religious, godly, holy, orthodox, pious, prayerful, pure, reverent, saintly

dexterity noun **1** skill, adroitness, deftness, expertise, finesse, nimbleness, proficiency, touch **2** cleverness, ability, aptitude, ingenuity

diabolical adjective Informal dreadful, abysmal, appalling, atrocious, hellish, outrageous, shocking, terrible

diagnose verb identify, analyse,

determine, distinguish, interpret, pinpoint, pronounce, recognize

diagnosis noun 1 examination, analysis, investigation, scrutiny 2 opinion, conclusion, interpretation, pronouncement

diagonal adjective slanting, angled, cross, crossways, crosswise, oblique

diagonally adverb aslant, at an angle, cornerwise, crosswise, obliquely

diagram noun plan, chart, drawing, figure, graph, representation, sketch

dialect noun language, brogue, idiom, jargon, patois, provincialism, speech, vernacular

dialogue noun conversation, communication, conference, discourse, discussion

diary noun journal, appointment book, chronicle, daily record, engagement book, Filofax (Trademark)

dicky adjective Brit. informal weak, fluttery, shaky, unreliable, unsound, unsteady

dictate verb 1 speak, read out, say, utter 2 order, command, decree, demand, direct, impose, lay down the law, pronounce ♦ noun 3 command, decree, demand, direction, edict, fiat, injunction, order 4 principle, code, law, rule

dictator noun absolute ruler, autocrat, despot, oppressor, tyrant

dictatorial adjective 1 absolute, arbitrary, autocratic, despotic, totalitarian, tyrannical, unlimited, unrestricted 2 domineering,

authoritarian, bossy (informal), imperious, oppressive, overbearing

dictatorship noun absolute rule, absolutism, authoritarianism, autocracy, despotism, totalitarianism, tyranny

diction noun pronunciation, articulation, delivery, elocution, enunciation, fluency, inflection, intonation, speech

dictionary noun wordbook, glossary, lexicon, vocabulary

die verb 1 pass away, breathe one's last, croak (slang), expire, give up the ghost, kick the bucket (slang), peg out (informal), perish, snuff it (slang) 2 dwindle, decay, decline, fade, sink, subside, wane, wilt, wither 3 stop, break down, fade out or away, fail, fizzle out, halt, lose power, peter out, run down 4 be dying long, ache, be eager, desire, hunger, pine for, yearn

die-hard noun reactionary, fanatic, old fogey, stick-in-the-mud (informal)

diet¹ noun 1 food, fare, nourishment, nutriment, provisions, rations, sustenance, victuals 2 regime, abstinence, fast, regimen ♦ verb 3 slim, abstain, eat sparingly, fast, lose weight

diet² noun council, chamber, congress, convention, legislature, meeting, parliament

differ verb 1 be dissimilar, contradict, contrast, depart from, diverge, run counter to, stand apart, vary 2 disagree, clash, contend, debate, demur, dispute, dissent, oppose, take exception, take issue

difference noun 1 dissimilarity, alteration, change, contrast, discrepancy, disparity, diversity, variation, variety
2 disagreement, argument, clash, conflict, contretemps, debate, dispute, quarrel
3 remainder, balance, rest, result

different adjective 1 unlike, altered, changed, contrasting, disparate, dissimilar, divergent, inconsistent, opposed 2 various, assorted, diverse, miscellaneous, sundry, varied 3 unusual, atypical, distinctive, extraordinary, peculiar, singular, special, strange, uncommon

differentiate verb 1 distinguish, contrast, discriminate, make a distinction, mark off, separate, set off or apart, tell apart 2 make different, adapt, alter, change, convert, modify, transform

difficult adjective 1 hard, arduous, demanding, formidable, laborious, onerous, strenuous, uphill
2 problematical, abstruse, baffling, complex, complicated, intricate, involved, knotty, obscure 3 hard to please, demanding, fastidious, fussy, perverse, refractory, unaccommodating

difficulty noun 1 laboriousness, arduousness, awkwardness, hardship, strain, strenuousness, tribulation 2 predicament, dilemma, embarrassment, hot water (informal), jam (informal), mess, plight, quandary, trouble
3 problem, complication, hindrance, hurdle, impediment, obstacle, pitfall, snag, stumbling block

diffidence noun shyness, bashfulness, hesitancy, insecurity, modesty, reserve, self-consciousness, timidity

diffident adjective shy, bashful, doubtful, hesitant, insecure, modest, reserved, self-conscious, timid, unassertive, unassuming

dig verb 1 excavate, burrow, delve, hollow out, mine, quarry, scoop, tunnel 2 investigate, delve, dig down, go into, probe, research, search 3 with out or up find, discover, expose, uncover, unearth, uproot 4 poke, drive, jab, prod, punch, thrust ♦ noun
5 poke, jab, prod, punch, thrust
6 cutting remark, barb, crack (slang), gibe, insult, jeer, sneer, taunt, wisecrack (informal)

digest verb 1 ingest, absorb, assimilate, dissolve, incorporate
2 take in, absorb, consider, contemplate, grasp, study, understand ♦ noun 3 summary, abridgment, abstract, epitome, précis, résumé, synopsis

digestion noun ingestion, absorption, assimilation, conversion, incorporation, transformation

dignified adjective distinguished, formal, grave, imposing, noble, reserved, solemn, stately

dignitary noun public figure, bigwig (informal), high-up (informal), notable, personage, pillar of society, V.I.P., worthy

dignity noun 1 decorum, courtliness, grandeur, gravity, loftiness, majesty, nobility, solemnity, stateliness 2 honour, eminence, importance, rank, respectability, standing, status **3** self-importance, pride, self-esteem, self-respect

digress verb wander, depart, deviate, diverge, drift, get off the point or subject, go off at a tangent, ramble, stray

digression noun departure, aside, detour, deviation, divergence, diversion, straying, wandering

dilapidated adjective ruined, broken-down, crumbling, decrepit, in ruins, ramshackle, rickety, run-down, tumbledown

dilate verb enlarge, broaden, expand, puff out, stretch, swell, widen

dilatory adjective time-wasting, delaying, lingering, procrastinating, slow, sluggish, tardy, tarrying

dilemma noun predicament, difficulty, mess, plight, problem, puzzle, quandary, spot (informal)

dilettante noun amateur, aesthete, dabbler, trifler

diligence noun application, attention, care, industry, laboriousness, perseverance

diligent adjective hard-working, assiduous, attentive, careful, conscientious, industrious, painstaking, persistent, studious, tireless

dilute verb **1** water down, adulterate, cut, make thinner, thin (out), weaken **2** reduce, attenuate, decrease, diffuse, diminish, lessen, mitigate, temper, weaken

dim adjective **1** poorly lit, cloudy,

dark, grey, overcast, shadowy, tenebrous **2** unclear, bleary, blurred, faint, fuzzy, ill-defined, indistinct, obscured, shadowy **3** Informal stupid, dense, dozy (Brit. informal), dull, dumb (informal), obtuse, slow on the uptake (informal), thick **4 take a dim view** disapprove, be displeased, be sceptical, look askance, reject, suspect, take exception, view with disfavour ♦ verb **5** dull, blur, cloud, darken, fade, obscure

dimension noun, often plural measurement, amplitude, bulk, capacity, extent, proportions, size, volume

diminish verb **1** decrease, curtail, cut, lessen, lower, reduce, shrink **2** dwindle, decline, die out, recede, subside, wane

diminutive adjective small, little, mini, miniature, minute, petite, tiny, undersized

din noun **1** noise, clamour, clatter, commotion, crash, pandemonium, racket, row, uproar ♦ verb **2 din (something) into (someone)** instil, drum into, go on at, hammer into, inculcate, instruct, teach

dine verb eat, banquet, feast, lunch, sup

dingy adjective dull, dark, dim, drab, dreary, gloomy, murky, obscure, sombre

dinner noun meal, banquet, feast, main meal, repast, spread (informal)

dip verb **1** plunge, bathe, douse, duck, dunk, immerse **2** slope, decline, descend, drop (down), fall, lower, sink, subside ♦ noun

3 plunge, douche, drenching, ducking, immersion, soaking 4 bathe, dive, plunge, swim 5 hollow, basin, concavity, depression, hole, incline, slope 6 drop, decline, fall, lowering, sag, slip, slump

dip into verb sample, browse, glance at, peruse, skim

diplomacy noun 1 statesmanship, international negotiation, statecraft 2 tact, artfulness, craft, delicacy, discretion, finesse, savoir-faire, skill, subtlety

diplomat noun negotiator, conciliator, go-between, mediator, moderator, politician, tactician

diplomatic adjective tactful, adept, discreet, polite, politic, prudent, sensitive, subtle

dire adjective 1 disastrous, awful, calamitous, catastrophic, horrible, ruinous, terrible, woeful 2 desperate, critical, crucial, drastic, extreme, now or never, pressing, urgent 3 grim, dismal, dreadful, fearful, gloomy, ominous, portentous

direct adjective 1 straight, nonstop, not crooked, shortest, through, unbroken, uninterrupted 2 immediate, face-to-face, first-hand, head-on, personal 3 honest, candid, frank, open, plain-spoken, straight, straightforward, upfront (informal) 4 explicit, absolute, blunt, categorical, downright, express, plain, point-blank, unambiguous, unequivocal ♦ verb 5 control, conduct, guide, handle, lead, manage, oversee,

run, supervise 6 order, bid, charge, command, demand, dictate, instruct 7 guide, indicate, lead, point in the direction of, point the way, show 8 address, label, mail, route, send 9 aim, focus, level, point, train

direction noun 1 way, aim, bearing, course, line, path, road, route, track 2 management, administration, charge, command, control, guidance, leadership, order, supervision

directions plural noun instructions, briefing, guidance, guidelines, plan, recommendation, regulations

directive noun order, command, decree, edict, injunction, instruction, mandate, regulation, ruling

directly adverb 1 straight, by the shortest route, exactly, in a beeline, precisely, unswervingly, without deviation 2 honestly, openly, plainly, point-blank, straightforwardly, truthfully, unequivocally 3 at once, as soon as possible, forthwith, immediately, promptly, right away, straightaway

director noun controller, administrator, chief, executive, governor, head, leader, manager, supervisor

dirge noun lament, dead march, elegy, funeral song, requiem, threnody

dirt noun 1 filth, dust, grime, impurity, muck, mud 2 soil, clay, earth, loam 3 obscenity, indecency, pornography, sleaze, smut

dirty adjective 1 filthy, foul, grimy, grubby, messy, mucky, muddy, polluted, soiled, unclean 2 dishonest, crooked, fraudulent, illegal, treacherous, unfair, unscrupulous, unsporting 3 obscene, blue, indecent, pornographic, salacious, sleazy, smutty 4 As in **a dirty look** angry, annoyed, bitter, choked, indignant, offended, resentful, scorching ♦ verb 5 soil, blacken, defile, foul, muddy, pollute, smirch, spoil, stain

disability noun 1 handicap, affliction, ailment, complaint, defect, disorder, impairment, infirmity, malady 2 incapacity, inability, unfitness

disable verb 1 handicap, cripple, damage, enfeeble, immobilize, impair, incapacitate, paralyse 2 disqualify, invalidate, render or declare incapable

disabled adjective handicapped, crippled, incapacitated, infirm, lame, paralysed, weakened

disadvantage noun 1 harm, damage, detriment, disservice, hurt, injury, loss, prejudice 2 drawback, downside, handicap, inconvenience, nuisance, snag, trouble

disagree verb 1 differ (in opinion), argue, clash, cross swords, dispute, dissent, object, quarrel, take issue with 2 conflict, be dissimilar, contradict, counter, differ, diverge, run counter to, vary 3 make ill, bother, discomfort, distress, hurt, nauseate, sicken, trouble, upset

disagreeable adjective 1 nasty,

disgusting, displeasing, distasteful, objectionable, obnoxious, offensive, repugnant, repulsive, unpleasant 2 rude, bad-tempered, churlish, difficult, disobliging, irritable, surly, unpleasant

disagreement noun 1 incompatibility, difference, discrepancy, disparity, dissimilarity, divergence, incongruity, variance 2 argument, altercation, clash, conflict, dispute, dissent, quarrel, row, squabble

disallow verb reject, disavow, dismiss, disown, rebuff, refuse, repudiate

disappear verb 1 vanish, evanesce, fade away, pass, recede 2 cease, die out, dissolve, evaporate, leave no trace, melt away, pass away, perish

disappearance noun vanishing, departure, eclipse, evanescence, evaporation, going, melting, passing

disappoint verb let down, disenchant, disgruntle, dishearten, disillusion, dismay, dissatisfy, fail

disappointed adjective let down, cast down, despondent, discouraged, disenchanted, disgruntled, dissatisfied, downhearted, frustrated

disappointing adjective unsatisfactory, depressing, disconcerting, discouraging, inadequate, insufficient, sad, sorry

disappointment noun 1 frustration, chagrin, discontent, discouragement, disenchantment, disillusionment, dissatisfaction, regret 2 letdown, blow, calamity, choker (*informal*), misfortune, setback

disapproval *noun* displeasure, censure, condemnation, criticism, denunciation, dissatisfaction, objection, reproach

disapprove *verb* condemn, deplore, dislike, find unacceptable, frown on, look down one's nose at (*informal*), object to, reject, take a dim view of, take exception to

disarm *verb* 1 render defenceless, disable 2 win over, persuade, set at ease 3 demilitarize, deactivate, demobilize, disband

disarmament *noun* arms reduction, arms limitation, de-escalation, demilitarization, demobilization

disarming *adjective* charming, irresistible, likable *or* likeable, persuasive, winning

disarrange *verb* disorder, confuse, disorganize, disturb, jumble (up), mess (up), scatter, shake (up), shuffle

disarray *noun* 1 confusion, disorder, disorganization, disunity, indiscipline, unruliness 2 untidiness, chaos, clutter, hotchpotch, jumble, mess, muddle, shambles

disaster *noun* catastrophe, adversity, calamity, cataclysm, misfortune, ruin, tragedy, trouble

disastrous *adjective* terrible, calamitous, cataclysmic, catastrophic, devastating, fatal, ruinous, tragic

disbelief *noun* scepticism,

distrust, doubt, dubiety, incredulity, mistrust, unbelief

discard *verb* get rid of, abandon, cast aside, dispense with, dispose of, drop, dump (*informal*), jettison, reject, throw away *or* out

discharge *verb* 1 release, allow to go, clear, free, liberate, pardon, set free 2 dismiss, cashier, discard, expel, fire (*informal*), oust, remove, sack (*informal*) 3 fire, detonate, explode, let loose (*informal*), let off, set off, shoot 4 pour forth, dispense, emit, exude, give off, leak, ooze, release 5 carry out, accomplish, do, execute, fulfil, observe, perform 6 pay, clear, honour, meet, relieve, satisfy, settle, square up ♦ *noun* 7 release, acquittal, clearance, liberation, pardon 8 dismissal, demobilization, ejection 9 firing, blast, burst, detonation, explosion, report, salvo, shot, volley 10 emission, excretion, ooze, pus, secretion, seepage, suppuration

disciple *noun* follower, adherent, apostle, devotee, pupil, student, supporter

disciplinarian *noun* authoritarian, despot, martinet, stickler, taskmaster, tyrant

discipline *noun* 1 training, drill, exercise, method, practice, regimen, regulation 2 punishment, castigation, chastisement, correction 3 self-control, conduct, control, orderliness, regulation, restraint, strictness 4 field of study, area, branch of knowledge, course,

curriculum, speciality, subject
♦ verb 5 <u>train</u>, bring up, drill, educate, exercise, prepare 6 <u>punish</u>, bring to book, castigate, chasten, chastise, correct, penalize, reprimand, reprove

disclose verb 1 <u>make known</u>, broadcast, communicate, confess, divulge, let slip, publish, relate, reveal 2 <u>show</u>, bring to light, expose, lay bare, reveal, uncover, unveil

disclosure noun <u>revelation</u>, acknowledgment, admission, announcement, confession, declaration, divulgence, leak, publication

discolour verb stain, fade, mark, soil, streak, tarnish, tinge

discomfort noun 1 <u>pain</u>, ache, hurt, irritation, malaise, soreness 2 <u>uneasiness</u>, annoyance, distress, hardship, irritation, nuisance, trouble

disconcert verb <u>disturb</u>, faze, fluster, perturb, rattle (informal), take aback, unsettle, upset, worry

disconcerting adjective <u>disturbing</u>, alarming, awkward, bewildering, confusing, distracting, embarrassing, off-putting (Brit. informal), perplexing, upsetting

disconnect verb <u>cut off</u>, detach, disengage, divide, part, separate, sever, take apart, uncouple

disconnected adjective <u>illogical</u>, confused, disjointed, incoherent, jumbled, mixed-up, rambling, unintelligible

disconsolate adjective <u>inconsolable</u>, crushed, dejected, desolate, forlorn, grief-stricken, heartbroken, miserable, wretched

discontent noun <u>dissatisfaction</u>, displeasure, envy, regret, restlessness, uneasiness, unhappiness

discontented adjective <u>dissatisfied</u>, disaffected, disgruntled, displeased, exasperated, fed up, unhappy, vexed

discontinue verb <u>stop</u>, abandon, break off, cease, drop, end, give up, quit, suspend, terminate

discord noun 1 <u>disagreement</u>, conflict, dissension, disunity, division, friction, incompatibility, strife 2 <u>disharmony</u>, cacophony, din, dissonance, harshness, jarring, racket, tumult

discordant adjective 1 <u>disagreeing</u>, at odds, clashing, conflicting, contradictory, contrary, different, incompatible 2 <u>inharmonious</u>, cacophonous, dissonant, grating, harsh, jarring, shrill, strident

discount verb 1 <u>leave out</u>, brush off (slang), disbelieve, disregard, ignore, overlook, pass over 2 <u>deduct</u>, lower, mark down, reduce, take off ♦ noun 3 <u>deduction</u>, concession, cut, rebate, reduction

discourage verb 1 <u>dishearten</u>, dampen, deject, demoralize, depress, dispirit, intimidate, overawe, put a damper on 2 <u>put off</u>, deter, dissuade, inhibit, prevent, talk out of

discouraged adjective <u>put off</u>, crestfallen, deterred, disheartened, dismayed, dispirited, downcast, down in the mouth, glum

discouragement noun 1 <u>loss of confidence</u>, dejection, depression, despair, despondency, disappointment, dismay, downheartedness 2 <u>deterrent</u>, damper, disincentive, hindrance, impediment, obstacle, opposition, setback

discouraging adjective <u>disheartening</u>, dampening, daunting, depressing, disappointing, dispiriting, off-putting (*Brit. informal*), unfavourable

discourse noun 1 <u>conversation</u>, chat, communication, dialogue, discussion, seminar, speech, talk 2 <u>speech</u>, dissertation, essay, homily, lecture, oration, sermon, treatise ♦ verb 3 <u>hold forth</u>, expatiate, speak, talk

discourteous adjective <u>rude</u>, bad-mannered, boorish, disrespectful, ill-mannered, impolite, insolent, offhand, ungentlemanly, ungracious

discourtesy noun 1 <u>rudeness</u>, bad manners, disrespectfulness, impertinence, impoliteness, incivility, insolence 2 <u>insult</u>, affront, cold shoulder, kick in the teeth (*slang*), rebuff, slight, snub

discover verb 1 <u>find</u>, come across, come upon, dig up, locate, turn up, uncover, unearth 2 <u>find out</u>, ascertain, detect, learn, notice, perceive, realize, recognize, uncover

discovery noun 1 <u>finding</u>, detection, disclosure, exploration, location, revelation, uncovering 2 <u>breakthrough</u>, find, innovation, invention, secret

discredit verb 1 <u>disgrace</u>, bring into disrepute, defame, dishonour, disparage, slander, smear, vilify 2 <u>doubt</u>, challenge, deny, disbelieve, discount, dispute, distrust, mistrust, question ♦ noun 3 <u>disgrace</u>, dishonour, disrepute, ignominy, ill-repute, scandal, shame, stigma

discreditable adjective <u>disgraceful</u>, dishonourable, ignominious, reprehensible, scandalous, shameful, unworthy

discreet adjective <u>tactful</u>, careful, cautious, circumspect, considerate, diplomatic, guarded, judicious, prudent, wary

discrepancy noun <u>disagreement</u>, conflict, contradiction, difference, disparity, divergence, incongruity, inconsistency, variation

discretion noun 1 <u>tact</u>, carefulness, caution, consideration, diplomacy, judiciousness, prudence, wariness 2 <u>choice</u>, inclination, pleasure, preference, volition, will

discriminate verb 1 <u>show prejudice</u>, favour, show bias, single out, treat as inferior, treat differently, victimize 2 <u>differentiate</u>, distinguish, draw a distinction, segregate, separate, tell the difference

discriminating adjective <u>discerning</u>, cultivated, fastidious, particular, refined, selective, tasteful

discrimination noun 1 <u>prejudice</u>, bias, bigotry, favouritism, intolerance, unfairness 2 <u>discernment</u>, judgment, perception, refinement, subtlety, taste

discuss verb <u>talk about</u>, argue, confer, consider, converse, debate, deliberate, examine

discussion noun <u>talk</u>, analysis, argument, conference, consultation, conversation, debate, deliberation, dialogue, discourse

disdain noun 1 <u>contempt</u>, arrogance, derision, haughtiness, scorn, superciliousness ♦ verb 2 <u>scorn</u>, deride, disregard, look down on, reject, slight, sneer at, spurn

disdainful adjective <u>contemptuous</u>, aloof, arrogant, derisive, haughty, proud, scornful, sneering, supercilious, superior

disease noun <u>illness</u>, affliction, ailment, complaint, condition, disorder, infection, infirmity, malady, sickness

diseased adjective <u>sick</u>, ailing, infected, rotten, sickly, unhealthy, unsound, unwell, unwholesome

disembark verb <u>land</u>, alight, arrive, get off, go ashore, step out of

disenchanted adjective <u>disillusioned</u>, cynical, disappointed, indifferent, jaundiced, let down, sick of, soured

disenchantment noun <u>disillusionment</u>, disappointment, disillusion, rude awakening

disengage verb <u>release</u>, disentangle, extricate, free, loosen, set free, unloose, untie

disentangle verb <u>untangle</u>,

disconnect, disengage, extricate, free, loose, unravel

disfavour noun <u>disapproval</u>, disapprobation, dislike, displeasure

disfigure verb <u>damage</u>, blemish, deface, deform, distort, mar, mutilate, scar

disgorge verb <u>vomit</u>, discharge, eject, empty, expel

disgrace noun 1 <u>shame</u>, degradation, dishonour, disrepute, ignominy, infamy, odium, opprobrium 2 <u>stain</u>, blemish, blot, reproach, scandal, slur, stigma ♦ verb 3 <u>bring shame upon</u>, degrade, discredit, dishonour, humiliate, shame, sully, taint

disgraceful adjective <u>shameful</u>, contemptible, detestable, dishonourable, disreputable, ignominious, scandalous, shocking, unworthy

disgruntled adjective <u>discontented</u>, annoyed, displeased, dissatisfied, grumpy, irritated, peeved, put out, vexed

disguise verb 1 <u>hide</u>, camouflage, cloak, conceal, cover, mask, screen, shroud, veil 2 <u>misrepresent</u>, fake, falsify ♦ noun 3 <u>costume</u>, camouflage, cover, mask, screen, veil 4 <u>façade</u>, deception, dissimulation, front, pretence, semblance, trickery, veneer

disguised adjective <u>in disguise</u>, camouflaged, covert, fake, false, feigned, incognito, masked, undercover

disgust noun 1 <u>loathing</u>, abhorrence, aversion, dislike, distaste, hatred, nausea,

repugnance, repulsion, revulsion
♦ *verb* 2 **sicken**, displease, nauseate, offend, put off, repel, revolt

disgusted *adjective* sickened, appalled, nauseated, offended, repulsed, scandalized

disgusting *adjective* sickening, foul, gross, loathsome, nauseating, offensive, repellent, repugnant, revolting

dish *noun* 1 **bowl**, plate, platter, salver 2 **food**, fare, recipe

dishearten *verb* discourage, cast down, deject, depress, deter, dismay, dispirit, put a damper on

dishevelled *adjective* untidy, bedraggled, disordered, messy, ruffled, rumpled, tousled, uncombed, unkempt

dishonest *adjective* deceitful, bent (*slang*), cheating, corrupt, crooked (*informal*), disreputable, double-dealing, false, lying, treacherous

dishonesty *noun* deceit, cheating, chicanery, corruption, fraud, treachery, trickery, unscrupulousness

dishonour *verb* 1 **shame**, debase, debauch, defame, degrade, discredit, disgrace, sully
♦ *noun* 2 **shame**, discredit, disgrace, disrepute, ignominy, infamy, obloquy, reproach, scandal 3 **insult**, abuse, affront, discourtesy, indignity, offence, outrage, sacrilege, slight

dishonourable *adjective*
1 **shameful**, contemptible, despicable, discreditable, disgraceful, ignominious, infamous, scandalous
2 untrustworthy, blackguardly,

corrupt, disreputable, shameless, treacherous, unprincipled, unscrupulous

disillusioned *adjective* disenchanted, disabused, disappointed, enlightened, undeceived

disinclination *noun* reluctance, aversion, dislike, hesitance, objection, opposition, repugnance, resistance, unwillingness

disinclined *adjective* reluctant, averse, hesitating, loath, not in the mood, opposed, resistant, unwilling

disinfect *verb* sterilize, clean, cleanse, decontaminate, deodorize, fumigate, purify, sanitize

disinfectant *noun* antiseptic, germicide, sterilizer

disinherit *verb Law* cut off, disown, dispossess, oust, repudiate

disintegrate *verb* break up, break apart, crumble, fall apart, go to pieces, separate, shatter, splinter

disinterest *noun* impartiality, detachment, fairness, neutrality

disinterested *adjective* impartial, detached, dispassionate, even-handed, impersonal, neutral, objective, unbiased, unprejudiced

disjointed *adjective* incoherent, confused, disconnected, disordered, rambling

dislike *verb* 1 be averse to, despise, detest, disapprove, hate, loathe, not be able to bear or abide or stand, object to, take a dim view of ♦ *noun* 2 aversion, animosity, antipathy, disapproval, disinclination, displeasure, distaste, enmity, hostility, repugnance

dislodge *verb* displace, disturb, extricate, force out, knock loose, oust, remove, uproot

disloyal *adjective* treacherous, faithless, false, subversive, traitorous, two-faced, unfaithful, untrustworthy

disloyalty *noun* treachery, breach of trust, deceitfulness, double-dealing, falseness, inconstancy, infidelity, treason, unfaithfulness

dismal *adjective* gloomy, bleak, cheerless, dark, depressing, discouraging, dreary, forlorn, sombre, wretched

dismantle *verb* take apart, demolish, disassemble, strip, take to pieces

dismay *verb* 1 alarm, appal, distress, frighten, horrify, paralyse, scare, terrify, unnerve 2 disappoint, daunt, discourage, dishearten, disillusion, dispirit, put off ♦ *noun* 3 alarm, anxiety, apprehension, consternation, dread, fear, horror, trepidation 4 disappointment, chagrin, discouragement, disillusionment

dismember *verb* cut into pieces, amputate, dissect, mutilate, sever

dismiss *verb* 1 sack (*informal*), axe (*informal*), cashier, discharge, fire (*informal*), give notice to, give (someone) their marching orders, lay off, remove 2 let go, disperse, dissolve, free, release, send away 3 put out of one's mind, banish, discard, dispel,

disregard, lay aside, reject, set aside

dismissal *noun* the sack (*informal*), expulsion, marching orders (*informal*), notice, removal, the boot (*slang*), the push (*slang*)

disobedience *noun* defiance, indiscipline, insubordination, mutiny, noncompliance, nonobservance, recalcitrance, revolt, unruliness, waywardness

disobedient *adjective* defiant, contrary, disorderly, insubordinate, intractable, naughty, refractory, undisciplined, unruly, wayward

disobey *verb* refuse to obey, contravene, defy, disregard, flout, ignore, infringe, rebel, violate

disorder *noun* 1 untidiness, chaos, clutter, confusion, disarray, jumble, mess, muddle, shambles 2 disturbance, commotion, riot, turmoil, unrest, unruliness, uproar 3 illness, affliction, ailment, complaint, disease, malady, sickness

disorderly *adjective* 1 untidy, chaotic, confused, disorganized, higgledy-piggledy (*informal*), jumbled, messy, shambolic (*informal*) 2 unruly, disruptive, indiscipline, lawless, riotous, rowdy, tumultuous, turbulent, ungovernable

disorganized *adjective* muddled, chaotic, confused, disordered, haphazard, jumbled, unsystematic

disown *verb* deny, cast off, disavow, disclaim, reject, renounce, repudiate

disparage verb run down, belittle, denigrate, deprecate, deride, malign, put down, ridicule, slander, vilify

dispassionate adjective
1 unemotional, calm, collected, composed, cool, imperturbable, serene, unruffled **2** objective, detached, disinterested, fair, impartial, impersonal, neutral, unbiased, unprejudiced

dispatch, despatch verb
1 send, consign, dismiss, hasten **2** carry out, discharge, dispose of, finish, perform, settle **3** murder, assassinate, execute, kill, slaughter, slay ♦ noun **4** message, account, bulletin, communication, communiqué, news, report, story

dispel verb drive away, banish, chase away, dismiss, disperse, eliminate, expel

dispense verb **1** distribute, allocate, allot, apportion, assign, deal out, dole out, share **2** prepare, measure, mix, supply **3** administer, apply, carry out, discharge, enforce, execute, implement, operate **4** dispense with a do away with, abolish, brush aside, cancel, dispose of, get rid of **b** do without, abstain from, forgo, give up, relinquish

disperse verb **1** scatter, broadcast, diffuse, disseminate, distribute, spread, strew **2** break up, disband, dissolve, scatter, separate

dispirited adjective disheartened, crestfallen, dejected, depressed, despondent, discouraged, downcast, gloomy, glum, sad

displace verb **1** move, disturb, misplace, shift, transpose **2** replace, oust, succeed, supersede, supplant, take the place of

display verb **1** show, demonstrate, disclose, exhibit, expose, manifest, present, reveal **2** show off, flash (informal), flaunt, flourish, parade, vaunt ♦ noun **3** exhibition, array, demonstration, presentation, revelation, show **4** show, flourish, ostentation, pageant, parade, pomp, spectacle

displease verb annoy, anger, irk, irritate, offend, pique, put out, upset, vex

displeasure noun annoyance, anger, disapproval, dissatisfaction, distaste, indignation, irritation, resentment

disposable adjective
1 throwaway, biodegradable, nonreturnable **2** available, consumable, expendable

disposal noun **1** throwing away, discarding, dumping (informal), ejection, jettisoning, removal, riddance, scrapping **2** at one's disposal available, at one's service, consumable, expendable, free for use

dispose verb arrange, array, distribute, group, marshal, order, place, put

dispose of verb **1** get rid of, destroy, discard, dump (informal), jettison, scrap, throw out or away, unload **2** deal with, decide, determine, end, finish with, settle

disposition noun **1** character, constitution, make-up, nature, spirit, temper, temperament

2 tendency, bent, bias, habit, inclination, leaning, proclivity, propensity **3** arrangement, classification, distribution, grouping, ordering, organization, placement

disproportion noun inequality, asymmetry, discrepancy, disparity, imbalance, lopsidedness, unevenness

disproportionate adjective unequal, excessive, inordinate, out of proportion, unbalanced, uneven, unreasonable

disprove verb prove false, contradict, discredit, expose, give the lie to, invalidate, negate, rebut, refute

dispute noun **1** disagreement, altercation, argument, conflict, feud, quarrel **2** argument, contention, controversy, debate, discussion, dissension ◆ verb **3** doubt, challenge, contest, contradict, deny, impugn, question, rebut **4** argue, clash, cross swords, debate, quarrel, squabble

disqualification noun ban, elimination, exclusion, ineligibility, rejection

disqualified adjective ineligible, debarred, eliminated, knocked out, out of the running

disqualify verb ban, debar, declare ineligible, preclude, prohibit, rule out

disquiet noun **1** uneasiness, alarm, anxiety, concern, disturbance, foreboding, nervousness, trepidation, worry ◆ verb **2** make uneasy, bother, concern, disturb, perturb, trouble, unsettle, upset, worry

disregard verb **1** ignore, brush aside or away, discount, make light of, neglect, overlook, pass over, pay no heed to, turn a blind eye to ◆ noun **2** inattention, contempt, disdain, disrespect, indifference, neglect, negligence, oversight

disrepair noun dilapidation, collapse, decay, deterioration, ruination

disreputable adjective discreditable, dishonourable, ignominious, infamous, louche, notorious, scandalous, shady (informal), shameful

disrepute noun discredit, disgrace, dishonour, ignominy, ill repute, infamy, obloquy, shame, unpopularity

disrespect noun contempt, cheek, impertinence, impoliteness, impudence, insolence, irreverence, lack of respect, rudeness, sauce

disrespectful adjective contemptuous, cheeky, discourteous, impertinent, impolite, impudent, insolent, insulting, irreverent, rude

disrupt verb **1** disturb, confuse, disorder, disorganize, spoil, upset **2** interrupt, break up or into, interfere with, intrude, obstruct, unsettle, upset

disruption noun disturbance, interference, interruption, stoppage

disruptive adjective disturbing, disorderly, distracting, troublesome, unruly, unsettling, upsetting

dissatisfaction noun discontent, annoyance, chagrin,

disappointment, displeasure, frustration, irritation, resentment, unhappiness

dissatisfied adjective discontented, disappointed, disgruntled, displeased, fed up, frustrated, unhappy, unsatisfied

dissect verb 1 cut up or apart, anatomize, dismember, lay open 2 analyse, break down, explore, inspect, investigate, research, scrutinize, study

disseminate verb spread, broadcast, circulate, disperse, distribute, publicize, scatter

dissension noun disagreement, conflict, discord, dispute, dissent, friction, quarrel, row, strife

dissent verb 1 disagree, differ, object, protest, refuse, withhold assent or approval ♦ noun 2 disagreement, discord, dissension, objection, opposition, refusal, resistance

dissenter noun objector, dissident, nonconformist

dissertation noun thesis, critique, discourse, disquisition, essay, exposition, treatise

disservice noun bad turn, harm, injury, injustice, unkindness, wrong

dissident adjective 1 dissenting, disagreeing, discordant, heterodox, nonconformist ♦ noun 2 protester, agitator, dissenter, rebel

dissimilar adjective different, disparate, divergent, diverse, heterogeneous, unlike, unrelated, various

dissipate verb 1 squander,

consume, deplete, expend, fritter away, run through, spend, waste 2 disperse, disappear, dispel, dissolve, drive away, evaporate, scatter, vanish

dissipation noun 1 dispersal, disappearance, disintegration, dissolution, scattering, vanishing 2 debauchery, dissoluteness, excess, extravagance, indulgence, intemperance, prodigality, profligacy, wantonness, waste

dissociate verb 1 break away, break off, part company, quit 2 separate, detach, disconnect, distance, divorce, isolate, segregate, set apart

dissolute adjective immoral, debauched, degenerate, depraved, dissipated, profligate, rakish, wanton, wild

dissolution noun 1 breaking up, disintegration, division, parting, separation 2 adjournment, discontinuation, end, finish, suspension, termination

dissolve verb 1 melt, deliquesce, fuse, liquefy, soften, thaw 2 end, break up, discontinue, suspend, terminate, wind up

dissuade verb deter, advise against, discourage, put off, remonstrate, talk out of, warn

distance noun 1 space, extent, gap, interval, length, range, span, stretch 2 reserve, aloofness, coldness, coolness, remoteness, restraint, stiffness 3 in the distance far off, afar, far away, on the horizon, yonder ♦ verb 4 distance oneself separate oneself, be distanced from, dissociate oneself

distant adjective **1** far-off, abroad, far, faraway, far-flung, outlying, out-of-the-way, remote **2** apart, dispersed, distinct, scattered, separate **3** reserved, aloof, cool, reticent, standoffish, unapproachable, unfriendly, withdrawn

distaste noun dislike, aversion, disgust, horror, loathing, odium, repugnance, revulsion

distasteful adjective unpleasant, disagreeable, objectionable, offensive, repugnant, repulsive, uninviting, unpalatable, unsavoury

distil verb extract, condense, purify, refine

distinct adjective **1** different, detached, discrete, individual, separate, unconnected **2** definite, clear, decided, evident, marked, noticeable, obvious, palpable, unmistakable, well-defined

distinction noun
1 differentiation, discernment, discrimination, perception, separation **2** feature, characteristic, distinctiveness, individuality, mark, particularity, peculiarity, quality **3** difference, contrast, differential, division, separation **4** excellence, eminence, fame, greatness, honour, importance, merit, prominence, repute

distinctive adjective characteristic, idiosyncratic, individual, original, peculiar, singular, special, typical, unique

distinctly adverb definitely, clearly, decidedly, markedly, noticeably, obviously, patently, plainly, unmistakably

distinguish verb **1** differentiate, ascertain, decide, determine, discriminate, judge, tell apart, tell the difference **2** characterize, categorize, classify, mark, separate, set apart, single out **3** make out, discern, know, perceive, pick out, recognize, see, tell

distinguished adjective eminent, acclaimed, celebrated, famed, famous, illustrious, noted, renowned, well-known

distort verb **1** misrepresent, bias, colour, falsify, pervert, slant, twist **2** deform, bend, buckle, contort, disfigure, misshape, twist, warp

distortion noun
1 misrepresentation, bias, falsification, perversion, slant **2** deformity, bend, buckle, contortion, crookedness, malformation, twist, warp

distract verb **1** divert, draw away, sidetrack, turn aside **2** amuse, beguile, engross, entertain, occupy

distracted adjective agitated, at sea, flustered, harassed, in a flap (informal), perplexed, puzzled, troubled

distraction noun **1** diversion, disturbance, interference, interruption **2** entertainment, amusement, diversion, pastime, recreation **3** agitation, bewilderment, commotion, confusion, discord, disorder, disturbance

distraught adjective frantic, agitated, beside oneself, desperate, distracted, distressed, out of one's mind, overwrought, worked-up

distress noun 1 worry, grief, heartache, misery, pain, sorrow, suffering, torment, wretchedness 2 need, adversity, difficulties, hardship, misfortune, poverty, privation, trouble ♦ verb 3 upset, disturb, grieve, harass, sadden, torment, trouble, worry

distressed adjective 1 upset, agitated, distracted, distraught, tormented, troubled, worried, wretched 2 poverty-stricken, destitute, down at heel, indigent, needy, poor, straitened

distressing adjective upsetting, disturbing, harrowing, heart-breaking, painful, sad, worrying

distribute verb 1 hand out, circulate, convey, deliver, pass round 2 share, allocate, allot, apportion, deal, dispense, dole out

distribution noun 1 delivery, dealing, handling, mailing, transportation 2 sharing, allocation, allotment, apportionment, division 3 classification, arrangement, grouping, organization, placement

district noun area, locale, locality, neighbourhood, parish, quarter, region, sector, vicinity

distrust verb 1 suspect, be suspicious of, be wary of, disbelieve, doubt, mistrust, question, smell a rat (informal) ♦ noun 2 suspicion, disbelief, doubt, misgiving, mistrust, question, scepticism, wariness

disturb verb 1 interrupt, bother,

butt in on, disrupt, interfere with, intrude on, pester 2 upset, alarm, distress, fluster, harass, perturb, trouble, unnerve, unsettle, worry 3 muddle, disarrange, disorder

disturbance noun 1 interruption, annoyance, bother, distraction, intrusion 2 disorder, brawl, commotion, fracas, fray, rumpus

disturbed adjective 1 Psychiatry unbalanced, disordered, maladjusted, neurotic, troubled, upset 2 worried, anxious, apprehensive, bothered, concerned, nervous, troubled, uneasy, upset

disturbing adjective worrying, alarming, disconcerting, distressing, frightening, harrowing, startling, unsettling, upsetting

disuse noun neglect, abandonment, decay, idleness

ditch noun 1 channel, drain, dyke, furrow, gully, moat, trench, watercourse ♦ verb 2 Slang get rid of, abandon, discard, dispose of, drop, dump (informal), jettison, scrap, throw out or overboard

dither verb 1 Chiefly Brit. vacillate, faff about (Brit. informal), hesitate, hum and haw, shillyshally (informal), teeter, waver ♦ noun 2 Chiefly Brit. flutter, flap (informal), fluster, tizzy (informal)

dive verb 1 plunge, descend, dip, drop, duck, nose-dive, plummet, swoop ♦ noun 2 plunge, jump, leap, lunge, nose dive, spring

diverge verb 1 separate, branch, divide, fork, part, split, spread

2 underline, depart, digress,
meander, stray, turn aside,
wander

diverse adjective 1 various,
assorted, manifold,
miscellaneous, of every
description, several, sundry,
varied 2 different, discrete,
disparate, dissimilar, distinct,
divergent, separate, unlike,
varying

diversify verb vary, branch out,
change, expand, have a finger in
every pie, spread out

diversion noun 1 Chiefly Brit.
detour, departure, deviation,
digression 2 pastime,
amusement, distraction,
entertainment, game, recreation,
relaxation, sport

diversity noun difference,
distinctiveness, diverseness,
heterogeneity, multiplicity,
range, variety

divert verb 1 redirect, avert,
deflect, switch, turn aside
2 distract, draw or lead away
from, lead astray, sidetrack
3 entertain, amuse, beguile,
delight, gratify, regale

diverting adjective entertaining,
amusing, beguiling, enjoyable,
fun, humorous, pleasant

divide verb 1 separate, bisect, cut
(up), part, partition, segregate,
split 2 share, allocate, allot, deal
out, dispense, distribute 3 cause
to disagree, break up, come
between, estrange, split

dividend noun bonus, cut
(informal), divvy (informal), extra,
gain, plus, portion, share, surplus

divine adjective 1 heavenly,
angelic, celestial, godlike, holy,

spiritual, superhuman,
supernatural 2 sacred,
consecrated, holy, religious,
sanctified, spiritual 3 Informal
wonderful, beautiful, excellent,
glorious, marvellous, perfect,
splendid, superlative ♦ verb
4 infer, apprehend, deduce,
discern, guess, perceive,
suppose, surmise

divinity noun 1 theology,
religion, religious studies 2 god
or goddess, deity, guardian
spirit, spirit 3 godliness, deity,
divine nature, holiness, sanctity

divisible adjective dividable,
separable, splittable

division noun 1 separation,
cutting up, dividing, partition,
splitting up 2 sharing, allotment,
apportionment, distribution
3 part, branch, category, class,
department, group, section
4 disagreement, difference of
opinion, discord, rupture, split,
variance

divorce noun 1 separation,
annulment, dissolution, split-up
♦ verb 2 separate, disconnect,
dissociate, dissolve (marriage),
divide, part, sever, split up

divulge verb make known,
confess, declare, disclose, let slip,
proclaim, reveal, tell

dizzy adjective 1 giddy, faint,
light-headed, off balance,
reeling, shaky, swimming,
wobbly, woozy (informal)
2 confused, at sea, befuddled,
bemused, bewildered, dazed,
dazzled, muddled

do verb 1 perform, accomplish,
achieve, carry out, complete,
execute 2 be adequate, be

sufficient, cut the mustard, pass muster, satisfy, suffice **3** get ready, arrange, fix, look after, prepare, see to **4** solve, decipher, decode, figure out, puzzle out, resolve, work out **5** cause, bring about, create, effect, produce ♦ *noun* **6** *Informal, chiefly Brit. & N.Z.* event, affair, function, gathering, occasion, party

do away with *verb* **1** kill, exterminate, murder, slay **2** get rid of, abolish, discard, discontinue, eliminate, put an end to, put paid to, remove

docile *adjective* submissive, amenable, biddable, compliant, manageable, obedient, pliant

docility *noun* submissiveness, compliance, manageability, meekness, obedience

dock[1] *noun* **1** wharf, harbour, pier, quay, waterfront ♦ *verb* **2** moor, anchor, berth, drop anchor, land, put in, tie up **3** *Of spacecraft* link up, couple, hook up, join, rendezvous, unite

dock[2] *verb* **1** deduct, decrease, diminish, lessen, reduce, subtract, withhold **2** cut off, clip, crop, curtail, cut short, shorten

doctor *noun* **1** G.P., general practitioner, medic (*informal*), medical practitioner, physician ♦ *verb* **2** change, alter, disguise, falsify, misrepresent, pervert, tamper with **3** add to, adulterate, cut, dilute, mix with, spike, water down

doctrinaire *adjective* dogmatic, biased, fanatical, inflexible, insistent, opinionated, rigid

doctrine *noun* teaching, article of

faith, belief, conviction, creed, dogma, opinion, precept, principle, tenet

document *noun* **1** paper, certificate, record, report ♦ *verb* **2** support, authenticate, certify, corroborate, detail, substantiate, validate, verify

dodge *verb* **1** duck, dart, sidestep, swerve, turn aside **2** evade, avoid, elude, get out of, shirk ♦ *noun* **3** trick, device, ploy, ruse, scheme, stratagem, subterfuge, wheeze (*Brit. slang*)

dog *noun* **1** hound, canine, cur, man's best friend, pooch (*slang*) **2** go to the dogs *Informal* go to ruin, degenerate, deteriorate, go down the drain, go to pot ♦ *verb* **3** trouble, follow, haunt, hound, plague, pursue, track, trail

dogged *adjective* determined, indefatigable, obstinate, persistent, resolute, steadfast, stubborn, tenacious, unflagging, unshakable

dogma *noun* doctrine, belief, credo, creed, opinion, teachings

dogmatic *adjective* opinionated, arrogant, assertive, doctrinaire, emphatic, obdurate, overbearing

doldrums *noun* the doldrums inactivity, depression, dumps (*informal*), gloom, listlessness, malaise

dole *noun* **1** *Brit. & Austral. informal* benefit, allowance, gift, grant, handout ♦ *verb* **2** dole out give out, administer, allot, apportion, assign, dispense, distribute, hand out

dollop *noun* lump, helping, portion, scoop, serving

dolt noun idiot, ass, blockhead, chump (informal), clot (Brit. informal), dope (informal), dunce, fool, oaf

domestic adjective 1 home, family, household, private 2 home-loving, domesticated, homely, housewifely, stay-at-home 3 domesticated, house-trained, pet, tame, trained 4 native, indigenous, internal ♦ noun 5 servant, char (informal), charwoman, daily, help, maid

dominant adjective 1 controlling, assertive, authoritative, commanding, governing, ruling, superior, supreme 2 main, chief, predominant, pre-eminent, primary, principal, prominent

dominate verb 1 control, direct, govern, have the whip hand over, monopolize, rule, tyrannize 2 tower above, loom over, overlook, stand head and shoulders above, stand over, survey

domination noun control, ascendancy, authority, command, influence, power, rule, superiority, supremacy

domineering adjective overbearing, arrogant, authoritarian, bossy (informal), dictatorial, high-handed, imperious, oppressive, tyrannical

dominion noun 1 control, authority, command, jurisdiction, power, rule, sovereignty, supremacy 2 kingdom, country, domain, empire, realm, territory

don verb put on, clothe oneself in, dress in, get into, pull on, slip on or into

donate verb give, contribute,

make a gift of, present, subscribe

donation noun contribution, gift, grant, hand-out, offering, present, subscription

donor noun giver, benefactor, contributor, donator, philanthropist

doom noun 1 destruction, catastrophe, downfall, fate, fortune, ruin ♦ verb 2 condemn, consign, damn, destine, sentence

doomed adjective condemned, bewitched, cursed, fated, hopeless, ill-fated, ill-omened, luckless, star-crossed

door noun opening, doorway, entrance, entry, exit

dope noun 1 Slang drug, narcotic, opiate 2 Informal idiot, dimwit (informal), dunce, fool, nitwit (informal), numbskull or numskull, simpleton, twit (informal, chiefly Brit.) ♦ verb 3 drug, anaesthetize, knock out, narcotize, sedate, stupefy

dormant adjective inactive, asleep, hibernating, inert, inoperative, latent, sleeping, slumbering, suspended

dose noun quantity, dosage, draught, measure, portion, potion, prescription

dot noun 1 spot, fleck, jot, mark, point, speck, speckle 2 **on the dot** on time, exactly, on the button (informal), precisely, promptly, punctually, to the minute ♦ verb 3 spot, dab, dabble, fleck, speckle, sprinkle, stipple, stud

dotage noun senility, decrepitude, feebleness, imbecility, old age, second childhood, weakness

dote on or **upon** verb adore, admire, hold dear, idolize, lavish affection on, prize, treasure

doting adjective adoring, devoted, fond, foolish, indulgent, lovesick

double adjective 1 twice, coupled, dual, duplicate, in pairs, paired, twin, twofold ♦ verb 2 multiply, duplicate, enlarge, grow, increase, magnify ♦ noun 3 twin, clone, dead ringer (slang), Doppelgänger, duplicate, lookalike, replica, spitting image (informal) 4 at or on the double quickly, at full speed, briskly, immediately, posthaste, without delay

double-cross verb betray, cheat, defraud, hoodwink, mislead, swindle, trick, two-time (informal)

doubt noun 1 uncertainty, hesitancy, hesitation, indecision, irresolution, lack of conviction, suspense 2 suspicion, apprehension, distrust, misgiving, mistrust, qualm, scepticism ♦ verb 3 be uncertain, be dubious, demur, fluctuate, hesitate, scruple, vacillate, waver 4 suspect, discredit, distrust, fear, lack confidence in, mistrust, query, question

doubtful adjective 1 unlikely, debatable, dubious, equivocal, improbable, problematic(al), questionable, unclear 2 unsure, distrustful, hesitating, in two minds (informal), sceptical, suspicious, tentative, uncertain, unconvinced, wavering

doubtless adverb 1 certainly, assuredly, indisputably, of course, surely, undoubtedly, unquestionably, without doubt 2 probably, apparently, most likely, ostensibly, presumably, seemingly, supposedly

dour adjective gloomy, dismal, dreary, forbidding, grim, morose, sour, sullen, unfriendly

dowdy adjective frumpy, dingy, drab, frowzy, old-fashioned, shabby, unfashionable

do without verb manage without, abstain from, dispense with, forgo, get along without, give up, kick (informal)

down adjective 1 depressed, dejected, disheartened, downcast, low, miserable, sad, unhappy ♦ verb 2 Informal swallow, drain, drink (down), gulp, put away, toss off ♦ noun 3 have a down on Informal be antagonistic or hostile to, bear a grudge towards, be prejudiced against, be set against, have it in for (slang)

down-and-out noun 1 tramp, bag lady, beggar, derelict, dosser (Brit. slang), pauper, vagabond, vagrant ♦ adjective 2 destitute, derelict, impoverished, on one's uppers (informal), penniless, short, without two pennies to rub together (informal)

downcast adjective dejected, crestfallen, depressed, despondent, disappointed, disconsolate, discouraged, disheartened, dismayed, dispirited

downfall noun ruin, collapse, comeuppance (slang), destruction, disgrace, fall, overthrow, undoing

downgrade verb <u>demote</u>, degrade, humble, lower or reduce in rank, take down a peg (informal)

downhearted adjective <u>dejected</u>, crestfallen, depressed, despondent, discouraged, disheartened, dispirited, downcast, sad, unhappy

downpour noun <u>rainstorm</u>, cloudburst, deluge, flood, inundation, torrential rain

downright adjective <u>complete</u>, absolute, out-and-out, outright, plain, thoroughgoing, total, undisguised, unqualified, utter

down-to-earth adjective <u>sensible</u>, matter-of-fact, no-nonsense, plain-spoken, practical, realistic, sane, unsentimental

downtrodden adjective <u>oppressed</u>, exploited, helpless, subjugated, subservient, tyrannized

downward adjective <u>descending</u>, declining, earthward, heading down, sliding, slipping

doze verb 1 <u>nap</u>, kip (Brit. slang), nod off (informal), sleep, slumber, snooze (informal) ♦ noun 2 <u>nap</u>, catnap, forty winks (informal), kip (Brit. slang), shuteye (slang), siesta, snooze (informal)

drab adjective <u>dull</u>, dingy, dismal, dreary, flat, gloomy, shabby, sombre

draft noun 1 <u>outline</u>, abstract, plan, rough, sketch, version 2 <u>order</u>, bill (of exchange), cheque, postal order ♦ verb 3 <u>outline</u>, compose, design, draw, draw up, formulate, plan, sketch

drag verb 1 <u>pull</u>, draw, haul, lug, tow, trail, tug 2 **drag on** or **out** <u>last</u>, draw out, extend, keep going, lengthen, persist, prolong, protract, spin out, stretch out ♦ noun 3 Slang <u>nuisance</u>, annoyance, bore, bother, pain (informal), pest

dragoon verb <u>force</u>, browbeat, bully, coerce, compel, constrain, drive, impel, intimidate, railroad (informal)

drain noun 1 <u>pipe</u>, channel, conduit, culvert, ditch, duct, sewer, sink, trench 2 <u>reduction</u>, depletion, drag, exhaustion, sap, strain, withdrawal ♦ verb 3 <u>remove</u>, bleed, draw off, dry, empty, pump off or out, tap, withdraw 4 <u>flow out</u>, effuse, exude, leak, ooze, seep, trickle, well out 5 <u>drink up</u>, finish, gulp down, quaff, swallow 6 <u>exhaust</u>, consume, deplete, dissipate, empty, sap, strain, use up

drama noun 1 <u>play</u>, dramatization, show, stage show 2 <u>theatre</u>, acting, dramaturgy, stagecraft 3 <u>excitement</u>, crisis, histrionics, scene, spectacle, turmoil

dramatic adjective 1 <u>theatrical</u>, dramaturgical, Thespian 2 <u>powerful</u>, expressive, impressive, moving, striking, vivid 3 <u>exciting</u>, breathtaking, climactic, electrifying, melodramatic, sensational, suspenseful, tense, thrilling

dramatist noun <u>playwright</u>, dramaturge, screenwriter, scriptwriter

dramatize verb <u>exaggerate</u>, lay it on (thick) (slang), overdo, overstate, play to the gallery

drape verb cover, cloak, fold, swathe, wrap

drastic adjective extreme, desperate, dire, forceful, harsh, radical, severe, strong

draught noun 1 breeze, current, flow, movement, puff 2 drink, cup, dose, potion, quantity

draw verb 1 sketch, depict, design, map out, mark out, outline, paint, portray, trace 2 pull, drag, haul, tow, tug 3 take out, extract, pull out 4 attract, allure, elicit, entice, evoke, induce, influence, invite, persuade 5 deduce, derive, infer, make, take ♦ noun 6 Informal attraction, enticement, lure, pull (informal) 7 tie, dead heat, deadlock, impasse, stalemate

drawback noun disadvantage, deficiency, difficulty, downside, flaw, handicap, hitch, snag, stumbling block

drawing noun picture, cartoon, depiction, illustration, outline, portrayal, representation, sketch, study

drawn adjective tense, haggard, pinched, stressed, strained, worn

draw on verb make use of, employ, exploit, extract, fall back on, have recourse to, rely on, take from, use

draw out verb extend, drag out, lengthen, make longer, prolong, protract, spin out, stretch, string out

draw up verb 1 draft, compose, formulate, frame, prepare, write out 2 halt, bring to a stop, pull up, stop

dread verb 1 fear, cringe at, have cold feet (informal), quail, shrink from, shudder, tremble ♦ noun 2 fear, alarm, apprehension, dismay, fright, horror, terror, trepidation

dreadful adjective terrible, abysmal, appalling, atrocious, awful, fearful, frightful, hideous, horrible, shocking

dream noun 1 vision, delusion, hallucination, illusion, imagination, trance 2 daydream, fantasy, pipe dream 3 ambition, aim, aspiration, desire, goal, hope, wish 4 delight, beauty, gem, joy, marvel, pleasure, treasure ♦ verb 5 have dreams, conjure up, envisage, fancy, hallucinate, imagine, think, visualize 6 daydream, build castles in the air or in Spain, fantasize, stargaze

dreamer noun idealist, daydreamer, escapist, fantasist, utopian, visionary, Walter Mitty

dreamy adjective 1 vague, absent, abstracted, daydreaming, faraway, pensive, preoccupied, with one's head in the clouds 2 impractical, airy-fairy, fanciful, imaginary, quixotic, speculative

dreary adjective dull, boring, drab, humdrum, monotonous, tedious, tiresome, uneventful, wearisome

dregs plural noun 1 sediment, deposit, dross, grounds, lees, residue, residuum, scum, waste 2 scum, good-for-nothings, rabble, ragtag and bobtail, riffraff

drench verb soak, drown, flood, inundate, saturate, souse, steep, swamp, wet

dress noun 1 frock, gown, outfit, robe 2 clothing, apparel, attire, clothes, costume, garb, garments, togs ◆ verb 3 put on, attire, change, clothe, don, garb, robe, slip on or into 4 bandage, bind up, plaster, treat 5 arrange, adjust, align, get ready, prepare, straighten

dressmaker noun seamstress, couturier, tailor

dribble verb 1 run, drip, drop, fall in drops, leak, ooze, seep, trickle 2 drool, drivel, slaver, slobber

drift verb 1 float, be carried along, coast, go (aimlessly), meander, stray, waft, wander 2 pile up, accumulate, amass, bank up, drive, gather ◆ noun 3 pile, accumulation, bank, heap, mass, mound 4 meaning, direction, gist, import, intention, purport, significance, tendency, thrust

drifter noun wanderer, beachcomber, bum (informal), hobo (U.S.), itinerant, rolling stone, vagrant

drill noun 1 boring tool, bit, borer, gimlet 2 training, discipline, exercise, instruction, practice, preparation, repetition ◆ verb 3 bore, penetrate, perforate, pierce, puncture, sink in 4 train, coach, discipline, exercise, instruct, practise, rehearse, teach

drink verb 1 swallow, gulp, guzzle, imbibe, quaff, sip, suck, sup 2 booze (informal), hit the bottle (informal), tipple, tope ◆ noun 3 beverage, liquid,

potion, refreshment 4 alcohol, booze (informal), hooch or hootch (informal, chiefly U.S. & Canad.), liquor, spirits, the bottle (informal) 5 glass, cup, draught

drip verb 1 drop, dribble, exude, plop, splash, sprinkle, trickle ◆ noun 2 drop, dribble, leak, trickle 3 Informal weakling, mummy's boy (informal), namby-pamby, softie (informal), weed (informal), wet (Brit. informal)

drive verb 1 operate, direct, guide, handle, manage, motor, ride, steer, travel 2 goad, coerce, constrain, force, press, prod, prompt, spur 3 push, herd, hurl, impel, propel, send, urge 4 push, hammer, ram, thrust ◆ noun 5 run, excursion, jaunt, journey, outing, ride, spin (informal), trip 6 campaign, action, appeal, crusade, effort, push (informal) 7 initiative, ambition, energy, enterprise, get-up-and-go (informal), motivation, vigour, zip (informal)

drivel noun 1 nonsense, garbage (informal), gibberish, hogwash, hot air (informal), poppycock (informal), rubbish, trash, twaddle, waffle (informal, chiefly Brit.) ◆ verb 2 babble, blether, gab (informal), prate, ramble, waffle (informal, chiefly Brit.)

driving adjective 1 forceful, compelling, dynamic, energetic, sweeping, vigorous, violent

drizzle noun 1 fine rain, Scotch mist ◆ verb 2 rain, shower, spot or spit with rain, spray, sprinkle

droll adjective amusing, comical, entertaining, funny, humorous, jocular, waggish, whimsical

drone verb 1 <u>hum</u>, buzz, purr, thrum, vibrate, whirr 2 **drone on** <u>speak monotonously</u>, be boring, chant, intone, spout, talk interminably ♦noun 3 <u>hum</u>, buzz, murmuring, purr, thrum, vibration, whirring

drool verb 1 <u>dribble</u>, drivel, salivate, slaver, slobber, water at the mouth 2 **drool over** <u>gloat over</u>, dote on, gush, make much of, rave about (informal)

droop verb <u>sag</u>, bend, dangle, drop, fall down, hang (down), sink

drop verb 1 <u>fall</u>, decline, descend, diminish, plummet, plunge, sink, tumble 2 <u>drip</u>, dribble, fall in drops, trickle 3 <u>discontinue</u>, axe (informal), give up, kick (informal), quit, relinquish ♦noun 4 <u>droplet</u>, bead, bubble, drip, globule, pearl, tear 5 <u>dash</u>, mouthful, shot (informal), sip, spot, tot, trace, trickle 6 <u>decrease</u>, cut, decline, deterioration, downturn, fall-off, lowering, reduction, slump 7 <u>fall</u>, descent, plunge

drop off verb 1 <u>set down</u>, deliver, leave, let off 2 Informal <u>fall asleep</u>, doze (off), have forty winks (informal), nod (off), snooze (informal) 3 <u>decrease</u>, decline, diminish, dwindle, fall off, lessen, slacken

drop out verb <u>leave</u>, abandon, fall by the wayside, give up, quit, stop, withdraw

drought noun <u>dry spell</u>, aridity, dehydration, dryness

drove noun <u>herd</u>, collection, company, crowd, flock, horde,

mob, multitude, swarm, throng

drown verb 1 <u>drench</u>, deluge, engulf, flood, go under, immerse, inundate, sink, submerge, swamp 2 <u>overpower</u>, deaden, muffle, obliterate, overcome, overwhelm, stifle, swallow up, wipe out

drowsy adjective <u>sleepy</u>, dopey (slang), dozy, half asleep, heavy, lethargic, somnolent, tired, torpid

drudge noun <u>menial</u>, dogsbody (informal), factotum, servant, skivvy (chiefly Brit.), slave, toiler, worker

drudgery noun <u>menial labour</u>, donkey-work, fag (informal), grind (informal), hard work, labour, skivvying (Brit.), slog, toil

drug noun 1 <u>medication</u>, medicament, medicine, physic, poison, remedy 2 <u>dope</u> (slang), narcotic, opiate, stimulant ♦verb 3 <u>dose</u>, administer a drug, dope (slang), medicate, treat 4 <u>knock out</u>, anaesthetize, deaden, numb, poison, stupefy

drum verb 1 <u>beat</u>, pulsate, rap, reverberate, tap, tattoo, throb 2 **drum into** <u>drive home</u>, din into, hammer away, harp on, instil into, reiterate

drunk adjective 1 <u>intoxicated</u>, drunken, inebriated, legless (informal), merry (Brit. informal), plastered (slang), tipsy, under the influence (informal) ♦noun 2 <u>drunkard</u>, alcoholic, boozer (informal), inebriate, lush (slang), wino (informal)

drunkard noun <u>drinker</u>, alcoholic, dipsomaniac, drunk, lush (slang), tippler, wino (informal)

drunkenness noun <u>intoxication</u>,

alcoholism, bibulousness,
dipsomania, inebriation,
insobriety, intemperance

dry *adjective* **1** <u>dehydrated</u>, arid,
barren, desiccated, dried up,
parched, thirsty **2** <u>dull</u>, boring,
dreary, monotonous, plain,
tedious, tiresome, uninteresting
3 <u>sarcastic</u>, deadpan, droll,
low-key, sly ♦ *verb* **4** <u>dehydrate</u>,
dehumidify, desiccate, drain,
make dry, parch, sear

dry out *or* **up** *verb* <u>become dry</u>,
harden, shrivel up, wilt, wither,
wizen

dual *adjective* <u>twofold</u>, binary,
double, duplex, duplicate,
matched, paired, twin

dubious *adjective* **1** <u>suspect</u>, fishy
(*informal*), questionable,
suspicious, unreliable,
untrustworthy **2** <u>unsure</u>,
doubtful, hesitant, sceptical,
uncertain, unconvinced,
undecided, wavering

duck *verb* **1** <u>bob</u>, bend, bow,
crouch, dodge, drop, lower,
stoop **2** <u>plunge</u>, dip, dive,
douse, dunk, immerse, souse,
submerge, wet **3** *Informal* <u>dodge</u>,
avoid, escape, evade, shirk,
shun, sidestep

dud *Informal* ♦ *noun* **1** <u>failure</u>, flop
(*informal*), washout (*informal*)
♦ *adjective* **2** <u>useless</u>, broken, duff
(*Brit. informal*), failed, inoperative,
worthless

dudgeon *noun* **in high dudgeon**
<u>indignant</u>, angry, choked,
fuming, offended, resentful,
vexed

due *adjective* **1** <u>expected</u>,
scheduled **2** <u>payable</u>, in arrears,
outstanding, owed, owing,

unpaid **3** <u>fitting</u>, appropriate,
deserved, justified, merited,
proper, rightful, suitable,
well-earned ♦ *noun* **4** <u>right(s)</u>,
comeuppance (*slang*), deserts,
merits, privilege ♦ *adverb*
5 <u>directly</u>, dead, exactly,
straight, undeviatingly

duel *noun* **1** <u>single combat</u>, affair
of honour **2** <u>contest</u>, clash,
competition, encounter,
engagement, fight,
head-to-head, rivalry ♦ *verb*
3 <u>fight</u>, clash, compete,
contend, contest, lock horns,
rival, struggle, vie with

dues *plural noun* <u>membership fee</u>,
charge, charges, contribution,
fee, levy

dull *adjective* **1** <u>boring</u>, dreary,
flat, humdrum, monotonous,
plain, run-of-the-mill, tedious,
uninteresting **2** <u>stupid</u>, dense,
dim-witted (*informal*), dozy (*Brit.
informal*), slow, thick,
unintelligent **3** <u>cloudy</u>, dim,
dismal, gloomy, leaden, overcast
4 <u>lifeless</u>, apathetic, blank,
indifferent, listless, passionless,
unresponsive **5** <u>blunt</u>, blunted,
unsharpened ♦ *verb* **6** <u>relieve</u>,
allay, alleviate, blunt, lessen,
moderate, soften, take the edge
off

duly *adverb* **1** <u>properly</u>,
accordingly, appropriately,
befittingly, correctly, decorously,
deservedly, fittingly, rightfully,
suitably **2** <u>on time</u>, at the proper
time, punctually

dumb *adjective* **1** <u>mute</u>, mum,
silent, soundless, speechless,
tongue-tied, voiceless, wordless
2 *Informal* <u>stupid</u>, asinine, dense,

dim-witted (*informal*), dull, foolish, thick, unintelligent

dumbfounded *adjective* amazed, astonished, astounded, flabbergasted (*informal*), lost for words, nonplussed, overwhelmed, speechless, staggered, stunned

dummy *noun* 1 model, figure, form, manikin, mannequin 2 copy, counterfeit, duplicate, imitation, sham, substitute 3 *Slang* fool, blockhead, dunce, idiot, nitwit (*informal*), numbskull or numskull, oaf, simpleton ♦ *adjective* 4 imitation, artificial, bogus, fake, false, mock, phoney or phony (*informal*), sham, simulated

dump *verb* 1 drop, deposit, fling down, let fall, throw down 2 get rid of, dispose of, ditch (*slang*), empty out, jettison, scrap, throw away or out, tip, unload ♦ *noun* 3 rubbish tip, junkyard, refuse heap, rubbish heap, tip 4 *Informal* pigsty, hole (*informal*), hovel, mess, slum

dunce *noun* simpleton, blockhead, duffer (*informal*), dunderhead, ignoramus, moron, nincompoop, numbskull or numskull, thickhead

dungeon *noun* prison, cage, cell, oubliette, vault

duplicate *adjective* 1 identical, corresponding, matched, matching, twin, twofold ♦ *noun* 2 copy, carbon copy, clone, double, facsimile, photocopy, replica, reproduction ♦ *verb* 3 copy, clone, double, repeat, replicate, reproduce

durability *noun* durableness,

constancy, endurance, imperishability, permanence, persistence

durable *adjective* long-lasting, dependable, enduring, hard-wearing, persistent, reliable, resistant, strong, sturdy, tough

duration *noun* length, extent, period, span, spell, stretch, term, time

duress *noun* pressure, coercion, compulsion, constraint, threat

dusk *noun* twilight, dark, evening, eventide, gloaming (*Scot. or poetic*), nightfall, sundown, sunset

dusky *adjective* 1 dark, dark-complexioned, sable, swarthy 2 dim, cloudy, gloomy, murky, obscure, shadowy, shady, tenebrous, twilit

dust *noun* 1 grime, grit, particles, powder ♦ *verb* 2 sprinkle, cover, dredge, powder, scatter, sift, spray, spread

dusty *adjective* dirty, grubby, sooty, unclean, unswept

dutiful *adjective* conscientious, devoted, obedient, respectful, reverential, submissive

duty *noun* 1 responsibility, assignment, function, job, obligation, role, task, work 2 loyalty, allegiance, deference, obedience, respect, reverence 3 tax, excise, levy, tariff, toll 4 on duty at work, busy, engaged, on active service

dwarf *verb* 1 tower above or over, diminish, dominate, overshadow ♦ *adjective* 2 miniature, baby, bonsai, diminutive, small, tiny, undersized ♦ noun 3 midget, Lilliputian, pygmy or pigmy, Tom Thumb

dwell verb Formal, literary live, abide, inhabit, lodge, reside

dwelling noun Formal, literary home, abode, domicile, habitation, house, lodging, quarters, residence

dwindle verb lessen, decline, decrease, die away, diminish, fade, peter out, shrink, subside, taper off, wane

dye noun 1 colouring, colorant, colour, pigment, stain, tinge, tint ♦ verb 2 colour, pigment, stain, tinge, tint

dying adjective expiring, at death's door, failing, in extremis, moribund, not long for this world

dynamic adjective energetic, forceful, go-ahead, go-getting (informal), high-powered, lively, powerful, vital

dynasty noun empire, government, house, regime, rule, sovereignty

E e

each adjective 1 every ♦ pronoun 2 every one, each and every one, each one, one and all ♦ adverb 3 apiece, for each, individually, per capita, per head, per person, respectively, to each

eager adjective keen, agog, anxious, athirst, avid, enthusiastic, fervent, hungry, impatient, longing

eagerness noun keenness, ardour, enthusiasm, fervour, hunger, impatience, thirst, yearning, zeal

ear noun sensitivity, appreciation, discrimination, taste

early adjective 1 premature, advanced, forward, untimely 2 primitive, primeval, primordial, undeveloped, young ♦ adverb 3 too soon, ahead of time, beforehand, in advance, in good time, prematurely

earmark verb set aside, allocate, designate, flag, label, mark out, reserve

earn verb 1 make, bring in, collect, gain, get, gross, net, receive 2 deserve, acquire, attain, be entitled to, be worthy of, merit, rate, warrant, win

earnest adjective 1 serious, grave, intent, resolute, resolved, sincere, solemn, thoughtful ♦ noun 2 As in in earnest seriousness, sincerity, truth

earnings plural noun income, pay, proceeds, profits, receipts, remuneration, salary, takings, wages

earth noun 1 world, globe, orb, planet, sphere 2 soil, clay, dirt, ground, land, turf

earthenware noun crockery, ceramics, pots, pottery, terracotta

earthly adjective 1 worldly, human, material, mortal, secular, temporal 2 Informal possible, conceivable, feasible, imaginable, likely, practical

earthy adjective crude, bawdy, coarse, raunchy (slang), ribald, robust, uninhibited, unsophisticated

ease noun 1 easiness, effortlessness, facility, readiness, simplicity 2 content, comfort, happiness, peace, peace of mind, quiet, serenity, tranquillity 3 rest, leisure, relaxation, repose, restfulness ◆ verb 4 relieve, alleviate, calm, comfort, lessen, lighten, relax, soothe 5 move carefully, edge, inch, manoeuvre, slide, slip

easily adverb without difficulty, comfortably, effortlessly, readily, smoothly, with ease, with one hand tied behind one's back

easy adjective 1 not difficult, a piece of cake (informal), child's play (informal), effortless, no trouble, painless, plain sailing, simple, straightforward, uncomplicated, undemanding 2 carefree, comfortable, cushy (informal), leisurely, peaceful, quiet, relaxed, serene, tranquil, untroubled 3 tolerant, easy-going, indulgent, lenient, mild, permissive, unoppressive

easy-going adjective relaxed, carefree, casual, easy, even-tempered, happy-go-lucky, laid-back (informal), nonchalant, placid, tolerant, undemanding

eat verb 1 consume, chew, devour, gobble, ingest, munch, scoff (slang), swallow 2 have a meal, dine, feed, take nourishment 3 destroy, corrode, decay, dissolve, erode, rot, waste away, wear away

eavesdrop verb listen in, earwig (informal), monitor, overhear, snoop (informal), spy

ebb verb 1 flow back, go out, recede, retire, retreat, subside,

wane, withdraw 2 decline, decrease, diminish, dwindle, fade away, fall away, flag, lessen, peter out ◆ noun 3 flowing back, going out, low tide, low water, retreat, subsidence, wane, withdrawal

eccentric adjective 1 odd, freakish, idiosyncratic, irregular, outlandish, peculiar, quirky, strange, unconventional ◆ noun 2 crank (informal), character (informal), nonconformist, oddball (informal), weirdo or weirdie (informal)

eccentricity noun oddity, abnormality, caprice, capriciousness, foible, idiosyncrasy, irregularity, peculiarity, quirk

ecclesiastic noun 1 clergyman, churchman, cleric, holy man, man of the cloth, minister, parson, pastor, priest ◆ adjective 2 Also **ecclesiastical** clerical, divine, holy, pastoral, priestly, religious, spiritual

echo noun 1 repetition, answer, reverberation 2 copy, imitation, mirror image, parallel, reflection, reiteration, reproduction ◆ verb 3 repeat, resound, reverberate 4 copy, ape, imitate, mirror, parallel, recall, reflect, resemble

eclipse noun 1 obscuring, darkening, dimming, extinction, shading ◆ verb 2 surpass, exceed, excel, outdo, outshine, put in the shade (informal), transcend

economic adjective 1 financial, commercial, industrial 2 profitable, money-making, productive, profit-making, remunerative, viable 3 Informal

Also **economical** inexpensive, cheap, low-priced, modest, reasonable

economical adjective **1** thrifty, careful, frugal, prudent, scrimping, sparing **2** cost-effective, efficient, money-saving, sparing, time-saving

economize verb cut back, be economical, be frugal, draw in one's horns, retrench, save, scrimp, tighten one's belt

economy noun thrift, frugality, husbandry, parsimony, prudence, restraint

ecstasy noun rapture, bliss, delight, elation, euphoria, fervour, joy, seventh heaven

ecstatic adjective rapturous, blissful, elated, enraptured, entranced, euphoric, in seventh heaven, joyous, on cloud nine (informal), overjoyed

eddy noun **1** swirl, counter-current, counterflow, undertow, vortex, whirlpool ♦ verb **2** swirl, whirl

edge noun **1** border, boundary, brink, fringe, limit, outline, perimeter, rim, side, verge **2** sharpness, bite, effectiveness, force, incisiveness, keenness, point **3** As in have the edge on advantage, ascendancy, dominance, lead, superiority, upper hand **4** on edge nervous, apprehensive, edgy, ill at ease, impatient, irritable, keyed up, on tenterhooks, tense ♦ verb **5** border, fringe, hem **6** inch, creep, ease, sidle, steal

edgy adjective nervous, anxious, ill at ease, irritable, keyed up, on edge, on tenterhooks, restive, tense

edible adjective eatable, digestible, fit to eat, good, harmless, palatable, wholesome

edict noun decree, act, command, injunction, law, order, proclamation, ruling

edifice noun building, construction, erection, house, structure

edify verb instruct, educate, enlighten, guide, improve, inform, nurture, school, teach

edit verb revise, adapt, condense, correct, emend, polish, rewrite

edition noun version, copy, impression, issue, number, printing, programme (TV, Radio), volume

educate verb teach, civilize, develop, discipline, enlighten, improve, inform, instruct, school, train, tutor

educated adjective **1** taught, coached, informed, instructed, nurtured, schooled, tutored **2** cultured, civilized, cultivated, enlightened, knowledgeable, learned, refined, sophisticated

education noun teaching, development, discipline, enlightenment, instruction, nurture, schooling, training, tuition

educational adjective instructive, cultural, edifying, educative, enlightening, improving, informative

eerie adjective frightening, creepy (informal), ghostly, mysterious, scary (informal), spooky (informal), strange, uncanny, unearthly, weird

efface verb obliterate, blot out, cancel, delete, destroy, eradicate, erase, rub out, wipe out

effect noun 1 result, conclusion, consequence, end result, event, outcome, upshot 2 operation, action, enforcement, execution, force, implementation 3 impression, essence, impact, sense, significance, tenor ♦ verb 4 bring about, accomplish, achieve, complete, execute, fulfil, perform, produce

effective adjective 1 efficient, active, adequate, capable, competent, productive, serviceable, useful 2 in operation, active, current, in effect, in force, operative 3 powerful, cogent, compelling, convincing, forceful, impressive, persuasive, telling

effects plural noun belongings, gear, goods, paraphernalia, possessions, property, things

effeminate adjective womanly, camp (informal), feminine, sissy, soft, tender, unmanly, weak, womanish

effervescent adjective 1 bubbling, carbonated, fizzy, foaming, frothy, sparkling 2 lively, animated, bubbly, ebullient, enthusiastic, exuberant, irrepressible, vivacious

effete adjective decadent, dissipated, enfeebled, feeble, ineffectual, spoiled, weak

efficacious adjective effective, adequate, efficient, operative, potent, powerful, productive, successful, useful

efficiency noun competence, adeptness, capability, economy, effectiveness, power, productivity, proficiency

efficient adjective competent, businesslike, capable, economic, effective, organized, productive, proficient, well-organized, workmanlike

effigy noun likeness, dummy, figure, guy, icon, idol, image, picture, portrait, representation, statue

effluent noun waste, effluvium, pollutant, sewage

effort noun 1 exertion, application, elbow grease (facetious), endeavour, energy, pains, struggle, toil, trouble, work 2 attempt, endeavour, essay, go (informal), shot (informal), stab (informal), try

effortless adjective easy, painless, plain sailing, simple, smooth, uncomplicated, undemanding

effrontery noun insolence, arrogance, audacity, brazenness, cheek (informal), impertinence, impudence, nerve, presumption, temerity

effusive adjective demonstrative, ebullient, expansive, exuberant, gushing, lavish, unreserved, unrestrained

egg on verb encourage, exhort, goad, incite, prod, prompt, push, spur, urge

egocentric adjective self-centred, egoistic, egoistical, egotistic, egotistical, selfish

egotism, egoism noun self-centredness, conceitedness, narcissism, self-absorption,

egotist self-esteem, self-importance, self-interest, selfishness, vanity

egotist, egoist noun egomaniac, bighead (informal), boaster, braggart, narcissist

egotistic, egotistical, egoistic or egoistical adjective self-centred, boasting, conceited, egocentric, full of oneself, narcissistic, self-absorbed, self-important, vain

egress noun Formal exit, departure, exodus, way out, withdrawal

eject verb throw out, banish, drive out, evict, expel, oust, remove, turn out

ejection noun expulsion, banishment, deportation, eviction, exile, removal

eke out verb be sparing with, economize on, husband, stretch out

elaborate adjective 1 detailed, intricate, minute, painstaking, precise, studied, thorough 2 complicated, complex, fancy, fussy, involved, ornamented, ornate ♦ verb 3 expand (upon), add detail, amplify, develop, embellish, enlarge, flesh out

elapse verb pass, glide by, go by, lapse, roll by, slip away

elastic adjective 1 stretchy, plastic, pliable, pliant, resilient, rubbery, springy, supple, tensile 2 adaptable, accommodating, adjustable, compliant, flexible, supple, tolerant, variable, yielding

elated adjective joyful, cock-a-hoop, delighted, ecstatic, euphoric, exhilarated, gleeful, jubilant, overjoyed

elation noun joy, bliss, delight, ecstasy, euphoria, exhilaration, glee, high spirits, jubilation, rapture

elbow noun 1 joint, angle ♦ verb 2 push, jostle, knock, nudge, shove

elbow room noun scope, freedom, latitude, leeway, play, room, space

elder adjective 1 older, first-born, senior ♦ noun 2 older person, senior

elect verb choose, appoint, determine, opt for, pick, prefer, select, settle on, vote

election noun voting, appointment, choice, judgment, preference, selection, vote

elector noun voter, constituent, selector

electric adjective charged, dynamic, exciting, rousing, stimulating, stirring, tense, thrilling

electrify verb startle, astound, excite, galvanize, invigorate, jolt, shock, stir, thrill

elegance noun style, dignity, exquisiteness, grace, gracefulness, grandeur, luxury, refinement, taste

elegant adjective stylish, chic, delicate, exquisite, fine, graceful, handsome, polished, refined, tasteful

element noun 1 component, constituent, factor, ingredient, part, section, subdivision, unit 2 As in in one's element environment, domain, field, habitat, medium, milieu, sphere

elementary adjective simple,

clear, easy, plain, rudimentary, straightforward, uncomplicated

elements plural noun **1** <u>basics</u>, essentials, foundations, fundamentals, nuts and bolts (informal), principles, rudiments **2** <u>weather conditions</u>, atmospheric conditions, powers of nature

elevate verb **1** <u>raise</u>, heighten, hoist, lift, lift up, uplift **2** <u>promote</u>, advance, aggrandize, exalt, prefer, upgrade

elevated adjective <u>high-minded</u>, dignified, exalted, grand, high-flown, inflated, lofty, noble, sublime

elevation noun **1** <u>promotion</u>, advancement, aggrandizement, exaltation, preferment, upgrading **2** <u>altitude</u>, height

elicit verb **1** <u>bring about</u>, bring forth, bring to light, call forth, cause, derive, evolve, give rise to **2** <u>obtain</u>, draw out, evoke, exact, extort, extract, wrest

eligible adjective <u>qualified</u>, acceptable, appropriate, desirable, fit, preferable, proper, suitable, worthy

eliminate verb <u>get rid of</u>, cut out, dispose of, do away with, eradicate, exterminate, remove, stamp out, take out

elite noun <u>best</u>, aristocracy, cream, crème de la crème, flower, nobility, pick, upper class

elitist adjective <u>snobbish</u>, exclusive, selective

elixir noun <u>panacea</u>, nostrum

elocution noun <u>diction</u>, articulation, declamation, delivery, enunciation, oratory, pronunciation, speech, speechmaking

elongate verb <u>make longer</u>, draw out, extend, lengthen, prolong, protract, stretch

elope verb <u>run away</u>, abscond, bolt, decamp, disappear, escape, leave, run off, slip away, steal away

eloquence noun <u>expressiveness</u>, expression, fluency, forcefulness, oratory, persuasiveness, rhetoric, way with words

eloquent adjective **1** <u>silver-tongued</u>, articulate, fluent, forceful, moving, persuasive, stirring, well-expressed **2** <u>expressive</u>, meaningful, suggestive, telling, vivid

elsewhere adverb <u>in or to another place</u>, abroad, away, hence (archaic), not here, somewhere else

elucidate verb <u>clarify</u>, clear up, explain, explicate, expound, illuminate, illustrate, make plain, shed or throw light upon, spell out

elude verb **1** <u>escape</u>, avoid, dodge, duck (informal), evade, flee, get away from, outrun **2** <u>baffle</u>, be beyond (someone), confound, escape, foil, frustrate, puzzle, stump, thwart

elusive adjective **1** <u>difficult to catch</u>, shifty, slippery, tricky **2** <u>indefinable</u>, fleeting, intangible, subtle, transient, transitory

emaciated adjective <u>skeletal</u>, cadaverous, gaunt, haggard, lean, pinched, scrawny, thin, undernourished, wasted

emanate verb flow, arise, come forth, derive, emerge, issue, originate, proceed, spring, stem

emancipate verb free, deliver, liberate, release, set free, unchain, unfetter

emancipation noun freedom, deliverance, liberation, liberty, release

embalm verb preserve, mummify

embargo noun 1 ban, bar, boycott, interdiction, prohibition, restraint, restriction, stoppage ♦ verb 2 ban, bar, block, boycott, prohibit, restrict, stop

embark verb 1 go aboard, board ship, take ship 2 embark on or upon begin, commence, enter, launch, plunge into, set about, set out, start, take up

embarrass verb shame, discomfit, disconcert, distress, fluster, humiliate, mortify, show up (informal)

embarrassed adjective ashamed, awkward, blushing, discomfited, disconcerted, humiliated, mortified, red-faced, self-conscious, sheepish

embarrassing adjective humiliating, awkward, compromising, discomfiting, disconcerting, mortifying, sensitive, shameful, toe-curling (informal), uncomfortable

embarrassment noun 1 shame, awkwardness, bashfulness, distress, humiliation, mortification, self-consciousness, showing up (informal) 2 predicament, bind (informal),

difficulty, mess, pickle (informal), scrape (informal)

embellish verb decorate, adorn, beautify, elaborate, embroider, enhance, enrich, festoon, ornament

embellishment noun decoration, adornment, elaboration, embroidery, enhancement, enrichment, exaggeration, ornament, ornamentation

embezzle verb misappropriate, appropriate, filch, misuse, peculate, pilfer, purloin, rip off (slang), steal

embezzlement noun misappropriation, appropriation, filching, fraud, misuse, peculation, pilfering, stealing, theft

embittered adjective resentful, angry, bitter, disaffected, disillusioned, rancorous, soured, with a chip on one's shoulder (informal)

emblem noun symbol, badge, crest, image, insignia, mark, sign, token

embodiment noun personification, epitome, example, exemplar, expression, incarnation, representation, symbol

embody verb 1 personify, exemplify, manifest, represent, stand for, symbolize, typify 2 incorporate, collect, combine, comprise, contain, include

embolden verb encourage, fire, inflame, invigorate, rouse, stimulate, stir, strengthen

embrace verb 1 hug, clasp,

cuddle, envelop, hold, seize, squeeze, take *or* hold in one's arms **2** accept, adopt, espouse, seize, take on board, take up, welcome **3** include, comprehend, comprise, contain, cover, encompass, involve, take in ♦ *noun* **4** hug, clasp, clinch (*slang*), cuddle, squeeze

embroil *verb* involve, enmesh, ensnare, entangle, implicate, incriminate, mire, mix up

embryo *noun* germ, beginning, nucleus, root, rudiment

emend *verb* revise, amend, correct, edit, improve, rectify

emendation *noun* revision, amendment, correction, editing, improvement, rectification

emerge *verb* **1** come into view, appear, arise, come forth, emanate, issue, rise, spring up, surface **2** become apparent, become known, come out, come out in the wash, come to light, crop up, transpire

emergence *noun* coming, advent, appearance, arrival, development, materialization, rise

emergency *noun* crisis, danger, difficulty, extremity, necessity, plight, predicament, quandary, scrape (*informal*)

emigrate *verb* move abroad, migrate, move

emigration *noun* departure, exodus, migration

eminence *noun* prominence, distinction, esteem, fame, greatness, importance, note, prestige, renown, repute

eminent *adjective* prominent, celebrated, distinguished,

esteemed, famous, high-ranking, illustrious, noted, renowned, well-known

emission *noun* giving off *or* out, discharge, ejaculation, ejection, exhalation, radiation, shedding, transmission

emit *verb* give off, cast out, discharge, eject, emanate, exude, radiate, send out, transmit

emotion *noun* feeling, ardour, excitement, fervour, passion, sensation, sentiment, vehemence, warmth

emotional *adjective* **1** sensitive, demonstrative, excitable, hot-blooded, passionate, sentimental, temperamental **2** moving, affecting, emotive, heart-warming, poignant, sentimental, stirring, touching

emotive *adjective* sensitive, controversial, delicate, touchy

emphasis *noun* stress, accent, attention, force, importance, priority, prominence, significance, weight

emphasize *verb* stress, accentuate, dwell on, give priority to, highlight, lay stress on, play up, press home, underline

emphatic *adjective* forceful, categorical, definite, insistent, positive, pronounced, resounding, unequivocal, unmistakable, vigorous

empire *noun* kingdom, commonwealth, domain, realm

empirical, empiric *adjective* first-hand, experiential, experimental, observed, practical, pragmatic

employ verb **1** hire, commission, engage, enlist, retain, take on **2** keep busy, engage, fill, make use of, occupy, take up, use up **3** use, apply, bring to bear, exercise, exert, make use of, ply, put to use, utilize ♦ noun **4** As in in the employ of service, employment, engagement, hire

employed adjective working, active, busy, engaged, in a job, in employment, in work, occupied

employee noun worker, hand, job-holder, staff member, wage-earner, workman

employer noun boss (informal), company, firm, gaffer (informal, chiefly Brit.), owner, patron, proprietor

employment noun **1** taking on, engagement, enlistment, hire, retaining **2** use, application, exercise, exertion, utilization **3** job, line, occupation, profession, trade, vocation, work

emporium noun Old-fashioned shop, bazaar, market, mart, store, warehouse

empower verb enable, allow, authorize, commission, delegate, entitle, license, permit, qualify, sanction, warrant

emptiness noun **1** bareness, blankness, desolation, vacancy, vacuum, void, waste **2** purposelessness, banality, futility, hollowness, inanity, meaninglessness, senselessness, vanity, worthlessness **3** insincerity, cheapness, hollowness, idleness

empty adjective **1** bare, blank, clear, deserted, desolate, hollow, unfurnished, uninhabited, unoccupied, vacant, void **2** purposeless, banal, fruitless, futile, hollow, inane, meaningless, senseless, vain, worthless **3** insincere, cheap, hollow, idle ♦ verb **4** As in evacuate, clear, drain, exhaust, pour out, unload, vacate, void

empty-headed adjective scatterbrained, brainless, dizzy (informal), featherbrained, harebrained, silly, vacuous

emulate verb imitate, compete with, copy, echo, follow, mimic, rival

enable verb allow, authorize, empower, entitle, license, permit, qualify, sanction, warrant

enact verb **1** establish, authorize, command, decree, legislate, ordain, order, proclaim, sanction **2** perform, act out, depict, play, play the part of, portray, represent

enamoured adjective in love, captivated, charmed, enraptured, fond, infatuated, smitten, taken

encampment noun camp, base, bivouac, camping ground, campsite, cantonment, quarters, tents

encapsulate verb sum up, abridge, compress, condense, digest, epitomize, précis, summarize

enchant verb fascinate, beguile, bewitch, captivate, charm, delight, enrapture, enthral, ravish

enchanter noun sorcerer, conjuror, magician, magus, necromancer, warlock, witch, wizard

enchanting adjective <u>fascinating</u>, alluring, attractive, bewitching, captivating, charming, delightful, entrancing, lovely, pleasant

enclose verb 1 <u>surround</u>, bound, encase, encircle, fence, hem in, shut in, wall in 2 <u>send with</u>, include, insert, put in

encompass verb 1 <u>surround</u>, circle, encircle, enclose, envelop, ring 2 <u>include</u>, admit, comprise, contain, cover, embrace, hold, incorporate, take in

encounter verb 1 <u>meet</u>, bump into (informal), chance upon, come upon, confront, experience, face, run across ♦ noun 2 <u>meeting</u>, brush, confrontation, rendezvous 3 <u>battle</u>, clash, conflict, contest, head-to-head, run-in (informal)

encourage verb 1 <u>inspire</u>, buoy up, cheer, comfort, console, embolden, hearten, reassure 2 <u>spur</u>, advocate, egg on, foster, promote, prompt, support, urge

encouragement noun <u>inspiration</u>, cheer, incitement, promotion, reassurance, stimulation, stimulus, support

encouraging adjective <u>promising</u>, bright, cheerful, comforting, good, heartening, hopeful, reassuring, rosy

encroach verb <u>intrude</u>, impinge, infringe, invade, make inroads, overstep, trespass, usurp

encumber verb <u>burden</u>, hamper, handicap, hinder, impede, inconvenience, obstruct, saddle, weigh down

end noun 1 <u>extremity</u>, boundary, edge, extent, extreme, limit, point, terminus, tip 2 <u>finish</u>,

cessation, close, closure, ending, expiration, expiry, stop, termination 3 <u>conclusion</u>, culmination, denouement, ending, finale, resolution 4 <u>remnant</u>, butt, fragment, leftover, oddment, remainder, scrap, stub 5 <u>destruction</u>, death, demise, doom, extermination, extinction, ruin 6 <u>purpose</u>, aim, goal, intention, object, objective, point, reason ♦ verb 7 <u>finish</u>, cease, close, conclude, culminate, stop, terminate, wind up

endanger verb <u>put at risk</u>, compromise, imperil, jeopardize, put in danger, risk, threaten

endearing adjective <u>attractive</u>, captivating, charming, cute, engaging, lovable, sweet, winning

endearment noun <u>loving word</u>, sweet nothing

endeavour Formal ♦ verb 1 <u>try</u>, aim, aspire, attempt, labour, make an effort, strive, struggle, take pains ♦ noun 2 <u>effort</u>, attempt, enterprise, trial, try, undertaking, venture

ending noun <u>finish</u>, cessation, close, completion, conclusion, culmination, denouement, end, finale

endless adjective <u>eternal</u>, boundless, continual, everlasting, incessant, infinite, interminable, unlimited

endorse verb 1 <u>approve</u>, advocate, authorize, back, champion, promote, ratify, recommend, support 2 <u>sign</u>, countersign

endorsement noun 1 <u>approval</u>,

advocacy, approbation, authorization, backing, favour, ratification, recommendation, seal of approval, support **2** signature, countersignature

endow verb provide, award, bequeath, bestow, confer, donate, finance, fund, give

endowment noun provision, award, benefaction, bequest, donation, gift, grant, legacy

endurable adjective bearable, acceptable, sufferable, sustainable, tolerable

endurance noun **1** staying power, fortitude, patience, perseverance, persistence, resolution, stamina, strength, tenacity, toleration **2** permanence, continuity, durability, duration, longevity, stability

endure verb **1** bear, cope with, experience, stand, suffer, sustain, undergo, withstand **2** last, continue, live on, persist, remain, stand, stay, survive

enduring adjective long-lasting, abiding, continuing, lasting, perennial, persistent, steadfast, unfaltering, unwavering

enemy noun foe, adversary, antagonist, competitor, opponent, rival, the opposition, the other side

energetic adjective vigorous, active, animated, dynamic, forceful, indefatigable, lively, strenuous, tireless

energy noun vigour, drive, forcefulness, get-up-and-go (informal), liveliness, stamina, verve, vitality

enforce verb impose, administer, apply, carry out, execute, implement, insist on, prosecute, put into effect

engage verb **1** participate, embark on, enter into, join, set about, take part, undertake **2** occupy, absorb, engross, grip, involve, preoccupy **3** captivate, arrest, catch, fix, gain **4** employ, appoint, enlist, enrol, hire, retain, take on **5** Military begin battle with, assail, attack, encounter, fall on, join battle with, meet, take on **6** set going, activate, apply, bring into operation, energize, switch on

engaged adjective **1** betrothed (archaic), affianced, pledged, promised, spoken for **2** occupied, busy, employed, in use, tied up, unavailable

engagement noun **1** appointment, arrangement, commitment, date, meeting **2** betrothal, troth (archaic) **3** battle, action, combat, conflict, encounter, fight

engaging adjective charming, agreeable, attractive, fetching (informal), likable or likeable, pleasing, winning, winsome

engender verb produce, breed, cause, create, generate, give rise to, induce, instigate, lead to

engine noun machine, mechanism, motor

engineer verb bring about, contrive, create, devise, effect, mastermind, plan, plot, scheme

engrave verb **1** carve, chisel, cut, etch, inscribe **2** fix, embed, impress, imprint, ingrain, lodge

engraving noun carving,

etching, inscription, plate, woodcut

engross verb 1 absorb, engage, immerse, involve, occupy, preoccupy

engrossed adjective absorbed, caught up, enthralled, fascinated, gripped, immersed, lost, preoccupied, rapt, riveted

engulf verb immerse, envelop, inundate, overrun, overwhelm, submerge, swallow up, swamp

enhance verb improve, add to, boost, heighten, increase, lift, reinforce, strengthen, swell

enigma noun mystery, conundrum, problem, puzzle, riddle, teaser

enigmatic adjective mysterious, ambiguous, cryptic, equivocal, inscrutable, obscure, puzzling, unfathomable

enjoy verb 1 take pleasure in or from, appreciate, be entertained by, be pleased with, delight in, like, relish 2 have, be blessed or favoured with, experience, have the benefit of, own, possess, reap the benefits of, use

enjoyable adjective pleasurable, agreeable, delightful, entertaining, gratifying, pleasant, satisfying, to one's liking

enjoyment noun pleasure, amusement, delectation, delight, entertainment, fun, gratification, happiness, joy, relish

enlarge verb 1 increase, amplify, broaden, expand, extend, grow, magnify, swell, widen 2 enlarge on expand on, descant on, develop, elaborate on, expatiate on, give further

details about

enlighten verb inform, advise, cause to understand, counsel, edify, educate, instruct, make aware, teach

enlightened adjective informed, aware, civilized, cultivated, educated, knowledgeable, open-minded, reasonable, sophisticated

enlightenment noun understanding, awareness, comprehension, education, insight, instruction, knowledge, learning, wisdom

enlist verb 1 join up, enrol, enter (into), join, muster, register, sign up, volunteer 2 obtain, engage, procure, recruit

enliven verb cheer up, animate, excite, inspire, invigorate, pep up, rouse, spark, stimulate, vitalize

enmity noun hostility, acrimony, animosity, bad blood, bitterness, hatred, ill will, malice

ennoble verb dignify, aggrandize, elevate, enhance, exalt, glorify, honour, magnify, raise

enormity noun 1 wickedness, atrocity, depravity, monstrousness, outrageousness, vileness, villainy 2 atrocity, abomination, crime, disgrace, evil, horror, monstrosity, outrage 3 Informal hugeness, greatness, immensity, magnitude, vastness

enormous adjective huge, colossal, gigantic, gross, immense, mammoth, massive, mountainous, tremendous, vast

enough adjective 1 sufficient,

enquire *see* INQUIRE

enquiry *see* INQUIRY

enrage *verb* anger, exasperate, incense, inflame, infuriate, madden

enrich *verb* 1 enhance, augment, develop, improve, refine, supplement 2 make rich, make wealthy

enrol *verb* enlist, accept, admit, join up, recruit, register, sign up or on, take on

enrolment *noun* enlistment, acceptance, admission, engagement, matriculation, recruitment, registration

en route *adverb* on or along the way, in transit, on the road

ensemble *noun* 1 whole, aggregate, collection, entirety, set, sum, total, totality 2 outfit, costume, get-up (*informal*), suit 3 group, band, cast, chorus, company, troupe

ensign *noun* flag, banner, colours, jack, pennant, pennon, standard, streamer

ensue *verb* follow, arise, come next, derive, flow, issue, proceed, result, stem

ensure *verb* 1 make certain, certify, confirm, effect, guarantee, make sure, secure, warrant 2 protect, guard, make safe, safeguard, secure

entail *verb* involve, bring about,

abundant, adequate, ample, plenty ♦ *noun* 2 sufficiency, abundance, adequacy, ample supply, plenty, right amount ♦ *adverb* 3 sufficiently, abundantly, adequately, amply, reasonably, satisfactorily, tolerably

call for, demand, give rise to, necessitate, occasion, require

entangle *verb* 1 tangle, catch, embroil, enmesh, ensnare, entrap, implicate, snag, snare, trap 2 mix up, complicate, confuse, jumble, muddle, perplex, puzzle

enter *verb* 1 come or go in or into, arrive, make an entrance, pass into, penetrate, pierce 2 join, commence, embark upon, enlist, enrol, set out on, start, take up 3 record, inscribe, list, log, note, register, set down, take down

enterprise *noun* 1 firm, business, company, concern, establishment, operation 2 undertaking, adventure, effort, endeavour, operation, plan, programme, project, venture 3 initiative, adventurousness, boldness, daring, drive, energy, enthusiasm, resourcefulness

enterprising *adjective* resourceful, adventurous, bold, daring, energetic, enthusiastic, go-ahead, intrepid, spirited

entertain *verb* 1 amuse, charm, cheer, delight, please, regale 2 show hospitality to, accommodate, be host to, harbour, have company, lodge, put up, treat 3 consider, conceive, contemplate, imagine, keep in mind, think about

entertaining *adjective* enjoyable, amusing, cheering, diverting, funny, humorous, interesting, pleasant, pleasurable

entertainment *noun* enjoyment, amusement, fun, leisure activity, pastime, pleasure, recreation, sport, treat

enthral verb <u>fascinate</u>, captivate, charm, enchant, enrapture, entrance, grip, mesmerize

enthusiasm noun <u>keenness</u>, eagerness, fervour, interest, passion, relish, zeal, zest

enthusiast noun <u>lover</u>, aficionado, buff (informal), devotee, fan, fanatic, follower, supporter

enthusiastic adjective <u>keen</u>, avid, eager, fervent, passionate, vigorous, wholehearted, zealous

entice verb <u>attract</u>, allure, cajole, coax, lead on, lure, persuade, seduce, tempt

entire adjective <u>whole</u>, complete, full, gross, total

entirely adverb <u>completely</u>, absolutely, altogether, fully, in every respect, thoroughly, totally, utterly, wholly

entitle verb 1 <u>give the right to</u>, allow, authorize, empower, enable, license, permit 2 <u>call</u>, christen, dub, label, name, term, title

entity noun <u>thing</u>, being, creature, individual, object, organism, substance

entourage noun <u>retinue</u>, associates, attendants, company, court, escort, followers, staff, train

entrails plural noun <u>intestines</u>, bowels, guts, innards (informal), insides (informal), offal, viscera

entrance¹ noun 1 <u>way in</u>, access, door, doorway, entry, gate, opening, passage 2 <u>appearance</u>, arrival, coming in, entry, introduction 3 <u>admission</u>, access, admittance, entrée, entry, permission to enter

entrance² verb 1 <u>enchant</u>, bewitch, captivate, charm, delight, enrapture, enthral, fascinate 2 <u>mesmerize</u>, hypnotize, put in a trance

entrant noun <u>competitor</u>, candidate, contestant, entry, participant, player

entreaty noun <u>plea</u>, appeal, earnest request, exhortation, petition, prayer, request, supplication

entrenched adjective <u>fixed</u>, deep-rooted, deep-seated, ineradicable, ingrained, rooted, set, unshakable, well-established

entrepreneur noun <u>businessman or businesswoman</u>, impresario, industrialist, magnate, tycoon

entrust verb <u>give custody of</u>, assign, commit, confide, delegate, deliver, hand over, turn over

entry noun 1 <u>way in</u>, access, door, doorway, entrance, gate, opening, passage 2 <u>coming in</u>, appearance, entering, entrance, initiation, introduction 3 <u>admission</u>, access, entrance, entrée, permission to enter 4 <u>record</u>, account, item, listing, note

entwine verb <u>twist</u>, interlace, interweave, knit, plait, twine, weave, wind

enumerate verb <u>list</u>, cite, itemize, mention, name, quote, recite, recount, relate, spell out

enunciate verb 1 <u>pronounce</u>, articulate, enounce, say, sound, speak, utter, vocalize, voice

2 state, declare, proclaim, promulgate, pronounce, propound, publish

envelop verb enclose, cloak, cover, encase, encircle, engulf, shroud, surround, wrap

envelope noun wrapping, case, casing, cover, covering, jacket, wrapper

enviable adjective desirable, advantageous, favoured, fortunate, lucky, privileged, to die for (informal)

envious adjective covetous, green with envy, grudging, jealous, resentful

environment noun surroundings, atmosphere, background, conditions, habitat, medium, setting, situation

environmental adjective ecological, green

environmentalist noun conservationist, ecologist, green

environs plural noun surrounding area, district, locality, neighbourhood, outskirts, precincts, suburbs, vicinity

envisage verb **1** imagine, conceive (of), conceptualize, contemplate, fancy, picture, think up, visualize **2** foresee, anticipate, envision, predict, see

envoy noun messenger, agent, ambassador, courier, delegate, diplomat, emissary, intermediary, representative

envy noun **1** covetousness, enviousness, jealousy, resentfulness, resentment ♦ verb **2** covet, be envious (of), begrudge, be jealous (of), grudge, resent

ephemeral adjective brief, fleeting, momentary, passing, short-lived, temporary, transient, transitory

epidemic noun spread, contagion, growth, outbreak, plague, rash, upsurge, wave

epigram noun witticism, aphorism, bon mot, quip

epilogue noun conclusion, coda, concluding speech, postscript

episode noun **1** event, adventure, affair, escapade, experience, happening, incident, matter, occurrence **2** part, chapter, instalment, passage, scene, section

epistle noun letter, communication, message, missive, note

epitaph noun monument, inscription

epithet noun name, appellation, description, designation, moniker or monicker (slang), nickname, sobriquet, tag, title

epitome noun personification, archetype, embodiment, essence, quintessence, representation, type, typical example

epitomize verb typify, embody, exemplify, illustrate, personify, represent, symbolize

epoch noun era, age, date, period, time

equable adjective even-tempered, calm, composed, easy-going, imperturbable, level-headed, placid, serene, unflappable (informal)

equal adjective **1** identical, alike, corresponding, equivalent, the same, uniform **2** regular, symmetrical, uniform, unvarying **3** even, balanced, evenly matched, fifty-fifty (*informal*), level pegging (*Brit. informal*) **4** fair, egalitarian, even-handed, impartial, just, unbiased **5 equal to** capable of, competent to, fit for, good enough for, ready for, strong enough, suitable for, up to ♦ *noun* **6** match, counterpart, equivalent, rival, twin ♦ *verb* **7** match, amount to, be tantamount to, correspond to, equate, level, parallel, tie with

equality *noun* **1** sameness, balance, correspondence, equivalence, evenness, identity, likeness, similarity, uniformity **2** fairness, egalitarianism, equal opportunity, parity

equalize *verb* make equal, balance, equal, even up, level, match, regularize, smooth, square, standardize

equate *verb* make or be equal, be commensurate, compare, correspond with or to, liken, mention in the same breath, parallel

equation *noun* equating, comparison, correspondence, parallel

equilibrium *noun* stability, balance, equipoise, evenness, rest, steadiness, symmetry

equip *verb* supply, arm, array, fit out, furnish, kit out, provide, stock

equipment *noun* tools, accoutrements, apparatus, gear, paraphernalia, stuff, supplies, tackle

equitable *adjective* fair,

even-handed, honest, impartial, just, proper, reasonable, unbiased

equivalence *noun* equality, correspondence, evenness, likeness, parity, sameness, similarity

equivalent *noun* **1** equal, counterpart, match, opposite number, parallel, twin ♦ *adjective* **2** equal, alike, commensurate, comparable, corresponding, interchangeable, of a piece, same, similar, tantamount

equivocal *adjective* ambiguous, evasive, indefinite, indeterminate, misleading, oblique, obscure, uncertain, vague

era *noun* age, date, day or days, epoch, generation, period, time

eradicate *verb* wipe out, annihilate, destroy, eliminate, erase, exterminate, extinguish, obliterate, remove, root out

erase *verb* wipe out, blot, cancel, delete, expunge, obliterate, remove, rub out

erect *verb* **1** build, construct, put up, raise, set up **2** found, create, establish, form, initiate, institute, organize, set up ♦ *adjective* **3** upright, elevated, perpendicular, pricked-up, stiff, straight, vertical

erode *verb* wear down or away, abrade, consume, corrode, destroy, deteriorate, disintegrate, eat away, grind down

erosion *noun* deterioration, abrasion, attrition, destruction, disintegration, eating away, grinding down, wearing down or away

erotic adjective <u>sexual</u>, amatory, carnal, lustful, seductive, sensual, sexy (informal), voluptuous

err verb <u>make a mistake</u>, blunder, go wrong, miscalculate, misjudge, mistake, slip up (informal)

errand noun <u>job</u>, charge, commission, message, mission, task

erratic adjective <u>unpredictable</u>, changeable, inconsistent, irregular, uneven, unreliable, unstable, variable, wayward

erroneous adjective <u>incorrect</u>, fallacious, false, faulty, flawed, invalid, mistaken, unsound, wrong

error noun <u>mistake</u>, bloomer (Brit. informal), blunder, howler (informal), miscalculation, oversight, slip, solecism

erstwhile adjective <u>former</u>, bygone, late, old, once, one-time, past, previous, sometime

erudite adjective <u>learned</u>, cultivated, cultured, educated, knowledgeable, scholarly, well-educated, well-read

erupt verb 1 <u>explode</u>, belch forth, blow up, burst out, gush, pour forth, spew forth or out, spout, throw off 2 Medical <u>break out</u>, appear

eruption noun 1 <u>explosion</u>, discharge, ejection, flare-up, outbreak, outburst 2 Medical <u>inflammation</u>, outbreak, rash

escalate verb <u>increase</u>, expand, extend, grow, heighten, intensify, mount, rise

escapade noun <u>adventure</u>, antic, caper, prank, scrape (informal), stunt

escape verb 1 <u>get away</u>, abscond, bolt, break free or out, flee, fly, make one's getaway, run away or off, slip away 2 <u>avoid</u>, dodge, duck, elude, evade, pass, shun, slip 3 <u>leak</u>, emanate, exude, flow, gush, issue, pour forth, seep ♦ noun 4 <u>getaway</u>, break, break-out, flight 5 <u>avoidance</u>, circumvention, evasion 6 <u>relaxation</u>, distraction, diversion, pastime, recreation 7 <u>leak</u>, emanation, emission, seepage

escort noun 1 <u>guard</u>, bodyguard, convoy, cortege, entourage, retinue, train 2 <u>companion</u>, attendant, beau, chaperon, guide, partner ♦ verb 3 <u>accompany</u>, chaperon, conduct, guide, lead, partner, shepherd, usher

especial adjective Formal <u>exceptional</u>, noteworthy, outstanding, principal, special, uncommon, unusual

especially adverb <u>exceptionally</u>, conspicuously, markedly, notably, outstandingly, remarkably, specially, strikingly, uncommonly, unusually

espionage noun <u>spying</u>, counter-intelligence, intelligence, surveillance, undercover work

espousal noun <u>support</u>, adoption, advocacy, backing, championing, defence, embracing, promotion, taking up

espouse verb <u>support</u>, adopt, advocate, back, champion, embrace, promote, stand up for, take up, uphold

essay noun 1 composition, article, discourse, dissertation, paper, piece, tract, treatise ◆ verb 2 Formal attempt, aim, endeavour, try, undertake

essence noun 1 fundamental nature, being, core, heart, nature, quintessence, soul, spirit, substance 2 concentrate, distillate, extract, spirits, tincture

essential adjective 1 vital, crucial, important, indispensable, necessary, needed, requisite 2 fundamental, basic, cardinal, elementary, innate, intrinsic, main, principal ◆ noun 3 prerequisite, basic, fundamental, must, necessity, rudiment, sine qua non

establish verb 1 create, constitute, form, found, ground, inaugurate, institute, settle, set up 2 prove, authenticate, certify, confirm, corroborate, demonstrate, substantiate, verify

establishment noun 1 creation, formation, foundation, founding, inauguration, installation, institution, organization, setting up 2 organization, business, company, concern, corporation, enterprise, firm, institution, outfit (informal) 3 the Establishment the authorities, ruling class, the powers that be, the system

estate noun 1 lands, area, domain, holdings, manor, property 2 Law property, assets, belongings, effects, fortune, goods, possessions, wealth

esteem noun 1 respect, admiration, credit, estimation, good opinion, honour, regard,

reverence, veneration ◆ verb 2 respect, admire, love, prize, regard highly, revere, think highly of, treasure, value 3 Formal consider, believe, deem, estimate, judge, reckon, regard, think, view

estimate verb 1 calculate roughly, assess, evaluate, gauge, guess, judge, number, reckon, value 2 form an opinion, believe, conjecture, consider, judge, rank, rate, reckon, surmise ◆ noun 3 approximate calculation, assessment, ballpark figure (informal), guess, guesstimate (informal), judgment, valuation 4 opinion, appraisal, assessment, belief, estimation, judgment

estimation noun opinion, appraisal, appreciation, assessment, belief, consideration, considered opinion, judgment, view

estuary noun inlet, creek, firth, fjord, mouth

et cetera adverb 1 and so on, and so forth ◆ noun 2 and the rest, and others, and the like, et al.

etch verb cut, carve, eat into, engrave, impress, imprint, inscribe, stamp

etching noun print, carving, engraving, impression, imprint, inscription

eternal adjective 1 everlasting, endless, immortal, infinite, never-ending, perpetual, timeless, unceasing, unending 2 permanent, deathless, enduring, immutable, imperishable, indestructible, lasting, unchanging

eternity noun 1 infinity, ages, endlessness, immortality, perpetuity, timelessness 2 *Theology* the afterlife, heaven, paradise, the hereafter, the next world

ethical adjective moral, conscientious, fair, good, honourable, just, principled, proper, right, upright, virtuous

ethics plural noun moral code, conscience, morality, moral philosophy, moral values, principles, rules of conduct, standards

ethnic, ethnical adjective cultural, folk, indigenous, national, native, racial, traditional

etiquette noun good or proper behaviour, civility, courtesy, decorum, formalities, manners, politeness, propriety, protocol

euphoria noun elation, ecstasy, exaltation, exhilaration, intoxication, joy, jubilation, rapture

evacuate verb clear, abandon, desert, forsake, leave, move out, pull out, quit, vacate, withdraw

evade verb 1 avoid, dodge, duck, elude, escape, get away from, sidestep, steer clear of 2 avoid answering, equivocate, fend off, fudge, hedge, parry

evaluate verb assess, appraise, calculate, estimate, gauge, judge, rate, reckon, size up (*informal*), weigh

evaporate verb 1 dry up, dehydrate, desiccate, dry, vaporize 2 disappear, dematerialize, dissolve, fade

away, melt away, vanish

evasion noun 1 avoidance, dodging, escape 2 deception, equivocation, evasiveness, prevarication

evasive adjective deceptive, cagey (*informal*), equivocating, indirect, oblique, prevaricating, shifty, slippery

eve noun 1 night before, day before, vigil 2 brink, edge, point, threshold, verge

even adjective 1 level, flat, horizontal, parallel, smooth, steady, straight, true, uniform 2 regular, constant, smooth, steady, unbroken, uniform, uninterrupted, unvarying, unwavering 3 equal, comparable, fifty-fifty (*informal*), identical, level, like, matching, neck and neck, on a par, similar, tied 4 calm, composed, cool, even-tempered, imperturbable, placid, unruffled, well-balanced 5 get even (with) *Informal* pay back, get one's own back, give tit for tat, reciprocate, repay, requite

evening noun dusk, gloaming (*Scot. or poetic*), twilight

event noun 1 incident, affair, business, circumstance, episode, experience, happening, occasion, occurrence 2 competition, bout, contest, game, tournament

even-tempered adjective calm, composed, cool, imperturbable, level-headed, placid, tranquil, unexcitable, unruffled

eventful adjective exciting, active, busy, dramatic, full, lively, memorable, remarkable

eventual *adjective* final, concluding, overall, ultimate

eventuality *noun* possibility, case, chance, contingency, event, likelihood, probability

eventually *adverb* in the end, after all, at the end of the day, finally, one day, some time, ultimately, when all is said and done

ever *adverb* **1** at any time, at all, at any period, at any point, by any chance, in any case, on any occasion **2** always, at all times, constantly, continually, evermore, for ever, perpetually

everlasting *adjective* eternal, endless, immortal, indestructible, never-ending, perpetual, timeless, undying

evermore *adverb* for ever, always, eternally, ever, to the end of time

every *adjective* each, all, each one

everybody *pronoun* everyone, all and sundry, each one, each person, every person, one and all, the whole world

everyday *adjective* common, customary, mundane, ordinary, routine, run-of-the-mill, stock, usual, workaday

everyone *pronoun* everybody, all and sundry, each one, each person, every person, one and all, the whole world

everything *pronoun* all, each thing, the lot, the whole lot

everywhere *adverb* to or in every place, all around, all over, far and wide or near, high and low, in every nook and cranny, the world over, ubiquitously

evict *verb* expel, boot out (*informal*), eject, kick out (*informal*), oust, remove, throw out, turf out (*informal*), turn out

evidence *noun* **1** proof, confirmation, corroboration, demonstration, grounds, indication, sign, substantiation, testimony ♦ *verb* **2** show, demonstrate, display, exhibit, indicate, prove, reveal, signify, witness

evident *adjective* obvious, apparent, clear, manifest, noticeable, perceptible, plain, unmistakable, visible

evidently *adverb* **1** obviously, clearly, manifestly, plainly, undoubtedly, unmistakably, without question **2** apparently, ostensibly, outwardly, seemingly, to all appearances

evil *noun* **1** wickedness, badness, depravity, malignity, sin, vice, villainy, wrongdoing **2** harm, affliction, disaster, hurt, ill, injury, mischief, misfortune, suffering, woe ♦ *adjective* **3** wicked, bad, depraved, immoral, malevolent, malicious, sinful, villainous **4** harmful, calamitous, catastrophic, destructive, dire, disastrous, pernicious, ruinous **5** offensive, foul, noxious, pestilential, unpleasant, vile

evoke *verb* recall, arouse, awaken, call, give rise to, induce, rekindle, stir up, summon up

evolution *noun* development, expansion, growth, increase, maturation, progress, unfolding, working out

evolve *verb* develop, expand,

grow, increase, mature,
progress, unfold, work out

exact adjective 1 <u>accurate</u>,
correct, definite, faultless,
precise, right, specific, true,
unerring ◆ verb 2 <u>demand</u>, claim,
command, compel, extort,
extract, force

exacting adjective <u>demanding</u>,
difficult, hard, harsh, rigorous,
severe, strict, stringent, taxing,
tough

exactly adverb 1 <u>precisely</u>,
accurately, correctly, explicitly,
faithfully, scrupulously, truthfully,
unerringly 2 <u>in every respect</u>,
absolutely, indeed, precisely,
quite, specifically, to the letter

exactness noun <u>precision</u>,
accuracy, correctness,
exactitude, rigorousness,
scrupulousness, strictness,
veracity

exaggerate verb <u>overstate</u>,
amplify, embellish, embroider,
enlarge, overemphasize,
overestimate

exaggeration noun
<u>overstatement</u>, amplification,
embellishment, enlargement,
hyperbole, overemphasis,
overestimation

exalt verb 1 <u>praise</u>, acclaim,
extol, glorify, idolize, set on a
pedestal, worship 2 <u>raise</u>,
advance, elevate, ennoble,
honour, promote, upgrade

exaltation noun 1 <u>praise</u>,
acclaim, glorification, idolization,
reverence, tribute, worship
2 <u>rise</u>, advancement, elevation,
ennoblement, promotion,
upgrading

exalted adjective <u>high-ranking</u>,

dignified, eminent, grand,
honoured, lofty, prestigious

examination noun 1 <u>inspection</u>,
analysis, exploration,
interrogation, investigation,
research, scrutiny, study, test
2 <u>questioning</u>, inquiry,
inquisition, probe, quiz, test

examine verb 1 <u>inspect</u>, analyse,
explore, investigate, peruse,
scrutinize, study, survey
2 <u>question</u>, cross-examine, grill
(informal), inquire, interrogate,
quiz, test

example noun 1 <u>specimen</u>, case,
illustration, instance, sample
2 <u>model</u>, archetype, ideal,
paradigm, paragon, prototype,
standard 3 <u>warning</u>, caution,
lesson

exasperate verb <u>irritate</u>, anger,
annoy, enrage, incense, inflame,
infuriate, madden, pique

exasperation noun <u>irritation</u>,
anger, annoyance, fury, pique,
provocation, rage, wrath

excavate verb <u>dig out</u>, burrow,
delve, dig up, mine, quarry,
tunnel, uncover, unearth

exceed verb 1 <u>surpass</u>, beat,
better, cap (informal), eclipse,
outdo, outstrip, overtake, pass,
top 2 <u>go over the limit of</u>, go
over the top, overstep

exceedingly adverb <u>extremely</u>,
enormously, exceptionally,
extraordinarily, hugely,
superlatively, surpassingly,
unusually, very

excel verb 1 <u>be superior</u>, beat,
eclipse, outdo, outshine, surpass,
transcend 2 <u>excel in</u> or <u>at be</u>
<u>good at</u>, be proficient in, be
skilful at, be talented at, shine

at, show talent in

excellence noun high quality, distinction, eminence, goodness, greatness, merit, pre-eminence, superiority, supremacy

excellent adjective outstanding, brilliant, exquisite, fine, first-class, first-rate, good, great, superb, superlative, world-class

except preposition **1** Also **except for** apart from, barring, besides, but, excepting, excluding, omitting, other than, saving, with the exception of ♦ verb **2** exclude, leave out, omit, pass over

exception noun **1** special case, anomaly, deviation, freak, inconsistency, irregularity, oddity, peculiarity **2** exclusion, leaving out, omission, passing over

exceptional adjective **1** special, abnormal, atypical, extraordinary, irregular, odd, peculiar, strange, unusual **2** remarkable, excellent, extraordinary, marvellous, outstanding, phenomenal, prodigious, special, superior

excerpt noun extract, fragment, part, passage, piece, quotation, section, selection

excess noun **1** surfeit, glut, overload, superabundance, superfluity, surplus, too much **2** overindulgence, debauchery, dissipation, dissoluteness, extravagance, intemperance, prodigality

excessive adjective immoderate, disproportionate, exaggerated, extreme, inordinate, overmuch, superfluous, too much, undue,

unfair, unreasonable

exchange verb **1** interchange, barter, change, convert into, swap, switch, trade ♦ noun **2** interchange, barter, quid pro quo, reciprocity, substitution, swap, switch, tit for tat, trade

excitable adjective nervous, emotional, highly strung, hot-headed, mercurial, quick-tempered, temperamental, volatile

excite verb arouse, animate, galvanize, inflame, inspire, provoke, rouse, stir up, thrill

excitement noun agitation, action, activity, animation, commotion, furore, passion, thrill

exciting adjective stimulating, dramatic, electrifying, exhilarating, rousing, sensational, stirring, thrilling

exclaim verb cry out, call out, declare, proclaim, shout, utter, yell

exclamation noun cry, call, interjection, outcry, shout, utterance, yell

exclude verb **1** keep out, ban, bar, boycott, disallow, forbid, prohibit, refuse, shut out **2** leave out, count out, eliminate, ignore, omit, pass over, reject, rule out, set aside

exclusion noun **1** ban, bar, boycott, disqualification, embargo, prohibition, veto **2** elimination, omission, rejection

exclusive adjective **1** sole, absolute, complete, entire, full, total, undivided, whole **2** limited, confined, peculiar, restricted, unique **3** select, chic, cliquish, fashionable, posh (*informal, chiefly Brit.*), restricted, snobbish, up-market

excommunicate *verb* expel, anathematize, ban, banish, cast out, denounce, exclude, repudiate

excruciating *adjective* agonizing, harrowing, insufferable, intense, piercing, severe, unbearable, violent

exculpate *verb* absolve, acquit, clear, discharge, excuse, exonerate, pardon, vindicate

excursion *noun* trip, day trip, expedition, jaunt, journey, outing, pleasure trip, ramble, tour

excusable *adjective* forgivable, allowable, defensible, justifiable, pardonable, permissible, understandable, warrantable

excuse *noun* 1 justification, apology, defence, explanation, grounds, mitigation, plea, reason, vindication ♦ *verb* 2 justify, apologize for, defend, explain, mitigate, vindicate 3 forgive, acquit, exculpate, exonerate, make allowances for, overlook, pardon, tolerate, turn a blind eye to 4 free, absolve, discharge, exempt, let off, release, relieve, spare

execute *verb* 1 put to death, behead, electrocute, guillotine, hang, kill, shoot 2 carry out, accomplish, administer, discharge, effect, enact, implement, perform, prosecute

execution *noun* 1 carrying out, accomplishment, administration, enactment, enforcement, implementation, operation, performance, prosecution

2 killing, capital punishment, hanging

executioner *noun* 1 hangman, headsman 2 killer, assassin, exterminator, hit man (*slang*), liquidator, murderer, slayer

executive *noun* 1 administrator, director, manager, official 2 administration, directorate, directors, government, hierarchy, leadership, management ♦ *adjective* 3 administrative, controlling, decision-making, directing, governing, managerial

exemplary *adjective* 1 ideal, admirable, commendable, excellent, fine, good, model, praiseworthy 2 warning, cautionary

exemplify *verb* show, demonstrate, display, embody, exhibit, illustrate, represent, serve as an example of

exempt *adjective* 1 immune, excepted, excused, free, not liable, released, spared ♦ *verb* 2 grant immunity, absolve, discharge, excuse, free, let off, release, relieve, spare

exemption *noun* immunity, absolution, discharge, dispensation, exception, exoneration, freedom, release

exercise *noun* 1 exertion, activity, effort, labour, toil, training, work, work-out 2 task, drill, lesson, practice, problem 3 use, application, discharge, fulfilment, implementation, practice, utilization ♦ *verb* 4 put to use, apply, bring to bear, employ, exert, use, utilize 5 train, practise, work out

exert *verb* 1 use, apply, bring to

bear, employ, exercise, make use of, utilize, wield **2 exert oneself** make an effort, apply oneself, do one's best, endeavour, labour, strain, strive, struggle, toil, work

exertion noun effort, elbow grease (facetious), endeavour, exercise, industry, strain, struggle, toil

exhaust verb **1** tire out, debilitate, drain, enervate, enfeeble, fatigue, sap, weaken, wear out **2** use up, consume, deplete, dissipate, expend, run through, spend, squander, waste

exhausted adjective **1** worn out, all in (slang), debilitated, done in (informal), drained, fatigued, knackered (slang), spent, tired out **2** used up, consumed, depleted, dissipated, expended, finished, spent, squandered, wasted

exhausting adjective tiring, backbreaking, debilitating, gruelling, laborious, punishing, sapping, strenuous, taxing

exhaustion noun **1** tiredness, debilitation, fatigue, weariness **2** depletion, consumption, emptying, using up

exhaustive adjective thorough, all-embracing, complete, comprehensive, extensive, full-scale, in-depth, intensive

exhibit verb display, demonstrate, express, indicate, manifest, parade, put on view, reveal, show

exhibition noun display, demonstration, exposition, performance, presentation, representation, show, spectacle

exhilarating adjective exciting, breathtaking, enlivening, invigorating, stimulating, thrilling

exhort verb Formal urge, advise, beseech, call upon, entreat, persuade, press, spur

exhume verb Formal dig up, disentomb, disinter, unearth

exigency, exigence noun need, constraint, demand, necessity, requirement

exile noun **1** banishment, deportation, expatriation, expulsion **2** expatriate, deportee, émigré, outcast, refugee ♦ verb **3** banish, deport, drive out, eject, expatriate, expel

exist verb **1** be, be present, endure, live, occur, survive **2** survive, eke out a living, get along or by, keep one's head above water, stay alive, subsist

existence noun being, actuality, life, subsistence

existent adjective in existence, alive, existing, extant, living, present, standing, surviving

exit noun **1** way out, door, gate, outlet **2** departure, exodus, farewell, going, goodbye, leave-taking, retreat, withdrawal ♦ verb **3** depart, go away, go offstage (Theatre), go out, leave, make tracks, retire, retreat, take one's leave, withdraw

exodus noun departure, evacuation, exit, flight, going out, leaving, migration, retreat, withdrawal

exonerate verb clear, absolve, acquit, discharge, exculpate, excuse, justify, pardon, vindicate

exorbitant adjective excessive, extortionate, extravagant, immoderate, inordinate, outrageous, preposterous, unreasonable

exorcise verb drive out, cast out, deliver (from), expel, purify

exotic adjective 1 unusual, colourful, fascinating, glamorous, mysterious, strange, striking, unfamiliar 2 foreign, alien, external, imported, naturalized

expand verb 1 increase, amplify, broaden, develop, enlarge, extend, grow, magnify, swell, widen 2 spread (out), diffuse, stretch (out), unfold, unfurl, unravel, unroll 3 expand on go into detail about, amplify, develop, elaborate on, embellish, enlarge on, expatiate on, expound on, flesh out

expanse noun area, breadth, extent, range, space, stretch, sweep, tract

expansion noun increase, amplification, development, enlargement, growth, magnification, opening out, spread

expansive adjective 1 wide, broad, extensive, far-reaching, voluminous, wide-ranging, widespread 2 talkative, affable, communicative, effusive, friendly, loquacious, open, outgoing, sociable, unreserved

expatriate adjective 1 exiled, banished, emigrant, émigré ♦ noun 2 exile, emigrant, émigré, refugee

expect verb 1 think, assume, believe, imagine, presume, reckon, suppose, surmise, trust 2 look forward to, anticipate, await, contemplate, envisage,

hope for, predict, watch for 3 require, call for, demand, insist on, want

expectant adjective 1 expecting, anticipating, apprehensive, eager, hopeful, in suspense, ready, watchful 2 pregnant, expecting (informal), gravid

expectation noun 1 probability, assumption, belief, conjecture, forecast, likelihood, presumption, supposition 2 anticipation, apprehension, expectancy, hope, promise, suspense

expediency noun suitability, advisability, benefit, convenience, pragmatism, profitability, prudence, usefulness, utility

expedient noun 1 means, contrivance, device, makeshift, measure, method, resort, scheme, stopgap ♦ adjective 2 advantageous, appropriate, beneficial, convenient, effective, helpful, opportune, practical, suitable, useful

expedition noun journey, excursion, mission, quest, safari, tour, trek, voyage

expel verb 1 drive out, belch, cast out, discharge, eject, remove, spew out 2 dismiss, ban, banish, drum out, evict, exclude, exile, throw out, turf out (informal)

expend verb Formal spend, consume, dissipate, exhaust, go through, pay out, use (up)

expendable adjective dispensable, inessential, nonessential, replaceable, unimportant, unnecessary

expenditure noun spending,

consumption, cost, expense, outgoings, outlay, output, payment

expense noun <u>cost</u>, charge, expenditure, loss, outlay, payment, spending

expensive adjective <u>dear</u>, costly, exorbitant, extravagant, high-priced, lavish, overpriced, steep (informal), stiff

experience noun 1 <u>knowledge</u>, contact, exposure, familiarity, involvement, participation, practice, training 2 <u>event</u>, adventure, affair, encounter, episode, happening, incident, occurrence ♦ verb 3 <u>undergo</u>, encounter, endure, face, feel, go through, live through, sample, taste

experienced adjective <u>knowledgeable</u>, accomplished, expert, practised, seasoned, tested, tried, veteran, well-versed

experiment noun 1 <u>test</u>, examination, experimentation, investigation, procedure, proof, research, trial, trial run ♦ verb 2 <u>test</u>, examine, investigate, put to the test, research, sample, try, verify

experimental adjective <u>test</u>, exploratory, pilot, preliminary, probationary, provisional, speculative, tentative, trial, trial-and-error

expert noun 1 <u>master</u>, authority, connoisseur, dab hand (Brit. informal), past master, professional, specialist, virtuoso ♦ adjective 2 <u>skilful</u>, adept, adroit, experienced, masterly, practised, professional, proficient, qualified, virtuoso

expertise noun <u>skill</u>, adroitness, command, facility, judgment, know-how (informal), knowledge, mastery, proficiency

expire verb 1 <u>finish</u>, cease, close, come to an end, conclude, end, lapse, run out, stop, terminate 2 <u>breathe out</u>, emit, exhale, expel 3 <u>die</u>, depart, kick the bucket (informal), pass away or on, perish

explain verb 1 <u>make clear or plain</u>, clarify, clear up, define, describe, elucidate, expound, resolve, teach 2 <u>account for</u>, excuse, give a reason for, justify

explanation noun 1 <u>reason</u>, account, answer, excuse, justification, motive, vindication 2 <u>description</u>, clarification, definition, elucidation, illustration, interpretation

explanatory adjective <u>descriptive</u>, illustrative, interpretive

explicit adjective <u>clear</u>, categorical, definite, frank, precise, specific, straightforward, unambiguous

explode verb 1 <u>blow up</u>, burst, detonate, discharge, erupt, go off, set off, shatter 2 <u>disprove</u>, debunk, discredit, give the lie to, invalidate, refute, repudiate

exploit verb 1 <u>take advantage of</u>, abuse, manipulate, milk, misuse, play on or upon 2 <u>make the best use of</u>, capitalize on, cash in on (informal), profit by or from, use, utilize ♦ noun 3 <u>feat</u>, accomplishment, achievement, adventure, attainment, deed, escapade, stunt

exploitation noun <u>misuse</u>, abuse, manipulation

exploration noun
1 <u>investigation</u>, analysis, examination, inquiry, inspection, research, scrutiny, search
2 <u>expedition</u>, reconnaissance, survey, tour, travel, trip

exploratory adjective
<u>investigative</u>, experimental, fact-finding, probing, searching, trial

explore verb 1 <u>investigate</u>, examine, inquire into, inspect, look into, probe, research, search
2 <u>travel</u>, reconnoitre, scout, survey, tour

explosion noun 1 <u>bang</u>, blast, burst, clap, crack, detonation, discharge, report 2 <u>outburst</u>, eruption, fit, outbreak

explosive adjective 1 <u>unstable</u>, volatile 2 <u>violent</u>, fiery, stormy, touchy, vehement

exponent noun 1 <u>advocate</u>, backer, champion, defender, promoter, proponent, supporter, upholder 2 <u>performer</u>, player

expose verb 1 <u>uncover</u>, display, exhibit, present, reveal, show, unveil 2 <u>make vulnerable</u>, endanger, imperil, jeopardize, lay open, leave open, subject

exposed adjective 1 <u>unconcealed</u>, bare, on display, on show, on view, revealed, uncovered
2 <u>unsheltered</u>, open, unprotected 3 <u>vulnerable</u>, in peril, laid bare, susceptible, wide open

exposure noun <u>publicity</u>, display, exhibition, presentation, revelation, showing, uncovering, unveiling

expound verb <u>explain</u>, describe, elucidate, interpret, set forth, spell out, unfold

express verb 1 <u>state</u>, articulate, communicate, declare, phrase, put into words, say, utter, voice, word 2 <u>show</u>, convey, exhibit, indicate, intimate, make known, represent, reveal, signify, stand for, symbolize ♦ adjective
3 <u>explicit</u>, categorical, clear, definite, distinct, plain, unambiguous 4 <u>specific</u>, clear-cut, especial, particular, singular, special 5 <u>fast</u>, direct, high-speed, nonstop, rapid, speedy, swift

expression noun 1 <u>statement</u>, announcement, communication, declaration, utterance
2 <u>indication</u>, demonstration, exhibition, manifestation, representation, show, sign, symbol, token 3 <u>look</u>, air, appearance, aspect, countenance, face 4 <u>phrase</u>, idiom, locution, remark, term, turn of phrase, word

expressive adjective <u>vivid</u>, eloquent, moving, poignant, striking, telling

expressly adverb 1 <u>definitely</u>, categorically, clearly, distinctly, explicitly, in no uncertain terms, plainly, unambiguously
2 <u>specifically</u>, especially, particularly, specially

expulsion noun <u>ejection</u>, banishment, dismissal, eviction, exclusion, removal

exquisite adjective 1 <u>beautiful</u>, attractive, charming, comely, lovely, pleasing, striking 2 <u>fine</u>, beautiful, dainty, delicate, elegant, lovely, precious
3 <u>intense</u>, acute, keen, sharp

extempore adverb, adjective impromptu, ad lib, freely, improvised, offhand, off the cuff (informal), spontaneously, unpremeditated, unprepared

extend verb 1 make longer, drag out, douse, quench, smother, prolong, spin out, spread out, stretch 2 last, carry on, continue, go on 3 widen, add to, augment, broaden, enhance, enlarge, expand, increase, supplement 4 offer, confer, impart, present, proffer

extension noun 1 annexe, addition, appendage, appendix, supplement 2 lengthening, broadening, development, enlargement, expansion, increase, spread, widening

extensive adjective wide, broad, far-flung, far-reaching, large-scale, pervasive, spacious, vast, voluminous, widespread

extent noun size, amount, area, breadth, expanse, length, stretch, volume, width

extenuating adjective mitigating, justifying, moderating, qualifying

exterior noun 1 outside, coating, covering, facade, face, shell, skin, surface ♦ adjective 2 outside, external, outer, outermost, outward, surface

exterminate verb destroy, abolish, annihilate, eliminate, eradicate

external adjective 1 outer, exterior, outermost, outside, outward, surface 2 outside, alien, extrinsic, foreign

extinct adjective dead, defunct, gone, lost, vanished

extinction noun dying out, abolition, annihilation, destruction, eradication, extermination, obliteration, oblivion

extinguish verb 1 put out, blow out, douse, quench, smother, snuff out, stifle 2 destroy, annihilate, eliminate, end, eradicate, exterminate, remove, wipe out

extol verb praise, acclaim, commend, eulogize, exalt, glorify, sing the praises of

extort verb force, blackmail, bully, coerce, extract, squeeze

extortionate adjective exorbitant, excessive, extravagant, inflated, outrageous, preposterous, sky-high, unreasonable

extra adjective 1 additional, added, ancillary, auxiliary, further, more, supplementary 2 surplus, excess, leftover, redundant, spare, superfluous, unused ♦ noun 3 addition, accessory, attachment, bonus, extension, supplement ♦ adverb 4 exceptionally, especially, extraordinarily, extremely, particularly, remarkably, uncommonly, unusually

extract verb 1 pull out, draw, pluck out, pull, remove, take out, uproot, withdraw 2 derive, draw, elicit, glean, obtain ♦ noun 3 passage, citation, clipping, cutting, excerpt, quotation, selection 4 essence, concentrate, distillation, juice

extraneous adjective irrelevant, beside the point, immaterial, inappropriate, off the subject, unconnected, unrelated

extraordinary adjective unusual, amazing, exceptional, fantastic, outstanding, phenomenal, remarkable, strange, uncommon

extravagance noun 1 waste, lavishness, overspending, prodigality, profligacy, squandering, wastefulness 2 excess, exaggeration, outrageousness, preposterousness, wildness

extravagant adjective 1 wasteful, lavish, prodigal, profligate, spendthrift 2 excessive, outrageous, over the top (slang), preposterous, reckless, unreasonable

extreme adjective 1 maximum, acute, great, highest, intense, severe, supreme, ultimate, utmost 2 severe, drastic, harsh, radical, rigid, strict, uncompromising 3 excessive, fanatical, immoderate, radical 4 farthest, far-off, most distant, outermost, remotest ♦noun 5 limit, boundary, edge, end, extremity, pole

extremely adverb very, awfully (informal), exceedingly, exceptionally, extraordinarily, severely, terribly, uncommonly, unusually

extremist noun fanatic, die-hard, radical, zealot

extremity noun 1 limit, border, boundary, edge, extreme, frontier, pinnacle, tip 2 crisis, adversity, dire straits, disaster, emergency, exigency, trouble 3 extremities hands and feet, fingers and toes, limbs

extricate verb free, disengage, disentangle, get out, release, remove, rescue, wriggle out of

extrovert adjective outgoing, exuberant, gregarious, sociable

exuberance noun 1 high spirits, cheerfulness, ebullience, enthusiasm, liveliness, spirit, vitality, vivacity, zest 2 luxuriance, abundance, copiousness, lavishness, profusion

exuberant adjective 1 high-spirited, animated, cheerful, ebullient, energetic, enthusiastic, lively, spirited, vivacious 2 luxuriant, abundant, copious, lavish, plentiful, profuse

exult verb be joyful, be overjoyed, celebrate, jump for joy, rejoice

eye noun 1 eyeball, optic (informal) 2 appreciation, discernment, discrimination, judgment, perception, recognition, taste ♦verb 3 look at, check out (informal), contemplate, inspect, study, survey, view, watch

eyesight noun vision, perception, sight

eyesore noun mess, blemish, blot, disfigurement, horror, monstrosity, sight (informal)

eyewitness noun observer, bystander, onlooker, passer-by, spectator, viewer, witness

F f

fable noun 1 story, allegory, legend, myth, parable, tale 2 fiction, fabrication, fantasy, invention, tall story (informal), urban legend, yarn (informal)

fabric noun 1 <u>cloth</u>, material, stuff, textile, web 2 <u>framework</u>, constitution, construction, foundations, make-up, organization, structure

fabricate verb 1 <u>make up</u>, concoct, devise, fake, falsify, feign, forge, invent, trump up 2 <u>build</u>, assemble, construct, erect, form, make, manufacture, shape

fabrication noun 1 <u>forgery</u>, concoction, fake, falsehood, fiction, invention, lie, myth 2 <u>construction</u>, assembly, building, erection, manufacture, production

fabulous adjective 1 Informal <u>wonderful</u>, brilliant, fantastic (informal), marvellous, out-of-this-world (informal), sensational (informal), spectacular, superb 2 <u>astounding</u>, amazing, breathtaking, inconceivable, incredible, phenomenal, unbelievable 3 <u>legendary</u>, apocryphal, fantastic, fictitious, imaginary, invented, made-up, mythical, unreal

façade noun <u>appearance</u>, exterior, face, front, guise, mask, pretence, semblance, show

face noun 1 <u>countenance</u>, features, mug (slang), visage 2 <u>expression</u>, appearance, aspect, look 3 <u>scowl</u>, frown, grimace, pout, smirk 4 <u>façade</u>, appearance, display, exterior, front, mask, show 5 <u>side</u>, exterior, front, outside, surface 6 <u>self-respect</u>, authority, dignity, honour, image, prestige, reputation, standing, status ♦ verb 7 <u>meet</u>, brave, come up against, confront, deal with, encounter, experience, oppose, tackle 8 <u>look onto</u>, be opposite, front onto, overlook 9 <u>coat</u>, clad, cover, dress, finish

faceless adjective <u>impersonal</u>, anonymous, remote

facet noun <u>aspect</u>, angle, face, part, phase, plane, side, slant, surface

facetious adjective <u>funny</u>, amusing, comical, droll, flippant, frivolous, humorous, jocular, playful, tongue in cheek

face up to verb <u>accept</u>, acknowledge, come to terms with, confront, cope with, deal with, meet head-on, tackle

facile adjective <u>superficial</u>, cursory, glib, hasty, shallow, slick

facilitate verb <u>promote</u>, expedite, forward, further, help, make easy, pave the way for, speed up

facility noun 1 <u>skill</u>, ability, adroitness, dexterity, ease, efficiency, effortlessness, fluency, proficiency 2 often plural <u>equipment</u>, advantage, aid, amenity, appliance, convenience, means, opportunity, resource

facsimile noun <u>copy</u>, carbon copy, duplicate, fax, photocopy, print, replica, reproduction, transcript

fact noun 1 <u>event</u>, act, deed, fait accompli, happening, incident, occurrence, performance 2 <u>truth</u>, certainty, reality

faction noun 1 <u>group</u>, bloc, cabal, clique, contingent, coterie, gang, party, set, splinter group **2** <u>dissension</u>, conflict, disagreement, discord, disunity, division, infighting, rebellion

factor *noun* <u>element</u>, aspect, cause, component, consideration, influence, item, part

factory *noun* <u>works</u>, mill, plant

factual *adjective* <u>true</u>, authentic, correct, exact, genuine, precise, real, true-to-life

faculties *plural noun* <u>powers</u>, capabilities, intelligence, reason, senses, wits

faculty *noun* **1** <u>ability</u>, aptitude, capacity, facility, power, propensity, skill **2** <u>department</u>, school

fad *noun* <u>craze</u>, fashion, mania, rage, trend, vogue, whim

fade *verb* **1** <u>pale</u>, bleach, discolour, lose colour, wash out **2** <u>dwindle</u>, decline, die away, disappear, dissolve, melt away, vanish, wane

faded *adjective* <u>discoloured</u>, bleached, dull, indistinct, pale, washed out

fading *adjective* <u>declining</u>, decreasing, disappearing, dying, on the decline, vanishing

fail *verb* **1** <u>be unsuccessful</u>, bite the dust, break down, come to grief, come unstuck, fall, fizzle out (*informal*), flop (*informal*), founder, miscarry, misfire **2** <u>disappoint</u>, abandon, desert, forget, forsake, let down, neglect, omit **3** <u>give out</u>, conk out (*informal*), cut out, die, peter out, stop working **4** <u>go bankrupt</u>, become insolvent, close down, fold (*informal*), go

broke (*informal*), go bust (*informal*), go into receivership, go out of business, go to the wall, go under ♦ *noun* **5** <u>without fail</u> regularly, conscientiously, constantly, dependably, like clockwork, punctually, religiously, without exception

failing *noun* **1** <u>weakness</u>, blemish, defect, deficiency, drawback, fault, flaw, imperfection, shortcoming ♦ *preposition* **2** <u>in the absence of</u>, in default of, lacking

failure *noun* **1** <u>defeat</u>, breakdown, collapse, downfall, fiasco, lack of success, miscarriage, overthrow **2** <u>loser</u>, black sheep, dead duck (*slang*), disappointment, dud (*informal*), flop (*informal*), nonstarter, washout (*informal*) **3** <u>bankruptcy</u>, crash, downfall, insolvency, liquidation, ruin

faint *adjective* **1** <u>dim</u>, distant, faded, indistinct, low, muted, soft, subdued, vague **2** <u>slight</u>, feeble, remote, unenthusiastic, weak **3** <u>dizzy</u>, exhausted, giddy, light-headed, muzzy, weak, woozy (*informal*) ♦ *verb* **4** <u>pass out</u>, black out, collapse, flake out (*informal*), keel over (*informal*), lose consciousness, swoon (*literary*) ♦ *noun* **5** <u>blackout</u>, collapse, swoon (*literary*), unconsciousness

faintly *adverb* **1** <u>softly</u>, feebly, in a whisper, indistinctly, weakly **2** <u>slightly</u>, a little, dimly, somewhat

fair[1] *adjective* **1** <u>unbiased</u>, above board, equitable, even-handed, honest, impartial, just, lawful,

legitimate, proper, unprejudiced
2 light, blond, blonde,
fair-haired, flaxen-haired,
towheaded **3** respectable,
adequate, average, decent,
moderate, O.K. or okay
(informal), passable, reasonable,
satisfactory, tolerable **4** beautiful,
bonny, comely, handsome,
lovely, pretty **5** fine, bright,
clear, cloudless, dry, sunny,
unclouded

fair² noun carnival, bazaar,
festival, fête, gala, show

fairly adverb **1** moderately,
adequately, pretty well, quite,
rather, reasonably, somewhat,
tolerably **2** deservedly, equitably,
honestly, impartially, justly,
objectively, properly, without
fear or favour **3** positively,
absolutely, really

fairness noun impartiality,
decency, disinterestedness,
equitableness, equity, justice,
legitimacy, rightfulness

fairy noun sprite, brownie, elf,
leprechaun, peri, pixie, Robin
Goodfellow

fairy tale or **fairy story** noun
1 folk tale, romance **2** lie,
cock-and-bull story (informal),
fabrication, fiction, invention, tall
story, untruth

faith noun **1** confidence,
assurance, conviction, credence,
credit, dependence, reliance,
trust **2** religion, belief, church,
communion, creed,
denomination, dogma,
persuasion **3** allegiance,
constancy, faithfulness, fidelity,
loyalty

faithful adjective **1** loyal,

constant, dependable, devoted,
reliable, staunch, steadfast, true,
trusty **2** accurate, close, exact,
precise, strict, true

faithless adjective disloyal, false,
fickle, inconstant, traitorous,
treacherous, unfaithful, unreliable

fake verb **1** forge, copy,
counterfeit, fabricate, feign,
pretend, put on, sham, simulate
♦ noun **2** impostor, charlatan,
copy, forgery, fraud, hoax,
imitation, reproduction, sham
♦ adjective **3** artificial, counterfeit,
false, forged, imitation, mock,
phoney or phony (informal), sham

fall verb **1** descend, cascade,
collapse, dive, drop, plummet,
plunge, sink, subside, tumble
2 decrease, decline, diminish,
drop, dwindle, go down, lessen,
slump, subside **3** be overthrown,
capitulate, pass into enemy
hands, succumb, surrender
4 die, be killed, meet one's end,
perish **5** occur, befall, chance,
come about, come to pass,
happen, take place **6** slope, fall
away, incline **7** lapse, err, go
astray, offend, sin, transgress,
trespass ♦ noun **8** descent, dive,
drop, nose dive, plummet,
plunge, slip, tumble **9** decrease,
cut, decline, dip, drop,
lessening, lowering, reduction,
slump **10** collapse, capitulation,
defeat, destruction, downfall,
overthrow, ruin **11** lapse, sin,
transgression

fallacy noun error, delusion,
falsehood, flaw,
misapprehension,
misconception, mistake, untruth

fallible adjective imperfect, erring,

frail, ignorant, uncertain, weak

fall out verb argue, clash, come to blows, differ, disagree, fight, quarrel, squabble

fallow adjective uncultivated, dormant, idle, inactive, resting, unplanted, unused

false adjective **1** incorrect, erroneous, faulty, inaccurate, inexact, invalid, mistaken, wrong **2** untrue, lying, unreliable, unsound, untruthful **3** artificial, bogus, counterfeit, fake, forged, imitation, sham, simulated **4** deceptive, deceitful, fallacious, fraudulent, hypocritical, misleading, trumped up

falsehood noun **1** untruthfulness, deceit, deception, dishonesty, dissimulation, mendacity **2** lie, fabrication, fib, fiction, story, untruth

falsify verb forge, alter, counterfeit, distort, doctor, fake, misrepresent, tamper with

falter verb hesitate, stammer, stumble, stutter, totter, vacillate, waver

faltering adjective hesitant, broken, irresolute, stammering, tentative, timid, uncertain, weak

fame noun prominence, celebrity, glory, honour, renown, reputation, repute, stardom

familiar adjective **1** well-known, accustomed, common, customary, frequent, ordinary, recognizable, routine **2** friendly, amicable, close, easy, intimate, relaxed **3** disrespectful, bold, forward, impudent, intrusive, presumptuous

familiarity noun **1** acquaintance,

awareness, experience, grasp, understanding **2** friendliness, ease, informality, intimacy, openness, sociability **3** disrespect, boldness, forwardness, presumption

familiarize verb accustom, habituate, instruct, inure, school, season, train

family noun **1** relations, folk (informal), household, kin, kith and kin, one's nearest and dearest, one's own flesh and blood, relatives **2** clan, dynasty, house, race, tribe **3** group, class, genre, network, subdivision, system

famine noun hunger, dearth, scarcity, starvation

famished adjective starving, ravenous, voracious

famous adjective well-known, acclaimed, celebrated, distinguished, eminent, illustrious, legendary, noted, prominent, renowned

fan[1] noun **1** blower, air conditioner, ventilator ♦ verb **2** blow, air-condition, cool, refresh, ventilate

fan[2] noun supporter, admirer, aficionado, buff (informal), devotee, enthusiast, follower, lover

fanatic noun extremist, bigot, militant, zealot

fanatical adjective passionate, bigoted, extreme, fervent, frenzied, immoderate, obsessive, overenthusiastic, wild, zealous

fanciful adjective unreal, imaginary, mythical, romantic, visionary, whimsical, wild

fancy adjective 1 elaborate, baroque, decorative, embellished, extravagant, intricate, ornamental, ornate ♦ noun 2 whim, caprice, desire, humour, idea, impulse, inclination, notion, thought, urge 3 delusion, chimera, daydream, dream, fantasy, vision ♦ verb 4 suppose, believe, conjecture, imagine, reckon, think, think likely 5 wish for, crave, desire, hanker after, hope for, long for, thirst for, yearn for 6 Informal be attracted to, be captivated by, like, lust after, take a liking to

fantasize verb daydream, dream, envision, imagine

fantastic adjective 1 Informal excellent, awesome (slang), first-rate, marvellous, sensational (informal), superb, wonderful 2 strange, fanciful, grotesque, outlandish 3 unrealistic, extravagant, far-fetched, ludicrous, ridiculous, wild 4 implausible, absurd, cock-and-bull (informal), incredible, preposterous, unlikely

fantasy noun 1 imagination, creativity, fancy, invention, originality 2 daydream, dream, flight of fancy, illusion, mirage, pipe dream, reverie, vision

far adverb 1 a long way, afar, a good way, a great distance, deep, miles 2 much, considerably, decidedly, extremely, greatly, incomparably, very much ♦ adjective 3 remote, distant, faraway, far-flung, far-off, outlying, out-of-the-way

farce noun 1 comedy, buffoonery, burlesque, satire, slapstick 2 mockery, joke, nonsense, parody, sham, travesty

farcical adjective ludicrous, absurd, comic, derisory, laughable, nonsensical, preposterous, ridiculous, risible

fare noun 1 charge, price, ticket money 2 food, provisions, rations, sustenance, victuals ♦ verb 3 get on, do, get along, make out, manage, prosper

farewell noun goodbye, adieu, departure, leave-taking, parting, sendoff (informal), valediction

far-fetched adjective unconvincing, cock-and-bull (informal), fantastic, implausible, incredible, preposterous, unbelievable, unlikely, unrealistic

farm noun 1 smallholding, croft (Scot.), farmstead, grange, homestead, plantation, ranch (chiefly North American) ♦ verb 2 cultivate, plant, work

fascinate verb intrigue, absorb, beguile, captivate, engross, enthral, entrance, hold spellbound, rivet, transfix

fascinating adjective gripping, alluring, captivating, compelling, engaging, engrossing, enticing, intriguing, irresistible, riveting

fascination noun attraction, allure, charm, enchantment, lure, magic, magnetism, pull

fashion noun 1 style, craze, custom, fad, look, mode, rage, trend, vogue 2 method, manner, mode, style, way ♦ verb 3 make, construct, create, forge, form, manufacture, mould, shape

fashionable *adjective* popular, à la mode, chic, in (*informal*), in vogue, modern, stylish, trendy (*Brit. informal*), up-to-date, with it (*informal*)

fast[1] *adjective* **1** quick, brisk, fleet, flying, hasty, nippy (*Brit. informal*), rapid, speedy, swift **2** fixed, close, fastened, firm, immovable, secure, sound, steadfast, tight **3** dissipated, dissolute, extravagant, loose, profligate, reckless, self-indulgent, wanton, wild ◆ *adverb* **4** quickly, hastily, hurriedly, in haste, like lightning, rapidly, speedily, swiftly **5** soundly, deeply, firmly, fixedly, securely, tightly

fast[2] *verb* **1** go hungry, abstain, deny oneself, go without food ◆ *noun* **2** fasting, abstinence

fasten *verb* fix, affix, attach, bind, connect, join, link, secure, tie

fat *adjective* **1** overweight, corpulent, heavy, obese, plump, podgy, portly, rotund, stout, tubby **2** fatty, adipose, greasy, oily, oleaginous ◆ *noun* **3** fatness, blubber, bulk, corpulence, flab, flesh, obesity, paunch

fatal *adjective* **1** lethal, deadly, final, incurable, killing, malignant, mortal, terminal **2** ruinous, baleful, baneful, calamitous, catastrophic, disastrous

fatality *noun* death, casualty, loss, mortality

fate *noun* **1** destiny, chance, divine will, fortune, kismet, nemesis, predestination, providence **2** fortune, cup,

horoscope, lot, portion, stars

fated *adjective* destined, doomed, foreordained, inescapable, inevitable, predestined, preordained, sure, written

fateful *adjective* **1** crucial, critical, decisive, important, portentous, significant **2** disastrous, deadly, destructive, fatal, lethal, ominous, ruinous

father *noun* **1** daddy (*informal*), dad (*informal*), old man (*informal*), papa (*old-fashioned informal*), pater, pop (*informal*) **2** forefather, ancestor, forebear, predecessor, progenitor **3** founder, architect, author, creator, inventor, maker, originator, prime mover **4** priest, padre (*informal*), pastor ◆ *verb* **5** sire, beget, get, procreate

fatherland *noun* homeland, motherland, native land

fatherly *adjective* paternal, affectionate, benevolent, benign, kindly, patriarchal, protective, supportive

fathom *verb* understand, comprehend, get to the bottom of, grasp, interpret

fatigue *noun* **1** tiredness, heaviness, languor, lethargy, listlessness ◆ *verb* **2** tire, drain, exhaust, knacker (*slang*), take it out of (*informal*), weaken, wear out, weary

fatten *verb* **1** grow fat, expand, gain weight, put on weight, spread, swell, thicken **2** *often with up* feed up, build up, feed, nourish, overfeed, stuff

fatty *adjective* greasy, adipose, fat, oily, oleaginous, rich

fatuous adjective foolish, brainless, idiotic, inane, ludicrous, mindless, moronic, silly, stupid, witless

fault noun 1 flaw, blemish, defect, deficiency, failing, imperfection, shortcoming, weakness, weak point 2 mistake, blunder, error, indiscretion, lapse, oversight, slip 3 responsibility, accountability, culpability, liability 4 **at fault** guilty, answerable, blamable, culpable, in the wrong, responsible, to blame 5 **find fault with** criticize, carp at, complain, pick holes in, pull to pieces, quibble, take to task 6 **to a fault** excessively, immoderately, in the extreme, overmuch, unduly ◆ verb 7 criticize, blame, censure, find fault with, hold (someone) responsible, impugn

faultless adjective flawless, correct, exemplary, foolproof, impeccable, model, perfect, unblemished

faulty adjective defective, broken, damaged, flawed, impaired, imperfect, incorrect, malfunctioning, out of order, unsound

favour noun 1 approval, approbation, backing, good opinion, goodwill, patronage, support 2 good turn, benefit, boon, courtesy, indulgence, kindness, service ◆ verb 3 side with, indulge, reward, smile upon 4 advocate, approve, champion, commend, encourage, incline towards, prefer, support

favourable adjective 1 advantageous, auspicious, beneficial, encouraging, helpful, opportune, promising, propitious, suitable 2 positive, affirmative, agreeable, approving, encouraging, enthusiastic, reassuring, sympathetic

favourably adverb 1 advantageously, auspiciously, conveniently, fortunately, opportunely, profitably, to one's advantage, well 2 positively, approvingly, enthusiastically, helpfully, with approval

favourite adjective 1 preferred, best-loved, choice, dearest, esteemed, favoured ◆ noun 2 darling, beloved, blue-eyed boy (informal), idol, pet, teacher's pet, the apple of one's eye

fawn[1] verb, often with **on** or **upon** curry favour, crawl, creep, cringe, dance attendance, flatter, grovel, ingratiate oneself, kowtow, pander to

fawn[2] adjective beige, buff, greyish-brown, neutral

fawning adjective obsequious, crawling, cringing, deferential, flattering, grovelling, servile, sycophantic

fear noun 1 alarm, apprehensiveness, dread, fright, horror, panic, terror, trepidation 2 bugbear, bête noire, bogey, horror, nightmare, spectre ◆ verb 3 be afraid, dread, shake in one's shoes, shudder at, take fright, tremble at 4 **fear for** worry about, be anxious about, feel concern for

fearful adjective 1 <u>scared</u>, afraid, alarmed, frightened, jumpy, nervous, timid, timorous, uneasy 2 <u>frightful</u>, awful, dire, dreadful, gruesome, hair-raising, horrendous, horrific, terrible

fearfully adverb 1 <u>nervously</u>, apprehensively, diffidently, timidly, timorously, uneasily 2 <u>very</u>, awfully, exceedingly, excessively, frightfully, terribly, tremendously

fearless adjective <u>brave</u>, bold, courageous, dauntless, indomitable, intrepid, plucky, unafraid, undaunted, valiant

fearsome adjective <u>terrifying</u>, awe-inspiring, daunting, formidable, frightening, horrifying, menacing, unnerving

feasible adjective <u>possible</u>, achievable, attainable, likely, practicable, reasonable, viable, workable

feast noun 1 <u>banquet</u>, dinner, repast, spread (informal), treat 2 <u>festival</u>, celebration, fête, holiday, holy day, red-letter day, saint's day 3 <u>treat</u>, delight, enjoyment, gratification, pleasure ♦ verb 4 <u>eat one's fill</u>, gorge, gormandize, indulge, overindulge, pig out (slang), wine and dine

feat noun <u>accomplishment</u>, achievement, act, attainment, deed, exploit, performance

feathers plural noun <u>plumage</u>, down, plumes

feature noun 1 <u>aspect</u>, characteristic, facet, factor, hallmark, peculiarity, property, quality, trait 2 <u>highlight</u>, attraction, main item, speciality

3 <u>article</u>, column, item, piece, report, story ♦ verb 4 <u>spotlight</u>, emphasize, foreground, give prominence to, play up, present, star

features plural noun <u>face</u>, countenance, lineaments, physiognomy

feckless adjective <u>irresponsible</u>, good-for-nothing, hopeless, incompetent, ineffectual, shiftless, worthless

federation noun <u>union</u>, alliance, amalgamation, association, coalition, combination, league, syndicate

fed up adjective <u>dissatisfied</u>, bored, brassed off (Brit. slang), depressed, discontented, down in the mouth, glum, sick and tired (informal), tired

fee noun <u>charge</u>, bill, payment, remuneration, toll

feeble adjective 1 <u>weak</u>, debilitated, doddering, effete, frail, infirm, puny, sickly, weedy (informal) 2 <u>unconvincing</u>, flimsy, inadequate, insufficient, lame, paltry, pathetic, poor, tame, thin

feebleness noun <u>weakness</u>, effeteness, frailty, infirmity, languor, lassitude, sickliness

feed verb 1 <u>cater for</u>, nourish, provide for, provision, supply, sustain, victual, wine and dine 2 sometimes with **on** <u>eat</u>, devour, exist on, live on, partake of ♦ noun 3 <u>food</u>, fodder, pasturage, provender 4 Informal <u>meal</u>, feast, nosh (slang), repast, spread (informal)

feel verb 1 <u>touch</u>, caress, finger, fondle, handle, manipulate, paw, stroke 2 <u>experience</u>, be aware

of, notice, observe, perceive
3 sense, be convinced, intuit
4 believe, consider, deem, hold,
judge, think ♦ *noun* **5** texture,
finish, surface, touch
6 impression, air, ambience,
atmosphere, feeling, quality,
sense

feeler *noun* **1** antenna, tentacle,
whisker **2** approach, advance,
probe

feeling *noun* **1** emotion, ardour,
fervour, intensity, passion,
sentiment, warmth **2** impression,
hunch, idea, inkling, notion,
presentiment, sense, suspicion
3 opinion, inclination, instinct,
point of view, view **4** sympathy,
compassion, concern, empathy,
pity, sensibility, sensitivity,
understanding **5** sense of touch,
perception, sensation
6 atmosphere, air, ambience,
aura, feel, mood, quality

fell *verb* cut down, cut, demolish,
hew, knock down, level

fellow *noun* **1** man, bloke (*Brit.
informal*), chap (*informal*),
character, guy (*informal*),
individual, person **2** associate,
colleague, companion, comrade,
partner, peer

fellowship *noun* **1** camaraderie,
brotherhood, companionship,
sociability **2** society, association,
brotherhood, club, fraternity,
guild, league, order

feminine *adjective* womanly,
delicate, gentle, ladylike, soft,
tender

femme fatale *noun* seductress,
enchantress, siren, vamp
(*informal*)

fen *noun* marsh, bog, morass,

quagmire, slough, swamp

fence *noun* **1** barrier, barricade,
defence, hedge, palisade,
railings, rampart, wall ♦ *verb*
2 *often with* **in** *or* **off** enclose,
bound, confine, encircle, pen,
protect, surround **3** evade,
dodge, equivocate, flannel (*Brit.
informal*), parry

ferment *noun* commotion,
disruption, excitement, frenzy,
furore, stir, tumult, turmoil,
unrest, uproar

ferocious *adjective* **1** fierce,
predatory, rapacious, ravening,
savage, violent, wild **2** cruel,
bloodthirsty, brutal, ruthless,
vicious

ferocity *noun* savagery,
bloodthirstiness, brutality,
cruelty, fierceness, viciousness,
wildness

ferret out *verb* track down, dig
up, discover, elicit, root out,
search out, trace, unearth

ferry *noun* **1** ferry boat, packet,
packet boat ♦ *verb* **2** carry,
chauffeur, convey, run, ship,
shuttle, transport

fertile *adjective* rich, abundant,
fecund, fruitful, luxuriant,
plentiful, productive, prolific,
teeming

fertility *noun* fruitfulness,
abundance, fecundity,
luxuriance, productiveness,
richness

fertilizer *noun* compost,
dressing, dung, manure

fervent, fervid *adjective* ardent,
devout, earnest, enthusiastic,
heartfelt, impassioned, intense,
vehement

fervour noun intensity, ardour, enthusiasm, excitement, passion, vehemence, warmth, zeal

fester verb 1 decay, putrefy, suppurate, ulcerate 2 intensify, aggravate, smoulder

festival noun 1 celebration, carnival, entertainment, fête, gala, jubilee 2 holy day, anniversary, commemoration, feast, fête, fiesta, holiday, red-letter day, saint's day

festive adjective celebratory, cheery, convivial, happy, jovial, joyful, joyous, jubilant, merry

festivity noun, often plural celebration, entertainment, festival, party

festoon verb decorate, array, deck, drape, garland, hang, swathe, wreathe

fetch verb 1 bring, carry, convey, deliver, get, go for, obtain, retrieve, transport 2 sell for, bring in, earn, go for, make, realize, yield

fetching adjective attractive, alluring, captivating, charming, cute, enticing, winsome

fetish noun 1 fixation, mania, obsession, thing (informal) 2 talisman, amulet

feud noun 1 hostility, argument, conflict, disagreement, enmity, quarrel, rivalry, row, vendetta ♦ verb 2 quarrel, bicker, clash, contend, dispute, fall out, row, squabble, war

fever noun excitement, agitation, delirium, ferment, fervour, frenzy, restlessness

feverish adjective 1 hot, febrile, fevered, flushed, inflamed, pyretic (Medical) 2 excited, agitated, frantic, frenetic, frenzied, overwrought, restless

few adjective not many, meagre, negligible, rare, scanty, scarcely any, sparse, sporadic

fiasco noun debacle, catastrophe, cock-up (Brit. slang), disaster, failure, mess, washout (informal)

fib noun lie, fiction, story, untruth, white lie

fibre noun 1 thread, filament, pile, strand, texture, wisp 2 essence, nature, quality, spirit, substance 3 As in moral fibre resolution, stamina, strength, toughness

fickle adjective changeable, capricious, faithless, inconstant, irresolute, temperamental, unfaithful, variable, volatile

fiction noun 1 tale, fantasy, legend, myth, novel, romance, story, yarn (informal) 2 lie, cock and bull story (informal), fabrication, falsehood, invention, tall story, untruth, urban legend

fictional adjective imaginary, invented, legendary, made-up, nonexistent, unreal

fictitious adjective false, bogus, fabricated, imaginary, invented, made-up, make-believe, mythical, untrue

fiddle verb 1 fidget, finger, interfere with, mess about or around, play, tamper with, tinker 2 Informal cheat, cook the books (informal), diddle (informal), fix, swindle, wangle (informal) ♦ noun 3 violin 4 Informal fraud, fix, racket, scam (slang), swindle 5 fit as a fiddle healthy, blooming, hale and hearty, in fine fettle, in good form, in good shape, in rude health, in the pink, sound, strong

fiddling *adjective* trivial, futile, insignificant, pettifogging, petty, trifling

fidelity *noun* 1 loyalty, allegiance, constancy, dependability, devotion, faithfulness, staunchness, trustworthiness 2 accuracy, closeness, correspondence, exactness, faithfulness, precision, scrupulousness

fidget *verb* 1 move restlessly, fiddle (*informal*), fret, squirm, twitch ◆ *noun* 2 the fidgets restlessness, fidgetiness, jitters (*informal*), nervousness, unease, uneasiness

fidgety *adjective* restless, impatient, jittery (*informal*), jumpy, nervous, on edge, restive, twitchy (*informal*), uneasy

field *noun* 1 meadow, grassland, green, lea (*poetic*), pasture 2 competitors, applicants, candidates, competition, contestants, entrants, possibilities, runners 3 speciality, area, department, discipline, domain, line, province, territory ◆ *verb* 4 retrieve, catch, pick up, return, stop 5 deal with, deflect, handle, turn aside

fiend *noun* 1 demon, devil, evil spirit 2 brute, barbarian, beast, ghoul, monster, ogre, savage 3 *Informal* enthusiast, addict, fanatic, freak (*informal*), maniac

fiendish *adjective* wicked, cruel, devilish, diabolical, hellish, infernal, malignant, monstrous, satanic, unspeakable

fierce *adjective* 1 wild, brutal, cruel, dangerous, ferocious, fiery, menacing, savage, vicious 2 strong, furious, howling, inclement, powerful, raging, stormy, tempestuous, violent 3 intense, cut-throat, keen, relentless, strong

fiercely *adverb* ferociously, furiously, passionately, savagely, tempestuously, tigerishly, tooth and nail, viciously, with no holds barred

fiery *adjective* 1 burning, ablaze, afire, aflame, blazing, flaming, on fire 2 excitable, fierce, hot-headed, impetuous, irascible, irritable, passionate

fight *verb* 1 battle, box, clash, combat, do battle, grapple, spar, struggle, tussle, wrestle 2 oppose, contest, defy, dispute, make a stand against, resist, stand up to, withstand 3 engage in, carry on, conduct, prosecute, wage ◆ *noun* 4 conflict, action, clash, contest, dispute, duel, encounter, struggle, tussle 5 resistance, belligerence, militancy, pluck, spirit

fighter *noun* 1 soldier, fighting man, man-at-arms, warrior 2 boxer, prize fighter, pugilist

fight off *verb* repel, beat off, keep or hold at bay, repress, repulse, resist, stave off, ward off

figure *noun* 1 number, character, digit, numeral, symbol 2 amount, cost, price, sum, total, value 3 shape, body, build, frame, physique, proportions 4 diagram, design, drawing, illustration, pattern, representation, sketch

5 <u>character</u>, big name, celebrity, dignitary, personality ♦ *verb* **6** <u>calculate</u>, compute, count, reckon, tally, tot up, work out **7** *usually with* **in** feature, act, appear, be featured, contribute to, play a part

figurehead *noun* front man, mouthpiece, puppet, titular *or* nominal head

figure out *verb* **1** <u>calculate</u>, compute, reckon, work out **2** <u>understand</u>, comprehend, decipher, fathom, make out, see

filch *verb* <u>steal</u>, embezzle, misappropriate, pilfer, pinch (*informal*), take, thieve, walk off with

file[1] *noun* **1** <u>folder</u>, case, data, documents, dossier, information, portfolio **2** <u>line</u>, column, queue, row ♦ *verb* **3** <u>register</u>, document, enter, pigeonhole, put in place, record **4** <u>march</u>, parade, troop

file[2] *verb* <u>smooth</u>, abrade, polish, rasp, rub, scrape, shape

fill *verb* **1** <u>stuff</u>, cram, crowd, glut, pack, stock, supply, swell **2** <u>saturate</u>, charge, imbue, impregnate, pervade, suffuse **3** <u>plug</u>, block, bung, close, cork, seal, stop **4** <u>perform</u>, carry out, discharge, execute, fulfil, hold, occupy ♦ *verb* **5** **one's fill** <u>sufficient</u>, all one wants, ample, enough, plenty

filler *noun* padding, makeweight, stopgap

fill in *verb* **1** <u>complete</u>, answer, fill out (*U.S.*), fill up **2** *Informal* <u>inform</u>, acquaint, apprise, bring up to date, give the facts *or* background **3** <u>replace</u>, deputize, represent, stand in, sub,

substitute, take the place of

filling *noun* **1** <u>stuffing</u>, contents, filler, inside, insides, padding, wadding ♦ *adjective* **2** <u>satisfying</u>, ample, heavy, square, substantial

film *noun* **1** <u>movie</u>, flick (*slang*), motion picture **2** <u>layer</u>, coating, covering, dusting, membrane, skin, tissue ♦ *verb* **3** <u>photograph</u>, shoot, take, video, videotape

filter *noun* **1** <u>sieve</u>, gauze, membrane, mesh, riddle, strainer ♦ *verb* **2** <u>purify</u>, clarify, filtrate, refine, screen, sieve, sift, strain, winnow **3** <u>trickle</u>, dribble, escape, exude, leak, ooze, penetrate, percolate, seep

filth *noun* **1** <u>dirt</u>, excrement, grime, muck, refuse, sewage, slime, sludge, squalor **2** <u>obscenity</u>, impurity, indecency, pornography, smut, vulgarity

filthy *adjective* **1** <u>dirty</u>, foul, polluted, putrid, slimy, squalid, unclean **2** <u>muddy</u>, begrimed, blackened, grimy, grubby **3** <u>obscene</u>, corrupt, depraved, impure, indecent, lewd, licentious, pornographic, smutty

final *adjective* **1** <u>last</u>, closing, concluding, latest, terminal, ultimate **2** <u>definitive</u>, absolute, conclusive, decided, definite, incontrovertible, irrevocable, settled

finale *noun* <u>ending</u>, climax, close, conclusion, culmination, denouement, epilogue

finalize *verb* <u>complete</u>, clinch, conclude, decide, settle, tie up, work out, wrap up (*informal*)

finally *adverb* **1** <u>eventually</u>, at last, at length, at long last, in the end, lastly, ultimately **2** in conclusion, in summary, to conclude

finance noun **1** economics, accounts, banking, business, commerce, investment, money ♦ verb **2** fund, back, bankroll (U.S.), guarantee, pay for, subsidize, support, underwrite

finances plural noun resources, affairs, assets, capital, cash, funds, money, wherewithal

financial adjective economic, fiscal, monetary, pecuniary

find verb **1** discover, come across, encounter, hit upon, locate, meet, recognize, spot, uncover **2** perceive, detect, discover, learn, note, notice, observe, realise ♦ noun **3** discovery, acquisition, asset, bargain, catch, good buy

find out verb **1** learn, detect, discover, note, observe, perceive, realize **2** detect, catch, disclose, expose, reveal, uncover, unmask

fine[1] adjective **1** excellent, accomplished, exceptional, exquisite, first-rate, magnificent, masterly, outstanding, splendid, superior **2** sunny, balmy, bright, clear, clement, cloudless, dry, fair, pleasant **3** satisfactory, acceptable, all right, convenient, good, O.K. or okay (informal), suitable **4** delicate, dainty, elegant, expensive, exquisite, fragile, quality **5** subtle, abstruse, acute, hairsplitting, minute, nice, precise, sharp **6** slender, diaphanous, flimsy, gauzy, gossamer, light, sheer, thin

fine[2] noun **1** penalty, damages, forfeit, punishment ♦ verb **2** penalize, mulct, punish

finery noun splendour, frippery, gear (informal), glad rags (informal), ornaments, showiness, Sunday best, trappings, trinkets

finesse noun skill, adeptness, adroitness, craft, delicacy, diplomacy, discretion, savoir-faire, sophistication, subtlety, tact

finger verb touch, feel, fiddle with (informal), handle, manipulate, maul, paw (informal), toy with

finish verb **1** stop, cease, close, complete, conclude, end, round off, terminate, wind up, wrap up **2** consume, devour, dispose of, eat, empty, exhaust, use up **3** destroy, bring down, defeat, dispose of, exterminate, overcome, put an end to, put paid to, rout, ruin **4** perfect, polish, refine **5** coat, gild, lacquer, polish, stain, texture, veneer, wax ♦ noun **6** end, cessation, close, completion, conclusion, culmination, denouement, finale, run-in **7** defeat, annihilation, curtains (informal), death, end, end of the road, ruin **8** surface, lustre, patina, polish, shine, smoothness, texture

finished adjective **1** polished, accomplished, perfected, professional, refined **2** over, closed, complete, done, ended, finalized, through **3** spent, done, drained, empty, exhausted, used up **4** ruined, defeated, done for (informal), doomed, lost, through, undone, wiped out

finite adjective limited, bounded, circumscribed, delimited, demarcated, restricted

fire noun **1** flames, blaze, combustion, conflagration, inferno **2** bombardment, barrage, cannonade, flak, fusillade, hail, salvo, shelling, sniping, volley **3** passion, ardour, eagerness, enthusiasm, excitement, fervour, intensity, sparkle, spirit, verve, vigour ♦ verb **4** shoot, detonate, discharge, explode, let off, pull the trigger, set off, shell **5** inspire, animate, enliven, excite, galvanize, impassion, inflame, rouse, stir **6** Informal dismiss, cashier, discharge, make redundant, sack (informal), show the door

firebrand noun rabble-rouser, agitator, demagogue, incendiary, instigator, tub-thumper

fireworks plural noun **1** pyrotechnics, illuminations **2** rage, hysterics, row, storm, trouble, uproar

firm¹ adjective **1** hard, dense, inflexible, rigid, set, solid, solidified, stiff, unyielding **2** secure, embedded, fast, fixed, immovable, rooted, stable, steady, tight, unshakable **3** definite, adamant, inflexible, resolute, resolved, set on, unbending, unshakable, unyielding

firm² noun company, association, business, concern, conglomerate, corporation, enterprise, organization, partnership

firmly adverb **1** securely, immovably, like a rock, steadily, tightly, unflinchingly, unshakably **2** resolutely, staunchly,

steadfastly, unchangeably, unwaveringly

firmness noun **1** hardness, inelasticity, inflexibility, resistance, rigidity, solidity, stiffness **2** resolve, constancy, inflexibility, resolution, staunchness, steadfastness

first adjective **1** foremost, chief, head, highest, leading, pre-eminent, prime, principal, ruling **2** earliest, initial, introductory, maiden, opening, original, premier, primordial **3** elementary, basic, cardinal, fundamental, key, primary, rudimentary ♦ noun **4** As in from the first start, beginning, commencement, inception, introduction, outset, starting point ♦ adverb **5** beforehand, at the beginning, at the outset, firstly, initially, in the first place, to begin with, to start with

first-rate adjective excellent, crack (slang), elite, exceptional, first class, outstanding, superb, superlative, top-notch (informal), world-class

fishy adjective **1** Informal suspicious, dodgy (Brit., Austral., & N.Z. informal), dubious, funny (informal), implausible, odd, questionable, suspect, unlikely **2** fishlike, piscatorial, piscatory, piscine

fissure noun crack, breach, cleft, crevice, fault, fracture, opening, rift, rupture, split

fit¹ verb **1** match, accord, belong, conform, correspond, meet, suit, tally **2** prepare, arm, equip, fit out, kit out, provide **3** adapt, adjust, alter, arrange, customize,

modify, shape, tweak (*informal*)
♦ *adjective* **4** appropriate, apt, becoming, correct, fitting, proper, right, seemly, suitable **5** healthy, able-bodied, hale, in good shape, robust, strapping, trim, well

fit² *noun* **1** seizure, attack, bout, convulsion, paroxysm, spasm **2** outbreak, bout, burst, outburst, spell

fitful *adjective* irregular, broken, desultory, disturbed, inconstant, intermittent, spasmodic, sporadic, uneven

fitness *noun* **1** appropriateness, aptness, competence, eligibility, propriety, readiness, suitability **2** health, good condition, good health, robustness, strength, vigour

fitting *adjective* **1** appropriate, apposite, becoming, correct, decent, proper, right, seemly, suitable ♦ *noun* **2** accessory, attachment, component, part, piece, unit

fix *verb* **1** place, embed, establish, implant, install, locate, plant, position, set **2** fasten, attach, bind, connect, link, secure, stick, tie **3** decide, agree on, arrange, arrive at, determine, establish, set, settle, specify **4** repair, correct, mend, patch up, put to rights, see to **5** focus, direct **6** *Informal* manipulate, fiddle (*informal*), influence, rig ♦ *noun* **7** *Informal* predicament, difficulty, dilemma, embarrassment, mess, pickle (*informal*), plight, quandary

fixation *noun* preoccupation, complex, hang-up (*informal*), idée

fixe, infatuation, mania, obsession, thing (*informal*)

fixed *adjective* **1** permanent, established, immovable, rigid, rooted, secure, set **2** intent, resolute, steady, unwavering **3** agreed, arranged, decided, definite, established, planned, resolved, settled

fix up *verb* **1** arrange, agree on, fix, organize, plan, settle, sort out **2** *often with* with provide, arrange for, bring about, lay on

fizz *verb* bubble, effervesce, fizzle, froth, hiss, sparkle, sputter

fizzy *adjective* bubbly, bubbling, carbonated, effervescent, gassy, sparkling

flabbergasted *adjective* astonished, amazed, astounded, dumbfounded, lost for words, overwhelmed, speechless, staggered, stunned

flabby *adjective* limp, baggy, drooping, flaccid, floppy, loose, pendulous, sagging

flag¹ *noun* **1** banner, colours, ensign, pennant, pennon, standard, streamer ♦ *verb* **2** mark, indicate, label, note **3** *sometimes with* down hail, signal, warn, wave

flag² *verb* weaken, abate, droop, fade, languish, peter out, sag, wane, weary, wilt

flagging *adjective* fading, declining, deteriorating, faltering, waning, weakening, wilting

flagrant *adjective* outrageous, barefaced, blatant, brazen, glaring, heinous, scandalous, shameless

flagstone noun <u>paving stone</u>, block, flag, slab

flail verb <u>thrash</u>, beat, thresh, windmill

flair noun 1 <u>ability</u>, aptitude, faculty, feel, genius, gift, knack, mastery, talent 2 <u>style</u>, chic, dash, discernment, elegance, panache, stylishness, taste

flake noun 1 <u>wafer</u>, layer, peeling, scale, shaving, sliver ♦ verb 2 <u>blister</u>, chip, peel (off)

flake out verb <u>collapse</u>, faint, keel over, pass out

flamboyant adjective
1 <u>extravagant</u>, dashing, elaborate, florid, ornate, ostentatious, showy, swashbuckling, theatrical 2 <u>colourful</u>, brilliant, dazzling, glamorous, glitzy (slang)

flame noun 1 <u>fire</u>, blaze, brightness, light 2 Informal <u>sweetheart</u>, beau, boyfriend, girlfriend, heart-throb (Brit.), lover ♦ verb 3 <u>burn</u>, blaze, flare, flash, glare, glow, shine

flaming adjective <u>burning</u>, ablaze, blazing, fiery, glowing, raging, red-hot

flank noun 1 <u>side</u>, hip, loin, thigh 2 <u>wing</u>, side

flap verb 1 <u>flutter</u>, beat, flail, shake, thrash, vibrate, wag, wave ♦ noun 2 <u>flutter</u>, beating, shaking, swinging, swish, waving 3 Informal <u>panic</u>, agitation, commotion, fluster, state (informal), sweat (informal), tizzy (informal)

flare verb 1 <u>blaze</u>, burn up, flicker, glare 2 <u>widen</u>, broaden, spread out ♦ noun 3 <u>flame</u>, blaze,

burst, flash, flicker, glare

flare up verb <u>lose one's temper</u>, blow one's top (informal), boil over, explode, fly off the handle (informal), throw a tantrum

flash noun 1 <u>blaze</u>, burst, dazzle, flare, flicker, gleam, shimmer, spark, streak 2 <u>moment</u>, instant, jiffy (informal), second, split second, trice, twinkling of an eye ♦ adjective 3 Informal <u>ostentatious</u>, tacky (informal), tasteless, vulgar ♦ verb 4 <u>blaze</u>, flare, flicker, glare, gleam, shimmer, sparkle, twinkle 5 <u>speed</u>, dart, dash, fly, race, shoot, streak, whistle, zoom 6 <u>show</u>, display, exhibit, expose, flaunt, flourish

flashy adjective <u>showy</u>, flamboyant, garish, gaudy, glitzy (slang), jazzy (informal), ostentatious, snazzy (informal)

flat¹ adjective 1 <u>even</u>, horizontal, level, levelled, low, smooth 2 <u>dull</u>, boring, dead, lacklustre, lifeless, monotonous, tedious, tiresome, uninteresting 3 <u>absolute</u>, categorical, downright, explicit, out-and-out, positive, unequivocal 4 <u>punctured</u>, blown out, burst, collapsed, deflated, empty ♦ adverb 5 <u>completely</u>, absolutely, categorically, exactly, point blank, precisely, utterly 6 <u>flat out</u> at full speed, all out, at full pelt, at full tilt, for all one is worth, hell for leather (informal)

flat² noun <u>apartment</u>, rooms

flatly adverb <u>absolutely</u>, categorically, completely, positively, unhesitatingly

flatness noun 1 <u>evenness</u>, smoothness, uniformity

2 <u>dullness</u>, monotony, tedium

flatten verb <u>level</u>, compress, even out, iron out, raze, smooth off, squash, trample

flatter verb 1 <u>praise</u>, butter up, compliment, pander to, soft-soap (*informal*), sweet-talk (*informal*), wheedle 2 <u>suit</u>, become, do something for, enhance, set off, show to advantage

flattering adjective 1 <u>becoming</u>, effective, enhancing, kind, well-chosen 2 <u>ingratiating</u>, adulatory, complimentary, fawning, fulsome, laudatory

flattery noun <u>obsequiousness</u>, adulation, blandishment, fawning, servility, soft-soap (*informal*), sweet-talk (*informal*), sycophancy

flaunt verb <u>show off</u>, brandish, display, exhibit, flash about, flourish, parade, sport (*informal*)

flavour noun 1 <u>taste</u>, aroma, flavouring, piquancy, relish, savour, seasoning, smack, tang, zest 2 <u>quality</u>, character, essence, feel, feeling, style, tinge, tone ♦ verb 3 <u>season</u>, ginger up, imbue, infuse, leaven, spice

flaw noun <u>weakness</u>, blemish, chink in one's armour, defect, failing, fault, imperfection, weak spot

flawed adjective <u>damaged</u>, blemished, defective, erroneous, faulty, imperfect, unsound

flawless adjective <u>perfect</u>, faultless, impeccable, spotless, unblemished, unsullied

flee verb <u>run away</u>, bolt, depart,

escape, fly, make one's getaway, scarper (*Brit. slang*), take flight, take off (*informal*), take to one's heels, turn tail

fleet noun <u>navy</u>, armada, flotilla, task force

fleeting adjective <u>momentary</u>, brief, ephemeral, passing, short-lived, temporary, transient, transitory

flesh noun 1 <u>meat</u>, brawn, fat, tissue, weight 2 <u>human nature</u>, carnality, flesh and blood 3 **one's own flesh and blood** <u>family</u>, blood, kin, kinsfolk, kith and kin, relations, relatives

flexibility noun <u>adaptability</u>, adjustability, elasticity, give (*informal*), pliability, pliancy, resilience, springiness

flexible adjective 1 <u>pliable</u>, elastic, lithe, plastic, pliant, springy, stretchy, supple 2 <u>adaptable</u>, adjustable, discretionary, open, variable

flick verb 1 <u>strike</u>, dab, flip, hit, tap, touch 2 **flick through** <u>browse</u>, flip through, glance at, skim, skip, thumb

flicker verb 1 <u>twinkle</u>, flare, flash, glimmer, gutter, shimmer, sparkle 2 <u>flutter</u>, quiver, vibrate, waver ♦ noun 3 <u>glimmer</u>, flare, flash, gleam, spark 4 <u>trace</u>, breath, glimmer, iota, spark

flight[1] noun 1 *Of air travel* <u>journey</u>, trip, voyage 2 <u>aviation</u>, aeronautics, flying 3 <u>flock</u>, cloud, formation, squadron, swarm, unit

flight[2] noun <u>escape</u>, departure, exit, exodus, fleeing, getaway, retreat, running away

flimsy adjective 1 <u>fragile</u>, delicate,

frail, insubstantial, makeshift, rickety, shaky **2** thin, gauzy, gossamer, light, sheer, transparent **3** unconvincing, feeble, implausible, inadequate, pathetic, poor, unsatisfactory, weak

flinch verb recoil, cower, cringe, draw back, quail, shirk, shrink, shy away, wince

fling verb **1** throw, cast, catapult, heave, hurl, propel, sling, toss ♦ noun **2** binge (informal), bash, good time, party, rave-up (Brit. slang), spree

flip verb, noun toss, flick, snap, spin, throw

flippancy noun frivolity, impertinence, irreverence, levity, pertness, sauciness

flippant adjective frivolous, cheeky, disrespectful, glib, impertinent, irreverent, offhand, superficial

flirt verb **1** lead on, chat up (informal), make advances, make eyes at, make sheep's eyes at, philander **2** usually with with toy with, consider, dabble in, entertain, expose oneself to, give a thought to, play with, trifle with ♦ noun **3** tease, coquette, heart-breaker, philanderer

flirtatious adjective teasing, amorous, come-hither, coquettish, coy, enticing, flirty, provocative, sportive

float verb **1** be buoyant, hang, hover **2** glide, bob, drift, move gently, sail, slide, slip along **3** launch, get going, promote, set up

floating adjective **1** buoyant, afloat, buoyed up, sailing, swimming **2** fluctuating, free, movable, unattached, variable, wandering

flock noun **1** herd, colony, drove, flight, gaggle, skein **2** crowd, collection, company, congregation, gathering, group, herd, host, mass ♦ verb **3** gather, collect, congregate, converge, crowd, herd, huddle, mass, throng

flog verb beat, flagellate, flay, lash, scourge, thrash, trounce, whack, whip

flood noun **1** deluge, downpour, inundation, overflow, spate, tide, torrent **2** abundance, flow, glut, profusion, rush, stream, torrent ♦ verb **3** immerse, drown, inundate, overflow, pour over, submerge, swamp **4** engulf, overwhelm, surge, swarm, sweep **5** oversupply, choke, fill, glut, saturate

floor noun **1** tier, level, stage, storey ♦ verb **2** knock down, deck (slang), prostrate **3** Informal bewilder, baffle, confound, defeat, disconcert, dumbfound, perplex, puzzle, stump, throw (informal)

flop verb **1** fall, collapse, dangle, droop, drop, sag, slump **2** Informal fail, come unstuck, fall flat, fold (informal), founder, go belly-up (slang), misfire ♦ noun **3** Informal failure, debacle, disaster, fiasco, nonstarter, washout (informal)

floppy adjective droopy, baggy, flaccid, limp, loose, pendulous, sagging, soft

floral adjective flowery, flower-patterned

florid adjective 1 flushed, blowsy, high-coloured, rubicund, ruddy 2 flowery, baroque, flamboyant, fussy, high-flown, ornate, overelaborate

flotsam noun debris, detritus, jetsam, junk, odds and ends, wreckage

flounder verb fumble, grope, struggle, stumble, thrash, toss

flourish verb 1 prosper, bloom, blossom, boom, flower, grow, increase, succeed, thrive 2 wave, brandish, display, flaunt, shake, wield ♦ noun 3 wave, display, fanfare, parade, show 4 ornamentation, curlicue, decoration, embellishment, plume, sweep

flourishing adjective successful, blooming, going places, in the pink, luxuriant, prospering, rampant, thriving

flout verb defy, laugh in the face of, mock, scoff at, scorn, sneer at, spurn

flow verb 1 run, circulate, course, move, roll 2 pour, cascade, flood, gush, rush, stream, surge, sweep 3 result, arise, emanate, emerge, issue, proceed, spring ♦ noun 4 tide, course, current, drift, flood, flux, outpouring, spate, stream

flower noun 1 bloom, blossom, efflorescence 2 elite, best, cream, crème de la crème, pick ♦ verb 3 blossom, bloom, flourish, mature, open, unfold

flowery adjective ornate, baroque, embellished, fancy, florid, high-flown

flowing adjective 1 streaming, falling, gushing, rolling, rushing, smooth, sweeping 2 fluent, continuous, easy, smooth, unbroken, uninterrupted

fluctuate verb change, alternate, oscillate, seesaw, shift, swing, vary, veer, waver

fluency noun ease, articulateness, assurance, command, control, facility, readiness, slickness, smoothness

fluent adjective smooth, articulate, easy, effortless, flowing, natural, voluble, well-versed

fluff noun 1 fuzz, down, nap, pile ♦ verb 2 Informal spoil, bungle, make a mess off, mess up (informal), muddle

fluffy adjective soft, downy, feathery, fleecy, fuzzy

fluid noun 1 liquid, liquor, solution ♦ adjective 2 liquid, flowing, liquefied, melted, molten, runny, watery

fluke noun lucky break, accident, chance, coincidence, quirk of fate, serendipity, stroke of luck

flurry noun 1 commotion, ado, bustle, disturbance, excitement, flutter, fuss, stir 2 gust, squall

flush[1] verb 1 blush, colour, glow, go red, redden 2 rinse out, cleanse, flood, hose down, wash out ♦ noun 3 blush, colour, glow, redness, rosiness

flush[2] adjective 1 level, even, flat, square, true 2 Informal wealthy, in the money (informal), moneyed, rich, well-heeled (informal), well-off

flushed adjective blushing, crimson, embarrassed, glowing, hot, red, rosy, ruddy

fluster verb 1 upset, agitate, bother, confuse, disturb, perturb, rattle (informal), ruffle, unnerve ◆ noun 2 turmoil, disturbance, dither (chiefly Brit.), flap (informal), flurry, flutter, furore, state (informal)

flutter verb 1 beat, flap, palpitate, quiver, ripple, tremble, vibrate, waver ◆ noun 2 vibration, palpitation, quiver, shiver, shudder, tremble, tremor, twitching 3 agitation, commotion, confusion, dither (chiefly Brit.), excitement, fluster, state (informal)

fly verb 1 take wing, flit, flutter, hover, sail, soar, wing 2 pilot, control, manoeuvre, operate 3 display, flap, float, flutter, show, wave 4 pass, elapse, flit, glide, pass swiftly, roll on, run its course, slip away 5 rush, career, dart, dash, hurry, race, shoot, speed, sprint, tear 6 flee, escape, get away, run for it, skedaddle (informal), take to one's heels

flying adjective hurried, brief, fleeting, hasty, rushed, short-lived, transitory

foam noun 1 froth, bubbles, head, lather, spray, spume, suds ◆ verb 2 bubble, boil, effervesce, fizz, froth, lather

focus noun 1 centre, focal point, heart, hub, target ◆ verb 2 concentrate, aim, centre, direct, fix, pinpoint, spotlight, zoom in

foe noun enemy, adversary, antagonist, opponent, rival

fog noun mist, gloom, miasma, murk, peasouper (informal), smog

foggy adjective misty, cloudy,

dim, hazy, indistinct, murky, smoggy, vaporous

foil¹ verb thwart, balk, counter, defeat, disappoint, frustrate, nullify, stop

foil² noun contrast, antithesis, complement

foist verb impose, fob off, palm off, pass off, sneak in, unload

fold verb 1 bend, crease, double over 2 Informal go bankrupt, collapse, crash, fail, go bust (informal), go to the wall, go under, shut down ◆ noun 3 crease, bend, furrow, overlap, pleat, wrinkle

folder noun file, binder, envelope, portfolio

folk noun people, clan, family, kin, kindred, race, tribe

follow verb 1 come after, come next, succeed, supersede, supplant, take the place of 2 pursue, chase, dog, hound, hunt, shadow, stalk, track, trail 3 accompany, attend, escort, tag along 4 obey, be guided by, conform, heed, observe 5 understand, appreciate, catch on (informal), comprehend, fathom, grasp, realize, take in 6 result, arise, develop, ensue, flow, issue, proceed, spring 7 be interested in, cultivate, keep abreast of, support

follower noun supporter, adherent, apostle, devotee, disciple, fan, pupil

following adjective 1 next, consequent, ensuing, later, subsequent, succeeding, successive ◆ noun 2 supporters, clientele, coterie, entourage, fans, retinue, suite, train

folly noun <u>foolishness</u>, imprudence, indiscretion, lunacy, madness, nonsense, rashness, stupidity

fond adjective **1** <u>loving</u>, adoring, affectionate, amorous, caring, devoted, doting, indulgent, tender, warm **2** <u>foolish</u>, deluded, delusive, empty, naive, overoptimistic, vain **3** fond of <u>keen on</u>, addicted to, attached to, enamoured of, having a soft spot for, hooked on, into (informal), partial to

fondle verb <u>caress</u>, cuddle, dandle, pat, pet, stroke

fondly adverb **1** <u>lovingly</u>, affectionately, dearly, indulgently, possessively, tenderly, with affection **2** <u>foolishly</u>, credulously, naively, stupidly, vainly

fondness noun **1** <u>liking</u>, attachment, fancy, love, partiality, penchant, soft spot, taste, weakness **2** <u>devotion</u>, affection, attachment, kindness, love, tenderness

food noun <u>nourishment</u>, cuisine, diet, fare, grub (slang), nutrition, rations, refreshment

fool noun **1** <u>simpleton</u>, blockhead, dunce, halfwit, idiot, ignoramus, imbecile (informal), numbskull or numskull, twit (informal, chiefly Brit.) **2** <u>dupe</u>, fall guy (informal), laughing stock, mug (Brit. slang), stooge (slang), sucker (slang) **3** <u>clown</u>, buffoon, harlequin, jester ♦ verb **4** <u>deceive</u>, beguile, con (informal), delude, dupe, hoodwink, mislead, take in, trick

foolhardy adjective <u>rash</u>,

hot-headed, impetuous, imprudent, irresponsible, reckless

foolish adjective <u>unwise</u>, absurd, ill-judged, imprudent, injudicious, senseless, silly

foolishly adverb <u>unwisely</u>, idiotically, ill-advisedly, imprudently, injudiciously, mistakenly, stupidly

foolishness noun <u>stupidity</u>, absurdity, folly, imprudence, indiscretion, irresponsibility, silliness, weakness

foolproof adjective <u>infallible</u>, certain, guaranteed, safe, sure-fire (informal), unassailable, unbreakable

footing noun **1** <u>basis</u>, foundation, groundwork **2** <u>relationship</u>, grade, position, rank, standing, status

footling adjective <u>trivial</u>, fiddling, hairsplitting, insignificant, minor, petty, silly, trifling, unimportant

footstep noun <u>step</u>, footfall, tread

forage verb **1** <u>search</u>, cast about, explore, hunt, rummage, scour, seek ♦ noun **2** Cattle, etc. <u>fodder</u>, feed, food, provender

foray noun <u>raid</u>, incursion, inroad, invasion, sally, sortie, swoop

forbear verb <u>refrain</u>, abstain, cease, desist, hold back, keep from, restrain oneself, stop

forbearance noun <u>patience</u>, long-suffering, moderation, resignation, restraint, self-control, temperance, tolerance

forbearing adjective <u>patient</u>, forgiving, indulgent, lenient, long-suffering, merciful, moderate, tolerant

forbid verb prohibit, ban, disallow, exclude, outlaw, preclude, rule out, veto

forbidden adjective prohibited, banned, outlawed, out of bounds, proscribed, taboo, vetoed

forbidding adjective threatening, daunting, frightening, hostile, menacing, ominous, sinister, unfriendly

force noun 1 power, energy, impulse, might, momentum, pressure, strength, vigour 2 compulsion, arm-twisting (informal), coercion, constraint, duress, pressure, violence 3 intensity, emphasis, fierceness, vehemence, vigour 4 army, host, legion, patrol, regiment, squad, troop, unit 5 in force: **a** valid, binding, current, effective, in operation, operative, working **b** in great numbers, all together, in full strength ♦ verb 6 compel, coerce, constrain, drive, impel, make, oblige, press, pressurize 7 break open, blast, prise, wrench, wrest 8 push, propel, thrust

forced adjective 1 compulsory, conscripted, enforced, involuntary, mandatory, obligatory 2 false, affected, artificial, contrived, insincere, laboured, stiff, strained, unnatural, wooden

forceful adjective powerful, cogent, compelling, convincing, dynamic, effective, persuasive

forcible adjective 1 violent, aggressive, armed, coercive, compulsory 2 strong,

compelling, energetic, forceful, potent, powerful, weighty

forebear noun ancestor, father, forefather, forerunner, predecessor

foreboding noun dread, anxiety, apprehension, apprehensiveness, chill, fear, misgiving, premonition, presentiment

forecast verb 1 predict, anticipate, augur, divine, foresee, foretell, prophesy ♦ noun 2 prediction, conjecture, guess, prognosis, prophecy

forefather noun ancestor, father, forebear, forerunner, predecessor

forefront noun lead, centre, fore, foreground, front, prominence, spearhead, vanguard

foregoing adjective preceding, above, antecedent, anterior, former, previous, prior

foreign adjective alien, exotic, external, imported, remote, strange, unfamiliar, unknown

foreigner noun alien, immigrant, incomer, stranger

foremost adjective leading, chief, highest, paramount, pre-eminent, primary, prime, principal, supreme

forerunner noun precursor, envoy, harbinger, herald, prototype

foresee verb anticipate, envisage, forecast, foretell, predict, prophesy

foreshadow verb predict, augur, forebode, indicate, portend, prefigure, presage, promise, signal

foresight noun anticipation, far-sightedness, forethought, precaution, preparedness, prescience, prudence

foretell verb predict, forecast, forewarn, presage, prognosticate, prophesy

forethought noun anticipation, far-sightedness, foresight, precaution, providence, provision, prudence

forever adverb 1 evermore, always, for all time, for keeps, in perpetuity, till Doomsday, till the cows come home (informal) 2 constantly, all the time, continually, endlessly, eternally, incessantly, interminably, perpetually, unremittingly

forewarn verb caution, advise, alert, apprise, give fair warning, put on guard, tip off

forfeit noun 1 penalty, damages, fine, forfeiture, loss, mulct ♦ verb 2 lose, be deprived of, be stripped of, give up, relinquish, renounce, say goodbye to, surrender

forge verb 1 create, construct, devise, fashion, form, frame, make, mould, shape, work 2 falsify, copy, counterfeit, fake, feign, imitate

forgery noun 1 fraudulence, coining, counterfeiting, falsification, fraudulent imitation 2 fake, counterfeit, falsification, imitation, phoney or phony (informal), sham

forget verb neglect, leave behind, lose sight of, omit, overlook

forgetful adjective absent-minded, careless, inattentive, neglectful, oblivious, unmindful, vague

forgive verb excuse, absolve, acquit, condone, exonerate, let bygones be bygones, let off (informal), pardon

forgiveness noun pardon, absolution, acquittal, amnesty, exoneration, mercy, remission

forgiving adjective merciful, clement, compassionate, forbearing, lenient, magnanimous, soft-hearted, tolerant

forgo verb give up, abandon, do without, relinquish, renounce, resign, surrender, waive, yield

forgotten adjective left behind, bygone, lost, omitted, past, past recall, unremembered

fork verb branch, bifurcate, diverge, divide, part, split

forked adjective branching, angled, bifurcate(d), branched, divided, pronged, split, zigzag

forlorn adjective miserable, disconsolate, down in the dumps (informal), helpless, hopeless, pathetic, pitiful, unhappy, woebegone, wretched

form noun 1 shape, appearance, configuration, formation, pattern, structure 2 type, kind, sort, style, variety 3 condition, fettle, fitness, health, shape, trim 4 procedure, convention, custom, etiquette, protocol 5 document, application, paper, sheet 6 class, grade, rank ♦ verb 7 make, build, construct, fashion, forge, mould, produce, shape 8 arrange, combine, draw up, organize 9 take shape, appear, become visible, come into being, crystallize, grow, materialize, rise 10 develop, acquire, contract, cultivate, pick up **11** constitute, compose, comprise, make up

formal adjective **1** official, ceremonial, ritualistic, solemn **2** conventional, affected, correct, precise, stiff, unbending

formality noun **1** convention, custom, procedure, red tape, rite, ritual **2** correctness, decorum, etiquette, protocol

format noun style, appearance, arrangement, construction, form, layout, look, make-up, plan, type

formation noun **1** establishment, constitution, development, forming, generation, genesis, manufacture, production **2** pattern, arrangement, configuration, design, grouping, structure

formative adjective developmental, influential

former adjective previous, earlier, erstwhile, one-time, prior

formerly adverb previously, at one time, before, lately, once

formidable adjective **1** intimidating, daunting, dismaying, fearful, frightful, menacing, terrifying, threatening **2** impressive, awesome, great, mighty, powerful, redoubtable, terrific, tremendous

formula noun method, blueprint, precept, principle, procedure, recipe, rule

formulate verb **1** define, detail, express, frame, give form to, set down, specify, systematize **2** devise, develop, forge, invent, map out, originate, plan, work out

forsake verb **1** desert, abandon, disown, leave in the lurch, strand **2** give up, forgo, relinquish, renounce, set aside, surrender, yield

forsaken adjective deserted, abandoned, disowned, forlorn, left in the lurch, marooned, outcast, stranded

fort noun **1** fortress, blockhouse, camp, castle, citadel, fortification, garrison, stronghold **2 hold the fort** stand in, carry on, keep things on an even keel, take over the reins

forte noun speciality, gift, long suit (informal), métier, strength, strong point, talent

forth adverb forward, ahead, away, onward, out, outward

forthcoming adjective **1** approaching, coming, expected, future, imminent, impending, prospective, upcoming **2** accessible, at hand, available, in evidence, obtainable, on tap (informal), ready **3** communicative, chatty, expansive, free, informative, open, sociable, talkative, unreserved

forthright adjective outspoken, blunt, candid, direct, frank, open, plain-spoken, straightforward, upfront (informal)

forthwith adverb at once, directly, immediately, instantly, quickly, right away, straightaway, without delay

fortification noun **1** defence, bastion, fastness, fort, fortress, protection, stronghold **2** strengthening, reinforcement

fortify verb strengthen, augment,

buttress, protect, reinforce, shore up, support

fortitude noun <u>courage</u>, backbone, bravery, fearlessness, grit, perseverance, resolution, strength, valour

fortress noun <u>castle</u>, citadel, fastness, fort, redoubt, stronghold

fortunate adjective **1** <u>lucky</u>, favoured, in luck, jammy (Brit. slang), successful, well-off **2** <u>favourable</u>, advantageous, convenient, expedient, felicitous, fortuitous, helpful, opportune, providential, timely

fortunately adverb <u>luckily</u>, by a happy chance, by good luck, happily, providentially

fortune noun **1** <u>wealth</u>, affluence, opulence, possessions, property, prosperity, riches, treasure **2** <u>luck</u>, chance, destiny, fate, kismet, providence **3** <u>fortunes</u> destiny, adventures, experiences, history, lot, success

forward adjective **1** <u>leading</u>, advance, first, foremost, front, head **2** <u>presumptuous</u>, bold, brash, brazen, cheeky, familiar, impertinent, impudent, pushy (informal) **3** <u>well-developed</u>, advanced, precocious, premature ♦ adverb **4** <u>ahead</u>, forth, on, onward ♦ verb **5** <u>promote</u>, advance, assist, expedite, further, hasten, hurry **6** <u>send</u>, dispatch, post, send on

foster verb **1** <u>promote</u>, cultivate, encourage, feed, nurture, stimulate, support, uphold **2** <u>bring up</u>, mother, nurse, raise, rear, take care of

foul adjective **1** <u>dirty</u>, fetid, filthy, malodorous, nauseating, putrid,

repulsive, squalid, stinking, unclean **2** <u>obscene</u>, abusive, blue, coarse, indecent, lewd, profane, scurrilous, vulgar **3** <u>offensive</u>, abhorrent, despicable, detestable, disgraceful, scandalous, shameful, wicked **4** <u>unfair</u>, crooked, dishonest, fraudulent, shady (informal), underhand, unscrupulous ♦ verb **5** <u>pollute</u>, besmirch, contaminate, defile, dirty, stain, sully, taint

found verb <u>establish</u>, constitute, create, inaugurate, institute, organize, originate, set up, start

foundation noun **1** <u>groundwork</u>, base, basis, bedrock, bottom, footing, substructure, underpinning **2** <u>setting up</u>, endowment, establishment, inauguration, institution, organization, settlement

founder¹ noun <u>initiator</u>, architect, author, beginner, father, inventor, originator

founder² verb **1** <u>sink</u>, be lost, go down, go to the bottom, submerge **2** <u>fail</u>, break down, collapse, come to grief, come unstuck, fall through, miscarry, misfire **3** <u>stumble</u>, lurch, sprawl, stagger, trip

foundling noun <u>stray</u>, orphan, outcast, waif

fountain noun **1** <u>jet</u>, font, fount, reservoir, spout, spray, spring, well **2** <u>source</u>, cause, derivation, fount, fountainhead, origin, wellspring

foyer noun <u>entrance hall</u>, antechamber, anteroom, lobby, reception area, vestibule

fracas noun <u>brawl</u>, affray (Law),

disturbance, melee or mêlée, riot, rumpus, scuffle, skirmish

fraction noun piece, part, percentage, portion, section, segment, share, slice

fractious adjective irritable, captious, cross, petulant, querulous, refractory, testy, tetchy, touchy

fracture noun 1 break, cleft, crack, fissure, opening, rift, rupture, split ♦ verb 2 break, crack, rupture, splinter, split

fragile adjective delicate, breakable, brittle, dainty, fine, flimsy, frail, frangible, weak

fragment noun 1 piece, bit, chip, particle, portion, scrap, shred, sliver ♦ verb 2 break, break up, come apart, come to pieces, crumble, disintegrate, shatter, splinter, split up

fragmentary adjective incomplete, bitty, broken, disconnected, incoherent, partial, piecemeal, scattered, scrappy, sketchy

fragrance noun scent, aroma, balm, bouquet, fragrancy, perfume, redolence, smell, sweet odour

fragrant adjective perfumed, aromatic, balmy, odorous, redolent, sweet-scented, sweet-smelling

frail adjective weak, delicate, feeble, flimsy, fragile, infirm, insubstantial, puny, vulnerable

frailty noun feebleness, fallibility, frailness, infirmity, susceptibility, weakness

frame noun 1 casing, construction, framework, shell,

structure 2 physique, anatomy, body, build, carcass 3 **frame of mind** mood, attitude, disposition, humour, outlook, state, temper ♦ verb 4 construct, assemble, build, make, manufacture, put together 5 draft, compose, devise, draw up, formulate, map out, sketch 6 mount, case, enclose, surround

framework noun structure, foundation, frame, groundwork, plan, shell, skeleton, the bare bones

frank adjective honest, blunt, candid, direct, forthright, open, outspoken, plain-spoken, sincere, straightforward, truthful

frankly adverb honestly, candidly, in truth, to be honest 2 openly, bluntly, directly, freely, plainly, without reserve

frankness noun outspokenness, bluntness, candour, forthrightness, openness, plain speaking, truthfulness

frantic adjective 1 furious, at the end of one's tether, berserk, beside oneself, distracted, distraught, wild 2 hectic, desperate, fraught (informal), frenetic, frenzied

fraternity noun 1 club, association, brotherhood, circle, company, guild, league, union 2 companionship, brotherhood, camaraderie, fellowship, kinship

fraternize verb associate, consort, cooperate, hobnob, keep company, mingle, mix, socialize

fraud noun 1 deception, chicanery, deceit, double-dealing, duplicity, sharp practice, swindling, treachery, trickery **2** impostor, charlatan, fake, fraudster, hoaxer, phoney or phony (informal), pretender, swindler

fraudulent adjective deceitful, crooked (informal), dishonest, double-dealing, duplicitous, sham, swindling, treacherous

fray verb wear thin, chafe, rub, wear

freak noun **1** oddity, aberration, anomaly, malformation, monstrosity, weirdo or weirdie (informal) **2** enthusiast, addict, aficionado, buff (informal), devotee, fan, fanatic, fiend (informal), nut (slang) ◆ adjective **3** abnormal, exceptional, unparalleled, unusual

free adjective **1** for nothing, complimentary, for free (informal), free of charge, gratis, gratuitous, on the house, unpaid, without charge **2** at liberty, at large, footloose, independent, liberated, loose, on the loose, unfettered **3** allowed, able, clear, permitted, unimpeded, unrestricted **4** available, empty, idle, spare, unemployed, unoccupied, unused, vacant **5** generous, lavish, liberal, unsparing, unstinting ◆ verb **6** release, deliver, let out, liberate, loose, set free, turn loose, unchain, untie **7** extricate, cut loose, disengage, disentangle, rescue

freedom noun **1** liberty, deliverance, emancipation, independence, release **2** opportunity, blank cheque, carte blanche, discretion, free

rein, latitude, licence

free-for-all noun fight, brawl, dust-up (informal), fracas, melee or mêlée, riot, row, scrimmage

freely adverb **1** willingly, of one's own accord, of one's own free will, spontaneously, voluntarily, without prompting **2** openly, candidly, frankly, plainly, unreservedly, without reserve **3** abundantly, amply, copiously, extravagantly, lavishly, liberally, unstintingly

freeze verb **1** chill, harden, ice over or up, stiffen **2** suspend, fix, hold up, inhibit, peg, stop

freezing adjective icy, arctic, biting, bitter, chill, frosty, glacial, raw, wintry

freight noun **1** transportation, carriage, conveyance, shipment **2** cargo, burden, consignment, goods, load, merchandise, payload

French adjective Gallic

frenzied adjective furious, distracted, feverish, frantic, frenetic, rabid, uncontrolled, wild

frenzy noun fury, derangement, hysteria, paroxysm, passion, rage, seizure

frequent adjective **1** common, customary, everyday, familiar, habitual, persistent, recurrent, repeated, usual ◆ verb **2** visit, attend, be found at, hang out at (informal), haunt, patronize

frequently adverb often, commonly, habitually, many times, much, not infrequently, repeatedly

fresh adjective **1** new, different, modern, novel, original, recent, up-to-date **2** <u>additional</u>, added, auxiliary, extra, further, more, other, supplementary **3** <u>invigorating</u>, bracing, brisk, clean, cool, crisp, pure, refreshing, unpolluted **4** <u>lively</u>, alert, energetic, keen, refreshed, sprightly, spry, vigorous **5** <u>natural</u>, unprocessed **6** *Informal* <u>cheeky</u>, disrespectful, familiar, forward, impudent, insolent, presumptuous

freshen verb <u>refresh</u>, enliven, freshen up, liven up, restore, revitalize

freshness noun **1** <u>novelty</u>, inventiveness, newness, originality **2** <u>cleanness</u>, brightness, clearness, glow, shine, sparkle, vigour, wholesomeness

fret verb <u>worry</u>, agonize, brood, grieve, lose sleep over, upset or distress oneself

fretful adjective <u>irritable</u>, crotchety (*informal*), edgy, fractious, querulous, short-tempered, testy, touchy, uneasy

friction noun **1** <u>rubbing</u>, abrasion, chafing, grating, rasping, resistance, scraping **2** <u>hostility</u>, animosity, bad blood, conflict, disagreement, discord, dissension, resentment

friend noun **1** <u>companion</u>, buddy (*informal*), chum (*informal*), comrade, mate (*informal*), pal, playmate **2** <u>supporter</u>, ally, associate, patron, well-wisher

friendliness noun <u>kindliness</u>, affability, amiability, congeniality, conviviality, geniality, neighbourliness, sociability, warmth

friendly adjective <u>sociable</u>, affectionate, amicable, close, familiar, helpful, intimate, neighbourly, on good terms, pally (*informal*), sympathetic, welcoming

friendship noun <u>goodwill</u>, affection, amity, attachment, concord, familiarity, friendliness, harmony, intimacy

fright noun <u>fear</u>, alarm, consternation, dread, horror, panic, scare, shock, trepidation

frighten verb <u>scare</u>, alarm, intimidate, petrify, shock, startle, terrify, terrorize, unnerve

frightened adjective <u>afraid</u>, alarmed, petrified, scared, scared stiff, startled, terrified, terrorized, terror-stricken

frightening adjective <u>terrifying</u>, alarming, fearful, fearsome, horrifying, menacing, scary (*informal*), shocking, unnerving

frightful adjective <u>terrifying</u>, alarming, awful, dreadful, fearful, ghastly, horrendous, horrible, terrible, traumatic

frigid adjective **1** <u>cold</u>, arctic, frosty, frozen, glacial, icy, wintry **2** <u>forbidding</u>, aloof, austere, formal, unapproachable, unfeeling, unresponsive

frills plural noun <u>trimmings</u>, additions, bells and whistles, embellishments, extras, frippery, fuss, ornamentation, ostentation

fringe noun **1** <u>border</u>, edging, hem, trimming **2** <u>edge</u>, borderline, limits, margin, outskirts, perimeter, periphery ♦ adjective **3** <u>unofficial</u>, unconventional, unorthodox

frisk verb 1 frolic, caper, cavort, gambol, jump, play, prance, skip, trip 2 Informal search, check, inspect, run over, shake down (U.S. slang)

frisky adjective lively, coltish, frolicsome, high-spirited, kittenish, playful, sportive

fritter away verb waste, dissipate, idle away, misspend, run through, spend like water, squander

frivolity noun fun, flippancy, frivolousness, gaiety, levity, light-heartedness, silliness, superficiality, triviality

frivolous adjective 1 flippant, childish, foolish, idle, juvenile, puerile, silly, superficial 2 trivial, footling (informal), minor, petty, shallow, trifling, unimportant

frolic verb 1 play, caper, cavort, frisk, gambol, lark, make merry, romp, sport ♦ noun 2 revel, antic, game, lark, spree

frolicsome adjective playful, coltish, frisky, kittenish, lively, merry, sportive

front noun 1 exterior, façade, face, foreground, frontage 2 forefront, front line, head, lead, vanguard 3 disguise, blind, cover, cover-up, façade, mask, pretext, show ♦ adjective 4 first, foremost, head, lead, leading, topmost ♦ verb 5 face onto, look over or onto, overlook

frontier noun boundary, borderline, edge, limit, perimeter, verge

frost noun hoarfrost, freeze, rime

frosty adjective 1 cold, chilly, frozen, icy, wintry 2 unfriendly, discouraging, frigid, off-putting (Brit. informal), standoffish, unenthusiastic, unwelcoming

froth noun 1 foam, bubbles, effervescence, head, lather, scum, spume, suds ♦ verb 2 fizz, bubble over, come to a head, effervesce, foam, lather

frothy adjective foamy, foaming, sudsy

frown verb 1 scowl, glare, glower, knit one's brows, look daggers, lour or lower 2 **frown on** disapprove of, discourage, dislike, look askance at, take a dim view of

frozen adjective icy, arctic, chilled, frigid, frosted, icebound, ice-cold, ice-covered, numb

frugal adjective thrifty, abstemious, careful, economical, niggardly, parsimonious, prudent, sparing

fruit noun 1 produce, crop, harvest, product, yield 2 result, advantage, benefit, consequence, effect, end result, outcome, profit, return, reward

fruitful adjective useful, advantageous, beneficial, effective, productive, profitable, rewarding, successful, worthwhile

fruition noun maturity, attainment, completion, fulfilment, materialization, perfection, realization, ripeness

fruitless adjective useless, futile, ineffectual, pointless, profitless, unavailing, unproductive, unprofitable, unsuccessful, vain

frustrate verb thwart, balk, block, check, counter, defeat, disappoint, foil, forestall, nullify, stymie

frustrated adjective <u>disappointed</u>, discouraged, disheartened, embittered, resentful

frustration noun 1 <u>obstruction</u>, blocking, circumvention, foiling, thwarting 2 <u>annoyance</u>, disappointment, dissatisfaction, grievance, irritation, resentment, vexation

fuddy-duddy noun <u>conservative</u>, (old) fogey, square (informal), stick-in-the-mud (informal), stuffed shirt (informal)

fudge verb <u>hedge</u>, equivocate, flannel (Brit. informal), stall

fuel noun <u>incitement</u>, ammunition, provocation

fugitive noun 1 <u>runaway</u>, deserter, escapee, refugee ♦ adjective 2 <u>momentary</u>, brief, ephemeral, fleeting, passing, short-lived, temporary, transient, transitory

fulfil verb 1 <u>achieve</u>, accomplish, carry out, complete, perform, realise, satisfy 2 <u>comply with</u>, answer, conform to, fill, meet, obey, observe

fulfilment noun <u>achievement</u>, accomplishment, attainment, completion, consummation, implementation, realization

full adjective 1 <u>saturated</u>, brimming, complete, filled, loaded, replete, satiated, stocked 2 <u>plentiful</u>, abundant, adequate, ample, comprehensive, extensive, generous 3 <u>rich</u>, clear, deep, distinct, loud, resonant, rounded 4 <u>plump</u>, buxom, curvaceous, rounded, voluptuous 5 <u>loose</u>, baggy,

capacious, large, puffy, voluminous ♦ noun 6 **in full** <u>completely</u>, in its entirety, in total, without exception

full-blooded adjective <u>vigorous</u>, hearty, lusty, red-blooded, virile

fullness noun 1 <u>plenty</u>, abundance, copiousness, fill, profusion, satiety, saturation, sufficiency 2 <u>richness</u>, clearness, loudness, resonance, strength

full-scale adjective <u>major</u>, all-out, comprehensive, exhaustive, in-depth, sweeping, thorough, thoroughgoing, wide-ranging

fully adverb <u>totally</u>, altogether, completely, entirely, in all respects, one hundred per cent, perfectly, thoroughly, utterly, wholly

fulsome adjective <u>insincere</u>, excessive, extravagant, immoderate, inordinate, sycophantic, unctuous

fumble verb <u>grope</u>, feel around, flounder, scrabble

fume verb <u>rage</u>, get hot under the collar (informal), rant, see red (informal), seethe, smoulder, storm

fumes plural noun <u>smoke</u>, exhaust, gas, pollution, smog, vapour

fumigate verb <u>disinfect</u>, clean out or up, cleanse, purify, sanitize, sterilize

fuming adjective <u>angry</u>, enraged, in a rage, incensed, on the warpath (informal), raging, seething, up in arms

fun noun 1 <u>enjoyment</u>, amusement, entertainment, jollity, merriment, mirth,

pleasure, recreation, sport
2 make fun of mock, lampoon,
laugh at, parody, poke fun at,
ridicule, satirize, send up (*Brit.
informal*) ♦ *adjective* **3** enjoyable,
amusing, convivial, diverting,
entertaining, lively, witty

function *noun* **1** purpose,
business, duty, job, mission,
raison d'être, responsibility, role,
task **2** reception, affair, do
(*informal*), gathering, social
occasion ♦ *verb* **3** work, act,
behave, do duty, go, operate,
perform, run

functional *adjective* **1** practical,
hard-wearing, serviceable, useful,
utilitarian **2** working, operative

fund *noun* **1** reserve, kitty, pool,
stock, store, supply ♦ *verb*
2 finance, pay for, subsidize,
support

fundamental *adjective*
1 essential, basic, cardinal,
central, elementary, key,
primary, principal, rudimentary,
underlying ♦ *noun* **2** principle,
axiom, cornerstone, law,
rudiment, rule

fundamentally *adverb*
essentially, at bottom, at heart,
basically, intrinsically, primarily,
radically

funds *plural noun* money, capital,
cash, finance, ready money,
resources, savings, the
wherewithal

funeral *noun* burial, cremation,
inhumation, interment, obsequies

funnel *verb* channel, conduct,
convey, direct, filter, move, pass,
pour

funny *adjective* **1** humorous,
amusing, comic, comical, droll,

entertaining, hilarious, riotous,
side-splitting, witty **2** peculiar,
curious, mysterious, odd, queer,
strange, suspicious, unusual,
weird

furious *adjective* **1** angry, beside
oneself, enraged, fuming,
incensed, infuriated, livid
(*informal*), raging, up in arms
2 violent, fierce, intense, savage,
turbulent, unrestrained,
vehement

furnish *verb* **1** decorate, equip,
fit out, stock **2** supply, give,
grant, hand out, offer, present,
provide

furniture *noun* household goods,
appliances, fittings, furnishings,
goods, possessions, things
(*informal*)

furore *noun* disturbance,
commotion, hullabaloo, outcry,
stir, to-do, uproar

furrow *noun* **1** groove, channel,
crease, hollow, line, rut, seam,
trench, wrinkle ♦ *verb* **2** wrinkle,
corrugate, crease, draw
together, knit

further *adverb* **1** in addition,
additionally, also, besides,
furthermore, into the bargain,
moreover, to boot ♦ *adjective*
2 additional, extra, fresh, more,
new, other, supplementary ♦ *verb*
3 promote, advance, assist,
encourage, forward, help, lend
support to, work for

furthermore *adverb* besides,
additionally, as well, further, in
addition, into the bargain,
moreover, to boot, too

furthest *adjective* most distant,
extreme, farthest, furthermost,
outmost, remotest, ultimate

furtive adjective <u>sly</u>, clandestine, conspiratorial, secretive, sneaky, stealthy, surreptitious, underhand, under-the-table

fury noun 1 <u>anger</u>, frenzy, impetuosity, madness, passion, rage, wrath 2 <u>violence</u>, ferocity, fierceness, force, intensity, savagery, severity, vehemence

fuss noun 1 <u>bother</u>, ado, commotion, excitement, hue and cry, palaver, stir, to-do 2 <u>argument</u>, complaint, furore, objection, row, squabble, trouble ♦ verb 3 <u>worry</u>, fidget, flap (informal), fret, get worked up, take pains

fussy adjective 1 <u>hard to please</u>, choosy (informal), difficult, fastidious, finicky, nit-picking (informal), particular, pernickety, picky (informal) 2 <u>overelaborate</u>, busy, cluttered, overworked, rococo

fusty adjective <u>stale</u>, airless, damp, mildewed, mouldering, musty, stuffy

futile adjective <u>useless</u>, fruitless, ineffectual, unavailing, unprofitable, unsuccessful, vain, worthless

futility noun <u>uselessness</u>, emptiness, hollowness, ineffectiveness

future noun 1 <u>hereafter</u>, time to come 2 <u>outlook</u>, expectation, prospect ♦ adjective 3 <u>forthcoming</u>, approaching, coming, fated, impending, later, subsequent, to come

fuzzy adjective 1 <u>fluffy</u>, downy, frizzy, woolly 2 <u>indistinct</u>, bleary, blurred, distorted, ill-defined, out of focus, unclear, vague

G g

gabble verb 1 <u>prattle</u>, babble, blabber, gibber, gush, jabber, spout ♦ noun 2 <u>gibberish</u>, babble, blabber, chatter, drivel, prattle, twaddle

gadabout noun <u>pleasure-seeker</u>, gallivanter, rambler, rover, wanderer

gadget noun <u>device</u>, appliance, contraption (informal), contrivance, gizmo (slang, chiefly U.S.), instrument, invention, thing, tool

gaffe noun <u>blunder</u>, bloomer (informal), clanger (informal), faux pas, howler, indiscretion, lapse, mistake, slip, solecism

gaffer noun 1 Informal <u>manager</u>, boss (informal), foreman, overseer, superintendent, supervisor 2 <u>old man</u>, granddad, greybeard, old boy (informal), old fellow, old-timer (U.S.)

gag¹ verb 1 <u>suppress</u>, curb, muffle, muzzle, quiet, silence, stifle, stop up 2 <u>retch</u>, heave, puke (slang), spew, throw up (informal), vomit

gag² noun <u>joke</u>, crack (slang), funny (informal), hoax, jest, wisecrack (informal), witticism

gaiety noun 1 <u>cheerfulness</u>, blitheness, exhilaration, glee, high spirits, jollity, light-heartedness, merriment, mirth 2 <u>merrymaking</u>, conviviality, festivity, fun, jollification, revelry

gaily adverb 1 <u>cheerfully</u>, blithely,

gleefully, happily, joyfully, light-heartedly, merrily 2 **colourfully**, brightly, brilliantly, flamboyantly, flashily, gaudily, showily

gain verb 1 **obtain**, acquire, attain, capture, collect, gather, get, land, pick up, secure, win 2 **reach**, arrive at, attain, come to, get to 3 **gain on** **get nearer**, approach, catch up with, close, narrow the gap, overtake ◆noun 4 **profit**, advantage, benefit, dividend, return, yield 5 **increase**, advance, growth, improvement, progress, rise

gainful adjective **profitable**, advantageous, beneficial, fruitful, lucrative, productive, remunerative, rewarding, useful, worthwhile

gains plural noun **profits**, earnings, prize, proceeds, revenue, takings, winnings

gainsay verb **contradict**, contravene, controvert, deny, disagree with, dispute, rebut, retract

gait noun **walk**, bearing, carriage, pace, step, stride, tread

gala noun **festival**, carnival, celebration, festivity, fête, jamboree, pageant

gale noun 1 **storm**, blast, cyclone, hurricane, squall, tempest, tornado, typhoon 2 Informal **outburst**, burst, eruption, explosion, fit, howl, outbreak, peal, shout, shriek

gall¹ noun 1 Informal **impudence**, brazenness, cheek (informal), chutzpah (U.S. & Canad. informal), effrontery, impertinence, insolence, nerve

(informal) 2 **bitterness**, acrimony, animosity, bile, hostility, rancour

gall² verb 1 **scrape**, abrade, chafe, irritate 2 **annoy**, exasperate, irk, irritate, provoke, rankle, vex

gallant adjective 1 **brave**, bold, courageous, heroic, honourable, intrepid, manly, noble, valiant 2 **chivalrous**, attentive, courteous, gentlemanly, gracious, noble, polite

gallantry noun 1 **bravery**, boldness, courage, heroism, intrepidity, manliness, spirit, valour 2 **attentiveness**, chivalry, courteousness, courtesy, gentlemanliness, graciousness, nobility, politeness

galling adjective **annoying**, bitter, exasperating, irksome, irritating, provoking, vexatious

gallivant verb **wander**, gad about, ramble, roam, rove

gallop verb **run**, bolt, career, dash, hurry, race, rush, speed, sprint

galore adverb **in abundance**, all over the place, aplenty, everywhere, in great quantity, in numbers, in profusion, to spare

galvanize verb **stimulate**, electrify, excite, inspire, invigorate, jolt, provoke, spur, stir

gamble verb 1 **bet**, game, have a flutter (informal), play, punt, wager 2 **risk**, chance, hazard, speculate, stick one's neck out (informal), take a chance ◆noun 3 **risk**, chance, leap in the dark, lottery, speculation, uncertainty, venture 4 **bet**, flutter (informal), punt, wager

gambol verb 1 **frolic**, caper,

game cavort, frisk, hop, jump, prance, skip ♦ *noun* 2 frolic, caper, hop, jump, prance, skip

game *noun* 1 pastime, amusement, distraction, diversion, entertainment, lark, recreation, sport 2 match, competition, contest, event, head-to-head, meeting, tournament 3 wild animals, prey, quarry 4 scheme, design, plan, plot, ploy, stratagem, tactic, trick ♦ *adjective* 5 brave, courageous, gallant, gritty, intrepid, persistent, plucky, spirited 6 willing, desirous, eager, interested, keen, prepared, ready

gamut *noun* range, area, catalogue, compass, field, scale, scope, series, sweep

gang *noun* group, band, clique, club, company, coterie, crowd, mob, pack, squad, team

gangling *adjective* tall, angular, awkward, lanky, rangy, rawboned, spindly

gangster *noun* racketeer, crook (*informal*), hood (*U.S. slang*), hoodlum (*chiefly U.S.*), mobster (*U.S. slang*)

gap *noun* 1 opening, break, chink, cleft, crack, hole, space 2 interval, breathing space, hiatus, interlude, intermission, interruption, lacuna, lull, pause, respite 3 difference, disagreement, disparity, divergence, inconsistency

gape *verb* 1 stare, gawk, gawp (*Brit. slang*), goggle, wonder 2 open, crack, split, yawn

gaping *adjective* wide, broad, cavernous, great, open, vast, wide open, yawning

garbage *noun* rubbish, refuse, trash (*chiefly U.S.*), waste

garbled *adjective* jumbled, confused, distorted, double-Dutch, incomprehensible, mixed up, unintelligible

garish *adjective* gaudy, brash, brassy, flashy, loud, showy, tacky (*informal*), tasteless, vulgar

garland *noun* 1 wreath, bays, chaplet, crown, festoon, honours, laurels ♦ *verb* 2 adorn, crown, deck, festoon, wreathe

garments *plural noun* clothes, apparel, attire, clothing, costume, dress, garb, gear (*slang*), outfit, uniform

garner *verb* collect, accumulate, amass, gather, hoard, save, stockpile, store, stow away

garnish *verb* 1 decorate, adorn, embellish, enhance, ornament, set off, trim ♦ *noun* 2 decoration, adornment, embellishment, enhancement, ornamentation, trimming

garrison *noun* 1 troops, armed force, command, detachment, unit 2 fort, base, camp, encampment, fortification, fortress, post, station, stronghold ♦ *verb* 3 station, assign, position, post, put on duty

garrulous *adjective* talkative, chatty, gossiping, loquacious, prattling, verbose, voluble

gash *verb* 1 cut, gouge, lacerate, slash, slit, split, tear, wound ♦ *noun* 2 cut, gouge, incision, laceration, slash, slit, split, tear, wound

gasp *verb* 1 gulp, blow, catch

one's breath, choke, pant, puff
♦ *noun* 2 <u>gulp</u>, exclamation,
pant, puff, sharp intake of breath

gate *noun* <u>barrier</u>, door, entrance,
exit, gateway, opening, passage,
portal

gather *verb* 1 <u>assemble</u>,
accumulate, amass, collect,
garner, mass, muster, stockpile
2 <u>learn</u>, assume, conclude,
deduce, hear, infer, surmise,
understand 3 <u>pick</u>, cull, garner,
glean, harvest, pluck, reap,
select 4 <u>intensify</u>, deepen,
expand, grow, heighten,
increase, rise, swell, thicken
5 <u>fold</u>, pleat, tuck

gathering *noun* <u>assembly</u>,
company, conclave, congress,
convention, crowd, group,
meeting

gauche *adjective* <u>awkward</u>,
clumsy, ill-mannered, inelegant,
tactless, unsophisticated

gaudy *adjective* <u>garish</u>, bright,
flashy, loud, showy, tacky
(*informal*), tasteless, vulgar

gauge *verb* 1 <u>measure</u>, ascertain,
calculate, check, compute,
count, determine, weigh
2 <u>judge</u>, adjudge, appraise,
assess, estimate, evaluate, guess,
rate, reckon, value ♦ *noun*
3 <u>indicator</u>, criterion, guide,
guideline, measure, meter,
standard, test, touchstone,
yardstick

gaunt *adjective* <u>thin</u>, angular,
bony, haggard, lean, pinched,
scrawny, skinny, spare

gawky *adjective* <u>awkward</u>,
clumsy, gauche, loutish,
lumbering, maladroit, ungainly

gay *adjective* 1 <u>homosexual</u>,

lesbian, queer (*informal*,
derogatory) 2 <u>carefree</u>, blithe,
cheerful, jovial, light-hearted,
lively, merry, sparkling
3 <u>colourful</u>, bright, brilliant,
flamboyant, flashy, rich, showy,
vivid ♦ *noun* 4 <u>homosexual</u>,
lesbian

gaze *verb* 1 <u>stare</u>, gape, look,
regard, view, watch, wonder
♦ *noun* 2 <u>stare</u>, fixed look, look

gazette *noun* <u>newspaper</u>, journal,
news-sheet, paper, periodical

gear *noun* 1 <u>cog</u>, cogwheel,
gearwheel 2 <u>mechanism</u>, cogs,
machinery, works 3 <u>equipment</u>,
accoutrements, apparatus,
instruments, paraphernalia,
supplies, tackle, tools 4 <u>clothing</u>,
clothes, costume, dress,
garments, outfit, togs, wear
♦ *verb* 5 <u>equip</u>, adapt, adjust, fit

gelatinous *adjective* <u>jelly-like</u>,
glutinous, gummy, sticky, viscous

gelid *adjective* <u>cold</u>, arctic, chilly,
freezing, frigid, frosty, frozen,
glacial, ice-cold, icy

gem *noun* 1 <u>precious stone</u>,
jewel, stone 2 <u>prize</u>, jewel,
masterpiece, pearl, treasure

general *adjective* 1 <u>common</u>,
accepted, broad, extensive,
popular, prevalent, public,
universal, widespread
2 <u>imprecise</u>, approximate,
ill-defined, indefinite, inexact,
loose, unspecific, vague
3 <u>universal</u>, across-the-board,
blanket, collective,
comprehensive, indiscriminate,
miscellaneous, sweeping, total

generally *adverb* 1 <u>usually</u>, as a
rule, by and large, customarily,
normally, on the whole,

ordinarily, typically **2** commonly, extensively, popularly, publicly, universally, widely

generate verb produce, breed, cause, create, engender, give rise to, make, propagate

generation noun **1** production, creation, formation, genesis, propagation, reproduction **2** age group, breed, crop **3** age, epoch, era, period, time

generic adjective collective, blanket, common, comprehensive, general, inclusive, universal, wide

generosity noun **1** charity, beneficence, bounty, kindness, largesse or largess, liberality, munificence, open-handedness **2** unselfishness, goodness, high-mindedness, magnanimity, nobleness

generous adjective **1** charitable, beneficent, bountiful, hospitable, kind, lavish, liberal, open-handed, unstinting **2** unselfish, big-hearted, good, high-minded, lofty, magnanimous, noble **3** plentiful, abundant, ample, copious, full, lavish, liberal, rich, unstinting

genesis noun beginning, birth, creation, formation, inception, origin, start

genial adjective cheerful, affable, agreeable, amiable, congenial, friendly, good-natured, jovial, pleasant, warm

geniality noun cheerfulness, affability, agreeableness, amiability, conviviality, cordiality, friendliness, good cheer, joviality, warmth

genius noun **1** master, brainbox,

expert, hotshot (informal), maestro, mastermind, virtuoso, whiz (informal) **2** brilliance, ability, aptitude, bent, capacity, flair, gift, knack, talent

genre noun type, category, class, group, kind, sort, species, style

genteel adjective refined, courteous, cultured, elegant, gentlemanly, ladylike, polite, respectable, urbane, well-mannered

gentle adjective
1 sweet-tempered, compassionate, humane, kindly, meek, mild, placid, tender **2** moderate, light, mild, muted, slight, soft, soothing **3** gradual, easy, imperceptible, light, mild, moderate, slight, slow **4** tame, biddable, broken, docile, manageable, placid, tractable

gentlemanly adjective polite, civil, courteous, gallant, genteel, honourable, refined, urbane, well-mannered

gentleness noun tenderness, compassion, kindness, mildness, softness, sweetness

gentry noun nobility, aristocracy, elite, upper class, upper crust (informal)

genuine adjective **1** authentic, actual, bona fide, legitimate, real, the real McCoy, true, veritable **2** sincere, candid, earnest, frank, heartfelt, honest, unaffected, unfeigned

germ noun **1** microbe, bacterium, bug (informal), microorganism, virus **2** beginning, embryo, origin, root, rudiment, seed, source, spark

germane adjective relevant, apposite, appropriate, apropos, connected, fitting, material, pertinent, related, to the point or purpose

germinate verb sprout, bud, develop, generate, grow, originate, shoot, swell, vegetate

gesticulate verb signal, gesture, indicate, make a sign, motion, sign, wave

gesture noun 1 signal, action, gesticulation, indication, motion, sign ♦ verb 2 signal, gesticulate, indicate, motion, sign, wave

get verb 1 obtain, acquire, attain, fetch, gain, land, net, pick up, procure, receive, secure, win 2 contract, catch, come down with, fall victim to, take 3 capture, grab, lay hold of, nab (informal), seize, take 4 become, come to be, grow, turn 5 understand, catch, comprehend, fathom, follow, perceive, see, take in, work out 6 persuade, convince, induce, influence, prevail upon 7 Informal annoy, bug (informal), gall, irritate, upset, vex

get across verb 1 cross, ford, negotiate, pass over, traverse 2 communicate, bring home to, convey, impart, make clear or understood, put over, transmit

get at verb 1 gain access to, acquire, attain, come to grips with, get hold of, reach 2 imply, hint, intend, lead up to, mean, suggest 3 criticize, attack, blame, find fault with, nag, pick on

getaway noun escape, break, break-out, flight

get by verb manage, cope, exist, fare, get along, keep one's head above water, make both ends meet, survive

get off verb leave, alight, depart, descend, disembark, dismount, escape, exit

get on verb 1 board, ascend, climb, embark, mount 2 be friendly, be compatible, concur, get along, hit it off (informal)

get over verb recover from, come round, get better, mend, pull through, rally, revive, survive

ghastly adjective horrible, dreadful, frightful, gruesome, hideous, horrendous, loathsome, shocking, terrible, terrifying

ghost noun 1 spirit, apparition, phantom, soul, spectre, spook (informal), wraith 2 trace, glimmer, hint, possibility, semblance, shadow, suggestion

ghostly adjective supernatural, eerie, ghostlike, phantom, spectral, spooky (informal), unearthly, wraithlike

ghoulish adjective macabre, disgusting, grisly, gruesome, morbid, sick (informal), unwholesome

giant noun 1 ogre, colossus, monster, titan ♦ adjective 2 huge, colossal, enormous, gargantuan, gigantic, immense, mammoth, titanic, vast

gibberish noun nonsense, babble, drivel, gobbledegook (informal), mumbo jumbo, twaddle

gibe, jibe verb 1 taunt, jeer, make fun of, mock, poke fun at, ridicule, scoff, scorn, sneer

♦ *noun* **2** taunt, barb, crack (*slang*), dig, jeer, sarcasm, scoffing, sneer

giddiness *noun* dizziness, faintness, light-headedness, vertigo

giddy *adjective* dizzy, dizzying, faint, light-headed, reeling, unsteady, vertiginous

gift *noun* **1** donation, bequest, bonus, contribution, grant, hand-out, legacy, offering, present **2** talent, ability, capability, capacity, flair, genius, knack, power

gifted *adjective* talented, able, accomplished, brilliant, capable, clever, expert, ingenious, masterly, skilled

gigantic *adjective* enormous, colossal, giant, huge, immense, mammoth, stupendous, titanic, tremendous

giggle *verb, noun* laugh, cackle, chortle, chuckle, snigger, titter, twitter

gild *verb* embellish, adorn, beautify, brighten, coat, dress up, embroider, enhance, ornament

gimmick *noun* stunt, contrivance, device, dodge, ploy, scheme

gingerly *adverb* cautiously, carefully, charily, circumspectly, hesitantly, reluctantly, suspiciously, timidly, warily

gird *verb* surround, encircle, enclose, encompass, enfold, hem in, ring

girdle *noun* **1** belt, band, cummerbund, sash, waistband
♦ *verb* **2** surround, bound,

encircle, enclose, encompass, gird, ring

girl *noun* female child, damsel (*archaic*), daughter, lass, lassie (*informal*), maid (*archaic*), maiden (*archaic*), miss

girth *noun* circumference, bulk, measure, size

gist *noun* point, core, essence, force, idea, meaning, sense, significance, substance

give *verb* **1** present, award, contribute, deliver, donate, grant, hand over *or* out, provide, supply **2** announce, communicate, issue, notify, pronounce, transmit, utter **3** concede, grant, hand over, relinquish, surrender, yield **4** produce, cause, engender, make, occasion

give away *verb* reveal, betray, disclose, divulge, expose, leak, let out, let slip, uncover

give in *verb* admit defeat, capitulate, collapse, concede, quit, submit, succumb, surrender, yield

give off *verb* emit, discharge, exude, produce, release, send out, throw out

give out *verb* emit, discharge, exude, produce, release, send out, throw out

give up *verb* abandon, call it a day *or* night, cease, desist, leave off, quit, relinquish, renounce, stop, surrender

glad *adjective* **1** happy, contented, delighted, gratified, joyful, overjoyed, pleased **2** pleasing, cheerful, cheering, gratifying, pleasant

gladden verb please, cheer, delight, gratify, hearten

gladly adverb happily, cheerfully, freely, gleefully, readily, willingly, with pleasure

gladness noun happiness, cheerfulness, delight, gaiety, glee, high spirits, joy, mirth, pleasure

glamorous adjective elegant, attractive, dazzling, exciting, fascinating, glittering, glossy, prestigious, smart

glamour noun charm, allure, appeal, attraction, beauty, enchantment, fascination, prestige

glance verb 1 look, glimpse, peek, peep, scan, view 2 gleam, flash, glimmer, glint, glisten, glitter, reflect, shimmer, shine, twinkle ♦ noun 3 look, dekko (slang), glimpse, peek, peep, view

glare verb 1 scowl, frown, glower, look daggers, lour or lower 2 dazzle, blaze, flame, flare ♦ noun 3 scowl, black look, dirty look, frown, glower, lour or lower 4 dazzle, blaze, brilliance, flame, glow

glaring adjective 1 conspicuous, blatant, flagrant, gross, manifest, obvious, outrageous, unconcealed 2 dazzling, blazing, bright, garish, glowing

glassy adjective 1 transparent, clear, glossy, shiny, slippery, smooth 2 expressionless, blank, cold, dull, empty, fixed, glazed, lifeless, vacant

glaze verb 1 coat, enamel, gloss, lacquer, polish, varnish ♦ noun 2 coat, enamel, finish, gloss, lacquer, lustre, patina, polish,

shine, varnish

gleam noun 1 glow, beam, flash, glimmer, ray, sparkle 2 trace, flicker, glimmer, hint, inkling, suggestion ♦ verb 3 shine, flash, glimmer, glint, glisten, glitter, glow, shimmer, sparkle

glee noun delight, elation, exhilaration, exuberance, exultation, joy, merriment, triumph

gleeful adjective delighted, cock-a-hoop, elated, exuberant, exultant, joyful, jubilant, overjoyed, triumphant

glib adjective smooth, easy, fluent, insincere, plausible, quick, ready, slick, suave, voluble

glide verb slide, coast, drift, float, flow, roll, run, sail, skate, slip

glimmer verb 1 flicker, blink, gleam, glisten, glitter, glow, shimmer, shine, sparkle, twinkle ♦ noun 2 gleam, blink, flicker, glow, ray, shimmer, sparkle, twinkle 3 trace, flicker, gleam, hint, inkling, suggestion

glimpse noun 1 look, glance, peek, peep, sight, sighting ♦ verb 2 catch sight of, espy, sight, spot, spy, view

glint verb 1 gleam, flash, glimmer, glitter, shine, sparkle, twinkle ♦ noun 2 gleam, flash, glimmer, glitter, shine, sparkle, twinkle, twinkling

glisten verb gleam, flash, glance, glare, glimmer, glint, glitter, shimmer, shine, sparkle, twinkle

glitch noun problem, blip, difficulty, gremlin, hitch, interruption, malfunction, snag

glitter verb 1 shine, flash, glare,

gleam, glimmer, glint, glisten, shimmer, sparkle, twinkle ♦ *noun* **2** shine, brightness, flash, glare, gleam, radiance, sheen, shimmer, sparkle **3** glamour, display, gaudiness, pageantry, show, showiness, splendour, tinsel

gloat *verb* relish, crow, drool, exult, glory, revel in, rub it in (*informal*), triumph

global *adjective* **1** worldwide, international, universal, world **2** comprehensive, all-inclusive, exhaustive, general, total, unlimited

globe *noun* sphere, ball, earth, orb, planet, world

globule *noun* droplet, bead, bubble, drop, particle, pearl, pellet

gloom *noun* **1** darkness, blackness, dark, dusk, murk, obscurity, shade, shadow, twilight **2** depression, dejection, despondency, low spirits, melancholy, sorrow, unhappiness, woe

gloomy *adjective* **1** dark, black, dim, dismal, dreary, dull, grey, murky, sombre **2** depressing, bad, cheerless, disheartening, dispiriting, dreary, sad, sombre **3** miserable, crestfallen, dejected, dispirited, downcast, downhearted, glum, melancholy, morose, pessimistic, sad

glorify *verb* **1** enhance, aggrandize, dignify, elevate, ennoble, magnify **2** worship, adore, bless, exalt, honour, idolize, pay homage to, revere, venerate **3** praise, celebrate, eulogize, extol, sing *or* sound

the praises of

glorious *adjective* **1** famous, celebrated, distinguished, eminent, honoured, illustrious, magnificent, majestic, renowned **2** splendid, beautiful, brilliant, dazzling, gorgeous, shining, superb **3** delightful, excellent, fine, gorgeous, marvellous, wonderful

glory *noun* **1** honour, dignity, distinction, eminence, fame, praise, prestige, renown **2** splendour, grandeur, greatness, magnificence, majesty, nobility, pageantry, pomp ♦ *verb* **3** triumph, boast, exult, pride oneself, relish, revel, take delight

gloss[1] *noun* shine, brightness, gleam, lustre, patina, polish, sheen, veneer

gloss[2] *noun* **1** comment, annotation, commentary, elucidation, explanation, footnote, interpretation, note, translation ♦ *verb* **2** interpret, annotate, comment, elucidate, explain, translate

glossy *adjective* shiny, bright, glassy, glazed, lustrous, polished, shining, silky

glow *verb* **1** shine, brighten, burn, gleam, glimmer, redden, smoulder ♦ *noun* **2** light, burning, gleam, glimmer, luminosity, phosphorescence **3** radiance, brightness, brilliance, effulgence, splendour, vividness

glower *verb* **1** scowl, frown, give a dirty look, glare, look daggers, lour *or* lower ♦ *noun* **2** scowl, black look, dirty look, frown, glare, lour *or* lower

glowing adjective **1** bright, aglow, flaming, luminous, radiant **2** complimentary, adulatory, ecstatic, enthusiastic, laudatory, rave (informal), rhapsodic

glue noun **1** adhesive, cement, gum, paste ♦ verb **2** stick, affix, cement, fix, gum, paste, seal

glum adjective gloomy, crestfallen, dejected, doleful, low, morose, pessimistic, sullen

glut noun **1** surfeit, excess, oversupply, plethora, saturation, superfluity, surplus ♦ verb **2** saturate, choke, clog, deluge, flood, inundate, overload, oversupply

glutton noun gourmand, gannet (slang), pig (informal)

gluttonous adjective greedy, gormandizing, insatiable, piggish, ravenous, voracious

gluttony noun greed, gormandizing, greediness, voracity

gnarled adjective twisted, contorted, knotted, knotty, rough, rugged, weather-beaten, wrinkled

gnaw verb bite, chew, munch, nibble

go verb **1** move, advance, journey, make for, pass, proceed, set off, travel **2** leave, depart, make tracks, move out, slope off, withdraw **3** function, move, operate, perform, run, work **4** contribute, lead to, serve, tend, work towards **5** harmonize, agree, blend, chime, complement, correspond, fit, match, suit **6** elapse, expire, flow, lapse, pass, slip away

♦ noun **7** attempt, bid, crack (informal), effort, shot (informal), try, turn **8** Informal energy, drive, force, life, spirit, verve, vigour, vitality, vivacity

goad verb **1** provoke, drive, egg on, exhort, incite, prod, prompt, spur ♦ noun **2** provocation, impetus, incentive, incitement, irritation, spur, stimulus, urge

goal noun aim, ambition, end, intention, object, objective, purpose, target

gobble verb devour, bolt, cram, gorge, gulp, guzzle, stuff, swallow, wolf

gobbledegook noun nonsense, babble, cant, gabble, gibberish, hocus-pocus, jargon, mumbo jumbo, twaddle

go-between noun intermediary, agent, broker, dealer, mediator, medium, middleman

godforsaken adjective desolate, abandoned, bleak, deserted, dismal, dreary, forlorn, gloomy, lonely, remote, wretched

godlike adjective divine, celestial, heavenly, superhuman, transcendent

godly adjective devout, god-fearing, good, holy, pious, religious, righteous, saintly

godsend noun blessing, boon, manna, stroke of luck, windfall

go for verb **1** favour, admire, be attracted to, be fond of, choose, like, prefer **2** attack, assail, assault, launch oneself at, rush upon, set about or upon, spring upon

golden adjective **1** yellow, blond or blonde, flaxen **2** successful, flourishing, glorious, halcyon, happy, prosperous, rich **3** promising, excellent, favourable, opportune

gone adjective **1** finished, elapsed, ended, over, past **2** missing, absent, astray, away, lacking, lost, vanished

good adjective **1** pleasing, acceptable, admirable, excellent, fine, first-class, first-rate, great, satisfactory, splendid, superior **2** praiseworthy, admirable, ethical, honest, honourable, moral, righteous, trustworthy, upright, virtuous, worthy **3** expert, able, accomplished, adept, adroit, clever, competent, proficient, skilled, talented **4** beneficial, advantageous, convenient, favourable, fitting, helpful, profitable, suitable, useful, wholesome **5** kind, altruistic, benevolent, charitable, friendly, humane, kind-hearted, kindly, merciful, obliging **6** valid, authentic, bona fide, genuine, legitimate, proper, real, true **7** well-behaved, dutiful, obedient, orderly, polite, well-mannered **8** full, adequate, ample, complete, considerable, extensive, large, substantial, sufficient ♦ noun **9** benefit, advantage, gain, interest, profit, use, usefulness, welfare, wellbeing **10** virtue, excellence, goodness, merit, morality, rectitude, right, righteousness, worth **11 for good** permanently, finally, for ever, irrevocably, once and for all

goodbye noun farewell, adieu, leave-taking, parting

good-for-nothing noun

1 layabout, black sheep, idler, ne'er-do-well, skiver (*Brit. slang*), slacker (*informal*), waster, wastrel ♦ adjective **2** worthless, feckless, idle, irresponsible, useless

goodly adjective considerable, ample, large, significant, sizable or sizeable, substantial, tidy (*informal*)

goodness noun **1** excellence, merit, quality, superiority, value, worth **2** kindness, benevolence, friendliness, generosity, goodwill, humaneness, kind-heartedness, kindliness, mercy **3** virtue, honesty, honour, integrity, merit, morality, probity, rectitude, righteousness, uprightness **4** benefit, advantage, salubriousness, wholesomeness

goods plural noun **1** property, belongings, chattels, effects, gear, paraphernalia, possessions, things, trappings **2** merchandise, commodities, stock, stuff, wares

goodwill noun friendliness, amity, benevolence, friendship, heartiness, kindliness

go off verb **1** explode, blow up, detonate, fire **2** leave, decamp, depart, go away, move out, part, quit, slope off **3** *Informal* rot, go bad, go stale

go out verb **1** leave, depart, exit **2** be extinguished, die out, expire, fade out

go over verb examine, inspect, rehearse, reiterate, review, revise, study, work over

gore[1] noun blood, bloodshed, butchery, carnage, slaughter

gore[2] verb pierce, impale, transfix, wound

gorge noun 1 ravine, canyon, chasm, cleft, defile, fissure, pass ♦ verb 2 overeat, cram, devour, feed, glut, gobble, gulp, guzzle, stuff, wolf

gorgeous adjective 1 beautiful, dazzling, elegant, magnificent, ravishing, splendid, stunning (informal), sumptuous, superb 2 Informal pleasing, delightful, enjoyable, exquisite, fine, glorious, good, lovely

gory adjective bloodthirsty, blood-soaked, bloodstained, bloody, murderous, sanguinary

gospel noun 1 truth, certainty, fact, the last word 2 doctrine, credo, creed, message, news, revelation, tidings

gossip noun 1 idle talk, blether, chinwag (Brit. informal), chitchat, hearsay, scandal, small talk, tittle-tattle 2 busybody, chatterbox (informal), chatterer, gossipmonger, scandalmonger, tattler, telltale ♦ verb 3 chat, blether, gabble, jaw (slang), prate, prattle, tattle

go through verb 1 suffer, bear, brave, endure, experience, tolerate, undergo, withstand 2 examine, check, explore, forage, hunt, look, search

gouge verb 1 scoop, chisel, claw, cut, dig (out), hollow (out) ♦ noun 2 gash, cut, furrow, groove, hollow, scoop, scratch, trench

gourmet noun connoisseur, bon vivant, epicure, foodie (informal), gastronome

govern verb 1 rule, administer, command, control, direct, guide, handle, lead, manage, order 2 restrain, check, control, curb, discipline, hold in check, master, regulate, subdue, tame

government noun 1 rule, administration, authority, governance, sovereignty, statecraft 2 executive, administration, ministry, powers-that-be, regime

governor noun leader, administrator, chief, commander, controller, director, executive, head, manager, ruler

gown noun dress, costume, frock, garb, garment, habit, robe

grab verb snatch, capture, catch, catch or take hold of, clutch, grasp, grip, pluck, seize, snap up

grace noun 1 elegance, attractiveness, beauty, charm, comeliness, ease, gracefulness, poise, polish, refinement, tastefulness 2 goodwill, benefaction, benevolence, favour, generosity, goodness, kindliness, kindness 3 manners, consideration, decency, decorum, etiquette, propriety, tact 4 indulgence, mercy, pardon, reprieve 5 prayer, benediction, blessing, thanks, thanksgiving ♦ verb 6 honour, adorn, decorate, dignify, embellish, enhance, enrich, favour, ornament, set off

graceful adjective elegant, beautiful, charming, comely, easy, pleasing, tasteful

gracious adjective kind, charitable, civil, considerate, cordial, courteous, friendly, polite, well-mannered

grade noun 1 level, category, class, degree, echelon, group, rank, stage ♦ verb **2** classify, arrange, class, group, order, range, rank, rate, sort

gradient noun slope, bank, declivity, grade, hill, incline, rise

gradual adjective steady, gentle, graduated, piecemeal, progressive, regular, slow, unhurried

gradually adverb steadily, by degrees, gently, little by little, progressively, slowly, step by step, unhurriedly

graduate verb **1** mark off, calibrate, grade, measure out, proportion, regulate **2** classify, arrange, grade, group, order, rank, sort

graft noun **1** shoot, bud, implant, scion, splice, sprout ♦ verb **2** transplant, affix, implant, ingraft, insert, join, splice

grain noun **1** cereals, corn **2** seed, grist, kernel **3** bit, fragment, granule, modicum, morsel, particle, piece, scrap, speck, trace **4** texture, fibre, nap, pattern, surface, weave **5** As in **go against the grain** inclination, character, disposition, humour, make-up, temper

grand adjective **1** impressive, dignified, grandiose, great, imposing, large, magnificent, regal, splendid, stately, sublime **2** excellent, fine, first-class, great (*informal*), outstanding, smashing (*informal*), splendid, wonderful

grandeur noun splendour, dignity, magnificence, majesty, nobility, pomp, stateliness, sublimity

grandiose adjective

1 pretentious, affected, bombastic, extravagant, flamboyant, high-flown, ostentatious, pompous, showy **2** imposing, grand, impressive, lofty, magnificent, majestic, monumental, stately

grant verb **1** consent to, accede to, agree to, allow, permit **2** give, allocate, allot, assign, award, donate, hand out, present **3** admit, acknowledge, concede ♦ noun **4** award, allowance, donation, endowment, gift, hand-out, present, subsidy

granule noun grain, atom, crumb, fragment, molecule, particle, scrap, speck

graphic adjective **1** vivid, clear, detailed, explicit, expressive, lively, lucid, striking **2** pictorial, diagrammatic, visual

grapple verb **1** grip, clutch, grab, grasp, seize, wrestle **2** deal with, address oneself to, confront, get to grips with, struggle, tackle, take on

grasp verb **1** grip, catch, clasp, clinch, clutch, grab, grapple, hold, lay or take hold of, seize, snatch **2** understand, catch on, catch or get the drift of, comprehend, get, realize, see, take in ♦ noun **3** grip, clasp, clutches, embrace, hold, possession, tenure **4** control, power, reach, scope **5** understanding, awareness, comprehension, grip, knowledge, mastery

grasping adjective greedy, acquisitive, avaricious, covetous, rapacious

grate verb **1** <u>shred</u>, mince, pulverize, triturate **2** <u>scrape</u>, creak, grind, rasp, rub, scratch **3** <u>annoy</u>, exasperate, get on one's nerves (informal), irritate, jar, rankle, set one's teeth on edge

grateful adjective <u>thankful</u>, appreciative, beholden, indebted, obliged

gratification noun <u>satisfaction</u>, delight, enjoyment, fulfilment, indulgence, pleasure, relish, reward, thrill

gratify verb <u>please</u>, delight, give pleasure, gladden, humour, requite, satisfy

grating[1] adjective <u>irritating</u>, annoying, discordant, displeasing, harsh, jarring, offensive, raucous, strident, unpleasant

grating[2] noun <u>grille</u>, grate, grid, gridiron, lattice, trellis

gratitude noun <u>thankfulness</u>, appreciation, gratefulness, indebtedness, obligation, recognition, thanks

gratuitous adjective **1** <u>free</u>, complimentary, gratis, spontaneous, unasked-for, unpaid, unrewarded, voluntary **2** <u>unjustified</u>, baseless, causeless, groundless, needless, superfluous, uncalled-for, unmerited, unnecessary, unwarranted, wanton

gratuity noun <u>tip</u>, bonus, donation, gift, largesse or largess, reward

grave[1] noun <u>burying place</u>, crypt, mausoleum, pit, sepulchre, tomb, vault

grave[2] adjective **1** <u>solemn</u>, dignified, dour, earnest, serious, sober, sombre, unsmiling **2** <u>important</u>, acute, critical, dangerous, pressing, serious, severe, threatening, urgent

graveyard noun <u>cemetery</u>, burial ground, charnel house, churchyard, necropolis

gravity noun **1** <u>importance</u>, acuteness, momentousness, perilousness, seriousness, severity, significance, urgency, weightiness **2** <u>solemnity</u>, dignity, earnestness, gravitas, seriousness, sobriety

graze[1] verb <u>feed</u>, browse, crop, pasture

graze[2] verb **1** <u>touch</u>, brush, glance off, rub, scrape, shave, skim **2** <u>scratch</u>, abrade, chafe, scrape, skin ◆ noun **3** <u>scratch</u>, abrasion, scrape

greasy adjective <u>fatty</u>, oily, oleaginous, slimy, slippery

great adjective **1** <u>large</u>, big, enormous, gigantic, huge, immense, prodigious, vast, voluminous **2** <u>important</u>, crucial, momentous, serious, significant **3** <u>famous</u>, eminent, illustrious, noteworthy, outstanding, prominent, remarkable, renowned **4** Informal <u>excellent</u>, fantastic (informal), fine, marvellous (informal), superb, terrific (informal), tremendous (informal), wonderful

greatly adverb <u>very much</u>, considerably, enormously, exceedingly, hugely, immensely, remarkably, tremendously, vastly

greatness noun **1** <u>immensity</u>, enormity, hugeness, magnitude,

prodigiousness, size, vastness
2 importance, gravity,
momentousness, seriousness,
significance, urgency, weight
3 fame, celebrity, distinction,
eminence, glory, grandeur,
illustriousness, note, renown

greed, greediness noun
1 gluttony, edacity, esurience,
gormandizing, hunger, voracity
2 avarice, acquisitiveness,
avidity, covetousness, craving,
desire, longing, selfishness

greedy adjective **1** gluttonous,
gormandizing, hungry,
insatiable, piggish, ravenous,
voracious **2** grasping, acquisitive,
avaricious, avid, covetous,
craving, desirous, rapacious,
selfish

green adjective **1** leafy, grassy,
verdant **2** ecological,
conservationist,
environment-friendly,
non-polluting, ozone-friendly
3 immature, gullible,
inexperienced, naive, new, raw,
untrained, wet behind the ears
(informal) **4** jealous, covetous,
envious, grudging, resentful
♦ noun **5** lawn, common, sward,
turf

greet verb welcome, accost,
address, compliment, hail, meet,
receive, salute

greeting noun welcome, address,
reception, salutation, salute

gregarious adjective outgoing,
affable, companionable,
convivial, cordial, friendly,
sociable, social

grey adjective **1** pale, ashen,
pallid, wan **2** dismal, dark,
depressing, dim, drab, dreary,

dull, gloomy **3** characterless,
anonymous, colourless, dull

gridlock noun standstill,
deadlock, impasse, stalemate

grief noun sadness, anguish,
distress, heartache, misery,
regret, remorse, sorrow,
suffering, woe

grievance noun complaint, axe
to grind, gripe (informal), injury,
injustice

grieve verb **1** mourn, complain,
deplore, lament, regret, rue,
suffer, weep **2** sadden, afflict,
distress, hurt, injure, pain, wound

grievous adjective **1** painful,
dreadful, grave, harmful, severe
2 deplorable, atrocious, dreadful,
monstrous, offensive,
outrageous, shameful, shocking

grim adjective forbidding,
formidable, harsh, merciless,
ruthless, severe, sinister, stern,
terrible

grimace noun **1** scowl, face,
frown, sneer ♦ verb **2** scowl,
frown, lour or lower, make a face
or faces, sneer

grime noun dirt, filth, grot
(slang), smut, soot

grimy adjective dirty, filthy, foul,
grubby, soiled, sooty, unclean

grind verb **1** crush, abrade,
granulate, grate, mill, pound,
powder, pulverize, triturate
2 smooth, polish, sand, sharpen,
whet **3** scrape, gnash, grate
♦ noun **4** Informal hard work,
chore, drudgery, labour, sweat
(informal), toil

grip noun **1** clasp, hold **2** control,
clutches, domination, influence,
possession, power

3 underlined, command, comprehension, grasp, mastery
♦ *verb* **4** grasp, clasp, clutch, hold, seize, take hold of **5** engross, absorb, enthral, entrance, fascinate, hold, mesmerize, rivet

gripping *adjective* fascinating, compelling, engrossing, enthralling, entrancing, exciting, riveting, spellbinding, thrilling

grisly *adjective* gruesome, appalling, awful, dreadful, ghastly, horrible, macabre, shocking, terrifying

grit *noun* **1** gravel, dust, pebbles, sand **2** courage, backbone, determination, fortitude, guts (*informal*), perseverance, resolution, spirit, tenacity ♦ *verb* **3** grind, clench, gnash, grate

gritty *adjective* **1** rough, dusty, granular, gravelly, rasping, sandy **2** courageous, brave, determined, dogged, plucky, resolute, spirited, steadfast, tenacious

groan *noun* **1** moan, cry, sigh, whine **2** *Informal* complaint, gripe (*informal*), grouse, grumble, objection, protest
♦ *verb* **3** moan, cry, sigh, whine **4** *Informal* complain, bemoan, gripe (*informal*), grouse, grumble, lament, object

groggy *adjective* dizzy, confused, dazed, faint, shaky, unsteady, weak, wobbly

groom *noun* **1** stableman, hostler or ostler (*archaic*), stableboy
♦ *verb* **2** smarten up, clean, preen, primp, spruce up, tidy **3** rub down, brush, clean, curry, tend **4** train, coach, drill,

educate, make ready, nurture, prepare, prime, ready

groove *noun* indentation, channel, cut, flute, furrow, hollow, rut, trench, trough

grope *verb* feel, cast about, fish, flounder, forage, fumble, scrabble, search

gross *adjective* **1** fat, corpulent, hulking, obese, overweight **2** total, aggregate, before deductions, before tax, entire, whole **3** vulgar, coarse, crude, indelicate, obscene, offensive **4** blatant, flagrant, grievous, heinous, rank, sheer, unmitigated, utter ♦ *verb* **5** earn, bring in, make, rake in (*informal*), take

grotesque *adjective* unnatural, bizarre, deformed, distorted, fantastic, freakish, outlandish, preposterous, strange

ground *noun* **1** earth, dry land, land, soil, terra firma, terrain, turf **2** stadium, arena, field, park (*informal*), pitch **3** *often plural* land, estate, fields, gardens, terrain, territory **4** *usually plural* dregs, deposit, lees, sediment **5** grounds reason, basis, cause, excuse, foundation, justification, motive, occasion, pretext, rationale ♦ *verb* **6** base, establish, fix, found, set, settle **7** instruct, acquaint with, familiarize with, initiate, teach, train, tutor

groundless *adjective* unjustified, baseless, empty, idle, uncalled-for, unfounded, unwarranted

groundwork *noun* preliminaries, foundation, fundamentals, preparation, spadework, underpinnings

group noun **1** set, band, bunch, cluster, collection, crowd, gang, pack, party ♦ verb **2** arrange, bracket, class, classify, marshal, order, sort

grouse verb **1** complain, bellyache (slang), carp, gripe (informal), grumble, moan, whine, whinge (informal) ♦ noun **2** complaint, grievance, gripe (informal), grouch (informal), grumble, moan, objection, protest

grove noun wood, coppice, copse, covert, plantation, spinney, thicket

grovel verb humble oneself, abase oneself, bow and scrape, crawl, creep, cringe, demean oneself, fawn, kowtow, toady

grow verb **1** increase, develop, enlarge, expand, get bigger, multiply, spread, stretch, swell **2** originate, arise, issue, spring, stem **3** improve, advance, flourish, progress, prosper, succeed, thrive **4** become, come to be, get, turn **5** cultivate, breed, farm, nurture, produce, propagate, raise

grown-up adjective **1** mature, adult, fully-grown, of age ♦ noun **2** adult, man, woman

growth noun **1** increase, development, enlargement, expansion, multiplication, proliferation, stretching **2** improvement, advance, expansion, progress, prosperity, rise, success **3** Medical tumour, lump

grub noun **1** larva, caterpillar, maggot **2** Slang food, nosh

(slang), rations, sustenance, victuals ♦ verb **3** dig up, burrow, pull up, root (informal) **4** search, ferret, forage, hunt, rummage, scour, uncover, unearth

grubby adjective dirty, filthy, grimy, messy, mucky, scruffy, seedy, shabby, sordid, squalid, unwashed

grudge verb **1** resent, begrudge, complain, covet, envy, mind ♦ noun **2** resentment, animosity, antipathy, bitterness, dislike, enmity, grievance, rancour

gruelling adjective exhausting, arduous, backbreaking, demanding, laborious, punishing, severe, strenuous, taxing, tiring

gruesome adjective horrific, ghastly, grim, grisly, horrible, macabre, shocking, terrible

gruff adjective **1** surly, bad-tempered, brusque, churlish, grumpy, rough, rude, sullen, ungracious **2** hoarse, croaking, guttural, harsh, husky, low, rasping, rough, throaty

grumble verb **1** complain, bleat, carp, gripe (informal), grouch (informal), grouse, moan, whine, whinge (informal) **2** rumble, growl, gurgle, murmur, mutter, roar ♦ noun **3** complaint, grievance, gripe (informal), grouch (informal), grouse, moan, objection, protest **4** rumble, growl, gurgle, murmur, muttering, roar

grumpy adjective irritable, cantankerous, crotchety (informal), ill-tempered, peevish, sulky, sullen, surly, testy

guarantee noun **1** assurance,

bond, certainty, pledge, promise, security, surety, warranty, word of honour ♦ *verb* **2** make certain, assure, certify, ensure, pledge, promise, secure, vouch for, warrant

guard *verb* **1** watch over, defend, mind, preserve, protect, safeguard, secure, shield ♦ *noun* **2** protector, custodian, defender, lookout, picket, sentinel, sentry, warder, watch, watchman **3** protection, buffer, defence, safeguard, screen, security, shield **4 off guard** unprepared, napping, unready, unwary **5 on guard** prepared, alert, cautious, circumspect, on the alert, on the lookout, ready, vigilant, wary, watchful

guarded *adjective* cautious, cagey (*informal*), careful, circumspect, noncommittal, prudent, reserved, reticent, suspicious, wary

guardian *noun* keeper, champion, curator, custodian, defender, guard, protector, warden

guerrilla *noun* freedom fighter, partisan, underground fighter

guess *verb* **1** estimate, conjecture, hypothesize, predict, speculate, work out **2** suppose, believe, conjecture, fancy, imagine, judge, reckon, suspect, think ♦ *noun* **3** prediction, conjecture, hypothesis, shot in the dark, speculation, supposition, theory

guesswork *noun* speculation, conjecture, estimation, supposition, surmise, theory

guest *noun* visitor, boarder, caller, company, lodger, visitant

guidance *noun* advice, counselling, direction, help, instruction, leadership, management, teaching

guide *noun* **1** escort, adviser, conductor, counsellor, leader, mentor, teacher, usher **2** model, example, ideal, inspiration, paradigm, standard **3** pointer, beacon, guiding light, landmark, lodestar, marker, sign, signpost **4** guidebook, Baedeker, catalogue, directory, handbook, instructions, key, manual ♦ *verb* **5** lead, accompany, conduct, direct, escort, shepherd, show the way, usher **6** steer, command, control, direct, handle, manage, manoeuvre **7** supervise, advise, counsel, influence, instruct, oversee, superintend, teach, train

guild *noun* society, association, brotherhood, club, company, corporation, fellowship, fraternity, league, lodge, order, organization, union

guile *noun* cunning, artifice, cleverness, craft, deceit, slyness, trickery, wiliness

guilt *noun* **1** culpability, blame, guiltiness, misconduct, responsibility, sinfulness, wickedness, wrongdoing **2** remorse, contrition, guilty conscience, regret, self-reproach, shame, stigma

guiltless *adjective* innocent, blameless, clean (*slang*), irreproachable, pure, sinless, spotless, squeaky-clean, untainted

guilty *adjective* **1** responsible, at fault, blameworthy, culpable, reprehensible, sinful, to blame, wrong **2** <u>remorseful</u>, ashamed, conscience-stricken, contrite, regretful, rueful, shamefaced, sheepish, sorry

guise noun <u>form</u>, appearance, aspect, demeanour, disguise, mode, pretence, semblance, shape

gulf noun **1** <u>bay</u>, bight, sea inlet **2** <u>chasm</u>, abyss, gap, opening, rift, separation, split, void

gullibility noun <u>credulity</u>, innocence, naïveté, simplicity

gullible adjective <u>naive</u>, born yesterday, credulous, innocent, simple, trusting, unsuspecting, wet behind the ears (informal)

gully noun <u>channel</u>, ditch, gutter, watercourse

gulp verb **1** <u>swallow</u>, devour, gobble, guzzle, quaff, swig (informal), swill, wolf **2** <u>gasp</u>, choke, swallow ♦ noun **3** <u>swallow</u>, draught, mouthful, swig (informal)

gum noun **1** <u>glue</u>, adhesive, cement, paste, resin ♦ verb **2** <u>stick</u>, affix, cement, glue, paste

gumption noun <u>resourcefulness</u>, acumen, astuteness, common sense, enterprise, initiative, mother wit, savvy (slang), wit(s)

gun noun <u>firearm</u>, handgun, piece (slang), shooter (slang)

gunman noun <u>terrorist</u>, bandit, gunslinger (U.S. slang), killer

gurgle verb **1** <u>murmur</u>, babble, bubble, lap, plash, purl, ripple, splash ♦ noun **2** <u>murmur</u>, babble, purl, ripple

guru noun <u>teacher</u>, authority, leader, master, mentor, sage, Svengali, tutor

gush verb **1** <u>flow</u>, cascade, flood, pour, run, rush, spout, spurt, stream **2** <u>enthuse</u>, babble, chatter, effervesce, effuse, overstate, spout ♦ noun **3** <u>stream</u>, cascade, flood, flow, jet, rush, spout, spurt, torrent

gust noun **1** <u>blast</u>, blow, breeze, puff, rush, squall ♦ verb **2** <u>blow</u>, blast, squall

gusto noun <u>relish</u>, delight, enjoyment, enthusiasm, fervour, pleasure, verve, zeal

gut noun **1** Informal <u>paunch</u>, belly, potbelly, spare tyre (Brit. slang) **2 guts: a** <u>intestines</u>, belly, bowels, entrails, innards (informal), insides (informal), stomach, viscera **b** Informal <u>courage</u>, audacity, backbone, bottle (slang), daring, mettle, nerve, pluck, spirit ♦ verb **3** <u>disembowel</u>, clean **4** <u>ravage</u>, clean out, despoil, empty ♦ adjective **5** As in **gut reaction** <u>instinctive</u>, basic, heartfelt, intuitive, involuntary, natural, spontaneous, unthinking, visceral

gutsy adjective <u>brave</u>, bold, courageous, determined, gritty, indomitable, plucky, resolute, spirited

gutter noun <u>drain</u>, channel, conduit, ditch, sluice, trench, trough

guttural adjective <u>throaty</u>, deep, gravelly, gruff, hoarse, husky, rasping, rough, thick

guy noun Informal <u>man</u>, bloke (Brit. informal), chap, fellow, lad, person

guzzle verb <u>devour</u>, bolt, cram, drink, gobble, stuff (oneself), swill, wolf

Gypsy, Gipsy noun traveller, Bohemian, nomad, rambler, roamer, Romany, rover, wanderer

H h

habit noun **1** mannerism, custom, practice, proclivity, propensity, quirk, tendency, way **2** addiction, dependence

habitation noun **1** dwelling, abode, domicile, home, house, living quarters, lodging, quarters, residence **2** occupancy, inhabitance, occupation, tenancy

habitual adjective customary, accustomed, familiar, normal, regular, routine, standard, traditional, usual

hack[1] verb cut, chop, hew, lacerate, mangle, mutilate, slash

hack[2] noun **1** scribbler, literary hack, penny-a-liner **2** horse, crock, nag

hackneyed adjective unoriginal, clichéd, commonplace, overworked, stale, stereotyped, stock, threadbare, tired, trite

hag noun witch, crone, harridan

haggard adjective gaunt, careworn, drawn, emaciated, pinched, thin, wan

haggle verb bargain, barter, beat down

hail[1] noun **1** bombardment, barrage, downpour, rain, shower, storm, volley ♦ verb **2** rain down on, batter, beat down upon, bombard, pelt, rain, shower

hail[2] verb **1** greet, acclaim, acknowledge, applaud, cheer, honour, salute, welcome **2** flag down, signal to, wave down **3** hail from come from, be a native of, be born in, originate in

hair noun locks, head of hair, mane, mop, shock, tresses

hairdresser noun stylist, barber, coiffeur or coiffeuse

hair-raising adjective frightening, alarming, bloodcurdling, horrifying, scary, shocking, spine-chilling, terrifying

hairstyle noun haircut, coiffure, cut, hairdo, style

hairy adjective **1** shaggy, bushy, furry, hirsute, stubbly, unshaven, woolly **2** Slang dangerous, difficult, hazardous, perilous, risky

halcyon adjective **1** peaceful, calm, gentle, quiet, serene, tranquil, undisturbed **2** As in **halcyon days** happy, carefree, flourishing, golden, palmy, prosperous

hale adjective healthy, able-bodied, fit, flourishing, in the pink, robust, sound, strong, vigorous, well

half noun **1** equal part, fifty per cent, hemisphere, portion, section ♦ adjective **2** partial, halved, limited, moderate ♦ adverb **3** partially, in part, partly

half-baked adjective ill-judged, ill-conceived, impractical, poorly planned, short-sighted, unformed, unthought out or through

half-hearted adjective unenthusiastic, apathetic, indifferent, lacklustre, listless, lukewarm, perfunctory, tame

halfway adverb **1** midway, to or in the middle ♦ adjective **2** midway, central, equidistant, intermediate, mid, middle

halfwit noun fool, airhead (slang), dunderhead, idiot, imbecile (informal), moron, numbskull or numskull, simpleton, twit (informal, chiefly Brit.)

hall noun **1** entrance hall, corridor, entry, foyer, hallway, lobby, passage, passageway, vestibule **2** meeting place, assembly room, auditorium, chamber, concert hall

hallmark noun **1** seal, device, endorsement, mark, sign, stamp, symbol **2** indication, sure sign, telltale sign

hallucination noun illusion, apparition, delusion, dream, fantasy, figment of the imagination, mirage, vision

halo noun ring of light, aura, corona, nimbus, radiance

halt verb **1** stop, break off, cease, come to an end, desist, rest, stand still, wait **2** end, block, bring to an end, check, curb, cut short, nip in the bud, terminate ♦ noun **3** stop, close, end, pause, standstill, stoppage

halting adjective faltering, awkward, hesitant, laboured, stammering, stumbling, stuttering

halve verb bisect, cut in half, divide equally, share equally, split in two

hammer verb **1** hit, bang, beat, drive, knock, strike, tap **2** Informal defeat, beat, drub, run

rings around (informal), thrash, trounce, wipe the floor with (informal)

hamper verb hinder, frustrate, hamstring, handicap, impede, interfere with, obstruct, prevent, restrict

hand noun **1** palm, fist, mitt (slang), paw (informal) **2** hired man, artisan, craftsman, employee, labourer, operative, worker, workman **3** penmanship, calligraphy, handwriting, script **4** ovation, clap, round of applause **5** at or on hand nearby, at one's fingertips, available, close, handy, near, ready, within reach ♦ verb **6** pass, deliver, hand over

handbook noun guidebook, Baedeker, guide, instruction book, manual

handcuff verb shackle, fetter, manacle

handcuffs plural noun shackles, cuffs (informal), fetters, manacles

handful noun few, small number, smattering, sprinkling

handicap noun **1** disadvantage, barrier, drawback, hindrance, impediment, limitation, obstacle, restriction, stumbling block **2** advantage, head start **3** disability, defect, impairment ♦ verb **4** restrict, burden, encumber, hamper, hamstring, hinder, hold back, impede, limit

handicraft noun craftsmanship, art, craft, handiwork, skill, workmanship

handiwork noun creation, achievement, design, invention, product, production

handle noun 1 <u>grip</u>, haft, hilt, stock ◆ verb 2 <u>hold</u>, feel, finger, grasp, pick up, touch 3 <u>control</u>, direct, guide, manage, manipulate, manoeuvre 4 <u>deal with</u>, cope with, manage

hand-out noun 1 <u>charity</u>, alms, dole 2 <u>leaflet</u>, bulletin, circular, literature (informal), mailshot, press release

handsome adjective 1 <u>good-looking</u>, attractive, comely, dishy (informal, chiefly Brit.), elegant, gorgeous, personable, well-proportioned 2 <u>large</u>, abundant, ample, considerable, generous, liberal, plentiful, sizable or sizeable

handwriting noun <u>penmanship</u>, calligraphy, hand, scrawl, script

handy adjective 1 <u>available</u>, accessible, at hand, at one's fingertips, close, convenient, nearby, on hand, within reach 2 <u>useful</u>, convenient, easy to use, helpful, manageable, neat, practical, serviceable, user-friendly 3 <u>skilful</u>, adept, adroit, deft, dexterous, expert, proficient, skilled

hang verb 1 <u>suspend</u>, dangle, droop 2 <u>execute</u>, lynch, string up (informal) ◆ noun 3 <u>get the hang of</u> grasp, comprehend, understand

hang back verb <u>hesitate</u>, be reluctant, demur, hold back, recoil

hangdog adjective <u>guilty</u>, cowed, cringing, defeated, downcast, furtive, shamefaced, wretched

hangover noun <u>aftereffects</u>, crapulence, morning after (informal)

hang-up noun <u>preoccupation</u>, block, difficulty, inhibition, obsession, problem, thing (informal)

hank noun <u>coil</u>, length, loop, piece, roll, skein

hanker verb, with **for** or **after** <u>desire</u>, crave, hunger, itch, long, lust, pine, thirst, yearn

haphazard adjective <u>disorganized</u>, aimless, casual, hit or miss (informal), indiscriminate, slapdash

happen verb 1 <u>occur</u>, come about, come to pass, develop, result, take place, transpire (informal) 2 <u>chance</u>, turn out

happening noun <u>event</u>, affair, episode, experience, incident, occurrence, proceeding

happily adverb 1 <u>willingly</u>, freely, gladly, with pleasure 2 <u>joyfully</u>, blithely, cheerfully, gaily, gleefully, joyously, merrily 3 <u>luckily</u>, fortunately, opportunely, providentially

happiness noun <u>joy</u>, bliss, cheerfulness, contentment, delight, ecstasy, elation, jubilation, pleasure, satisfaction

happy adjective 1 <u>joyful</u>, blissful, cheerful, content, delighted, ecstatic, elated, glad, jubilant, merry, overjoyed, pleased, thrilled 2 <u>fortunate</u>, advantageous, auspicious, favourable, lucky, timely

happy-go-lucky adjective <u>carefree</u>, blithe, easy-going, light-hearted, nonchalant, unconcerned, untroubled

harangue verb 1 <u>rant</u>, address, declaim, exhort, hold forth,

lecture, spout (*informal*) ♦ *noun*
2 speech, address, declaration,
diatribe, exhortation, tirade

harass *verb* annoy, bother, harry,
hassle (*informal*), hound,
persecute, pester, plague,
trouble, vex

harassed *adjective* worried,
careworn, distraught, hassled
(*informal*), strained, tormented,
troubled, under pressure, vexed

harassment *noun* trouble,
annoyance, bother, hassle
(*informal*), irritation, nuisance,
persecution, pestering

harbour *noun* 1 port, anchorage,
haven ♦ *verb* 2 shelter, hide,
protect, provide refuge, shield
3 maintain, cling to, entertain,
foster, hold, nurse, nurture, retain

hard *adjective* 1 solid, firm,
inflexible, rigid, rocklike, stiff,
strong, tough, unyielding
2 strenuous, arduous,
backbreaking, exacting,
exhausting, laborious, rigorous,
tough 3 difficult, complicated,
intricate, involved, knotty,
perplexing, puzzling, thorny
4 unfeeling, callous, cold, cruel,
hardhearted, pitiless, stern,
unkind, unsympathetic 5 painful,
disagreeable, distressing,
grievous, intolerable, unpleasant
♦ *adverb* 6 energetically, fiercely,
forcefully, forcibly, heavily,
intensely, powerfully, severely,
sharply, strongly, vigorously,
violently, with all one's might,
with might and main
7 diligently, doggedly,
industriously, persistently,
steadily, untiringly

hard-bitten or **hard-boiled**

adjective tough, cynical,
hard-nosed (*informal*),
matter-of-fact, practical, realistic,
unsentimental

harden *verb* 1 solidify, anneal,
bake, cake, freeze, set, stiffen
2 accustom, habituate, inure,
season, train

hardened *adjective* 1 habitual,
chronic, incorrigible, inveterate,
shameless 2 accustomed,
habituated, inured, seasoned,
toughened

hard-headed *adjective* sensible,
level-headed, practical,
pragmatic, realistic, shrewd,
tough, unsentimental

hardhearted *adjective*
unsympathetic, callous, cold,
hard, heartless, insensitive,
uncaring, unfeeling

hardiness *noun* resilience,
resolution, robustness,
ruggedness, sturdiness, toughness

hardly *adverb* barely, just, only
just, scarcely, with difficulty

hardship *noun* suffering,
adversity, difficulty, misfortune,
need, privation, tribulation

hard up *adjective* poor, broke
(*informal*), impecunious,
impoverished, on the breadline,
out of pocket, penniless, short,
skint (*Brit. slang*), strapped for
cash (*informal*)

hardy *adjective* strong, robust,
rugged, sound, stout, sturdy,
tough

harm *verb* 1 injure, abuse,
damage, hurt, ill-treat, maltreat,
ruin, spoil, wound ♦ *noun*
2 injury, abuse, damage, hurt,
ill, loss, mischief, misfortune

harmful *adjective* <u>destructive</u>, damaging, deleterious, detrimental, hurtful, injurious, noxious, pernicious

harmless *adjective* <u>innocuous</u>, gentle, innocent, inoffensive, nontoxic, safe, unobjectionable

harmonious *adjective*
1 <u>melodious</u>, agreeable, concordant, consonant, dulcet, mellifluous, musical, sweet-sounding, tuneful
2 <u>friendly</u>, agreeable, amicable, compatible, congenial, cordial, sympathetic

harmonize *verb* <u>blend</u>, chime with, cohere, coordinate, correspond, match, tally, tone in with

harmony *noun* 1 <u>agreement</u>, accord, amicability, compatibility, concord, cooperation, friendship, peace, rapport, sympathy 2 <u>tunefulness</u>, euphony, melody, tune, unison

harness *noun* 1 <u>equipment</u>, gear, tack, tackle ♦ *verb* 2 <u>exploit</u>, channel, control, employ, mobilize, utilize

harrowing *adjective* <u>distressing</u>, agonizing, disturbing, heart-rending, nerve-racking, painful, terrifying, tormenting, traumatic

harry *verb* <u>pester</u>, badger, bother, chivvy, harass, hassle (*informal*), molest, plague

harsh *adjective* 1 <u>raucous</u>, discordant, dissonant, grating, guttural, rasping, rough, strident 2 <u>severe</u>, austere, cruel, Draconian, drastic, pitiless, punitive, ruthless, stern

harshly *adverb* <u>severely</u>, brutally,

cruelly, roughly, sternly, strictly

harshness *noun* <u>severity</u>, asperity, austerity, brutality, rigour, roughness, sternness

harvest *noun* 1 <u>crop</u>, produce, yield ♦ *verb* 2 <u>gather</u>, mow, pick, pluck, reap

hash *noun* **make a hash of** *Informal* <u>mess up</u>, botch, bungle, make a pig's ear of (*informal*), mishandle, mismanage, muddle

hassle *noun* 1 <u>argument</u>, bickering, disagreement, dispute, fight, quarrel, row, squabble 2 <u>trouble</u>, bother, difficulty, grief (*informal*), inconvenience, problem ♦ *verb* 3 <u>bother</u>, annoy, badger, bug (*informal*), harass, hound, pester

haste *noun* 1 <u>speed</u>, alacrity, quickness, rapidity, swiftness, urgency, velocity 2 <u>rush</u>, hurry, hustle, impetuosity

hasten *verb* <u>rush</u>, dash, fly, hurry (up), make haste, race, scurry, speed

hastily *adverb* 1 <u>speedily</u>, promptly, quickly, rapidly 2 <u>hurriedly</u>, impetuously, precipitately, rashly

hasty *adjective* 1 <u>speedy</u>, brisk, hurried, prompt, rapid, swift, urgent 2 <u>impetuous</u>, impulsive, precipitate, rash, thoughtless

hatch *verb* 1 <u>incubate</u>, breed, bring forth, brood 2 <u>devise</u>, conceive, concoct, contrive, cook up (*informal*), design, dream up (*informal*), think up

hate *verb* 1 <u>detest</u>, abhor, despise, dislike, loathe, recoil from 2 <u>be unwilling</u>, be loath, be reluctant, be sorry, dislike,

feel disinclined, shrink from
♦ *noun* **3** dislike, animosity,
antipathy, aversion, detestation,
enmity, hatred, hostility, loathing

hateful *adjective* despicable,
abhorrent, detestable, horrible,
loathsome, obnoxious, odious,
offensive, repellent, repugnant,
repulsive

hatred *noun* dislike, animosity,
antipathy, aversion, detestation,
enmity, hate, repugnance,
revulsion

haughty *adjective* proud,
arrogant, conceited,
contemptuous, disdainful,
imperious, scornful, snooty
(*informal*), stuck-up (*informal*),
supercilious

haul *verb* **1** drag, draw, heave,
lug, pull, tug ♦ *noun* **2** gain,
booty, catch, harvest, loot,
spoils, takings, yield

haunt *verb* **1** plague, obsess,
possess, prey on, recur, stay
with, torment, trouble, weigh on
♦ *noun* **2** meeting place, hangout
(*informal*), rendezvous, stamping
ground

haunted *adjective* **1** possessed,
cursed, eerie, ghostly, jinxed,
spooky (*informal*) **2** preoccupied,
obsessed, plagued, tormented,
troubled, worried

haunting *adjective* poignant,
evocative, nostalgic, persistent,
unforgettable

have *verb* **1** possess, hold, keep,
obtain, own, retain **2** receive,
accept, acquire, gain, get,
obtain, procure, secure, take
3 experience, endure, enjoy,
feel, meet with, suffer, sustain,
undergo **4** *Slang* cheat, deceive,

dupe, fool, outwit, swindle, take
in (*informal*), trick **5** give birth
to, bear, beget, bring forth,
deliver **6 have to** be obliged, be
bound, be compelled, be forced,
have got to, must, ought, should

haven *noun* sanctuary, asylum,
refuge, retreat, sanctum, shelter

have on *verb* **1** wear, be clothed
in, be dressed in **2** tease,
deceive, kid (*informal*), pull
someone's leg, take the mickey,
trick, wind up (*Brit. slang*)

havoc *noun* disorder, chaos,
confusion, disruption, mayhem,
shambles

haywire *adjective* As in **go
haywire** topsy-turvy, chaotic,
confused, disordered,
disorganized, mixed up, out of
order, shambolic (*informal*)

hazard *noun* **1** danger, jeopardy,
peril, pitfall, risk, threat ♦ *verb*
2 jeopardize, endanger, expose,
imperil, risk, threaten **3** As in
hazard a guess conjecture,
advance, offer, presume, throw
out, venture, volunteer

hazardous *adjective* dangerous,
dicey (*informal, chiefly Brit.*),
difficult, insecure, perilous,
precarious, risky, unsafe

haze *noun* mist, cloud, fog,
obscurity, vapour

hazy *adjective* **1** misty, cloudy,
dim, dull, foggy, overcast
2 vague, fuzzy, ill-defined,
indefinite, indistinct, muddled,
nebulous, uncertain, unclear

head *noun* **1** skull, crown, loaf
(*slang*), nut (*slang*), pate
2 leader, boss (*informal*), captain,
chief, commander, director,
manager, master, principal,

supervisor **3** top, crest, crown, peak, pinnacle, summit, tip **4** brain, brains (*informal*), intellect, intelligence, mind, thought, understanding **5 go to one's head** excite, intoxicate, make conceited, puff up **6 head over heels** uncontrollably, completely, intensely, thoroughly, utterly, wholeheartedly ♦ *adjective* **7** chief, arch, first, leading, main, pre-eminent, premier, prime, principal, supreme ♦ *verb* **8** lead, be *or* go first, cap, crown, lead the way, precede, top **9** control, be in charge of, command, direct, govern, guide, lead, manage, run **10** make for, aim, go to, make a beeline for, point, set off for, set out, start towards, steer, turn

headache *noun* **1** migraine, head (*informal*), neuralgia **2** problem, bane, bother, inconvenience, nuisance, trouble, vexation, worry

heading *noun* title, caption, headline, name, rubric

headlong *adverb, adjective* **1** headfirst, head-on ♦ *adverb* **2** hastily, heedlessly, helter-skelter, hurriedly, pell-mell, precipitately, rashly, thoughtlessly ♦ *adjective* **3** hasty, breakneck, dangerous, impetuous, impulsive, inconsiderate, precipitate, reckless, thoughtless

headstrong *adjective* obstinate, foolhardy, heedless, impulsive, perverse, pig-headed, self-willed, stubborn, unruly, wilful

headway *noun* progress, advance, improvement,

progression, way

heady *adjective* **1** inebriating, intoxicating, potent, strong **2** exciting, exhilarating, intoxicating, stimulating, thrilling

heal *verb* cure, make well, mend, regenerate, remedy, restore, treat

health *noun* **1** wellbeing, fitness, good condition, healthiness, robustness, soundness, strength, vigour **2** condition, constitution, fettle, shape, state

healthy *adjective* **1** well, active, fit, hale and hearty, in fine fettle, in good shape (*informal*), in the pink, robust, strong **2** wholesome, beneficial, hygienic, invigorating, nourishing, nutritious, salubrious, salutary

heap *noun* **1** pile, accumulation, collection, hoard, lot, mass, mound, stack **2** *often plural* a lot, great deal, load(s) (*informal*), lots (*informal*), mass, plenty, pot's (*informal*), stack(s), tons ♦ *verb* **3** pile, accumulate, amass, collect, gather, hoard, stack **4** confer, assign, bestow, load, shower upon

hear *verb* **1** listen to, catch, overhear **2** learn, ascertain, discover, find out, gather, get wind of (*informal*), pick up **3** *Law* try, examine, investigate, judge

hearing *noun* inquiry, industrial tribunal, investigation, review, trial

hearsay *noun* rumour, gossip, idle talk, report, talk, tittle-tattle, word of mouth

heart *noun* **1** nature, character, disposition, soul, temperament **2** bravery, courage, fortitude, pluck, purpose, resolution, spirit, will **3** centre, core, hub, middle, nucleus, quintessence **4 by heart** by memory, by rote, off pat, parrot-fashion (*informal*), pat, word for word

heartache *noun* sorrow, agony, anguish, despair, distress, grief, heartbreak, pain, remorse, suffering, torment, torture

heartbreak *noun* grief, anguish, desolation, despair, misery, pain, sorrow, suffering

heartbreaking *adjective* tragic, agonizing, distressing, harrowing, heart-rending, pitiful, poignant, sad

heartbroken *adjective* miserable, brokenhearted, crushed, desolate, despondent, disconsolate, dispirited, heartsick

heartfelt *adjective* sincere, deep, devout, earnest, genuine, honest, profound, unfeigned, wholehearted

heartily *adverb* enthusiastically, eagerly, earnestly, resolutely, vigorously, zealously

heartless *adjective* cruel, callous, cold, hard, hardhearted, merciless, pitiless, uncaring, unfeeling

heart-rending *adjective* moving, affecting, distressing, harrowing, heartbreaking, poignant, sad, tragic

hearty *adjective* **1** friendly, back-slapping, ebullient, effusive, enthusiastic, genial, jovial, warm **2** substantial, ample, filling, nourishing, sizable *or* sizeable, solid, square

heat *verb* **1** warm up, make hot, reheat ♦ *noun* **2** hotness, high temperature, warmth **3** intensity, excitement, fervour, fury, passion, vehemence

heated *adjective* angry, excited, fierce, frenzied, furious, impassioned, intense, passionate, stormy, vehement

heathen *noun* **1** unbeliever, infidel, pagan ♦ *adjective* **2** pagan, godless, idolatrous, irreligious

heave *verb* **1** lift, drag (up), haul (up), hoist, pull (up), raise, tug **2** throw, cast, fling, hurl, pitch, send, sling, toss **3** sigh, groan, puff **4** vomit, be sick, gag, retch, spew, throw up (*informal*)

heaven *noun* **1** paradise, bliss, Elysium *or* Elysian fields (*Greek myth*), hereafter, life everlasting, next world, nirvana (*Buddhism, Hinduism*), Zion (*Christianity*) **2** happiness, bliss, ecstasy, paradise, rapture, seventh heaven, utopia **3 the heavens** sky, ether, firmament

heavenly *adjective* **1** beautiful, blissful, delightful, divine (*informal*), exquisite, lovely, ravishing, sublime, wonderful **2** celestial, angelic, blessed, divine, holy, immortal

heavily *adverb* **1** ponderously, awkwardly, clumsily, weightily **2** densely, closely, compactly, thickly **3** considerably, a great deal, copiously, excessively, to excess, very much

heaviness *noun* weight, gravity, heftiness, ponderousness

heavy *adjective* **1** weighty, bulky, hefty, massive, ponderous **2** considerable, abundant, copious, excessive, large, profuse

heckle verb jeer, barrack (informal), boo, disrupt, interrupt, shout down, taunt

hectic adjective frantic, animated, chaotic, feverish, frenetic, heated, turbulent

hedge noun 1 barrier, boundary, screen, windbreak ♦ verb 2 dodge, duck, equivocate, evade, flannel (Brit. informal), prevaricate, sidestep, temporize 3 insure, cover, guard, protect, safeguard, shield

heed noun 1 care, attention, caution, mind, notice, regard, respect, thought ♦ verb 2 pay attention to, bear in mind, consider, follow, listen to, note, obey, observe, take notice of

heedless adjective careless, foolhardy, inattentive, oblivious, thoughtless, unmindful

heel noun Slang swine, bounder (old-fashioned Brit. slang), cad (Brit. informal), rotter (slang, chiefly Brit.)

heel over verb lean over, keel over, list, tilt

hefty adjective strong, big, burly, hulking, massive, muscular, robust, strapping

height noun 1 altitude, elevation, highness, loftiness, stature, tallness 2 peak, apex, crest, crown, pinnacle, summit, top, zenith 3 culmination, climax, limit, maximum, ultimate

heighten verb intensify, add to, amplify, enhance, improve, increase, magnify, sharpen, strengthen

heir noun successor, beneficiary,

heiress (fem.), inheritor, next in line

hell noun 1 underworld, abyss, fire and brimstone, Hades (Greek myth), hellfire, inferno, nether world 2 torment, agony, anguish, misery, nightmare, ordeal, suffering, wretchedness

hellish adjective devilish, damnable, diabolical, fiendish, infernal

hello interjection welcome, good afternoon, good evening, good morning, greetings

helm noun 1 tiller, rudder, wheel 2 at the helm in charge, at the wheel, in command, in control, in the driving seat, in the saddle

help verb 1 aid, abet, assist, cooperate, lend a hand, succour, support 2 improve, alleviate, ameliorate, ease, facilitate, mitigate, relieve 3 refrain from, avoid, keep from, prevent, resist ♦ noun 4 assistance, advice, aid, cooperation, guidance, helping hand, support

helper noun assistant, adjutant, aide, ally, attendant, collaborator, helpmate, mate, right-hand man, second, supporter

helpful adjective 1 useful, advantageous, beneficial, constructive, practical, profitable, timely 2 cooperative, accommodating, considerate, friendly, kind, neighbourly, supportive, sympathetic

helping noun portion, dollop (informal), piece, plateful, ration, serving

helpless adjective weak, disabled, impotent, incapable, infirm, paralysed, powerless

helter-skelter *adjective*
1 haphazard, confused,
disordered, higgledy-piggledy
(*informal*), hit-or-miss, jumbled,
muddled, random, topsy-turvy
♦ *adverb* **2** carelessly, anyhow,
hastily, headlong, hurriedly,
pell-mell, rashly, recklessly, wildly

hem *noun* **1** edge, border, fringe,
margin, trimming ♦ *verb* **2 hem
in** surround, beset, circumscribe,
confine, enclose, restrict, shut in

hence *conjunction* therefore, ergo,
for this reason, on that account,
thus

henchman *noun* attendant,
associate, bodyguard, follower,
minder (*slang*), right-hand man,
sidekick (*slang*), subordinate,
supporter

henpecked *adjective* bullied,
browbeaten, dominated, meek,
subjugated, timid

herald *noun* **1** messenger, crier
2 forerunner, harbinger,
indication, omen, precursor,
sign, signal, token ♦ *verb*
3 indicate, foretoken, portend,
presage, promise, show, usher in

herd *noun* **1** multitude,
collection, crowd, drove, flock,
horde, mass, mob, swarm,
throng ♦ *verb* **2** congregate,
assemble, collect, flock, gather,
huddle, muster, rally

hereafter *adverb* **1** in future,
from now on, hence,
henceforth, henceforward ♦ *noun*
2 afterlife, life after death, next
world

hereditary *adjective* **1** genetic,
inborn, inbred, inheritable,
transmissible **2** inherited,

ancestral, traditional

heredity *noun* genetics,
constitution, genetic make-up,
inheritance

heresy *noun* dissidence, apostasy,
heterodoxy, iconoclasm,
unorthodoxy

heretic *noun* dissident, apostate,
dissenter, nonconformist,
renegade, revisionist

heretical *adjective* unorthodox,
heterodox, iconoclastic,
idolatrous, impious, revisionist

heritage *noun* inheritance,
bequest, birthright, endowment,
legacy, tradition

hermit *noun* recluse, anchorite,
eremite, loner (*informal*), monk

hero *noun* **1** idol, champion,
conqueror, star, superstar, victor
2 leading man, protagonist

heroic *adjective* courageous,
brave, daring, fearless, gallant,
intrepid, lion-hearted, valiant

heroine *noun* leading lady, diva,
prima donna, protagonist

heroism *noun* bravery, courage,
courageousness, fearlessness,
gallantry, intrepidity, spirit, valour

hesitant *adjective* uncertain,
diffident, doubtful, half-hearted,
halting, irresolute, reluctant,
unsure, vacillating, wavering

hesitate *verb* **1** waver, delay,
dither (*chiefly Brit.*), doubt, hum
and haw, pause, vacillate, wait
2 be reluctant, balk, be
unwilling, demur, hang back,
scruple, shrink from, think twice

hesitation *noun* **1** indecision,
delay, doubt, hesitancy,
irresolution, uncertainty,
vacillation **2** reluctance,

misgiving(s), qualm(s), scruple(s), unwillingness

hew verb 1 <u>cut</u>, axe, chop, hack, lop, split 2 <u>carve</u>, fashion, form, make, model, sculpt, sculpture, shape, smooth

heyday noun <u>prime</u>, bloom, pink, prime of life, salad days

hiatus noun <u>pause</u>, break, discontinuity, gap, interruption, interval, respite, space

hidden adjective <u>concealed</u>, clandestine, covert, latent, secret, under wraps, unseen, veiled

hide[1] verb 1 <u>conceal</u>, secrete, stash (informal) 2 <u>go into hiding</u>, go to ground, go underground, hole up, lie low, take cover 3 <u>disguise</u>, camouflage, cloak, conceal, cover, mask, obscure, shroud, veil 4 <u>suppress</u>, draw a veil over, hush up, keep dark, keep secret, keep under one's hat, withhold

hide[2] noun <u>skin</u>, pelt

hidebound adjective <u>conventional</u>, narrow-minded, rigid, set in one's ways, strait-laced, ultraconservative

hideous adjective <u>ugly</u>, ghastly, grim, grisly, grotesque, gruesome, monstrous, repulsive, revolting, unsightly

hide-out noun <u>hideaway</u>, den, hiding place, lair, shelter

hiding noun <u>beating</u>, drubbing, licking (informal), spanking, thrashing, walloping (informal), whipping

hierarchy noun <u>grading</u>, pecking order, ranking

high adjective 1 <u>tall</u>, elevated,

lofty, soaring, steep, towering 2 <u>extreme</u>, excessive, extraordinary, great, intensified, sharp, strong 3 <u>important</u>, arch, chief, eminent, exalted, powerful, superior 4 Informal <u>intoxicated</u>, stoned (slang), tripping (informal) 5 <u>high-pitched</u>, acute, penetrating, piercing, piping, sharp, shrill, strident ◆ adverb 6 <u>aloft</u>, at great height, far up, way up

highbrow noun 1 <u>intellectual</u>, aesthete, egghead (informal), scholar ◆ adjective 2 <u>intellectual</u>, bookish, cultivated, cultured, sophisticated

high-flown adjective <u>extravagant</u>, elaborate, exaggerated, florid, grandiose, inflated, lofty, overblown, pretentious

high-handed adjective <u>dictatorial</u>, despotic, domineering, imperious, oppressive, overbearing, tyrannical, wilful

highlight noun 1 <u>feature</u>, climax, focal point, focus, high point, high spot, peak ◆ verb 2 <u>emphasize</u>, accent, accentuate, bring to the fore, show up, spotlight, stress, underline

highly adverb <u>extremely</u>, exceptionally, greatly, immensely, tremendously, vastly, very, very much

highly strung adjective <u>nervous</u>, edgy, excitable, neurotic, sensitive, stressed, temperamental, tense

hijack verb <u>seize</u>, commandeer, expropriate, take over

hike noun 1 <u>walk</u>, march, ramble, tramp, trek ◆ verb 2 <u>walk</u>, back-pack, ramble, tramp **3 hike up** raise, hitch up, jack up, lift, pull up

hilarious adjective funny, amusing, comical, entertaining, humorous, rollicking, side-splitting, uproarious

hilarity noun laughter, amusement, exhilaration, glee, high spirits, jollity, merriment, mirth

hill noun mount, fell, height, hillock, hilltop, knoll, mound, tor

hillock noun mound, hummock, knoll

hilly adjective mountainous, rolling, undulating

hilt noun handle, grip, haft, handgrip

hinder verb obstruct, block, check, delay, encumber, frustrate, hamper, handicap, hold up or back, impede, interrupt, stop

hindmost adjective last, final, furthest, furthest behind, rearmost, trailing

hindrance noun obstacle, barrier, deterrent, difficulty, drawback, handicap, hitch, impediment, obstruction, restriction, snag, stumbling block

hinge verb depend, be contingent, hang, pivot, rest, revolve around, turn

hint noun 1 indication, allusion, clue, implication, innuendo, insinuation, intimation, suggestion 2 advice, help, pointer, suggestion, tip 3 trace, dash, suggestion, suspicion, tinge, touch, undertone ◆ verb 4 suggest, imply, indicate,

insinuate, intimate

hippy noun bohemian, beatnik, dropout

hire verb 1 employ, appoint, commission, engage, sign up, take on 2 rent, charter, engage, lease, let ◆ noun 3 rental, charge, cost, fee, price, rent

hiss noun 1 sibilation, buzz, hissing 2 catcall, boo, jeer ◆ verb 3 whistle, sibilate, wheeze, whirr, whiz 4 jeer, boo, deride, hoot, mock

historic adjective significant, epoch-making, extraordinary, famous, ground-breaking, momentous, notable, outstanding, remarkable

historical adjective factual, actual, attested, authentic, documented, real

history noun 1 chronicle, account, annals, narrative, recital, record, story 2 the past, antiquity, olden days, yesterday, yesteryear

hit verb 1 strike, bang, beat, clout (informal), knock, slap, smack, thump, wallop (informal), whack 2 collide with, bang into, bump, clash with, crash against, run into, smash into 3 reach, accomplish, achieve, arrive at, attain, gain 4 affect, damage, devastate, impact on, influence, leave a mark on, overwhelm, touch 5 **hit it off** Informal get on (well) with, be on good terms, click (slang), get on like a house on fire (informal) ◆ noun 6 stroke, belt (informal), blow, clout (informal), knock, rap, slap, smack, wallop (informal) 7 success, sensation, smash (*informal*), triumph, winner

hit-and-miss *adjective*
haphazard, aimless, casual,
disorganized, indiscriminate,
random, undirected, uneven

hitch *noun* **1** problem, catch,
difficulty, drawback, hindrance,
hold-up, impediment, obstacle,
snag ♦ *verb* **2** fasten, attach,
connect, couple, harness, join,
tether, tie **3** *Informal* hitchhike,
thumb a lift **4 hitch up** pull up,
jerk, tug, yank

hitherto *adverb* previously,
heretofore, so far, thus far, until
now

hit on *verb* think up, arrive at,
discover, invent, light upon,
strike upon, stumble on

hoard *noun* **1** store,
accumulation, cache, fund, pile,
reserve, stockpile, supply,
treasure-trove ♦ *verb* **2** save,
accumulate, amass, collect,
gather, lay up, put by, stash
away (*informal*), stockpile, store

hoarse *adjective* raucous, croaky,
grating, gravelly, gruff, guttural,
husky, rasping, rough, throaty

hoax *noun* **1** trick, con (*informal*),
deception, fraud, practical joke,
prank, spoof (*informal*), swindle
♦ *verb* **2** deceive, con (*slang*),
dupe, fool, hoodwink, swindle,
take in (*informal*), trick

hobby *noun* pastime, diversion,
(leisure) activity, leisure pursuit,
relaxation

hobnob *verb* socialize, associate,
consort, fraternize, hang about,
hang out (*informal*), keep
company, mingle, mix

hoist *verb* **1** raise, elevate, erect,

heave, lift ♦ *noun* **2** lift, crane,
elevator, winch

hold *verb* **1** own, have, keep,
maintain, occupy, possess, retain
2 grasp, clasp, cling, clutch,
cradle, embrace, enfold, grip
3 restrain, confine, detain,
impound, imprison **4** consider,
assume, believe, deem, judge,
presume, reckon, regard, think
5 convene, call, conduct, preside
over, run **6** accommodate,
contain, have a capacity for,
seat, take **7** grip, clasp,
grasp **8** foothold, footing,
support **9** control, influence,
mastery

holder *noun* **1** owner, bearer,
keeper, possessor, proprietor
2 case, container, cover

hold forth *verb* speak, declaim,
discourse, go on, lecture,
preach, spiel (*informal*), spout
(*informal*)

hold-up *noun* **1** delay,
bottleneck, hitch, setback, snag,
stoppage, traffic jam, wait
2 robbery, mugging (*informal*),
stick-up (*slang, chiefly U.S.*), theft

hold up *verb* **1** delay, detain,
hinder, retard, set back, slow
down, stop **2** support, prop,
shore up, sustain **3** rob, mug
(*informal*), waylay

hold with *verb* approve of, agree
to *or* with, be in favour of,
countenance, subscribe to,
support

hole *noun* **1** opening, aperture,
breach, crack, fissure, gap,
orifice, perforation, puncture,
tear, vent **2** cavity, cave, cavern,
chamber, hollow, pit **3** burrow,
den, earth, lair, shelter **4** *Informal*

hovel, dive (slang), dump (informal), slum **5** Informal **predicament**, dilemma, fix (informal), hot water (informal), jam (informal), mess, scrape (informal), spot (informal), tight spot

holiday noun **1** vacation, break, leave, recess, time off **2** festival, celebration, feast, fête, gala

holiness noun divinity, godliness, piety, purity, righteousness, sacredness, saintliness, sanctity, spirituality

hollow adjective **1** empty, unfilled, vacant, void **2** reverberant, deep, dull, low, muted **3** worthless, fruitless, futile, meaningless, pointless, useless, vain ♦ noun **4** cavity, basin, bowl, crater, depression, hole, pit, trough **5** valley, dale, dell, dingle, glen ♦ verb **6** scoop, dig, excavate, gouge

holocaust noun genocide, annihilation, conflagration, destruction, devastation, massacre

holy adjective **1** devout, god-fearing, godly, pious, pure, religious, righteous, saintly, virtuous **2** sacred, blessed, consecrated, hallowed, sacrosanct, sanctified, venerable

homage noun respect, adoration, adulation, deference, devotion, honour, reverence, worship

home noun **1** house, abode, domicile, dwelling, habitation, pad (slang), residence **2** birthplace, home town **3** at **home: a** in, available, present **b** at ease, comfortable, familiar, relaxed **4** bring home to make

clear, drive home, emphasize, impress upon, press home ♦ adjective **5** domestic, familiar, internal, local, native

homeland noun native land, country of origin, fatherland, mother country, motherland

homeless adjective **1** destitute, displaced, dispossessed, down-and-out ♦ noun **2** the **homeless** vagrants, squatters

homely adjective comfortable, cosy, friendly, homespun, modest, ordinary, plain, simple, welcoming

homespun adjective unsophisticated, coarse, homely, home-made, plain, rough

homicidal adjective murderous, deadly, lethal, maniacal, mortal

homicide noun **1** murder, bloodshed, killing, manslaughter, slaying **2** murderer, killer, slayer

homily noun sermon, address, discourse, lecture, preaching

homogeneity noun uniformity, consistency, correspondence, sameness, similarity

homogeneous adjective uniform, akin, alike, analogous, comparable, consistent, identical, similar, unvarying

hone verb sharpen, edge, file, grind, point, polish, whet

honest adjective **1** trustworthy, ethical, honourable, law-abiding, reputable, scrupulous, truthful, upright, virtuous **2** open, candid, direct, forthright, frank, plain, sincere, upfront (informal)

honestly adverb **1** ethically, by fair means, cleanly, honourably, lawfully, legally **2** frankly, candidly, in all sincerity, plainly, straight (out), to one's face, truthfully

honesty noun **1** integrity, honour, incorruptibility, morality, probity, rectitude, scrupulousness, trustworthiness, truthfulness, uprightness, virtue **2** frankness, bluntness, candour, openness, outspokenness, sincerity, straightforwardness

honorary adjective nominal, complimentary, in name or title only, titular, unofficial, unpaid

honour noun **1** glory, credit, dignity, distinction, fame, prestige, renown, reputation **2** tribute, accolade, commendation, homage, praise, recognition **3** fairness, decency, goodness, honesty, integrity, morality, probity, rectitude **4** privilege, compliment, credit, pleasure ♦ verb **5** respect, adore, appreciate, esteem, prize, value **6** fulfil, be true to, carry out, discharge, keep, live up to, observe **7** acclaim, commemorate, decorate, praise **8** accept, acknowledge, pass, pay, take

honourable adjective respected, creditable, estimable, reputable, respectable, virtuous

hoodwink verb deceive, con (informal), delude, dupe, fool, mislead, swindle, trick

hook noun **1** fastener, catch, clasp, link, peg ♦ verb **2** fasten, clasp, fix, secure **3** catch, ensnare, entrap, snare, trap

hooked adjective **1** bent, aquiline, curved, hook-shaped **2** addicted, devoted, enamoured, obsessed,

taken, turned on (slang)

hooligan noun delinquent, lager lout, ruffian, vandal, yob or yobbo (Brit. slang)

hooliganism noun delinquency, disorder, loutishness, rowdiness, vandalism, violence

hoop noun ring, band, circlet, girdle, loop, wheel

hoot noun **1** cry, call, toot **2** catcall, boo, hiss, jeer ♦ verb **3** jeer, boo, hiss, howl down

hop verb **1** jump, bound, caper, leap, skip, spring, trip, vault ♦ noun **2** jump, bounce, bound, leap, skip, spring, step, vault

hope verb **1** desire, aspire, cross one's fingers, long, look forward to, set one's heart on ♦ noun **2** desire, ambition, assumption, dream, expectation, longing

hopeful adjective **1** optimistic, buoyant, confident, expectant, looking forward to, sanguine **2** promising, auspicious, bright, encouraging, heartening, reassuring, rosy

hopefully adverb optimistically, confidently, expectantly

hopeless adjective pointless, futile, impossible, no-win, unattainable, useless, vain

horde noun crowd, band, drove, gang, host, mob, multitude, pack, swarm, throng

horizon noun skyline, vista

horizontal adjective level, flat, parallel

horrible adjective **1** terrifying, appalling, dreadful, frightful, ghastly, grim, grisly, gruesome, hideous, repulsive, revolting, shocking **2** unpleasant, awful,

horrid cruel, disagreeable, dreadful, horrid, mean, nasty, terrible

horrid adjective **1** unpleasant, awful, disagreeable, dreadful, horrible, terrible **2** Informal unkind, beastly (informal), cruel, mean, nasty

horrific adjective terrifying, appalling, awful, dreadful, frightful, ghastly, grisly, horrendous, horrifying, shocking

horrify verb **1** terrify, alarm, frighten, intimidate, make one's hair stand on end, petrify, scare **2** shock, appal, dismay, outrage, sicken

horror noun **1** terror, alarm, consternation, dread, fear, fright, panic **2** hatred, aversion, detestation, disgust, loathing, odium, repugnance, revulsion

horse noun nag, colt, filly, gee-gee (slang), mare, mount, stallion, steed (archaic or literary)

horseman noun rider, cavalier, cavalryman, dragoon, equestrian

horseplay noun buffoonery, clowning, fooling around, high jinks, pranks, romping, rough-and-tumble, skylarking (informal)

hospitable adjective welcoming, cordial, friendly, generous, gracious, kind, liberal, sociable

hospitality noun welcome, conviviality, cordiality, friendliness, neighbourliness, sociability, warmth

host[1] noun **1** master of ceremonies, entertainer, innkeeper, landlord or landlady, proprietor **2** presenter, anchorman or anchorwoman,

compere (Brit.) ♦ verb **3** present, compere (Brit.), front (informal), introduce

host[2] noun multitude, army, array, drove, horde, legion, myriad, swarm, throng

hostage noun prisoner, captive, pawn

hostile adjective **1** opposed, antagonistic, belligerent, contrary, ill-disposed, rancorous **2** unfriendly, adverse, inhospitable, unsympathetic, unwelcoming

hostilities plural noun warfare, conflict, fighting, war

hostility noun opposition, animosity, antipathy, enmity, hatred, ill will, malice, resentment, unfriendliness

hot adjective **1** heated, boiling, roasting, scalding, scorching, searing, steaming, sultry, sweltering, torrid, warm **2** spicy, biting, peppery, piquant, pungent, sharp **3** fierce, fiery, intense, passionate, raging, stormy, violent **4** recent, fresh, just out, latest, new, up to the minute **5** popular, approved, favoured, in demand, in vogue, sought-after

hot air noun empty talk, bombast, claptrap (informal), guff (slang), verbiage, wind

hot-blooded adjective passionate, ardent, excitable, fiery, impulsive, spirited, temperamental, wild

hotchpotch noun mixture, farrago, jumble, medley, mélange, mess, mishmash, potpourri

hot-headed adjective rash, fiery, foolhardy, hasty, hot-tempered, impetuous, quick-tempered, reckless, volatile

hound verb harass, badger, goad, harry, impel, persecute, pester, provoke

house noun 1 home, abode, domicile, dwelling, habitation, homestead, pad (slang), residence 2 family, household 3 dynasty, clan, tribe 4 firm, business, company, organization, outfit (informal) 5 assembly, Commons, legislative body, parliament 6 on the house free, for nothing, gratis ♦ verb 7 accommodate, billet, harbour, lodge, put up, quarter, take in 8 contain, cover, keep, protect, sheathe, shelter, store

household noun family, home, house

householder noun occupant, homeowner, resident, tenant

housing noun 1 accommodation, dwellings, homes, houses 2 case, casing, container, cover, covering, enclosure, sheath

hovel noun hut, cabin, den, hole, shack, shanty, shed

hover verb 1 float, drift, flutter, fly, hang 2 linger, hang about 3 waver, dither (chiefly Brit.), fluctuate, oscillate, vacillate

however adverb nevertheless, after all, anyhow, but, nonetheless, notwithstanding, still, though, yet

howl noun 1 cry, bawl, bay, clamour, groan, roar, scream, shriek, wail ♦ verb 2 cry, bawl, bellow, roar, scream, shriek, wail, weep, yell

howler noun mistake, bloomer (Brit. informal), blunder, boob (Brit. slang), clanger (informal), error, malapropism

hub noun centre, core, focal point, focus, heart, middle, nerve centre

huddle verb 1 crowd, cluster, converge, flock, gather, press, throng 2 curl up, crouch, hunch up ♦ noun 3 Informal conference, confab (informal), discussion, meeting, powwow

hue noun colour, dye, shade, tinge, tint, tone

hug verb 1 clasp, cuddle, embrace, enfold, hold close, squeeze, take in one's arms ♦ noun 2 embrace, bear hug, clasp, clinch (slang), squeeze

huge adjective large, colossal, enormous, gigantic, immense, mammoth, massive, monumental, tremendous, vast

hulk noun 1 wreck, frame, hull, shell, shipwreck 2 oaf, lout, lubber, lump (informal)

hull noun frame, body, casing, covering, framework

hum verb 1 murmur, buzz, drone, purr, throb, thrum, vibrate, whir 2 be busy, bustle, buzz, pulsate, pulse, stir

human adjective 1 mortal, manlike ♦ noun 2 human being, creature, individual, man or woman, mortal, person, soul

humane adjective kind, benign, compassionate, forgiving, good-natured, merciful, sympathetic, tender, understanding

humanitarian adjective

1 compassionate, altruistic, benevolent, charitable, humane, philanthropic, public-spirited ♦ *noun* **2** philanthropist, altruist, benefactor, Good Samaritan

humanity *noun* **1** human race, Homo sapiens, humankind, man, mankind, people **2** human nature, mortality **3** sympathy, charity, compassion, fellow feeling, kind-heartedness, kindness, mercy, philanthropy

humanize *verb* civilize, educate, enlighten, improve, soften, tame

humble *adjective* **1** modest, meek, self-effacing, unassuming, unostentatious, unpretentious **2** lowly, mean, modest, obscure, ordinary, plebeian, poor, simple, undistinguished ♦ *verb* **3** humiliate, chasten, crush, disgrace, put (someone) in their place, subdue, take down a peg (*informal*)

humbug *noun* **1** fraud, charlatan, con man (*informal*), faker, impostor, phoney *or* phony (*informal*), swindler, trickster **2** nonsense, baloney (*informal*), cant, claptrap (*informal*), hypocrisy, quackery, rubbish

humdrum *adjective* dull, banal, boring, dreary, monotonous, mundane, ordinary, tedious, tiresome, uneventful

humid *adjective* damp, clammy, dank, moist, muggy, steamy, sticky, sultry, wet

humidity *noun* damp, clamminess, dampness, dankness, moistness, moisture, mugginess, wetness

humiliate *verb* embarrass, bring low, chasten, crush, degrade, humble, mortify, put down, put (someone) in their place, shame

humiliating *adjective* embarrassing, crushing, degrading, humbling, ignominious, mortifying, shaming

humiliation *noun* embarrassment, degradation, disgrace, dishonour, humbling, ignominy, indignity, loss of face, mortification, put-down, shame

humility *noun* modesty, humbleness, lowliness, meekness, submissiveness, unpretentiousness

humorist *noun* comedian, card (*informal*), comic, funny man, jester, joker, wag, wit

humorous *adjective* funny, amusing, comic, comical, droll, entertaining, jocular, playful, waggish, witty

humour *noun* **1** funniness, amusement, comedy, drollery, facetiousness, fun, jocularity, ludicrousness **2** joking, comedy, farce, jesting, pleasantry, wisecracks (*informal*), wit, witticisms **3** mood, disposition, frame of mind, spirits, temper ♦ *verb* **4** indulge, accommodate, flatter, go along with, gratify, mollify, pander to

hump *noun* **1** lump, bulge, bump, mound, projection, protrusion, protuberance, swelling ♦ *verb* **2** *Slang* carry, heave, hoist, lug, shoulder

hunch *noun* **1** feeling, idea, impression, inkling, intuition, premonition, presentiment, suspicion ♦ *verb* **2** draw in, arch, bend, curve

hunger *noun* **1** famine, starvation,

2 <u>appetite</u>, emptiness, hungriness, ravenousness **3** <u>desire</u>, ache, appetite, craving, itch, lust, thirst, yearning ♦ *verb* **4** <u>want</u>, ache, crave, desire, hanker, itch, long, thirst, wish, yearn

hungry *adjective* **1** <u>empty</u>, famished, peckish (*informal, chiefly Brit.*), ravenous, starved, starving, voracious **2** <u>eager</u>, athirst, avid, covetous, craving, desirous, greedy, keen, yearning

hunk *noun* <u>lump</u>, block, chunk, mass, nugget, piece, slab, wedge

hunt *verb* **1** <u>stalk</u>, chase, hound, pursue, track, trail **2** <u>search</u>, ferret about, forage, look, scour, seek ♦ *noun* **3** <u>search</u>, chase, hunting, investigation, pursuit, quest

hurdle *noun* **1** <u>fence</u>, barricade, barrier **2** <u>obstacle</u>, barrier, difficulty, handicap, hazard, hindrance, impediment, obstruction, stumbling block

hurl *verb* <u>throw</u>, cast, fling, heave, launch, let fly, pitch, propel, sling, toss

hurricane *noun* <u>storm</u>, cyclone, gale, tempest, tornado, twister (*U.S. informal*), typhoon

hurried *adjective* <u>hasty</u>, brief, cursory, perfunctory, quick, rushed, short, speedy, swift

hurry *verb* **1** <u>rush</u>, dash, fly, get a move on (*informal*), make haste, scoot, scurry, step on it (*informal*) ♦ *noun* **2** <u>urgency</u>, flurry, haste, quickness, rush, speed

hurt *verb* **1** <u>harm</u>, bruise, damage, disable, impair, injure, mar, spoil, wound **2** <u>ache</u>, be

sore, be tender, burn, smart, sting, throb **3** <u>sadden</u>, annoy, distress, grieve, pain, upset, wound ♦ *noun* **4** <u>distress</u>, discomfort, pain, pang, soreness, suffering ♦ *adjective* **5** <u>injured</u>, bruised, cut, damaged, harmed, scarred, wounded **6** <u>offended</u>, aggrieved, crushed, wounded

hurtful *adjective* <u>unkind</u>, cruel, cutting, damaging, destructive, malicious, nasty, spiteful, upsetting, wounding

hurtle *verb* <u>rush</u>, charge, crash, fly, plunge, race, shoot, speed, stampede, tear

husband *noun* **1** <u>partner</u>, better half (*humorous*), mate, spouse ♦ *verb* **2** <u>economize</u>, budget, conserve, hoard, save, store

husbandry *noun* **1** <u>farming</u>, agriculture, cultivation, tillage **2** <u>thrift</u>, economy, frugality

hush *verb* **1** <u>quieten</u>, mute, muzzle, shush, silence ♦ *noun* **2** <u>quiet</u>, calm, peace, silence, stillness, tranquillity

hush-hush *adjective* <u>secret</u>, classified, confidential, restricted, top-secret, under wraps

husky *adjective* **1** <u>hoarse</u>, croaky, gruff, guttural, harsh, raucous, rough, throaty **2** *Informal* <u>muscular</u>, burly, hefty, powerful, rugged, stocky, strapping, thickset

hustle *verb* <u>jostle</u>, elbow, force, jog, push, shove

hut *noun* <u>shed</u>, cabin, den, hovel, lean-to, shanty, shelter

hybrid *noun* <u>crossbreed</u>, amalgam, composite, compound, cross, half-breed, mixture, mongrel

hygiene noun <u>cleanliness</u>, sanitation

hygienic adjective <u>clean</u>, aseptic, disinfected, germ-free, healthy, pure, sanitary, sterile

hymn noun <u>anthem</u>, carol, chant, paean, psalm

hype noun <u>publicity</u>, ballyhoo (informal), brouhaha, plugging (informal), promotion, razzmatazz (slang)

hypnotic adjective <u>mesmeric</u>, mesmerizing, sleep-inducing, soothing, soporific, spellbinding

hypnotize verb <u>mesmerize</u>, put in a trance, put to sleep

hypocrisy noun <u>insincerity</u>, cant, deceitfulness, deception, duplicity, pretence

hypocrite noun <u>fraud</u>, charlatan, deceiver, impostor, phoney or phony (informal), pretender

hypocritical adjective <u>insincere</u>, canting, deceitful, duplicitous, false, fraudulent, phoney or phony (informal), sanctimonious, two-faced

hypothesis noun <u>assumption</u>, postulate, premise, proposition, supposition, theory, thesis

hypothetical adjective <u>theoretical</u>, academic, assumed, conjectural, imaginary, putative, speculative, supposed

hysteria noun <u>frenzy</u>, agitation, delirium, hysterics, madness, panic

hysterical adjective 1 <u>frenzied</u>, crazed, distracted, distraught, frantic, overwrought, raving 2 Informal <u>hilarious</u>, comical, side-splitting, uproarious

I i

icy adjective 1 <u>cold</u>, biting, bitter, chill, chilly, freezing, frosty, ice-cold, raw 2 <u>slippery</u>, glassy, slippy (informal or dialect) 3 <u>unfriendly</u>, aloof, cold, distant, frigid, frosty, unwelcoming

idea noun 1 <u>thought</u>, concept, impression, perception 2 <u>belief</u>, conviction, notion, opinion, teaching, view 3 <u>plan</u>, aim, intention, object, objective, purpose

ideal adjective 1 <u>perfect</u>, archetypal, classic, complete, consummate, model, quintessential, supreme ♦ noun 2 <u>model</u>, last word, paradigm, paragon, pattern, perfection, prototype, standard

idealist noun <u>romantic</u>, dreamer, Utopian, visionary

idealistic adjective <u>perfectionist</u>, impracticable, optimistic, romantic, starry-eyed, Utopian, visionary

idealize verb <u>romanticize</u>, apotheosize, ennoble, exalt, glorify, magnify, put on a pedestal, worship

ideally adverb <u>in a perfect world</u>, all things being equal, if one had one's way

identical adjective <u>alike</u>, duplicate, indistinguishable, interchangeable, matching, twin

identification noun 1 <u>recognition</u>, naming, pinpointing 2 <u>empathy</u>, association, connection, fellow feeling, involvement, rapport, relationship, sympathy

identify verb 1 <u>recognize</u>, diagnose, make out, name, pick out, pinpoint, place, put one's finger on (informal), spot 2 **identify with** <u>relate to</u>, associate with, empathize with, feel for, respond to

identity noun 1 <u>existence</u>, individuality, personality, self 2 <u>sameness</u>, correspondence, unity

idiocy noun <u>foolishness</u>, asininity, fatuousness, imbecility, inanity, insanity, lunacy, senselessness

idiom noun 1 <u>phrase</u>, expression, turn of phrase 2 <u>language</u>, jargon, parlance, style, vernacular

idiosyncrasy noun <u>peculiarity</u>, characteristic, eccentricity, mannerism, oddity, quirk, trick

idiot noun <u>fool</u>, chump, cretin, dunderhead, halfwit, imbecile, moron, nincompoop, numbskull or numskull, simpleton, twit (informal, chiefly Brit.)

idiotic adjective <u>foolish</u>, asinine, crazy, daft (informal), foolhardy, harebrained, insane, moronic, senseless, stupid

idle adjective 1 <u>inactive</u>, redundant, unemployed, unoccupied, unused, vacant 2 <u>lazy</u>, good-for-nothing, indolent, lackadaisical, shiftless, slothful, sluggish 3 <u>useless</u>, fruitless, futile, groundless, ineffective, pointless, unavailing, unsuccessful, vain, worthless ◆ verb 4 often with **away** <u>laze</u>, dally, dawdle, kill time, loaf, loiter, lounge, potter

idleness noun 1 <u>inactivity</u>,

inaction, leisure, time on one's hands, unemployment 2 <u>laziness</u>, inertia, shiftlessness, sloth, sluggishness, torpor

idol noun 1 <u>graven image</u>, deity, god 2 <u>hero</u>, beloved, darling, favourite, pet, pin-up (slang)

idolatry noun <u>adoration</u>, adulation, exaltation, glorification

idolize verb <u>worship</u>, adore, dote upon, exalt, glorify, hero-worship, look up to, love, revere, venerate

idyllic adjective <u>idealized</u>, charming, halcyon, heavenly, ideal, picturesque, unspoiled

if conjunction <u>provided</u>, assuming, on condition that, providing, supposing

ignite verb 1 <u>catch fire</u>, burn, burst into flames, flare up, inflame, take fire 2 <u>set fire to</u>, kindle, light, set alight, torch

ignominious adjective <u>humiliating</u>, discreditable, disgraceful, dishonourable, indecorous, inglorious, shameful, sorry, undignified

ignominy noun <u>disgrace</u>, discredit, dishonour, disrepute, humiliation, infamy, obloquy, shame, stigma

ignorance noun <u>unawareness</u>, inexperience, innocence, unconsciousness, unfamiliarity

ignorant adjective 1 <u>uninformed</u>, benighted, inexperienced, innocent, oblivious, unaware, unconscious, unenlightened, uninitiated, unwitting 2 <u>uneducated</u>, illiterate 3 <u>insensitive</u>, crass, half-baked (informal), rude

ignore verb <u>overlook</u>, discount, disregard, neglect, pass over, reject, take no notice of, turn a blind eye to

ill adjective **1** <u>unwell</u>, ailing, diseased, indisposed, infirm, off-colour, poorly (*informal*), sick, under the weather (*informal*), unhealthy **2** <u>harmful</u>, bad, damaging, deleterious, detrimental, evil, foul, injurious, unfortunate ♦ noun **3** <u>harm</u>, affliction, hardship, hurt, injury, misery, misfortune, trouble, unpleasantness, woe ♦ adverb **4** <u>badly</u>, inauspiciously, poorly, unfavourably, unfortunately, unluckily **5** <u>hardly</u>, barely, by no means, scantily

ill-advised adjective <u>misguided</u>, foolhardy, ill-considered, ill-judged, imprudent, incautious, injudicious, rash, reckless, thoughtless, unwise

ill-disposed adjective <u>unfriendly</u>, antagonistic, disobliging, hostile, inimical, uncooperative, unwelcoming

illegal adjective <u>unlawful</u>, banned, criminal, felonious, forbidden, illicit, outlawed, prohibited, unauthorized, unlicensed

illegality noun <u>crime</u>, felony, illegitimacy, lawlessness, wrong

illegible adjective <u>indecipherable</u>, obscure, scrawled, unreadable

illegitimate adjective **1** <u>unlawful</u>, illegal, illicit, improper, unauthorized **2** <u>born out of wedlock</u>, bastard

ill-fated adjective <u>doomed</u>, hapless, ill-omened, ill-starred, luckless, star-crossed, unfortunate, unhappy, unlucky

illicit adjective **1** <u>illegal</u>, criminal, felonious, illegitimate, prohibited, unauthorized, unlawful, unlicensed **2** <u>forbidden</u>, clandestine, furtive, guilty, immoral, improper

illiterate adjective <u>uneducated</u>, ignorant, uncultured, untaught, untutored

ill-mannered adjective <u>rude</u>, badly behaved, boorish, churlish, discourteous, impolite, insolent, loutish, uncouth

illness noun <u>disease</u>, affliction, ailment, disorder, infirmity, malady, sickness

illogical adjective <u>irrational</u>, absurd, inconsistent, invalid, meaningless, senseless, unreasonable, unscientific, unsound

ill-treat verb <u>abuse</u>, damage, harm, injure, maltreat, mishandle, misuse, oppress

illuminate verb **1** <u>light up</u>, brighten **2** <u>explain</u>, clarify, clear up, elucidate, enlighten, interpret, make clear, shed light on

illuminating adjective <u>informative</u>, enlightening, explanatory, helpful, instructive, revealing

illumination noun **1** <u>light</u>, brightness, lighting, radiance **2** <u>enlightenment</u>, clarification, insight, revelation

illusion noun **1** <u>fantasy</u>, chimera, daydream, figment of the imagination, hallucination, mirage, will-o'-the-wisp **2** <u>misconception</u>, deception, delusion, error, fallacy, misapprehension

illusory adjective unreal, chimerical, deceptive, delusive, fallacious, false, hallucinatory, mistaken, sham

illustrate verb demonstrate, bring home, elucidate, emphasize, explain, point up, show

illustrated adjective pictorial, decorated, graphic

illustration noun 1 example, case, instance, specimen 2 picture, decoration, figure, plate, sketch

illustrious adjective famous, celebrated, distinguished, eminent, glorious, great, notable, prominent, renowned

ill will noun hostility, animosity, bad blood, dislike, enmity, hatred, malice, rancour, resentment, venom

image noun 1 representation, effigy, figure, icon, idol, likeness, picture, portrait, statue 2 replica, counterpart, (dead) ringer (slang), Doppelgänger, double, facsimile, spitting image (informal) 3 concept, idea, impression, mental picture, perception

imaginable adjective possible, believable, comprehensible, conceivable, credible, likely, plausible

imaginary adjective fictional, fictitious, hypothetical, illusory, imagined, invented, made-up, nonexistent, unreal

imagination noun 1 creativity, enterprise, ingenuity, invention, inventiveness, originality, resourcefulness, vision 2 unreality, illusion, supposition

imaginative adjective creative, clever, enterprising, ingenious, inspired, inventive, original

imagine verb 1 envisage, conceive, conceptualize, conjure up, picture, plan, think of, think up, visualize 2 believe, assume, conjecture, fancy, guess (informal, chiefly U.S. & Canad.), infer, suppose, surmise, suspect, take it, think

imbecile noun 1 idiot, chump, cretin, fool, halfwit, moron, numbskull or numskull, thickhead, twit (informal, chiefly Brit.) ♦ adjective 2 stupid, asinine, fatuous, feeble-minded, foolish, idiotic, moronic, thick, witless

imbibe verb 1 drink, consume, knock back (informal), quaff, sink (informal), swallow, swig (informal) 2 Literary absorb, acquire, assimilate, gain, gather, ingest, receive, take in

imbroglio noun complication, embarrassment, entanglement, involvement, misunderstanding, quandary

imitate verb copy, ape, echo, emulate, follow, mimic, mirror, repeat, simulate

imitation noun 1 mimicry, counterfeiting, duplication, likeness, resemblance, simulation 2 replica, fake, forgery, impersonation, impression, reproduction, sham, substitution ♦ adjective 3 artificial, dummy, ersatz, man-made, mock, phoney or phony (informal), reproduction, sham, simulated, synthetic

imitative adjective derivative, copycat (informal), mimetic, parrot-like, second-hand, simulated, unoriginal

imitator noun impersonator, copier, copycat (informal), impressionist, mimic, parrot

immaculate adjective 1 clean, neat, spick-and-span, spotless, spruce, squeaky-clean 2 flawless, above reproach, faultless, impeccable, perfect, unblemished, unexceptionable, untarnished

immaterial adjective irrelevant, extraneous, inconsequential, inessential, insignificant, of no importance, trivial, unimportant

immature adjective 1 young, adolescent, undeveloped, unformed, unripe 2 childish, callow, inexperienced, infantile, juvenile, puerile

immaturity noun 1 unripeness, greenness, imperfection, rawness, unpreparedness 2 childishness, callowness, inexperience, puerility

immediate adjective 1 instant, instantaneous 2 nearest, close, direct, near, next

immediately adverb at once, directly, forthwith, instantly, now, promptly, right away, straight away, this instant, without delay

immense adjective huge, colossal, enormous, extensive, gigantic, great, massive, monumental, stupendous, tremendous, vast

immensity noun size, bulk, enormity, expanse, extent, greatness, hugeness, magnitude, vastness

immerse verb 1 plunge, bathe, dip, douse, duck, dunk, sink, submerge 2 engross, absorb, busy, engage, involve, occupy, take up

immersion noun 1 dipping, dousing, ducking, dunking, plunging, submerging 2 involvement, absorption, concentration, preoccupation

immigrant noun settler, incomer, newcomer

imminent adjective near, at hand, close, coming, forthcoming, gathering, impending, in the pipeline, looming

immobile adjective stationary, at a standstill, at rest, fixed, immovable, motionless, rigid, rooted, static, still, stock-still, unmoving

immobility noun stillness, fixity, inertness, motionlessness, stability, steadiness

immobilize verb paralyse, bring to a standstill, cripple, disable, freeze, halt, stop, transfix

immoderate adjective excessive, exaggerated, exorbitant, extravagant, extreme, inordinate, over the top (slang), undue, unjustified, unreasonable

immoral adjective wicked, bad, corrupt, debauched, depraved, dissolute, indecent, sinful, unethical, unprincipled, wrong

immorality noun wickedness, corruption, debauchery, depravity, dissoluteness, sin, vice, wrong

immortal adjective 1 eternal, deathless, enduring, everlasting, imperishable, lasting, perennial, undying ♦ *noun* **2** god, goddess **3** great, genius, hero

immortality *noun* **1** eternity, everlasting life, perpetuity **2** fame, celebrity, glory, greatness, renown

immortalize *verb* commemorate, celebrate, exalt, glorify

immovable *adjective* **1** fixed, firm, immutable, jammed, secure, set, stable, stationary, stuck **2** inflexible, adamant, obdurate, resolute, steadfast, unshakable, unwavering, unyielding

immune *adjective* exempt, clear, free, invulnerable, proof (against), protected, resistant, safe, unaffected

immunity *noun* **1** exemption, amnesty, freedom, indemnity, invulnerability, licence, release **2** resistance, immunization, protection

immunize *verb* vaccinate, inoculate, protect, safeguard

imp *noun* **1** demon, devil, sprite **2** rascal, brat, minx, rogue, scamp

impact *noun* **1** collision, blow, bump, contact, crash, jolt, knock, smash, stroke, thump **2** effect, consequences, impression, influence, repercussions, significance ♦ *verb* **3** hit, clash, collide, crash, crush, strike

impair *verb* worsen, blunt, damage, decrease, diminish, harm, hinder, injure, lessen, reduce, undermine, weaken

impaired *adjective* damaged,

defective, faulty, flawed, imperfect, unsound

impart *verb* **1** communicate, convey, disclose, divulge, make known, pass on, relate, reveal, tell **2** give, accord, afford, bestow, confer, grant, lend, yield

impartial *adjective* neutral, detached, disinterested, equitable, even-handed, fair, just, objective, open-minded, unbiased, unprejudiced

impartiality *noun* neutrality, detachment, disinterestedness, dispassion, equity, even-handedness, fairness, objectivity, open-mindedness

impassable *adjective* blocked, closed, impenetrable, obstructed

impasse *noun* deadlock, dead end, stalemate, standoff, standstill

impassioned *adjective* intense, animated, fervent, fiery, heated, inspired, passionate, rousing, stirring

impatience *noun* **1** haste, impetuosity, intolerance, rashness **2** restlessness, agitation, anxiety, eagerness, edginess, fretfulness, nervousness, uneasiness

impatient *adjective* **1** hasty, demanding, hot-tempered, impetuous, intolerant **2** restless, eager, edgy, fretful, straining at the leash

impeach *verb* charge, accuse, arraign, indict

impeccable *adjective* faultless, blameless, flawless, immaculate, irreproachable, perfect, unblemished, unimpeachable

impecunious *adjective* poor,

broke (*informal*), destitute, down and out, indigent, insolvent, penniless, poverty-stricken

impede *verb* hinder, block, check, disrupt, hamper, hold up, obstruct, slow (down), thwart

impediment *noun* obstacle, barrier, difficulty, encumbrance, hindrance, obstruction, snag, stumbling block

impel *verb* force, compel, constrain, drive, induce, oblige, push, require

impending *adjective* looming, approaching, coming, forthcoming, gathering, imminent, in the pipeline, near, upcoming

impenetrable *adjective* **1** solid, dense, impassable, impermeable, impervious, inviolable, thick **2** incomprehensible, arcane, enigmatic, inscrutable, mysterious, obscure, unfathomable, unintelligible

imperative *adjective* urgent, crucial, essential, pressing, vital

imperceptible *adjective* undetectable, faint, indiscernible, microscopic, minute, slight, small, subtle, tiny

imperfect *adjective* flawed, damaged, defective, faulty, impaired, incomplete, limited, unfinished

imperfection *noun* fault, blemish, defect, deficiency, failing, flaw, frailty, shortcoming, taint, weakness

imperial *adjective* royal, kingly, majestic, princely, queenly, regal, sovereign

imperil *verb* endanger, expose, jeopardize, risk

impersonal *adjective* remote, aloof, cold, detached, dispassionate, formal, inhuman, neutral

impersonate *verb* imitate, ape, do (*informal*), masquerade as, mimic, pass oneself off as, pose as (*informal*), take off (*informal*)

impersonation *noun* imitation, caricature, impression, mimicry, parody, takeoff (*informal*)

impertinence *noun* rudeness, brazenness, cheek (*informal*), disrespect, effrontery, front, impudence, insolence, nerve (*informal*), presumption

impertinent *adjective* rude, brazen, cheeky (*informal*), disrespectful, impolite, impudent, insolent, presumptuous

imperturbable *adjective* calm, collected, composed, cool, nerveless, self-possessed, serene, unexcitable, unflappable (*informal*), unruffled

impervious *adjective* **1** sealed, impassable, impenetrable, impermeable, resistant **2** unaffected, immune, invulnerable, proof against, unmoved, untouched

impetuosity *noun* haste, impulsiveness, precipitateness, rashness

impetuous *adjective* rash, hasty, impulsive, precipitate, unthinking

impetus *noun* **1** incentive, catalyst, goad, impulse, motivation, push, spur, stimulus **2** force, energy, momentum, power

impinge verb 1 encroach, infringe, invade, obtrude, trespass, violate 2 affect, bear upon, have a bearing on, impact, influence, relate to, touch

impious adjective sacrilegious, blasphemous, godless, irreligious, irreverent, profane, sinful, ungodly, unholy, wicked

impish adjective mischievous, devilish, puckish, rascally, roguish, sportive, waggish

implacable adjective unyielding, inflexible, intractable, merciless, pitiless, unbending, uncompromising, unforgiving

implant verb 1 instil, inculcate, infuse 2 insert, fix, graft

implement verb 1 carry out, bring about, complete, effect, enforce, execute, fulfil, perform, realize ♦ noun 2 tool, apparatus, appliance, device, gadget, instrument, utensil

implicate verb incriminate, associate, embroil, entangle, include, inculpate, involve

implication noun suggestion, inference, innuendo, meaning, overtone, presumption, significance

implicit adjective 1 implied, inferred, latent, tacit, taken for granted, undeclared, understood, unspoken 2 absolute, constant, firm, fixed, full, steadfast, unqualified, unreserved, wholehearted

implied adjective unspoken, hinted at, implicit, indirect, suggested, tacit, undeclared, unexpressed, unstated

implore verb beg, beseech, entreat, importune, plead with, pray

imply verb 1 hint, insinuate, intimate, signify, suggest 2 entail, indicate, involve, mean, point to, presuppose

impolite adjective bad-mannered, discourteous, disrespectful, ill-mannered, insolent, loutish, rude, uncouth

impoliteness noun bad manners, boorishness, churlishness, discourtesy, disrespect, insolence, rudeness

import verb 1 bring in, introduce ♦ noun 2 meaning, drift, gist, implication, intention, sense, significance, thrust 3 importance, consequence, magnitude, moment, significance, substance, weight

importance noun 1 significance, concern, consequence, import, interest, moment, substance, usefulness, value, weight 2 prestige, distinction, eminence, esteem, influence, prominence, standing, status

important adjective 1 significant, far-reaching, momentous, seminal, serious, substantial, urgent, weighty 2 powerful, eminent, high-ranking, influential, noteworthy, pre-eminent, prominent

importunate adjective persistent, demanding, dogged, insistent, pressing, urgent

impose verb 1 establish, decree, fix, institute, introduce, levy, ordain 2 inflict, appoint, enforce, saddle (someone) with

imposing adjective impressive, commanding, dignified, grand, majestic, stately, striking

imposition noun **1** <u>application</u>, introduction, levying **2** <u>intrusion</u>, liberty, presumption

impossibility noun <u>hopelessness</u>, impracticability, inability

impossible adjective
1 <u>unattainable</u>, impracticable, inconceivable, out of the question, unachievable, unobtainable, unthinkable
2 <u>absurd</u>, ludicrous, outrageous, preposterous, unreasonable

impostor noun <u>impersonator</u>, charlatan, deceiver, fake, fraud, phoney or phony (informal), pretender, sham, trickster

impotence noun <u>powerlessness</u>, feebleness, frailty, helplessness, inability, incapacity, incompetence, ineffectiveness, paralysis, uselessness, weakness

impotent adjective <u>powerless</u>, feeble, frail, helpless, incapable, incapacitated, incompetent, ineffective, paralysed, weak

impoverish verb **1** <u>bankrupt</u>, beggar, break, ruin **2** <u>diminish</u>, deplete, drain, exhaust, reduce, sap, use up, wear out

impoverished adjective <u>poor</u>, bankrupt, destitute, impecunious, needy, on one's uppers, penurious, poverty-stricken

impracticable adjective <u>unfeasible</u>, impossible, out of the question, unachievable, unattainable, unworkable

impractical adjective
1 <u>unworkable</u>, impossible, impracticable, inoperable, nonviable, unrealistic, wild

2 <u>idealistic</u>, romantic, starry-eyed, unrealistic

imprecise adjective <u>indefinite</u>, equivocal, hazy, ill-defined, indeterminate, inexact, inexplicit, loose, rough, vague, woolly

impregnable adjective <u>invulnerable</u>, impenetrable, indestructible, invincible, secure, unassailable, unbeatable, unconquerable

impregnate verb **1** <u>saturate</u>, infuse, permeate, soak, steep, suffuse **2** <u>fertilize</u>, inseminate, make pregnant

impress verb **1** <u>excite</u>, affect, inspire, make an impression, move, stir, strike, touch **2** <u>stress</u>, bring home to, emphasize, fix, inculcate, instil into **3** <u>imprint</u>, emboss, engrave, indent, mark, print, stamp

impression noun **1** <u>effect</u>, feeling, impact, influence, reaction **2** <u>idea</u>, belief, conviction, feeling, hunch, notion, sense, suspicion **3** <u>mark</u>, dent, hollow, imprint, indentation, outline, stamp **4** <u>imitation</u>, impersonation, parody, send-up (Brit. informal), takeoff (informal)

impressionable adjective <u>suggestible</u>, gullible, ingenuous, open, receptive, responsive, sensitive, susceptible, vulnerable

impressive adjective <u>grand</u>, awesome, dramatic, exciting, moving, powerful, stirring, striking

imprint noun **1** <u>mark</u>, impression, indentation, sign, stamp ♦ verb **2** <u>fix</u>, engrave, etch, impress, print, stamp

imprison verb jail, confine, detain, incarcerate, intern, lock up, put away, send down (informal)

imprisoned adjective jailed, behind bars, captive, confined, incarcerated, in jail, inside (slang), locked up, under lock and key

imprisonment noun custody, confinement, detention, incarceration, porridge (slang)

improbability noun doubt, dubiety, uncertainty, unlikelihood

improbable adjective doubtful, dubious, fanciful, far-fetched, implausible, questionable, unconvincing, unlikely, weak

impromptu adjective unprepared, ad-lib, extemporaneous, improvised, offhand, off the cuff (informal), spontaneous, unrehearsed, unscripted

improper adjective 1 indecent, risqué, smutty, suggestive, unbecoming, unseemly, untoward, vulgar 2 unwarranted, inappropriate, out of place, uncalled-for, unfit, unsuitable

impropriety noun indecency, bad taste, incongruity, vulgarity

improve verb 1 enhance, advance, better, correct, help, rectify, touch up, upgrade 2 progress, develop, make strides, pick up, rally, rise

improvement noun 1 enhancement, advancement, betterment 2 progress, development, rally, recovery, upswing

improvident adjective

imprudent, careless, negligent, prodigal, profligate, reckless, short-sighted, spendthrift, thoughtless, wasteful

improvisation noun 1 spontaneity, ad-libbing, extemporizing, invention 2 makeshift, ad-lib, expedient

improvise verb 1 extemporize, ad-lib, busk, invent, play it by ear (informal), speak off the cuff (informal), wing it (informal) 2 concoct, contrive, devise, throw together

imprudent adjective unwise, careless, foolhardy, ill-advised, ill-considered, ill-judged, injudicious, irresponsible, rash, reckless

impudence noun boldness, audacity, brazenness, cheek (informal), effrontery, impertinence, insolence, nerve (informal), presumption, shamelessness

impudent adjective bold, audacious, brazen, cheeky (informal), impertinent, insolent, presumptuous, rude, shameless

impulse noun urge, caprice, feeling, inclination, notion, whim, wish

impulsive adjective instinctive, devil-may-care, hasty, impetuous, intuitive, passionate, precipitate, rash, spontaneous

impunity noun security, dispensation, exemption, freedom, immunity, liberty, licence, permission

impure adjective 1 unrefined, adulterated, debased, mixed 2 contaminated, defiled, dirty, infected, polluted, tainted

3 immoral, corrupt, indecent, lascivious, lewd, licentious, obscene, unchaste

impurity noun contamination, defilement, dirtiness, infection, pollution, taint

imputation noun blame, accusation, aspersion, censure, insinuation, reproach, slander, slur

inability noun incapability, disability, disqualification, impotence, inadequacy, incapacity, incompetence, ineptitude, powerlessness

inaccessible adjective out of reach, impassable, out of the way, remote, unapproachable, unattainable, unreachable

inaccuracy noun error, defect, erratum, fault, lapse, mistake

inaccurate adjective incorrect, defective, erroneous, faulty, imprecise, mistaken, out, unreliable, unsound, wrong

inactive adjective unused, dormant, idle, inoperative, unemployed, unoccupied

inactivity noun immobility, dormancy, hibernation, inaction, passivity, unemployment

inadequacy noun **1** shortage, dearth, insufficiency, meagreness, paucity, poverty, scantiness **2** incompetence, deficiency, inability, incapacity, ineffectiveness **3** shortcoming, defect, failing, imperfection, weakness

inadequate adjective
1 insufficient, meagre, scant, sketchy, sparse **2** incompetent, deficient, faulty, found wanting,

incapable, not up to scratch (informal), unqualified

inadmissible adjective unacceptable, inappropriate, irrelevant, unallowable

inadvertently adverb unintentionally, accidentally, by accident, by mistake, involuntarily, mistakenly, unwittingly

inadvisable adjective unwise, ill-advised, impolitic, imprudent, inexpedient, injudicious

inane adjective senseless, empty, fatuous, frivolous, futile, idiotic, mindless, silly, stupid, vacuous

inanimate adjective lifeless, cold, dead, defunct, extinct, inert

inapplicable adjective irrelevant, inappropriate, unsuitable

inappropriate adjective unsuitable, improper, incongruous, out of place, unbecoming, unbefitting, unfitting, unseemly, untimely

inarticulate adjective faltering, halting, hesitant, poorly spoken

inattention noun neglect, absent-mindedness, carelessness, daydreaming, inattentiveness, preoccupation, thoughtlessness

inattentive adjective preoccupied, careless, distracted, dreamy, negligent, unobservant, vague

inaudible adjective indistinct, low, mumbling, out of earshot, stifled, unheard

inaugural adjective first, initial, introductory, maiden, opening

inaugurate verb **1** launch, begin, commence, get under way, initiate, institute, introduce, set in motion **2** invest, induct, install

inauguration noun **1** launch, initiation, institution, opening, setting up **2** investiture, induction, installation

inauspicious adjective unpromising, bad, discouraging, ill-omened, ominous, unfavourable, unfortunate, unlucky, unpropitious

inborn adjective natural, congenital, hereditary, inbred, ingrained, inherent, innate, instinctive, intuitive, native

inbred adjective natural, constitutional, deep-seated, ingrained, inherent, native, natural

incalculable adjective countless, boundless, infinite, innumerable, limitless, numberless, untold, vast

incantation noun chant, charm, formula, invocation, spell

incapable adjective
1 incompetent, feeble, inadequate, ineffective, inept, inexpert, insufficient, unfit, unqualified, weak **2** unable, helpless, impotent, powerless

incapacitate verb disable, cripple, immobilize, lay up (informal), paralyse, put out of action (informal)

incapacitated adjective indisposed, hors de combat, immobilized, laid up (informal), out of action (informal), unfit

incapacity noun inability, impotence, inadequacy, incapability, incompetency, ineffectiveness, powerlessness, unfitness, weakness

incarcerate verb imprison,

confine, detain, impound, intern, jail or gaol, lock up, throw in jail

incarceration noun imprisonment, captivity, confinement, detention, internment

incarnate adjective personified, embodied, typified

incarnation noun embodiment, epitome, manifestation, personification, type

incense verb anger, enrage, inflame, infuriate, irritate, madden, make one's hackles rise, rile (informal)

incensed adjective angry, enraged, fuming, furious, indignant, infuriated, irate, maddened, steamed up (slang), up in arms

incentive noun encouragement, bait, carrot (informal), enticement, inducement, lure, motivation, spur, stimulus

inception noun beginning, birth, commencement, dawn, initiation, origin, outset, start

incessant adjective endless, ceaseless, constant, continual, eternal, interminable, never-ending, nonstop, perpetual, unceasing, unending

incessantly adverb endlessly, ceaselessly, constantly, continually, eternally, interminably, nonstop, perpetually, persistently

incident noun **1** happening, adventure, episode, event, fact, matter, occasion, occurrence **2** disturbance, clash, commotion, confrontation, contretemps, scene

incidental adjective secondary, ancillary, minor, nonessential, occasional, subordinate, subsidiary

incidentally adverb parenthetically, by the bye, by the way, in passing

incinerate verb burn up, carbonize, char, cremate, reduce to ashes

incipient adjective beginning, commencing, developing, embryonic, inchoate, nascent, starting

incision noun cut, gash, notch, opening, slash, slit

incisive adjective penetrating, acute, keen, perspicacious, piercing, trenchant

incite verb provoke, encourage, foment, inflame, instigate, spur, stimulate, stir up, urge, whip up

incitement noun provocation, agitation, encouragement, impetus, instigation, prompting, spur, stimulus

incivility noun rudeness, bad manners, boorishness, discourteousness, discourtesy, disrespect, ill-breeding, impoliteness

inclement adjective stormy, foul, harsh, intemperate, rough, severe, tempestuous

inclination noun 1 tendency, disposition, liking, partiality, penchant, predilection, predisposition, proclivity, proneness, propensity 2 slope, angle, gradient, incline, pitch, slant, tilt

incline verb 1 predispose, influence, persuade, prejudice,

sway 2 slope, lean, slant, tilt, tip, veer ♦ noun 3 slope, ascent, descent, dip, grade, gradient, rise

inclined adjective disposed, apt, given, liable, likely, minded, predisposed, prone, willing

include verb 1 contain, comprise, cover, embrace, encompass, incorporate, involve, subsume, take in 2 introduce, add, enter, insert

inclusion noun addition, incorporation, insertion

inclusive adjective comprehensive, across-the-board, all-embracing, blanket, general, global, sweeping, umbrella

incognito adjective in disguise, disguised, under an assumed name, unknown, unrecognized

incoherence noun unintelligibility, disjointedness, inarticulateness

incoherent adjective unintelligible, confused, disjointed, disordered, inarticulate, inconsistent, jumbled, muddled, rambling, stammering, stuttering

income noun revenue, earnings, pay, proceeds, profits, receipts, salary, takings, wages

incoming adjective arriving, approaching, entering, homeward, landing, new, returning

incomparable adjective unequalled, beyond compare, inimitable, matchless, peerless, superlative, supreme, transcendent, unmatched, unparalleled, unrivalled

incompatible adjective
inconsistent, conflicting,
contradictory, incongruous,
mismatched, unsuited

incompetence noun ineptitude,
inability, inadequacy,
incapability, incapacity,
ineffectiveness, unfitness,
uselessness

incompetent adjective inept,
bungling, floundering,
incapable, ineffectual, inexpert,
unfit, useless

incomplete adjective unfinished,
deficient, fragmentary,
imperfect, partial, wanting

incomprehensible adjective
unintelligible, baffling, beyond
one's grasp, impenetrable,
obscure, opaque, perplexing,
puzzling, unfathomable

inconceivable adjective
unimaginable, beyond belief,
incomprehensible, incredible,
mind-boggling (informal), out of
the question, unbelievable,
unheard-of, unthinkable

inconclusive adjective indecisive,
ambiguous, indeterminate,
open, unconvincing, undecided,
up in the air (informal), vague

incongruity noun
inappropriateness, conflict,
discrepancy, disparity,
incompatibility, inconsistency,
unsuitability

incongruous adjective
inappropriate, discordant,
improper, incompatible, out of
keeping, out of place,
unbecoming, unsuitable

inconsiderable adjective
insignificant, inconsequential,
minor, negligible, slight, small,
trifling, trivial, unimportant

inconsiderate adjective selfish,
indelicate, insensitive, rude,
tactless, thoughtless, unkind,
unthinking

inconsistency noun
1 incompatibility, disagreement,
discrepancy, disparity,
divergence, incongruity, variance
2 unreliability, fickleness,
instability, unpredictability,
unsteadiness

inconsistent adjective
1 incompatible, at odds,
conflicting, contradictory,
discordant, incongruous,
irreconcilable, out of step
2 changeable, capricious, erratic,
fickle, unpredictable, unstable,
unsteady, variable

inconsolable adjective
heartbroken, brokenhearted,
desolate, despairing

inconspicuous adjective
unobtrusive, camouflaged,
hidden, insignificant, ordinary,
plain, unassuming, unnoticeable,
unostentatious

incontrovertible adjective
indisputable, certain, established,
incontestable, indubitable,
irrefutable, positive, sure,
undeniable, unquestionable

inconvenience noun 1 trouble,
awkwardness, bother, difficulty,
disadvantage, disruption,
disturbance, fuss, hindrance,
nuisance ♦ verb 2 trouble,
bother, discommode, disrupt,
disturb, put out, upset

inconvenient adjective
troublesome, awkward,
bothersome, disadvantageous,
disturbing, inopportune,

unsuitable, untimely

incorporate *verb* <u>include</u>, absorb, assimilate, blend, combine, integrate, merge, subsume

incorrect *adjective* <u>false</u>, erroneous, faulty, flawed, inaccurate, mistaken, untrue, wrong

incorrigible *adjective* <u>incurable</u>, hardened, hopeless, intractable, inveterate, irredeemable, unreformed

incorruptible *adjective* **1** <u>honest</u>, above suspicion, straight, trustworthy, upright **2** <u>imperishable</u>, everlasting, undecaying

increase *verb* **1** <u>grow</u>, advance, boost, develop, enlarge, escalate, expand, extend, multiply, raise, spread, swell ♦ *noun* **2** <u>growth</u>, development, enlargement, escalation, expansion, extension, gain, increment, rise, upturn

increasingly *adverb* <u>progressively</u>, more and more

incredible *adjective* **1** <u>implausible</u>, beyond belief, far-fetched, improbable, inconceivable, preposterous, unbelievable, unimaginable, unthinkable **2** *Informal* <u>amazing</u>, astonishing, astounding, extraordinary, prodigious, sensational (*informal*), wonderful

incredulity *noun* <u>disbelief</u>, distrust, doubt, scepticism

incredulous *adjective* <u>disbelieving</u>, distrustful, doubtful, dubious, sceptical, suspicious, unbelieving, unconvinced

increment *noun* <u>increase</u>,

accrual, addition, advancement, augmentation, enlargement, gain, step up, supplement

incriminate *verb* <u>implicate</u>, accuse, blame, charge, impeach, inculpate, involve

incumbent *adjective* <u>obligatory</u>, binding, compulsory, mandatory, necessary

incur *verb* <u>earn</u>, arouse, bring (upon oneself), draw, expose oneself to, gain, meet with, provoke

incurable *adjective* <u>fatal</u>, inoperable, irremediable, terminal

indebted *adjective* <u>grateful</u>, beholden, in debt, obligated, obliged, under an obligation

indecency *noun* <u>obscenity</u>, immodesty, impropriety, impurity, indelicacy, lewdness, licentiousness, pornography, vulgarity

indecent *adjective* **1** <u>lewd</u>, crude, dirty, filthy, immodest, improper, impure, licentious, pornographic, salacious **2** <u>unbecoming</u>, in bad taste, indecorous, unseemly, vulgar

indecipherable *adjective* <u>illegible</u>, indistinguishable, unintelligible, unreadable

indecision *noun* <u>hesitation</u>, dithering (*chiefly Brit.*), doubt, indecisiveness, shilly-shallying (*informal*), uncertainty, vacillation, wavering

indecisive *adjective* <u>hesitating</u>, dithering (*chiefly Brit.*), faltering, in two minds (*informal*), tentative, uncertain, undecided, vacillating, wavering

indeed *adverb* <u>really</u>, actually,

certainly, in truth, truly, undoubtedly

indefensible *adjective*
unforgivable, inexcusable, unjustifiable, unpardonable, untenable, unwarrantable, wrong

indefinable *adjective*
inexpressible, impalpable, indescribable

indefinite *adjective* unclear, doubtful, equivocal, ill-defined, imprecise, indeterminate, inexact, uncertain, unfixed, vague

indefinitely *adverb* endlessly, ad infinitum, continually, for ever

indelible *adjective* permanent, enduring, indestructible, ineradicable, ingrained, lasting

indelicate *adjective* offensive, coarse, crude, embarrassing, immodest, risqué, rude, suggestive, tasteless, vulgar

indemnify *verb* 1 insure, guarantee, protect, secure, underwrite 2 compensate, reimburse, remunerate, repair, repay

indemnity *noun* 1 insurance, guarantee, protection, security 2 compensation, redress, reimbursement, remuneration, reparation, restitution

independence *noun* freedom, autonomy, liberty, self-reliance, self-rule, self-sufficiency, sovereignty

independent *adjective* 1 free, liberated, separate, unconstrained, uncontrolled 2 self-governing, autonomous, nonaligned, self-determining, sovereign 3 self-sufficient, liberated, self-contained,

self-reliant, self-supporting

independently *adverb*
separately, alone, autonomously, by oneself, individually, on one's own, solo, unaided

indescribable *adjective*
unutterable, beyond description, beyond words, indefinable, inexpressible

indestructible *adjective*
permanent, enduring, everlasting, immortal, imperishable, incorruptible, indelible, indissoluble, lasting, unbreakable

indeterminate *adjective*
uncertain, imprecise, indefinite, inexact, undefined, unfixed, unspecified, unstipulated, vague

indicate *verb* 1 signify, betoken, denote, imply, manifest, point to, reveal, suggest 2 point out, designate, specify 3 show, display, express, read, record, register

indication *noun* sign, clue, evidence, hint, inkling, intimation, manifestation, mark, suggestion, symptom

indicative *adjective* suggestive, pointing to, significant, symptomatic

indicator *noun* sign, gauge, guide, mark, meter, pointer, signal, symbol

indict *verb* charge, accuse, arraign, impeach, prosecute, summon

indictment *noun* charge, accusation, allegation, impeachment, prosecution, summons

indifference *noun* disregard,

aloofness, apathy, coldness, coolness, detachment, inattention, negligence, nonchalance, unconcern

indifferent *adjective*
1 underline: unconcerned, aloof, callous, cold, cool, detached, impervious, inattentive, uninterested, unmoved, unsympathetic
2 mediocre, moderate, no great shakes (*informal*), ordinary, passable, so-so (*informal*), undistinguished

indigestion *noun* heartburn, dyspepsia, upset stomach

indignant *adjective* resentful, angry, disgruntled, exasperated, incensed, irate, peeved (*informal*), riled, scornful, up in arms (*informal*)

indignation *noun* resentment, anger, exasperation, pique, rage, scorn, umbrage

indignity *noun* humiliation, affront, dishonour, disrespect, injury, insult, opprobrium, slight, snub

indirect *adjective* **1** circuitous, long-drawn-out, meandering, oblique, rambling, roundabout, tortuous, wandering
2 incidental, secondary, subsidiary, unintended

indiscreet *adjective* tactless, impolitic, imprudent, incautious, injudicious, naive, rash, reckless, unwise

indiscretion *noun* mistake, error, faux pas, folly, foolishness, gaffe, lapse, slip

indiscriminate *adjective* random, careless, desultory, general, uncritical, undiscriminating, unsystematic, wholesale

indispensable *adjective* essential, crucial, imperative, key, necessary, needed, requisite, vital

indisposed *adjective* ill, ailing, poorly (*informal*), sick, under the weather, unwell

indisposition *noun* illness, ailment, ill health, sickness

indisputable *adjective* undeniable, beyond doubt, certain, incontestable, incontrovertible, indubitable, irrefutable, unquestionable

indistinct *adjective* unclear, blurred, faint, fuzzy, hazy, ill-defined, indeterminate, shadowy, undefined, vague

individual *adjective* **1** personal, characteristic, distinctive, exclusive, idiosyncratic, own, particular, peculiar, singular, special, specific, unique ♦ *noun*
2 person, being, character, creature, soul, unit

individualist *noun* maverick, freethinker, independent, loner, lone wolf, nonconformist, original

individuality *noun* distinctiveness, character, originality, personality, separateness, singularity, uniqueness

individually *adverb* separately, apart, independently, one at a time, one by one, singly

indoctrinate *verb* train, brainwash, drill, ground, imbue, initiate, instruct, school, teach

indoctrination *noun* training, brainwashing, drilling, grounding, inculcation, instruction, schooling

indolent *adjective* lazy, idle,

inactive, inert, languid, lethargic, listless, slothful, sluggish, workshy

indomitable *adjective* invincible, bold, resolute, staunch, steadfast, unbeatable, unconquerable, unflinching, unyielding

indubitable *adjective* certain, incontestable, incontrovertible, indisputable, irrefutable, obvious, sure, undeniable, unquestionable

induce *verb* 1 persuade, convince, encourage, incite, influence, instigate, prevail upon, prompt, talk into 2 cause, bring about, effect, engender, generate, give rise to, lead to, occasion, produce

inducement *noun* incentive, attraction, bait, carrot (*informal*), encouragement, incitement, lure, reward

indulge *verb* 1 gratify, feed, give way to, pander to, satisfy, yield to 2 spoil, cosset, give in to, go along with, humour, mollycoddle, pamper

indulgence *noun* 1 gratification, appeasement, fulfilment, satiation, satisfaction 2 luxury, extravagance, favour, privilege, treat 3 tolerance, forbearance, patience, understanding

indulgent *adjective* lenient, compliant, easy-going, forbearing, kindly, liberal, permissive, tolerant, understanding

industrialist *noun* capitalist, big businessman, captain of industry, magnate, manufacturer, tycoon

industrious *adjective* hard-working, busy,

conscientious, diligent, energetic, persistent, purposeful, tireless, zealous

industry *noun* 1 business, commerce, manufacturing, production, trade 2 effort, activity, application, diligence, labour, tirelessness, toil, zeal

inebriated *adjective* drunk, half-cut (*informal*), intoxicated, legless (*informal*), merry (*Brit. informal*), paralytic (*informal*), plastered (*slang*), tight (*informal*), tipsy, under the influence (*informal*)

ineffective *adjective* useless, fruitless, futile, idle, impotent, inefficient, unavailing, unproductive, vain, worthless

ineffectual *adjective* weak, feeble, impotent, inadequate, incompetent, ineffective, inept

inefficiency *noun* incompetence, carelessness, disorganization, muddle, slackness, sloppiness

inefficient *adjective* incompetent, disorganized, ineffectual, inept, wasteful, weak

ineligible *adjective* unqualified, disqualified, ruled out, unacceptable, unfit, unsuitable

inept *adjective* incompetent, bumbling, bungling, clumsy, inexpert, maladroit

ineptitude *noun* incompetence, clumsiness, inexpertness, unfitness

inequality *noun* disparity, bias, difference, disproportion, diversity, irregularity, prejudice, unevenness

inequitable *adjective* unfair, biased, discriminatory,

inert *adjective* inactive, dead, dormant, immobile, lifeless, motionless, static, still, unreactive, unresponsive

inertia *noun* inactivity, apathy, immobility, lethargy, listlessness, passivity, sloth, unresponsiveness

inescapable *adjective* unavoidable, certain, destined, fated, ineluctable, inevitable, inexorable, sure

inestimable *adjective* incalculable, immeasurable, invaluable, precious, priceless, prodigious

inevitable *adjective* unavoidable, assured, certain, destined, fixed, ineluctable, inescapable, inexorable, sure

inevitably *adverb* unavoidably, as a result, automatically, certainly, necessarily, of necessity, perforce, surely, willy-nilly

inexcusable *adjective* unforgivable, indefensible, outrageous, unjustifiable, unpardonable, unwarrantable

inexorable *adjective* unrelenting, inescapable, relentless, remorseless, unbending, unyielding

inexpensive *adjective* cheap, bargain, budget, economical, modest, reasonable

inexperience *noun* unfamiliarity, callowness, greenness, ignorance, newness, rawness

inexperienced *adjective* immature, callow, green, new, raw, unpractised, untried, unversed

inexpert *adjective* amateurish, bungling, cack-handed (*informal*), clumsy, inept, maladroit, unpractised, unprofessional, unskilled

inexplicable *adjective* unaccountable, baffling, enigmatic, incomprehensible, insoluble, mysterious, mystifying, strange, unfathomable, unintelligible

inextricably *adverb* inseparably, indissolubly, indistinguishably, intricately, irretrievably, totally

infallibility *noun* perfection, impeccability, omniscience, supremacy, unerringness

infallible *adjective* foolproof, certain, dependable, reliable, sure, sure-fire (*informal*), trustworthy, unbeatable, unfailing

infamous *adjective* notorious, disreputable, ignominious, ill-famed

infancy *noun* beginnings, cradle, dawn, inception, origins, outset, start

infant *noun* baby, babe, bairn (*Scot.*), child, toddler, tot

infantile *adjective* childish, babyish, immature, puerile

infatuate *verb* obsess, besot, bewitch, captivate, enchant, enrapture, fascinate

infatuated *adjective* obsessed, besotted, bewitched, captivated, carried away, enamoured, enraptured, fascinated, possessed, smitten (*informal*), spellbound

infatuation *noun* obsession, crush (*informal*), fixation, madness, passion, thing (*informal*)

infect verb contaminate, affect, blight, corrupt, defile, poison, pollute, taint

infection noun contamination, contagion, corruption, defilement, poison, pollution, virus

infectious adjective catching, communicable, contagious, spreading, transmittable, virulent

infer verb deduce, conclude, derive, gather, presume, surmise, understand

inference noun deduction, assumption, conclusion, presumption, reading, surmise

inferior adjective **1** lower, lesser, menial, minor, secondary, subordinate, subsidiary ♦ noun **2** underling, junior, menial, subordinate

inferiority noun **1** inadequacy, deficiency, imperfection, insignificance, mediocrity, shoddiness, worthlessness **2** subservience, abasement, lowliness, subordination

infernal adjective devilish, accursed, damnable, damned, diabolical, fiendish, hellish, satanic

infertile adjective barren, sterile, unfruitful, unproductive

infertility noun sterility, barrenness, infecundity, unproductiveness

infest verb overrun, beset, invade, penetrate, permeate, ravage, swarm, throng

infested adjective overrun, alive, crawling, ravaged, ridden, swarming, teeming

infiltrate verb penetrate, filter

through, insinuate oneself, make inroads (into), percolate, permeate, pervade, sneak in (informal)

infinite adjective never-ending, boundless, eternal, everlasting, illimitable, immeasurable, inexhaustible, limitless, measureless, unbounded

infinitesimal adjective microscopic, insignificant, minuscule, minute, negligible, teeny, tiny, unnoticeable

infinity noun eternity, boundlessness, endlessness, immensity, vastness

infirm adjective frail, ailing, debilitated, decrepit, doddering, enfeebled, failing, feeble, weak

infirmity noun frailty, decrepitude, ill health, sickliness, vulnerability

inflame verb enrage, anger, arouse, excite, incense, infuriate, madden, provoke, rouse, stimulate

inflamed adjective sore, fevered, hot, infected, red, swollen

inflammable adjective flammable, combustible, incendiary

inflammation noun soreness, painfulness, rash, redness, tenderness

inflammatory adjective provocative, explosive, fiery, intemperate, like a red rag to a bull, rabble-rousing

inflate verb expand, bloat, blow up, dilate, distend, enlarge, increase, puff up or out, pump up, swell

inflated adjective exaggerated,

ostentatious, overblown, swollen

inflation noun expansion, enlargement, escalation, extension, increase, rise, spread, swelling

inflexibility noun obstinacy, intransigence, obduracy

inflexible adjective 1 obstinate, implacable, intractable, obdurate, resolute, set in one's ways, steadfast, stubborn, unbending, uncompromising 2 inelastic, hard, rigid, stiff, taut

inflict verb impose, administer, apply, deliver, levy, mete or deal out, visit, wreak

infliction noun imposition, administration, perpetration, wreaking

influence noun 1 effect, authority, control, domination, magnetism, pressure, weight 2 power, clout (informal), hold, importance, leverage, prestige, pull (informal) ♦ verb 3 affect, control, direct, guide, manipulate, sway

influential adjective important, authoritative, instrumental, leading, potent, powerful, significant, telling, weighty

influx noun arrival, incursion, inrush, inundation, invasion, rush

inform verb 1 tell, advise, communicate, enlighten, instruct, notify, teach, tip off 2 incriminate, betray, blow the whistle on (informal), denounce, grass (Brit. slang), inculpate, shop (slang, chiefly Brit.), squeal (slang)

informal adjective relaxed, casual, colloquial, cosy, easy, familiar, natural, simple, unofficial

informality noun familiarity, casualness, ease, naturalness, relaxation, simplicity

information noun facts, data, intelligence, knowledge, message, news, notice, report

informative adjective instructive, chatty, communicative, edifying, educational, enlightening, forthcoming, illuminating, revealing

informed adjective knowledgeable, enlightened, erudite, expert, familiar, in the picture, learned, up to date, versed, well-read

informer noun betrayer, accuser, Judas, sneak, shout pigeon

infrequent adjective occasional, few and far between, once in a blue moon, rare, sporadic, uncommon, unusual

infringe verb break, contravene, disobey, transgress, violate

infringement noun contravention, breach, infraction, transgression, trespass, violation

infuriate verb enrage, anger, exasperate, incense, irritate, madden, provoke, rile

infuriating adjective annoying, exasperating, galling, irritating, maddening, mortifying, provoking, vexatious

ingenious adjective creative, bright, brilliant, clever, crafty, inventive, original, resourceful, shrewd

ingenuity noun originality, cleverness, flair, genius, gift, inventiveness, resourcefulness, sharpness, shrewdness

ingenuous adjective naive,

artless, guileless, honest, innocent, open, plain, simple, sincere, trusting, unsophisticated

inglorious adjective dishonourable, discredited, disgraceful, disreputable, ignoble, ignominious, infamous, shameful, unheroic

ingratiate verb pander to, crawl, curry favour, fawn, flatter, grovel, insinuate oneself, toady

ingratiating adjective sycophantic, crawling, fawning, flattering, humble, obsequious, servile, toadying, unctuous

ingratitude noun ungratefulness, thanklessness

ingredient noun component, constituent, element, part

inhabit verb live, abide, dwell, occupy, populate, reside

inhabitant noun dweller, citizen, denizen, inmate, native, occupant, occupier, resident, tenant

inhabited adjective populated, colonized, developed, occupied, peopled, settled, tenanted

inhale verb breathe in, draw in, gasp, respire, suck in

inherent adjective innate, essential, hereditary, inborn, inbred, inbuilt, ingrained, inherited, intrinsic, native, natural

inherit verb be left, come into, fall heir to, succeed to

inheritance noun legacy, bequest, birthright, heritage, patrimony

inhibit verb restrain, check, constrain, curb, discourage, frustrate, hinder, hold back or in, impede, obstruct

inhibited adjective shy, constrained, guarded, repressed, reserved, reticent, self-conscious, subdued

inhibition noun shyness, block, hang-up (informal), reserve, restraint, reticence, self-consciousness

inhospitable adjective 1 unwelcoming, cool, uncongenial, unfriendly, unreceptive, unsociable, xenophobic 2 bleak, barren, desolate, forbidding, godforsaken, hostile

inhuman adjective cruel, barbaric, brutal, cold-blooded, heartless, merciless, pitiless, ruthless, savage, unfeeling

inhumane adjective cruel, brutal, heartless, pitiless, unfeeling, unkind, unsympathetic

inhumanity noun cruelty, atrocity, barbarism, brutality, heartlessness, pitilessness, ruthlessness, unkindness

inimical adjective hostile, adverse, antagonistic, ill-disposed, opposed, unfavourable, unfriendly, unwelcoming

inimitable adjective unique, consummate, incomparable, matchless, peerless, unparalleled, unrivalled

iniquitous adjective wicked, criminal, evil, immoral, reprehensible, sinful, unjust

iniquity noun wickedness, abomination, evil, injustice, sin, wrong

initial adjective first, beginning, incipient, introductory, opening, primary

initially adverb at first, at or in the beginning, first, firstly, originally, primarily

initiate verb 1 begin, commence, get under way, kick off (informal), launch, open, originate, set in motion, start 2 induct, indoctrinate, introduce, invest 3 instruct, acquaint with, coach, familiarize with, teach, train ♦ noun 4 novice, beginner, convert, entrant, learner, member, probationer

initiation noun introduction, debut, enrolment, entrance, inauguration, induction, installation, investiture

initiative noun 1 first step, advantage, first move, lead 2 resourcefulness, ambition, drive, dynamism, enterprise, get-up-and-go (informal), leadership

inject verb 1 vaccinate, inoculate 2 introduce, bring in, infuse, insert, instil

injection noun 1 vaccination, inoculation, jab (informal), shot (informal) 2 introduction, dose, infusion, insertion

injudicious adjective unwise, foolish, ill-advised, ill-judged, impolitic, imprudent, incautious, inexpedient, rash, unthinking

injure verb hurt, damage, harm, impair, ruin, spoil, undermine, wound

injured adjective hurt, broken, damaged, disabled, undermined, weakened, wounded

injury noun harm, damage, detriment, disservice, hurt, ill, trauma (Pathology), wound, wrong

injustice noun unfairness, bias, discrimination, inequality, inequity, iniquity, oppression, partisanship, prejudice, wrong

inkling noun suspicion, clue, conception, hint, idea, indication, intimation, notion, suggestion, whisper

inland adjective interior, domestic, internal, upcountry

inlet noun bay, bight, creek, firth or frith (Scot.), fjord, passage

inmost or **innermost** adjective deepest, basic, central, essential, intimate, personal, private, secret

innate adjective inborn, congenital, constitutional, essential, inbred, ingrained, inherent, instinctive, intuitive, native, natural

inner adjective 1 inside, central, interior, internal, inward, middle 2 private, hidden, intimate, personal, repressed, secret, unrevealed

innkeeper noun publican, host or hostess, hotelier, landlord or landlady, mine host

innocence noun 1 guiltlessness, blamelessness, clean hands, incorruptibility, probity, purity, uprightness, virtue 2 harmlessness, innocuousness, inoffensiveness 3 inexperience, artlessness, credulousness, gullibility, ingenuousness, naïveté, simplicity, unworldliness

innocent adjective 1 not guilty, blameless, guiltless, honest, in the clear, uninvolved **2** <u>harmless</u>, innocuous, inoffensive, unobjectionable, well-intentioned, well-meant **3** <u>naive</u>, artless, childlike, credulous, gullible, ingenuous, open, simple, unworldly

innovation noun <u>modernization</u>, alteration, change, departure, introduction, newness, novelty, variation

innuendo noun <u>insinuation</u>, aspersion, hint, implication, imputation, intimation, overtone, suggestion, whisper

innumerable adjective <u>countless</u>, beyond number, incalculable, infinite, multitudinous, myriad, numberless, numerous, unnumbered, untold

inoffensive adjective <u>harmless</u>, innocent, innocuous, mild, quiet, retiring, unobjectionable, unobtrusive

inoperative adjective <u>out of action</u>, broken, defective, ineffective, invalid, null and void, out of order, out of service, useless

inopportune adjective <u>inconvenient</u>, ill-chosen, ill-timed, inappropriate, unfavourable, unfortunate, unpropitious, unseasonable, unsuitable, untimely

inordinate adjective <u>excessive</u>, disproportionate, extravagant, immoderate, intemperate, preposterous, unconscionable, undue, unreasonable, unwarranted

inorganic adjective <u>artificial</u>, chemical, man-made

inquest noun <u>inquiry</u>, inquisition,

investigation, probe

inquire verb **1** <u>investigate</u>, examine, explore, look into, make inquiries, probe, research **2** Also **enquire** <u>ask</u>, query, question

inquiry noun **1** <u>investigation</u>, examination, exploration, inquest, interrogation, probe, research, study, survey **2** Also **enquiry** <u>question</u>, query

inquisition noun <u>investigation</u>, cross-examination, examination, grilling (informal), inquest, inquiry, questioning, third degree (informal)

inquisitive adjective <u>curious</u>, inquiring, nosy (informal), probing, prying, questioning

insane adjective **1** <u>mad</u>, crazed, crazy, demented, deranged, mentally ill, out of one's mind, unhinged **2** <u>stupid</u>, daft (informal), foolish, idiotic, impractical, irrational, irresponsible, preposterous, senseless

insanitary adjective <u>unhealthy</u>, dirty, disease-ridden, filthy, infested, insalubrious, polluted, unclean, unhygienic

insanity noun **1** <u>madness</u>, delirium, dementia, mental disorder, mental illness **2** <u>stupidity</u>, folly, irresponsibility, lunacy, senselessness

insatiable adjective <u>unquenchable</u>, greedy, intemperate, rapacious, ravenous, voracious

inscribe verb <u>carve</u>, cut, engrave, etch, impress, imprint

inscription noun <u>engraving</u>,

dedication, legend, words

inscrutable adjective
1 enigmatic, blank, deadpan, impenetrable, poker-faced (informal) **2** mysterious, hidden, incomprehensible, inexplicable, unexplainable, unfathomable, unintelligible

insecure adjective **1** anxious, afraid, uncertain, unsure **2** unsafe, defenceless, exposed, unguarded, unprotected, vulnerable, wide-open

insecurity noun anxiety, fear, uncertainty, worry

insensible adjective unaware, impervious, oblivious, unaffected, unconscious, unmindful

insensitive adjective unfeeling, callous, hardened, indifferent, thick-skinned, tough, uncaring, unconcerned

inseparable adjective
1 indivisible, indissoluble **2** devoted, bosom, close, intimate

insert verb enter, embed, implant, introduce, place, put, stick in

insertion noun inclusion, addition, implant, interpolation, introduction, supplement

inside adjective **1** inner, interior, internal, inward **2** confidential, classified, exclusive, internal, private, restricted, secret ♦ adverb **3** indoors, under cover, within ♦ noun **4** interior, contents **5** insides Informal stomach, belly, bowels, entrails, guts, innards (informal), viscera, vitals

insidious adjective stealthy,

deceptive, sly, smooth, sneaking, subtle, surreptitious

insight noun understanding, awareness, comprehension, discernment, judgment, observation, penetration, perception, perspicacity, vision

insignia noun badge, crest, emblem, symbol

insignificance noun unimportance, inconsequence, irrelevance, meaninglessness, pettiness, triviality, worthlessness

insignificant adjective unimportant, inconsequential, irrelevant, meaningless, minor, nondescript, paltry, petty, trifling, trivial

insincere adjective deceitful, dishonest, disingenuous, duplicitous, false, hollow, hypocritical, lying, two-faced, untruthful

insincerity noun deceitfulness, dishonesty, dissimulation, duplicity, hypocrisy, pretence, untruthfulness

insinuate verb **1** imply, allude, hint, indicate, intimate, suggest **2** ingratiate, curry favour, get in with, worm or work one's way in

insinuation noun implication, allusion, aspersion, hint, innuendo, slur, suggestion

insipid adjective **1** bland, anaemic, characterless, colourless, prosaic, uninteresting, vapid, wishy-washy (informal) **2** tasteless, bland, flavourless, unappetizing, watery

insist verb **1** demand, lay down the law, put one's foot down (informal), require **2** assert, aver, claim, maintain, reiterate, repeat, swear, vow

insistence noun persistence, emphasis, importunity, stress

insistent adjective persistent, dogged, emphatic, importunate, incessant, persevering, unrelenting, urgent

insolence noun rudeness, boldness, cheek (informal), disrespect, effrontery, impertinence, impudence

insolent adjective rude, bold, contemptuous, impertinent, impudent, insubordinate, insulting

insoluble adjective inexplicable, baffling, impenetrable, indecipherable, mysterious, unaccountable, unfathomable, unsolvable

insolvency noun bankruptcy, failure, liquidation, ruin

insolvent adjective bankrupt, broke (informal), failed, gone bust (informal), gone to the wall, in receivership, ruined

insomnia noun sleeplessness, wakefulness

inspect verb examine, check, go over or through, investigate, look over, scrutinize, survey, vet

inspection noun examination, check, checkup, investigation, once-over (informal), review, scrutiny, search, survey

inspector noun examiner, censor, investigator, overseer, scrutinizer, superintendent, supervisor

inspiration noun 1 influence, muse, spur, stimulus 2 revelation, creativity,

illumination, insight

inspire verb 1 stimulate, animate, encourage, enliven, galvanize, influence, spur 2 arouse, enkindle, excite, give rise to, produce

inspired adjective 1 brilliant, dazzling, impressive, memorable, outstanding, superlative, thrilling, wonderful 2 uplifted, elated, enthused, exhilarated, stimulated

inspiring adjective uplifting, exciting, exhilarating, heartening, moving, rousing, stimulating, stirring

instability noun unpredictability, changeableness, fickleness, fluctuation, impermanence, inconstancy, insecurity, unsteadiness, variability, volatility

install verb 1 set up, fix, lay, lodge, place, position, put in, station 2 induct, establish, inaugurate, institute, introduce, invest 3 settle, ensconce, position

installation noun 1 setting up, establishment, fitting, instalment, placing, positioning 2 induction, inauguration, investiture 3 equipment, machinery, plant, system

instalment noun portion, chapter, division, episode, part, repayment, section

instance noun 1 example, case, illustration, occasion, occurrence, situation ♦ verb 2 quote, adduce, cite, mention, name, specify

instant noun 1 second, flash, jiffy (informal), moment, split second, trice, twinkling of an eye (informal) 2 juncture, moment, occasion, point, time ♦ adjective

3 <u>immediate</u>, direct, instantaneous, on-the-spot, prompt, quick, split-second
4 <u>precooked</u>, convenience, fast, ready-mixed

instantaneous adjective <u>immediate</u>, direct, instant, on-the-spot, prompt

instantaneously adverb <u>immediately</u>, at once, instantly, in the twinkling of an eye (informal), on the spot, promptly, straight away

instantly adverb <u>immediately</u>, at once, directly, instantaneously, now, right away, straight away, this minute

instead adverb 1 <u>rather</u>, alternatively, in lieu, in preference, on second thoughts, preferably 2 **instead of** <u>in place of</u>, in lieu of, rather than

instigate verb <u>provoke</u>, bring about, incite, influence, initiate, prompt, set off, start, stimulate, trigger

instigation noun <u>prompting</u>, behest, bidding, encouragement, incitement, urging

instigator noun <u>ringleader</u>, agitator, leader, motivator, prime mover, troublemaker

instil verb <u>introduce</u>, engender, imbue, implant, inculcate, infuse, insinuate

instinct noun <u>intuition</u>, faculty, gift, impulse, knack, predisposition, proclivity, talent, tendency

instinctive adjective <u>inborn</u>, automatic, inherent, innate, intuitive, involuntary, natural, reflex, spontaneous, unpremeditated, visceral

instinctively adverb <u>intuitively</u>, automatically, by instinct, involuntarily, naturally, without thinking

institute noun 1 <u>society</u>, academy, association, college, foundation, guild, institution, school ♦ verb 2 <u>establish</u>, fix, found, initiate, introduce, launch, organize, originate, pioneer, set up, start

institution noun 1 <u>establishment</u>, academy, college, foundation, institute, school, society 2 <u>custom</u>, convention, law, practice, ritual, rule, tradition

institutional adjective <u>conventional</u>, accepted, established, formal, orthodox

instruct verb 1 <u>order</u>, bid, charge, command, direct, enjoin, tell 2 <u>teach</u>, coach, drill, educate, ground, school, train, tutor

instruction noun 1 <u>teaching</u>, coaching, education, grounding, guidance, lesson(s), schooling, training, tuition 2 <u>order</u>, command, demand, directive, injunction, mandate, ruling

instructions plural noun <u>orders</u>, advice, directions, guidance, information, key, recommendations, rules

instructive adjective <u>informative</u>, edifying, educational, enlightening, helpful, illuminating, revealing, useful

instructor noun <u>teacher</u>, adviser, coach, demonstrator, guide, mentor, trainer, tutor

instrument noun 1 <u>tool</u>, apparatus, appliance, contraption (*informal*), device, gadget, implement, mechanism 2 <u>means</u>, agency, agent, mechanism, medium, organ, vehicle

instrumental adjective <u>active</u>, contributory, helpful, influential, involved, useful

insubordinate adjective <u>disobedient</u>, defiant, disorderly, mutinous, rebellious, recalcitrant, refractory, undisciplined, ungovernable, unruly

insubordination noun <u>disobedience</u>, defiance, indiscipline, insurrection, mutiny, rebellion, recalcitrance, revolt

insubstantial adjective <u>flimsy</u>, feeble, frail, poor, slight, tenuous, thin, weak

insufferable adjective <u>unbearable</u>, detestable, dreadful, impossible, insupportable, intolerable, unendurable

insufficient adjective <u>inadequate</u>, deficient, incapable, lacking, scant, short

insular adjective <u>narrow-minded</u>, blinkered, circumscribed, inward-looking, limited, narrow, parochial, petty, provincial

insulate verb <u>isolate</u>, close off, cocoon, cushion, cut off, protect, sequester, shield

insult verb 1 <u>offend</u>, abuse, affront, call names, put down, slander, slight, snub ♦ noun 2 <u>abuse</u>, affront, aspersion, insolence, offence, put-down, slap in the face (*informal*), slight, snub

insulting adjective <u>offensive</u>, abusive, contemptuous, degrading, disparaging, insolent, rude, scurrilous

insuperable adjective <u>insurmountable</u>, impassable, invincible, unconquerable

insupportable adjective 1 <u>intolerable</u>, insufferable, unbearable, unendurable 2 <u>unjustifiable</u>, indefensible, untenable

insurance noun <u>protection</u>, assurance, cover, guarantee, indemnity, safeguard, security, warranty

insure verb <u>protect</u>, assure, cover, guarantee, indemnify, underwrite, warrant

insurgent noun 1 <u>rebel</u>, insurrectionist, mutineer, revolutionary, rioter ♦ adjective 2 <u>rebellious</u>, disobedient, insubordinate, mutinous, revolting, revolutionary, riotous, seditious

insurmountable adjective <u>insuperable</u>, hopeless, impassable, impossible, invincible, overwhelming, unconquerable

insurrection noun <u>rebellion</u>, coup, insurgency, mutiny, revolt, revolution, riot, uprising

intact adjective <u>undamaged</u>, complete, entire, perfect, sound, unbroken, unharmed, unimpaired, unscathed, whole

integral adjective <u>essential</u>, basic, component, constituent, fundamental, indispensable, intrinsic, necessary

integrate verb <u>combine</u>,

amalgamate, assimilate, blend, fuse, incorporate, join, merge, unite

integration noun assimilation, amalgamation, blending, combining, fusing, incorporation, mixing, unification

integrity noun 1 honesty, goodness, honour, incorruptibility, principle, probity, purity, rectitude, uprightness, virtue 2 unity, coherence, cohesion, completeness, soundness, wholeness

intellect noun intelligence, brains (informal), judgment, mind, reason, sense, understanding

intellectual adjective 1 scholarly, bookish, cerebral, highbrow, intelligent, studious, thoughtful ♦ noun 2 thinker, academic, egghead (informal), highbrow

intelligence noun 1 understanding, acumen, brain power, brains (informal), cleverness, comprehension, intellect, perception, sense 2 information, data, facts, findings, knowledge, news, notification, report

intelligent adjective clever, brainy (informal), bright, enlightened, perspicacious, quick-witted, sharp, smart, well-informed

intelligentsia noun intellectuals, highbrows, literati

intelligible adjective understandable, clear, comprehensible, distinct, lucid, open, plain

intemperate adjective excessive, extreme, immoderate, profligate, self-indulgent, unbridled,

unrestrained, wild

intend verb plan, aim, have in mind or view, mean, propose, purpose

intense adjective 1 extreme, acute, deep, excessive, fierce, great, powerful, profound, severe 2 passionate, ardent, fanatical, fervent, fierce, heightened, impassioned, vehement

intensify verb increase, add to, aggravate, deepen, escalate, heighten, magnify, redouble, reinforce, sharpen, strengthen

intensity noun force, ardour, emotion, fanaticism, fervour, fierceness, passion, strength, vehemence

intensive adjective concentrated, comprehensive, demanding, exhaustive, in-depth, thorough, thoroughgoing

intent noun 1 intention, aim, design, end, goal, meaning, object, objective, plan, purpose ♦ adjective 2 attentive, absorbed, determined, eager, engrossed, preoccupied, rapt, resolved, steadfast, watchful

intention noun purpose, aim, design, end, goal, idea, object, objective, point, target

intentional adjective deliberate, calculated, intended, meant, planned, premeditated, wilful

intentionally adverb deliberately, designedly, on purpose, wilfully

inter verb bury, entomb, lay to rest

intercede verb mediate, arbitrate, intervene, plead

intercept verb seize, block,

catch, cut off, head off, interrupt, obstruct, stop

interchange verb 1 <u>switch</u>, alternate, exchange, reciprocate, swap ♦ noun 2 <u>junction</u>, intersection

interchangeable adjective <u>identical</u>, equivalent, exchangeable, reciprocal, synonymous

intercourse noun 1 <u>communication</u>, commerce, contact, dealings 2 <u>sexual intercourse</u>, carnal knowledge, coitus, copulation, sex (informal)

interest noun 1 <u>curiosity</u>, attention, concern, notice, regard 2 <u>hobby</u>, activity, diversion, pastime, preoccupation, pursuit 3 <u>advantage</u>, benefit, good, profit 4 <u>stake</u>, claim, investment, right, share ♦ verb 5 <u>intrigue</u>, attract, catch one's eye, divert, engross, fascinate

interested adjective 1 <u>curious</u>, attracted, drawn, excited, fascinated, keen 2 <u>involved</u>, concerned, implicated

interesting adjective <u>intriguing</u>, absorbing, appealing, attractive, compelling, engaging, engrossing, gripping, stimulating, thought-provoking

interface noun <u>connection</u>, border, boundary, frontier, link

interfere verb 1 <u>intrude</u>, butt in, intervene, meddle, stick one's oar in (informal), tamper 2 often with **with** <u>conflict</u>, clash, hamper, handicap, hinder, impede, inhibit, obstruct

interference noun 1 <u>intrusion</u>, intervention, meddling, prying

2 <u>conflict</u>, clashing, collision, obstruction, opposition

interim adjective <u>temporary</u>, acting, caretaker, improvised, makeshift, provisional, stopgap

interior noun 1 <u>inside</u>, centre, core, heart ♦ adjective 2 <u>inside</u>, inner, internal, inward 3 <u>mental</u>, hidden, inner, intimate, personal, private, secret, spiritual

interloper noun <u>trespasser</u>, gate-crasher (informal), intruder, meddler

interlude noun <u>interval</u>, break, breathing space, delay, hiatus, intermission, pause, respite, rest, spell, stoppage

intermediary noun <u>mediator</u>, agent, broker, go-between, middleman

intermediate adjective <u>middle</u>, halfway, in-between (informal), intervening, mid, midway, transitional

interment noun <u>burial</u>, funeral

interminable adjective <u>endless</u>, ceaseless, everlasting, infinite, long-drawn-out, long-winded, never-ending, perpetual, protracted

intermingle verb <u>mix</u>, blend, combine, fuse, interlace, intermix, interweave, merge

intermission noun <u>interval</u>, break, interlude, pause, recess, respite, rest, stoppage

intermittent adjective <u>periodic</u>, broken, fitful, irregular, occasional, spasmodic, sporadic

intern verb <u>imprison</u>, confine, detain, hold, hold in custody

internal adjective 1 <u>inner</u>, inside, interior 2 <u>domestic</u>, civic, home, in-house, intramural

international adjective <u>universal</u>, cosmopolitan, global, intercontinental, worldwide

Internet noun <u>information superhighway</u>, cyberspace, the net (informal), the web (informal), World Wide Web

interpose verb <u>interrupt</u>, insert, interject, put one's oar in

interpret verb <u>explain</u>, construe, decipher, decode, elucidate, make sense of, render, translate

interpretation noun <u>explanation</u>, analysis, clarification, elucidation, exposition, portrayal, rendition, translation, version

interpreter noun <u>translator</u>, commentator

interrogate verb <u>question</u>, cross-examine, examine, grill (informal), investigate, pump, quiz

interrogation noun <u>questioning</u>, cross-examination, examination, grilling (informal), inquiry, inquisition, third degree (informal)

interrupt verb 1 <u>intrude</u>, barge in (informal), break in, butt in, disturb, heckle, interfere (with) 2 <u>suspend</u>, break off, cut short, delay, discontinue, hold up, lay aside, stop

interruption noun <u>stoppage</u>, break, disruption, disturbance, hitch, intrusion, pause, suspension

intersection noun <u>junction</u>, crossing, crossroads, interchange

interval noun <u>break</u>, delay, gap, interlude, intermission, pause, respite, rest, space, spell

intervene verb 1 <u>involve oneself</u>, arbitrate, intercede, interfere,

intrude, mediate, step in (informal), take a hand (informal) 2 <u>happen</u>, befall, come to pass, ensue, occur, take place

intervention noun <u>mediation</u>, agency, interference, intrusion

interview noun 1 <u>meeting</u>, audience, conference, consultation, dialogue, press conference, talk ♦ verb 2 <u>question</u>, examine, interrogate, talk to

interviewer noun <u>questioner</u>, examiner, interrogator, investigator, reporter

intestines plural noun <u>guts</u>, bowels, entrails, innards (informal), insides (informal), viscera

intimacy noun <u>familiarity</u>, closeness, confidentiality

intimate[1] adjective 1 <u>close</u>, bosom, confidential, dear, near, thick (informal) 2 <u>personal</u>, confidential, private, secret 3 <u>detailed</u>, deep, exhaustive, first-hand, immediate, in-depth, profound, thorough 4 <u>snug</u>, comfy (informal), cosy, friendly, warm ♦ noun 5 <u>friend</u>, close friend, confidant or confidante, (constant) companion, crony

intimate[2] verb 1 <u>suggest</u>, hint, imply, indicate, insinuate 2 <u>announce</u>, communicate, declare, make known, state

intimately adverb 1 <u>confidingly</u>, affectionately, confidentially, familiarly, personally, tenderly, warmly 2 <u>in detail</u>, fully, inside out, thoroughly, very well

intimation noun 1 <u>hint</u>, allusion, indication, inkling, insinuation, reminder, suggestion, warning

2 announcement,
communication, declaration,
notice

intimidate *verb* frighten,
browbeat, bully, coerce, daunt,
overawe, scare, subdue,
terrorize, threaten

intimidation *noun* bullying,
arm-twisting (*informal*),
browbeating, coercion, menaces,
pressure, terrorization, threat(s)

intolerable *adjective* unbearable,
excruciating, impossible,
insufferable, insupportable,
painful, unendurable

intolerance *noun*
narrow-mindedness, bigotry,
chauvinism, discrimination,
dogmatism, fanaticism,
illiberality, prejudice

intolerant *adjective*
narrow-minded, bigoted,
chauvinistic, dictatorial,
dogmatic, fanatical, illiberal,
prejudiced, small-minded

intone *verb* recite, chant

intoxicated *adjective* 1 drunk,
drunken, inebriated, legless
(*informal*), paralytic (*informal*),
plastered (*slang*), tipsy, under
the influence 2 euphoric, dizzy,
elated, enraptured, excited,
exhilarated, high (*informal*)

intoxicating *adjective*
1 alcoholic, strong 2 exciting,
exhilarating, heady, thrilling

intoxication *noun*
1 drunkenness, inebriation,
insobriety, tipsiness
2 excitement, delirium, elation,
euphoria, exhilaration

intransigent *adjective*
uncompromising, hardline,

intractable, obdurate, obstinate,
stiff-necked, stubborn,
unbending, unyielding

intrepid *adjective* fearless,
audacious, bold, brave,
courageous, daring, gallant,
plucky, stouthearted, valiant

intricacy *noun* complexity,
complication, convolutions,
elaborateness

intricate *adjective* complicated,
complex, convoluted, elaborate,
fancy, involved, labyrinthine,
tangled, tortuous

intrigue *verb* 1 interest, attract,
fascinate, rivet, titillate 2 plot,
connive, conspire, machinate,
manoeuvre, scheme ♦ *noun*
3 plot, chicanery, collusion,
conspiracy, machination,
manoeuvre, scheme, stratagem,
wile 4 affair, amour, intimacy,
liaison, romance

intriguing *adjective* interesting,
beguiling, compelling, diverting,
exciting, fascinating, tantalizing,
titillating

intrinsic *adjective* inborn, basic,
built-in, congenital,
constitutional, essential,
fundamental, inbred, inherent,
native, natural

introduce *verb* 1 present,
acquaint, familiarize, make
known 2 bring in, establish,
found, initiate, institute, launch,
pioneer, set up, start 3 bring up,
advance, air, broach, moot, put
forward, submit 4 insert, add,
inject, put in, throw in (*informal*)

introduction *noun* 1 launch,
establishment, inauguration,
institution, pioneering
2 opening, foreword, intro

(*informal*), lead-in, preamble, preface, prelude, prologue

introductory *adjective*
<u>preliminary</u>, first, inaugural, initial, opening, preparatory

introspective *adjective*
<u>inward-looking</u>, brooding, contemplative, introverted, meditative, pensive

introverted *adjective*
<u>introspective</u>, inner-directed, inward-looking, self-contained, withdrawn

intrude *verb* <u>interfere</u>, butt in, encroach, infringe, interrupt, meddle, push in, trespass

intruder *noun* <u>trespasser</u>, gate-crasher (*informal*), infiltrator, interloper, invader, prowler

intrusion *noun* <u>invasion</u>, encroachment, infringement, interference, interruption, trespass

intrusive *adjective* <u>interfering</u>, impertinent, importunate, meddlesome, nosy (*informal*), presumptuous, pushy (*informal*), uncalled-for, unwanted

intuition *noun* <u>instinct</u>, hunch, insight, perception, presentiment, sixth sense

intuitive *adjective* <u>instinctive</u>, innate, spontaneous, untaught

inundate *verb* <u>flood</u>, drown, engulf, immerse, overflow, overrun, overwhelm, submerge, swamp

invade *verb* <u>attack</u>, assault, burst in, descend upon, encroach, infringe, make inroads, occupy, raid, violate **2** <u>infest</u>, overrun, permeate, pervade, swarm over

invader *noun* <u>attacker</u>, aggressor, plunderer, raider, trespasser

invalid[1] *adjective* **1** <u>disabled</u>, ailing, bedridden, frail, ill, infirm, sick ◆ *noun* **2** <u>patient</u>, convalescent, valetudinarian

invalid[2] *adjective* <u>null and void</u>, fallacious, false, illogical, inoperative, irrational, unfounded, unsound, void, worthless

invalidate *verb* <u>nullify</u>, annul, cancel, overthrow, undermine, undo

invaluable *adjective* <u>precious</u>, inestimable, priceless, valuable, worth one's or its weight in gold

invariably *adverb* <u>consistently</u>, always, customarily, day in, day out, habitually, perpetually, regularly, unfailingly, without exception

invasion *noun* **1** <u>attack</u>, assault, campaign, foray, incursion, inroad, offensive, onslaught, raid **2** <u>intrusion</u>, breach, encroachment, infraction, infringement, usurpation, violation

invective *noun* <u>abuse</u>, censure, denunciation, diatribe, tirade, tongue-lashing, vilification, vituperation

invent *verb* **1** <u>create</u>, coin, conceive, design, devise, discover, formulate, improvise, originate, think up **2** <u>make up</u>, concoct, cook up (*informal*), fabricate, feign, forge, manufacture, trump up

invention *noun* **1** <u>creation</u>, brainchild (*informal*), contraption, contrivance, design, device, discovery, gadget, instrument **2** creativity, genius, imagination, ingenuity, inventiveness, originality, resourcefulness **3** fiction, fabrication, falsehood, fantasy, forgery, lie, untruth, yarn

inventive adjective creative, fertile, imaginative, ingenious, innovative, inspired, original, resourceful

inventor noun creator, architect, author, coiner, designer, maker, originator

inventory noun list, account, catalogue, file, record, register, roll, roster

inverse adjective opposite, contrary, converse, reverse, reversed, transposed

invert verb overturn, reverse, transpose, upset, upturn

invest verb **1** spend, advance, devote, lay out, put in, sink **2** empower, authorize, charge, license, sanction, vest

investigate verb examine, explore, go into, inquire into, inspect, look into, probe, research, study

investigation noun examination, exploration, inquest, inquiry, inspection, probe, review, search, study, survey

investigator noun examiner, inquirer, (private) detective, private eye (informal), researcher, sleuth

investiture noun installation, enthronement, inauguration, induction, ordination

investment noun **1** transaction, speculation, venture **2** stake, ante (informal), contribution

inveterate adjective long-standing, chronic, confirmed, deep-seated, dyed-in-the-wool, entrenched, habitual, hardened, incorrigible, incurable

invidious adjective undesirable, hateful

invigilate verb watch over, conduct, keep an eye on, oversee, preside over, run, superintend, supervise

invigorate verb refresh, energize, enliven, exhilarate, fortify, galvanize, liven up, revitalize, stimulate

invincible adjective unbeatable, impregnable, indestructible, indomitable, insuperable, invulnerable, unassailable, unconquerable

inviolable adjective sacrosanct, hallowed, holy, inalienable, sacred, unalterable

inviolate adjective intact, entire, pure, unbroken, undefiled, unhurt, unpolluted, unsullied, untouched, whole

invisible adjective unseen, imperceptible, indiscernible

invitation noun request, call, invite (informal), summons

invite verb **1** request, ask, beg, bid, summon **2** encourage, ask for (informal), attract, court, entice, provoke, tempt, welcome

inviting adjective tempting, alluring, appealing, attractive, enticing, mouthwatering, seductive, welcoming

invocation noun appeal, entreaty, petition, prayer, supplication

invoke verb 1 <u>call upon</u>, appeal to, beg, beseech, entreat, implore, petition, pray, supplicate 2 <u>apply</u>, implement, initiate, put into effect, resort to, use

involuntary adjective <u>unintentional</u>, automatic, instinctive, reflex, spontaneous, unconscious, uncontrolled, unthinking

involve verb 1 <u>entail</u>, imply, mean, necessitate, presuppose, require 2 <u>concern</u>, affect, draw in, implicate, touch

involved adjective 1 <u>complicated</u>, complex, confusing, convoluted, elaborate, intricate, labyrinthine, tangled, tortuous 2 <u>concerned</u>, caught (up), implicated, mixed up in or with, participating, taking part

involvement noun <u>connection</u>, association, commitment, interest, participation

invulnerable adjective <u>safe</u>, impenetrable, indestructible, insusceptible, invincible, proof against, secure, unassailable

inward adjective 1 <u>incoming</u>, entering, inbound, ingoing 2 <u>internal</u>, inner, inside, interior 3 <u>private</u>, confidential, hidden, inmost, innermost, personal, secret

inwardly adverb <u>privately</u>, at heart, deep down, inside, secretly

irate adjective <u>angry</u>, annoyed, cross, enraged, furious, incensed, indignant, infuriated, livid

irksome adjective <u>irritating</u>, annoying, bothersome, disagreeable, exasperating, tiresome, troublesome, trying, vexing, wearisome

iron adjective 1 <u>ferrous</u>, chalybeate, ferric 2 <u>inflexible</u>, adamant, hard, implacable, indomitable, rigid, steely, strong, tough, unbending, unyielding

ironic, ironical adjective 1 <u>sarcastic</u>, double-edged, mocking, sardonic, satirical, with tongue in cheek, wry 2 <u>paradoxical</u>, incongruous

iron out verb <u>settle</u>, clear up, get rid of, put right, reconcile, resolve, smooth over, sort out, straighten out

irony noun 1 <u>sarcasm</u>, mockery, satire 2 <u>paradox</u>, incongruity

irrational adjective <u>illogical</u>, absurd, crazy, nonsensical, preposterous, unreasonable

irrefutable adjective <u>undeniable</u>, certain, incontestable, incontrovertible, indisputable, indubitable, sure, unquestionable

irregular adjective 1 <u>variable</u>, erratic, fitful, haphazard, occasional, random, spasmodic, sporadic, unsystematic 2 <u>unconventional</u>, abnormal, exceptional, extraordinary, peculiar, unofficial, unorthodox, unusual 3 <u>uneven</u>, asymmetrical, bumpy, crooked, jagged, lopsided, ragged, rough

irregularity noun 1 <u>uncertainty</u>, desultoriness, disorganization, haphazardness 2 <u>abnormality</u>, anomaly, oddity, peculiarity, unorthodoxy 3 <u>unevenness</u>, asymmetry, bumpiness, jaggedness, lopsidedness, raggedness, roughness

irrelevant adjective <u>unconnected</u>, beside the point, extraneous, immaterial, impertinent, inapplicable, inappropriate, neither here nor there, unrelated

irreparable adjective <u>beyond repair</u>, incurable, irremediable, irretrievable, irreversible

irrepressible adjective <u>ebullient</u>, boisterous, buoyant, effervescent, unstoppable

irreproachable adjective <u>blameless</u>, beyond reproach, faultless, impeccable, innocent, perfect, pure, unimpeachable

irresistible adjective <u>overwhelming</u>, compelling, compulsive, overpowering, urgent

irresponsible adjective <u>immature</u>, careless, reckless, scatterbrained, shiftless, thoughtless, unreliable, untrustworthy

irreverent adjective <u>disrespectful</u>, cheeky (informal), flippant, iconoclastic, impertinent, impudent, mocking, tongue-in-cheek

irreversible adjective <u>irrevocable</u>, final, incurable, irreparable, unalterable

irrevocable adjective <u>fixed</u>, fated, immutable, irreversible, predestined, predetermined, settled, unalterable

irrigate verb <u>water</u>, flood, inundate, moisten, wet

irritability noun <u>bad temper</u>, ill humour, impatience, irascibility, prickliness, testiness, tetchiness, touchiness

irritable adjective <u>bad-tempered</u>, cantankerous, crotchety (informal), ill-tempered, irascible, oversensitive, prickly, testy, tetchy, touchy

irritate verb 1 <u>annoy</u>, anger, bother, exasperate, get on one's nerves (informal), infuriate, needle (informal), nettle, rankle with, try one's patience 2 <u>rub</u>, chafe, inflame, pain

irritated adjective <u>annoyed</u>, angry, bothered, cross, exasperated, nettled, piqued, put out, vexed

irritating adjective <u>annoying</u>, disturbing, infuriating, irksome, maddening, nagging, troublesome, trying

irritation noun 1 <u>annoyance</u>, anger, displeasure, exasperation, indignation, resentment, testiness, vexation 2 <u>nuisance</u>, drag (informal), irritant, pain in the neck (informal), thorn in one's flesh

island noun <u>isle</u>, ait or eyot (dialect), atoll, cay or key, islet

isolate verb <u>separate</u>, cut off, detach, disconnect, insulate, segregate, set apart

isolated adjective <u>remote</u>, hidden, lonely, off the beaten track, outlying, out-of-the-way, secluded

isolation noun <u>separation</u>, detachment, remoteness, seclusion, segregation, solitude

issue noun 1 <u>topic</u>, bone of contention, matter, point, problem, question, subject 2 <u>outcome</u>, consequence, effect, end result, result, upshot 3 <u>edition</u>, copy, number, printing 4 <u>children</u>, descendants, heirs, offspring, progeny 5 <u>take issue</u> disagree, challenge, dispute, object, oppose, raise an objection, take exception ♦ *verb* **6** publish, announce, broadcast, circulate, deliver, distribute, give out, put out, release

isthmus *noun* strip, spit

itch *noun* **1** irritation, itchiness, prickling, tingling **2** desire, craving, hankering, hunger, longing, lust, passion, yearning, yen (*informal*) ♦ *verb* **3** prickle, irritate, tickle, tingle **4** long, ache, crave, hanker, hunger, lust, pine, yearn

itching *adjective* longing, avid, eager, impatient, mad keen (*informal*), raring, spoiling for

itchy *adjective* impatient, eager, edgy, fidgety, restive, restless, unsettled

item *noun* **1** detail, article, component, entry, matter, particular, point, thing **2** report, account, article, bulletin, dispatch, feature, note, notice, paragraph, piece

itinerant *adjective* wandering, migratory, nomadic, peripatetic, roaming, roving, travelling, vagrant

itinerary *noun* schedule, programme, route, timetable

J j

jab *verb, noun* poke, dig, lunge, nudge, prod, punch, stab, tap, thrust

jabber *verb* chatter, babble, blether, gabble, mumble, prate, rabbit (on) (*Brit. informal*), ramble, yap (*informal*)

jacket *noun* covering, case, casing, coat, sheath, skin, wrapper, wrapping

jackpot *noun* prize, award, bonanza, reward, winnings

jack up *verb* raise, elevate, hoist, lift, lift up

jaded *adjective* tired, exhausted, fatigued, spent, weary

jagged *adjective* uneven, barbed, craggy, indented, ragged, serrated, spiked, toothed

jail *noun* **1** prison, nick (*Brit. slang*), penitentiary (*U.S.*), reformatory, slammer (*slang*) ♦ *verb* **2** imprison, confine, detain, incarcerate, lock up, send down

jailer *noun* guard, keeper, warden, warder

jam *verb* **1** pack, cram, force, press, ram, squeeze, stuff, wedge **2** crowd, crush, throng **3** congest, block, clog, obstruct, stall, stick ♦ *noun* **4** predicament, deep water, fix (*informal*), hole (*slang*), hot water, pickle (*informal*), tight spot, trouble

jamboree *noun* festival, carnival, celebration, festivity, fête, revelry

jangle *verb* rattle, chime, clank, clash, clatter, jingle, vibrate

janitor *noun* caretaker, concierge, custodian, doorkeeper, porter

jar¹ *noun* pot, container, crock, jug, pitcher, urn, vase

jar² *verb* **1** jolt, bump, convulse, rattle, rock, shake, vibrate **2** irritate, annoy, get on one's nerves (*informal*), grate, irk, nettle, offend ♦ *noun* **3** jolt, bump, convulsion, shock, vibration

jargon noun parlance, argot, idiom, usage

jaundiced adjective 1 cynical, sceptical 2 bitter, envious, hostile, jealous, resentful, spiteful, suspicious

jaunt noun outing, airing, excursion, expedition, ramble, stroll, tour, trip

jaunty adjective sprightly, buoyant, carefree, high-spirited, lively, perky, self-confident, sparky

jaw verb talk, chat, chatter, gossip, spout

jaws plural noun opening, entrance, mouth

jazz up verb enliven, animate, enhance, improve

jazzy adjective flashy, fancy, gaudy, snazzy (informal)

jealous adjective 1 envious, covetous, desirous, green, grudging, resentful 2 wary, mistrustful, protective, suspicious, vigilant, watchful

jealousy noun envy, covetousness, mistrust, possessiveness, resentment, spite, suspicion

jeans plural noun denims, Levis (Trademark)

jeer verb 1 scoff, barrack, deride, gibe, heckle, mock, ridicule, taunt ♦ noun 2 taunt, abuse, boo, catcall, derision, gibe, ridicule

jell verb 1 solidify, congeal, harden, set, thicken 2 take shape, come together, crystallise, materialize

jeopardize verb endanger, chance, expose, gamble, imperil,

risk, stake, venture

jeopardy noun danger, insecurity, peril, risk, vulnerability

jerk verb, noun tug, jolt, lurch, pull, thrust, twitch, wrench, yank

jerky adjective bumpy, convulsive, jolting, jumpy, shaky, spasmodic, twitchy

jerry-built adjective ramshackle, cheap, defective, flimsy, rickety, shabby, slipshod, thrown together

jest noun 1 joke, bon mot, crack (slang), jape, pleasantry, prank, quip, wisecrack (informal), witticism ♦ verb 2 joke, kid (informal), mock, quip, tease

jester noun clown, buffoon, fool, harlequin

jet[1] adjective black, coal-black, ebony, inky, pitch-black, raven, sable

jet[2] noun 1 stream, flow, fountain, gush, spout, spray, spring 2 nozzle, atomizer, sprayer, sprinkler ♦ verb 3 fly, soar, zoom

jettison verb abandon, discard, dump, eject, expel, scrap, throw overboard, unload

jetty noun pier, breakwater, dock, groyne, mole, quay, wharf

jewel noun 1 gemstone, ornament, rock (slang), sparkler (informal) 2 rarity, collector's item, find, gem, humdinger (slang), pearl, treasure, wonder

jewellery noun jewels, finery, gems, ornaments, regalia, treasure, trinkets

jib verb refuse, balk, recoil, retreat, shrink, stop short

jibe see GIBE

jig *verb* skip, bob, bounce, caper, prance, wiggle

jingle *noun* 1 rattle, clang, clink, reverberation, ringing, tinkle 2 song, chorus, ditty, melody, tune ♦ *verb* 3 ring, chime, clatter, clink, jangle, rattle, tinkle

jinx *noun* 1 curse, hex (*U.S. & Canad. informal*), hoodoo (*informal*), nemesis ♦ *verb* 2 curse, bewitch, hex (*U.S. & Canad. informal*)

jitters *plural noun* nerves, anxiety, butterflies (in one's stomach) (*informal*), cold feet (*informal*), fidgets, nervousness, the shakes (*informal*)

jittery *adjective* nervous, agitated, anxious, fidgety, jumpy, shaky, trembling, twitchy (*informal*)

job *noun* 1 task, assignment, chore, duty, enterprise, errand, undertaking, venture 2 occupation, business, calling, career, employment, livelihood, profession, vocation

jobless *adjective* unemployed, idle, inactive, out of work, unoccupied

jocular *adjective* humorous, amusing, droll, facetious, funny, joking, jovial, playful, sportive, teasing, waggish

jog *verb* 1 nudge, prod, push, shake, stir 2 run, canter, lope, trot

joie de vivre *noun* enthusiasm, ebullience, enjoyment, gusto, relish, zest

join *verb* 1 connect, add, append, attach, combine, couple, fasten, link, unite 2 enrol, enlist, enter, sign up

joint *adjective* 1 shared, collective, combined, communal, cooperative, joined, mutual, united ♦ *noun* 2 junction, connection, hinge, intersection, nexus, node ♦ *verb* 3 divide, carve, cut up, dissect, segment, sever

jointly *adverb* collectively, as one, in common, in conjunction, in league, in partnership, mutually, together

joke *noun* 1 jest, gag (*informal*), jape, prank, pun, quip, wisecrack (*informal*), witticism 2 clown, buffoon, laughing stock ♦ *verb* 3 jest, banter, kid (*informal*), mock, play the fool, quip, taunt, tease

joker *noun* comedian, buffoon, clown, comic, humorist, jester, prankster, trickster, wag, wit

jolly *adjective* happy, cheerful, chirpy (*informal*), genial, jovial, merry, playful, sprightly, upbeat (*informal*)

jolt *noun* 1 jerk, bump, jar, jog, jump, lurch, shake, start 2 surprise, blow, bolt from the blue, bombshell, setback, shock ♦ *verb* 3 jerk, jar, jog, jostle, knock, push, shake, shove 4 surprise, discompose, disturb, perturb, stagger, startle, stun

jostle *verb* push, bump, elbow, hustle, jog, jolt, shake, shove

jot *verb* 1 note down, list, record, scribble ♦ *noun* 2 bit, fraction, grain, morsel, scrap, speck

journal *noun* 1 newspaper, daily, gazette, magazine, monthly, periodical, weekly 2 diary, chronicle, log, record

journalist *noun* reporter,

broadcaster, columnist, commentator, correspondent, hack, journo (*slang*), newsman *or* newswoman, pressman

journey *noun* **1** trip, excursion, expedition, odyssey, pilgrimage, tour, trek, voyage ◆ *verb* **2** travel, go, proceed, roam, rove, tour, traverse, trek, voyage, wander

jovial *adjective* cheerful, animated, cheery, convivial, happy, jolly, merry, mirthful

joy *noun* delight, bliss, ecstasy, elation, gaiety, glee, pleasure, rapture, satisfaction

joyful *adjective* delighted, elated, enraptured, glad, gratified, happy, jubilant, merry, pleased

joyless *adjective* unhappy, cheerless, depressed, dismal, dreary, gloomy, miserable, sad

joyous *adjective* joyful, festive, merry, rapturous

jubilant *adjective* overjoyed, elated, enraptured, euphoric, exuberant, exultant, thrilled, triumphant

jubilation *noun* joy, celebration, ecstasy, elation, excitement, exultation, festivity, triumph

jubilee *noun* celebration, festival, festivity, holiday

judge *noun* **1** referee, adjudicator, arbiter, arbitrator, moderator, umpire **2** critic, arbiter, assessor, authority, connoisseur, expert **3** magistrate, beak (*Brit. slang*), justice ◆ *verb* **4** arbitrate, adjudicate, decide, mediate, referee, umpire **5** consider, appraise, assess, esteem, estimate, evaluate, rate, value

judgment *noun* **1** sense, acumen, discernment, discrimination, prudence, shrewdness, understanding, wisdom **2** verdict, arbitration, decision, decree, finding, ruling, sentence **3** opinion, appraisal, assessment, belief, diagnosis, estimate, finding, valuation, view

judicial *adjective* legal, official

judicious *adjective* sensible, astute, careful, discriminating, enlightened, prudent, shrewd, thoughtful, well-judged, wise

jug *noun* container, carafe, crock, ewer, jar, pitcher, urn, vessel

juggle *verb* manipulate, alter, change, manoeuvre, modify

juice *noun* liquid, extract, fluid, liquor, nectar, sap

juicy *adjective* **1** moist, lush, succulent **2** interesting, colourful, provocative, racy, risqué, sensational, spicy (*informal*), suggestive, vivid

jumble *noun* **1** muddle, clutter, confusion, disarray, disorder, mess, mishmash, mixture ◆ *verb* **2** mix, confuse, disorder, disorganize, mistake, muddle, shuffle

jumbo *adjective* giant, gigantic, huge, immense, large, oversized

jump *verb* **1** leap, bounce, bound, hop, hurdle, skip, spring, vault **2** recoil, flinch, jerk, start, wince **3** miss, avoid, evade, omit, skip **4** increase, advance, ascend, escalate, rise, surge ◆ *noun* **5** leap, bound, hop, skip, spring, vault **6** interruption, break, gap, hiatus, lacuna, space **7** rise, advance, increase, increment, upsurge, upturn

jumped-up adjective <u>conceited</u>, arrogant, insolent, overbearing, pompous, presumptuous

jumper noun <u>sweater</u>, jersey, pullover, woolly

jumpy adjective <u>nervous</u>, agitated, anxious, apprehensive, fidgety, jittery (*informal*), on edge, restless, tense

junction noun <u>connection</u>, coupling, linking, union

juncture noun <u>moment</u>, occasion, point, time

junior adjective <u>minor</u>, inferior, lesser, lower, secondary, subordinate, younger

junk noun <u>rubbish</u>, clutter, debris, litter, odds and ends, refuse, scrap, trash, waste

jurisdiction noun <u>authority</u>, command, control, influence, power, rule 2 <u>range</u>, area, bounds, compass, field, province, scope, sphere

just adverb 1 <u>exactly</u>, absolutely, completely, entirely, perfectly, precisely 2 <u>recently</u>, hardly, lately, only now, scarcely 3 <u>merely</u>, by the skin of one's teeth, only, simply, solely ♦ adjective 4 <u>fair</u>, conscientious, equitable, fair-minded, good, honest, upright, virtuous 5 <u>proper</u>, appropriate, apt, deserved, due, fitting, justified, merited, rightful

justice noun 1 <u>fairness</u>, equity, honesty, integrity, law, legality, legitimacy, right 2 <u>judge</u>, magistrate

justifiable adjective <u>reasonable</u>, acceptable, defensible, excusable, legitimate, sensible,

understandable, valid, warrantable

justification noun 1 <u>explanation</u>, defence, excuse, rationalization, vindication 2 <u>reason</u>, basis, grounds, warrant

justify verb <u>explain</u>, defend, exculpate, excuse, exonerate, support, uphold, vindicate, warrant

justly adverb <u>properly</u>, correctly, equitably, fairly, lawfully

jut verb <u>stick out</u>, bulge, extend, overhang, poke, project, protrude

juvenile adjective 1 <u>young</u>, babyish, childish, immature, inexperienced, infantile, puerile, youthful ♦ noun 2 <u>child</u>, adolescent, boy, girl, infant, minor, youth

juxtaposition noun <u>proximity</u>, closeness, contact, nearness, propinquity, vicinity

K k

kamikaze adjective <u>self-destructive</u>, foolhardy, suicidal

keel over verb <u>collapse</u>, black out (*informal*), faint, pass out

keen adjective 1 <u>eager</u>, ardent, avid, enthusiastic, impassioned, intense, zealous 2 <u>sharp</u>, cutting, incisive, razor-like 3 <u>astute</u>, canny, clever, perceptive, quick, shrewd, wise

keenness noun <u>eagerness</u>, ardour, enthusiasm, fervour, intensity, passion, zeal, zest

keep verb 1 <u>retain</u>, conserve,

control, hold, maintain, possess, preserve **2** store, carry, deposit, hold, place, stack, stock **3** look after, care for, guard, maintain, manage, mind, protect, tend, watch over **4** support, feed, maintain, provide for, subsidize, sustain **5** detain, delay, hinder, hold back, keep back, obstruct, prevent, restrain ♦ noun **6** board, food, living, maintenance **7** tower, castle

keeper noun guardian, attendant, caretaker, curator, custodian, guard, preserver, steward, warden

keeping noun **1** care, charge, custody, guardianship, possession, protection, safekeeping **2** As in **in keeping with** agreement, accord, balance, compliance, conformity, correspondence, harmony, observance, proportion

keepsake noun souvenir, memento, relic, reminder, symbol, token

keep up verb maintain, continue, keep pace, preserve, sustain

keg noun barrel, cask, drum, vat

kernel noun essence, core, germ, gist, nub, pith, substance

key noun **1** opener, latchkey **2** answer, explanation, solution ♦ adjective **3** essential, crucial, decisive, fundamental, important, leading, main, major, pivotal, principal

key in verb type, enter, input, keyboard

keynote noun heart, centre, core, essence, gist, substance, theme

kick verb **1** boot, punt **2** Informal

give up, abandon, desist from, leave off, quit, stop ♦ noun **3** Informal thrill, buzz (slang), pleasure, stimulation

kick off verb Informal begin, commence, get the show on the road, initiate, open, start

kick out verb dismiss, eject, evict, expel, get rid of, remove, sack (informal)

kid[1] noun Informal child, baby, bairn, infant, teenager, tot, youngster, youth

kid[2] verb tease, delude, fool, hoax, jest, joke, pretend, trick, wind up (Brit. slang)

kidnap verb abduct, capture, hijack, hold to ransom, seize

kill verb **1** slay, assassinate, butcher, destroy, execute, exterminate, liquidate, massacre, murder, slaughter **2** suppress, extinguish, halt, quash, quell, scotch, smother, stifle, stop

killer noun assassin, butcher, cut-throat, executioner, exterminator, gunman, hit man (slang), murderer, slayer

killing adjective **1** Informal tiring, debilitating, exhausting, fatiguing, punishing **2** Informal hilarious, comical, ludicrous, uproarious ♦ noun **3** slaughter, bloodshed, carnage, extermination, homicide, manslaughter, massacre, murder, slaying **4** Informal bonanza, bomb (slang), cleanup (informal), coup, gain, profit, success, windfall

killjoy noun spoilsport, dampener, wet blanket (informal)

kin noun family, kindred, kinsfolk,

relations, relatives

kind¹ adjective <u>considerate</u>, benign, charitable, compassionate, courteous, friendly, generous, humane, kindly, obliging, philanthropic, tender-hearted

kind² noun <u>class</u>, brand, breed, family, set, sort, species, variety

kind-hearted adjective <u>sympathetic</u>, altruistic, compassionate, considerate, generous, good-natured, helpful, humane, kind, tender-hearted

kindle verb 1 <u>set fire to</u>, ignite, inflame, light 2 <u>arouse</u>, awaken, induce, inspire, provoke, rouse, stimulate, stir

kindliness noun <u>kindness</u>, amiability, benevolence, charity, compassion, friendliness, gentleness, humanity, kind-heartedness

kindly adjective 1 <u>good-natured</u>, benevolent, benign, compassionate, helpful, kind, pleasant, sympathetic, warm ♦ adverb 2 <u>politely</u>, agreeably, cordially, graciously, tenderly, thoughtfully

kindness noun <u>goodwill</u>, benevolence, charity, compassion, generosity, humanity, kindliness, philanthropy, understanding

kindred adjective 1 <u>similar</u>, akin, corresponding, like, matching, related ♦ noun 2 <u>family</u>, kin, kinsfolk, relations, relatives

king noun <u>ruler</u>, emperor, monarch, sovereign

kingdom noun <u>country</u>, nation, realm, state, territory

kink noun 1 <u>twist</u>, bend, coil, wrinkle 2 <u>quirk</u>, eccentricity, fetish, foible, idiosyncrasy, vagary, whim

kinky adjective 1 <u>weird</u>, eccentric, odd, outlandish, peculiar, queer, quirky, strange 2 <u>twisted</u>, coiled, curled, tangled

kinship noun 1 <u>relation</u>, consanguinity, kin, ties of blood 2 <u>similarity</u>, affinity, association, connection, correspondence, relationship

kiosk noun <u>booth</u>, bookstall, counter, newsstand, stall, stand

kiss verb 1 <u>osculate</u>, neck (informal), peck (informal) 2 <u>brush</u>, glance, graze, scrape, touch ♦ noun 3 <u>osculation</u>, peck (informal), smacker (slang)

kit noun <u>equipment</u>, apparatus, gear, paraphernalia, tackle, tools

kit out verb <u>equip</u>, accoutre, arm, deck out, fit out, fix up, furnish, provide with, supply

knack noun <u>skill</u>, ability, aptitude, capacity, expertise, facility, gift, propensity, talent, trick

knave noun <u>rogue</u>, blackguard, bounder (old-fashioned Brit. slang), rascal, rotter (slang, chiefly Brit.), scoundrel, villain

knead verb <u>squeeze</u>, form, manipulate, massage, mould, press, rub, shape, work

kneel verb <u>genuflect</u>, stoop

knell noun <u>ringing</u>, chime, peal, sound, toll

knickers plural noun <u>underwear</u>, bloomers, briefs, drawers, panties, smalls

knick-knack noun <u>trinket</u>, bagatelle, bauble, bric-a-brac, plaything, trifle

knife noun 1 blade, cutter ♦ verb 2 cut, lacerate, pierce, slash, stab, wound

knit verb 1 join, bind, fasten, intertwine, link, tie, unite, weave 2 wrinkle, crease, furrow, knot, pucker

knob noun lump, bump, hump, knot, projection, protrusion, stud

knock verb 1 hit, belt (informal), cuff, punch, rap, smack, strike, thump 2 Informal criticize, abuse, belittle, censure, condemn, denigrate, deprecate, disparage, find fault, run down ♦ noun 3 blow, clip, clout (informal), cuff, rap, slap, smack, thump 4 setback, defeat, failure, rebuff, rejection, reversal

knockabout adjective boisterous, farcical, riotous, rollicking, slapstick

knock about or **around** verb 1 wander, ramble, range, roam, rove, travel 2 hit, abuse, batter, beat up (informal), maltreat, manhandle, maul, mistreat, strike

knock down verb demolish, destroy, fell, level, raze

knock off verb 1 stop work, clock off, clock out, finish 2 steal, nick (slang, chiefly Brit.), pinch, rob, thieve

knockout noun 1 killer blow, coup de grâce, KO or K.O. (slang) 2 success, hit, sensation, smash, smash hit, triumph, winner

knot noun 1 connection, bond, joint, ligature, loop, tie 2 cluster, bunch, clump, collection ♦ verb 3 tie, bind, loop, secure, tether

know verb 1 realize,

comprehend, feel certain, notice, perceive, recognize, see, understand 2 be acquainted with, be familiar with, have dealings with, have knowledge of, recognize

know-how noun capability, ability, aptitude, expertise, ingenuity, knack, knowledge, savoir-faire, skill, talent

knowing adjective meaningful, expressive, significant

knowingly adverb deliberately, consciously, intentionally, on purpose, purposely, wilfully, wittingly

knowledge noun 1 learning, education, enlightenment, erudition, instruction, intelligence, scholarship, wisdom 2 acquaintance, familiarity, intimacy

knowledgeable adjective 1 well-informed, au fait, aware, clued-up (informal), cognizant, conversant, experienced, familiar, in the know (informal) 2 intelligent, educated, erudite, learned, scholarly

known adjective famous, acknowledged, avowed, celebrated, noted, recognized, well-known

L l

label noun 1 tag, marker, sticker, ticket ♦ verb 2 mark, stamp, tag

laborious adjective hard, arduous, backbreaking, exhausting, onerous, strenuous, tiring, tough, wearisome

labour noun 1 work, industry, toil 2 workers, employees, hands, labourers, workforce 3 childbirth, delivery, parturition ♦ verb 4 work, endeavour, slave, strive, struggle, sweat (informal), toil 5 usually with under be disadvantaged, be a victim of, be burdened by, suffer 6 overemphasize, dwell on, elaborate, overdo, strain

laboured adjective forced, awkward, difficult, heavy, stiff, strained

labourer noun worker, blue-collar worker, drudge, hand, manual worker, navvy (Brit. informal)

labyrinth noun maze, intricacy, jungle, tangle

lace noun 1 netting, filigree, openwork 2 cord, bootlace, shoelace, string, tie ♦ verb 3 fasten, bind, do up, thread, tie 4 mix in, add to, fortify, spike

lacerate verb tear, claw, cut, gash, mangle, rip, slash, wound

laceration noun cut, gash, rent, rip, slash, tear, wound

lack noun 1 shortage, absence, dearth, deficiency, need, scarcity, want ♦ verb 2 need, be deficient in, be short of, be without, miss, require, want

lackadaisical adjective 1 lethargic, apathetic, dull, half-hearted, indifferent, languid, listless 2 lazy, abstracted, dreamy, idle, indolent, inert

lackey noun 1 hanger-on, flatterer, minion, sycophant, toady, yes man 2 manservant, attendant, flunky, footman, valet

lacklustre adjective flat, drab,

dull, leaden, lifeless, muted, prosaic, uninspired, vapid

laconic adjective terse, brief, concise, curt, monosyllabic, pithy, short, succinct

lad noun boy, fellow, guy (informal), juvenile, kid (informal), youngster, youth

laden adjective loaded, burdened, charged, encumbered, full, weighed down

lady noun 1 gentlewoman, dame 2 woman, female

lady-killer noun womanizer, Casanova, Don Juan, heartbreaker, ladies' man, libertine, philanderer, rake, roué

ladylike adjective refined, elegant, genteel, modest, polite, proper, respectable, sophisticated, well-bred

lag verb hang back, dawdle, delay, linger, loiter, straggle, tarry, trail

laggard noun straggler, dawdler, idler, loiterer, slowcoach (Brit. informal), sluggard, snail

laid-back adjective relaxed, casual, easy-going, free and easy, unflappable (informal), unhurried

lair noun nest, burrow, den, earth, hole

laissez faire noun nonintervention, free enterprise, free trade

lake noun pond, lagoon, loch (Scot.), lough (Irish), mere, reservoir, tarn

lame adjective 1 disabled, crippled, game, handicapped, hobbling, limping 2 unconvincing, feeble, flimsy, inadequate, pathetic, poor, thin, unsatisfactory, weak

lament verb 1 complain, bemoan, bewail, deplore, grieve, mourn, regret, sorrow, wail, weep ♦ noun 2 complaint, lamentation, moan, wailing 3 dirge, elegy, requiem, threnody

lamentable adjective regrettable, deplorable, distressing, grievous, mournful, tragic, unfortunate, woeful

lampoon noun 1 satire, burlesque, caricature, parody, send-up (Brit. informal), skit, takeoff (informal) ♦ verb 2 ridicule, caricature, make fun of, mock, parody, satirize, send up (Brit. informal), take off (informal)

land noun 1 ground, dry land, earth, terra firma 2 soil, dirt, ground, loam 3 countryside, farmland 4 property, estate, grounds, realty 5 country, district, nation, province, region, territory, tract ♦ verb 6 arrive, alight, come to rest, disembark, dock, touch down 7 end up, turn up, wind up 8 Informal obtain, acquire, gain, get, secure, win

landlord noun 1 innkeeper, host, hotelier 2 owner, freeholder, lessor, proprietor

landmark noun 1 feature, monument 2 milestone, turning point, watershed

landscape noun scenery, countryside, outlook, panorama, prospect, scene, view, vista

landslide noun 1 rockfall, avalanche, landslip ♦ adjective 2 overwhelming, conclusive,

decisive, runaway

lane noun road, alley, footpath, passageway, path, pathway, street, way

language noun 1 speech, communication, discourse, expression, parlance, talk 2 tongue, dialect, patois, vernacular

languid adjective 1 lazy, indifferent, lackadaisical, languorous, listless, unenthusiastic 2 lethargic, dull, heavy, sluggish, torpid

languish verb 1 weaken, decline, droop, fade, fail, faint, flag, wilt, wither 2 often with for pine, desire, hanker, hunger, long, yearn 3 be neglected, be abandoned, rot, suffer, waste away

lank adjective 1 limp, lifeless, straggling 2 thin, emaciated, gaunt, lean, scrawny, skinny, slender, slim, spare

lanky adjective gangling, angular, bony, gaunt, rangy, spare, tall

lap[1] noun circuit, circle, loop, orbit, tour

lap[2] verb 1 ripple, gurgle, plash, purl, splash, swish, wash 2 drink, lick, sip, sup

lapse noun 1 mistake, error, failing, fault, indiscretion, negligence, omission, oversight, slip 2 interval, break, breathing space, gap, intermission, interruption, lull, pause 3 drop, decline, deterioration, fall ♦ verb 4 drop, decline, degenerate, deteriorate, fall, sink, slide, slip 5 end, expire, run out, stop, terminate

lapsed *adjective* out of date, discontinued, ended, expired, finished, invalid, run out

large *adjective* **1** big, considerable, enormous, gigantic, great, huge, immense, massive, monumental, sizable or sizeable, substantial, vast **2 at large: a** free, at liberty, on the loose, on the run, unconfined **b** in general, as a whole, chiefly, generally, in the main, mainly **c** at length, exhaustively, greatly, in full detail

largely *adverb* mainly, as a rule, by and large, chiefly, generally, mostly, predominantly, primarily, principally, to a great extent

large-scale *adjective* wide-ranging, broad, extensive, far-reaching, global, sweeping, vast, wholesale, wide

lark *noun* **1** prank, caper, escapade, fun, game, jape, mischief ♦ *verb* **2 lark about** play, caper, cavort, have fun, make mischief

lash[1] *noun* **1** blow, hit, stripe, stroke, swipe (*informal*) ♦ *verb* **2** whip, beat, birch, flog, scourge, thrash **3** pound, beat, buffet, dash, drum, hammer, smack, strike **4** scold, attack, blast, censure, criticize, put down, slate (*informal, chiefly Brit.*), tear into (*informal*), upbraid

lash[2] *verb* fasten, bind, make fast, secure, strap, tie

lass *noun* girl, damsel, lassie (*informal*), maid, maiden, young woman

last[1] *adjective* **1** hindmost, at the end, rearmost **2** most recent, latest **3** final, closing, concluding, terminal, ultimate ♦ *adverb* **4** in the rear, after, behind, bringing up the rear, in or at the end

last[2] *verb* continue, abide, carry on, endure, keep on, persist, remain, stand up, survive

lasting *adjective* continuing, abiding, durable, enduring, long-standing, long-term, perennial, permanent

latch *noun* **1** fastening, bar, bolt, catch, hasp, hook, lock ♦ *verb* **2** fasten, bar, bolt, make fast, secure

late *adjective* **1** overdue, behind, behindhand, belated, delayed, last-minute, tardy **2** recent, advanced, fresh, modern, new **3** dead, deceased, defunct, departed, former, past ♦ *adverb* **4** belatedly, at the last minute, behindhand, behind time, dilatorily, tardily

lately *adverb* recently, in recent times, just now, latterly, not long ago, of late

lateness *noun* delay, belatedness, tardiness

latent *adjective* hidden, concealed, dormant, invisible, potential, undeveloped, unrealized

later *adverb* afterwards, after, by and by, in a while, in time, later on, subsequently, thereafter

lateral *adjective* sideways, edgeways, flanking

latest *adjective* up-to-date, current, fashionable, modern, most recent, newest, up-to-the-minute

lather *noun* **1** froth, bubbles,

foam, soapsuds, suds **2** *Informal* fluster, dither (*chiefly Brit.*), flap (*informal*), fuss, state (*informal*), sweat, tizzy (*informal*) ♦ *verb* **3** froth, foam, soap

latitude *noun* scope, elbowroom, freedom, laxity, leeway, liberty, licence, play

latter *adjective* last-mentioned, closing, concluding, last, second

latterly *adverb* recently, lately, of late

lattice *noun* grid, grating, grille, trellis

laudable *adjective* praiseworthy, admirable, commendable, creditable, excellent, meritorious, of note, worthy

laugh *verb* **1** chuckle, be in stitches, chortle, giggle, guffaw, snigger, split one's sides, titter ♦ *noun* **2** chuckle, chortle, giggle, guffaw, snigger, titter **3** *Informal* clown, card (*informal*), entertainer, hoot (*informal*), scream (*informal*) **4** *Informal* joke, hoot (*informal*), lark, scream (*informal*)

laughable *adjective* ridiculous, absurd, derisory, farcical, ludicrous, nonsensical, preposterous, risible

laughing stock *noun* figure of fun, Aunt Sally (*Brit.*), butt, target, victim

laugh off *verb* disregard, brush aside, dismiss, ignore, minimize, pooh-pooh, shrug off

laughter *noun* amusement, glee, hilarity, merriment, mirth

launch *verb* **1** propel, discharge, dispatch, fire, project, send off, set in motion **2** begin,

commence, embark upon, inaugurate, initiate, instigate, introduce, open, start

laurels *plural noun* glory, credit, distinction, fame, honour, praise, prestige, recognition, renown

lavatory *noun* toilet, bathroom, cloakroom (*Brit.*), latrine, loo (*Brit. informal*), powder room, (public) convenience, washroom, water closet, W.C.

lavish *adjective* **1** plentiful, abundant, copious, profuse, prolific **2** generous, bountiful, free, liberal, munificent, open-handed, unstinting **3** extravagant, exaggerated, excessive, immoderate, prodigal, unrestrained, wasteful, wild ♦ *verb* **4** spend, deluge, dissipate, expend, heap, pour, shower, squander, waste

law *noun* **1** constitution, charter, code **2** rule, act, command, commandment, decree, edict, order, ordinance, regulation, statute **3** principle, axiom, canon, precept

law-abiding *adjective* obedient, compliant, dutiful, good, honest, honourable, lawful, orderly, peaceable

law-breaker *noun* criminal, convict, crook (*informal*), culprit, delinquent, felon, miscreant, offender, villain, wrongdoer

lawful *adjective* legal, authorized, constitutional, legalized, legitimate, licit, permissible, rightful, valid, warranted

lawless *adjective* disorderly, anarchic, chaotic, rebellious, riotous, unruly, wild

lawlessness *noun* anarchy,

chaos, disorder, mob rule

lawsuit noun <u>case</u>, action, dispute, industrial tribunal, litigation, proceedings, prosecution, suit, trial

lawyer noun <u>legal adviser</u>, advocate, attorney, barrister, counsel, counsellor, solicitor

lax adjective <u>slack</u>, careless, casual, lenient, negligent, overindulgent, remiss, slapdash, slipshod

lay¹ verb 1 <u>place</u>, deposit, leave, plant, put, set, set down, spread 2 <u>arrange</u>, organize, position, set out 3 <u>produce</u>, bear, deposit 4 <u>put forward</u>, advance, bring forward, lodge, offer, present, submit 5 <u>attribute</u>, allocate, allot, ascribe, assign, impute 6 <u>devise</u>, concoct, contrive, design, hatch, plan, plot, prepare, work out 7 <u>bet</u>, gamble, give odds, hazard, risk, stake, wager

lay² adjective 1 <u>nonclerical</u>, secular 2 <u>nonspecialist</u>, amateur, inexpert, nonprofessional

layabout noun <u>idler</u>, couch potato (slang), good-for-nothing, loafer, lounger, ne'er-do-well, skiver (Brit. slang), wastrel

layer noun <u>tier</u>, row, seam, stratum, thickness

layman noun <u>amateur</u>, lay person, nonprofessional, outsider

lay-off noun <u>dismissal</u>, discharge, unemployment

lay off verb <u>dismiss</u>, discharge, let go, make redundant, pay off

lay on verb <u>provide</u>, cater (for), furnish, give, purvey, supply

layout noun <u>arrangement</u>, design, formation, outline, plan

lay out verb 1 <u>arrange</u>, design, display, exhibit, plan, spread out 2 Informal <u>spend</u>, disburse, expend, fork out (slang), invest, pay, shell out (informal) 3 Informal <u>knock out</u>, knock for six (informal), knock unconscious, KO or K.O. (slang)

laziness noun <u>idleness</u>, inactivity, indolence, slackness, sloth, sluggishness

lazy adjective 1 <u>idle</u>, inactive, indolent, inert, slack, slothful, slow, workshy 2 <u>lethargic</u>, drowsy, languid, languorous, sleepy, slow-moving, sluggish, somnolent, torpid

leach verb <u>extract</u>, drain, filter, percolate, seep, strain

lead verb 1 <u>guide</u>, conduct, escort, pilot, precede, show the way, steer, usher 2 <u>persuade</u>, cause, dispose, draw, incline, induce, influence, prevail, prompt 3 <u>command</u>, direct, govern, head, manage, preside over, supervise 4 <u>be ahead (of)</u>, blaze a trail, come first, exceed, excel, outdo, outstrip, surpass, transcend 5 <u>live</u>, experience, have, pass, spend, undergo 6 <u>result in</u>, bring on, cause, contribute, produce ♦ noun 7 <u>first place</u>, precedence, primacy, priority, supremacy, vanguard 8 <u>advantage</u>, edge, margin, start 9 <u>example</u>, direction, guidance, leadership, model 10 <u>clue</u>, hint, indication, suggestion 11 <u>leading role</u>, principal, protagonist, title role ♦ adjective 12 <u>main</u>, chief, first, foremost, head, leading, premier, primary, prime, principal

leader noun <u>principal</u>, boss (informal), captain, chief, chieftain, commander, director, guide, head, ringleader, ruler

leadership noun 1 <u>guidance</u>, direction, domination, management, running, superintendency 2 <u>authority</u>, command, control, influence, initiative, pre-eminence, supremacy

leading adjective <u>main</u>, chief, dominant, first, foremost, greatest, highest, primary, principal

lead on verb <u>entice</u>, beguile, deceive, draw on, lure, seduce, string along (informal), tempt

lead up to verb <u>introduce</u>, pave the way, prepare for

leaf noun 1 <u>frond</u>, blade 2 <u>page</u>, folio, sheet ♦ verb 3 **leaf through** <u>browse</u>, flip, glance, riffle, skim, thumb (through)

leaflet noun <u>booklet</u>, brochure, circular, pamphlet

leafy adjective <u>green</u>, bosky (literary), shaded, shady, verdant

league noun 1 <u>association</u>, alliance, coalition, confederation, consortium, federation, fraternity, group, guild, partnership, union 2 <u>class</u>, category, level

leak noun 1 <u>hole</u>, aperture, chink, crack, crevice, fissure, opening, puncture 2 <u>drip</u>, leakage, percolation, seepage 3 <u>disclosure</u>, divulgence ♦ verb 4 <u>drip</u>, escape, exude, ooze, pass, percolate, seep, spill, trickle 5 <u>disclose</u>, divulge, give away,

let slip, make known, make public, pass on, reveal, tell

leaky adjective <u>punctured</u>, cracked, holey, leaking, perforated, porous, split

lean[1] verb 1 <u>rest</u>, be supported, prop, recline, repose 2 <u>bend</u>, heel, incline, slant, slope, tilt, tip 3 <u>tend</u>, be disposed to, be prone to, favour, prefer 4 **lean on** <u>depend on</u>, count on, have faith in, rely on, trust

lean[2] adjective 1 <u>slim</u>, angular, bony, gaunt, rangy, skinny, slender, spare, thin, wiry 2 <u>unproductive</u>, barren, meagre, poor, scanty, unfruitful

leaning noun <u>tendency</u>, bent, bias, disposition, inclination, partiality, penchant, predilection, proclivity, propensity

leap verb 1 <u>jump</u>, bounce, bound, hop, skip, spring ♦ noun 2 <u>jump</u>, bound, spring, vault 3 <u>increase</u>, escalation, rise, surge, upsurge, upswing

learn verb 1 <u>master</u>, grasp, pick up 2 <u>memorize</u>, commit to memory, get off pat, learn by heart 3 <u>discover</u>, ascertain, detect, discern, find out, gather, hear, understand

learned adjective <u>scholarly</u>, academic, erudite, highbrow, intellectual, versed, well-informed, well-read

learner noun <u>beginner</u>, apprentice, neophyte, novice, tyro

learning noun <u>knowledge</u>, culture, education, erudition, information, lore, scholarship, study, wisdom

lease verb hire, charter, let, loan, rent

leash noun lead, rein, tether

least adjective smallest, fewest, lowest, meanest, minimum, poorest, slightest, tiniest

leathery adjective tough, hard, rough

leave¹ verb 1 depart, decamp, disappear, exit, go away, make tracks, move, pull out, quit, retire, slope off, withdraw 2 forget, leave behind, mislay 3 cause, deposit, generate, produce, result in 4 give up, abandon, drop, relinquish, renounce, surrender 5 entrust, allot, assign, cede, commit, consign, give over, refer 6 bequeath, hand down, will

leave² noun 1 permission, allowance, authorization, concession, consent, dispensation, freedom, liberty, sanction 2 holiday, furlough, leave of absence, sabbatical, time off, vacation 3 parting, adieu, departure, farewell, goodbye, leave-taking, retirement, withdrawal

leave out verb omit, cast aside, disregard, exclude, ignore, neglect, overlook, reject

lecherous adjective lustful, lascivious, lewd, libidinous, licentious, prurient, randy (informal, chiefly Brit.), salacious

lecture noun 1 talk, address, discourse, instruction, lesson, speech 2 rebuke, dressing-down (informal), reprimand, reproof, scolding, talking-to (informal), telling off (informal) ♦ verb 1 talk, address, discourse, expound, hold forth, speak, spout, teach 4 scold, admonish, berate, castigate, censure, reprimand, reprove, tell off (informal)

ledge noun shelf, mantle, projection, ridge, sill, step

leer noun, verb grin, gloat, goggle, ogle, smirk, squint, stare

lees plural noun sediment, deposit, dregs, grounds

leeway noun room, elbowroom, latitude, margin, play, scope, space

left adjective 1 left-hand, larboard (Nautical), port, sinistral 2 Of politics socialist, leftist, left-wing, radical

leftover noun remnant, oddment, scrap

left-wing adjective socialist, communist, radical, red (informal)

leg noun 1 limb, lower limb, member, pin (informal), stump (informal) 2 support, brace, prop, upright 3 stage, lap, part, portion, section, segment, stretch 4 pull someone's leg Informal tease, fool, kid (informal), make fun of, trick, wind up (Brit. slang)

legacy noun bequest, estate, gift, heirloom, inheritance

legal adjective 1 legitimate, allowed, authorized, constitutional, lawful, licit, permissible, sanctioned, valid 2 judicial, forensic, juridical

legality noun legitimacy, lawfulness, rightfulness, validity

legalize verb allow, approve, authorize, decriminalize, legitimate, legitimize, license, permit, sanction, validate

legation noun delegation, consulate, embassy, representation

legend noun 1 myth, fable, fiction, folk tale, saga, story, tale 2 celebrity, luminary, megastar (informal), phenomenon, prodigy 3 inscription, caption, motto

legendary adjective 1 mythical, apocryphal, fabled, fabulous, fictitious, romantic, traditional 2 famous, celebrated, famed, illustrious, immortal, renowned, well-known

legibility noun clarity, neatness, readability

legible adjective clear, decipherable, distinct, easy to read, neat, readable

legion noun 1 army, brigade, company, division, force, troop 2 multitude, drove, horde, host, mass, myriad, number, throng

legislation noun 1 lawmaking, enactment, prescription, regulation 2 law, act, bill, charter, measure, regulation, ruling, statute

legislative adjective law-making, judicial, law-giving

legislator noun lawmaker, lawgiver

legislature noun parliament, assembly, chamber, congress, senate

legitimate adjective 1 legal, authentic, authorized, genuine, kosher (informal), lawful, licit, rightful 2 reasonable, admissible, correct, justifiable, logical, sensible, valid, warranted, well-founded ♦ verb 3 authorize, legalize, legitimize, permit,

pronounce lawful, sanction

legitimize verb legalize, authorize, permit, sanction

leisure noun spare time, ease, freedom, free time, liberty, recreation, relaxation, rest

leisurely adjective unhurried, comfortable, easy, gentle, lazy, relaxed, slow

lend verb 1 loan, advance 2 add, bestow, confer, give, grant, impart, provide, supply 3 **lend itself to** suit, be appropriate, be serviceable

length noun 1 Of linear extent distance, extent, longitude, measure, reach, span 2 Of time duration, period, space, span, stretch, term 3 piece, measure, portion, section, segment 4 **at length: a** in detail, completely, fully, in depth, thoroughly, to the full **b** for a long time, for ages, for hours, interminably **c** at last, at long last, eventually, finally, in the end

lengthen verb extend, continue, draw out, elongate, expand, increase, prolong, protract, spin out, stretch

lengthy adjective long, drawn-out, extended, interminable, long-drawn-out, long-winded, prolonged, protracted, tedious

leniency noun tolerance, clemency, compassion, forbearance, indulgence, mercy, moderation, pity, quarter

lenient adjective tolerant, compassionate, forbearing, forgiving, indulgent, kind, merciful, sparing

lesbian adjective homosexual, gay, sapphic

less adjective 1 smaller, shorter ♦ preposition 2 minus, excepting, lacking, subtracting, without

lessen verb reduce, contract, decrease, diminish, ease, lower, minimize, narrow, shrink

lesser adjective minor, inferior, less important, lower, secondary

lesson noun 1 class, coaching, instruction, period, schooling, teaching, tutoring 2 example, deterrent, message, moral

let¹ verb 1 allow, authorize, entitle, give permission, give the go-ahead, permit, sanction, tolerate 2 lease, hire, rent

let² noun hindrance, constraint, impediment, interference, obstacle, obstruction, prohibition, restriction

letdown noun disappointment, anticlimax, blow, comedown (informal), setback, washout (informal)

let down verb disappoint, disenchant, disillusion, dissatisfy, fail, fall short, leave in the lurch, leave stranded

lethal adjective deadly, dangerous, destructive, devastating, fatal, mortal, murderous, virulent

lethargic adjective sluggish, apathetic, drowsy, dull, languid, listless, sleepy, slothful

lethargy noun sluggishness, apathy, drowsiness, inertia, languor, lassitude, listlessness, sleepiness, sloth

let off verb 1 fire, detonate, discharge, explode 2 emit,

exude, give off, leak, release 3 excuse, absolve, discharge, exempt, exonerate, forgive, pardon, release, spare

let on verb reveal, admit, disclose, divulge, give away, let the cat out of the bag (informal), make known, say

let out verb 1 emit, give vent to, produce 2 release, discharge, free, let go, liberate

letter noun 1 character, sign, symbol 2 message, communication, dispatch, epistle, line, missive, note

let-up noun lessening, break, breathing space, interval, lull, pause, remission, respite, slackening

let up verb stop, abate, decrease, diminish, ease (up), moderate, relax, slacken, subside

level adjective 1 horizontal, flat 2 even, consistent, plain, smooth, uniform 3 equal, balanced, commensurate, comparable, equivalent, even, neck and neck, on a par, proportionate ♦ verb 4 flatten, even off or out, plane, smooth 5 equalize, balance, even up 6 raze, bulldoze, demolish, destroy, devastate, flatten, knock down, pull down, tear down 7 direct, aim, focus, point, train ♦ noun 8 position, achievement, degree, grade, rank, stage, standard, standing, status 9 **on the level** Informal honest, above board, fair, genuine, square, straight

level-headed adjective steady, balanced, calm, collected, composed, cool, sensible, unflappable (*informal*)

lever noun 1 handle, bar ♦ verb 2 prise, force

leverage noun influence, authority, clout (*informal*), pull (*informal*), weight

levity noun light-heartedness, facetiousness, flippancy, frivolity, silliness, skittishness, triviality

levy verb 1 impose, charge, collect, demand, exact 2 conscript, call up, mobilize, muster, raise ♦ noun 3 imposition, assessment, collection, exaction, gathering 4 tax, duty, excise, fee, tariff, toll

lewd adjective indecent, bawdy, lascivious, libidinous, licentious, lustful, obscene, pornographic, smutty, wanton

lewdness noun indecency, bawdiness, carnality, debauchery, depravity, lasciviousness, lechery, licentiousness, obscenity, pornography, wantonness

liability noun 1 responsibility, accountability, answerability, culpability 2 debt, debit, obligation 3 disadvantage, burden, drawback, encumbrance, handicap, hindrance, inconvenience, millstone, nuisance

liable adjective 1 responsible, accountable, answerable, obligated 2 vulnerable, exposed, open, subject, susceptible 3 likely, apt, disposed, inclined, prone, tending

liaise verb link, communicate, keep contact, mediate

liaison noun 1 communication,

connection, contact, hook-up, interchange 2 affair, amour, entanglement, intrigue, love affair, romance

liar noun falsifier, fabricator, fibber, perjurer

libel noun 1 defamation, aspersion, calumny, denigration, smear ♦ verb 2 defame, blacken, malign, revile, slur, smear, vilify

libellous adjective defamatory, derogatory, false, injurious, malicious, scurrilous, untrue

liberal adjective 1 progressive, libertarian, radical, reformist 2 generous, beneficent, bountiful, charitable, kind, open-handed, open-hearted, unstinting 3 tolerant, broad-minded, indulgent, permissive 4 abundant, ample, bountiful, copious, handsome, lavish, munificent, plentiful, profuse, rich

liberality noun 1 generosity, beneficence, benevolence, bounty, charity, kindness, largesse or largess, munificence, philanthropy 2 toleration, broad-mindedness, latitude, liberalism, libertarianism, permissiveness

liberalize verb relax, ease, loosen, moderate, modify, slacken, soften

liberate verb free, deliver, emancipate, let loose, let out, release, rescue, set free

liberation noun deliverance, emancipation, freedom, freeing, liberty, release

liberator noun deliverer, emancipator, freer, redeemer, rescuer, saviour

libertine noun reprobate, debauchee, lecher, profligate, rake, roué, sensualist, voluptuary, womanizer

liberty noun 1 freedom, autonomy, emancipation, immunity, independence, liberation, release, self-determination, sovereignty 2 impertinence, impropriety, impudence, insolence, presumption 3 **at liberty** free, on the loose, unrestricted

libidinous adjective lustful, carnal, debauched, lascivious, lecherous, randy (informal, chiefly Brit.), sensual, wanton

licence noun 1 certificate, charter, permit, warrant 2 permission, authority, authorization, blank cheque, carte blanche, dispensation, entitlement, exemption, immunity, leave, liberty, right 3 latitude, freedom, independence, leeway, liberty 4 laxity, excess, immoderation, indulgence, irresponsibility

license verb permit, accredit, allow, authorize, certify, empower, sanction, warrant

licentious adjective promiscuous, abandoned, debauched, dissolute, immoral, lascivious, lustful, sensual, wanton

lick verb 1 taste, lap, tongue 2 Of flames flicker, dart, flick, play over, ripple, touch 3 Slang beat, defeat, master, outdo, outstrip, overcome, rout, trounce, vanquish ◆ noun 4 dab, bit, stroke, touch 5 Informal pace, clip (informal), rate, speed

lie¹ verb 1 falsify, dissimulate, equivocate, fabricate, fib, prevaricate, tell untruths ◆ noun 2 falsehood, deceit, fabrication, fib, fiction, invention, prevarication, untruth

lie² verb 1 recline, loll, lounge, repose, rest, sprawl, stretch out 2 be situated, be, be placed, exist, remain

life noun 1 being, sentience, vitality 2 existence, being, lifetime, span, time 3 biography, autobiography, confessions, history, life story, memoirs, story 4 behaviour, conduct, life style, way of life 5 liveliness, animation, energy, high spirits, spirit, verve, vigour, vitality, vivacity, zest

lifeless adjective 1 dead, deceased, defunct, extinct, inanimate 2 dull, colourless, flat, lacklustre, lethargic, listless, sluggish, wooden 3 unconscious, comatose, dead to the world (informal), insensible

lifelike adjective realistic, authentic, exact, faithful, natural, true-to-life, vivid

lifelong adjective long-standing, enduring, lasting, long-lasting, perennial, persistent

lifetime noun existence, career, day(s), span, time

lift verb 1 raise, draw up, elevate, hoist, pick up, uplift, upraise 2 revoke, annul, cancel, countermand, end, remove, rescind, stop, terminate 3 disappear, be dispelled, disperse, dissipate, vanish ◆ noun 4 boost, drive, run 5 boost, encouragement, fillip, pick-me-up, shot in the arm (*informal*) **6** elevator (chiefly U.S.)

light¹ *noun* **1** brightness, brilliance, glare, gleam, glint, glow, illumination, luminosity, radiance, shine **2** lamp, beacon, candle, flare, lantern, taper, torch **3** aspect, angle, context, interpretation, point of view, slant, vantage point, viewpoint **4** match, flame, lighter ◆ *adjective* **5** bright, brilliant, illuminated, luminous, lustrous, shining, well-lit **6** pale, bleached, blond, faded, fair, pastel ◆ *verb* **7** ignite, inflame, kindle **8** illuminate, brighten, light up

light² *adjective* **1** insubstantial, airy, buoyant, flimsy, portable, slight, underweight **2** weak, faint, gentle, indistinct, mild, moderate, slight, soft **3** insignificant, inconsequential, inconsiderable, scanty, slight, small, trifling, trivial **4** nimble, agile, graceful, lithe, sprightly, sylphlike **5** light-hearted, amusing, entertaining, frivolous, funny, humorous, witty **6** digestible, frugal, modest ◆ *verb* **7** settle, alight, land, perch **8** light on or upon come across, chance upon, discover, encounter, find, happen upon, hit upon, stumble on

lighten¹ *verb* brighten, become light, illuminate, irradiate, light up

lighten² *verb* **1** ease, allay, alleviate, ameliorate, assuage, lessen, mitigate, reduce, relieve **2** cheer, brighten, buoy up, lift, perk up, revive

light-headed *adjective* faint, dizzy, giddy, hazy, vertiginous,

woozy (*informal*)

light-hearted *adjective* carefree, blithe, cheerful, happy-go-lucky, jolly, jovial, playful, upbeat (*informal*)

lightly *adverb* **1** gently, delicately, faintly, slightly, softly **2** moderately, sparingly, sparsely, thinly **3** easily, effortlessly, readily, simply **4** carelessly, breezily, flippantly, frivolously, heedlessly, thoughtlessly

lightweight *adjective* unimportant, inconsequential, insignificant, paltry, petty, slight, trifling, trivial, worthless

likable, likeable *adjective* attractive, agreeable, amiable, appealing, charming, engaging, nice, pleasant, sympathetic

like¹ *adjective* similar, akin, alike, analogous, corresponding, equivalent, identical, parallel, same

like² *verb* **1** enjoy, be fond of, be keen on, be partial to, delight in, go for, love, relish, revel in **2** admire, appreciate, approve, cherish, esteem, hold dear, prize, take to **3** wish, care to, choose, desire, fancy, feel inclined, prefer, want

likelihood *noun* probability, chance, possibility, prospect

likely *adjective* **1** inclined, apt, disposed, liable, prone, tending **2** probable, anticipated, expected, odds-on, on the cards, to be expected **3** plausible, believable, credible, feasible, possible, reasonable **4** promising, hopeful, up-and-coming

liken verb compare, equate, match, parallel, relate, set beside

likeness noun 1 resemblance, affinity, correspondence, similarity 2 portrait, depiction, effigy, image, picture, representation

likewise adverb similarly, in like manner, in the same way

liking noun fondness, affection, inclination, love, partiality, penchant, preference, soft spot, taste, weakness

limb noun 1 part, appendage, arm, extremity, leg, member, wing 2 branch, bough, offshoot, projection, spur

limelight noun publicity, attention, celebrity, fame, prominence, public eye, recognition, stardom, the spotlight

limit noun 1 breaking point, deadline, end, ultimate 2 boundary, border, edge, frontier, perimeter ♦ verb 3 restrict, bound, check, circumscribe, confine, curb, ration, restrain

limitation noun restriction, check, condition, constraint, control, curb, qualification, reservation, restraint

limited adjective restricted, bounded, checked, circumscribed, confined, constrained, controlled, curbed, finite

limitless adjective infinite, boundless, countless, endless, inexhaustible, unbounded, unlimited, untold, vast

limp¹ verb 1 hobble, falter, hop, shamble, shuffle ♦ noun 2 lameness, hobble

limp² adjective floppy, drooping, flabby, flaccid, pliable, slack, soft

line noun 1 stroke, band, groove, mark, score, scratch, streak, stripe 2 wrinkle, crease, crow's foot, furrow, mark 3 boundary, border, borderline, edge, frontier, limit 4 string, cable, cord, rope, thread, wire 5 trajectory, course, direction, path, route, track 6 job, area, business, calling, employment, field, occupation, profession, specialization, trade 7 row, column, file, procession, queue, rank 8 in line for due for, in the running for ♦ verb 9 mark, crease, furrow, rule, score 10 border, bound, edge, fringe

lineaments plural noun features, countenance, face, physiognomy

lined adjective 1 ruled, feint 2 wrinkled, furrowed, wizened, worn

lines plural noun words, part, script

line-up noun arrangement, array, row, selection, team

linger verb 1 stay, hang around, loiter, remain, stop, tarry, wait 2 delay, dally, dawdle, drag one's feet or heels, idle, take one's time

link noun 1 component, constituent, element, member, part, piece 2 connection, affinity, association, attachment, bond, relationship, tie-up ♦ verb 3 fasten, attach, bind, connect, couple, join, tie, unite 4 associate, bracket, connect, identify, relate

lip noun 1 edge, brim, brink, margin, rim 2 *Slang* impudence, backchat (*informal*), cheek (*informal*), effrontery, impertinence, insolence

liquid noun 1 fluid, juice, solution ♦ *adjective* 2 fluid, aqueous, flowing, melted, molten, running, runny 3 *Of assets* convertible, negotiable

liquidate verb 1 pay, clear, discharge, honour, pay off, settle, square 2 dissolve, abolish, annul, cancel, terminate 3 kill, destroy, dispatch, eliminate, exterminate, get rid of, murder, wipe out (*informal*)

liquor noun 1 alcohol, booze (*informal*), drink, hard stuff (*informal*), spirits, strong drink 2 juice, broth, extract, liquid, stock

list[1] noun 1 register, catalogue, directory, index, inventory, record, roll, series, tally ♦ verb 2 tabulate, catalogue, enter, enumerate, itemize, record, register

list[2] verb 1 lean, careen, heel over, incline, tilt, tip ♦ noun 2 tilt, cant, leaning, slant

listen verb 1 hear, attend, lend an ear, prick up one's ears 2 pay attention, heed, mind, obey, observe, take notice

listless adjective languid, apathetic, indifferent, indolent, lethargic, sluggish

literacy noun education, knowledge, learning

literal adjective 1 exact, accurate, close, faithful, strict, verbatim, word for word 2 actual, bona fide, genuine, plain, real, simple, true, unvarnished

literally adverb strictly, actually, exactly, faithfully, precisely, really, to the letter, truly, verbatim, word for word

literary adjective well-read, bookish, erudite, formal, learned, scholarly

literate adjective educated, informed, knowledgeable

literature noun writings, letters, lore

lithe adjective supple, flexible, limber, lissom(e), loose-limbed, pliable

litigant noun claimant, party, plaintiff

litigate verb sue, go to court, press charges, prosecute

litigation noun lawsuit, action, case, prosecution

litter noun 1 rubbish, debris, detritus, garbage (*chiefly U.S.*), muck, refuse, trash 2 brood, offspring, progeny, young ♦ verb 3 clutter, derange, disarrange, disorder, mess up 4 scatter, strew

little adjective 1 small, diminutive, miniature, minute, petite, short, tiny, wee 2 young, babyish, immature, infant, junior, undeveloped ♦ adverb 3 hardly, barely 4 rarely, hardly ever, not often, scarcely, seldom ♦ noun 5 bit, fragment, hint, particle, speck, spot, touch, trace

live[1] verb 1 exist, be, be alive, breathe 2 persist, last, prevail 3 dwell, abide, inhabit, lodge, occupy, reside, settle 4 survive, endure, get along, make ends meet, subsist, support oneself 5 thrive, flourish, prosper

live² *adjective* **1** living, alive, animate, breathing **2** topical, burning, controversial, current, hot, pertinent, pressing, prevalent **3** burning, active, alight, blazing, glowing, hot, ignited, smouldering

livelihood *noun* occupation, bread and butter (*informal*), employment, job, living, work

liveliness *noun* energy, animation, boisterousness, dynamism, spirit, sprightliness, vitality, vivacity

lively *adjective* **1** vigorous, active, agile, alert, brisk, energetic, keen, perky, quick, sprightly **2** animated, cheerful, chirpy (*informal*), sparky, spirited, upbeat (*informal*), vivacious **3** vivid, bright, colourful, exciting, forceful, invigorating, refreshing, stimulating

liven up *verb* stir, animate, brighten, buck up (*informal*), enliven, perk up, rouse

liverish *adjective* **1** sick, bilious, queasy **2** irritable, crotchety (*informal*), crusty, disagreeable, grumpy, ill-humoured, irascible, splenetic, tetchy

livery *noun* costume, attire, clothing, dress, garb, regalia, suit, uniform

livid *adjective* **1** *Informal* angry, beside oneself, enraged, fuming, furious, incensed, indignant, infuriated, outraged **2** discoloured, black-and-blue, bruised, contused, purple

living *adjective* **1** alive, active, breathing, existing **2** current, active, contemporary, extant, in use ♦ *noun* **3** existence, being,

existing, life, subsistence **4** life style, way of life

load *noun* **1** cargo, consignment, freight, shipment **2** burden, albatross, encumbrance, millstone, onus, trouble, weight, worry ♦ *verb* **3** fill, cram, freight, heap, pack, pile, stack, stuff **4** burden, encumber, oppress, saddle with, weigh down, worry **5** *Of firearms* make ready, charge, prime

loaded *adjective* **1** weighted, biased, distorted **2** tricky, artful, insidious, manipulative, prejudicial **3** *Slang* rich, affluent, flush (*informal*), moneyed, wealthy, well-heeled (*informal*), well off, well-to-do

loaf¹ *noun* **1** lump, block, cake, cube, slab **2** *Slang* head, gumption (*Brit. informal*), nous (*Brit. slang*), sense

loaf² *verb* idle, laze, lie around, loiter, lounge around, take it easy

loan *noun* **1** advance, credit ♦ *verb* **2** lend, advance, let out

loath, loth *adjective* unwilling, averse, disinclined, opposed, reluctant

loathe *verb* hate, abhor, abominate, despise, detest, dislike

loathing *noun* hatred, abhorrence, antipathy, aversion, detestation, disgust, repugnance, repulsion, revulsion

loathsome *adjective* hateful, abhorrent, detestable, disgusting, nauseating, obnoxious, odious, offensive, repugnant, repulsive, revolting, vile

lobby *noun* **1** corridor, entrance

hall, foyer, hallway, passage, porch, vestibule **2** <u>pressure</u> <u>group</u> ♦ *verb* **3** <u>campaign</u>, influence, persuade, press, pressure, promote, push, urge

local *adjective* **1** <u>regional</u>, provincial **2** <u>restricted</u> (*chiefly U.S.*), confined, limited ♦ *noun* **3** <u>resident</u>, inhabitant, native

locality *noun* **1** <u>neighbourhood</u>, area, district, neck of the woods (*informal*), region, vicinity **2** <u>site</u>, locale, location, place, position, scene, setting, spot

localize *verb* <u>restrict</u>, circumscribe, confine, contain, delimit, limit

locate *verb* **1** <u>find</u>, come across, detect, discover, pin down, pinpoint, track down, unearth **2** <u>place</u>, establish, fix, put, seat, set, settle, situate

location *noun* <u>position</u>, locale, place, point, site, situation, spot, venue

lock[1] *noun* **1** <u>fastening</u>, bolt, clasp, padlock ♦ *verb* **2** <u>fasten</u>, bolt, close, seal, secure, shut **3** <u>unite</u>, clench, engage, entangle, entwine, join, link **4** <u>embrace</u>, clasp, clutch, encircle, enclose, grasp, hug, press

lock[2] *noun* <u>strand</u>, curl, ringlet, tress, tuft

lockup *noun* <u>prison</u>, cell, jail or gaol

lock up *verb* <u>imprison</u>, cage, confine, detain, incarcerate, jail, put behind bars, shut up

lodge *noun* **1** <u>cabin</u>, chalet, cottage, gatehouse, hut, shelter **2** <u>society</u>, branch, chapter, club,

group ♦ *verb* **3** <u>stay</u>, board, room **4** <u>stick</u>, come to rest, imbed, implant **5** <u>register</u>, file, put on record, submit

lodger *noun* <u>tenant</u>, boarder, paying guest, resident

lodging *noun, often plural* <u>accommodation</u>, abode, apartments, digs (*Brit. informal*), quarters, residence, rooms, shelter

lofty *adjective* **1** <u>high</u>, elevated, raised, soaring, towering **2** <u>noble</u>, dignified, distinguished, elevated, exalted, grand, illustrious, renowned **3** <u>haughty</u>, arrogant, condescending, disdainful, patronizing, proud, supercilious

log *noun* **1** <u>stump</u>, block, chunk, trunk **2** <u>record</u>, account, journal, logbook ♦ *verb* **3** <u>chop</u>, cut, fell, hew **4** <u>record</u>, chart, note, register, set down

loggerheads *plural noun* **at loggerheads** <u>quarrelling</u>, at daggers drawn, at each other's throats, at odds, feuding, in dispute, opposed

logic *noun* <u>reason</u>, good sense, sense

logical *adjective* **1** <u>rational</u>, clear, cogent, coherent, consistent, sound, valid, well-organized **2** <u>reasonable</u>, plausible, sensible, wise

loiter *verb* <u>linger</u>, dally, dawdle, dilly-dally (*informal*), hang about or around, idle, loaf, skulk

loll *verb* **1** <u>lounge</u>, loaf, recline, relax, slouch, slump, sprawl **2** <u>droop</u>, dangle, drop, flap, flop, hang, sag

lone adjective solitary, one, only, single, sole, unaccompanied

loneliness noun solitude, desolation, isolation, seclusion

lonely adjective **1** abandoned, destitute, forlorn, forsaken, friendless, lonesome **2** solitary, alone, apart, companionless, isolated, lone, single, withdrawn **3** remote, deserted, desolate, godforsaken, isolated, out-of-the-way, secluded, unfrequented, uninhabited

loner noun individualist, lone wolf, maverick, outsider, recluse

lonesome adjective lonely, companionless, desolate, dreary, forlorn, friendless, gloomy

long[1] adjective **1** elongated, expanded, extended, extensive, far-reaching, lengthy, spread out, stretched **2** prolonged, interminable, lengthy, lingering, long-drawn-out, protracted, sustained

long[2] verb desire, crave, hanker, itch, lust, pine, want, wish, yearn

longing noun desire, ambition, aspiration, craving, hope, itch, thirst, urge, wish, yearning, yen (informal)

long-lived adjective long-lasting, enduring

long shot noun outsider, dark horse

long-standing adjective established, abiding, enduring, fixed, long-established, long-lasting, time-honoured

long-suffering adjective uncomplaining, easy-going, forbearing, forgiving, patient, resigned, stoical, tolerant

long-winded adjective rambling, lengthy, long-drawn-out, prolix, prolonged, repetitious, tedious, tiresome, verbose, wordy

look verb **1** see, contemplate, examine, eye, gaze, glance, observe, scan, study, survey, view, watch **2** seem, appear, look like, strike one as **3** face, front, overlook **4** hope, anticipate, await, expect, reckon on **5** search, forage, hunt, seek ♦ noun **6** view, examination, gaze, glance, glimpse, inspection, observation, peek, sight **7** appearance, air, aspect, bearing, countenance, demeanour, expression, manner, semblance

look after verb take care of, attend to, care for, guard, keep an eye on, mind, nurse, protect, supervise, take charge of, tend

look down on verb disdain, contemn, despise, scorn, sneer, spurn

look forward to verb anticipate, await, expect, hope for, long for, look for, wait for

lookout noun **1** vigil, guard, readiness, watch **2** watchman, guard, sentinel, sentry **3** watchtower, observation post, observatory, post **4** Informal concern, business, worry

look out verb be careful, beware, keep an eye out, pay attention, watch out

look up verb **1** research, find, hunt for, search for, seek out, track down **2** improve, get better, perk up, pick up, progress, shape up (informal) **3** visit, call on, drop in on (*informal*), look in on **4 look up to** respect, admire, defer to, esteem, honour, revere

loom *verb* appear, bulk, emerge, hover, impend, menace, take shape, threaten

loop *noun* **1** curve, circle, coil, curl, ring, spiral, twirl, twist, whorl ♦ *verb* **2** twist, coil, curl, knot, roll, spiral, turn, wind round

loophole *noun* let-out, escape, excuse

loose *adjective* **1** untied, free, insecure, unattached, unbound, unfastened, unfettered, unrestricted **2** slack, easy, relaxed, sloppy **3** vague, ill-defined, imprecise, inaccurate, indistinct, inexact, rambling, random **4** promiscuous, abandoned, debauched, dissipated, dissolute, fast, immoral, profligate ♦ *verb* **5** free, detach, disconnect, liberate, release, set free, unfasten, unleash, untie

loosen *verb* **1** untie, detach, separate, undo, unloose **2** free, liberate, release, set free **3 loosen up** relax, ease up *or* off, go easy (*informal*), let up, soften

loot *noun* **1** plunder, booty, goods, haul, prize, spoils, swag (*slang*) ♦ *verb* **2** plunder, despoil, pillage, raid, ransack, ravage, rifle, rob, sack

lopsided *adjective* crooked, askew, asymmetrical, awry, cockeyed, disproportionate, skewwhiff (*Brit. informal*), squint, unbalanced, uneven, warped

lord *noun* **1** master, commander,

governor, leader, liege, overlord, ruler, superior **2** nobleman, earl, noble, peer, viscount **3 Our Lord** *or* **the Lord** Jesus Christ, Christ, God, Jehovah, the Almighty ♦ *verb* **4 lord it over** order around, boss around (*informal*), domineer, pull rank, put on airs, swagger

lordly *adjective* proud, arrogant, condescending, disdainful, domineering, haughty, high-handed, imperious, lofty, overbearing

lore *noun* traditions, beliefs, doctrine, sayings, teaching, wisdom

lose *verb* **1** mislay, be deprived of, drop, forget, misplace **2** forfeit, miss, pass up (*informal*), yield **3** be defeated, come to grief, lose out

loser *noun* failure, also-ran, dud (*informal*), flop (*informal*)

loss *noun* **1** defeat, failure, forfeiture, mislaying, squandering, waste **2** damage, cost, destruction, harm, hurt, injury, ruin **3** *sometimes plural* deficit, debit, debt, deficiency, depletion **4 at a loss** confused, at one's wits' end, baffled, bewildered, helpless, nonplussed, perplexed, puzzled, stumped

lost *adjective* **1** missing, disappeared, mislaid, misplaced, vanished, wayward **2** off-course, adrift, astray, at sea, disoriented, off-track

lot *noun* **1** collection, assortment, batch, bunch (*informal*), consignment, crowd, group, quantity, set **2** destiny, accident,

chance, doom, fate, fortune **3 a
lot** *or* **lots** plenty, abundance, a
great deal, heap(s), load(s)
(*informal*), masses (*informal*), piles
(*informal*), scores, stack(s)

loth *see* LOATH

lotion *noun* cream, balm,
embrocation, liniment, salve,
solution

lottery *noun* **1** raffle, draw,
sweepstake **2** gamble, chance,
hazard, risk, toss-up (*informal*)

loud *adjective* **1** noisy, blaring,
booming, clamorous, deafening,
ear-splitting, forte (*Music*),
resounding, thundering,
tumultuous, vociferous **2** garish,
brash, flamboyant, flashy, gaudy,
glaring, lurid, showy

loudly *adverb* noisily, deafeningly,
fortissimo (*Music*), lustily, shrilly,
uproariously, vehemently,
vigorously, vociferously

lounge *verb* relax, laze, lie about,
loaf, loiter, loll, sprawl, take it
easy

lout *noun* oaf, boor, dolt,
lummox (*informal*), yob *or* yobbo
(*Brit. slang*)

lovable, loveable *adjective*
endearing, adorable, amiable,
charming, cute, delightful,
enchanting, likable *or* likeable,
lovely, sweet

love *verb* **1** adore, cherish, dote
on, hold dear, idolize, prize,
treasure, worship **2** enjoy,
appreciate, delight in, like, relish,
savour, take pleasure in ◆ *noun*
3 passion, adoration, affection,
ardour, attachment, devotion,
infatuation, tenderness, warmth
4 liking, devotion, enjoyment,
fondness, inclination, partiality,

relish, soft spot, taste, weakness
5 beloved, darling, dear, dearest,
lover, sweetheart, truelove **6 in
love** enamoured, besotted,
charmed, enraptured, infatuated,
smitten

love affair *noun* romance, affair,
amour, intrigue, liaison,
relationship

lovely *adjective* **1** attractive,
adorable, beautiful, charming,
comely, exquisite, graceful,
handsome, pretty **2** enjoyable,
agreeable, delightful, engaging,
nice, pleasant, pleasing

lover *noun* sweetheart, admirer,
beloved, boyfriend *or* girlfriend,
flame (*informal*), mistress, suitor

loving *adjective* affectionate,
amorous, dear, devoted, doting,
fond, tender, warm-hearted

low *adjective* **1** small, little, short,
squat, stunted **2** inferior,
deficient, inadequate, poor,
second-rate, shoddy **3** coarse,
common, crude, disreputable,
rough, rude, undignified, vulgar
4 dejected, depressed,
despondent, disheartened,
downcast, down in the dumps
(*informal*), fed up, gloomy, glum,
miserable **5** ill, debilitated, frail,
stricken, weak **6** quiet, gentle,
hushed, muffled, muted, soft,
subdued, whispered

lowdown *noun Informal*
information, gen (*Brit. informal*),
info (*informal*), inside story,
intelligence

lower *adjective* **1** minor, inferior,
junior, lesser, secondary,
second-class, smaller,
subordinate **2** reduced, curtailed,
decreased, diminished, lessened

verb **3** drop, depress, fall, let down, sink, submerge, take down **4** lessen, cut, decrease, diminish, minimize, prune, reduce, slash

low-key *adjective* subdued, muted, quiet, restrained, toned down, understated

lowly *adjective* humble, meek, mild, modest, unassuming

low-spirited *adjective* depressed, dejected, despondent, dismal, down, down-hearted, fed up, low, miserable, sad

loyal *adjective* faithful, constant, dependable, devoted, dutiful, staunch, steadfast, true, trustworthy, trusty, unwavering

loyalty *noun* faithfulness, allegiance, constancy, dependability, devotion, fidelity, staunchness, steadfastness, trustworthiness

lubricate *verb* oil, grease, smear

lucid *adjective* **1** clear, comprehensible, explicit, intelligible, transparent **2** translucent, clear, crystalline, diaphanous, glassy, limpid, pellucid, transparent **3** clear-headed, all there, *compos mentis*, in one's right mind, rational, sane

luck *noun* **1** fortune, accident, chance, destiny, fate **2** good fortune, advantage, blessing, godsend, prosperity, serendipity, success, windfall

luckily *adverb* fortunately, favourably, happily, opportunely, propitiously, providentially

luckless *adjective* ill-fated, cursed, doomed, hapless, hopeless,

jinxed, unfortunate, unlucky

lucky *adjective* fortunate, advantageous, blessed, charmed, favoured, jammy (*Brit. slang*), serendipitous, successful

lucrative *adjective* profitable, advantageous, fruitful, productive, remunerative, well-paid

lucre *noun* money, gain, mammon, pelf, profit, riches, spoils, wealth

ludicrous *adjective* ridiculous, absurd, crazy, farcical, laughable, nonsensical, outlandish, preposterous, silly

luggage *noun* baggage, bags, cases, gear, impedimenta, paraphernalia, suitcases, things

lugubrious *adjective* gloomy, doleful, melancholy, mournful, sad, serious, sombre, sorrowful, woebegone

lukewarm *adjective* **1** tepid, warm **2** half-hearted, apathetic, cool, indifferent, unenthusiastic, unresponsive

lull *verb* **1** calm, allay, pacify, quell, soothe, subdue, tranquillize *noun* **2** respite, calm, hush, let-up (*informal*), pause, quiet, silence

lumber[1] *noun* **1** junk, clutter, jumble, refuse, rubbish, trash *verb* **2** *Informal* burden, encumber, land, load, saddle

lumber[2] *verb* plod, shamble, shuffle, stump, trudge, trundle, waddle

lumbering *adjective* awkward, clumsy, heavy, hulking, ponderous, ungainly

luminous *adjective* bright,

glowing, illuminated, luminescent, lustrous, radiant, shining

lump noun **1** piece, ball, chunk, hunk, mass, nugget **2** swelling, bulge, bump, growth, hump, protrusion, tumour ♦ verb **3** group, collect, combine, conglomerate, consolidate, mass, pool

lumpy adjective bumpy, knobbly, uneven

lunacy noun **1** insanity, dementia, derangement, madness, mania, psychosis **2** foolishness, absurdity, craziness, folly, foolhardiness, madness, stupidity

lunatic adjective **1** irrational, crackbrained, crackpot (*informal*), crazy, daft, deranged, insane, mad ♦ noun **2** madman, maniac, nutcase (*slang*), psychopath

lunge noun **1** thrust, charge, jab, pounce, spring, swing ♦ verb **2** pounce, charge, dive, leap, plunge, thrust

lurch verb **1** tilt, heave, heel, lean, list, pitch, rock, roll **2** stagger, reel, stumble, sway, totter, weave

lure verb **1** tempt, allure, attract, draw, ensnare, entice, invite, seduce ♦ noun **2** temptation, allurement, attraction, bait, carrot (*informal*), enticement, incentive, inducement

lurid adjective **1** sensational, graphic, melodramatic, shocking, vivid **2** glaring, intense

lurk verb hide, conceal oneself, lie in wait, prowl, skulk, slink, sneak

luscious adjective delicious,

appetizing, juicy, mouth-watering, palatable, succulent, sweet, toothsome

lush adjective **1** abundant, dense, flourishing, green, rank, verdant **2** luxurious, elaborate, extravagant, grand, lavish, opulent, ornate, palatial, plush (*informal*), sumptuous

lust noun **1** lechery, lasciviousness, lewdness, sensuality **2** appetite, craving, desire, greed, longing, passion, thirst ♦ verb **3** desire, covet, crave, hunger for or after, want, yearn

lustre noun **1** sparkle, gleam, glint, glitter, gloss, glow, sheen, shimmer, shine **2** glory, distinction, fame, honour, prestige, renown

lusty adjective vigorous, energetic, healthy, hearty, powerful, robust, strong, sturdy, virile

luxurious adjective sumptuous, comfortable, expensive, lavish, magnificent, opulent, plush (*informal*), rich, splendid

luxury noun **1** opulence, affluence, hedonism, richness, splendour, sumptuousness **2** extravagance, extra, frill, indulgence, treat

lying noun **1** dishonesty, deceit, mendacity, perjury, untruthfulness ♦ adjective **2** deceitful, dishonest, false, mendacious, perfidious, treacherous, two-faced, untruthful

lyrical adjective enthusiastic, effusive, impassioned, inspired, poetic, rhapsodic

M m

macabre *adjective* <u>gruesome</u>, dreadful, eerie, frightening, ghastly, ghostly, ghoulish, grim, grisly, morbid

machiavellian *adjective* <u>scheming</u>, astute, crafty, cunning, cynical, double-dealing, opportunist, sly, underhand, unscrupulous

machine *noun* 1 <u>appliance</u>, apparatus, contraption, contrivance, device, engine, instrument, mechanism, tool 2 <u>system</u>, machinery, organization, setup (*informal*), structure

machinery *noun* <u>equipment</u>, apparatus, gear, instruments, tackle, tools

macho *adjective* <u>manly</u>, chauvinist, masculine, virile

mad *adjective* 1 <u>insane</u>, crazy (*informal*), demented, deranged, *non compos mentis*, nuts (*slang*), of unsound mind, out of one's mind, psychotic, raving, unhinged, unstable 2 <u>foolish</u>, absurd, asinine, daft (*informal*), foolhardy, irrational, nonsensical, preposterous, senseless, wild 3 *Informal* <u>angry</u>, berserk, enraged, furious, incensed, livid (*informal*), wild 4 <u>enthusiastic</u>, ardent, avid, crazy (*informal*), fanatical, infatuated, wild 5 <u>frenzied</u>, excited, frenetic, uncontrolled, unrestrained, wild 6 <u>like mad</u> *Informal* <u>energetically</u>,

enthusiastically, excitedly, furiously, rapidly, speedily, violently, wildly

madcap *adjective* <u>reckless</u>, crazy, foolhardy, hare-brained, imprudent, impulsive, rash, thoughtless

madden *verb* <u>infuriate</u>, annoy, derange, drive one crazy, enrage, incense, inflame, irritate, upset

madly *adverb* 1 <u>insanely</u>, crazily, deliriously, distractedly, frantically, frenziedly, hysterically 2 <u>foolishly</u>, absurdly, irrationally, ludicrously, senselessly, wildly 3 <u>energetically</u>, excitedly, furiously, like mad (*informal*), recklessly, speedily, wildly 4 *Informal* <u>passionately</u>, desperately, devotedly, intensely, to distraction

madman *or* **madwoman** *noun* <u>lunatic</u>, maniac, nutcase (*slang*), psycho (*slang*), psychopath

madness *noun* 1 <u>insanity</u>, aberration, craziness, delusion, dementia, derangement, distraction, lunacy, mania, mental illness, psychopathy, psychosis 2 <u>foolishness</u>, absurdity, daftness (*informal*), folly, foolhardiness, idiocy, nonsense, preposterousness, wildness

maelstrom *noun* 1 <u>whirlpool</u>, vortex 2 <u>turmoil</u>, chaos, confusion, disorder, tumult, upheaval

maestro *noun* <u>master</u>, expert, genius, virtuoso

magazine *noun* 1 <u>journal</u>, pamphlet, periodical 2 <u>storehouse</u>, arsenal, depot, store, warehouse

magic noun 1 <u>sorcery</u>, black art, enchantment, necromancy, witchcraft, wizardry 2 <u>conjuring</u>, illusion, legerdemain, prestidigitation, sleight of hand, trickery 3 <u>charm</u>, allurement, enchantment, fascination, glamour, magnetism, power ♦ adjective 4 Also **magical** <u>miraculous</u>, bewitching, charming, enchanting, entrancing, fascinating, marvellous, spellbinding

magician noun <u>sorcerer</u>, conjuror or conjuror, enchanter or enchantress, illusionist, necromancer, warlock, witch, wizard

magisterial adjective <u>authoritative</u>, commanding, lordly, masterful

magistrate noun <u>judge</u>, J.P., justice, justice of the peace

magnanimity noun <u>generosity</u>, benevolence, big-heartedness, largesse or largess, nobility, selflessness, unselfishness

magnanimous adjective <u>generous</u>, big-hearted, bountiful, charitable, kind, noble, selfless, unselfish

magnate noun <u>tycoon</u>, baron, captain of industry, mogul, plutocrat

magnetic adjective <u>attractive</u>, captivating, charismatic, charming, fascinating, hypnotic, irresistible, mesmerizing, seductive

magnetism noun <u>charm</u>, allure, appeal, attraction, charisma, drawing power, magic, pull, seductiveness

magnification noun <u>increase</u>, amplification, enhancement, enlargement, expansion, heightening, intensification

magnificence noun <u>splendour</u>, brilliance, glory, grandeur, majesty, nobility, opulence, stateliness, sumptuousness

magnificent adjective 1 <u>splendid</u>, glorious, gorgeous, imposing, impressive, majestic, regal, sublime, sumptuous 2 <u>excellent</u>, brilliant, fine, outstanding, splendid, superb

magnify verb 1 <u>enlarge</u>, amplify, blow up (informal), boost, dilate, expand, heighten, increase, intensify 2 <u>overstate</u>, exaggerate, inflate, overemphasize, overplay

magnitude noun 1 <u>importance</u>, consequence, greatness, moment, note, significance, weight 2 <u>size</u>, amount, amplitude, extent, mass, quantity, volume

maid noun 1 <u>girl</u>, damsel, lass, lassie (informal), maiden, wench 2 <u>servant</u>, housemaid, maidservant, serving-maid

maiden noun 1 <u>girl</u>, damsel, lass, lassie (informal), maid, virgin, wench ♦ adjective 2 <u>unmarried</u>, unwed 3 <u>first</u>, inaugural, initial, introductory

maidenly adjective <u>modest</u>, chaste, decent, decorous, demure, pure, virginal

mail noun 1 <u>post</u>, correspondence, letters ♦ verb 2 <u>post</u>, dispatch, forward, send

maim verb <u>cripple</u>, disable, hurt, injure, mutilate, wound

main adjective 1 <u>chief</u>, central,

essential, foremost, head, leading, pre-eminent, primary, principal ♦ *noun* 2 conduit, cable, channel, duct, line, pipe 3 **in the main** on the whole, for the most part, generally, in general, mainly, mostly

mainly *adverb* chiefly, for the most part, in the main, largely, mostly, on the whole, predominantly, primarily, principally

mainstay *noun* pillar, anchor, backbone, bulwark, buttress, lynchpin, prop

mainstream *adjective* conventional, accepted, current, established, general, orthodox, prevailing, received

maintain *verb* 1 keep up, carry on, continue, perpetuate, preserve, prolong, retain, sustain 2 support, care for, look after, provide for, supply, take care of 3 assert, avow, claim, contend, declare, insist, profess, state

maintenance *noun* 1 continuation, carrying-on, perpetuation, prolongation 2 upkeep, care, conservation, keeping, nurture, preservation, repairs 3 allowance, alimony, keep, support

majestic *adjective* grand, grandiose, impressive, magnificent, monumental, regal, splendid, stately, sublime, superb

majesty *noun* grandeur, glory, magnificence, nobility, pomp, splendour, stateliness

major *adjective* 1 main, bigger, chief, greater, higher, leading, senior, supreme 2 important, critical, crucial, great, notable, outstanding, serious, significant

majority *noun* 1 preponderance, best part, bulk, greater number, mass, most 2 adulthood, manhood *or* womanhood, maturity, seniority

make *verb* 1 create, assemble, build, construct, fashion, form, manufacture, produce, put together, synthesize 2 produce, accomplish, bring about, cause, create, effect, generate, give rise to, lead to 3 force, cause, compel, constrain, drive, impel, induce, oblige, prevail upon, require 4 amount to, add up to, compose, constitute, form 5 perform, carry out, do, effect, execute 6 earn, clear, gain, get, net, obtain, win 7 **make it** *Informal* succeed, arrive (*informal*), crack it (*informal*), get on, prosper ♦ *noun* 8 brand, kind, model, sort, style, type, variety

make-believe *noun* fantasy, imagination, play-acting, pretence, unreality

make for *verb* head for, aim for, be bound for, head towards

make off *verb* 1 flee, bolt, clear out (*informal*), run away or off, take to one's heels 2 **make off with** steal, abduct, carry off, filch, kidnap, nick (*slang, chiefly Brit.*), pinch (*informal*), run away or off with

make out *verb* 1 see, detect, discern, discover, distinguish, perceive, recognize 2 understand, comprehend, decipher, fathom, follow, grasp, work out 3 write out, complete, draw up, fill in or out 4 pretend,

assert, claim, let on, make as if
or though **5** fare, get on, manage

maker noun manufacturer,
builder, constructor, producer

makeshift adjective temporary,
expedient, provisional, stopgap,
substitute

make-up noun **1** cosmetics, face
(informal), greasepaint (Theatre),
paint (informal), powder
2 structure, arrangement,
assembly, composition,
configuration, constitution,
construction, format,
organization **3** nature, character,
constitution, disposition,
temperament

make up verb **1** form, compose,
comprise, constitute **2** invent,
coin, compose, concoct,
construct, create, devise, dream
up, formulate, frame, originate
3 complete, fill, supply **4** settle,
bury the hatchet, call it quits,
reconcile **5** **make up for**
compensate for, atone for,
balance, make amends for,
offset, recompense

making noun creation, assembly,
building, composition,
construction, fabrication,
manufacture, production

makings plural noun beginnings,
capacity, ingredients, potential

maladjusted adjective disturbed,
alienated, neurotic, unstable

maladministration noun
mismanagement, corruption,
dishonesty, incompetence,
inefficiency, malpractice, misrule

maladroit adjective clumsy,
awkward, cack-handed
(informal), ham-fisted or
ham-handed (informal), inept,

inexpert, unskilful

malady noun disease, affliction,
ailment, complaint, disorder,
illness, infirmity, sickness

malaise noun unease, anxiety,
depression, disquiet, melancholy

malcontent noun troublemaker,
agitator, mischief-maker, rebel,
stirrer (informal)

male adjective masculine, manly,
virile

malefactor noun wrongdoer,
criminal, delinquent, evildoer,
miscreant, offender, villain

malevolence noun malice, hate,
hatred, ill will, rancour, spite,
vindictiveness

malevolent adjective spiteful,
hostile, ill-natured, malicious,
malign, vengeful, vindictive

malformation noun deformity,
distortion, misshapenness

malformed adjective misshapen,
abnormal, crooked, deformed,
distorted, irregular, twisted

malfunction verb **1** break down,
fail, go wrong ♦ noun **2** fault,
breakdown, defect, failure, flaw,
glitch

malice noun ill will, animosity,
enmity, evil intent, hate, hatred,
malevolence, spite, vindictiveness

malicious adjective spiteful,
ill-disposed, ill-natured,
malevolent, rancorous, resentful,
vengeful

malign verb **1** disparage, abuse,
defame, denigrate, libel, run
down, slander, smear, vilify
♦ adjective **2** evil, bad,
destructive, harmful, hostile,
injurious, malevolent, malignant,
pernicious, wicked

malignant adjective **1** harmful, destructive, hostile, hurtful, malevolent, malign, pernicious, spiteful **2** Medical uncontrollable, cancerous, dangerous, deadly, fatal, irremediable

malleable adjective **1** workable, ductile, plastic, soft, tensile **2** manageable, adaptable, biddable, compliant, impressionable, pliable, tractable

malodorous adjective smelly, fetid, mephitic, nauseating, noisome, offensive, putrid, reeking, stinking

malpractice noun misconduct, abuse, dereliction, mismanagement, negligence

maltreat verb abuse, bully, harm, hurt, ill-treat, injure, mistreat

mammoth adjective colossal, enormous, giant, gigantic, huge, immense, massive, monumental, mountainous, prodigious

man noun **1** male, bloke (Brit. informal), chap (informal), gentleman, guy (informal) **2** human, human being, individual, person, soul **3** mankind, Homo sapiens, humanity, humankind, human race, people **4** manservant, attendant, retainer, servant, valet ◆ verb **5** staff, crew, garrison, occupy, people

manacle noun **1** handcuff, bond, chain, fetter, iron, shackle ◆ verb **2** handcuff, bind, chain, fetter, put in chains, shackle

manage verb **1** administer, be in charge (of), command, conduct, direct, handle, run, supervise **2** succeed, accomplish, arrange, contrive, effect, engineer

3 handle, control, manipulate, operate, use **4** cope, carry on, get by (informal), make do, muddle through, survive

manageable adjective docile, amenable, compliant, easy, submissive

management noun **1** directors, administration, board, employers, executive(s) **2** administration, command, control, direction, handling, operation, running, supervision

manager noun supervisor, administrator, boss (informal), director, executive, governor, head, organizer

mandate noun command, commission, decree, directive, edict, instruction, order

mandatory adjective compulsory, binding, obligatory, required, requisite

manfully adverb bravely, boldly, courageously, determinedly, gallantly, hard, resolutely, stoutly, valiantly

mangle verb crush, deform, destroy, disfigure, distort, mutilate, ruin, spoil, tear, wreck

mangy adjective scruffy, dirty, moth-eaten, seedy, shabby, shoddy, squalid

manhandle verb rough up, knock about or around, maul, paw (informal)

manhood noun manliness, masculinity, virility

mania noun **1** madness, delirium, dementia, derangement, insanity, lunacy **2** obsession, craze, fad (informal), fetish, fixation, passion, preoccupation, thing (*informal*)

maniac noun **1** madman or madwoman, headcase (*informal*), lunatic, psycho, psychopath **2** fanatic, enthusiast, fan, fiend (*informal*), freak (*informal*)

manifest adjective **1** obvious, apparent, blatant, clear, conspicuous, evident, glaring, noticeable, palpable, patent ♦ verb **2** display, demonstrate, exhibit, expose, express, reveal, show

manifestation noun display, demonstration, exhibition, expression, indication, mark, show, sign, symptom

manifold adjective numerous, assorted, copious, diverse, many, multifarious, multiple, varied, various

manipulate verb **1** work, handle, operate, use **2** influence, control, direct, engineer, manoeuvre

mankind noun people, Homo sapiens, humanity, humankind, human race, man

manliness noun virility, boldness, bravery, courage, fearlessness, masculinity, valour, vigour

manly adjective virile, bold, brave, courageous, fearless, manful, masculine, strapping, strong, vigorous

man-made adjective artificial, ersatz, manufactured, mock, synthetic

manner noun **1** behaviour, air, aspect, bearing, conduct, demeanour **2** style, custom, fashion, method, mode, way **3** type, brand, category, form,

kind, sort, variety

mannered adjective affected, artificial, pretentious, stilted

mannerism noun habit, characteristic, foible, idiosyncrasy, peculiarity, quirk, trait, trick

manners plural noun **1** behaviour, conduct, demeanour **2** politeness, courtesy, decorum, etiquette, p's and q's, refinement

manoeuvre noun **1** stratagem, dodge, intrigue, machination, ploy, ruse, scheme, subterfuge, tactic, trick **2** movement, exercise, operation ♦ verb **3** manipulate, contrive, engineer, machinate, pull strings, scheme, wangle (*informal*) **4** move, deploy, exercise

mansion noun residence, hall, manor, seat, villa

mantle noun **1** cloak, cape, hood, shawl, wrap **2** covering, blanket, canopy, curtain, pall, screen, shroud, veil

manual adjective **1** hand-operated, human, physical ♦ noun **2** handbook, bible, instructions

manufacture verb **1** make, assemble, build, construct, create, mass-produce, produce, put together, turn out **2** concoct, cook up (*informal*), devise, fabricate, invent, make up, think up, trump up ♦ noun **3** making, assembly, construction, creation, production

manufacturer noun maker, builder, constructor, creator, industrialist, producer

manure noun compost, droppings, dung, excrement, fertilizer, muck, ordure

many adjective 1 numerous, abundant, countless, innumerable, manifold, myriad, umpteen (informal), various ◆ noun 2 a lot, heaps (informal), lots (informal), plenty, scores

mar verb spoil, blemish, damage, detract from, disfigure, hurt, impair, ruin, scar, stain, taint, tarnish

maraud verb raid, forage, loot, pillage, plunder, ransack, ravage

marauder noun raider, bandit, brigand, buccaneer, outlaw, plunderer

march verb 1 walk, file, pace, parade, stride, strut ◆ noun 2 walk, routemarch, trek 3 progress, advance, development, evolution, progression

margin noun edge, border, boundary, brink, perimeter, periphery, rim, side, verge

marginal adjective 1 borderline, bordering, on the edge, peripheral 2 insignificant, minimal, minor, negligible, slight, small

marijuana noun cannabis, dope (slang), grass (slang), hemp, pot (slang)

marine adjective nautical, maritime, naval, seafaring, seagoing

mariner noun sailor, salt, sea dog, seafarer, seaman

marital adjective matrimonial, conjugal, connubial, nuptial

maritime adjective 1 nautical,

marine, naval, oceanic, seafaring 2 coastal, littoral, seaside

mark noun 1 spot, blemish, blot, line, scar, scratch, smudge, stain, streak 2 sign, badge, device, emblem, flag, hallmark, label, symbol, token 3 criterion, measure, norm, standard, yardstick 4 target, aim, goal, object, objective, purpose ◆ verb 5 scar, blemish, blot, scratch, smudge, stain, streak 6 characterize, brand, flag, identify, label, stamp 7 distinguish, denote, exemplify, illustrate, show 8 observe, attend, mind, note, notice, pay attention, pay heed, watch 9 grade, appraise, assess, correct, evaluate

marked adjective noticeable, blatant, clear, conspicuous, decided, distinct, obvious, patent, prominent, pronounced, striking

markedly adverb noticeably, clearly, considerably, conspicuously, decidedly, distinctly, obviously, strikingly

market noun 1 fair, bazaar, mart ◆ verb 2 sell, retail, vend

marketable adjective sought after, in demand, saleable, wanted

marksman, markswoman noun sharpshooter, crack shot (informal), good shot

maroon verb abandon, desert, leave, leave high and dry (informal), strand

marriage noun wedding, match, matrimony, nuptials, wedlock

marry verb 1 wed, get hitched (slang), tie the knot (informal)

2 underline, ally, bond, join, knit, link, merge, unify, yoke

marsh noun swamp, bog, fen, morass, quagmire, slough

marshal verb 1 arrange, align, array, deploy, draw up, group, line up, order, organize 2 conduct, escort, guide, lead, shepherd, usher

marshy adjective swampy, boggy, quaggy, waterlogged, wet

martial adjective military, bellicose, belligerent, warlike

martinet noun disciplinarian, stickler

martyrdom noun persecution, ordeal, suffering

marvel verb 1 wonder, be amazed, be awed, gape ♦ noun 2 wonder, miracle, phenomenon, portent, prodigy

marvellous adjective 1 amazing, astonishing, astounding, breathtaking, brilliant, extraordinary, miraculous, phenomenal, prodigious, spectacular, stupendous 2 excellent, fabulous (informal), fantastic (informal), great (informal), splendid, superb, terrific (informal), wonderful

masculine adjective male, manlike, manly, mannish, virile

mask noun 1 disguise, camouflage, cover, façade, front, guise, screen, veil ♦ verb 2 disguise, camouflage, cloak, conceal, cover, hide, obscure, screen, veil

masquerade noun 1 masked ball, fancy dress party, revel 2 pretence, cloak, cover-up,

deception, disguise, mask, pose, screen, subterfuge ♦ verb 3 pose, disguise, dissemble, dissimulate, impersonate, pass oneself off, pretend (to be)

mass noun 1 piece, block, chunk, hunk, lump 2 lot, bunch, collection, heap, load, pile, quantity, stack 3 size, bulk, greatness, magnitude ♦ adjective 4 large-scale, extensive, general, indiscriminate, wholesale, widespread ♦ verb 5 gather, accumulate, assemble, collect, congregate, rally, swarm, throng

massacre noun 1 slaughter, annihilation, blood bath, butchery, carnage, extermination, holocaust, murder ♦ verb 2 slaughter, butcher, cut to pieces, exterminate, kill, mow down, murder, wipe out

massage noun 1 rub-down, manipulation ♦ verb 2 rub down, knead, manipulate

massive adjective huge, big, colossal, enormous, gigantic, hefty, immense, mammoth, monumental, whopping (informal)

master noun 1 ruler, boss (informal), chief, commander, controller, director, governor, lord, manager 2 expert, ace (informal), doyen, genius, maestro, past master, virtuoso, wizard 3 teacher, guide, guru, instructor, tutor ♦ adjective 4 main, chief, foremost, leading, predominant, prime, principal ♦ verb 5 learn, get the hang of (informal), grasp 6 overcome, conquer, defeat, tame, triumph over, vanquish

masterful adjective 1 skilful, adroit, consummate, expert, fine, first-rate, masterly, superlative, supreme, world-class 2 domineering, arrogant, bossy (informal), high-handed, imperious, overbearing, overweening

masterly adjective skilful, adroit, consummate, crack (informal), expert, first-rate, masterful, supreme, world-class

mastermind verb 1 plan, conceive, devise, direct, manage, organize ♦ noun 2 organizer, architect, brain(s) (informal), director, engineer, manager, planner

masterpiece noun classic, jewel, magnum opus, pièce de résistance, tour de force

mastery noun 1 expertise, finesse, know-how (informal), proficiency, prowess, skill, virtuosity 2 control, ascendancy, command, domination, superiority, supremacy, upper hand, whip hand

match noun 1 game, bout, competition, contest, head-to-head, test, trial 2 equal, counterpart, peer, rival 3 marriage, alliance, pairing, partnership ♦ verb 4 correspond, accord, agree, fit, go with, harmonize, tally 5 rival, compare, compete, emulate, equal, measure up to

matching adjective identical, coordinating, corresponding, equivalent, like, twin

matchless adjective unequalled, incomparable, inimitable,

superlative, supreme, unmatched, unparalleled, unrivalled, unsurpassed

mate noun 1 partner, husband or wife, spouse 2 Informal friend, buddy (informal), chum (informal), comrade, crony, pal (informal) 3 colleague, associate, companion 4 assistant, helper, subordinate ♦ verb 5 pair, breed, couple

material noun 1 substance, matter, stuff 2 information, data, evidence, facts, notes 3 cloth, fabric ♦ adjective 4 physical, bodily, concrete, corporeal, palpable, substantial, tangible 5 important, essential, meaningful, momentous, serious, significant, vital, weighty 6 relevant, applicable, apposite, apropos, germane, pertinent

materialize verb occur, appear, come about, come to pass, happen, take shape, turn up

materially adverb significantly, essentially, gravely, greatly, much, seriously, substantially

maternal adjective motherly

maternity noun motherhood, motherliness

matey adjective friendly, chummy (informal), hail-fellow-well-met, intimate, pally (informal), sociable, thick (informal)

matrimonial adjective marital, conjugal, connubial, nuptial

matrimony noun marriage, nuptials, wedding ceremony, wedlock

matted adjective tangled, knotted, tousled, uncombed

matter noun 1 substance, body,

material, stuff **2** situation, affair, business, concern, event, incident, proceeding, question, subject, topic **3** As in **what's the matter?** problem, difficulty, distress, trouble, worry ♦ verb **4** be important, carry weight, count, make a difference, signify

matter-of-fact adjective unsentimental, deadpan, down-to-earth, emotionless, mundane, plain, prosaic, sober, unimaginative

mature adjective **1** grown-up, adult, full-grown, fully fledged, mellow, of age, ready, ripe, seasoned ♦ verb **2** develop, age, bloom, blossom, come of age, grow up, mellow, ripen

maturity noun adulthood, experience, manhood or womanhood, ripeness, wisdom

maudlin adjective sentimental, mawkish, overemotional, slushy (informal), soppy (Brit. informal), tearful, weepy (informal)

maul verb **1** ill-treat, abuse, manhandle, molest, paw **2** tear, batter, claw, lacerate, mangle

maverick noun **1** rebel, dissenter, eccentric, heretic, iconoclast, individualist, nonconformist, protester, radical ♦ adjective **2** rebel, dissenting, eccentric, heretical, iconoclastic, individualistic, nonconformist, radical

mawkish adjective sentimental, emotional, maudlin, schmaltzy (slang), slushy (informal), soppy (Brit. informal)

maxim noun saying, adage, aphorism, axiom, dictum, motto, proverb, rule

maximum noun **1** top, ceiling, height, peak, pinnacle, summit, upper limit, utmost, zenith ♦ adjective **2** greatest, highest, most, paramount, supreme, topmost, utmost

maybe adverb perhaps, perchance (archaic), possibly

mayhem noun chaos, commotion, confusion, destruction, disorder, fracas, havoc, trouble, violence

maze noun **1** labyrinth **2** web, confusion, imbroglio, tangle

meadow noun field, grassland, lea (poetic), pasture

meagre adjective insubstantial, inadequate, measly, paltry, poor, puny, scanty, slight, small

mean[1] verb **1** signify, convey, denote, express, imply, indicate, represent, spell, stand for, symbolize **2** intend, aim, aspire, design, desire, plan, set out, want, wish

mean[2] adjective **1** miserly, mercenary, niggardly, parsimonious, penny-pinching, stingy, tight-fisted, ungenerous **2** despicable, callous, contemptible, hard-hearted, petty, shabby, shameful, sordid, vile

mean[3] noun **1** average, balance, compromise, happy medium, middle, midpoint, norm ♦ adjective **2** average, middle, standard

meander verb **1** wind, snake, turn, zigzag **2** wander, ramble, stroll ♦ noun **3** curve, bend, coil, loop, turn, twist, zigzag

meaning noun sense, connotation, drift, gist, message, significance, substance

meaningful adjective significant, important, material, purposeful, relevant, useful, valid, worthwhile

meaningless adjective pointless, empty, futile, inane, inconsequential, insignificant, senseless, useless, vain, worthless

meanness noun 1 miserliness, niggardliness, parsimony, selfishness, stinginess 2 pettiness, disgracefulness, ignobility, narrow-mindedness, shabbiness, shamefulness

means plural noun 1 method, agency, instrument, medium, mode, process, way 2 money, affluence, capital, fortune, funds, income, resources, wealth, wherewithal 3 by all means certainly, definitely, doubtlessly, of course, surely 4 by no means in no way, definitely not, not in the least, on no account

meantime, meanwhile adverb at the same time, concurrently, in the interim, simultaneously

measly adjective meagre, miserable, paltry, pathetic, pitiful, poor, puny, scanty, skimpy

measurable adjective quantifiable, assessable, perceptible, significant

measure noun 1 quantity, allotment, allowance, amount, portion, quota, ration, share 2 gauge, metre, rule, scale, yardstick 3 action, act, deed, expedient, manoeuvre, means, procedure, step 4 law, act, bill, resolution, statute 5 rhythm, beat, cadence, metre, verse ♦ verb 6 quantify, assess, calculate, calibrate, compute, determine, evaluate, gauge, weigh

measured adjective 1 steady, dignified, even, leisurely, regular, sedate, slow, solemn, stately, unhurried 2 considered, calculated, deliberate, reasoned, sober, studied, well-thought-out

measurement noun calculation, assessment, calibration, computation, evaluation, mensuration, valuation

measure up to verb fulfil the expectations, be equal to, be suitable, come up to scratch (informal), fit or fill the bill, make the grade (informal)

meat noun flesh

meaty adjective 1 brawny, beefy (informal), burly, heavily built, heavy, muscular, solid, strapping, sturdy 2 interesting, meaningful, profound, rich, significant, substantial

mechanical adjective 1 automatic, automated 2 unthinking, automatic, cursory, impersonal, instinctive, involuntary, perfunctory, routine, unfeeling

mechanism noun 1 machine, apparatus, appliance, contrivance, device, instrument, tool 2 process, agency, means, method, operation, procedure, system, technique

meddle verb interfere, butt in, intervene, intrude, pry, tamper

meddlesome adjective interfering, intrusive, meddling, mischievous, officious, prying

mediate verb intervene, arbitrate, conciliate, intercede, reconcile, referee, step in (informal), umpire

mediation noun arbitration, conciliation, intercession, intervention, reconciliation

mediator noun negotiator, arbiter, arbitrator, go-between, honest broker, intermediary, middleman, peacemaker, referee, umpire

medicinal adjective therapeutic, curative, healing, medical, remedial, restorative

medicine noun remedy, cure, drug, medicament, medication, nostrum

mediocre adjective second-rate, average, indifferent, inferior, middling, ordinary, passable, pedestrian, run-of-the-mill, so-so (informal), undistinguished

mediocrity noun insignificance, indifference, inferiority, ordinariness, unimportance

meditate verb 1 reflect, cogitate, consider, contemplate, deliberate, muse, ponder, ruminate, think 2 plan, have in mind, intend, purpose, scheme

meditation noun reflection, cogitation, contemplation, musing, pondering, rumination, study, thought

medium adjective 1 middle, average, fair, intermediate, mean, median, mediocre, middling, midway ♦ noun 2 middle, average, centre, compromise, mean, midpoint 3 means, agency, channel, instrument, mode, organ, vehicle, way 4 environment, atmosphere, conditions, milieu,

setting, surroundings 5 spiritualist

medley noun mixture, assortment, farrago, hotchpotch, jumble, mélange, miscellany, mishmash, mixed bag (informal), potpourri

meek adjective submissive, acquiescent, compliant, deferential, docile, gentle, humble, mild, modest, timid, unassuming, unpretentious

meekness noun submissiveness, acquiescence, compliance, deference, docility, gentleness, humility, mildness, modesty, timidity

meet verb 1 encounter, bump into, chance on, come across, confront, contact, find, happen on, run across, run into 2 converge, come together, connect, cross, intersect, join, link up, touch 3 satisfy, answer, come up to, comply with, discharge, fulfil, match, measure up to 4 gather, assemble, collect, come together, congregate, convene, muster 5 experience, bear, encounter, endure, face, go through, suffer, undergo

meeting noun 1 encounter, assignation, confrontation, engagement, introduction, rendezvous, tryst 2 conference, assembly, conclave, congress, convention, gathering, get-together (informal), reunion, session

melancholy noun 1 sadness, dejection, depression, despondency, gloom, low spirits, misery, sorrow, unhappiness ♦ adjective 2 sad, depressed, despondent, dispirited, downhearted, gloomy, glum, miserable, mournful, sorrowful

melee, mêlée noun fight, brawl, fracas, free-for-all (informal), rumpus, scrimmage, scuffle, set-to (informal), skirmish, tussle

mellifluous adjective sweet, dulcet, euphonious, honeyed, silvery, smooth, soft, soothing, sweet-sounding

mellow adjective 1 soft, delicate, full-flavoured, mature, rich, ripe, sweet ♦ verb 2 mature, develop, improve, ripen, season, soften, sweeten

melodious adjective tuneful, dulcet, euphonious, harmonious, melodic, musical, sweet-sounding

melodramatic adjective sensational, blood-and-thunder, extravagant, histrionic, overdramatic, overemotional, theatrical

melody noun 1 tune, air, music, song, strain, theme 2 tunefulness, euphony, harmony, melodiousness, musicality

melt verb 1 dissolve, fuse, liquefy, soften, thaw 2 often with **away** disappear, disperse, dissolve, evanesce, evaporate, fade, vanish 3 soften, disarm, mollify, relax

member noun 1 representative, associate, fellow 2 limb, appendage, arm, extremity, leg, part

membership noun 1 members, associates, body, fellows 2 participation, belonging, enrolment, fellowship

memento noun souvenir,

keepsake, memorial, relic, remembrance, reminder, token, trophy

memoir noun account, biography, essay, journal, life, monograph, narrative, record

memoirs plural noun autobiography, diary, experiences, journals, life story, memories, recollections, reminiscences

memorable adjective noteworthy, celebrated, famous, historic, momentous, notable, remarkable, significant, striking, unforgettable

memorandum noun note, communication, jotting, memo, message, minute, reminder

memorial noun 1 monument, memento, plaque, record, remembrance, souvenir ♦ adjective 2 commemorative, monumental

memorize verb remember, commit to memory, learn, learn by heart, learn by rote

memory noun 1 recall, recollection, remembrance, reminiscence, retention 2 commemoration, honour, remembrance

menace noun 1 threat, intimidation, warning 2 Informal nuisance, annoyance, pest, plague, troublemaker ♦ verb 3 threaten, bully, frighten, intimidate, loom, lour or lower, terrorize

menacing adjective threatening, forbidding, frightening, intimidating, looming, louring or lowering, ominous

mend verb 1 repair, darn, fix, patch, refit, renew, renovate, restore, retouch 2 improve, ameliorate, amend, correct, emend, rectify, reform, revise 3 heal, convalesce, get better, recover, recuperate ♦ noun 4 repair, darn, patch, stitch 5 **on the mend** convalescent, getting better, improving, recovering, recuperating

mendacious adjective lying, deceitful, deceptive, dishonest, duplicitous, fallacious, false, fraudulent, insincere, untruthful

menial adjective 1 unskilled, boring, dull, humdrum, low-status, routine ♦ noun 2 servant, attendant, dogsbody (informal), drudge, flunky, lackey, skivvy (chiefly Brit.), underling

mental adjective 1 intellectual, cerebral 2 Informal insane, deranged, disturbed, mad, mentally ill, psychotic, unbalanced, unstable

mentality noun attitude, cast of mind, character, disposition, make-up, outlook, personality, psychology

mentally adverb in the mind, in one's head, intellectually, inwardly, psychologically

mention verb 1 refer to, bring up, declare, disclose, divulge, intimate, point out, reveal, state, touch upon ♦ noun 2 acknowledgment, citation, recognition, tribute 3 reference, allusion, indication, observation, remark

mentor noun guide, adviser, coach, counsellor, guru, instructor, teacher, tutor

menu noun bill of fare, carte du jour, tariff (chiefly Brit.)

mercantile adjective commercial, trading

mercenary adjective 1 greedy, acquisitive, avaricious, grasping, money-grubbing (informal), sordid, venal ♦ noun 2 hireling, soldier of fortune

merchandise noun goods, commodities, produce, products, stock, wares

merchant noun tradesman, broker, dealer, purveyor, retailer, salesman, seller, shopkeeper, supplier, trader, trafficker, vendor, wholesaler

merciful adjective compassionate, clement, forgiving, generous, gracious, humane, kind, lenient, sparing, sympathetic, tender-hearted

merciless adjective cruel, barbarous, callous, hard-hearted, harsh, heartless, pitiless, ruthless, unforgiving

mercurial adjective lively, active, capricious, changeable, impulsive, irrepressible, mobile, quicksilver, spirited, sprightly, unpredictable, volatile

mercy noun 1 compassion, clemency, forbearance, forgiveness, grace, kindness, leniency, pity 2 blessing, boon, godsend

mere adjective simple, bare, common, nothing more than, plain, pure, sheer

meretricious adjective trashy, flashy, garish, gaudy, gimcrack, showy, tawdry, tinsel

merge verb combine,

amalgamate, blend, coalesce, converge, fuse, join, meet, mingle, mix, unite

merger noun <u>union</u>, amalgamation, coalition, combination, consolidation, fusion, incorporation

merit noun 1 <u>worth</u>, advantage, asset, excellence, goodness, integrity, quality, strong point, talent, value, virtue ♦ verb 2 <u>deserve</u>, be entitled to, be worthy of, earn, have a right to, rate, warrant

meritorious adjective <u>praiseworthy</u>, admirable, commendable, creditable, deserving, excellent, good, laudable, virtuous, worthy

merriment noun <u>fun</u>, amusement, festivity, glee, hilarity, jollity, joviality, laughter, mirth, revelry

merry adjective 1 <u>cheerful</u>, blithe, carefree, convivial, festive, happy, jolly, joyous 2 Brit. informal <u>tipsy</u>, happy, mellow, squiffy (Brit. informal), tiddly (slang, chiefly Brit.)

mesh noun 1 <u>net</u>, netting, network, tracery, web ♦ verb 2 <u>engage</u>, combine, connect, coordinate, dovetail, harmonize, interlock, knit

mesmerize verb <u>entrance</u>, captivate, enthral, fascinate, grip, hold spellbound, hypnotize

mess noun 1 <u>disorder</u>, chaos, clutter, confusion, disarray, disorganization, hotchpotch, jumble, litter, shambles, untidiness 2 <u>difficulty</u>, deep water, dilemma, fix (informal), jam (informal), muddle, pickle

(informal), plight, predicament, tight spot ♦ verb 3 often with up <u>dirty</u>, clutter, disarrange, dishevel, muck up (Brit. slang), muddle, pollute, scramble 4 often with with <u>interfere</u>, fiddle (informal), meddle, play, tamper, tinker

mess about or **around** verb <u>potter</u>, amuse oneself, dabble, fool (about or around), muck about (informal), play about or around, trifle

message noun
1 <u>communication</u>, bulletin, communiqué, dispatch, letter, memorandum, note, tidings, word 2 <u>point</u>, idea, import, meaning, moral, purport, theme

messenger noun <u>courier</u>, carrier, delivery boy, emissary, envoy, errand-boy, go-between, herald, runner

messy adjective <u>untidy</u>, chaotic, cluttered, confused, dirty, dishevelled, disordered, disorganized, muddled, shambolic, sloppy (informal)

metamorphosis noun <u>transformation</u>, alteration, change, conversion, mutation, transmutation

metaphor noun <u>figure of speech</u>, allegory, analogy, image, symbol, trope

metaphorical adjective <u>figurative</u>, allegorical, emblematic, symbolic

mete verb <u>distribute</u>, administer, apportion, assign, deal, dispense, dole, portion

meteoric adjective <u>spectacular</u>, brilliant, dazzling, fast, overnight, rapid, speedy, sudden, swift

method noun 1 <u>manner</u>, approach, mode, modus operandi, procedure, process, routine, style, system, technique, way 2 <u>orderliness</u>, order, organization, pattern, planning, purpose, regularity, system

methodical adjective <u>orderly</u>, businesslike, deliberate, disciplined, meticulous, organized, precise, regular, structured, systematic

meticulous adjective <u>thorough</u>, exact, fastidious, fussy, painstaking, particular, precise, punctilious, scrupulous, strict

mettle noun <u>courage</u>, bravery, fortitude, gallantry, life, nerve, pluck, resolution, spirit, valour, vigour

microbe noun <u>microorganism</u>, bacillus, bacterium, bug (informal), germ, virus

microscopic adjective <u>tiny</u>, imperceptible, infinitesimal, invisible, minuscule, minute, negligible

midday noun <u>noon</u>, noonday, twelve o'clock

middle adjective 1 <u>central</u>, halfway, intermediate, intervening, mean, median, medium, mid ♦ noun 2 <u>centre</u>, focus, halfway point, heart, midpoint, midsection, midst

middle-class adjective <u>bourgeois</u>, conventional, traditional

middling adjective 1 <u>mediocre</u>, indifferent, run-of-the-mill, so-so (informal), tolerable, unexceptional, unremarkable 2 <u>moderate</u>, adequate, all right, average, fair, medium, modest, O.K. or okay (informal), ordinary, passable, serviceable

midget noun <u>dwarf</u>, pygmy or pigmy, shrimp (informal), Tom Thumb

midnight noun <u>twelve o'clock</u>, dead of night, middle of the night, the witching hour

midst noun **in the midst of** <u>among</u>, amidst, during, in the middle of, in the thick of, surrounded by

midway adjective, adverb <u>halfway</u>, betwixt and between, in the middle

might noun 1 <u>power</u>, energy, force, strength, vigour 2 **with might and main** <u>forcefully</u>, lustily, manfully, mightily, vigorously

mightily adverb 1 <u>very</u>, decidedly, exceedingly, extremely, greatly, highly, hugely, intensely, much 2 <u>powerfully</u>, energetically, forcefully, lustily, manfully, strongly, vigorously

mighty adjective <u>powerful</u>, forceful, lusty, robust, strapping, strong, sturdy, vigorous

migrant noun 1 <u>wanderer</u>, drifter, emigrant, immigrant, itinerant, nomad, rover, traveller ♦ adjective 2 <u>travelling</u>, drifting, immigrant, itinerant, migratory, nomadic, roving, shifting, transient, vagrant, wandering

migrate verb <u>move</u>, emigrate, journey, roam, rove, travel, trek, voyage, wander

migration noun <u>wandering</u>, emigration, journey, movement, roving, travel, trek, voyage

migratory adjective <u>nomadic</u>,

mild itinerant, migrant, peripatetic, roving, transient

mild adjective **1** gentle, calm, docile, easy-going, equable, meek, peaceable, placid **2** bland, smooth **3** calm, balmy, moderate, temperate, tranquil, warm

mildness noun gentleness, calmness, clemency, docility, moderation, placidity, tranquillity, warmth

milieu noun surroundings, background, element, environment, locale, location, scene, setting

militant adjective aggressive, active, assertive, combative, vigorous

military adjective **1** warlike, armed, martial, soldierly ♦ noun **2** armed forces, army, forces, services

militate verb **militate against** counteract, be detrimental to, conflict with, counter, oppose, resist, tell against, weigh against

milk verb exploit, extract, pump, take advantage of

mill noun **1** factory, foundry, plant, works **2** grinder, crusher ♦ verb **3** grind, crush, grate, pound, powder **4** swarm, crowd, throng

millstone noun **1** grindstone, quernstone **2** burden, affliction, albatross, encumbrance, load, weight

mime verb act out, gesture, represent, simulate

mimic verb **1** imitate, ape, caricature, do (informal), impersonate, parody, take off

(informal) ♦ noun **2** imitator, caricaturist, copycat (informal), impersonator, impressionist

mimicry noun imitation, burlesque, caricature, impersonation, mimicking, mockery, parody, take-off (informal)

mince verb **1** cut, chop, crumble, grind, hash **2** As in **mince one's words** tone down, moderate, soften, spare, weaken

mincing adjective affected, camp (informal), dainty, effeminate, foppish, precious, pretentious, sissy

mind noun **1** intelligence, brain(s) (informal), grey matter (informal), intellect, reason, sense, understanding, wits **2** memory, recollection, remembrance **3** intention, desire, disposition, fancy, inclination, leaning, notion, urge, wish **4** sanity, judgment, marbles (informal), mental balance, rationality, reason, senses, wits **5** **make up one's mind** decide, choose, determine, resolve ♦ verb **6** take offence, be affronted, be bothered, care, disapprove, dislike, object, resent **7** pay attention, heed, listen to, mark, note, obey, observe, pay heed to, take heed **8** guard, attend to, keep an eye on, look after, take care of, tend, watch **9** be careful, be cautious, be on (one's) guard, be wary, take care, watch

mindful adjective aware, alert, alive to, careful, conscious, heedful, wary, watchful

mindless adjective stupid, foolish,

idiotic, inane, moronic, thoughtless, unthinking, witless

mine *noun* **1** pit, colliery, deposit, excavation, shaft **2** <u>source</u>, abundance, fund, hoard, reserve, stock, store, supply, treasury, wealth ♦ *verb* **3** <u>dig up</u>, dig for, excavate, extract, hew, quarry, unearth

miner *noun* coalminer, collier (*Brit.*), pitman (*Brit.*)

mingle *verb* **1** <u>mix</u>, blend, combine, intermingle, interweave, join, merge, unite **2** <u>associate</u>, consort, fraternize, hang about *or* around, hobnob, rub shoulders (*informal*), socialize

miniature *adjective* <u>small</u>, diminutive, little, minuscule, minute, scaled-down, tiny, toy

minimal *adjective* <u>minimum</u>, least, least possible, nominal, slightest, smallest, token

minimize *verb* **1** <u>reduce</u>, curtail, decrease, diminish, miniaturize, prune, shrink **2** <u>play down</u>, belittle, decry, deprecate, discount, disparage, make light *or* little of, underrate

minimum *adjective* <u>least</u>, least possible, lowest, minimal, slightest, smallest ♦ *noun* **2** <u>least</u>, lowest, nadir

minion *noun* <u>follower</u>, flunky, hanger-on, henchman, hireling, lackey, underling, yes man

minister *noun* **1** <u>clergyman</u>, cleric, parson, pastor, preacher, priest, rector, vicar ♦ *verb* **2** <u>attend</u>, administer, cater to, pander to, serve, take care of, tend

ministry *noun* **1** <u>department</u>, bureau, council, office, quango **2** <u>the priesthood</u>, holy orders, the church

minor *adjective* <u>small</u>, inconsequential, insignificant, lesser, petty, slight, trivial, unimportant

minstrel *noun* <u>musician</u>, bard, singer, songstress, troubadour

mint *verb* <u>make</u>, cast, coin, produce, punch, stamp, strike

minuscule *adjective* <u>tiny</u>, diminutive, infinitesimal, little, microscopic, miniature, minute

minute[1] *noun* <u>moment</u>, flash, instant, jiffy (*informal*), second, tick (*Brit. informal*), trice

minute[2] *adjective* **1** <u>small</u>, diminutive, infinitesimal, little, microscopic, miniature, minuscule, tiny **2** <u>precise</u>, close, critical, detailed, exact, exhaustive, meticulous, painstaking, punctilious

minutes *plural noun* <u>record</u>, memorandum, notes, proceedings, transactions, transcript

minutiae *plural noun* <u>details</u>, finer points, ins and outs, niceties, particulars, subtleties, trifles, trivia

minx *noun* <u>flirt</u>, coquette, hussy

miracle *noun* <u>wonder</u>, marvel, phenomenon, prodigy

miraculous *adjective* <u>wonderful</u>, amazing, astonishing, astounding, extraordinary, incredible, phenomenal, prodigious, unaccountable, unbelievable

mirage *noun* <u>illusion</u>, hallucination, optical illusion

mire *noun* **1** <u>swamp</u>, bog, marsh,

morass, quagmire **2** <u>mud</u>, dirt, muck, ooze, slime

mirror noun **1** <u>looking-glass</u>, glass, reflector ♦ verb **2** <u>reflect</u>, copy, echo, emulate, follow

mirth noun <u>merriment</u>, amusement, cheerfulness, fun, gaiety, glee, hilarity, jollity, joviality, laughter, revelry

mirthful adjective <u>merry</u>, blithe, cheerful, cheery, festive, happy, jolly, jovial, light-hearted, playful, sportive

misadventure noun <u>misfortune</u>, accident, bad luck, calamity, catastrophe, debacle, disaster, mishap, reverse, setback

misanthropic adjective <u>antisocial</u>, cynical, malevolent, unfriendly

misapprehend verb <u>misunderstand</u>, misconstrue, misinterpret, misread, mistake

misapprehension noun <u>misunderstanding</u>, delusion, error, fallacy, misconception, misinterpretation, mistake

misappropriate verb <u>steal</u>, embezzle, misspend, misuse, peculate, pocket

miscalculate verb <u>misjudge</u>, blunder, err, overestimate, overrate, slip up, underestimate, underrate

miscarriage noun <u>failure</u>, breakdown, error, mishap, perversion

miscarry verb <u>fail</u>, come to grief, fall through, go awry, go wrong, misfire

miscellaneous adjective <u>mixed</u>, assorted, diverse, jumbled, motley, sundry, varied, various

miscellany noun <u>assortment</u>,

anthology, collection, hotchpotch, jumble, medley, *mélange*, mixed bag, mixture, potpourri, variety

mischance noun <u>misfortune</u>, accident, calamity, disaster, misadventure, mishap

mischief noun **1** <u>trouble</u>, impishness, misbehaviour, monkey business (*informal*), naughtiness, shenanigans (*informal*), waywardness **2** <u>harm</u>, damage, evil, hurt, injury, misfortune, trouble

mischievous adjective **1** <u>naughty</u>, impish, playful, puckish, rascally, roguish, sportive, troublesome, wayward **2** <u>malicious</u>, damaging, destructive, evil, harmful, hurtful, spiteful, vicious, wicked

misconception noun <u>delusion</u>, error, fallacy, misapprehension, misunderstanding

misconduct noun <u>immorality</u>, impropriety, malpractice, mismanagement, wrongdoing

miscreant noun <u>wrongdoer</u>, blackguard, criminal, rascal, reprobate, rogue, scoundrel, sinner, vagabond, villain

misdeed noun <u>offence</u>, crime, fault, misconduct, sin, transgression, wrong

misdemeanour noun <u>offence</u>, fault, infringement, misdeed, peccadillo, transgression

miser noun <u>skinflint</u>, cheapskate (*informal*), niggard, penny-pincher (*informal*), Scrooge

miserable adjective **1** <u>unhappy</u>, dejected, depressed,

despondent, disconsolate,
forlorn, gloomy, sorrowful,
woebegone, wretched **2** squalid,
deplorable, lamentable,
shameful, sordid, sorry, wretched

miserly adjective mean,
avaricious, grasping, niggardly,
parsimonious, penny-pinching
(informal), stingy, tightfisted,
ungenerous

misery noun **1** unhappiness,
anguish, depression, desolation,
despair, distress, gloom, grief,
sorrow, suffering, torment, woe
2 Brit. informal moaner, killjoy,
pessimist, prophet of doom,
sourpuss (informal), spoilsport,
wet blanket (informal)

misfire verb fail, fall through, go
wrong, miscarry

misfit noun nonconformist,
eccentric, fish out of water
(informal), oddball (informal),
square peg (in a round hole)
(informal)

misfortune noun **1** bad luck,
adversity, hard luck, ill luck,
infelicity **2** mishap, affliction,
calamity, disaster, reverse,
setback, tragedy, tribulation,
trouble

misgiving noun unease, anxiety,
apprehension, distrust, doubt,
qualm, reservation, suspicion,
trepidation, uncertainty, worry

misguided adjective unwise,
deluded, erroneous, ill-advised,
imprudent, injudicious,
misplaced, mistaken,
unwarranted

mishandle verb mismanage,
botch, bungle, make a mess of,
mess up (informal), muff

mishap noun accident, calamity,

misadventure, mischance,
misfortune

misinform verb mislead, deceive,
misdirect, misguide

misinterpret verb
misunderstand, distort,
misapprehend, misconceive,
misconstrue, misjudge, misread,
misrepresent, mistake

misjudge verb miscalculate,
overestimate, overrate,
underestimate, underrate

mislay verb lose, lose track of,
misplace

mislead verb deceive, delude,
fool, hoodwink, misdirect,
misguide, misinform, take in
(informal)

misleading adjective confusing,
ambiguous, deceptive,
disingenuous, evasive, false

mismanage verb mishandle,
botch, bungle, make a mess of,
mess up, misconduct, misdirect,
misgovern

misplace verb lose, lose track of,
mislay

misprint noun mistake,
corrigendum, erratum, literal,
typo (informal)

misquote verb misrepresent,
falsify, twist

misrepresent verb distort,
disguise, falsify, misinterpret

misrule noun disorder, anarchy,
chaos, confusion, lawlessness,
turmoil

miss verb **1** omit, leave out, let
go, overlook, pass over, skip
2 avoid, escape, evade **3** long
for, pine for, yearn for ◆ noun
4 mistake, blunder, error, failure,
omission, oversight

misshapen *adjective* deformed, contorted, crooked, distorted, grotesque, malformed, twisted, warped

missile *noun* rocket, projectile, weapon

missing *adjective* absent, astray, lacking, left out, lost, mislaid, misplaced, unaccounted-for

mission *noun* task, assignment, commission, duty, errand, job, quest, undertaking, vocation

missionary *noun* evangelist, apostle, preacher

missive *noun* letter, communication, dispatch, epistle, memorandum, message, note, report

misspent *adjective* wasted, dissipated, imprudent, profitless, squandered

mist *noun* fog, cloud, film, haze, smog, spray, steam, vapour

mistake *noun* 1 error, blunder, erratum, fault, faux pas, gaffe, howler (*informal*), miscalculation, oversight, slip ♦*verb* 2 misunderstand, misapprehend, misconstrue, misinterpret, misjudge, misread 3 confuse with, mix up with, take for

mistaken *adjective* wrong, erroneous, false, faulty, inaccurate, incorrect, misguided, unsound, wide of the mark

mistakenly *adverb* incorrectly, by mistake, erroneously, fallaciously, falsely, inaccurately, misguidedly, wrongly

mistimed *adjective* inopportune, badly timed, ill-timed, untimely

mistreat *verb* abuse, harm, ill-treat, injure, knock about or around, maltreat, manhandle, misuse, molest

mistress *noun* lover, concubine, girlfriend, kept woman, paramour

mistrust *verb* 1 doubt, be wary of, distrust, fear, suspect ♦*noun* 2 suspicion, distrust, doubt, misgiving, scepticism, uncertainty, wariness

mistrustful *adjective* suspicious, chary, cynical, distrustful, doubtful, fearful, hesitant, sceptical, uncertain, wary

misty *adjective* foggy, blurred, cloudy, dim, hazy, indistinct, murky, obscure, opaque, overcast

misunderstand *verb* misinterpret, be at cross-purposes, get the wrong end of the stick, misapprehend, misconstrue, misjudge, misread, mistake

misunderstanding *noun* mistake, error, misconception, misinterpretation, misjudgment, mix-up

misuse *noun* 1 waste, abuse, desecration, misapplication, squandering ♦*verb* 2 waste, abuse, desecrate, misapply, prostitute, squander

mitigate *verb* ease, extenuate, lessen, lighten, moderate, soften, subdue, temper

mitigation *noun* relief, alleviation, diminution, extenuation, moderation, remission

mix *verb* 1 combine, blend, cross, fuse, intermingle, interweave, join, jumble, merge, mingle 2 socialize, associate, consort, fraternize, hang out (*informal*),

hobnob, mingle ♦ *noun*
3 mixture, alloy, amalgam, assortment, blend, combination, compound, fusion, medley

mixed *adjective* **1** combined, amalgamated, blended, composite, compound, joint, mingled, united **2** varied, assorted, cosmopolitan, diverse, heterogeneous, miscellaneous, motley

mixed-up *adjective* confused, at sea, bewildered, distraught, disturbed, maladjusted, muddled, perplexed, puzzled, upset

mixture *noun* blend, amalgam, assortment, brew, compound, fusion, jumble, medley, mix, potpourri, variety

mix-up *noun* confusion, mess, mistake, misunderstanding, muddle, tangle

mix up *verb* **1** combine, blend, mix **2** confuse, confound, muddle

moan *noun* **1** groan, lament, sigh, sob, wail, whine **2** *Informal* grumble, complaint, gripe (*informal*), grouch (*informal*), grouse, protest, whine ♦ *verb* **3** groan, lament, sigh, sob, whine **4** *Informal* grumble, bleat, carp, complain, groan, grouse, whine, whinge (*informal*)

mob *noun* **1** crowd, drove, flock, horde, host, mass, multitude, pack, swarm, throng **2** *Slang* gang, crew (*informal*), group, lot, set ♦ *verb* **3** surround, crowd around, jostle, set upon, swarm around

mobile *adjective* movable, itinerant, moving, peripatetic, portable, travelling, wandering

mobilize *verb* prepare, activate, call to arms, call up, get or make ready, marshal, organize, rally, ready

mock *verb* **1** laugh at, deride, jeer, make fun of, poke fun at, ridicule, scoff, scorn, sneer, taunt, tease **2** mimic, ape, caricature, imitate, lampoon, parody, satirize, send up (*Brit. informal*) ♦ *adjective* **3** imitation, artificial, dummy, fake, false, feigned, phoney *or* phony (*informal*), pretended, sham, spurious

mockery *noun* **1** derision, contempt, disdain, disrespect, insults, jeering, ridicule, scoffing, scorn **2** farce, apology (*informal*), disappointment, joke, letdown

mocking *adjective* scornful, contemptuous, derisive, disdainful, disrespectful, sarcastic, sardonic, satirical, scoffing

mode *noun* **1** method, form, manner, procedure, process, style, system, technique, way **2** fashion, craze, look, rage, style, trend, vogue

model *noun* **1** representation, copy, dummy, facsimile, image, imitation, miniature, mock-up, replica **2** pattern, archetype, example, ideal, original, paradigm, paragon, prototype, standard **3** sitter, poser, subject ♦ *verb* **4** shape, carve, design, fashion, form, mould, sculpt **5** show off, display, sport (*informal*), wear

moderate *adjective* **1** mild, controlled, gentle, limited, middle-of-the-road, modest, reasonable, restrained, steady **2** average, fair, indifferent, mediocre, middling, ordinary, passable, so-so (*informal*), unexceptional ♦ *verb* **3** regulate, control, curb, ease, modulate, restrain, soften, subdue, temper, tone down

moderately *adverb* reasonably, fairly, passably, quite, rather, slightly, somewhat, tolerably

moderation *noun* restraint, fairness, reasonableness, temperance

modern *adjective* current, contemporary, fresh, new, newfangled, novel, present-day, recent, up-to-date

modernity *noun* novelty, currency, freshness, innovation, newness

modernize *verb* update, make over, rejuvenate, remake, remodel, renew, renovate, revamp

modest *adjective*
1 unpretentious, bashful, coy, demure, diffident, reserved, reticent, retiring, self-effacing, shy **2** moderate, fair, limited, middling, ordinary, small, unexceptional

modesty *noun* reserve, bashfulness, coyness, demureness, humility, reticence, shyness, timidity

modicum *noun* little, bit, crumb, drop, fragment, scrap, shred, touch

modification *noun* change, adjustment, alteration, qualification, refinement, revision, variation

modify *verb* **1** change, adapt, adjust, alter, convert, reform, remodel, revise, rework **2** tone down, ease, lessen, lower, moderate, qualify, restrain, soften, temper

modish *adjective* fashionable, contemporary, current, in, smart, stylish, trendy (*Brit. informal*), up-to-the-minute, voguish

modulate *verb* adjust, attune, balance, regulate, tune, vary

mogul *noun* tycoon, baron, big noise (*informal*), big shot (*informal*), magnate, V.I.P.

moist *adjective* damp, clammy, dewy, humid, soggy, wet

moisten *verb* dampen, damp, moisturize, soak, water, wet

moisture *noun* damp, dew, liquid, water, wetness

molecule *noun* particle, jot, speck

molest *verb* **1** annoy, badger, beset, bother, disturb, harass, persecute, pester, plague, torment, worry **2** abuse, attack, harm, hurt, ill-treat, interfere with, maltreat

mollify *verb* pacify, appease, calm, conciliate, placate, quiet, soothe, sweeten

mollycoddle *verb* pamper, baby, cosset, indulge, spoil

moment *noun* **1** instant, flash, jiffy (*informal*), second, split second, trice, twinkling **2** time, juncture, point, stage

momentarily *adverb* briefly, for a moment, temporarily

momentary *adjective* short-lived, brief, fleeting, passing, short, temporary, transitory

momentous adjective significant, critical, crucial, fateful, historic, important, pivotal, vital, weighty

momentum noun impetus, drive, energy, force, power, propulsion, push, strength, thrust

monarch noun ruler, emperor or empress, king, potentate, prince or princess, queen, sovereign

monarchy noun 1 sovereignty, autocracy, kingship, monocracy, royalism 2 kingdom, empire, principality, realm

monastery noun abbey, cloister, convent, friary, nunnery, priory

monastic adjective monkish, ascetic, cloistered, contemplative, hermit-like, reclusive, secluded, sequestered, withdrawn

monetary adjective financial, budgetary, capital, cash, fiscal, pecuniary

money noun cash, capital, coin, currency, hard cash, legal tender, readies (informal), riches, silver, wealth

mongrel noun 1 hybrid, cross, crossbreed, half-breed ◆ adjective 2 hybrid, crossbred

monitor noun 1 watchdog, guide, invigilator, prefect (Brit.), supervisor ◆ verb 2 check, follow, keep an eye on, keep tabs on, keep track of, observe, survey, watch

monk noun friar, brother

monkey noun 1 simian, primate 2 rascal, devil, imp, rogue, scamp ◆ verb 3 fool, meddle, mess, play, tinker

monolithic adjective huge, colossal, impenetrable, intractable, massive, monumental, solid

monologue noun speech, harangue, lecture, sermon, soliloquy

monopolize verb control, corner the market in, dominate, hog (slang), keep to oneself, take over

monotonous adjective tedious, boring, dull, humdrum, mind-numbing, repetitive, tiresome, unchanging, wearisome

monotony noun tedium, boredom, monotonousness, repetitiveness, routine, sameness, tediousness

monster noun 1 brute, beast, demon, devil, fiend, villain 2 freak, monstrosity, mutant 3 giant, colossus, mammoth, titan ◆ adjective 4 huge, colossal, enormous, gigantic, immense, mammoth, massive, stupendous, tremendous

monstrosity noun eyesore, freak, horror, monster

monstrous adjective 1 unnatural, fiendish, freakish, frightful, grotesque, gruesome, hideous, horrible 2 outrageous, diabolical, disgraceful, foul, inhuman, intolerable, scandalous, shocking 3 huge, colossal, enormous, immense, mammoth, massive, prodigious, stupendous, tremendous

monument noun memorial, cairn, cenotaph, commemoration, gravestone, headstone, marker, mausoleum, shrine, tombstone

monumental adjective 1 important, awesome, enormous, epoch-making,

mood *noun* historic, majestic, memorable, significant, unforgettable **2** *Informal* immense, colossal, great, massive, staggering

mood *noun* state of mind, disposition, frame of mind, humour, spirit, temper

moody *adjective* **1** sullen, gloomy, glum, ill-tempered, irritable, morose, sad, sulky, temperamental, touchy **2** changeable, capricious, erratic, fickle, flighty, impulsive, mercurial, temperamental, unpredictable, volatile

moon *noun* **1** satellite ♦ *verb* **2** idle, daydream, languish, mope, waste time

moor[1] *noun* moorland, fell (*Brit.*), heath

moor[2] *verb* tie up, anchor, berth, dock, lash, make fast, secure

moot *adjective* **1** debatable, arguable, contestable, controversial, disputable, doubtful, undecided, unresolved, unsettled ♦ *verb* **2** bring up, broach, propose, put forward, suggest

mop *noun* **1** squeegee, sponge, swab **2** mane, shock, tangle, thatch

mope *verb* brood, fret, languish, moon, pine, pout, sulk

mop up *verb* clean up, soak up, sponge, swab, wash, wipe

moral *adjective* **1** good, decent, ethical, high-minded, honourable, just, noble, principled, right, virtuous ♦ *noun* **2** lesson, meaning, message, point, significance

morale *noun* confidence, esprit de corps, heart, self-esteem, spirit

morality *noun* **1** integrity, decency, goodness, honesty, justice, righteousness, virtue **2** standards, conduct, ethics, manners, morals, mores, philosophy, principles

morals *plural noun* morality, behaviour, conduct, ethics, habits, integrity, manners, mores, principles, scruples, standards

morass *noun* **1** marsh, bog, fen, quagmire, slough, swamp **2** mess, confusion, mix-up, muddle, tangle

moratorium *noun* postponement, freeze, halt, standstill, suspension

morbid *adjective* **1** unwholesome, ghoulish, gloomy, melancholy, sick, sombre, unhealthy **2** gruesome, dreadful, ghastly, grisly, hideous, horrid, macabre

mordant *adjective* sarcastic, biting, caustic, cutting, incisive, pungent, scathing, stinging, trenchant

more *adjective* **1** extra, added, additional, further, new, other, supplementary ♦ *adverb* **2** to a greater extent, better, further, longer

moreover *adverb* furthermore, additionally, also, as well, besides, further, in addition, too

morgue *noun* mortuary

moribund *adjective* declining, on its last legs, stagnant, waning, weak

morning *noun* dawn, a.m., break of day, daybreak, forenoon, morn (*poetic*), sunrise

moron noun <u>fool</u>, blockhead, cretin, dunce, dunderhead, halfwit, idiot, imbecile, oaf

moronic adjective <u>idiotic</u>, cretinous, foolish, halfwitted, imbecilic, mindless, stupid, unintelligent

morose adjective <u>sullen</u>, depressed, dour, gloomy, glum, ill-tempered, moody, sour, sulky, surly, taciturn

morsel noun <u>piece</u>, bit, bite, crumb, mouthful, part, scrap, soupçon, taste, titbit

mortal adjective 1 <u>human</u>, ephemeral, impermanent, passing, temporal, transient, worldly 2 <u>fatal</u>, deadly, death-dealing, destructive, killing, lethal, murderous, terminal ♦ noun 3 <u>human being</u>, being, earthling, human, individual, man, person, woman

mortality noun 1 <u>humanity</u>, impermanence, transience 2 <u>killing</u>, bloodshed, carnage, death, destruction, fatality

mortification noun 1 <u>humiliation</u>, annoyance, chagrin, discomfiture, embarrassment, shame, vexation 2 <u>discipline</u>, abasement, chastening, control, denial, subjugation 3 Medical <u>gangrene</u>, corruption, festering

mortified adjective <u>humiliated</u>, ashamed, chagrined, chastened, crushed, deflated, embarrassed, humbled, shamed

mortify verb 1 <u>humiliate</u>, chagrin, chasten, crush, deflate, embarrass, humble, shame 2 <u>discipline</u>, abase, chasten, control, deny, subdue 3 Of flesh putrefy, deaden, die, fester

mortuary noun <u>morgue</u>, funeral parlour

mostly adverb <u>generally</u>, as a rule, chiefly, largely, mainly, on the whole, predominantly, primarily, principally, usually

moth-eaten adjective <u>decayed</u>, decrepit, dilapidated, ragged, shabby, tattered, threadbare, worn-out

mother noun 1 <u>parent</u>, dam, ma (informal), mater, mum (Brit. informal), mummy (Brit. informal) ♦ adjective 2 <u>native</u>, inborn, innate, natural ♦ verb 3 <u>nurture</u>, care for, cherish, nurse, protect, raise, rear, tend

motherly adjective <u>maternal</u>, affectionate, caring, comforting, loving, protective, sheltering

motif noun 1 <u>theme</u>, concept, idea, leitmotif, subject 2 <u>design</u>, decoration, ornament, shape

motion noun 1 <u>movement</u>, flow, locomotion, mobility, move, progress, travel 2 <u>proposal</u>, proposition, recommendation, submission, suggestion ♦ verb 3 <u>gesture</u>, beckon, direct, gesticulate, nod, signal, wave

motionless adjective <u>still</u>, fixed, frozen, immobile, paralysed, standing, static, stationary, stock-still, transfixed, unmoving

motivate verb <u>inspire</u>, arouse, cause, drive, induce, move, persuade, prompt, stimulate, stir

motivation noun <u>incentive</u>, incitement, inducement, inspiration, motive, reason, spur, stimulus

motive noun <u>reason</u>, ground(s),

incentive, inducement, inspiration, object, purpose, rationale, stimulus

motley *adjective* **1** miscellaneous, assorted, disparate, heterogeneous, mixed, varied **2** multicoloured, chequered, variegated

mottled *adjective* blotchy, dappled, flecked, piebald, speckled, spotted, stippled, streaked

motto *noun* saying, adage, dictum, maxim, precept, proverb, rule, slogan, watchword

mould¹ *noun* **1** cast, pattern, shape **2** design, build, construction, fashion, form, format, kind, pattern, shape, style **3** nature, calibre, character, kind, quality, sort, stamp, type ♦ *verb* **4** shape, construct, create, fashion, forge, form, make, model, sculpt, work **5** influence, affect, control, direct, form, make, shape

mould² *noun* fungus, blight, mildew

mouldy *adjective* stale, bad, blighted, decaying, fusty, mildewed, musty, rotten

mound *noun* **1** heap, drift, pile, rick, stack **2** hill, bank, dune, embankment, hillock, knoll, rise

mount *verb* **1** climb, ascend, clamber up, go up, scale **2** bestride, climb onto, jump on **3** increase, accumulate, build, escalate, grow, intensify, multiply, pile up, swell ♦ *noun* **4** backing, base, frame, setting, stand, support **5** horse, steed (*literary*)

mountain *noun* **1** peak, alp, fell

(*Brit.*), mount **2** heap, abundance, mass, mound, pile, stack, ton

mountainous *adjective* **1** high, alpine, highland, rocky, soaring, steep, towering, upland **2** huge, daunting, enormous, gigantic, great, immense, mammoth, mighty, monumental

mourn *verb* grieve, bemoan, bewail, deplore, lament, rue, wail, weep

mournful *adjective* **1** sad, melancholy, piteous, plaintive, sorrowful, tragic, unhappy, woeful **2** dismal, disconsolate, downcast, gloomy, grieving, heavy-hearted, lugubrious, miserable, rueful, sombre

mourning *noun* **1** grieving, bereavement, grief, lamentation, weeping, woe **2** black, sackcloth and ashes, widow's weeds

mouth *noun* **1** lips, gob (*slang, especially Brit.*), jaws, maw **2** opening, aperture, door, entrance, gateway, inlet, orifice

mouthful *noun* taste, bit, bite, little, morsel, sample, spoonful, swallow

mouthpiece *noun* spokesperson, agent, delegate, representative, spokesman *or* spokeswoman

movable *adjective* portable, detachable, mobile, transferable, transportable

move *verb* **1** go, advance, budge, proceed, progress, shift, stir **2** change, shift, switch, transfer, transpose **3** leave, migrate, pack one's bags (*informal*), quit, relocate, remove **4** drive, activate, operate, propel, shift, start, turn **5** touch, affect, excite, impress **6** incite, cause, induce, influence, inspire, motivate, prompt, persuade, prompt, rouse **7** propose, advocate, put forward, recommend, suggest, urge ♦ *noun* **8** action, manoeuvre, measure, ploy, step, stratagem, stroke, turn **9** transfer, relocation, removal, shift

movement *noun* **1** motion, action, activity, change, development, flow, manoeuvre, progress, stirring **2** group, campaign, crusade, drive, faction, front, grouping, organization, party **3** workings, action, machinery, mechanism, works **4** *Music* section, division, part, passage

movie *noun* film, feature, flick (*slang*), picture

moving *adjective* **1** emotional, affecting, inspiring, pathetic, persuasive, poignant, stirring, touching **2** mobile, movable, portable, running, unfixed

mow *verb* cut, crop, scythe, shear, trim

mow down *verb* massacre, butcher, cut down, cut to pieces, shoot down, slaughter

much *adjective* **1** great, abundant, a lot of, ample, considerable, copious, plenty of, sizable *or* sizeable, substantial ♦ *noun* **2** a lot, a good deal, a great deal, heaps (*informal*), loads (*informal*), lots (*informal*), plenty ♦ *adverb* **3** greatly, a great deal, a lot, considerably, decidedly, exceedingly

muck *noun* **1** manure, dung, ordure **2** dirt, filth, gunge

(*informal*), mire, mud, ooze, slime, sludge

muck up *verb* ruin, blow (*slang*), botch, bungle, make a mess of, make a pig's ear of (*informal*), mess up, muff, spoil

mucky *adjective* dirty, begrimed, filthy, grimy, messy, muddy

mud *noun* dirt, clay, mire, ooze, silt, slime, sludge

muddle *verb* **1** jumble, disarrange, disorder, disorganize, mess, scramble, spoil, tangle **2** confuse, befuddle, bewilder, confound, daze, disorient, perplex, stupefy ♦ *noun* **3** confusion, chaos, disarray, disorder, disorganization, jumble, mess, mix-up, predicament, tangle

muddy *adjective* **1** dirty, bespattered, grimy, mucky, mud-caked, soiled **2** boggy, marshy, quaggy, swampy

muffle *verb* **1** wrap up, cloak, cover, envelop, shroud, swaddle, swathe **2** deaden, muzzle, quieten, silence, soften, stifle, suppress

muffled *adjective* indistinct, faint, muted, stifled, strangled, subdued, suppressed

mug[1] *noun* cup, beaker, pot, tankard

mug[2] *noun* **1** face, countenance, features, visage **1** fool, chump (*informal*), easy *or* soft touch (*slang*), simpleton, sucker (*slang*) ♦ *verb* **2** attack, assault, beat up, rob, set about *or* upon

muggy *adjective* humid, clammy, close, moist, oppressive, sticky, stuffy, sultry

mug up verb study, bone up on (informal), burn the midnight oil (informal), cram (informal), swot (Brit. informal)

mull verb ponder, consider, contemplate, deliberate, meditate, reflect on, ruminate, think over, weigh

multifarious adjective diverse, different, legion, manifold, many, miscellaneous, multiple, numerous, sundry, varied

multiple adjective many, manifold, multitudinous, numerous, several, sundry, various

multiply verb 1 increase, build up, expand, extend, proliferate, spread 2 reproduce, breed, propagate

multitude noun mass, army, crowd, horde, host, mob, myriad, swarm, throng

munch verb chew, champ, chomp, crunch

mundane adjective 1 ordinary, banal, commonplace, day-to-day, everyday, humdrum, prosaic, routine, workaday 2 earthly, mortal, secular, temporal, terrestrial, worldly

municipal adjective civic, public, urban

municipality noun town, borough, city, district, township

munificence noun generosity, beneficence, benevolence, bounty, largesse or largess, liberality, magnanimousness, philanthropy

munificent adjective generous, beneficent, benevolent, bountiful, lavish, liberal,

magnanimous, open-handed, philanthropic, unstinting

murder noun 1 killing, assassination, bloodshed, butchery, carnage, homicide, manslaughter, massacre, slaying ♦ verb 2 kill, assassinate, bump off (slang), butcher, eliminate (slang), massacre, slaughter, slay

murderer noun killer, assassin, butcher, cut-throat, hit man (slang), homicide, slaughterer, slayer

murderous adjective deadly, bloodthirsty, brutal, cruel, cut-throat, ferocious, lethal, savage

murky adjective dark, cloudy, dim, dull, gloomy, grey, misty, overcast

murmur verb 1 mumble, mutter, whisper 2 grumble, complain, moan (informal) ♦ noun 3 drone, buzzing, humming, purr, rumble, whisper

muscle noun 1 tendon, sinew 2 strength, brawn, clout (informal), forcefulness, might, power, stamina, weight ♦ verb 3 muscle in Informal impose oneself, butt in, force one's way in

muscular adjective strong, athletic, powerful, robust, sinewy, strapping, sturdy, vigorous

muse verb ponder, brood, cogitate, consider, contemplate, deliberate, meditate, mull over, reflect, ruminate

mushy adjective 1 soft, pulpy, semi-solid, slushy, squashy, squelchy, squidgy (informal) 2 Informal sentimental, maudlin, mawkish, saccharine, schmaltzy (*slang*), sloppy (*informal*), slushy (*informal*)

musical *adjective* <u>melodious</u>, dulcet, euphonious, harmonious, lyrical, melodic, sweet-sounding, tuneful

must *noun* <u>necessity</u>, essential, fundamental, imperative, prerequisite, requirement, requisite, sine qua non

muster *verb* 1 <u>assemble</u>, call together, convene, gather, marshal, mobilize, rally, summon ♦ *noun* 2 <u>assembly</u>, collection, congregation, convention, gathering, meeting, rally, roundup

musty *adjective* <u>stale</u>, airless, dank, fusty, mildewed, mouldy, old, smelly, stuffy

mutability *noun* <u>change</u>, alteration, evolution, metamorphosis, transition, variation, vicissitude

mutable *adjective* <u>changeable</u>, adaptable, alterable, fickle, inconsistent, inconstant, unsettled, unstable, variable, volatile

mutation *noun* <u>change</u>, alteration, evolution, metamorphosis, modification, transfiguration, transformation, variation

mute *adjective* <u>silent</u>, dumb, mum, speechless, unspoken, voiceless, wordless

mutilate *verb* 1 <u>maim</u>, amputate, cut up, damage, disfigure, dismember, injure, lacerate, mangle 2 <u>distort</u>, adulterate, bowdlerize, censor, cut, damage, expurgate

mutinous *adjective* <u>rebellious</u>, disobedient, insubordinate, insurgent, refractory, riotous, subversive, unmanageable, unruly

mutiny *noun* 1 <u>rebellion</u>, disobedience, insubordination, insurrection, revolt, revolution, riot, uprising ♦ *verb* 2 <u>rebel</u>, disobey, resist, revolt, rise up

mutter *verb* <u>grumble</u>, complain, grouse, mumble, murmur, rumble

mutual *adjective* <u>shared</u>, common, interchangeable, joint, reciprocal, requited, returned

muzzle *noun* 1 <u>jaws</u>, mouth, nose, snout 2 <u>gag</u>, guard ♦ *verb* 3 <u>suppress</u>, censor, curb, gag, restrain, silence, stifle

myopic *adjective* <u>short-sighted</u>, near-sighted

myriad *adjective* 1 <u>innumerable</u>, countless, immeasurable, incalculable, multitudinous, untold ♦ *noun* 2 <u>multitude</u>, army, horde, host, swarm

mysterious *adjective* <u>strange</u>, arcane, enigmatic, inexplicable, inscrutable, mystifying, perplexing, puzzling, secret, uncanny, unfathomable, weird

mystery *noun* <u>puzzle</u>, conundrum, enigma, problem, question, riddle, secret, teaser

mystic, mystical *adjective* <u>supernatural</u>, inscrutable, metaphysical, mysterious, occult, otherworldly, paranormal, preternatural, transcendental

mystify *verb* <u>puzzle</u>, baffle, bewilder, confound, confuse, flummox, nonplus, perplex, stump

mystique noun fascination, awe, charisma, charm, glamour, magic, spell

myth noun 1 legend, allegory, fable, fairy story, fiction, folk tale, saga, story 2 illusion, delusion, fancy, fantasy, figment, imagination, superstition, tall story

mythical adjective 1 legendary, fabled, fabulous, fairy-tale, mythological 2 imaginary, fictitious, invented, made-up, make-believe, nonexistent, pretended, unreal, untrue

mythological adjective legendary, fabulous, mythic, mythical, traditional

mythology noun legend, folklore, lore, tradition

N n

nab verb catch, apprehend, arrest, capture, collar (informal), grab, seize, snatch

nadir noun bottom, depths, lowest point, minimum, rock bottom

naevus noun birthmark, mole

naff adjective bad, duff (Brit. informal), inferior, low-grade, poor, rubbishy, second-rate, shabby, shoddy, worthless

nag¹ verb 1 scold, annoy, badger, harass, hassle (informal), henpeck, irritate, pester, plague, upbraid, worry ♦ noun 2 scold, harpy, shrew, tartar, virago

nag² noun horse, hack

nagging adjective irritating, persistent, scolding, shrewish, worrying

nail verb fasten, attach, fix, hammer, join, pin, secure, tack

naive adjective 1 gullible, callow, credulous, green, unsuspicious, wet behind the ears (informal) 2 innocent, artless, guileless, ingenuous, open, simple, trusting, unsophisticated, unworldly

naivety, naïveté noun 1 gullibility, callowness, credulity 2 innocence, artlessness, guilelessness, inexperience, ingenuousness, naturalness, openness, simplicity

naked adjective nude, bare, exposed, starkers (informal), stripped, unclothed, undressed, without a stitch on (informal)

nakedness noun nudity, bareness, undress

namby-pamby adjective feeble, insipid, sentimental, spineless, vapid, weak, weedy (informal), wimpish or wimpy (informal), wishy-washy (informal)

name noun 1 title, designation, epithet, handle (slang), moniker or monicker (slang), nickname, sobriquet, term 2 fame, distinction, eminence, esteem, honour, note, praise, renown, repute ♦ verb 3 call, baptize, christen, dub, entitle, label, style, term 4 nominate, appoint, choose, designate, select, specify

named adjective 1 called, baptized, christened, dubbed, entitled, known as, labelled, styled, termed 2 nominated, appointed, chosen, designated, mentioned, picked, selected, singled out, specified

nameless adjective
1 <u>anonymous</u>, unnamed, untitled **2** <u>unknown</u>, incognito, obscure, undistinguished, unheard-of, unsung **3** <u>horrible</u>, abominable, indescribable, unmentionable, unspeakable, unutterable

namely adverb <u>specifically</u>, to wit, viz.

nap¹ noun **1** <u>sleep</u>, catnap, forty winks (informal), kip (Brit. slang), rest, siesta ♦ verb **2** <u>sleep</u>, catnap, doze, drop off (informal), kip (Brit. slang), nod off (informal), rest, snooze (informal)

nap² noun <u>weave</u>, down, fibre, grain, pile

napkin noun <u>serviette</u>, cloth

narcissism noun <u>egotism</u>, self-love, vanity

narcotic noun **1** <u>drug</u>, anaesthetic, analgesic, anodyne, opiate, painkiller, sedative, tranquillizer ♦ adjective **2** <u>sedative</u>, analgesic, calming, hypnotic, painkilling, soporific

nark verb <u>annoy</u>, bother, exasperate, get on one's nerves (informal), irritate, nettle

narrate verb <u>tell</u>, chronicle, describe, detail, recite, recount, relate, report

narration noun <u>telling</u>, description, explanation, reading, recital, relation

narrative noun <u>story</u>, account, chronicle, history, report, statement, tale

narrator noun <u>storyteller</u>, author, chronicler, commentator, reporter, writer

narrow adjective **1** <u>thin</u>, attenuated, fine, slender, slim, spare, tapering **2** <u>limited</u>, close, confined, constricted, contracted, meagre, restricted, tight **3** <u>insular</u>, dogmatic, illiberal, intolerant, narrow-minded, partial, prejudiced, small-minded ♦ verb **4** <u>tighten</u>, constrict, limit, reduce

narrowly adverb <u>just</u>, barely, by the skin of one's teeth, only just, scarcely

narrow-minded adjective <u>intolerant</u>, bigoted, hidebound, illiberal, opinionated, parochial, prejudiced, provincial, small-minded

nastiness noun <u>unpleasantness</u>, malice, meanness, spitefulness

nasty adjective **1** <u>objectionable</u>, disagreeable, loathsome, obnoxious, offensive, unpleasant, vile **2** <u>spiteful</u>, despicable, disagreeable, distasteful, malicious, mean, unpleasant, vicious, vile **3** <u>painful</u>, bad, critical, dangerous, serious, severe

nation noun <u>country</u>, people, race, realm, society, state, tribe

national adjective **1** <u>nationwide</u>, countrywide, public, widespread ♦ noun **2** <u>citizen</u>, inhabitant, native, resident, subject

nationalism noun <u>patriotism</u>, allegiance, chauvinism, jingoism, loyalty

nationality noun <u>race</u>, birth, nation

nationwide adjective <u>national</u>, countrywide, general, widespread

native adjective **1** <u>local</u>, domestic, home, indigenous **2** <u>inborn</u>, congenital, hereditary, inbred, ingrained, innate, instinctive, intrinsic, natural ♦ *noun* 3 <u>inhabitant</u>, aborigine, citizen, countryman, dweller, national, resident

natter *verb* 1 <u>gossip</u>, blether, chatter, gabble, jaw (*slang*), prattle, rabbit (on) (*Brit. informal*), talk 2 <u>gossip</u>, chat, chinwag (*Brit. informal*), chitchat, conversation, gab (*informal*), jaw (*slang*), prattle, talk

natty *adjective* <u>smart</u>, dapper, elegant, fashionable, neat, snazzy (*informal*), spruce, stylish, trim

natural *adjective* 1 <u>normal</u>, common, everyday, legitimate, logical, ordinary, regular, typical, usual 2 <u>unaffected</u>, genuine, ingenuous, open, real, simple, spontaneous, unpretentious, unsophisticated 3 <u>innate</u>, characteristic, essential, inborn, inherent, instinctive, intuitive, native 4 <u>pure</u>, organic, plain, unrefined, whole

naturalist *noun* <u>biologist</u>, botanist, ecologist, zoologist

naturalistic *adjective* <u>realistic</u>, lifelike, true-to-life

naturally *adverb* 1 <u>of course</u>, certainly 2 <u>genuinely</u>, normally, simply, spontaneously, typically, unaffectedly, unpretentiously

nature *noun* 1 <u>creation</u>, cosmos, earth, environment, universe, world 2 <u>make-up</u>, character, complexion, constitution, essence 3 <u>kind</u>, category, description, sort, species, style, type, variety 4 <u>temperament</u>, disposition, humour, mood,

outlook, temper

naughty *adjective* 1 <u>disobedient</u>, bad, impish, misbehaved, mischievous, refractory, wayward, wicked, worthless 2 <u>obscene</u>, improper, lewd, ribald, risqué, smutty, vulgar

nausea *noun* <u>sickness</u>, biliousness, queasiness, retching, squeamishness, vomiting

nauseate *verb* <u>sicken</u>, disgust, offend, repel, repulse, revolt, turn one's stomach

nauseous *adjective* <u>sickening</u>, abhorrent, disgusting, distasteful, nauseating, offensive, repugnant, repulsive, revolting

nautical *adjective* <u>maritime</u>, marine, naval

naval *adjective* <u>nautical</u>, marine, maritime

navigable *adjective* 1 <u>passable</u>, clear, negotiable, unobstructed 2 <u>sailable</u>, controllable, dirigible

navigate *verb* <u>sail</u>, drive, guide, handle, manoeuvre, pilot, steer, voyage

navigation *noun* <u>sailing</u>, helmsmanship, seamanship, voyaging

navigator *noun* <u>pilot</u>, mariner, seaman

navvy *noun* <u>labourer</u>, worker, workman

navy *noun* <u>fleet</u>, armada, flotilla

near *adjective* 1 <u>close</u>, adjacent, adjoining, nearby, neighbouring 2 <u>forthcoming</u>, approaching, imminent, impending, in the offing, looming, nigh, upcoming

nearby *adjective* <u>neighbouring</u>, adjacent, adjoining, convenient, handy

nearly adverb almost, approximately, as good as, just about, practically, roughly, virtually, well-nigh

nearness noun closeness, accessibility, availability, handiness, proximity, vicinity

near-sighted adjective short-sighted, myopic

neat adjective 1 tidy, orderly, shipshape, smart, spick-and-span, spruce, systematic, trim 2 elegant, adept, adroit, deft, dexterous, efficient, graceful, nimble, skilful, stylish 3 Of alcoholic drinks straight, pure, undiluted, unmixed

neatly adverb 1 tidily, daintily, fastidiously, methodically, smartly, sprucely, systematically 2 elegantly, adeptly, adroitly, deftly, dexterously, efficiently, expertly, gracefully, nimbly, skilfully

neatness noun 1 tidiness, daintiness, orderliness, smartness, spruceness, trimness 2 elegance, adroitness, deftness, dexterity, efficiency, grace, nimbleness, skill, style

nebulous adjective vague, confused, dim, hazy, imprecise, indefinite, indistinct, shadowy, uncertain, unclear

necessarily adverb certainly, automatically, compulsorily, incontrovertibly, inevitably, inexorably, naturally, of necessity, undoubtedly

necessary adjective 1 needed, compulsory, essential, imperative, indispensable, mandatory, obligatory, required, requisite, vital 2 certain, fated, inescapable, inevitable, inexorable, unavoidable

necessitate verb compel, call for, coerce, constrain, demand, force, impel, oblige, require

necessities plural noun essentials, exigencies, fundamentals, needs, requirements

necessity noun 1 inevitability, compulsion, inexorableness, obligation 2 need, desideratum, essential, fundamental, prerequisite, requirement, requisite, sine qua non

necromancy noun magic, black magic, divination, enchantment, sorcery, witchcraft, wizardry

necropolis noun cemetery, burial ground, churchyard, graveyard

need verb 1 require, call for, demand, entail, lack, miss, necessitate, want ◆noun 2 poverty, deprivation, destitution, inadequacy, insufficiency, lack, paucity, penury, shortage 3 requirement, demand, desideratum, essential, requisite 4 emergency, exigency, necessity, obligation, urgency, want

needed adjective necessary, called for, desired, lacked, required, wanted

needful adjective necessary, essential, indispensable, needed, required, requisite, stipulated, vital

needle verb irritate, annoy, get on one's nerves (informal), goad, harass, nag, pester, provoke, rile, taunt

needless adjective unnecessary,

gratuitous, groundless, pointless, redundant, superfluous, uncalled-for, unwanted, useless

needlework noun embroidery, needlecraft, sewing, stitching, tailoring

needy adjective poor, deprived, destitute, disadvantaged, impoverished, penniless, poverty-stricken, underprivileged

ne'er-do-well noun layabout, black sheep, good-for-nothing, idler, loafer, loser, skiver (Brit. slang), wastrel

nefarious adjective wicked, criminal, depraved, evil, foul, heinous, infernal, villainous

negate verb 1 invalidate, annul, cancel, countermand, neutralize, nullify, obviate, reverse, wipe out 2 deny, contradict, disallow, disprove, gainsay (archaic or literary), oppose, rebut, refute

negation noun 1 cancellation, neutralization, nullification 2 denial, contradiction, converse, disavowal, inverse, opposite, rejection, renunciation, reverse

negative adjective
1 contradictory, contrary, denying, dissenting, opposing, refusing, rejecting, resisting
2 pessimistic, cynical, gloomy, jaundiced, uncooperative, unenthusiastic, unwilling ♦ noun
3 contradiction, denial, refusal

neglect verb 1 disregard, disdain, ignore, overlook, rebuff, scorn, slight, spurn 2 be remiss, evade, omit, pass over, shirk, skimp ♦ noun 3 disregard, disdain, inattention, indifference 4 negligence, carelessness,

dereliction, failure, laxity, oversight, slackness

neglected adjective
1 abandoned, derelict, overgrown 2 disregarded, unappreciated, underestimated, undervalued

neglectful adjective careless, heedless, inattentive, indifferent, lax, negligent, remiss, thoughtless, uncaring

negligence noun carelessness, dereliction, disregard, inattention, indifference, laxity, neglect, slackness, thoughtlessness

negligent adjective careless, forgetful, heedless, inattentive, neglectful, remiss, slack, slapdash, thoughtless, unthinking

negligible adjective insignificant, imperceptible, inconsequential, minor, minute, small, trifling, trivial, unimportant

negotiable adjective debatable, variable

negotiate verb 1 deal, arrange, bargain, conciliate, debate, discuss, mediate, transact, work out 2 get round, clear, cross, get over, get past, pass, surmount

negotiation noun bargaining, arbitration, debate, diplomacy, discussion, mediation, transaction, wheeling and dealing (informal)

negotiator noun mediator, ambassador, delegate, diplomat, honest broker, intermediary, moderator

neighbourhood noun district, community, environs, locale, locality, quarter, region, vicinity

neighbouring *adjective* <u>nearby</u>, adjacent, adjoining, bordering, connecting, near, next, surrounding

neighbourly *adjective* <u>helpful</u>, considerate, friendly, harmonious, hospitable, kind, obliging, sociable

nemesis *noun* <u>retribution</u>, destiny, destruction, fate, vengeance

nepotism *noun* <u>favouritism</u>, bias, partiality, patronage, preferential treatment

nerd, nurd *noun* <u>bore</u>, anorak (*informal*), dork (*slang*), drip (*informal*), geek (*informal*), obsessive, trainspotter (*informal*), wonk (*informal*)

nerve *noun* **1** <u>bravery</u>, bottle (*Brit. slang*), courage, daring, fearlessness, grit, guts (*informal*), pluck, resolution, will **2** <u>impudence</u>, audacity, boldness, brazenness, cheek (*informal*), impertinence, insolence, temerity ♦ *verb* **3 nerve oneself** <u>brace oneself</u>, fortify oneself, steel oneself

nerveless *adjective* <u>calm</u>, composed, controlled, cool, impassive, imperturbable, self-possessed, unemotional

nerve-racking *adjective* <u>tense</u>, difficult, distressing, frightening, harrowing, stressful, trying, worrying

nerves *plural noun* <u>tension</u>, anxiety, butterflies (in one's stomach) (*informal*), cold feet (*informal*), fretfulness, nervousness, strain, stress, worry

nervous *adjective* <u>apprehensive</u>, anxious, edgy, fearful, jumpy, on edge, tense, uneasy, uptight (*informal*), worried

nervousness *noun* <u>anxiety</u>, agitation, disquiet, excitability, fluster, tension, touchiness, worry

nervy *adjective* <u>anxious</u>, agitated, fidgety, jittery (*informal*), jumpy, nervous, on edge, tense, twitchy (*informal*)

nest *noun* <u>refuge</u>, den, haunt, hideaway, retreat

nest egg *noun* <u>reserve</u>, cache, deposit, fall-back, fund(s), savings, store

nestle *verb* <u>snuggle</u>, cuddle, curl up, huddle, nuzzle

nestling *noun* <u>chick</u>, fledgling

net[1] *noun* **1** <u>mesh</u>, lattice, netting, network, openwork, tracery, web ♦ *verb* **2** <u>catch</u>, bag, capture, enmesh, ensnare, entangle, trap

net[2], **nett** *adjective* **1** <u>final</u>, after taxes, clear, take-home ♦ *verb* **2** <u>earn</u>, accumulate, bring in, clear, gain, make, realize, reap

nether *adjective* <u>lower</u>, below, beneath, bottom, inferior, under, underground

nettled *adjective* <u>irritated</u>, annoyed, exasperated, galled, harassed, incensed, peeved, put out, riled, vexed

network *noun* <u>system</u>, arrangement, complex, grid, labyrinth, lattice, maze, organization, structure, web

neurosis *noun* <u>obsession</u>, abnormality, affliction, derangement, instability, maladjustment, mental illness, phobia

neurotic *adjective* <u>unstable</u>,

neuter *adjective* abnormal, compulsive, disturbed, maladjusted, manic, nervous, obsessive, unhealthy

neuter *verb* castrate, doctor (*informal*), emasculate, fix (*informal*), geld, spay

neutral *adjective* 1 unbiased, disinterested, even-handed, impartial, nonaligned, nonpartisan, uncommitted, uninvolved, unprejudiced 2 indeterminate, dull, indistinct, intermediate, undefined

neutrality *noun* impartiality, detachment, nonalignment, noninterference, noninvolvement, nonpartisanship

neutralize *verb* counteract, cancel, compensate for, counterbalance, frustrate, negate, nullify, offset, undo

never *adverb* at no time, not at all, on no account, under no circumstances

nevertheless *adverb* nonetheless, but, even so, (even) though, however, notwithstanding, regardless, still, yet

new *adjective* 1 modern, contemporary, current, fresh, ground-breaking, latest, novel, original, recent, state-of-the-art, unfamiliar, up-to-date 2 changed, altered, improved, modernized, redesigned, renewed, restored 3 extra, added, more, supplementary

newcomer *noun* novice, arrival, beginner, Johnny-come-lately (*informal*), parvenu

newfangled *adjective* new, contemporary, fashionable, gimmicky, modern, novel, recent, state-of-the-art

newly *adverb* recently, anew, freshly, just, lately, latterly

newness *noun* novelty, freshness, innovation, oddity, originality, strangeness, unfamiliarity, uniqueness

news *noun* information, bulletin, communiqué, exposé, gossip, hearsay, intelligence, latest (*informal*), report, revelation, rumour, story

newsworthy *adjective* interesting, important, notable, noteworthy, remarkable, significant, stimulating

next *adjective* 1 following, consequent, ensuing, later, subsequent, succeeding 2 nearest, adjacent, adjoining, closest, neighbouring ♦ *adverb* 3 afterwards, following, later, subsequently, thereafter

nibble *verb* 1 bite, eat, gnaw, munch, nip, peck, pick at ♦ *noun* 2 snack, bite, crumb, morsel, peck, soupçon, taste, titbit

nice *adjective* 1 pleasant, agreeable, attractive, charming, delightful, good, pleasurable 2 kind, courteous, friendly, likable *or* likeable, polite, well-mannered 3 neat, dainty, fine, tidy, trim 4 subtle, careful, delicate, fastidious, fine, meticulous, precise, strict

nicely *adverb* 1 pleasantly, acceptably, agreeably, attractively, charmingly, delightfully, pleasurably, well 2 kindly, amiably, commendably, courteously, politely 3 neatly, daintily, finely, tidily, trimly

nicety noun <u>subtlety</u>, daintiness, delicacy, discrimination, distinction, nuance, refinement

niche noun **1** <u>alcove</u>, corner, hollow, nook, opening, recess **2** <u>position</u>, calling, pigeonhole (*informal*), place, slot (*informal*), vocation

nick verb **1** <u>cut</u>, chip, dent, mark, notch, scar, score, scratch, snick **2** <u>steal</u>, pilfer, pinch (*informal*), swipe (*slang*) ♦ noun **3** <u>cut</u>, chip, dent, mark, notch, scar, scratch

nickname noun <u>pet name</u>, diminutive, epithet, label, moniker or monicker (*slang*), sobriquet

nifty adjective <u>neat</u>, attractive, chic, deft, pleasing, smart, stylish

niggard noun <u>miser</u>, cheapskate (*informal*), Scrooge, skinflint

niggardly adjective <u>stingy</u>, avaricious, frugal, grudging, mean, miserly, parsimonious, tightfisted, ungenerous

niggle verb **1** <u>worry</u>, annoy, irritate, rankle **2** <u>criticize</u>, carp, cavil, find fault, fuss

niggling adjective **1** <u>persistent</u>, gnawing, irritating, troubling, worrying **2** <u>petty</u>, finicky, fussy, nit-picking (*informal*), pettifogging, picky (*informal*), quibbling

night noun <u>darkness</u>, dark, night-time

nightfall noun <u>evening</u>, dusk, sundown, sunset, twilight

nightly adjective **1** <u>nocturnal</u>, night-time ♦ adverb **2** <u>every night</u>, each night, night after night, nights (*informal*)

nightmare noun **1** <u>bad dream</u>, hallucination **2** <u>ordeal</u>, horror, torment, trial, tribulation

nil noun <u>nothing</u>, love, naught, none, zero

nimble adjective <u>agile</u>, brisk, deft, dexterous, lively, quick, sprightly, spry, swift

nimbly adverb <u>quickly</u>, briskly, deftly, dexterously, easily, readily, smartly, spryly, swiftly

nincompoop noun <u>idiot</u>, blockhead, chump, fool, nitwit (*informal*), numbskull or numskull, twit (*informal, chiefly Brit.*)

nip[1] verb <u>pinch</u>, bite, squeeze, tweak

nip[2] noun <u>dram</u>, draught, drop, mouthful, shot (*informal*), sip, snifter (*informal*)

nipper noun *Informal* <u>child</u>, baby, boy, girl, infant, kid (*informal*), tot

nippy adjective **1** <u>chilly</u>, biting, sharp **2** *Informal* <u>quick</u>, active, agile, fast, nimble, spry

nirvana noun <u>paradise</u>, bliss, joy, peace, serenity, tranquillity

nit-picking adjective <u>fussy</u>, captious, carping, finicky, hairsplitting, pedantic, pettifogging, quibbling

nitty-gritty noun <u>basics</u>, brass tacks (*informal*), core, crux, essentials, fundamentals, gist, substance

nitwit noun *Informal* <u>fool</u>, dimwit (*informal*), dummy (*slang*), halfwit, nincompoop, oaf, simpleton

no interjection **1** <u>never</u>, nay, not at all, no way ♦ noun **2** <u>refusal</u>, denial, negation

nob noun <u>aristocrat</u>, bigwig

(*informal*), toff (*Brit. slang*), V.I.P.

nobble *verb* bribe, get at, influence, intimidate, win over

nobility *noun* 1 integrity, honour, incorruptibility, uprightness, virtue 2 aristocracy, elite, lords, nobles, patricians, peerage, upper class

noble *adjective* 1 worthy, generous, honourable, magnanimous, upright, virtuous 2 aristocratic, blue-blooded, highborn, lordly, patrician, titled 3 great, dignified, distinguished, grand, imposing, impressive, lofty, splendid, stately ♦ *noun* 4 lord, aristocrat, nobleman, peer

nobody *pronoun* 1 no-one ♦ *noun* 2 nonentity, cipher, lightweight (*informal*), menial

nocturnal *adjective* nightly, night-time

nod *verb* 1 acknowledge, bow, gesture, indicate, signal 2 sleep, doze, drowse, nap ♦ *noun* 3 gesture, acknowledgment, greeting, indication, sign, signal

noggin *noun* 1 cup, dram, mug, nip, tot 2 *Informal* head, block (*informal*), nut (*slang*)

no go *adjective* impossible, futile, hopeless, not on (*informal*), vain

noise *noun* sound, clamour, commotion, din, hubbub, racket, row, uproar

noiseless *adjective* silent, hushed, inaudible, mute, quiet, soundless, still

noisome *adjective* 1 poisonous, bad, harmful, pernicious, pestilential, unhealthy, unwholesome 2 offensive, disgusting, fetid, foul,

malodorous, noxious, putrid, smelly, stinking

noisy *adjective* loud, boisterous, cacophonous, clamorous, deafening, ear-splitting, strident, tumultuous, uproarious, vociferous

nomad *noun* wanderer, drifter, itinerant, migrant, rambler, rover, vagabond

nomadic *adjective* wandering, itinerant, migrant, peripatetic, roaming, roving, travelling, vagrant

nom de plume *noun* pseudonym, alias, assumed name, nom de guerre, pen name

nomenclature *noun* terminology, classification, codification, phraseology, taxonomy, vocabulary

nominal *adjective* 1 so-called, formal, ostensible, professed, puppet, purported, supposed, theoretical, titular 2 small, inconsiderable, insignificant, minimal, symbolic, token, trifling, trivial

nominate *verb* name, appoint, assign, choose, designate, elect, propose, recommend, select, suggest

nomination *noun* choice, appointment, designation, election, proposal, recommendation, selection, suggestion

nominee *noun* candidate, aspirant, contestant, entrant, protégé, runner

nonaligned *adjective* neutral, impartial, uncommitted, undecided

nonchalance noun indifference, calm, composure, equanimity, imperturbability, sang-froid, self-possession, unconcern

nonchalant adjective casual, blasé, calm, careless, indifferent, insouciant, laid-back (informal), offhand, unconcerned, unperturbed

noncombatant noun civilian, neutral, nonbelligerent

noncommittal adjective evasive, cautious, circumspect, equivocal, guarded, neutral, politic, temporizing, tentative, vague, wary

non compos mentis adjective insane, crazy, deranged, mentally ill, unbalanced, unhinged

nonconformist noun maverick, dissenter, eccentric, heretic, iconoclast, individualist, protester, radical, rebel

nonconformity noun dissent, eccentricity, heresy, heterodoxy

nondescript adjective ordinary, commonplace, dull, featureless, run-of-the-mill, undistinguished, unexceptional, unremarkable

none pronoun not any, nil, nobody, no-one, nothing, not one, zero

nonentity noun nobody, cipher, lightweight (informal), mediocrity, small fry

nonessential adjective unnecessary, dispensable, expendable, extraneous, inessential, peripheral, superfluous, unimportant

nonetheless adverb nevertheless, despite that, even so, however, in spite of that, yet

nonevent noun flop (informal), disappointment, dud (informal), failure, fiasco, washout

nonexistent adjective imaginary, chimerical, fictional, hypothetical, illusory, legendary, mythical, unreal

nonsense noun rubbish, balderdash, claptrap (informal), double Dutch (Brit. informal), drivel, gibberish, hot air (informal), stupidity, tripe (informal), twaddle

nonsensical adjective senseless, absurd, crazy, foolish, inane, incomprehensible, irrational, meaningless, ridiculous, silly

nonstarter noun dead loss, dud (informal), lemon (informal), loser, no-hoper (informal), turkey (informal), washout (informal)

nonstop adjective **1** continuous, constant, endless, incessant, interminable, relentless, unbroken, uninterrupted ♦ adverb **2** continuously, ceaselessly, constantly, endlessly, incessantly, interminably, perpetually, relentlessly

nook noun niche, alcove, corner, cubbyhole, hide-out, opening, recess, retreat

noon noun midday, high noon, noonday, noontide, twelve noon

norm noun standard, average, benchmark, criterion, par, pattern, rule, yardstick

normal adjective **1** usual, average, common, conventional, natural, ordinary, regular, routine, standard, typical **2** sane, rational, reasonable, well-adjusted

normality noun **1** regularity, conventionality, naturalness **2** sanity, balance, rationality, reason

normally adverb usually, as a rule, commonly, generally, habitually, ordinarily, regularly, typically

north adjective **1** northern, Arctic, boreal, northerly, polar ♦ adverb **2** northward(s), northerly

nose noun **1** snout, beak, bill, hooter (slang), proboscis ♦ verb **2** ease forward, nudge, nuzzle, push, shove **3** pry, meddle, snoop (informal)

nosegay noun posy, bouquet

nosey, nosy adjective inquisitive, curious, eavesdropping, interfering, intrusive, meddlesome, prying, snooping (informal)

nostalgia noun reminiscence, homesickness, longing, pining, regretfulness, remembrance, wistfulness, yearning

nostalgic adjective sentimental, emotional, homesick, longing, maudlin, regretful, wistful

nostrum noun medicine, cure, drug, elixir, panacea, potion, remedy, treatment

notability noun fame, celebrity, distinction, eminence, esteem, renown

notable adjective **1** remarkable, conspicuous, extraordinary, memorable, noteworthy, outstanding, rare, striking, uncommon, unusual ♦ noun **2** celebrity, big name, dignitary, personage, V.I.P.

notably adverb particularly, especially, outstandingly, strikingly

notation noun signs, characters, code, script, symbols, system

notch noun **1** cut, cleft, incision, indentation, mark, nick, score **2** Informal level, degree, grade, step ♦ verb **3** cut, indent, mark, nick, score, scratch

notch up verb register, achieve, gain, make, score

note noun **1** message, comment, communication, epistle, jotting, letter, memo, memorandum, minute, remark, reminder **2** indication, mark, sign, token ♦ verb **3** see, notice, observe, perceive **4** mark, denote, designate, indicate, record, register **5** mention, remark

notebook noun jotter, diary, exercise book, journal, notepad

noted adjective famous, acclaimed, celebrated, distinguished, eminent, illustrious, notable, prominent, renowned, well-known

noteworthy adjective remarkable, exceptional, extraordinary, important, notable, outstanding, significant, unusual

nothing noun nought, emptiness, nil, nothingness, nullity, void, zero

nothingness noun **1** oblivion, nonbeing, nonexistence, nullity **2** insignificance, unimportance, worthlessness

notice noun **1** observation, cognizance, consideration, heed, interest, note, regard

2 attention, civility, respect
3 announcement, advice, communication, instruction, intimation, news, notification, order, warning ♦ *verb* **4** observe, detect, discern, distinguish, mark, note, perceive, see, spot

noticeable *adjective* obvious, appreciable, clear, conspicuous, evident, manifest, perceptible, plain, striking

notification *noun* announcement, advice, declaration, information, intelligence, message, notice, statement, warning

notify *verb* inform, advise, alert, announce, declare, make known, publish, tell, warn

notion *noun* **1** idea, belief, concept, impression, inkling, opinion, sentiment, view
2 whim, caprice, desire, fancy, impulse, inclination, wish

notional *adjective* speculative, abstract, conceptual, hypothetical, imaginary, theoretical, unreal

notoriety *noun* scandal, dishonour, disrepute, infamy, obloquy, opprobrium

notorious *adjective* infamous, dishonourable, disreputable, opprobrious, scandalous

notoriously *adverb* infamously, dishonourably, disreputably, opprobriously, scandalously

notwithstanding *preposition* despite, in spite of

nought *noun* zero, nil, nothing

nourish *verb* **1** feed, nurse, nurture, supply, sustain, tend
2 encourage, comfort, cultivate,

foster, maintain, promote, support

nourishing *adjective* nutritious, beneficial, nutritive, wholesome

nourishment *noun* food, nutriment, nutrition, sustenance

novel[1] *noun* story, fiction, narrative, romance, tale

novel[2] *adjective* new, different, fresh, innovative, original, strange, uncommon, unfamiliar, unusual

novelty *noun* **1** newness, freshness, innovation, oddity, originality, strangeness, surprise, unfamiliarity, uniqueness
2 gimmick, curiosity, gadget
3 knick-knack, bauble, memento, souvenir, trifle, trinket

novice *noun* beginner, amateur, apprentice, learner, newcomer, probationer, pupil, trainee

now *adverb* **1** nowadays, any more, at the moment
2 immediately, at once, instantly, promptly, straightaway
3 now and then *or* **again** occasionally, from time to time, infrequently, intermittently, on and off, sometimes, sporadically

nowadays *adverb* now, any more, at the moment, in this day and age, today

noxious *adjective* harmful, deadly, destructive, foul, hurtful, injurious, poisonous, unhealthy, unwholesome

nuance *noun* subtlety, degree, distinction, gradation, nicety, refinement, shade, tinge

nubile *adjective* marriageable, ripe (*informal*)

nucleus *noun* centre, basis, core,

focus, heart, kernel, nub, pivot

nude adjective naked, bare, disrobed, stark-naked, stripped, unclad, unclothed, undressed, without a stitch on (informal)

nudge verb push, bump, dig, elbow, jog, poke, prod, shove, touch

nudity noun nakedness, bareness, deshabille, nudism, undress

nugget noun lump, chunk, clump, hunk, mass, piece

nuisance noun problem, annoyance, bother, drag (informal), hassle (informal), inconvenience, irritation, pain in the neck, pest, trouble

null adjective null and void invalid, inoperative, useless, valueless, void, worthless

nullify verb cancel, counteract, invalidate, negate, neutralize, obviate, render null and void, veto

nullity noun nonexistence, invalidity, powerlessness, uselessness, worthlessness

numb adjective 1 unfeeling, benumbed, dead, deadened, frozen, immobilized, insensitive, paralysed, torpid ♦ verb 2 deaden, benumb, dull, freeze, immobilize, paralyse

number noun 1 numeral, character, digit, figure, integer 2 quantity, aggregate, amount, collection, crowd, horde, multitude, throng 3 issue, copy, edition, imprint, printing ♦ verb 4 count, account, add, calculate, compute, enumerate, include, reckon, total

numberless adjective infinite,

countless, endless, innumerable, multitudinous, myriad, unnumbered, untold

numbness noun deadness, dullness, insensitivity, paralysis, torpor

numbskull, numskull noun fool, blockhead, clot (Brit. informal), dolt, dummy (slang), dunce, oaf, twit (informal)

numeral noun number, digit, figure, integer

numerous adjective many, abundant, copious, plentiful, profuse, several, thick on the ground

nuncio noun ambassador, envoy, legate, messenger

nunnery noun convent, abbey, cloister, house

nuptial adjective marital, bridal, conjugal, connubial, matrimonial

nuptials plural noun wedding, marriage, matrimony

nurse verb 1 look after, care for, minister to, tend, treat 2 breast-feed, feed, nourish, nurture, suckle, wet-nurse 3 foster, cherish, cultivate, encourage, harbour, preserve, promote, succour, support

nursery noun creche, kindergarten, playgroup

nurture noun 1 development, discipline, education, instruction, rearing, training, upbringing ♦ verb 2 develop, bring up, discipline, educate, instruct, rear, school, train

nut noun 1 Slang madman, crank (informal), lunatic, maniac, nutcase (slang), psycho (slang) 2 Slang head, brain, mind, reason, senses

nutrition noun food, nourishment, nutriment, sustenance

nutritious adjective nourishing, beneficial, health-giving, invigorating, nutritive, strengthening, wholesome

nuzzle verb snuggle, burrow, cuddle, fondle, nestle, pet

nymph noun sylph, dryad, girl, maiden, naiad

O o

oaf noun idiot, blockhead, clod, dolt, dunce, fool, goon, lout, moron, numbskull or numskull

oafish adjective moronic, dense, dim-witted (informal), doltish, dumb (informal), loutish, stupid, thick

oath noun 1 promise, affirmation, avowal, bond, pledge, vow, word 2 swearword, blasphemy, curse, expletive, profanity

obdurate adjective stubborn, dogged, hard-hearted, immovable, implacable, inflexible, obstinate, pig-headed, unyielding

obedience noun respect, acquiescence, compliance, docility, observance, reverence, submissiveness, subservience

obedient adjective respectful, acquiescent, biddable, compliant, deferential, docile, dutiful, submissive, subservient, well-trained

obelisk noun column, monolith,

monument, needle, pillar, shaft

obese adjective fat, corpulent, gross, heavy, overweight, paunchy, plump, portly, rotund, stout, tubby

obesity noun fatness, bulk, corpulence, grossness, portliness, stoutness, tubbiness

obey verb carry out, abide by, act upon, adhere to, comply, conform, follow, heed, keep, observe

obfuscate verb confuse, befog, cloud, darken, muddy the waters, obscure, perplex

object¹ noun 1 thing, article, body, entity, item, phenomenon 2 target, focus, recipient, victim 3 purpose, aim, design, end, goal, idea, intention, objective, point

object² verb protest, argue against, demur, draw the line (at something), expostulate, oppose, take exception

objection noun protest, counter-argument, demur, doubt, opposition, remonstrance, scruple

objectionable adjective unpleasant, deplorable, disagreeable, intolerable, obnoxious, offensive, regrettable, repugnant, unseemly

objective noun 1 purpose, aim, ambition, end, goal, intention, mark, object, target ♦ adjective 2 unbiased, detached, disinterested, dispassionate, even-handed, fair, impartial, open-minded, unprejudiced

objectively adverb impartially, disinterestedly, dispassionately, even-handedly, with an open mind

objectivity noun impartiality, detachment, disinterestedness, dispassion

obligation noun duty, accountability, burden, charge, compulsion, liability, requirement, responsibility

obligatory adjective compulsory, binding, de rigueur, essential, imperative, mandatory, necessary, required, requisite, unavoidable

oblige verb 1 compel, bind, constrain, force, impel, make, necessitate, require 2 indulge, accommodate, benefit, gratify, please

obliged adjective 1 grateful, appreciative, beholden, indebted, in (someone's) debt, thankful 2 bound, compelled, forced, required

obliging adjective cooperative, accommodating, agreeable, considerate, good-natured, helpful, kind, polite, willing

oblique adjective 1 slanting, angled, aslant, sloping, tilted 2 indirect, backhanded, circuitous, implied, roundabout, sidelong

obliterate verb destroy, annihilate, blot out, efface, eradicate, erase, expunge, extirpate, root out, wipe out

obliteration noun annihilation, elimination, eradication, extirpation, wiping out

oblivion noun 1 neglect, abeyance, disregard, forgetfulness 2 unconsciousness,

insensibility, obliviousness, unawareness

oblivious adjective unaware, forgetful, heedless, ignorant, insensible, neglectful, negligent, regardless, unconcerned, unconscious, unmindful

obloquy noun 1 abuse, aspersion, attack, blame, censure, criticism, invective, reproach, slander, vilification 2 discredit, disgrace, dishonour, humiliation, ignominy, infamy, shame, stigma

obnoxious adjective offensive, disagreeable, insufferable, loathsome, nasty, nauseating, objectionable, odious, repulsive, revolting, unpleasant

obscene adjective 1 indecent, dirty, filthy, immoral, improper, lewd, offensive, pornographic, salacious 2 sickening, atrocious, disgusting, evil, heinous, loathsome, outrageous, shocking, vile, wicked

obscenity noun 1 indecency, coarseness, dirtiness, impropriety, lewdness, licentiousness, pornography, smut 2 swearword, four-letter word, profanity, vulgarism 3 outrage, abomination, affront, atrocity, blight, evil, offence, wrong

obscure adjective 1 vague, ambiguous, arcane, confusing, cryptic, enigmatic, esoteric, mysterious, opaque, recondite 2 indistinct, blurred, cloudy, dim, faint, gloomy, murky, shadowy 3 little-known, humble, lowly, out-of-the-way, remote, undistinguished, unheard-of, unknown ♦ *verb* **4** <u>conceal</u>, cover, disguise, hide, obfuscate, screen, veil

obscurity *noun* **1** <u>darkness</u>, dimness, dusk, gloom, haze, shadows **2** <u>insignificance</u>, lowliness, unimportance

obsequious *adjective* <u>sycophantic</u>, cringing, deferential, fawning, flattering, grovelling, ingratiating, servile, submissive, unctuous

observable *adjective* <u>noticeable</u>, apparent, detectable, discernible, evident, obvious, perceptible, recognizable, visible

observance *noun* <u>honouring</u>, carrying out, compliance, fulfilment, performance

observant *adjective* <u>attentive</u>, alert, eagle-eyed, perceptive, quick, sharp-eyed, vigilant, watchful, wide-awake

observation *noun* **1** <u>study</u>, examination, inspection, monitoring, review, scrutiny, surveillance, watching **2** <u>remark</u>, comment, note, opinion, pronouncement, reflection, thought, utterance

observe *verb* **1** <u>see</u>, detect, discern, discover, note, notice, perceive, spot, witness **2** <u>watch</u>, check, keep an eye on (*informal*), keep track of, look at, monitor, scrutinize, study, survey, view **3** <u>remark</u>, comment, mention, note, opine, say, state **4** <u>honour</u>, abide by, adhere to, comply, conform to, follow, heed, keep, obey, respect

observer *noun* <u>spectator</u>, beholder, bystander, eyewitness, fly on the wall, looker-on,

onlooker, viewer, watcher, witness

obsessed *adjective* <u>preoccupied</u>, dominated, gripped, haunted, hung up on (*slang*), infatuated, troubled

obsession *noun* <u>preoccupation</u>, complex, fetish, fixation, hang-up (*informal*), infatuation, mania, phobia, thing (*informal*)

obsessive *adjective* <u>compulsive</u>, besetting, consuming, gripping, haunting

obsolescent *adjective* <u>waning</u>, ageing, declining, dying out, on the wane, on the way out, past its prime

obsolete *adjective* <u>extinct</u>, antiquated, archaic, discarded, disused, old, old-fashioned, outmoded, out of date, passé

obstacle *noun* <u>difficulty</u>, bar, barrier, block, hindrance, hitch, hurdle, impediment, obstruction, snag, stumbling block

obstinacy *noun* <u>stubbornness</u>, doggedness, inflexibility, intransigence, obduracy, persistence, pig-headedness, tenacity, wilfulness

obstinate *adjective* <u>stubborn</u>, determined, dogged, inflexible, intractable, intransigent, pig-headed, refractory, self-willed, strong-minded, wilful

obstreperous *adjective* <u>unruly</u>, disorderly, loud, noisy, riotous, rowdy, turbulent, unmanageable, wild

obstruct *verb* <u>block</u>, bar, barricade, check, hamper, hinder, impede, restrict, stop, thwart

...ruction noun obstacle, bar, barricade, barrier, blockage, difficulty, hindrance, impediment

obstructive adjective uncooperative, awkward, blocking, delaying, hindering, restrictive, stalling, unhelpful

obtain verb 1 get, achieve, acquire, attain, earn, gain, land, procure, secure 2 exist, be in force, be prevalent, be the case, hold, prevail

obtainable adjective available, achievable, attainable, on tap (informal), to be had

obtrusive adjective noticeable, blatant, obvious, prominent, protruding, protuberant, sticking out

obtuse adjective slow, dense, dull, stolid, stupid, thick, uncomprehending

obviate verb preclude, avert, prevent, remove

obvious adjective evident, apparent, clear, conspicuous, distinct, indisputable, manifest, noticeable, plain, self-evident, undeniable, unmistakable

obviously adverb clearly, manifestly, of course, palpably, patently, plainly, undeniably, unmistakably, unquestionably, without doubt

occasion noun 1 time, chance, moment, opening, opportunity, window 2 event, affair, celebration, experience, happening, occurrence 3 reason, call, cause, excuse, ground(s), justification, motive, prompting, provocation ♦ verb 4 cause, bring about, engender, generate, give rise to, induce, inspire, lead to,

produce, prompt, provoke

occasional adjective infrequent, incidental, intermittent, irregular, odd, rare, sporadic, uncommon

occasionally adverb sometimes, at times, from time to time, irregularly, now and again, once in a while, periodically

occult adjective supernatural, arcane, esoteric, magical, mysterious, mystical

occupancy noun tenure, possession, residence, tenancy, use

occupant noun inhabitant, incumbent, indweller, inmate, lessee, occupier, resident, tenant

occupation noun 1 profession, business, calling, employment, job, line (of work), pursuit, trade, vocation, walk of life 2 possession, control, holding, occupancy, residence, tenancy, tenure 3 invasion, conquest, seizure, subjugation

occupied adjective 1 busy, employed, engaged, working 2 in use, engaged, full, taken, unavailable 3 inhabited, lived-in, peopled, settled, tenanted

occupy verb 1 often passive take up, divert, employ, engage, engross, involve, monopolize, preoccupy, tie up 2 live in, dwell in, inhabit, own, possess, reside in 3 fill, cover, permeate, pervade, take up 4 invade, capture, overrun, seize, take over

occur verb 1 happen, befall, come about, crop up (informal), take place, turn up (informal) 2 exist, appear, be found, be present, develop, manifest itself, show itself 3 occur to come to mind, cross one's mind, dawn on, enter one's head, spring to mind, strike one, suggest itself

occurrence noun **1** incident, adventure, affair, circumstance, episode, event, happening, instance **2** existence, appearance, development, manifestation, materialization

odd adjective **1** unusual, bizarre, extraordinary, freakish, irregular, peculiar, rare, remarkable, singular, strange **2** occasional, casual, incidental, irregular, periodic, random, sundry, various **3** spare, leftover, remaining, solitary, surplus, unmatched, unpaired

oddity noun **1** irregularity, abnormality, anomaly, eccentricity, freak, idiosyncrasy, peculiarity, quirk **2** misfit, crank (informal), maverick, oddball (informal)

oddment noun leftover, bit, fag end, fragment, off cut, remnant, scrap, snippet

odds plural noun **1** probability, chances, likelihood **2** at odds in conflict, at daggers drawn, at loggerheads, at sixes and sevens, at variance, out of line

odds and ends plural noun scraps, bits, bits and pieces, debris, oddments, remnants

odious adjective offensive, detestable, horrid, loathsome, obnoxious, repulsive, revolting, unpleasant

odour noun smell, aroma, bouquet, essence, fragrance, perfume, redolence, scent, stench, stink

odyssey noun journey, crusade, pilgrimage, quest, trek, voyage

off adverb **1** away, apart, aside, elsewhere, out ♦ adjective **2** unavailable, cancelled, finished, gone, postponed **3** bad, mouldy, rancid, rotten, sour, turned

offbeat adjective unusual, eccentric, left-field (informal), novel, outré, strange, unconventional, unorthodox, way-out (informal)

off colour adjective ill, out of sorts, peaky, poorly (informal), queasy, run down, sick, under the weather (informal), unwell

offence noun **1** crime, fault, misdeed, misdemeanour, sin, transgression, trespass, wrongdoing **2** snub, affront, hurt, indignity, injustice, insult, outrage, slight **3** annoyance, anger, displeasure, indignation, pique, resentment, umbrage, wrath

offend verb insult, affront, annoy, displease, hurt (someone's) feelings, outrage, slight, snub, upset, wound

offended adjective resentful, affronted, disgruntled, displeased, outraged, piqued, put out (informal), smarting, stung, upset

offender noun criminal, crook, culprit, delinquent, lawbreaker, miscreant, sinner, transgressor, villain, wrongdoer

offensive adjective **1** insulting, abusive, discourteous, disrespectful, impertinent, insolent, objectionable, rude **2** disagreeable, disgusting, nauseating, obnoxious, odious, repellent, revolting, unpleasant, vile **3** <u>aggressive</u>, attacking, invading ♦ *noun* **4** <u>attack</u>, campaign, drive, onslaught, push (*informal*)

offer *verb* **1** <u>bid</u>, proffer, tender **2** <u>provide</u>, afford, furnish, present **3** <u>propose</u>, advance, submit, suggest **4** <u>volunteer</u>, come forward, offer one's services ♦ *noun* **5** <u>bid</u>, proposal, proposition, submission, suggestion, tender

offering *noun* <u>donation</u>, contribution, gift, hand-out, present, sacrifice, subscription

offhand *adjective* **1** <u>casual</u>, aloof, brusque, careless, curt, glib ♦ *adverb* **2** <u>impromptu</u>, ad lib, extempore, off the cuff (*informal*)

office *noun* <u>post</u>, function, occupation, place, responsibility, role, situation

officer *noun* <u>official</u>, agent, appointee, executive, functionary, office-holder, representative

official *adjective* **1** <u>authorized</u>, accredited, authentic, certified, formal, legitimate, licensed, proper, sanctioned ♦ *noun* **2** <u>officer</u>, agent, bureaucrat, executive, functionary, office bearer, representative

officiate *verb* <u>preside</u>, chair, conduct, manage, oversee, serve, superintend

officious *adjective* <u>interfering</u>, dictatorial, intrusive, meddlesome, obtrusive, overzealous, pushy (*informal*), self-important

offing *noun* **in the offing** <u>in prospect</u>, imminent, on the horizon, upcoming

off-putting *adjective* <u>discouraging</u>, daunting, disconcerting, dispiriting, disturbing, formidable, intimidating, unnerving, unsettling

offset *verb* <u>cancel out</u>, balance out, compensate for, counteract, counterbalance, make up for, neutralize

offshoot *noun* <u>by-product</u>, adjunct, appendage, development, spin-off

offspring *noun* **1** <u>child</u>, descendant, heir, scion, successor **2** <u>children</u>, brood, descendants, family, heirs, issue, progeny, young

often *adverb* <u>frequently</u>, generally, repeatedly, time and again

ogle *verb* <u>leer</u>, eye up (*informal*)

ogre *noun* <u>monster</u>, bogeyman, bugbear, demon, devil, giant, spectre

oil *verb* <u>lubricate</u>, grease

oily *adjective* <u>greasy</u>, fatty, oleaginous

ointment *noun* <u>lotion</u>, balm, cream, embrocation, emollient, liniment, salve, unguent

O.K., okay *interjection* **1** <u>all right</u>, agreed, right, roger, very good, very well, yes ♦ *adjective* **2** <u>all right</u>, acceptable, adequate, fine, good, in order, permitted, satisfactory, up to scratch (*informal*) ♦ *verb* **3** <u>approve</u>, agree to, authorize, endorse, give the green light, rubber-stamp (*informal*), sanction ♦ *noun* **4** <u>approval</u>, agreement, assent,